ADVENTURING
IN NORTH AFRICA

THE SIERRA CLUB ADVENTURE TRAVEL GUIDES

ADVENTURING
IN NORTH AFRICA

$\wp$

The Sierra Club Travel Guide to
Morocco, Algeria, Tunisia,
and the Maltese Islands

SCOTT WAYNE

Sierra Club Books
San Francisco

The Sierra Club, founded in 1892 by John Muir, has devoted itself to the study and protection of the earth's scenic and ecological resources — mountains, wetlands, woodlands, wild shores and rivers, deserts and plains. The publishing program of the Sierra Club offers books to the public as a nonprofit educational service in the hope that they may enlarge the public's understanding of the Club's basic concerns. The point of view expressed in each book, however, does not necessarily represent that of the Club. The Sierra Club has some sixty chapters coast to coast, in Canada, Hawaii, and Alaska. For information about how you may participate in its programs to preserve wilderness and the quality of life, please address inquiries to Sierra Club, 730 Polk Street, San Francisco, CA 94109.

The publisher gratefully acknowledges Faber and Faber, London, for permission to quote from *The Kasbahs of Southern Morocco*, by Rom Landau.

LIBRARY OF CONGRESS CATALOGING-IN-PUBLICATION DATA

Wayne, Scott.
    Adventuring in North Africa : the Sierra Club travel guide to Morocco, Algeria, Tunisia, and the Maltese Islands / by Scott Wayne.
    p. cm.
    Includes index.
    ISBN 0-87156-745-8
    1. Africa, North—Description and travel—1951- —Guide-books.
2. Malta—Description and travel—1981- —Guide-books.   I. Title.
DT184.W38 1991
916.104'49—dc20   90-45253
                                                                CIP

PRODUCTION	Eileen Max
COVER DESIGN	Bonnie Smetts
BOOK DESIGN	Susan Colen/Park Press
MAPS	Robert Bathrick

PRINTED IN THE UNITED STATES OF AMERICA ON RECYCLED PAPER

10 9 8 7 6 5 4 3 2 1

℘

This book is dedicated to my grandmother Nan
and to the memory of my grandmother Nana Pauline.

CONTENTS

PREFACE

Adventuring in North Africa is organized according to the adventure possibilities and ease of access in each country. Morocco receives an overwhelming majority of the North American travelers to the Maghreb— over 160,000 (an estimate) in 1989, compared to approximately 5,000 to 10,000 each for Algeria and Tunisia. For Morocco, this figure represents an almost threefold increase since 1986. Because of these statistics, this book emphasizes Morocco, followed by Algeria, Tunisia, and Malta.

The chapters covering each country include background sections such as history and culture, and practical information on where and how to travel and obtain additional information when necessary. Principal cities and possible self-guided tours or miniadventures are described. As much as possible, independent adventure travel options and some organized tours away from the usual tourist routes are also covered. In some sections you'll find anecdotes that will, I hope, provide you additional insight into the lives of local people and offer a traveler's perspective on getting around the country. Happy adventuring!

The regional organization of the book will also help guide you through variations in the way Arabic words have been treated. Please note that Arabic is spoken differently in different areas, and the overlay of European rule and other influences, such as French colonial rule of Algeria, has produced quite diverse local ways of rendering Arabic script into the Indo-European alphabet and now into American English. In addition, the publishing conventions used for books, maps, and signposts are not nearly as uniform as in the European and North American tradition. Thus it is possible to find the name Abd Al-Qādir in one place, and to find him elsewhere as el-Kader, Al-Kadir, Al Kader, or Al Qader—and so on. A street named after him may appear as Rue Abdelkader.

I have made certain choices to satisfy the eye of North American readers; for example, the French do not capitalize the word *rue* (street) in proper street names; but we do, as readers will thus more easily recognize that we are using the name of a street. Similarly, we have capitalized *Al, El, Bin, Ben,* and *Ibn,* but you should expect to sometimes find them lowercased on maps of the region, or on street signs and timetables. The flexibility of the written and spoken language will be richly evident in the spellings we have accepted in this book; we apologize to purists.

ACKNOWLEDGEMENTS

First and foremost, if it weren't for the endless love, patience and understanding of my wife and best friend Shirley, the many long months of research and writing that produced this book would not have been possible. And if it weren't for the friendship and enthusiastic support of Jim Cohee, Senior Editor of Sierra Club Books, this book would have never been born. Special thanks to Linda Purrington, the best copy editor a writer could have, Bob Bathrick who deserves a medal for his superb cartography, and Paul Gallese for sharing his photographs of Morocco.

Many other people in the USA helped me prepare for a super research trip to Morocco, Algeria, Tunisia and Malta. For Morocco I am grateful to the assistance of Issam Lamdouar, Director of the Moroccan Tourism Office (ONMT) in New York City; Driss Britel, Director of the Moroccan Tourism Office in Beverly Hills; and Hassania Bezzaz, Assistant Director of the Moroccan Tourism Office in Beverly Hills, who provided many details about travel in Morocco and Berber dialects. I am thankful, I think, to Piotr Kostrzewski of Cross Cultural Adventures who put me on Clyde the cud-spitting camel, an overladen beast of burden that gave me a crash course in how to be a camel jockey in a rainstorm.

For Algeria, I am grateful to Ambassador Mohammed Sahnoun and his staff in the Algerian Embassy in Washington, D.C. for meeting with me and providing information about Algeria. Special thanks to Benchaa Dani, Press Attache. I am also grateful to Dr. Nicolas Hetzer of Forum Travel International, who got me into the Sahara for one of the highlights of my travels—a seven day walk in the Tassili-n-Ajjer region of the Algerian Sahara. Dr. Hetzer also assisted me with several pages of detailed information about Tamanrasset

At the Tunisian Embassy in Washington, D.C., Madame Fatma Masmoudi, Cultural Affairs Attache, was particularly helpful in providing information and contacting the Tunisian Ministry of Information on my behalf.

In Morocco, thanks to Ait El Kadi Brahim, Natasha Haugnes and Farouk Bennani in Marrakesh for their assistance and hospitality.

In Algeria, my friends Farid Hamdi and Sakina Messabih (now Mr. and Mrs. Hamdi) of ONAT and their director A. Kassoussi were a tremendous help with research and travel. I hope that someday they will visit California so we may reciprocate their kindness. Also in Algeria, M. Cherif-Zahar of ONAT, M. Bensalem of the Ministry of Culture, Mohammed Belkheir of the Ministry of Information, Abdel Hak Rafiah of ONAT in Djanet, my friends Mostefa Hamouda and Hocine Benmhidi in Batna, and Toufik Boughali of Mzab Tours in Ghardaia.

In Tunisia, Tarek Aouadi of ONTT, Tunisia's national tourism organization, was a great help with expediting my research and travels around Tunisia.

In Malta, Louis Azzopardi of the National Tourism Organization provided incredible assistance with my research and travels. Thanks also to Ileana Curmi and Joseph Micallef for being two of the best guides a visitor could have.

PART
ONE

ɸ

The Maghreb

CHAPTER 1

Introduction

Adventuring in North Africa describes adventures in the Maghreb—Morocco, Algeria, and Tunisia—and the Mediterranean islands of Malta. When they first arrived in the late seventh century A.D., the Arabs called this region (excluding Malta, which isn't considered part of Africa) the Maghreb, which means "Land of the West" or "Land of the Setting Sun." In the name of Islam, they swept westward to the Atlantic coast of Morocco and northward to Spain. Attempts to convert and arabize the indigenous Berber tribes of the Maghreb were met with increasingly fierce resistance the farther west the Arabs traveled and proselytized. The varied Arab success—partially a result of the Maghreb's diverse geography—contributed greatly to making the Maghreb the cultural paradox of homogeneity and diversity that it is today. For travelers, the cultural and geographic diversity of the Maghreb make this a fascinating and challenging region for adventure travel.

As you'll quickly realize in your own sweep across the Maghreb, Islam is the common thread linking these countries, (except for Malta, which is predominantly Roman Catholic). Although there are some differences in how Islam is practiced in each country, certain characteristics and practices are essentially the same throughout most of the Islamic world.

ISLAM AND GEOGRAPHY IN THE MAGHREB

Through speakers atop minarets of various shapes and sizes, five times a day muezzins (Muslim criers) bellow out the call to prayer. Faithful Muslims follow the call and fill the mosques below for several minutes of elaborate prayers. With these prayers, a Muslim reaffirms his or her faith in Islam.

The following verse (no. 124) from Surah IV in *The Holy Qur'an* (translated by M. H. Shakir, Tahrike Tarsile Qur'an, Inc., Elmhurst, New York, 1982) is often interpreted throughout the Middle East and North Africa to mean that men and women are permitted to pray together in mosques: "And whoever does good deeds whether male or female and he

3

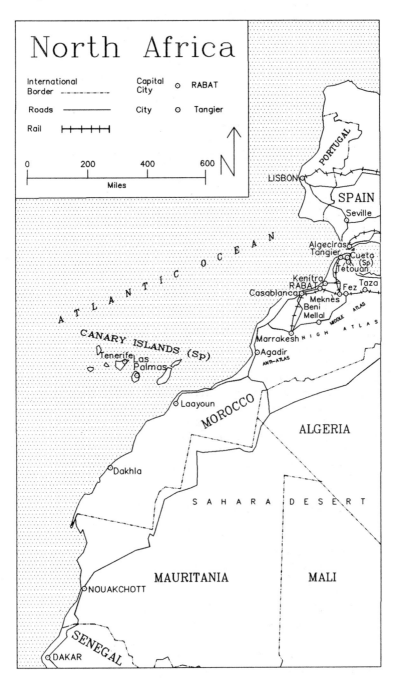

North Africa

International
Border ‑‑‑‑‑‑‑‑

Roads ‑‑‑‑‑‑‑

Rail ├─┼─┼─┼─┤

Capital
City ○ RABAT

City ○ Tangier

0   200   400   600

Miles

PORTUGAL

LISBON

SPAIN

Seville

A T L A N T I C   O C E A N

Algeciras
Tangier
Cueta
(Sp)
Tétouan
Kenitra
RABAT   Fez   Taza
Casablanca
Meknès
Beni
Mellal
MIDDLE   ATLAS
Marrakesh HIGH   ATLAS
Agadir
ANTI-ATLAS

CANARY ISLANDS (Sp)
Tenerife
Las
Palmas

Laayoun

MOROCCO

ALGERIA

Dakhla

S A H A R A   D E S E R T

MAURITANIA

MALI

NOUAKCHOTT

SENEGAL

DAKAR

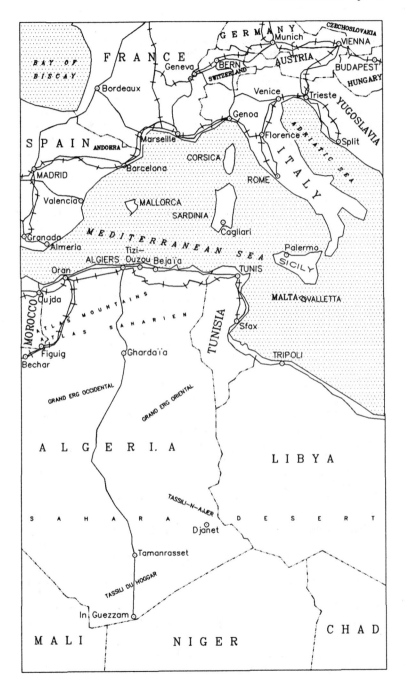

(or she) is a believer—these shall enter the garden, and they shall not be dealt with a jot unjustly." In practice, however, when women do pray in a mosque—which they do relatively rarely, compared to men—they pray behind the men or in a separate, adjoining room. It is rare because social tradition in the Maghreb deems that a woman's main role is to manage the household—thus to remain at home. In addition, many men believe that women can distract them from their prayers and that most women really don't know how to pray. It is more usual for men to be outside of the home than women. As women in the Maghreb become more educated, this situation is changing (see Chapter 2).

Islam shares its roots with two of the world's other major religions—Judaism and Christianity. Adam, Abraham, Noah, Moses, and Jesus are all accepted as Muslim prophets; however, Jesus is not recognized as the son of God. Muslim teachings correspond closely with the Torah, the Old Testament, and the Gospels, but the essence of Islam is the Qur'ān (Koran) and the Prophet Mohammed.

The Arabic term *islam* means submission to Allah (God), which is a fundamental precept of the religion Islam. Mohammed was the last and truest prophet to deliver this and other messages from Allah to the people. He was born in A.D. 570 in Mecca (now in Saudi Arabia) and received his first revelation from Allah in 610. He began to preach against the idolatry rampant in the region, particularly in Mecca, and proved a powerful and persuasive speaker. He quickly gained a fanatical following.

The Muslim faith was more than just a religion, as it also called on its followers to spread the word—by the sword, if necessary. Within two decades of the Prophet's death, most of Arabia had converted to Islam, and in succeeding centuries Islam spread over three continents. Mecca became the holiest city because it was there that Ibrahim (Abraham) built the first shrine to Allah. The building, known as the Kaaba, is still the holiest pilgrim shrine in Islam and contains the black stone given to Abraham by the angel Gabriel.

More than ten years after Mohammed's death in A.D. 632, his messages and revelations were compiled into the Muslim holy book, the Qur'ān. No changes to that text have been permitted since A.D. 651.

According to the Qur'ān, faithful Muslims must carry out five acts known formally as the Five Pillars of Faith:

- Publicly declare that "There is no God but Allah, and Mohammed is his Prophet."
- Pray five times a day: sunrise, noon, afternoon, sunset, and night.
- Pay *zakah* or charity for the propagation of Islam and for help to the needy.
- Fast during the day for the month of Ramadan.
- Make the *haj* or pilgrimage to Mecca.

The first pillar is accomplished through prayer, which is the second pillar. Since you will probably see quite a lot of praying during your travels in the Maghreb, here is a brief description of what happens:

As a Muslim enters the mosque he (or she) takes off his shoes and carries them, sole to sole, in his left hand. It is considered offensive to wear shoes in the House of God. He enters with his right foot first and then washes himself in a certain way before proceeding to pray.

Prayers are done in one- to two-minute cycles called *rek'ah*. Each worshiper faces the *mihrab* or pulpit, which is always directed toward Mecca. In fact, the entire mosque is built so that it too points towards Mecca. Part of the first rek'ah goes something like this: "*bism-allah wisallahtu wisalaamu rasulallah allahum ergferrli zenubi waftahli abwaba rahmatik....*"

Then he (or she) prays silently, and bows his head a number of times. This is followed by certain actions and prayers said aloud,

- "*Alla-hu Akbar*" (which means Allah is great)
- The first chapter of the Qur'ān
- Verses from another chapter
- "*Alla-hu Akbar*"

Then he (or she) bows, kneels, and places his palms on the ground, followed by his nose and forehead. (The foreheads of the most faithful Muslims have a slight but noticeable indentation created by this genuflection). Then he says, "I extol the perfection of Allah the Great" three times. Then he stands and says, "*Alla-hu Akbar.*" Now back to the ground, saying the same thing as before.

That is one *rek'ah*, and a good Muslim performs several in a single prayer session. The *rek'ah* requires a lot of concentration. To create the right conditions for this, the interior of most mosques is simple and devoid of elaborate decorations.

Visiting Mosques

In Morocco, mosques are off limits to non-Muslims. In Algeria, it's rare for non-Muslims to visit mosques, so ask before entering. In Tunisia, most are off limits, but a few are usually open for visits, particularly in tourist areas such as Sousse and Kairouan.

When you are able to visit a mosque (not on Fridays or during prayers), dress modestly. For men that means no shorts; for women that means no shorts, tight pants, open or loose-fitting shirts, or anything else even remotely suggestive. Just use common sense. Lastly, you must take off your shoes, or use the shoe coverings that are sometimes available.

Geography, mainly in the form of the Atlas mountain ranges of Algeria and Morocco, increasingly frayed this "thread" of Islam as the Arabs stretched it westward from Tunisia.

In Tunisia, arabization and Islamization were almost total; today more than 99 percent of Tunisians consider themselves Muslim Arabs. In Algeria, Islam melded somewhat with local traditional beliefs in spirits and saints (*marabouts*) and with Algerian nationalism. Also, many Berbers were not arabized or only partially arabized because for thousands of years they have resided in the once impregnable Atlas mountains and in desolate or closely guarded parts of the Sahara. In Morocco, the Berbers continue to form an even more distinct segment of the population—especially in the isolated parts of the Atlas mountains—local beliefs in saints, *baraka* (holiness, saintliness, good luck), and spirits sometimes overshadow traditional Islam.

French rule in this and the last century, particularly in Morocco and Algeria, took advantage of the cultural differences between Arabs and Berbers. In Algeria, the only country in the Maghreb that was actually colonized, the French attempted to pit Arabs and Berbers against each other and restrict Islamic influence by closing Islamic schools and converting some mosques to churches. Their objective was the Frenchification of the country and integration with France.

Arabs and Berbers were also pitted against each other in Morocco, but more for the sake of political control than frenchification and integration. The French also formed alliances with one Berber or Arab clan, faction, or tribe against another.

In Tunisia, French control was primarily over economic affairs. Without a substantial Berber population, there were no political factions built along ethnic or tribal lines, thus few impediments to a unified independent Tunisia. The French concentrated on building the economy and a local French-educated elite. In so doing, they laid the groundwork for an independent Tunisia. Consequently, transition from French rule to independence was a much smoother and more unified process than in Morocco and Algeria.

Malta has had long, but markedly different colonial experiences. Dominated for several centuries by the countries, empires, and kingdoms of the Mediterranean and only independent since 1964, the most amazing fact of Maltese history is that the Maltese people haven't been swallowed by another culture. They form a distinct culture that has been predominately Roman Catholic for several centuries. Although their ties to Europe, especially Sicily, have greatly overshadowed cultural ties to North Africa, the Maltese language is remarkably similar to Arabic. Malta is included in this book because throughout its history it has acted as a tiny, but significant bridge between Europe and North Africa. Not many North Americans venture to Malta, in part because so little is written about it in North America. Europeans have discovered Malta and, partially out of economic necessity, Malta has become much more amenable and organized for tourism than the countries of the Maghreb.

THE SOCIAL CONTEXT OF TRAVEL IN NORTH AFRICA

In varying degrees, each country in the Maghreb is prepared for travel and tourism. Morocco leads the African continent with the number of foreign tourists, which is not surprising, because King Hassan, Morocco's penultimate ruler, recognized the possible development value of tourism revenue. Accommodations from cheap to deluxe, restaurants, tour operators, and adventure travel companies are all plentiful. Opportunities for getting away from commercialized travel operations and into isolated locales are abundant. Adventure travel possibilities include a variety of mountain hikes, visits to isolated Berber villages, camel treks in the Sahara, mountain bike trips, and even skiing in the Atlas mountains. There are also, of course, miniadventures in the medieval imperial cities of Morocco.

In Algeria, commercial travel operations are quite limited compared to Morocco, a result perhaps of stifling government control. This control, in turn, can be traced to Algeria's history as a French colony for more than 130 years, during which Algerians who didn't assimilate to French culture were relegated to second-class status and limited mostly to servile jobs. After independence the Algerian government set out on the task of rebuilding an Algerian identity, a task that also entailed rebuilding the Algerian economy and hence the nationalization of many private enterprises. Service-oriented ventures, which are essential for developing a prosperous tourism sector, were virtually ignored because the colonial legacy left a negative attitude toward such jobs.

In the 1980s, after big price drops for petrochemicals, the government began to recognize tourism as a probable source of hard currency and thus capital for development projects. Eventually, the government hopes to correct the country's deficiencies in tourism-related sectors— accommodations, restaurants, transportation, tour operators—by increasing government investments and encouraging some private investment.

Opportunities, however, for tourism and adventure travel in Algeria are not in short supply. As the second largest country in Africa, Algeria offers a variety of adventure possibilities—hikes in the Sahara and the Atlas mountains, skiing, Land Rover expeditions and camel treks across the Sahara, and mountain bike trips in the mountains and valleys of the central Sahara. Unfortunately, since facilities, information, and access are limited, it's difficult to deviate from the usual tourist routes unless you have your own transport and/or are willing to hike long distances just to reach departure points (especially in the mountains). Several foreign— mainly French—and a few Algerian tour operators offer trips to most of Algeria, including parts of the Sahara.

Tunisia has a thriving tourism sector, due in large part to the modernization efforts of the postindependence government. In fact, tourism is so well developed and commercialized in Tunisia that relatively few parts of the country are "off the beaten track," thus far fewer opportunities exist for adventure travel. These are described in the Tunisia chapters.

CHAPTER 2

Practical Tips on Traveling in North Africa

This chapter covers those aspects of travel that all three countries of the Maghreb have in common: health considerations, practical matters (measurements and weights, money matters, and things to bring), and women traveling alone. There's also a short section highlighting the valuable work of SPANA (Society for the Protection of Animals in North Africa).

All information concerning Malta is in the Malta chapter.

HEALTH

Vaccinations should be obtained before you arrive in North Africa. According to the International Association for Medical Assistance to Travelers (IAMAT), the following vaccinations are recommended for all three countries of the Maghreb:

- All routine immunizations should be current: tetanus-diphtheria, polio, measles, mumps, and influenza (for the elderly and others with certain medical complications).
- Viral hepatitis A (immune globulin), also known as "gamma globulin."
- Typhoid fever.
- Selective vaccinations: viral hepatitis B (only for people who are working and/or residents), pre-exposure rabies vaccine ("advised for people planning an extended stay or on working assignments").

Algeria and Tunisia recommend typhoid and gamma globulin only for travelers who plan to venture off the beaten track.

Travel Insurance

Get some travel insurance! You may never need it, but if you do need it you'll be very glad you got it. Many different travel insurance policies

11

are available, which cover medical costs for illness or injury, the cost of getting home for medical treatment, life insurance, and baggage insurance. Some protect you against cancelation penalties on advance purchase tickets if you must change travel plans because of illness. Most travel and insurance agents should be able to recommend a policy but check the fine print, especially regarding baggage insurance.

Medical Kit

It is always a good idea to travel with a small first-aid kit. Some items that should be included are Band-Aids, a sterilized gauze bandage, Elastoplast, cotton wool, a thermometer, tweezers, scissors, antibiotic cream or ointment, an antiseptic agent (dettol or batadine), burn cream (Caladryl is good for sunburn, minor burns, and itchy bites), insect repellent and multivitamins.

Don't forget water sterilization tablets or iodine; antimalarial tablets; any medication you're already taking; and contraceptives, if necessary.

Recommended traveler's medications include diarrhea tablets, such as Lomotil or Imodium, paracetamol (Panadol) for pain and fever, and a course of antibiotics (check with your doctor). Erythromycin is recommended for respiratory, dental, and skin infections and is a safe alternative to penicillin. Tinidazole (Fasigyn) is recommended for treating amoebic dysentery and giardia.

Most of these items—other than contraceptives, water sterilization tablets, and insect repellent—are readily available in North African pharmacies.

Food and Water

Bottled water is recommended for most locales in North Africa, including the big cities. If in doubt, ask before drinking the tap water. Tap water that is definitely suspect should be boiled, filtered, or treated with tincture of iodine or purification tablets. You should also be sure to use clean water for brushing your teeth and rinsing your mouth.

There are also a few commonsense precautions to take with food in North Africa. Always wash and peel fruits and vegetables, and generally avoid salads. Fields are sometimes fertilized with human excrement, and this waste has a way of sticking to the produce. The food isn't always well washed before it reaches your plate. If you can't wash or peel it, don't eat it. Yet many travelers—including myself—have eaten salads regularly with few ill aftereffects. If you think that you are particularly susceptible to stomach troubles, then you should probably avoid salads.

Meat is safe as long as it has been thoroughly cooked. If you favor raw meat, keep in mind that conditions in North Africa can make the meat a nice and tasty home for worms. Your stomach and intestines are an even better habitat. Similar precautions should be taken with fish, which is more perishable than meat.

Avoid milk and cream that have not at least been boiled. Milk in sealed cartons is usually imported and is safe to drink because it has been pasteurized and homogenized. Most processed and packaged ice cream is safe.

Avoid anything raw, especially shellfish.

Contaminated food or water can cause dysentery, giardia, hepatitis A, cholera (increasingly rare), polio, and typhoid—all of which are best avoided!

Health Precautions

Common Ailments

Breathing can sometimes be bothersome in parts of North Africa. I know, that sounds odd because, of course, you have to breathe. However, the lack of humidity (especially in the desert regions), the contrast of heat outside and air conditioning indoors, and the abundance of [dust] can aggravate your eyes, nose, and throat. Although you can survive without eyedrops and throat lozenges when traveling through North Africa, they can be helpful. During hot periods, try to avoid frequently going in and out of air-conditioned rooms, or you'll catch a cold, which is particularly miserable when the weather is hot.

Almost every traveler who stays in North Africa for more than a week seems to be hit with diarrhea. There is usually nothing you can do to prevent the onslaught; it is simply your system trying to adjust to a different environment. It can happen anywhere. There is no "cure," but following certain regimens will eventually eliminate or suppress it. Avoid taking drugs if possible—it is much better to let the diarrhea run its course.

The regimen to follow is fairly basic: drink plenty of fluids but not milk, coffee, strong tea, soft drinks, or cocoa. Don't eat anything other than toast, boiled rice, or *fresh* yogurt. (Yogurt is sometimes recommended, but I'm not absolutely convinced about it as a remedy.)

If you are traveling, it may be difficult to follow this path. That is when Imodium, codeine phosphate tablets, a liquid derivative of opium prescribed by the doctor, or a medicine with pectin (such as Kaopectate) can be useful. If you are still ailing after all this, then you may have dysentery, and need a doctor.

Dysentery

Unfortunately, dysentery is quite common among travelers. There are two types of dysentery, characterized by diarrhea containing blood and lots of mucous.

Bacillary dysentery, the most common variety, is short, sharp, and nasty but rarely persistent. It hits suddenly and lays you out with fever, nausea, cramps, and diarrhea but as it's caused by bacteria, it responds well to antibiotics.

Amoebic dysentery—which, as its name suggests, is caused by amoebic parasites—is much more difficult to treat, is often persistent, and is more dangerous. It builds up more slowly, cannot be starved out, and if untreated it will get worse and permanently damage your intestines. Tinidazole (Fasigyn) is the recommended drug for treating amoebic dysentery.

Hepatitis

The liver disease hepatitis is caused by a virus. There are two types—infectious hepatitis (Type A) and serum hepatitis (Type B). Hepatitis A, the most common, can be caught from eating food, drinking water, or using cutlery or crockery contaminated by an infected person. Hepatitis B can only be contracted by having sex with an infected person or by using the same intravenous syringe. Symptoms appear 15 to 50 days after infection (generally around 25 days) and consist of fever, loss of appetite, nausea, depression, lack of energy, and pains around the base of your ribcage. Your skin turns yellow, the whites of your eyes turn yellow to orange, and your urine will be deep orange or brown. Do not take antibiotics. There is no cure for hepatitis except complete rest and good food. You should be over the worst in about ten days, but continue to take it easy after that. A gamma globulin injection is said to provide protection again Hepatitis A for three to six months but its effectiveness is still debatable.

Cholera

Cholera can be extremely dangerous, as it is very contagious and usually occurs in epidemics. The symptoms are very bad but painless, watery diarrhea (commonly known as "rice-water shits"); vomiting; quick, shallow breathing; fast, faint heartbeat; wrinkled skin; stomach cramps; and severe dehydration. Do not attempt to treat cholera yourself; see a doctor immediately. Cholera vaccinations are valid for six months, and if you're revaccinated before the expiration date that vaccination is immediately valid. The vaccine doesn't give 100 percent protection, but if you also take the usual precautions about food and water you should be safe. A last note about cholera: it is now considered quite rare.

Polio

Polio is another disease spread by unsanitary conditions and found more frequently in hot climates. There is an oral vaccine against polio—three doses of drops taken at 4- to 8-week intervals. If you were vaccinated as a child, you may only need a booster. Once again, take care with food and drink while traveling.

Typhoid Fever

Typhoid fever is a dangerous infection that starts in the gut and spreads to the whole body. It can be caught from contaminated food, water, or milk and, as its name suggests, the main feature is a high temperature. Another characteristic is rose-colored spots on the chest and abdomen, which may appear after about a week. Two vaccinations, a month apart, provide protection against typhoid for three years.

Malaria

Malaria, which is spread by mosquitoes, has a nasty habit of coming back in later years—and can be fatal. Protection is simple—a daily or weekly antimalarial tablet that you start taking before you travel. Malaria is a minimal risk, and only in Morocco and Algeria. Sleeping near a fan (mosquitos hate fast-moving air) and using insect repellent are usually adequate; antimalarial protection has not been regarded as essential.

Common symptoms are headache, fever, chills, and sweats.

The following excerpt is from a leaflet issued by the British Airways Medical Service, entitled "Guidelines for Malaria Prophylaxis":

> No tablet will completely prevent malaria; however, the tablets recommended will provide a useful degree of protection in addition to the following precautions. Malaria mosquitoes bite after dark. Exposure outdoors can be reduced by wearing clothing that adequately covers your arms and legs. Repellant creams and lotions can be applied to exposed skin. Indoors, aerosol knockdown spray can be used and, where there is no air conditioning, window screens and mosquito nets are advised. If none of this is available, then at least try to sleep under or next to a fan.
>
> Remember to take the tablets while you are in the malarial area and for at least six weeks afterward.

> *Malaria prevention drugs:*
> - **Paludrine**—two tablets daily after same meal each day.
> - **Daraprim**—one tablet weekly. Start one week prior to travel.
> - **Nivaquine or Avloclor (Chloroquine)**—Two tablets weekly, best taken after food starting one week prior to travel. Use for southern Sudan.

- **Maloprim**—one tablet weekly for adults starting one week before travel.
- **Fansidar**—one tablet weekly starting one week before travel. When two weekly tablets are advised to be taken concurrently—for example, Maloprim and Nivaquine—they should be taken on different days of the week, so that protection overlaps.

Recently, Maloprim has been recommended over Fansidar because of the latter's potentially serious side effects.

According to the "World Malaria Risk Chart" published by the International Association for Medical Assistance to Travellers (IAMAT), malaria is "present" in Morocco

> [in] certain risk areas: rural areas of the provinces of Kenitra, Sidi Kacem, Chefchaouen, Beni Mellal, Tetouan, Nador, and Al Hoceima. From May to October are the high-risk months. The *Anopheles labranchiae* mosquito is most prevalent; it breeds in fresh or saline water of swamps and marshes near the coast. It feeds on humans indoors.

In Algeria,

> the malaria risk is absent in most of the country, [but] exists only in specific areas...Adrar and Ouargla (from November to March) [and] Tamanrasset and Djanet (from March to October). The *Anopheles sergentii* mosquito or oasis mosquito is most prevalent; it breeds in small pools [and attacks] after dark.

A chloroquine regimen is recommended for both countries. Tunisia does not have malaria.

Yellow Fever

A serious, often fatal disease, yellow fever is transmitted by the mosquito. It is caused by a virus that produces severe inflammation of the liver. Yellow fever is entirely preventable. It requires one injection, at least 10 days before departure, which is valid for ten years.

Bilharzia (schistosomiasis)

Bilharzia is prevalent in warm, stagnant bodies of fresh water usually frequented by animals. The bilharzia parasite hitches a ride on a microscopic snail that enters humans by burrowing through the skin. They inhabit and breed in the blood vessels of the abdomen, pelvis, and sometimes the lungs and liver. The disease is painful and causes persistent and cumulative damage by repeated deposits of eggs. The main symptom is blood in the urine, and sometimes in the feces. The victim may suffer weakness, loss of appetite, sweating at night, and afternoon fevers. If you have contracted bilharzia, you will begin noticing these symptoms anywhere from one to four weeks after contact. Bilharzia can be treated, so see a specialist in tropical medicine as quickly as possible. Do not drink, wash, swim, paddle, or even stand in water that may be infected.

Rabies

If you are bitten, scratched, or even licked by a rabid animal and do not start treatment within a few days, you may die. Rabies affects the central nervous system and is certainly an unpleasant way to go. Typical signs of a rabid animal are mad or uncontrolled behavior, inability to eat, biting at anything, and frothing at the mouth. If you are bitten by an animal, react as if it had rabies—there are no second chances. Get to a doctor and begin the course of injections that will prevent the disease from developing.

Tetanus

A killer disease, tetanus can easily be prevented by immunization. It is caught through cuts and breaks in the skin caused by rusty or dirty objects, animal bites, or through contamination of wounds. Even if you have been vaccinated, wash the wound thoroughly.

Taking the Heat

Protect yourself against the sun's heat in desert regions. It is sometimes difficult to gauge how quickly you are losing body water, because the climate is dry. Headaches, dizziness, and nausea are signs that you have lost too much water and may have heat exhaustion. To prevent this, take a bit of extra salt with your food, drink plenty of fluids, and wear a hat and sunglasses. The salt helps keep you from getting dehydrated. Incidentally, the caffeine in coffee and tea also contributes to dehydration. Sunblock will keep the sun from frying your skin. Wearing long pants and long sleeves is cooler than wearing shorts and short sleeves, because your body moisture stays closer to your skin. Lastly, the sunshine on the beach and in the water is deceiving and will burn you quite quickly, so wear a shirt while snorkeling or swimming.

Doctors and Hospitals

There are hospitals throughout North Africa. Most of the doctors are well trained and often must deal with a greater variety of diseases and ailments than do their European and North American counterparts. Yet most medical facilities are not as well equipped, and consequently it is not unusual for diagnoses to be inaccurate. If for some reason you need an operation, don't have it in North Africa. London and other European cities are only a few hours away by plane.

Before you leave for North Africa, it is worthwhile writing to the International Association for Medical Assistance to Travellers (IAMAT) for its worldwide directory of English-speaking doctors. For their services, doctors who belong to this organization charge standard fees that are fair and reasonable. The fees are set by IAMAT. Its membership addresses are

Australia:	575 Bourke St, 12th floor, Melbourne 3000
Canada:	40 Regal Road, Guelph, Ontario N1K 1B5
New Zealand:	P.O. Box 5049, Christchurch 5
Switzerland:	57 Voirets, 1212 Grand-Lancy-Geneva
United States:	417 Center St, Lewiston, NY 14092

The following places have IAMAT representatives.

In Algeria:
- Algiers: Institut Pasteur d'Algerie (tel. 658860 and 608507); IAMAT coordinator, Dr. Smail Belazzoug

In Morocco:
- Rabat: Clinique Beauséjour (tel. 38824 and 38722), Triangle de la Gare, Salé; medical director, Dr. H. Moystad
- Tangier: Clinique California; medical director, Dr. Pierre Leonetti

In Tunisia:
- Carthage and Sidi Bou Saïd: Clinique Carthage (tel. 275720 and 731096); medical director, Dr. Rachid Ben Youssef
- Hammamet: IAMAT Center, Avenue Habib Bourguiba (tel. 80709); coordinator, Dr. Ismail Mami
- Jerba (Houmt-Souk): Hôpital Jerba (tel. 50018); IAMAT Center, 25 Avenue Abdelhamid El Kadi; coordinator, Dr. Abdelmoutaal Amin El Kaddossy
- Jerba (Midoun): IAMAT Center, 20 Avenue Habib Bourguiba (tel. 57305); coordinator, Dr. Habiba El Messabi
- Monastir: IAMAT Center, 12 Rue Trabelsia (tel. 62600); coordinator, Dr. Mohammed Naceur Tabka
- Sfax: University Hospital Hedi Chaker (tel. 42621); chief, intensive care unit, Dr. Habib Mokhtar Jeddi

- Sousse: University Hospital F. Hached (tel. 21411, ext. 311); Chief, intensive care unit: Dr. Saïd Rachid
- Tunis: IAMAT Center, 101 bis, Avenue de la Liberté (tel. 286032 and 263079)
- Zarzis: Hôpital Circonscription Sanitaire Zarzis (tel. 80302 and 80400); medical director, Dr. Ali Benali

The British, Canadian, and U.S. embassies in each country can also help you find a doctor.

General Thoughts

Make sure your teeth are in good shape before you leave home. If you have an emergency, however, there are English-speaking dentists in some North African cities and towns. In capital cities, consult your embassy.

If you wear eyeglasses, carry a second pair or at least a copy of your prescription in case of loss or breakage.

Public toilets are bad news—fly-infested, dirty, and stinky. Some toilets are still of the squat-over-a-hole-in-a-little-room variety. Always carry a roll of toilet paper with you; it's easy to buy throughout Morocco and Tunisia, somewhat less so in Algeria.

PRACTICAL MATTERS

The following sections describe various practical matters of concern to travelers. Unless otherwise indicated, these matters are common to all three countries of the Maghreb.

Electricity

Electric current is 220 volts AC, 50 cycles, across most of North Africa. Wall plugs are the round, two-prong European type. Bring adapter plugs and transformers if necessary; travel-size transformers are difficult to obtain in North Africa.

Time

Time in Morocco is Greenwich Mean Time, thus the same as London, which is five hours ahead of New York and eight ahead of Los Angeles. Algeria and Tunisia are one hour ahead of Morocco. However, all three countries convert to daylight savings time on different days. And when Ramadan is in the summer, one or more of the countries change their clocks an additional hour. As you'll quickly discover for yourself, time takes on new meaning in North Africa.

Weights and Measures

North African countries use the metric system. Here are basic conversion and equivalency charts:

To Convert	Multiply by
inches to centimeters	2.540
centimeters to inches	0.3937
feet to meters	0.3048
meters to feet	3.281
yards to meters	0.9144
meters to yards	1.094
miles to kilometers	1.609
kilometers to miles	0.6214
imperial gallons to liters	4.546
liters to imperial gallons	0.22
ounces to grams	28.35
grams to ounces	0.03527
pounds to kilograms	0.4536
kilograms to pounds	2.205

Temperature Conversion

Centigrade	Fahrenheit
50	122
45	113
40	104
35	95
30	86
25	75
20	68
15	59
10	50
5	41
0	32

Money

In Morocco and Tunisia, there are two convenient ways to receive money from home. If you have an American Express card and personal checks, American Express will cash your checks. If you have an American

Express green card, though, you are not permitted to cash more than US $1,000 every twenty-one days without authorization from American Express offices in London or the United States. If you have a VISA or MasterCard, you can get a cash advance from most major banks.

It is also possible to have money wired from home through American Express (only in Morocco and Tunisia) and most of the banks. In Algeria, this is about the only way to obtain money from overseas.

Travel in Morocco and Tunisia is cheap, compared to travel in Europe and North America. It is easy to get by on US $10 to $15 a day or even less if you're willing to endure certain inconveniences. Forgoing hot water or showers and taking crowded buses will save you quite a bit in daily expenses. For the most part, the amount of convenience and comfort varies according to how much you are willing to pay.

In Algeria, the costs of travel can be ridiculously high because of an overvalued currency. There's a flourishing black market in hard currencies, particularly in U.S. dollars and French francs, that offers exchange rates three or four times higher than official bank rates. Understandably, the government is not fond of the black market, so exercise caution if you decide to exchange money this way—it is illegal.

As most of you are probably aware, prices change, sometimes dramatically. They are subject to changing economic conditions— fluctuating exchange rates, two- or three-digit inflation rates, the rise and fall of the price of petrochemical products (especially important for Algeria) and of phosphates (important for Tunisia), the amount of interest owed on foreign debts, and so forth.

Business Hours

In Morocco, banks are usually open from 8:15 A.M. to 2:15 P.M. Monday to Friday; during Ramadan, from 9:30 A.M. to 2:30 P.M. Shops are usually open from 8:30 A.M. to 12 noon and 2:30 P.M. to 7 P.M.

In Algeria, banks are open from 8:30 A.M. to 12 noon Sunday to Thursday. Shops are usually open from 8 A.M. to 12 noon and from 2:30 P.M. to 6 P.M.

In Tunisia, banks are open from 8 A.M. to 11 A.M. and 2 P.M. to 4:15 P.M. in the winter and closed during summer afternoons. Shops have varying hours, generally 8:30 A.M. to 12 noon and 3 P.M. to 6 P.M.

Tipping in Morocco and Tunisia averages about 10 to 15 percent for restaurants, and various amounts (smaller than in Europe and North America) for services. Ask locals for some idea of the proper amount. In Algeria, tips are often factored into hotel and restaurant bills. Tipping can be a sensitive subject in Algeria because of cultural dislike (as a result of Algeria's historical experiences) of service positions.

Things to Bring

Bring sunglasses, flashlight, a collapsible drinking cup, a water bottle or canteen, sunscreen (sunblock), a hat, a flat drain-stopper (not a plug), pocket knife, two to three meters of nylon cord, plastic clothespins, a daypack, a small sewing kit, and a money belt or pouch (leather pouches can be made to order in the bazaars).

Although most toiletries can be found in Morocco and Tunisia, certain items can be expensive or difficult to find. So you may want to bring your own contact lens solutions, tampons, contraceptives, shaving cream in a can (in a tube it's readily available), any favorite brand of shampoo and deodorant (which is expensive). When available, toiletries in Algeria are expensive, especially at official exchange rates.

Women in North Africa

Moroccans, Algerians, and Tunisians (both male and female) are conservative, especially about matters concerning sex and women; Arab and Berber women, that is, not foreign women.

Unlike many Middle Eastern Muslims, the majority of North African women don't wear veils but they are still, for the most part, quite restricted in what they can do with their lives. Generally, they do not have the same degree of freedom that Western women have; this situation varies, however, from country to country.

Moroccan women are becoming increasingly liberated from traditional social restrictions, particularly in urban areas. In marriage, the future husband and wife are increasingly permitted to make their own arrangements rather than leave it up to the families. Previously, most marriages were arranged with almost no involvement of the couple in the decision making, including selection of one's spouse. Polygamy is rare, and nuclear families are increasingly common. European clothing styles, especially for women, can often be seen on city streets, although it is still not unusual to see veiled women in the cities and countryside. Enrollment of women in schools and universities is steadily increasing. All these factors have contributed to a gradual liberalization of Moroccan women.

In Algeria, independence from the French fostered ideas and expectations of freedom and equality for both men and women. Traditional Islam was often a principal source of unity for the independence struggle. Women often wore a head scarf and veil—traditional Islamic accouterments for women—to show their solidarity with the struggle and thus indirectly protest French colonialism. Both items are still worn by many Muslim Algerian women, but today the veil and scarf do not always symbolize conservatism or religiousness. They can also serve as a form of protection or shield from unwanted male attention.

After independence, changes in the status of women were quite limited. A progressive family code that restricted polygamy and gave women the right to divorce was adopted in the mid-1980s. Women's groups have been organized throughout Algeria to press for more comprehensive changes. My wife and I met the members of one such group in the dining room of a hotel in Constantine, a city known for its huge Islamic university and generally traditional populace. These women were demanding changes in labor laws so that they would receive the same salaries as men who were in the same or comparable jobs. If the diversity of clothing styles visible in the room can be considered an indication of the broad cross section of Algerian society represented there, then this particular movement has become quite pervasive.

Tunisia has the most progressive laws concerning the status of women. On independence in 1956, newly elected President Bourguiba instituted a status code that established a minimum age for marriage, abolished religious courts and polygamy, and legalized abortion and birth control and equal rights of divorce with men. However, prior to 1956 Tunisia had long been a male-dominated society, thus making full acceptance of these changes difficult for both men and women. Consequently, even though women have the same legal and social rights as men, traditional social mores have constrained women from fully exercising their rights and breaking away from their traditionally subordinate role.

All of the above is important for foreign women to keep in mind as they travel in North Africa. In addition to traditions, male attitudes toward women, especially foreign women, are shaped by the many Western television programs and films shown throughout North Africa. Foreign women are presented, by North African standards, as walking billboards for sex of all kinds. By those standards, it doesn't actually take much in the way of presentation to promote and perpetuate this belief— bare shoulders or shorts on a woman are proof enough. In Tunisia, however, it is not unusual to see European women sunbathing topless at hotel swimming pools and beaches.

Harassment of Western women travelers is practically a given in North Africa, but the degree of harassment can vary from country to country. In Tunisia, harassment is most likely, if it occurs at all, in the countryside where traditions are still fairly strong. The same applies to Morocco and Algeria, but attitudes in the cities and resort areas (except for the tourist-dominated Moroccan city Agadir) of both countries are still more conservative than in Tunisia. This means that harassment is also likely in the cities.

Harassment will usually consist of intense staring, a few choice words that you probably wouldn't want translated, touching, and being followed. For harassment to go beyond this depends, in part, on how a woman carries herself and avoids situations where physical harassment might occur.

A woman can travel independently if she follows a few common-sense tips:

- Avoid direct eye contact with a man unless you know him.
- Try not to respond to an obnoxious comment from a man—act as if you didn't hear it.
- Be careful in crowds where you are crammed among people, as it is not unusual for crude things to happen behind you.
- If you're in the countryside (off the beaten track), it's often a good idea to wear a scarf over your hair.
- Most of all, be careful about behaving in a flirtatious or suggestive manner—it could create more problems than you ever imagined.

Generally if you're alone with other women, the amount of harassment you get will be directly related to how you dress—the more skin that is exposed the more harassment you'll get. As hot as it can get in some parts of North Africa, you'll have fewer hassles if you don't dress for hot weather in the same way as you might back home.

Again, there are exceptions to this general rule. Beach resort areas in Morocco and Tunisia and hotel swimming pools in Tunisia are westernized, thus minimal dress is tolerated. Remember, though, toleration does not necessarily mean acceptance. In other words, North African men seem to consider topless bathing and minimal dress acceptable for Western women (in the above places), but totally *unacceptable* for North African women.

Another recommendation for women travelers is to befriend a woman. Apart from having someone totally non-threatening to show you around, you will probably also learn much more about life in North Africa from her. It helps if you can speak some French. The *hammams* or bathhouses are good places for women to meet women.

The Society for the Protection of Animals in North Africa

SPANA is the North African equivalent of the Humane Society in the United States. Its chief mission is to protect domesticated animals from mistreatment and to preserve existing wildlife reserves from human encroachment. Although their work isn't directly related to adventure travel in North Africa, it deserves as much exposure as possible. The following are excerpts from their literature explaining the organization and their programs in each country:

> In the winter of 1921, two British ladies, Mrs. Frances Kate Hosali and her daughter Nina set off for a six-month visit

to North Africa in search of sunshine. However, such were the appalling instances of neglect and ignorance toward pack and domestic animals which assailed them on all sides that on their return to Britain, Mrs. Hosali planned and later founded, in 1923, the Society for the Protection of Animals in North Africa. She herself went out alone that year and began work in Algeria, in the medinas (commercial quarters), souks (country markets), and fondouks (enclosures for pack animals), treating wounded and bleeding backs, saddle sores, and fistulous withers, some very large, with her own hands....

By 1939 Mrs. Hosali, steadily backed up by increasing support organised by her daughter in London, succeeded in setting up free treatment centres at 20 different places in Algeria and Tunisia, at the same time training local people to work as dressers....

There are now 18 permanent refuges and centres in North Africa and 3 more are planned for Tunisia this year...Over 100 markets, souks and fondouks are visited by our dressers. SPANA gives rest, refuge, and treatment to well over 300,000 animals each year; a figure which could be increased considerably were funds available...

Morocco Programs

In Morocco, SPANA operates through Société Protrectrice des Animaux de Rabat (SPAR) and in close collaboration with Union Marocaine pour la Protection des Animaux (UMPA). Both are recognised by Government decree of Public Utility. There are animal hospitals or refuges at Rabat, Khemisset, Meknes, Casablanca, Chemaïa, and Marrakesh.

SPANA Education Programme

In November 1986, SPANA and UMPA started an Animal Welfare Education Programme. This Education Programme has been officially approved by the Moroccan Ministry of Agriculture and Agrarian Reform. Its aim is to educate the public, by appropriate means, to protect wildlife as well as working and domestic animals and to provide them with adequate care and food....

Algeria Programs

Operations in Algeria are carried out at two centres, one at EL HARRACH (about 10 miles south of Algiers).

Here SPANA is mainly concerned with the rescue, treatment, and rehabilitation of cats and dogs. The other centre is at Touggourt (about 300 miles south-east of Algiers). Here treatment and care are given mainly to horses, mules, and donkeys.

Tunisia Programs

In Tunisia, where SPANA operates through Société Protectrice des Animaux de Tunisie (SPA), it has animal hospitals, refuges, or a resident dresser in the following places: Tunis, Sousse, Bizerte, Bousalem, Gafsa, Tozeur, Gabés, Jerba, Kasserine, and Sidi Bouzid.

SPANA is a registered charity in Great Britain that depends on contributions for a large share of its operating budget. Contact SPANA for more information: 15 Buckingham Gate, London SW1E 6LB England.

CHAPTER 3

Literary North Africa

The majority of literature on Morocco, Algeria, and Tunisia has been in French, but there is a growing body of translations and original works in English.

BOOKS ABOUT NORTH AFRICA

The classic (and probably one of the first) books on North Africa is *The History and Description of Africa and of the Notable Things Wherein Contained* by Leo Africanus (also known as al-Hassan ibn Mohammed al-Wezzaz and Giovanni Leone), who first visited North Africa in the early sixteenth century. All three volumes were translated in 1600 by J. Pory and published in 1896 by the Hakluyt Society, London. They can be found at most major university libraries.

There isn't a wealth of other material about the pre-Islamic Maghreb. However, *The North African Stones Speak* (London: Croom Helm, 1980) by Paul Mackendrick offers a good archeological and cultural history of the entire region, including coverage of the Carthaginian Empire.

Another book, *The History of the Maghrib* (Cambridge, England: Cambridge University Press, 1975), by Jamil M. Abun-Nasr, is a decent general reference on the history of North Africa from the days of Carthage in Tunisia to independence.

For the medieval period, there are several works on various topics, but most are articles in academic journals such as the *Journal of African History*, *Islamic Quarterly*, *International Journal of Middle Eastern Studies*, and *Bulletin of the School of Oriental and African Studies*—all of which can be found at most major university and a few public libraries.

Edited by Ernest Gellner and Charles Micaud, *Arabs and Berbers: From Tribe to Nation in North Africa* (London: Duckworth, 1973) considers and compares the political development of Morocco, Algeria, and Tunisia in terms of ethnic group differences. Most of the chapters cover political and social change in Morocco.

In *The Maghreb in the Modern World: Algeria, Tunisia, Morocco,*

Samir Amin (translated by Michael Perl; Harmondsworth: Penguin African Library, 1970) analyzes and compares the effects of French colonialism in terms of each country's social, economic, and political issues and problems. This book is an informative resource for understanding the contemporary cultural and political differences of each country.

BOOKS ABOUT MOROCCO

One of the best introductions to Morocco, *Morocco: A Country Study* (Washington, D.C.: Foreign Area Studies, American University, 1985) offers a current, comprehensive overview of Morocco, with sections on history, society, people, government, and military structure. Excellent bibliographical sections at the end of each chapter direct you to more comprehensive works on each topic.

Travelogues

Paul Bowles has been one of the most prolific authors and translators of fiction (see fiction section) and nonfiction works covering Morocco. In the travelogue category, Bowles's *Their Heads Are Green and Their Hands Are Blue* (New York: Random House, 1963) is a collection of nine travel essays chronicling his journeys around North Africa and other areas. In Morocco, he traveled around the country to collect samples of traditional music.

Elias Canetti's *The Voices of Marrakesh* (translated from the German by J. A. Underwood; New York: Continuum Press, 1981) is also a collection of anecdotes, impressions, and observations of life in Morocco, mainly Marrakesh in the early 1960s. It offers some interesting insights into the *mellah*— the Jewish quarter—and the camel market on the outskirts of Marrakesh. However, the text occasionally seems erratic, perhaps because of poor translating.

Elizabeth Warnock Fernea's *A Street in Marrakesh* (New York: Anchor Press, Doubleday, 1975) is an excellent account of her family's one-year stay in a house in the heart of the Marrakesh *medina*. She describes the lives of her Moroccan neighbors, particularly the women, first as the outsider she was during the first months and then as an insider, almost a full participant in the local culture. Fernea never assumes, however, that she could completely assimilate; friendship and understanding seems to have been her principal objective. Read this book for insight into the traditional separation of men and women in Moroccan society, the intricacies of wedding ceremonies, and popular superstitions and perceptions. A quick read!

Lady Agnes Grove's *Seventy-One Days Camping in Morocco* (London: Longman, 1902) is a remarkable description of a camping trip made by Lady Grove and friends in 1899. She traveled throughout Morocco and met with a variety of people, including the sultan. The photographs she took of unveiled women in their homes are especially interesting.

Lawrence Harris's *With Mulai Hafid at Fez: Behind the Scenes in Morocco* (Boston: Badger, 1910) is a wonderful description of his experiences at the court of Sultan Mulai Hafid. With typically dry wit, Harris writes about how his London newspaper sent him to Morocco to sketch the sultan and write about life in Morocco. A good, but strongly opinionated, anecdotal account of tribal and royal relations.

Walter Burton Harris, another British journalist, also wrote about late nineteenth- and early twentieth-century Morocco. His books include *The Land of the African Sultan: Travels in Morocco 1887, 1888, 1889* (London: Sampson, Low, Marston, Searle & Rivington, 1889) covering his journey through northern Morocco and on to Marrakesh; a summary of his Moroccan travels in *Morocco That Was* (Edinburgh: Blackwood, 1921), most of which was excerpted in Gavin Maxwell's *Lords of the Atlas*; and *Tafilelt: The Narrative of a Journey of Exploration in the Atlas Mountains and the Oases of the North-West Sahara* (London: Blackwood, 1895), which describes Harris's journey from Marrakesh over the High Atlas mountains and through the Dadés valley to the oasis region and traditional power center of Tafilelt. The latter book is full of minute details about the landscape and people that he encounters along the way.

Another interesting pair of works from the same period are by Robert Kerr, a medical missionary in Morocco from 1886 to 1892: *Morocco After Twenty-Five Years: A Description of the Country, Its Laws and Customs and the European Situation* (London: Murray & Evenden, 1912) and *Pioneering in Morocco: A Record of Seven Years' Medical Mission Work in the Palace and the Hut* (London: Allenson, 1894).

Another set of classic travelogues and historical accounts was written in the late nineteenth century and early twentieth century by Budgett Meakin, yet another British journalist. His principal works are crammed into three thick tomes: (1) *The Land of the Moors* (London: Swan Sonnenschein, 1901), a detailed description of almost every town and city in Morocco as well as the land; (2) *The Moorish Empire: A Historical Epitome*, (London: Swan Sonnenschein, 1901), tracing Morocco's history from the Roman period to the late nineteenth century, including an extensive bibliography and chapters on journalism in Morocco; and (3) *The Moors: A Comprehensive Description* (London: Swan Sonnenschein, 1902). Unlike the other two books, this last concentrates on daily life in Morocco and includes sections on etiquette, Berbers, Jews, marriage traditions and festivals. The latter book is fascinating and definitely worth a look if you can find a copy. The State Mutual Bank & Periodical Services (New York City) published a reprint of *Land of the Moors* in 1986.

Guidebooks

Robin G. Collomb's *The Atlas Mountains, Morocco* (Goring, Reading, Berkshire, England: West Col Productions, 1980) has been the only book in English covering mountaineering in the Atlas mountains. The introductory section includes sections on the flora and fauna, terrain, and local culture. However, its lack of maps—only four—is somewhat of a drawback.

The following books in French are more comprehensive and were supposed to be translated into English in 1989: *Le Haut Atlas Central*, a 376-page trail guide in French by resident Morocco explorer André Fougerolles that covers the High Central Atlas region in good, but somewhat technical detail. It costs about US $15 and is usually available at bookstores in Agadir, Rabat, and Marrakesh. *Ski dans le Haut Atlas de Marrakesh*, by Claude Cominelli, is a decent guide in French for those travelers with the time and wherewithal to ski along remote, unmarked trails in the High Atlas. The well-organized ski center at Oukaïmeden is also described. It's usually available in Rabat, Marrakesh, and Agadir bookstores for about US $10.

Mark Ellingham and Shaun McVeigh's *The Real Guide to Morocco* (Englewood Cliffs, N.J.: Prentice-Hall, 1989) is a good general low-budget guide to all Morocco. The first edition of this book was known as *The Rough Guide to Morocco*.

Fiction

Paul Bowles's *Sheltering Sky* is an existentialist novel set in North Africa, probably in southern Morocco. It's the type of book that you probably must read more than once to fully appreciate. The central characters are a U.S. couple whose lives seem totally futile. As they travel through North Africa, their personalities seem to disintegrate. The husband dies, leaving his wife alone in an isolated desert town where she begins a troubling journey in which she loses all sense of self. For travelers, its chief value lies in its detailed descriptions of the desert and its inhabitants.

Paul Bowles was also renowned for his translations of pre-eminent Moroccan poetry and literature, including several by Mohammed Mrabet: *A Boy Who Set the Fire & Other Stories* (Los Angeles: Black Sparrow Press, 1975), *Harmless Poisons, Blameless Sins* (Santa Barbara, Calif.: Black Sparrow Press, 1976), *The Lemon* (London: Peter Owen, 1969), *Look and Move On* (Los Angeles: Black Sparrow Press, 1976), *Love with a Few Hairs* (London: Peter Owen, 1967), and *M'hashish* (San Francisco: City Lights Books, 1969).

He has also translated a book titled *For Bread Alone* (London: Peter

Owen, 1973) by a Moroccan writer named Mohammed Choukri. Although this book was written as fiction, most of it is an autobiographical account of Choukri's childhood and struggle for survival.

History

One particularly noteworthy book is *Fez in the Age of the Marinides* (Norman: University of Oklahoma Press, 1961), by Roger Le Tourneau (translated by A. Clement). It describes several aspects of fourteenth-century Fez commercial and religious life, and thus gives some insight into daily urban life in medieval Morocco.

Nineteenth and Twentieth Centuries

One of the classic works covering the period from 1893 to 1956 is *Lords of the Atlas: The Rise and Fall of the House of Glaoua* (London: Longman, Pan Books, 1967), by Gavin Maxwell. This book is officially banned in Morocco because it covers a period in which the sultanate was made powerless by the collusion of the French Protectorate government and the Glaoua family. Under the leadership of T'hami El Glaoui, the family gained immense power and ostensibly ruled the country with French assistance from Marrakesh and their immense kasbah, or fortress, at Telouet. Do not attempt to bring a copy of this book into Morocco.

John Waterbury has written several books about Morocco, mostly works of political history and analysis. *The Commander of the Faithful: The Moroccan Political Elite—A Study in Segmented Politics* (London: Weidenfeld & Nicolson, 1970) isn't as pedantic as his other works. It traces the development of Morocco's political elite and shows how the king manages to maintain power.

Historian Douglas Porch's *The Conquest of Morocco* (New York: Fromm International, 1986; New York: Knopf, 1983) is a quite readable account of the French conquest of Morocco between 1903 and 1914. He presents a lively history replete with colorful prose describing people, places, and events.

A more comprehensive list of titles on the history and politics of Morocco can be found in Volume 47 of the World Bibliographical series, published by Clio Press of Santa Barbara, California, and Oxford, England.

BOOKS ABOUT ALGERIA

One of the best introductions to Algeria is *Algeria: A Country Study* (Washington D.C.: Foreign Area Studies, American University, 1985). The format is the same as that of the Country Studies of Morocco and

Tunisia. Consult the book's bibliographical sections for references to more comprehensive works on each topic.

A photographic introduction to the Sahara, Kazuyoshi Nomachi's *The Sahara* (Newton Abbot, England: Westbridge Books, 1978), will whet your appetite for exploring this part of Algeria. The author-photographer traveled throughout the great desert and compiled this book of sixty-three color and black and white photographs. It includes a brief introductory section on the land and its inhabitants.

Guidebooks

Jon and Valerie Stevens's *Algeria and the Sahara: A Handbook for Travellers* (London: Constable, 1977) is an outdated, but still somewhat useful, guidebook with details on forty possible routes through the Sahara. About the only other guidebook in English with information about Algeria is *Fodor's North Africa* guide. Some of Fodor's practical information, such as hotel and restaurant listings, can be helpful. New editions are published annually, but not all the information seems to be updated annually.

History

Medieval Period

William Spencer's *Algiers in the Age of the Corsairs* (Norman: University of Oklahoma Press, 1976) describes the rise of Algiers as a naval power, mainly for piracy, in the sixteenth and seventeenth centuries. Some of the more interesting parts include descriptions of the sources and revenues of the pirate states and a portrayal of Algiers as a cosmopolitan city.

Nineteenth and Twentieth Centuries

Isabelle Eberhardt's *The Oblivion Seekers & Other Writings* (San Francisco, Calif.: City Lights Books, 1975; translated by Paul Bowles) is a semiautobiographical account of her unusual life as a Muslim convert among the nomadic tribes of the Sahara.

At about the same time Eberhardt was seeking oblivion somewhere deep within the Sahara, the French were attempting to conquer the desert. In his book *The Conquest of the Sahara* (New York: Knopf, 1984), Douglas Porch describes in beautiful detail life in the Sahara; included are accounts of various French military expeditions, Tuareg caravans and raiders, villages and settlements. He has made a complicated period of Algerian history much more palatable for the average reader.

Not long after the French entered Algeria in 1830, an Algerian nationalism movement began to emerge. Abd El Kader, emir of Algeria, is considered one of the founders of this movement, a movement that really didn't gain full momentum until the 1950s, about a century after Abd El Kader's rule. In *The Phantom Caravan of Abd El Kader, Emir of Algeria* (Hicksville, N.Y.: Exposition Press, 1975), Vista Clayton presents a biography of Abd El Kader (also spelled Abdel Kader, Abd Al Kader, Abdel Qadir, Abd El Qadir, Abd Al Qadir, and probably a few other ways) and describes the rise of Algerian nationalism.

Algerian nationalism is also the focus of Edward Behr's *The Algerian Problem* (London: Greenwood Press, 1976). Behr recounts the history of French involvement in Algeria as it led to the rise of Algerian nationalism and the war for independence.

Alistair Horne's *A Savage War of Peace: Algeria 1954–1962* (New York: Penguin Books, 1987) and Mahfoud Bennoune's *The Making of Contemporary Algeria, 1830–1987: Colonial Upheavals and Post-Independence Development* (Cambridge, England: Cambridge University Press, 1988) both examine this pivotal period of Algerian history. To understand Algeria today requires some understanding of Algeria during the war for independence, which these books offer.

Frantz Fanon's *Wretched of the Earth* (New York: Grove Press, 1965) covers the war for independence from Fanon's vantage point as a psychiatrist who had been treating French and Algerian victims of the war. As a result of his experience after joining the war against the French, Fanon concludes that in a colonial struggle violence and freedom are connected. He also describes the difficulty of sustaining revolutionary fervor and ideals after independence and questions the formation of a new culture in a newly independent nation. Many of the issues he raises, particularly in regards to culture and identity, are germane to Algerian society today.

The People and the Land

Christopher Krüger edited *The Sahara* (New York: Putman, 1969), an introduction to the land and the people of the great desert. Although as a whole it's outdated, most of the book is still relevant, particularly the sections on flora, fauna, geology, and prehistory of the Sahara.

For more information on the region's fascinating ancient history, try to track down Henri Lhote's *The Search for the Tassili Frescoes: Story of the Prehistoric Rock-Paintings of the Sahara*, translated by Alan Houghton Brodrick (New York: Dutton Books, 1959). Lhote was one of the first explorers to "catalogue" thousands of the frescoes. This book is his analysis of the paintings and interpretation of prehistoric life in the Sahara.

In *The Tuareg* (London: Gentry Books, 1973), Kenneth and Julie

Flavin present the Tuareg, nomadic inhabitants of the Sahara, in a sympathetic light. This book examines the traditional Tuareg way of life and the changes that are threatening and, in some cases, destroying this society. In *The Tuareg: People of Ahaggar* (New York: St. Martin's Press, 1977), Jeremy H. Keenen focuses on the nomadic Kel Ahaggar Tuareg tribe of the Ahaggar (or Hoggar) mountains.

Farther north around Ghardaïa are found the Mozabite people. Their secretive community is examined—too briefly—in an article in the March-April 1976 edition of *Africa Report* (vol. 21, no. 2). At least, you can gain some insight into their community.

The Kabyles of the Kabylie mountains are described in the Family of Man series, no. 33 (1975), in a brief study by Richard I. Lawless.

BOOKS ABOUT TUNISIA

As with Morocco and Algeria, the Country Study on Tunisia, *Tunisia: A Country Study* (Washington D.C.: Foreign Area Studies, American University, 1986), is a comprehensive overview of the country, although a recent edition hasn't yet been published that covers the post-Bourguiba period. A new edition is due soon. The sections on history, society, people, government, and military structure are mostly still valid. Excellent bibliographical sections at the end of each chapter direct you to more comprehensive works on each topic.

Kenneth J. Perkins's *Tunisia: Crossroads of the Islamic and European Worlds* (Boulder, Colo.: Westview Press, 1986), is a well-written analysis of Tunisian history from the first millennium B.C. to the mid-1980s just before the demise of Bourguiba. It includes an important (increasingly timely) section on the rise of Islamic fundamentalism in Tunisia.

Dwight Ling's *Tunisia: From Protectorate to Republic* (Ann Arbor, Mich.: Books on Demand, 1967) is still an important introduction to Tunisian history.

The Rough Guide to Tunisia (New York: Routledge, Chapman & Hall, 1985), by Peter Morris, is similar to the *Real Guide to Morocco* (see above; it will probably be named the *Real Guide to Tunisia* by the time this is published). It's a good budget guide to just about every point of interest in Tunisia, with especially useful sections on hotels and restaurants.

For important historical insights into the Carthaginian Empire, read the classic the *Aeneid* by Virgil. Books I and IV of this epic Roman poem recount the love story of Queen Dido (founder of Carthage) and Aeneas (founder of Rome). By allusion, you can get a fairly good idea of life in Carthage before the Romans razed it.

PART TWO

ॐ

Morocco

CHAPTER 4

Morocco

Name:	Kingdom of Morocco (Al Mamlaka al-Maghribiyya)
Political status:	Constitutional monarchy with one legislative house
Capital:	Rabat
Population:	23.9 million (U.N. Bureau of Statistics, 1989)
Land area:	458,730 square kilometers (176,833 square miles) excluding the western Sahara, which is 178,000 square kilometers (68,725 square miles)
Other prominent Languages:	Berber dialects (three most prominent: Rif, Tamazight, and the Shleuh); French (especially in government and business); Spanish in northern region near the Rif mountains; Arabic
Currency:	Dirham (DH); and francs (100 francs = 1 dirham; but francs are seldom used)
Approximate exchange rate:	DH 8.26 = US $1

The Arabs call it the Maghreb, "Land Where the Sun Sets", "Land of the West". Morocco is a predominantly Arab and Muslim kingdom with a distinct history, culture, and geography. Situated at the western edge of the Middle East and the northwest corner of Africa, Morocco is a blend of Arab, African, and European influences. It's both developed and undeveloped, traditional and modern, hot and cold, frustrating and exhilarating, overall an often rocky marriage of East and West and North and South.

For travelers, the geography is also important in other ways. Morocco is a country between the Sahara and the sea with snow-capped mountains, deserts dotted with dunes and lush oases, and landscapes carved and sculpted by an eternity of rivers and once-active volcanoes. Adventuring in Morocco can be as diverse as the land and limited only by ability, imagination, and time—skiing and trekking through the mountains, a camel safari in the desert, visits to the ancient kasbahs and villages of the countryside, and miniexpeditions through the medieval walled medinas in many of Morocco's towns and cities.

THE NATURAL ENVIRONMENT

Physical Characteristics

Morocco is at the northwesternmost corner of the African continent with coastlines along both the Atlantic Ocean and the Mediterranean Sea. Most of the country lies at an average altitude of 800 m (2,600 ft) above sea level atop a plate margin. The margin is a seismically unstable area between two of the six major tectonic plates that comprise the top 80 km of Earth's crust. Geologists have theorized that all six plates, thus all seven continents, were connected about 200 million years ago and split into continents over the following 100 million years. About 60 million years ago, the Mediterranean (or Tethys Sea, as geologists call it) was much larger than it is today, but it was beginning to shrink as Europe and Africa moved closer together and gradually formed the two main mountain chains that now define much of Morocco. The main chains are the Rif along the northern coast, which was attached tens of millions of years ago to ranges across the Mediterranean on the Iberian peninsula, and the three chains of the Atlas mountains running through the center of Morocco. These chains divide the country into specific climatic and geographical zones, which have, in turn, significantly influenced Morocco's history, culture, and society.

The Rif mountains are a crescent of limestone peaks separated from the Mediterranean by a narrow coastal plain. The mountains shelter the plain from the cooler winds of the Atlantic Ocean, thus resulting in a temperate Mediterranean climate. Three rivers—the Oued Laou, the Oued Rhis, and the Oued Nakor—flow from the Rif across the plain and into the Mediterranean. From the southern slopes, the Oued Loukkos flows along the edge of the fertile Rharb plain, through the city of Larache and into the Atlantic. A tributary from the Rif feeds the Oued Sebou, one of Morocco's longest and strongest rivers. The Rif peaks average about 1,494 m (4,900 ft), with the highest—Jebel Tidirhine—rising to 2,458 m (8,058 ft). They are separated from the Atlas chain to the southeast by the Taza pass, which also connects much of eastern Morocco to the Atlantic plains.

The Atlas mountains form a great spinelike swath of ranges along a southwest to northeast axis in Morocco and then west to east in Algeria to the edge of Tunisia. In Morocco, there are three principal ranges: the High Atlas (Haut Atlas) is the longest (about 740 km, or 460 miles) and has the highest peaks (Mount Toubkal at 4,165 m, or 13,665 ft); the Middle Atlas (Moyen Atlas) between the Rif and the High Atlas ranges; and the lower Anti-Atlas range that stretches southwest from the High Atlas to the Atlantic. The Atlas mountains act as a barrier trapping most of the moist air and rain that flows off the Atlantic. Consequently, most

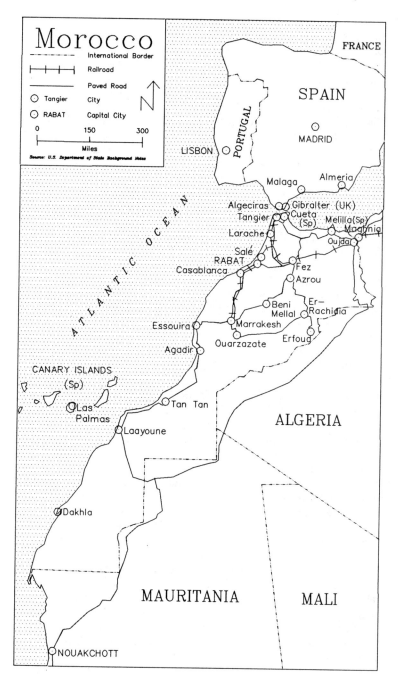

Morocco

- ─·─·─·─ International Border
- ├─┼─┼─┤ Railroad
- ─────── Paved Road
- ◯ Tangier   City
- ◎ RABAT   Capital City

0   150   300
Miles

Source: U.S. Department of State Background Notes

FRANCE

SPAIN

PORTUGAL

MADRID

LISBON

Malaga   Almeria

Algeciras   Gibralter (UK)
Tangier   Cueta
              (Sp)   Melilla(Sp)
Larache   Maghnia
                        Oujda
Salé
RABAT
Casablanca   Fez
                      Azrou

              Beni   Er-
              Mellal   Rachidia
Essouira   Marrakesh
Ouarzazate   Erfoud
Agadir

ATLANTIC OCEAN

CANARY ISLANDS
    (Sp)

Las
Palmas   Tan Tan

Laayoune   ALGERIA

Dakhla

MAURITANIA   MALI

NOUAKCHOTT

of Morocco southeast of the Atlas mountains is markedly hotter and dryer than the rest of the country.

The various rivers, streams, and tributaries that flow from the Atlas mountains have spawned several fertile plains on the Atlantic side and lush oasis valleys on the southeast side. The Rharb plain south of the Rif mountains merges with the Fez plain farther inland and a vast coastal plateau that stretches south almost as far as Sidi Ifni. The most fertile and strategically important parts of the plateau include the Tadla plain near Beni Mellal, the Haouz plain around Marrakesh, and the Sous plain around Agadir and Taroudannt. Until independence in 1956, many conflicts in Morocco were due to divergent claims over these plains.

Equally important have been the oasis valleys of the Drâa especially between Ouarzazate and Zagora, the Dadés from Ouarzazate to the Dadés and Tohdra gorges, and the Ziz from Er-Rachidia to Rissani at the edge of the Sahara. The Dadés and Tohdra gorges are an especially great area for hiking and exploring.

Two Spanish enclaves remain on Morocco's Mediterranean coast— Ceuta and Melilla, vestiges of the Spanish Protectorate that existed in the Rif region of northern Morocco until 1956. Morocco wants the territories returned; however, they remain part of Spain.

Climate

Although there are several climatic zones, Morocco's climate is easy to summarize because it varies with the terrain. Along the Mediterranean coastal plain, the weather is fairly stable all year, with temperatures averaging about 12°C (54°F) in the winter and 24°C (75°F) in the summer and sporadic rainfall in the autumn and winter. The Atlantic coastal plains have similar, sometimes lower, average temperatures with somewhat fewer inches of rain. Rainfall in the foothills and inland plains adjacent to the High Atlas mountains follows patterns similar to the Atlantic plains. The rainy season is generally from November to February or March with snow falling at higher than 1,981 m (6,500 ft) at about the same time. Many of the peaks of the High and Middle Atlas ranges remain snowcapped and cold (as low as -20°C or -4°F) often as late as June and rain is possible throughout the year.

In the desert regions around Ouarzazate, Zagora, and Er-Rachidia, temperature differentials can be extreme. Summers can be scorching; temperatures as high as 120°F have been recorded at Zagora. As with most desert environments, winter nights can be freezing. Rainfall is generally rare but has been known to occur, and when it does the results are spectacular—tiny plants sprout in the sand and coat the dunes with green splotches, rainbows appear on the horizon, and the camels screech and groan in confusion.

Flora & Fauna

With a variety of climatic zones, Morocco also has a variety of flora and fauna, but only the legendary *argan* tree is not also found in other Mediterranean and North African countries.

Morocco was once the habitat for animals now found only in zoos or other parts of Africa. Fossils and bones discovered show that elephants, lions, and giraffes once roamed throughout Morocco, but they have long since disappeared. Elephants, perhaps, haven't been seen in Morocco since about 218 B.C., when the Carthaginian general Hannibal passed through with an army of 40,000 soldiers and a force of elephants en route to crossing the Pyrenees and Alps to fight Roman forces at the Trebia river.

Today, the most common animals seen in Morocco are camels, horses, and donkeys. Camels and some types of horses were introduced to Morocco through trans-Saharan and trans-African trade caravans before the advent of Islam. As a mode of transport in Morocco, however, camels have generally been replaced by pickup trucks and four-wheel-drive vehicles. People still buy and sell camels in public markets such as Goulimine, but mostly for their meat, hair, skin, and occasionally milk. Camel milk continues to be a chief source of sustenance for the relatively few remaining nomads in North Africa. For more information about camels see Chapter 1.

Other commonly seen animals in Morocco include the *mouflon*, which is also known as the *aoudad*, wild sheep, or Barbary sheep and resembles the wild bighorn sheep of North America; the Edmi and Dorcas gazelles, which resemble each other, the *macaco* monkey, also known as the Barbary macaque or ape, which averages about 11 to 15 kilograms (24 to 34 pounds), and has yellow-gray to gray-brown fur; and the *fennec* or desert fox.

The fennec weighs a maximum of only about 3 pounds (1 1/4 kilos) and has disproportionately large ears. It's the smallest fox, and the only mammal out of fourteen species living in Sahara that can live away from water and oases for extended periods. The fox survives in the desert by digging burrows just beneath the surface. Its great ability to survive in a harsh environment has spawned a common proverb in North Africa that translates into something like "Two dogs make a fennec play, three dogs make him laugh, four make him run about, five make him flee, and six finally catch him."

Flora in Morocco is similar to that found on the Iberian peninsula and in other parts of the western Mediterranean. Only the argan tree, found primarily near the Atlantic coastal city of Essaouira, is unique to Morocco. Although its wood makes excellent charcoal and a popular oil can be extracted from its prune-sized nuts, the tree is best known for attracting goats that climb into its branches to chew on the leaves. Camels also like the leaves. Argan oil is used as lamp and heating oil and as an ingredient in making soap.

In the mountains, Atlas cedars, yew junipers, and firs are the most common trees. Atlas cedars, which are found only in Morocco and Algeria, are evergreens that can grow as tall as about 37 m (120 ft) and have cones as long as three inches. The yew juniper is a slow-growing evergreen that's also common in Europe and the Himalaya mountains. It can grow as tall as about 21 m (70 ft) and is distinguished by its red-brown bark and flat, inch-long leaves.

In the Rif mountains and on the Rharb plain, the cork oak (genus Quercus) is the most common tree. It reaches a maximum height of 18 m (60 ft) and bears an acornlike fruit. About every nine years, its thick bark is stripped and used as a principal source of cork. This tree is related to the evergreen oaks that cover about one-third of all forested areas in Morocco (holm and evergreen oaks) and are commonly found in California (live oak).

Most of Morocco's forested areas are found on the northern slopes of the Atlas mountains, while the southern slopes are much more arid and rocky and have less vegetation.

On the Tadla and Haouz plains, two species of the fruit-bearing jujube tree are prevalent—the *Zizyphus lotus* and the *Zizyphus spina-christi*. The former is also known as the jujube of the Lotus Eaters and is generally much smaller than jujube trees found in other parts of the world. In biblical times, the latter supposedly provided the thorny branches to make Christ's crown. Jujube fruit are the size of plums, and can be eaten fresh or cooked; little candies are made from the juice.

In the desert regions, particularly in oases, you'll see the famous date palm. Some palms reach as high as about 30.5 m (100 ft). Many of the palm trees around Marrakesh are date palms. Date palms grow about 23 m (75 ft) tall on the average, and each palm produces several bunches of dates. A bunch is about 1,000 dates (8 kg, or 18 lbs). Parts of the tree are used for basketry, timber, boxes, rope, animal feed, and fuel.

Eucalyptus trees (of which there are many species) are becoming increasingly common in the Moroccan desert. They were imported from Australia for use in antidesertification programs, particularly near Ouarzazate, because they retain water much better than most other trees. Eucalyptus leaves are also supposedly popular with camels.

Almost everywhere in Morocco, except at high elevations, you'll see esparto grass, which is distinguished by its short, feathery bristles. Its tough fibers are often used for making rope and cloth.

HISTORY

Morocco's early history is marked by the arrival of Berbers in about 2000 B.C. Linguists have been able to trace the origins of various Berber dialects to southwestern Asia; a second, simultaneous influx of Berbers is thought to have come from central Africa. After settling in Morocco, the Berbers were also influenced by contact with Phoenician traders who had established iron and salt stations along the Atlantic and Mediterranean coasts.

The Phoenician or Punic colony of Carthage, which was based in present-day Tunisia, became an independent empire by the fifth century B.C. The Carthaginians controlled most of present-day Morocco as far inland as the coastal plains, which had been settled by Punicized Berber farmers. In the mountains beyond the plains and trading stations, however, Berber tribes predominated.

Until the arrival of Arabs in the late seventh century, the Berber tribes were united in various loose confederations. Some semblance of tighter political organization had appeared by the second century B.C. with the establishment of Berber kingdoms, but they were still subject to the military whims and requirements of first the Carthaginian and then the Roman Empire. Rome divided North Africa into three provinces with the northern portion of present-day Morocco called Mauretania Tingitana. Their trading posts became towns such as Tingis, the capital and predecessor of modern-day Tangier, and Volubilis, near present-day Fez. Camels, Christianity, Jews exiled from Palestine after the destruction of the Temple in Jerusalem in A.D. 70, and Vandals (a Germanic tribe) were all introduced to the province during the Roman period. By the sixth century, the Roman Empire had vanished, to be replaced by the Byzantine Empire, which exercised limited control over present-day Morocco.

Stronger challenges to Berber autonomy came with the Arab invasions that began in A.D. 683, only 51 years after the Prophet Mohammed's death. By A.D. 710, Arab armies under Musa Ibn Nusayr were converting plains Berbers to Islam and gaining control of most of the low-lying areas of Morocco. With the help of Berber recruits, the Arab armies also conquered and converted the Iberians (present-day Spain and Portugal) and established Arab-Berber settlements throughout the peninsula.

The Arab conquest of Iberia created a crescent of Islam from present-day Spain across North Africa to Baghdad. Authority over this vast empire was exercised by the Umayyad caliphate at Damascus until about A.D. 750, when the Abbassid dynasty moved the caliphate to Baghdad. Their authority was challenged throughout the Islamic world, thus precipitating various dissident movements, such as the Alids in

Arabia. By 788 an Alid dissident named Moulay Idriss Ibn Abdallah had been forced to flee to the west; he settled among the Berber Arwaba tribe of Morocco.

Moulay Idriss gained the respect of the Islamized Arwaba Berbers, in part because he claimed to be a direct descendant of the Prophet Mohammed. Once his position as a religious and political leader was firmly established, he began working toward independence from the Abbassid caliphate. He was succeeded by his son Idriss II, whose mother was a Berber. Idriss II's cultural and political connections to both Arabs and Berbers allowed him to solidify his authority and lay the foundations for the walled city of Fez in the early ninth century. Fez became the capital of the first independent Islamic Moroccan state. Idriss II's efforts were short-lived, however, because his son Mohammed who succeeded him divided the state among family members and destroyed the Idrissid state.

After several years of chaos and anarchy, a group of Sanhaji nomads from the western Sahara region united in the eleventh century to re-create an Islamic state. At this time the foundations for the Marrakesh were laid and the Almoravid dynasty was spawned. The Almoravids remained in power only until 1147, when they were conquered by Almohads. The Almohads were even more fanatical than the Almoravids, more intent on creating a united Islamic state. Although this goal wasn't exactly attained, they did build up Marrakesh as one of North Africa's greatest centers of religious scholarship. Less than a century later, however, they were ejected from power by the Beni Merenid Berber tribe of eastern Morocco.

The Merenids also seemed to be religious fanatics clamoring for a unitary Islamic state. However, they claimed that their rule was a continuation of the ninth-century Idrissid state, so they abandoned Marrakesh for Fez, which was the Idrissid—thus original—capital of Morocco. Fez prospered as a cultural and religious center even as Arab-Berber control over Iberia was vanquished by Christian Crusaders in the Middle Ages. The last Muslim stronghold, Granada, fell in 1492; all Spanish Jews were expelled from Spain in 1492 and Muslims were likewise expelled by 1502. Most of the refugees flocked across the Mediterranean to Morocco and many of the best educated—architects, artists, scholars, and others—settled in Fez.

Spanish and Portuguese crusaders, though, didn't stop their conquests at the Iberian peninsula, but continued to the Moroccan coastal towns and settlements. Moroccan marabouts—leaders of religious cults that blended Islam with traditional Berber saint worship—were the only leaders capable of organizing resistance to the Christian invasions. Resistance was effective, but diffused because power was spread among several clanlike marabout groups. The lack of cohesive power among these predominately Berber marabout groups opened the way for an Arab tribe called the Saadians to seize power.

The Saadians ousted the Portuguese from Agadir, Safi, and Azzemmour in the early sixteenth century, captured Fez from the Berbers in 1559, and re-established Marrakesh as a capital. In 1578 the Portuguese invaded Morocco in an attempt to regain control over their lost settlements and expand their empire, but their forces were destroyed by Ksar El Kebir (Alcàzarquivir) in the Battle of the Three Kings. Sultan Abd Al Malik died in the battle and was succeeded by his brother Ahmed, who added the title "Al Mansur" (the Victorious) to his name.

Mansur united and expanded the empire as far as Timbuktu and the Niger river basin in present-day Nigeria. For Morocco the chief, though dubious, benefit of this expansion was an increase in the slave trade. The black-skinned Harratine people who today inhabit southern Morocco are believed to be descendants of these slaves. After Mansur's death in 1603, the empire disintegrated into rival city-states and autonomous tribal regions, and piracy thrived on the coast. The seventeenth century became the heyday of the infamous Barbary pirates.

In 1660 yet another phoenix, an Arab leader or *sharif* from Tafilelt named Moulay Rashid, rose from the ashes of the anarchy and established the Alawite dynasty. He claimed to be a descendant of Ali Ibn Abu Talib, son-in-law of the Prophet Mohammed, founder of Islam. His brother, Moulay Ismail, succeeded him in 1672, established Meknes as the dynasty's capital, and consolidated his control over Morocco by building a chain of *kasbahs* (fortresses) and an army of 150,000. He ruled Morocco with an iron fist, and—with the help of his piratical Salli Rovers— enslaved, tortured, and massacred most Europeans who wandered into Morocco. Again, however, the unity of his empire rested on his personal leadership, so after his death in 1727 the empire again collapsed.

A smaller unified empire rose under Sultan Mohammed III who ruled from 1757 to 1790. The most notable events of his rule were that Morocco became one of the first countries to recognize the independent United States and that a treaty of peace and friendship with the United States was signed in 1787. The treaty is still in effect, thus making it the oldest bilateral agreement in U.S. diplomatic history.

Through the nineteenth century, foreign intervention in Morocco increased, particularly in terms of the commercial privileges and exemptions from local laws granted to European traders. In 1880, Moulay Hassan I, who ruled from 1873 to 1894, organized the Madrid Conference to play European powers against each other and thereby maintain Morocco's independence. His suave diplomatic maneuvering, however, merely delayed rather than prevented European control over Morocco.

On his death, Hassan's chamberlain, a former slave named Bou Ahmed, installed the Sultan's 14-year-old son, Abd Al Aziz, in power.

Aziz was totally unprepared for ruling the country, so Bou Ahmed ruled through him. He diverted Aziz's attention from government by providing him with many of the latest European and U.S. toys and gadgets—bicycles, cameras, toy boats, clocks, and many other things. When Bou Ahmed died in 1900 and Aziz took full control, he was still unprepared for governing. Europeans were easily able to increase their commercial interests in Morocco and lend the government money for a variety of projects.

By 1907, Aziz had sunk Morocco heavily into debt to Europeans, thus opening the country up to further intervention. Europeans were hungering to gain control of Morocco because after the Berlin Conference of 1884 most of the rest of Africa had been divided among various European powers. France was ensconced in Algeria and Tunisia and most of West Africa. Great Britain effectively controlled much of eastern Africa from Cairo to Capetown. Germany had a strong presence in "German East Africa" or Tanganyika—Tanzania, Zanzibar, Burundi, and Rwanda. Italy, Spain, Portugal, and Belgium also had significant claims to parts of Africa. Morocco was the only African country that hadn't been assigned to a European power. However, a series of conferences and secret agreements between 1901 and 1906 changed that.

In 1901 France and Italy secretly agreed to respect each other's interests in North Africa; Italy had been jockeying for a claim on Tripolitania (present-day Libya). In 1904 the Entente Cordiale between France and Great Britain guaranteed (1) cooperation against Germany, (2) a British presence in Egypt and Gibraltar, and (3) French influence in Morocco. Later that year, France and Spain secretly agreed to similar spheres of influence; Spain was allotted northern Morocco. Germany was upset by these agreements and arrangements because it was excluded from exercising political influence in North Africa. At Germany's behest, another international conference was called in 1906 to discuss Morocco. Rather than weaken other European claims and strengthen Germany's claim on Morocco, the conference recognized Moroccan independence and, in a seemingly contradictory move, specified the terms of French and Spanish protectorates in Morocco.

By 1907 France had invaded Morocco from Algeria, on the pretext that tribal rebellions threatened the safety of Europeans in and around Oujda near the border. The invasion precipitated a massacre of European workers in Casablanca, thus in turn prompting the bombardment of Casablanca and the landing of more French troops, including many Foreign Legionnaires. Sultan Abd Al Aziz was powerless against the impending French and Spanish occupation and was, consequently, deposed by his brother Moulay Abd Al Hafid.

Moulay Abd Al Hafid also proved to be powerless against the growing strength of French and Spanish interests in Morocco. He was torn between securing foreign commercial interests in Morocco to prevent foreign political incursions and forcing foreigners out of Morocco to appease his people. He failed at both undertakings and instead sought to escape his troubles through drugs. By 1912 Hafid had been forced to sign the Treaty of Fez, which formally established the French and Spanish protectorates. However, he refused to implement the various provisions of the treaty and was therefore forced by the French to abdicate.

The Protectorates: 1912–1956

Establishment of a "protectorate" over Morocco was a lightly veiled way for the French to assume control over Morocco's government and economy. Great Britain, Italy, and other nations had at one time also established protectorates in other countries.

The French Protectorate

With the official establishment of the French Protectorate, Marshal Louis Lyautey arrived to serve as the protectorate's first "resident general". His main responsibilities were to pacify the countryside and centralize government authority. Lyautey quickly did the latter, but acceptance or at least recognition of this authority throughout the country didn't occur until 1934, when the tribal resistance in the Middle Atlas mountains was finally quashed.

The resident general followed a colonial policy of coercion instead of military force, although he used force when necessary. He strived to rule with the country, not against it, which meant respecting local traditions. In practice, this became a "divide and rule" policy, whereby Lyautey gained control by establishing alliances with cooperative tribal *qa'ids* (local leaders or rulers). The Glaoui family, which is described in the Telouet section, especially benefited from this policy and greatly increased its power and influence in southern Morocco. As a result, the sultan's power was diminished; he was coerced into transferring thousands of hectares of the best agricultural land to European ownership.

Two distinct societies evolved in Morocco—one European and the other Moroccan. Everything was divided—schools, political organizations, and living quarters. New colonial cities—still referred to as the "*villes nouvelles*"—were built outside the traditional medina (town, or old town) quarters, parts of town that Lyautey had strived to preserve. To succeed and advance in this society, an educated Moroccan had to adapt to and work through and with the more powerful Frenchified half of society. The consciousness of this second-class position spawned the beginnings of a Moroccan independence movement in the 1920s.

At first the independence movement comprised members of the French-educated Moroccan elite, but after 1930 it became a popular movement. In 1930, French Protectorate officials proposed a law referred to as the Berber *zahir* or *dahir*, which was intended to strengthen traditional Berber judicial institutions such as the community councils. The Arab majority in Morocco perceived this proposal as another attempt by the French to divide and rule, to diminish Arab authority and Islamic culture. The proposal was abandoned in 1934 and replaced with reform plans that were more agreeable to the Arab population.

By 1943, the Istiqlal or independence party had been formed with the support of Sultan Mohammed Ibn Yusuf, whose Alawite dynasty had been ruling most of Morocco since the mid-seventeenth century. The sultan attempted to resist pressure to ratify laws that benefited the French more than they did the Moroccans. The French, in turn, arrested him for dissension in 1953 and then exiled him to Madagascar. The Istiqlal Party was banned at the end of 1952 because of violent riots in Casablanca, but it had attained an active membership of approximately 80,000 and hundreds of thousands of supporters throughout the country. The sultan's departure precipitated two years of violent demonstrations and terrorism. The only solutions remaining for the French were to allow the sultan to return in 1955 and to grant Morocco independence in 1956.

The Spanish Protectorate

The Spanish began administering their protectorate zone—northern Morocco—at about the same time as the French. However, the Spanish didn't have the military forces and economic strength to overcome Riffian resistance in the mountains and develop the region. In fact, the Riffians were even able to form an autonomous Riffian Republic led by Abd El Krim. The republic was "overthrown" only after the Spanish formed a temporary military alliance with the French and the mountains were invaded from both sides. Spain also granted Morocco independence in 1956, but retained the enclaves of Sidi Ifni (until the mid-1970s) on the Atlantic coast, and Ceuta and Melilla on the Mediterranean, both of which are still Spanish territory.

Independent Morocco

On independence, the sultan took the title "King Mohammed V" and emphasized his close ties to the independence-nationalist movement. His assumption of power was perceived as a continuation of this movement, rather than a contradiction. He died in 1961 and was succeeded by his son Hassan II, the current ruler.

Although the king was the supreme authority of the land, the Istiqlal

Party was an important part of the decision-making process. However, in 1959 the party was divided over differences of opinion concerning the influence of the monarchy on its programs and proposals. A leftist party called the UNFP—Union Nationale des Forces Populaires —was formed while the Istiqlal became more nationalist and supportive of the monarchy. A new constitution was ratified by both parties in 1962, but subsequent parliamentary elections resulted in neither having the majority of seats necessary to run the government. King Hassan II declared a state of emergency, annulled the parliament for five years, and ruled independently of both parties.

In 1971, a referendum created yet another constitution. The king seemed popular and firmly in control, with great popular support and loyal armed forces. That year, though, his position was made untenable by an attempted coup. A group of army officers led an attack on the king's palace during his birthday celebrations.

The king tried to squelch the resistance by forming another government in 1972, but there was yet another coup attempt. While returning from an official visit to Paris, the king's plane was attacked over Khenitra by a group of his air force jets. His plane was damaged, but returned safely. This plot, which had been planned by his minister of defense, General Oufkir, made Hassan increasingly suspicious of many of the government officials around him. In an effort to bolster his political image and popular support, he implemented two major populist programs: the redistribution of land expropriated from foreigners and the 1975 Green March to the Spanish Sahara.

Morocco had claimed the Spanish Sahara since independence, so when the Spanish announced their intention to withdraw, King Hassan II was anxious to annex the territory. To expedite the withdrawal, Hassan marched 350,000 Moroccan civilians across the Spanish frontier as a show of popular support for the annexation. Spain left the area in 1976, but granted administrative responsibilities to both Morocco and Mauritania because both claimed the territory. Algeria, however, opposed both countries' claims and instead supported an independence movement called the Polisario—*Frente Popular para la Liberación de Saguía El Hamra y Río de Oro*. After a military coup toppled the government of Mauritania in 1978, Morocco claimed the entire Spanish or western Sahara, as they called it, and began a protracted war with the Polisario.

The Polisario's demands for self-determination and independence were approved by the United Nations and a majority of the member states of the Organization for African Unity. A government-in-exile for the Saharawi Arab Democratic Republic (SADR) was formed, and the Polisario forces were supplied and maintained by the Algerians.

The Polisario still exists today, but its struggle has almost been completely quashed by Morocco's construction of a berm (dike) of fortified sand across the Sahara. The berm has isolated Polisario forces and prevented serious attacks on Moroccan forces, thus safeguarding the precious phosphate reserves at Bou Kraa in the heart of the western Sahara. Algeria is now offering less support to the Polisario and has normalized relations with Morocco. For travelers, that means easier passage across the Moroccan-Algerian border.

Morocco Today

Although phosphates are a major export, economic growth in Morocco has also been closely linked to tourism, subcontracting of manufacturing and assembly processes for European companies, the repatriated salaries of emigré workers, and foreign capital investment. Morocco has been attempting to become industrialized, but so far only about one-sixth of the country's gross domestic product comes from industry. Most of that is from light industry such as textile plants, subcontracting assembly and manufacturing, and food processing. There's still relatively little heavy industry.

Most of Morocco's population works in agriculture and related fields. Morocco is an agriculturally rich country that has the potential to be self-sufficient in food production. Until the population exploded over the last few decades, Morocco was self-sufficient in production of barley, corn, and wheat, but now it must import approximately one-third of what it requires. It has been more successful growing fruits and vegetables, enough to export around the world. Production of industrial crops such as sugar cane, cotton, sugar beets, and sunflowers has also been successful. Afforestation projects have created a burgeoning cellulose and paper pulp export industry.

Comparable success can be claimed in livestock raising, particularly cattle and sheep. Morocco is self-sufficient in meat and milk production.

Other important sectors of the economy include fishing and development of fishing ports with foreign assistance; mining of iron, zinc, lead, manganese, and cobalt; a petroleum industry that supplies approximately half of the country's needs; and hydroelectric power, of which only half the potential has been tapped.

POPULATION, PEOPLE, AND CULTURE

Population

Morocco's population of approximately 23,565,000 is a fast-growing set of diverse groups spread almost equally between cities and villages, but unevenly split between mountains and plains and the two main ethnic groups—Arabs and Berbers. The population has increased about

31 percent since 1971 and continues to grow at an estimated annual rate of about 2.9 percent to 3.3 percent. That means the population will probably double in about 24 years, unless, of course, drastic birth control measures are instituted. However, birth control is a touchy issue among both Arabs and Berbers because of social and, to a lesser extent, Islamic strictures.

Over 43 percent of the population is concentrated in the urban areas of greater Casablanca, Fez, Rabat-Salé, Marrakesh, and Tangier. The rest of the population is spread around approximately five major areas of mountains and plains. The populations of Casablanca and Rabat are estimated to be growing at about 5 percent annually. Around Casablanca on the Haouz plain, there are seminomadic cattle breeders and settlements of peasant farmers. To the east and south on the Sous plain and in the High Atlas and Anti-Atlas mountains, most of the people are Shleuh Berbers, one of the three principal Berber groups in Morocco, in villages and hamlets of mud-walled kasbahs. South and east of the High Atlas mountains is the Tafilelt, a region of cultivated oases and oasis valleys occupied by Arabs, arabized Berbers, and Shleuh Berbers. Along the northern edge of Morocco are the Rif mountains, which are settled by clannish Riffian Berber farmers and pastoralists. South of the Rif mountains is the Rharb plain, which is dominated by prosperous farming settlements and the urban centers of Fez and Meknes.

People and Culture

Arabs and Berbers are the predominant ethnic groups in Morocco, followed by Harratines, and a dwindling group of Jews and European settlers. Although there are differences between the two groups, both Arabs and Berbers are overwhelmingly Sunni Muslims of the Maliki order. They practice a uniquely Moroccan form of Islam that reflects the melding of Arab and Berber society.

When the first Arabs arrived in Morocco in the late seventh century, they introduced a predominantly urban Islamic culture and an autocratic system of rule. The Berbers were predominantly rural mountain people with strong animist-polytheistic beliefs and a communal system of rule. Over time, these differences lessened as both groups intermarried, the Berbers were converted to Islam, and the Arabs adopted the Berbers' belief in *baraka* and veneration of saints (known as *marabouts*) and spirits. Today, the differences between Arabs and Berbers are more linguistic than racial and, to a lesser extent, constitute differences in lifestyle, particularly in the status of women.

Officially, Berbers comprise about one-third of the total population. Less than 25 percent of the Berbers still speak only Berber; the rest speak Arabic and—increasingly, as education improves in the mountain villages—French. There are three main Berber languages or dialects, which are similar, but almost distinct enough to be considered separate languages. The Rif dialect is spoken in northern Morocco, primarily in the Rif mountains; the Tamazight (pronounced *ta-ma-zeer-kcht*) in the Middle Atlas mountains; and the Shleuh in the High Atlas mountains and on the Sous plain. All three are quite distinct from Arabic, but show Arabic influences in some words and phrases.

The word *baraka* is one of the most important words and concepts in Moroccan Arabic and Berber dialects. It's a word of thanks: *Baraka law feek* means "Thank you." It also symbolizes the saintliness and spirituality of certain chosen individuals and objects. However, baraka is so much a part of traditional Moroccan culture and society that trying to fully explain it in Western terms is impossible. Certain objects such as gun powder and salt are imbued with baraka because they help to ward off bad *jinn*, or spirits. Similarly, some individuals have been considered imbued with baraka or holiness because of past deeds or family ties and have been elevated to saintly status. Throughout Morocco these individuals' tombs have become shrines and cult centers where pilgrims seek solace for and protection from certain health and familial problems.

At fixed times of the year, pilgrims flock to *moussems*, the grand religious-social events that are held in almost every city, town, and village to honor local or regional marabouts. Descendants of the saint are often active participants in the celebrations. In addition to shrine visits (usually by Muslims only), festivities often include horse races, folk dances, music, and feasts under traditional-style tents.

The moussem of Moulay Idriss, who is considered the founder of the Idrissid dynasty and the first Moroccan "state," is the largest and grandest in the country, with many of the celebrations concentrated in the cities of Moulay Idriss and Fez. Other important moussems include the following:

- **Goulimine Moussem**, usually celebrated in early June with a huge gathering of camels and performances of the local *guedra* dance at Goulimine in southern Morocco.
- **Sidi Mohammed M'a El Anin Moussem.** Also called the Tan Tan Moussem, it's usually held in Tan Tan at the end of May or in early June and offers a great opportunity to see members of the traditionally nomadic Berber Tuareg tribe.
- **Moulay Idriss of Zerhoun Moussem**, a huge mid-August celebration in Meknes with several folklore troupe processions.
- **Moulay Abdallah Moussem.** Held near El Jadida in the small town of Moulay Abdallah toward the end of August, this is an immense moussem famous for its magnificent fantasias (traditional shows of horsemanship).
- **Sidi Ahmed Ou Moussa Moussem**, a five-day moussem in Tiznit that usually begins the third Thursday of August.

- **Imilchil "Wedding" Moussem,** usually held about the third week in September. More than 30,000 people gather at Imilchil for this three-day festival. Among many Berbers of the High Atlas mountains, this was the traditional time for getting married. For more details, see the Imilchil-High Atlas section.

The following moussems may also be worth checking out:

In Agadir province:
- Sidi Bou Moussa—at Ouled Teima toward the end of June
- Sidi Bihi—at Biougra in August

In Beni Mellal province:
- Moulay Aïssa Ben Driss—at Aït Attab in March
- Nouar—at Zaouia Houar in early September

In El Jadida province:
- Sidi Beni Dghough—at Sidi Bennour toward the end of September

In Fez province:
- Sidi Ahmed El Bernoussi—in Fez toward the end of September
- Sidi Lachen Lyoussi—at Séfrou toward the end of August
- Moulay Bouchta El Khemmar—at Fez toward the end of September

In Khenitra province:
- Sidi Ahmed Ben Mansour—at Moulay Bousselham in September
- Sidi Boughaba—at Aïn El Aouda toward the end of August
- Sidi Kacem—at Sidi Kacem in mid-September

In Ksar es Souk province:
- Moulay Ali Cherif—at Moulay Ali Cherif in mid-September
- Sidi Bou Yacoub—at Goulmima in mid-November

In Marrakesh province:
- Setti Fatma—at Ourika in August
- El Aouina—at Asni in July
- Moulay Ibrahim—at Asni in June
- Sidi Abdelkader Ben Yassine—at Marrakesh in early September

In Khenifra province:
- Moulay Bouazza—at Khenifra in mid-September

In Nador:
- Zaouia Kadiria—at Driouch toward the end of July

In Oujda province:
- Sidi Ali Ben Salah—at Ouled Amran in September
  Sidi Ahmed Ou Driss—at Taza in mid-September

In Ouarzazate province:
* Moulay Abdelmalek—at Aït Yahya toward the end of February
* Sidi Ahmed Ou Driss—at Tazenakht in August

In Rabat province:
* Dar Zhirou—at Rabat in August
* Sidi Lachen—at Temara in mid-August

In Safi province:
* Sidi Muallahbab—at Ras El Aïn in August
* Zaouia El Kettania—at Essaouira in early May
* Sidi Moghdoul—at Essaouira toward the end of August

In Settat province:
* Sidi Loghlimi—at Settat in September
* Sidi Bouknifa—at Settat toward the end of August
* Sidi Moussa—at Sidi Moussa in mid-September

In Tangier province:
* Sidi Bou Araquia—at Tangier
* Dar Zhirou—at Tangier in early September

In Tan Tan province:
* Sidi Mohammed Laghdal—at Tan Tan in October

In Tetuan province:
* Moulay Abdelsalam Ben Mchich—at Beni Aros toward the end of September
* Outa Aammou—at Chaouch in early August
* Moulay Abdelkader Jilali—at Larache in early June

Aside from moussems, other ways to attract baraka and ward off evil jinn include the use of colors such as black, red, blue, and yellow in clothing or decoration and the use of symbolic representations of hands or of the number 5. Black is commonly used in the clothing of southern Morocco. Another important color throughout Morocco and most of the Islamic world is green, which is the holy color of Islam. Symbolic representations of hands and the number 5 can often be seen as decorations on buildings, in jewelry and in the facial and hand henna tattoos of Berber women, particularly in the mountains. The tattoos, however, are also sometimes done just for beauty's sake and seen not only in the countryside, but also in the cities.

Partially and fully veiled women are also seen in the towns and cities, but they tend to be predominantly Arab, arabized Berbers, and more traditionally orthodox Muslims. In the mountains, partial or full veils are rarely found among Berber women. Generally, unlike many urban women, they are not confined to their homes; they also work more closely with men in maintaining the household. Exceptions do exist, but more in the urban areas than in the countryside, because of greater urban access to education and increased contact with Western values of individualism.

The third largest ethnic group in Morocco is the Harratines, black-skinned descendants of the slaves brought in from West Africa and the Sudan. As with other groups, there has been some intermarriage with Berbers and Arabs, particularly with Shleuh Berbers, but not as much as other groups. One of the reasons for this isolation is that some rural Moroccan Berbers and Arabs have traditionally associated black skin with the evil jinn or spirits. This association is strengthened by the predominance of Harratines in mystical professions such as conjurer, spiritual healer, and seller of secret potions. Harratine mystics and spiritualists are especially prevalent in the Djemā'a El Fna, the main square of the Marrakesh medina.

The fourth group is a dwindling population of Jews, many of them descendants of a 1492 Inquisition during which most Muslims and Jews were expelled from Spain. Prior to Moroccan independence in 1956, the Jewish population was estimated to be more than 200,000. However, subsequent wars between Israel and Arab countries caused a mass exodus of Moroccan Jews to Israel, France, and the United States. Today, estimates of the numbers of Jews who remain in the country vary from 10,000 to 15,000, with most concentrated in Casablanca. There are still synagogues, albeit not all functioning, in almost every city and town and many villages in Morocco.

Language

Arabic is the official language of Morocco—the mother language for about two-thirds of the population, the language of Islam and most governmental and business affairs. Spoken Arabic in Morocco differs from Arabic in other Arab countries by accent and in many cases vocabulary, because of Berber influences. The three principal dialects of Berber mentioned earlier are spoken by the remaining one-third as first languages, but a majority of these people (approximately 75 percent) are equally fluent in Moroccan Arabic. French is also still a major language in Morocco, even though the French Protectorate ended in 1956. In fact, French continues to be the language of the government and business elite and necessary for advancement in either sector. Spanish is still widely spoken in northern Morocco, but its link to the country's modern sectors is increasingly tenuous.

For travelers, knowledge of French is helpful, but not essential if you plan to stay mostly in areas frequented by tourists. English is widely spoken by people in the tourism industry, particularly by the hordes of hustlers, would-be guides, and bazaar salespeople as well as tourism offices and many hotel employees. Outside the main tourist areas, though, French and even some words of Moroccan Arabic are useful. Here are a few words and phrases of Moroccan Arabic that will help you get around:

Pronunciation notes: In the following examples, the letter *x* is pronounced as a throaty *ch* or *kch* sound. The @ sounds like "ine" but it's formed at the back of your throat by tightening your larynx. Note that Arabic does not distinguish between capital and lowercase letters.

Greetings

Hello. (Peace on you.)	*la bahs* or *salaam alake koom*
Hello *or* How do you do?	*ash xchubarak*
Hello. (*response*)	*la bahs hamdililah*
Pleased to meet you.	*misharafane*
How are you?	
(*to individual*)	*ash xchubarak* or *la bahs alake*
(*to group*)	*ash xchubarakoom* or *la bahs alakoom*
Fine (*literally* "Thanks be to God").	*il hamdililah*
Good morning.	*sabah il xeer*
Good morning. (*response*)	*sabah il nuur*
Good night.	
(*to a man*)	*tissbah ala xeer*
(*to a woman*)	*tissbahee ala xeer*
(*to a group*)	*tissbahoo ala xeer*
Good night. (*response*)	
(*to a man*)	*wenta min il xeer*
(*to a woman*)	*wentee min il xeer*
(*to a group*)	*wentoo min il xeer*
Goodbye.	*bislamma*

General Expressions

Yes (*when being called*)	*naam*
Yes (*in agreement*)	*yeh*
No	*la*
Please.	
(*to an individual*)	*lech halake*
(*to a group*)	*lech halake koom*
Thank you.	*baraka law feek*
Thank you very much.	*baraka law feek bizaf*
You are welcome.	*blehj meel*
Excuse me.	
(*to a man*)	*semhellee*

(to a woman)	semelleeya
(to a group)	semholeeya
excellent	mizian bizaf
good	mizian
bad	xchayyib
How much?	shahhal?
How many?	hal breetee?
What do you want?	
(to an individual)	wesh briti?
(to a group)	wesh britoo?
I, me	ana
you (masculine)	enta
you (feminine)	entee
you (plural)	entuma
he, him	howa
she, her	hiyya
we, us	hehna
they, them	homa
my wife	me rahtee
my husband	jozee rajli
my sister	ukhtee
my brother	khooya
I am	ana
a student (m)	talab
a student (f)	taleeba
American (m)	merree kanee
American (f)	merree kaniyya
British (m)	ingleezee
British (f)	ingleezeeya
Australian (m)	australhlee
Australian (f)	australhliyya
Canadian (m)	canadee
Canadian (f)	canadiyya
I speak	ana kanhadar
English	ingleezeeya
French	fransaweeya
German	almaneeya
I understand you.	kan fahemek
I don't understand you.	mahfahhemtiksh
Do you understand me?	
(to m)	wash kat fehemnee?
(to f)	wash kat fehemenee?
What does this mean?	wash ma@na dee el hadshee?
We need an interpreter.	breena tarjman

Finding Your Way Around

here	henna
there	li hay
left	esree
right	yimeen
straight ahead	sertoll
Where?	feen?
police station	bolees
toilet	twahlet or bitellma
ticket window	guichet (French, pronounced gee-shay)
train station	la gare (French)
bus station	moda'a tobees
airport	mahtar
Give me a ticket to...	atenee waraka leh...
What bus goes to...?	tobees leh kay emshee leh...?

In the Hotel

hotel	fonduke or hotel
Do you have a room?	wash kayna shibate?
a double room (twin beds)	bate bee joojfrash
a single	brit wahid el bate
with hot water	el mahskune
cheaper	arkhes

Miscellaneous Essentials

customs	deewana
post office	el bohstah
I want to send this by	brit ensafet hadshee
air mail	bi tayarra
soap	sahboon
fluent	mizian (literally "excellent")
not fluent	la makan nahadarsh mizian
OK	waxcha
foreigner	ajnabee
thief	sarak

Numbers

Numbers	Pronunciation	Numbers	Pronunciation
0	sefar	30	talateen
1	wahid	40	arba'aeen
2	juje	50	khamseen
3	talata	60	sitt-teen
4	arba'a	70	saba'aeen
5	khamsa	80	taman-nee-yen

6	setta	90	sane
7	seba'a	100	meyah
8	temaniya	101	mayyah-wi-wahid
9	sa'ode	110	mayyah-wi-ashara
10	ashara	1,000	alf
11	hidash	2,000	alfane
12	itnash	3,000	talat-talaf
13	talatash	4,000	arba'a-talaf
14	arba'atash	5,000	khamas-talaf
15	khammahstahsh		
16	sittahsh		
17	saba'atahsh		
18	tamantahsh		
19	tissa'atahsh		
20	ayshreen		
21	wahi-wi-ayshreen		
22	itnane-wi-ayshreen		

For the sake of comparison and also novelty, the following are some travel-related words and phrases in the Tamazight (pronounced *ta-ma-zeer-kcht*) Berber dialect—a few of which are the same as or similar to Moroccan Arabic.

Hello. (Peace on you.)	la bahs or salaam alake koom
Hello. (*response*)	la bahs hamdililah
How are you?	mayteneet
Fine (*literally*, "Thanks be to God").	il hamdililah
Good morning.	sabah il xeer
Good morning. (*response*)	sabah il nuur
Good night.	
(*to a man*)	tissbah ala xeer
(*to a woman*)	tissbahee ala xeer
(*to a group*)	tissbahoo ala xeer
Good night. (*response*)	
(*to a man*)	wenta min il xeer
(*to a woman*)	wentee min il xeer
(*to a group*)	wentoo min il xeer
Goodbye.	bislamma
Where is…?	meneeg ilah…?
good	izzil
bad	show (like "how") rehhleeh
Yes (*when being called*)	naam
Yes (*in agreement*)	yeh
I, me	nkin

you	*kchee-yen*
he, him	*hee-yen*
she, her	*emtet*
we, us	*neknee*
they, them	*hen-neekch*
I speak	*sinach-ats-say-oulach*
English	*tengleezeet*
French	*tafransaweet*
Spanish	*taspanoleet*
German	*taleemaneet*
Do you speak?	*sint-ats-say-oulit?*
I understand.	*fehemach*
I don't understand.	*show* ("how") *fehemach*
We need an interpreter.	*nirah tarjmen*
bread	*arohm*
water	*amahn*

THE TRAVELER IN MOROCCO

Information

The Office National Marocain du Tourisme, or ONMT—Morocco's national tourism organization—is the principal source of tourist information about Morocco. There are offices in almost every major city and town as well as in several cities overseas. ONMT publishes and distributes a series of brochures on each major city and region of Morocco. Each offers brief descriptions of the city's history, tourist sights in and around the city, maps of the city and region, and lists of principal hotels, restaurants, sports facilities, and various services. ONMT also offers a free hotel guide that lists all but the very cheapest, unclassified hotels; this is definitely worth obtaining. If this book and the ONMT brochures and hotel guide can't answer your questions, then most branches of the ONMT have English-speaking staff who are usually well informed.

Overseas branches of the ONMT include the following:

Austria
20 Aegidi Gasse, 6th District 1060, Vienna (tel. 568-355)
Belgium
66 Rue du Marché aux Herbes, Bruxelles 1000 (tel. 512-2182 or 512-1286)
Canada
2001 Rue Université, Suite 1460, Montreal, PQ H3A 2A6 (tel. 514-842-8111 or 514-842-8112)
Dubaï
P.O. Box 1344, Dubaï (tel. 23-69-26 or 23-69-66)

England
174 Regent Street, London W1R GHB (tel. 437-0073 or 437-0074)

France
161 Rue Saint Honoré, Paris 1er (tel. 260-6350 or 260-4724)

Italy
23 Via Larga, 20122 Milano (tel. 860-927 or 861-256)

Portugal
Rua Artilharia UM 7985, 1200 Lisboa (tel. 68-00-77)

Spain
Edificio España, Plaza España, Primera Planta, Madrid 13 (tel. 241-25-63); Pasaje Pizarro 7, Torremolinos (tel. 386-644 or 386-659)

Sweden
Storgatan, 16-11436, Stockholm (tel. 67-94-85)

Switzerland
Schifflände 5, 8001 Zürich (tel. 252-77-52)

United States
California: 421 North Rodeo Drive, #T7, Beverly Hills, CA 90210 (tel. 213-271-8939); Florida: EPCOT Center, Walt Disney World, FL 32830 (tel. 407-827-5337); New York: 20 East 46th Street, Suite 1201, New York, NY 10017 (tel. 212-557-2520 or 212-557-2521)

West Germany
59 Graf Adolf Strasse 4000, Düsseldorf (tel. 37-05-51)

Another source of tourist information in Morocco is the Syndicat d'Initiative, which is approximately the equivalent of a city's chamber of commerce. The Syndicat offices are likely to have more specific information about the city or town. Many also distribute the same materials as the ONMT. Most Syndicats are the best places to visit first if you wish to hire an official guide. You will be charged officially set half-day or full-day rates that are about $5 and $10 respectively, regardless of the number of people in your group.

Unofficial guides are also easy—sometimes too easy—to arrange. They are quite adept at finding you, despite your attempts at avoiding them. Dealing with them is a continuous adventure that I describe through anecdotes in subsequent chapters.

Both unofficial and official guides are likely to steer you toward shops where they will receive a commission from the owners for whatever you buy. You don't have to buy anything, nor do you have to visit the shops. If you don't want to shop, politely but firmly insist that you want to see the sights, not the shops. Be prepared, however, to hear that certain shops, particularly those selling carpets, are actually "carpet museums."

Although the guides are trying to earn additional money from you, just remember that the unemployment rate in Morocco hovers between 22 and 30 percent of the employable population and that the World Bank has estimated that over 38 percent of the population is living in "absolute poverty." The guides—both official and unofficial—are merely trying to make a living.

Maps

A variety of maps is available in Morocco. In addition to the standard city and regional maps reproduced in ONMT brochures, there are also road maps sold at most big city newsstands and major hotels. The "Maroc—Carte Routière" published by Éditions Marcus of Paris, France, and sold throughout Morocco for about $4, is a good map. The best maps, however, for any sort of travel off the main roads are the ones published by the government map office—La Direction de la Conservation Foncière et des Travaux Topographiques, Division de la Carte—at 31 Avenue Moulay Al Hassan in Rabat. They sell a broad range of topographic maps for about $2 each. Unfortunately, though, they can only sell the maps over the counter, not by mail. You might have better luck trying to order the maps from two British companies: McCarta, 122 Kings Cross Road, WC1 London, England; and West Col Productions, Goring, Reading, Berkshire, England. The latter company is also the only publisher of English-language guidebooks to the Atlas mountains.

Money and Banks

Morocco's currency is the dirham (DH or Dhm), which is divided into centimes (100 centimes = 1 DH), but centimes are worth so little that you probably won't see many in circulation. Moroccan currency is basically inconvertible outside Morocco and isn't supposed to be exported out of Morocco. Consequently, you may be able to buy dirhams for a lower rate outside Morocco. In any case, that's not really necessary because Moroccan banks and their associated exchange counters do offer fair exchange rates.

Moroccan banks can also grant cash advances and cash checks for customers who have VISA, Access, Eurocheque, American Express, and International Giro Cheques. For financial services, VISA cards are better represented in Morocco than American Express; the former can be used at all branches of the SGMB (Société Génèrale Marocaine des Banques) while the latter is represented by the Voyages Schwarz travel agencies in a few cities. The Voyages Schwarz agencies can be found at the following addresses:

- Agadir—87 Place du Marché Municipal
- Casablanca—112 Rue Prince Moulay Abdullah

- Marrakesh—1 Rue Mauritania
- Tangier—54 Boulevard Pasteur

Costs, Accommodations, and Food

The costs of traveling around Morocco vary, depending on how much you want to spend on food and accommodations. At the lowest end of comfort and price are, of course, youth hostels and camping, which can cost you as little as $1 to $2 a night. At the other end is the palatial five-star deluxe La Mamounia Hotel in Marrakesh where an "average" room can cost about $245 per night.

In between are hundreds of hotels, most of them given official government ratings of one to five stars that approximately dictate how much they can charge for their rooms. I say "approximately" because there doesn't always seem to be a direct correlation between the room rates and the number of stars. If, for example, a two-star hotel is the only hotel in town, it may be charging as much as a three- or four-star hotel in Marrakesh. So, in addition to the typical criteria of cleanliness, comfort, and facilities, other criteria for determining the rates include location, competition, and availability. If you are ever uncertain about the price and standards of a hotel, all classified hotels post their star ratings and official room rates next to the reception desk. Also, the hotel guide published by the ONMT lists all classified hotels in the country and indicates what facilities and amenities are available at each.

The costs of food are similar to accommodations—you can spend a little or a lot depending on your budget and choice of restaurants or type of food. A basic, but typical, Moroccan meal of *harira* (sort of a bean soup), "brochettes" (chunks of grilled meat or chicken), and tea can cost less than $1 in a nontouristic restaurant or café. The same meal with a pastry or piece of fruit in a simple tourist-class restaurant may cost about $3 to $4. You can distinguish one from the other by the existence of a posted menu in French and possibly English near the front door and a glance at the clientele. More expensive and fancier restaurant almost always have the menu posted at the door.

In addition to *harira* and "brochettes," other popular Moroccan dishes include *tajines* (a beef, chicken, or fish stew cooked in a clay pot over a charcoal fire; sometimes includes raisins or prunes); *méchoui* (stuffed lamb); couscous (steamed semolina piled with chicken, lamb, and vegetables—served more in homes than in restaurants); *poulet aux olives et citron* (stewed chicken with olives and lemon cooked like a tajine); and *bastilla* (pigeon wrapped in a flaky pastry-like shell).

If you're looking for backpack food staples, then you'll want to head for the small grocery stores and public open-air markets known as *souks*. Prices at the grocery stores tend to be somewhat higher than souk prices, but the selection of canned and bottled goods and toiletries is usually much better; such stores are also open longer hours than the souks. Fresh produce, meat, chicken, and some dry goods such as flour and rice are often easily obtainable at the souks. Prices are usually marked and nonnegotiable at both stores and souks, but you will find this the cheapest way to eat.

Where to Go

Morocco is a country that takes time to explore. If you rush in and then out again in just a few days, you will have barely had time to recuperate from culture shock and jet lag. You should plan to spend one or two weeks at the very least for a fair visit to the country. In one week, however, it would be difficult to visit beyond just two or three "imperial" cities such as Fez and Marrakesh. In about 10 to 14 days, you can adequately visit a few cities and countryside destinations.

If you have only a week, my personal recommendations are the following itineraries:

Option One: To Fez
Day 1. Arrive Casablanca and fly or take the train to Fez.
Day 2. Arrange a half-day official tour of Fez and leave rest of the day at leisure.
Day 3. Walk around Fez on your own.
Day 4. Early morning bus to Azrou and half-day visit to Oum Er Rbia river and falls. Night at Azrou.
Day 5. Day visit from Azrou to Ifrane and Mischliffen for skiing or hiking. Night at Azrou.

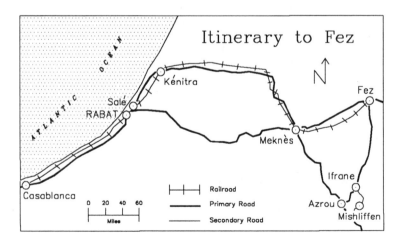

Day 6. Return to Fez and travel to Rabat by train. Half-day walk around Rabat and, possibly, Salé.

Day 7. Bus to Casablanca airport.

Option Two: To Marrakesh

Day 1. Arrive at Casablanca and take the train to Marrakesh.

Day 2. Half-day official tour of Marrakesh and rest of the day roaming the city on your own.

Day 3. Explore Marrakesh on your own.

Day 4. Rent a car or arrange transport by bus and collective taxi to the High Atlas village of Imlil. Short hikes through the villages and hamlets in the mountains and hills around Imlil. Night in Imlil or Aremd.

Day 5. Hike or hitch to the "refuge" of Tacheddîrt and hike in surrounding area for rest of the day. Or continue hike (four hours) to Oukaïmeden. This might be difficult in the winter because of snow.

Day 6. Return to Marrakesh.

Day 7. Train to Casablanca and bus to Casablanca airport.

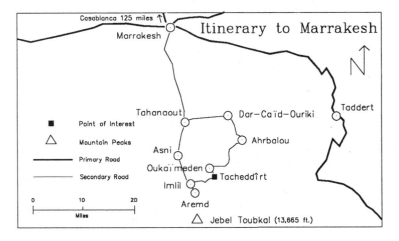

With more time available, a variety of extensions and adventure options are recommended, most of which are described in the following chapters. The following are a few highlights:

- To Azilal (on west side of High Atlas mountains) from Marrakesh for hikes and walks in the area around Aït Bougmez—plan on at least three or four days.

- To the Drâa valley via Ouarzazate from Marrakesh, continue to Zagora and beyond—at least three days.
- Dadés and Tohdra gorges via Ouarzazate from Marrakesh—three to four days.
- Hike to Mount Toubkal—five days from Marrakesh.

Various side trips are also possible from each of these itinerary extensions. Several of these are described in subsequent chapters.

Getting Around Morocco

By Air

Royal Air Inter, the domestic counterpart of Royal Air Maroc, services almost every major city in Morocco. There are frequent flights between Casablanca and the following cities: Agadir (several daily flights), Dakhla (6 flights weekly), Er-Rachidia (5), Fez (9), Laayoune (at least 2 daily), Marrakesh (at least 2 daily), Ouarzazate (6 weekly), Oujda (5), Tangier (at least 2 daily), and Tan Tan (10 weekly).

As of early 1989, there were also direct flights between Agadir and Dakhla, Laayoune, Marrakesh, Ouarzazate, Tangier, and Tan Tan; Dakhla and Laayoune; Er-Rachidia and Fez; Fez and Laayoune, Marrakesh and Tangier; Laayoune and Tan Tan; Marrakesh and Ouarzazate.

Royal Air Maroc flies some of these routes, sometimes as extensions of international flights. For the latest information about all routes, call or write to Royal Air Moroc and obtain a copy of its latest timetable.

By Bus

Buses are the most popular mode of transport around Morocco. They go to almost every city, town, and village in the country. Unless you really get off the beaten track, the buses you'll see most often are with the CTM company—the national line. CTM buses tend to be more comfortable, punctual, and slightly more expensive than private-line buses. In larger cities and towns, such as Marrakesh, CTM and private buses depart from the same terminal. Otherwise, there are separate terminals. Whether you go by CTM or another bus line, you'll find bus travel the cheapest way to tour Morocco.

By Grand Taxi

Faster, higher-priced, and second in popularity to buses are grand taxis, six-passenger Mercedes or Peugeot wagons (sometimes other types of vehicles as well), which make frequent daily runs between most cities, towns, and villages. These taxis only leave when there are six passengers, unless, of course, someone pays for the vacant seats. Everyone pays the same government-regulated price, so don't worry about having to haggle. Prices are negotiable, however, when you (or a group) wish to hire a grand taxi for a particular excursion.

By Train

Traveling by train in Morocco can be fast, easy, clean, and comfortable, particularly if you take first- and second-class express trains. Fares for these trains average about 20 to 40 percent higher than buses along the same routes. There are also second- and third-class regular trains, which can be cheaper, but also slower than intercity buses.

It is possible to take the train from Tangier all the way to Marrakesh, the southernmost terminus, or Oujda, the easternmost terminus at the Algerian border. Before Algerian and Moroccan disagreements over the western Sahara disrupted service between the two countries, there was a trans-Maghrebian line that continued from Oujda across Algeria through Oran, Algiers, and Constantine to Tunis. In 1988, the Moroccan and Algerian governments had begun to repair relations and reinitiate cargo train service across the border. Passenger train service followed in 1990.

If you plan to travel by train in Morocco, buy a copy of the ONCF (Office National des Chemins de Fer du Maroc) "Horaires des Trains" (timetable) pamphlet for about $0.15. Schedules for every first- and second-class express and regular train are listed, including the sleeper trains.

The most popular routes for sleepers, known officially as Wagons Lits, are between Marrakesh and Oujda via Fez and Casablanca and between Tangier and Oujda. Advance reservations and tickets are recommended. The sleeper compartments are European-style with full sinks and comfortable beds.

Transalpino and Eurotrain passes are valid on Moroccan and European trains and most ferries for six months. The tickets can only be purchased in Europe at Transalpino-Eurotrain offices and student travel agencies; the prices depend on which routes you select for traveling to and from Morocco. You can make any number of stops along a specified route within the time period of the ticket.

By Car

Touring Morocco by car is a convenient way to see the country. An extensive system of paved roads begun by the French during the days of the Protectorate facilitates travel to almost every city and major town. Many Europeans take advantage of this by ferrying their cars (by the thousands) and recreational vehicles across the Strait of Gibraltar and the Mediterranean. I also met a group of Australian surfers who had ferried across a cheap VW bus they had bought in West Germany. For ferry and hydrofoil information, see the "Getting There" section.

Renting a car is also an option, but it can be relatively expensive if you don't split the cost with other travelers. Avis, Budget, and Hertz have offices throughout Morocco—Agadir, Casablanca, Fez, Marrakesh, Ouarzazate (Budget and Hertz only), Oujda, Rabat, and Tangier. Rates for all three agencies are comparable, although each one's rates differ according to location. Daily and weekly rates for a Renault 4, the most inexpensive, are about US $22 per day plus $0.23 per km plus 19 percent tax plus insurance, or a weekly rate of $298 (Avis), $231 (Budget), and $288 (Hertz) plus 19 percent plus insurance, but with unlimited kilometers.

In every city, there are also many small car rental agencies that offer substantially lower rates than the Big Three agencies. For example, recently the Interlov agency of Marrakesh was renting a Renault 4 for about DH 95 (approximately US $11.60) per day plus DH 1.3 ($0.16) per km plus the usual other costs. You will probably not get the service guarantees of the Big Three, but it's worth shopping around and comparing rates and possible service if you have the time. Before renting a car, be sure that it has a spare tire. Also, get a list of telephone numbers to call in case of a breakdown or emergency, including after-hours numbers.

Although it is possible to take rented cars off the main road and onto some *pistes* (dirt roads and tracks), you may not want to stray too far from the beaten track and car mechanics.

Traveling by car in Morocco is faster and more convenient, but you also risk missing out on some contact with Moroccans. Some of my best experiences traveling around Morocco were conversations with and observations of Moroccans in trains, buses, and grand taxis. However, if your time is limited, a car does allow you to travel farther than if you were relying on public transport.

By Hitchhiking

If time isn't a concern, than you can try hitching rides. In cities and bigger towns, you may want to first visit campgrounds and gas stations and attempt to hitch rides with Europeans who have an extra place in their vehicles. I approached a French family at a gas station in Zagora and got a ride in their Land-Rover. If you hitch a ride with a truck or van, both of which often fill in for a lack of buses on certain rural routes, you may be expected to pay. You should pay at the end of your trip, and don't be surprised if a bit of bargaining is necessary. In several parts of the High Atlas mountains, trucks are the only means of transportation, other than donkeys and horses.

By Camel

As a mode of transport, camels now seem to be mostly for tourists. In the villages and hamlets near Zagora, you can rent a camel for a miniexcursion into the desert. Prices are definitely negotiable.

By Donkey and Horse

Donkeys and horses are now more common and easier to rent and handle than camels. In the High Atlas mountains, particularly around the village of Imlil, donkeys and horses are readily available for rent. Four of us once rented both donkeys and horses from Imlil to carry us and our packs over a steep hill and into a valley beyond the village of Aremd. Again, prices are negotiable.

By Foot

Except around Mount Toubkal, the highest mountain in Morocco and a favorite hiking destination, trails aren't specifically marked for hikers as they are in Europe and North America. Most trails are the products of centuries of Arab and Berber traders and travelers treading through villages and hamlets. Unless you somehow find someplace where no one has ever trekked before, you will probably never be on a trail that is more than a day's hike from a settlement, hamlet, or village.

For truly serious trekking, you should buy the necessary topographical maps from the government mapping division in Rabat (see that section) and consider buying one of the Atlas trail guidebooks published by West Col Productions (address: Goring, Reading, Berkshire, England). Also, if you can track them down, talk to members of Morocco's Club Alpin (Alpine Club) in Casablanca and Rabat. They supposedly have a branch club at Rabat University.

Hiking supplies are difficult to find in Morocco. So if you're missing, for example, tent stakes or packets of your favorite dehydrated food, you may have to improvise. Markets (souks) and small grocery stores stock most basic provisions and foods.

Getting There

Visas and Permits

Travelers holding U.S., Australian, British, Canadian, French, New Zealand, and West German passports do not need visas to enter Morocco for up to 90 days. Passports should be valid and, according to official Moroccan policy, should not contain Israeli or South African visa stamps. According to a consular official at the Moroccan Embassy in Washington, D.C., the ban on Israeli and South African passport stamps doesn't matter for U.S. citizens. However, you don't want to risk traveling all the way to Morocco and then be turned away because some Moroccan immigration official suddenly wants to enforce the ban. Get a clean passport.

Dutch and Belgian passport holders require visas to enter Morocco.

By Air

From Europe. Royal Air Maroc, Lufthansa, and several other European airlines offer frequent flights to Casablanca from almost every major city in Europe, including even a few Eastern European capitals such as East Berlin, Bucharest, and Budapest. A few airlines, such as Royal Air Maroc and Air France, also have direct flights to Marrakesh, Fez, Ouarzazate, Agadir, and Tangier. Throughout the year, there are also many charter flights, especially to Marrakesh and Agadir.

From North America. Royal Air Maroc is the only airline that flies direct from North America to Morocco. There are two flights weekly on Tuesdays and Saturdays from Montreal via New York (JFK Airport) to Casablanca.

Other Flights. There are also flights to and from most West African countries (including Mali and Senegal), the Canary islands (twice weekly from Casablanca), Algeria (daily to Algiers), Tunis, Cairo, Amman (Jordan), Moscow, and Rio de Janeiro.

By Sea

Ferries and hydrofoils from Europe use three major ports of entry into Morocco: Tangier, Ceuta (Sebta), and Melilla. The principal hydrofoil routes are from Spain (Tarifa and Algeciras) and Gibraltar to Tangier— three times daily from Tarifa (half an hour) and once daily from Algeciras (one hour) and Gibraltar (one hour). Since this is the fastest way to cross by sea, the hydrofoils tend to be crowded, especially in the summer.

Ferry departures are more numerous and frequent, but take longer than the hydrofoils. There are ferry crossings from Algeciras to Tangier (2 1/2 hours) and Ceuta (1 1/2 hours); Gibraltar to Tangier (two hours, Wednesdays and Fridays); Málaga (8 1/2 hours, daily) and Almeria (8 1/2 hours, daily except Sundays) to Melilla (a Spanish enclave in Morocco); and Sète (France) to Tangier, a weekly 14-hour trip.

If you don't have advance reservations, then taking one of the car ferries from Algeciras to Tangier or Ceuta is the easiest way to go. There are at least two ferries daily to Tangier at 12:30 P.M. and 8 P.M. between November 1 and March 31; three daily at 9 A.M., 1 P.M., and 6 P.M.

between April 1 and June 14; and sometimes as many as five or six daily the rest of the year. One-way fares are about $26 (Class A) and $21 (Class B). Bicycles and motorcycles cost an extra $19.50. From Algeciras to Ceuta, there are at least 12 ferries daily in the summer and eight in the winter on boats that are reputedly better than the Tangier boats.

The Gibraltar ferries are operated by the Bland Line, which has its offices in the Cloister Building, Gibraltar; tel. 79-200. The boats run on Wednesdays and Fridays departing Gibraltar at 6 P.M. and arriving Tangier at 8 P.M. Write to the company for more information.

The weekly ferry from Sète, France, is operated by Comanav, SNCM, 12 Rue Godot de Mauroy, Paris (tel. 2666-6019). If you can get them, reservations are essential.

By Land

The only possible ways to enter Morocco overland are through Oujda and the oasis of Figuig, 300 km (186 miles) to the south. In 1988 the border crossing became considerably easier because of closer relations between Morocco and Algeria. A train connection through Oujda was restored in 1988, but only for cargo; passenger service was reactivated in 1990.

Oujda is a compact place with most major facilities situated around or near the main square—Place du 16 Août 1953. In this area are the CTM and non-CTM bus terminals, the ONMT tourist office, the post office, and banks. The train station is within walking distance of the main square and most hotels are on Boulevard Zerktouni, which runs between the station and the Place.

Connections from Oujda to other parts of Morocco are easy. There are four trains daily to Fez (6 hours); three buses to Figuig (7 hours); and numerous grand taxis to Saïdia (fifty minutes) and Taza (2 1/2 hours). There are also daily flights from Oujda to Casablanca; for information, visit the Royal Air Maroc office at the Hotel Oujda.

The second border crossing between Morocco and Algeria is at the isolated oasis town of Figuig. Although the town is quite interesting, the seven-hour bus ride from Oujda or ten-hour ride from Er-Rachidia make this a long trek. Unless you are coming from the oases and dunes of the Grand Erg Occidental in western Algeria, it's much easier to pass via Oujda than Figuig. If you do make it here, you will see a town that comprises more than 200,000 palm trees and seven ksour (traditional mudbrick fortress-style architecture) villages, each with extensive palmeries encased in medieval walls. There's only one hotel in town—unclassified, quite basic—and a campsite. The town's only taxi makes frequently shuttle runs to the border, which is about 8 km (5 miles) away. Otherwise, you'll have to hitch a ride or walk.

By Tour or Organized Group

Cross-Cultural Adventures (P.O. Box 3285, Arlington, Virginia 22203; tel. 703-204-2717) offers unique trips to Morocco. The trips are organized and led by a former Peace Corps volunteer, Piotr Kostrzewski, who knows Morocco intimately. He offers an interesting set of itineraries that includes a Land-Rover expedition to the annual wedding "fair" at Imilchil, a High Atlas mountain trek, and home stays with Berber families.

Sherpa Expeditions, an English-based company, specializes in two-week mountain treks in Morocco. All four of its itineraries start in Marrakesh. Its address is 131A, Heston Road, Hounslow, Middlesex, TW5 ORD England; tel. 01-557-2717, fax 01-572-9788.

The University Research Expeditions Program (UREP) of the University of California, Berkeley, California 94720, occasionally organizes special research expeditions to Morocco. These scientific expeditions permit a limited number of travelers to assist with basic research projects. The 1988 Morocco trip was "A Study of Moroccan Sheep," which involved a field survey of farmed and nomadic sheep flocks over a range of 186-248 miles (300-400 km) between the coast and the Atlas mountains. According to UREP, a mineral deficiency that affects growth and fertility in sheep has recently been found. A comprehensive survey of various breeds of Moroccan sheep is the first step needed in a program to improve wool production and animal health that could greatly benefit not only the shepherds' livelihood but the country's economy as a whole. Excluding air fare, the price was US $1,285.

More standard group tours are offered by Maupintour (arranged through a travel agent), Jet Vacations, and Air France (California tel. 213-652-0999), and Travel Plans International (arranged through a travel agent).

CHAPTER 5

Casablanca, Rabat-Salé, and Tangier

Casablanca and the twin cities of Rabat and Salé form the economic and political heart of Morocco. With over 2.5 million inhabitants—and growing at a daily rate of 140, or 51,000 annually—Casablanca is Morocco's biggest city. It's also the country's biggest port and commercial center and second biggest port in Africa, the origins of which were with the French Protectorate. Rabat is the country's administrative center, with its unicameral parliament, main ministry offices, high courts, and foreign embassies. Salé, its sister city just across the Oued Bou Regreg river, is a whitewashed traditional medina city. For the traveler who wants to visit a place that's like Marseilles (France) or a Frenchified Long Beach, then Casablanca is a good choice. However, Rabat and Salé offer a much better introduction to Morocco. Rabat is a modern city with a traditional side, while Salé is predominantly a traditional medina town with medieval monuments and markets.

CASABLANCA

For the traveler expecting to find the Casablanca of Bogart fame, disappointment is certain. As in the film, there is a Rick's American Café in Casablanca, but it's a plush neon re-creation just off the lobby of the sparkling Hyatt Regency. In the café, the melancholy sounds of "As Time Goes By" conjure up images of the actual Rick's American Café in the film, but only with your eyes closed. Rick is probably groaning in his grave over this stainless steel art deco version of his fictional haven.

The Casablanca depicted in the film existed, at least partially, in the 1930s and 1940s. The city was a French creation forceably grafted onto the small medina town of Casablanca in 1907. French troops landed in Casablanca in 1907 ostensibly to protect the small European population from an angry Moroccan mob that had already killed ten Europeans. The troops included regular soldiers, Senegalese riflemen (called *tirailleurs*),

73

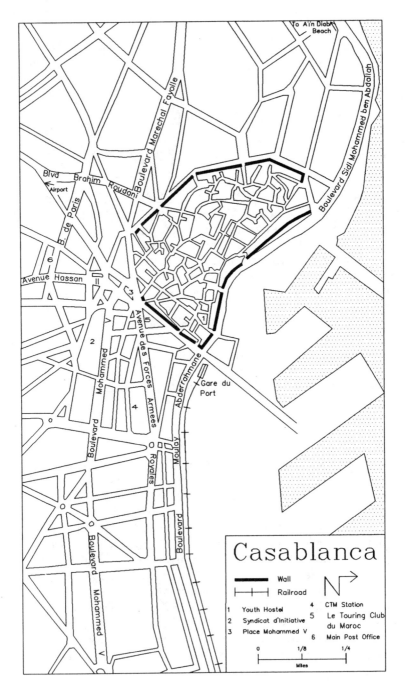

Casablanca

Wall
Railroad

1 Youth Hostel
2 Syndicat d'Initiative
3 Place Mohammed V
4 CTM Station
5 Le Touring Club du Maroc
6 Main Post Office

0   1/8   1/4
Miles

and Foreign Legionnaires, all of whom longed to avenge the murders. They did more than avenge—they went on a rampage, murdering many people, including women and children, and shelled the medina from a French ship offshore for several days in August 1907. Eventually the soldiers settled down and French colonial administrators arrived to begin the installation of the protectorate (finalized in 1912).

By the 1940s, Casablanca was a booming port and commercial center that attracted an increasing number of rural migrants and spawned many of the usual social problems and urban blight of a burgeoning city—unemployment, housing shortages, crime, and prostitution. A few of the seeds of Morocco's independence movement can be traced to discontented workers in Casablanca's *bidonvilles* (shantytowns). After independence in 1956, though, Casablanca continued to develop as a Westernized city complete with beach clubs, nightclubs, veilless women, French-style cafés and restaurants, and a rapidly increasing population of migrants searching for work. The population continues to increase, thus exacerbating unemployment and the housing shortage. The government has been trying to control the influx of migrants, but the city's existing problems are still enough to spark occasional violent protests.

For travelers, the city's social ills are seen in the proliferation of hustlers and con artists who approach you at the bus and train stations and on the street. They disappear, however, on royal holidays and events because then the police crack down on any Moroccan who is behaving "improperly." During all other times, listening to the con artists' scams can be something of an adventure.

One of the most common cons goes something like this: A man approaches and asks you to write a letter for him in English. He takes you to a café and recites a variety of sympathy stories hoping that "your kind heart" will allow you to help by giving him money. The usual money requests are for car breakdowns, gasoline to go home, train or bus ticket to go home, brother's wedding...you get the idea. If you believe the man's story and want to test his sincerity, then offer to go with him to his car or to the bus or train station. Don't be surprised if he starts making excuses about having to go later and instead just asks for your money. You can prevent these sorts of encounters whenever anyone approaches you uninvited. However, you could also be missing a typical Casablanca experience of meeting characters that you might not find back home. You can (and should) easily control the situation by selecting the café, asking lots of questions, not doing anything that you don't want to do, and politely but firmly leaving when you want to leave.

Arrival and Departure

By Air

Morocco's biggest and busiest airport—the Aeroport Mohammed V—is about 30 km (19 miles) south of Casablanca. Arrival at the airport is straightforward—through passport control to the baggage claim area and then through customs, which is usually little more than a cursory look at your bags. The money exchange windows are to your left once you're inside the terminal. If you need to leave any baggage at the airport, there is a baggage room just to your right.

A few words should be said about the money exchange windows. The employees are notoriously slow and never put up signs telling you which of two or three windows is the right one for changing foreign currency into Moroccan dirhams. It's a good idea to ask at the window before standing in one of the usually long lines.

Transportation between the airport and Casablanca and Rabat is easy. CTM buses run every half hour from in front of the terminal just outside the baggage claim area and from the CTM station in Casablanca (less frequently for Rabat, see that section).

Casablanca is Morocco's principal international and domestic airport. Most direct international flights to Morocco are via this airport. Flights to almost all domestic airports are easily arranged from the Casablanca airport.

By Bus

In addition to being a major air transit hub, Casablanca is also a major center for buses to just about everywhere in Morocco and even to a few European destinations. CTM buses use a large, centrally located terminal on Rue Léon l'Africain just off Avenue des Forces Armées Royales, and Boulevard Hassan Seghir. Non-CTM buses use a much less convenient terminal south of Place de la Victoire on Boulevard de Strasbourg, which is on the route to Marrakesh. From the CTM terminal, all buses except those to and from European destinations run daily.

By Train

Casablanca has two train stations—the centrally located Gare du Port just off Place Mohammed V and the Gare des Voyageurs at the east end of Boulevard Mohammed V. Most trains from Marrakesh stop at both stations. However, trains from Rabat and beyond often just stop at the Gare des Voyageurs. If you are coming into the city, try to get a train that stops at the Gare du Port because from there it's a much shorter walk into the city. From the Gare des Voyageurs it's a fight or a long wait for a taxi or a 50-minute (3 km or 2 mile) walk into town.

By Grand Taxi

Grand taxis for Rabat are stationed in a small lot on Boulevard Hassan Seghir about a block south of the CTM bus terminal.

First Things First

Information

There's an ONMT tourist information booth at the airport terminal, but it doesn't usually have a lot of information. At least you can pick up a copy of the ONMT's Casablanca map; most of the major streets and several of the major hotels and buildings are well marked. Near downtown Casablanca at 55 Rue Omar Slaoui, just off Avenue Hassan II and Rue d'Agadir, is the main ONMT office, where you can get brochures and information on most of Morocco. It's open in the summer Monday through Friday from 8 A.M. to 2 P.M., with flexible hours the rest of the year.

Information about Casablanca is also available from the Syndicat d'Initiative at the corner of Boulevard Mohammed V and Rue Colbert.

If you plan to tour Morocco by car, you may want to stop by the Le Touring Club du Maroc office on Avenue des Forces Armées Royales just east of Place Mohammed V. It's the Moroccan equivalent of the American Automobile Association club.

Hotels

Casablanca offers a good selection of hotels in every price range. Many of the budget hotels—three stars and below—are concentrated in an area that's bounded by Avenue Lalla Yacout on the south-southeast, Avenue Hassan II on the west, Avenue des Forces Armées Royales on the north, and Boulevard Hassan Seghir on the east. Some of the hotels in this area include the two-star Hotel Rialto at 9 Rue Claude, just across the street is the non-rated Hotel de France, the formerly opulent three-star Hotel Excelsior at Place Mohammed V, the one-star Hotel Lincoln at 1 Rue Ibn Batouta just off Boulevard Mohammed V, and the one-star Hotel Majestic at 57 Boulevard Lalla Yacout (one of the Bennani family hotels, see Marrakesh section). There's also a youth hostel at 6 Place

Amiral Philbert right inside the medina quarter near the Gare du Port train station and the intersection of Boulevard El Hansali and Boulevard des Almohades. The hostel is often recommended by travelers as a good, cheap place to stay. It's open all year from 8 A.M. to 2 P.M. and 5 P.M. to 11 P.M. A comprehensive list of accommodations is available from the ONMT or Syndicat d'Initiative offices.

Camping is possible at Camping Oasis on Avenue Mermoz several kilometers from downtown. Unless you are really set on camping, it's not worth the trip because nonrated and one-star hotels will cost about the same as camping for a night. To get here, take Bus 31 from the CTM terminal or follow Boulevard Brahim Roudani and, when it branches in two, Boulevard Yacoub El Mansour on the right side. The campground will be on your left about 328 feet (100 m) past the street division.

Restaurants and Cafés

As with hotels, Casablanca offers a broad selection of restaurants and cafés, most of which are concentrated in approximately the same area as the budget hotels—Avenue Lalla Yacout on the south-southeast, Avenue Hassan II on the west, Avenue des Forces Armées Royale on the north, and Boulevard Hassan Seghir on the east. The Restaurant Ouarzazate just off Rue Mohammed El Quori is highly recommended by travelers; look for the signs. Another low-budget-travelers' place is Restaurant Dallas around the corner from the Hotel Rialto, which claims to be a "Texas-style" restaurant, but actually it serves tajines and Moroccan-style grilled meat and fish dishes that are displayed in a refrigerated case in the front window. It's called Dallas because the walls are decorated with photographs and memorabilia related to the television program *Dallas*. There are several other grill-style places like Restaurant Dallas. For more upscale places, head out to the Aïn Diab beach area west of downtown and try the fish restaurants along the Corniche.

French-style cafés where you can have a good breakfast croissant and a cup of coffee are some of the most common establishments in downtown Casablanca. They all seem fairly similar, so just walk around and find one you like.

Getting Things Done and Shopping

Money

There are several banks where you can exchange foreign currency and travelers' checks near the main post and telephone offices on

Avenue Hassan II and around Place Mohammed V. A few banks also have after-hours exchange offices; there's one across from the post office.

American Express (tel. 73433) has an office in Casablanca at Voyages Schwarz, 112 Avenue du Prince Moulay Abdallah, that offers basic travel and financial services such as replacement of lost travelers' checks.

Post and Telephone Offices

The main post office is on Avenue Hassan II about a block from Place des Nations Unies; another post office is at 116 Boulevard Mohammed V across from the Syndicat d'Initiative. There are two telephone offices adjacent to the main post office—one is all pay phones and the other is a long-distance office for operator-assisted calls. Overseas calls can be made direct on a few pay phones in both offices, which is cheaper and more convenient than ordering your call through an operator. The poste restante cabinet is at the long-distance counter.

Shopping

Tourist souvenir and leather stores abound in the area east of Place Mohammed V between Avenue des Forces Armées Royales and Boulevard Mohammed V. Prices are definitely not the best here, so your bargaining skills should be good. Most of the shops' specialties seem to be leather goods.

More inexpensive shopping can be found across Place Mohammed V in the medina, but many of the items for sale are secondhand. Don't venture into this medina expecting to find a traditional-style souk or bazaar; it's more like a flea market or swap meet. Somewhere hidden in the labyrinth of stalls and shops of the medina is a wonderful section devoted to used books and magazines. Unfortunately, I couldn't begin to tell you how to find it because I quickly lost track of the route my guide and I had followed.

For new paperbacks and magazines as well as postcards and maps, there are several newsstands and bookstores on Place Mohammed V and the side streets just off the Place.

Things to See

Casablanca has a paucity of sights and things to do—no museums, monuments, or interesting markets. Most people head for the beach at Aïn Diab about 3 km (2 miles) west of downtown Casablanca. Although the beach is pleasant, there are better, less crowded beaches in Morocco. The chief attractions at Aïn Diab are its beach clubs, each with its own sports facilities, restaurants, and cafés of varying quality.

RABAT AND SALÉ

For travelers who are unaccustomed to the exotic chaos and crowds of the medinas of Marrakesh and Fez, the sister cities of Rabat and Salé are the perfect place to start your trip. Similar to Casablanca, Rabat is a modern city grafted on to a traditional town by the French during the Protectorate. In 1912 at the beginning of the Protectorate, the French made Rabat the political capital of Morocco in order to weaken the traditionally prominent political centers of Marrakesh and Fez. During the Protectorate period, they erected a compact set of Frenchified Moroccan administrative buildings adjacent to the medieval walls of the *ribat* or fortress and medina. The original *ribat* was built in an area that has been occupied successively by Phoenicians, Carthaginians, Romans, a semiautonomous Berber state in the eighth century, and Almohads in the twelfth century. About a century before the Almohads arrived, though, the town of Salé was founded just across the Oued Bou Regreg river.

Most of what is today the walled medina of Rabat was built by Yakub El Mansur toward the end of the twelfth century. On returning from military campaigns in the east, Mansur arrived at the Bou Regreg and set up his Ribat El Fatih, or "Camp of Victory." With the construction of more than 5 km (3 miles) of high walls, the Camp became a fortress and staging area for campaigns into Spain, and then the Almohad capital. By the thirteenth century, however, Mansur had gone, the cities of Marrakesh and Fez had begun to rise as political and religious centers, and Rabat entered a long period of decline and neglect.

Rabat and Salé seemed to fade from history until the sixteenth and seventeenth centuries when both—particularly Salé, though—acquired an infamous international reputation for piracy. Corsairs or pirate ships dubbed the Salli Rovers were harbored at the mouth of the Bou Regreg between attacks on the merchant ships that plied the waters between Europe, the Americas, and West Africa. By the mid-seventeenth century, they were able to form an independent city-state known as the Republic of Bou Regreg, but its power faded with the installation of the Alawite dynasty in Marrakesh in 1669. Through the rest of the seventeenth century and up to the late nineteenth century, Rabat and Salé again resumed relatively insignificant roles in Morocco's history.

By the late nineteenth century, French traders and government representatives had begun visiting Rabat intent on dominating this geopolitically significant land. Most of the rest of Africa had been carved into colonies and protectorates by fourteen European countries in 1884 during the Conference of Berlin. By 1912 France was able to maneuver itself into establishing a protectorate over most of Morocco. Rabat was made the administrative capital of first the Protectorate and then the independent country of Morocco in 1956.

Today, Rabat is still a city of two halves—the medieval walled medina and the French-built New City. However, an extension of the walls goes from the southern corner of the medina parallel to Avenue Ibn Toumerte to Bab Rouah, the gate at the northern corner of the royal palace complex. The wall continues from the Bab to encircle most of the palace. The heart of the New City is east of the wall that parallels Avenue Ibn Toumerte and includes most of the city's hotels, restaurants, cafés, and public buildings as well as foreign embassies. It's a well-kept, compact area with many of the trappings of "modern" life—computer stores, VCRs, videocassette rental stores, storefronts full of electronic gadgets, 24-hour automatic teller machines, and French-style cafés popular with both men and women. It's a break with tradition in Morocco to see women in cafés, which is a sign of Rabat's more liberal, perhaps Western or modern, ambience. For travelers, Rabat makes an easy introduction to Morocco, a good place from which to plan your trip through the rest of Morocco.

Arrival and Departure

By Air

Rabat has its own airport, but it handles relatively few domestic and international flights compared to the Casablanca airport.

Several daily buses connect Rabat directly to the Casablanca airport. The departure-arrival point is conveniently located just across from the train station, which is within walking distance of most of Rabat's hotels and restaurants. Departures from the airport to Rabat are at 6:45, 8:15, and 10:45 A.M. and at 1:30, 4, 6, and 9 P.M. for the 90-minute trip. From Rabat—at 5, 6:30, 8:30, and 10 A.M. and at 1, 3:30, and 6:30 P.M. A one-way ticket costs about $5.75.

By Train

Rabat is on the main train route between Fez, Casablanca, and

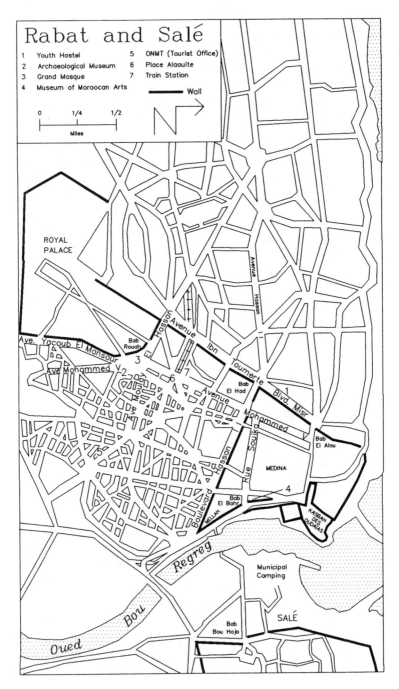

Rabat and Salé

1 Youth Hostel
2 Archaeological Museum
3 Grand Mosque
4 Museum of Moroocan Arts

5 ONMT (Tourist Office)
6 Place Alaouite
7 Train Station

━━━ Wall

0   1/4   1/2

Miles

ROYAL
PALACE

Ave. Yacoub El Mansour

Bab
Rouah

Ave Mohammed V

Avenue Hassan

Hassan Avenue

Ibn Toumerte

Blvd. Misr

3

7

2

6

Avenue

Bab
El Had

Mohammed

Bab
El Alou

Rue Souika

Hassan

MEDINA

Boulevard

MELLAH

Bab
El Bahr

4

KASBAH
DES
OUDAAS

Regreg

Municipal
Camping

Bou

SALÉ

Oued

Bab
Bou Haja

Marrakesh. There are nine trains daily to Fez, three of which continue all the way to Oujda and over the Algerian border. There are also nine to Casablanca with good connections to Marrakesh. The train station is well situated at Place Alaouite in the heart of the new city. It's easy and feasible to arrive on a morning train, leave your bags with the baggage office, and spend most of the day wandering around town before hopping a late afternoon or early evening train to another city.

By Bus

The main bus terminal is inconveniently located several kilometers from downtown on the road to Casablanca. CTM and private-line buses to almost everywhere in Morocco depart frequently from this terminal. To get there, take a petit taxi for about $0.75 or Bus 30 from Boulevard Hassan II. The following are a few CTM departure schedules, but use these only as a general guide: To Fez, Meknes, and Ifrane at 8:30 and 11:30 A.M. and 2:30, 4:30, 6:30, and 8:30 P.M.; to Tangier at 7:15 A.M., 12:30 and 4 P.M., midnight and 1 A.M.; to Oujda at 9:30 A.M. and 10:30 P.M. (via Taza); to Marrakesh at 7:30 P.M.

By Grand Taxis

The grand taxis also depart from the main bus terminal, but most of them only go to Casablanca.

First Things First

Information

The headquarters office for the Office National Marocain du Tourisme (ONMT) is at 22 Rue El Jazaïr, about a 15-minute walk from the train station. The reception desk is well stocked with ONMT brochures and maps, and the English-speaking receptionist seems helpful. Hours are Monday through Friday 8 A.M. to 2 P.M. and 2:30 P.M. to 6 P.M. in the winter, 8 A.M. to 2 P.M. in the summer and varying hours during Ramadan.

The Syndicat d'Initiative at Rue Patrice Lumumba and Rue Al Kahira is another source of tourist information, but its resources seem more limited than ONMT's. Hours are daily 8 A.M. to 7 P.M.

Map Information

For travelers planning to get off the beaten track in Morocco, a stop at the government map office—La Direction de la Conservation Foncière et des Travaux Topographiques, Division de la Carte—is an absolute must. The office is at 31 Avenue Moulay El Hassan at the corner of Zankat Ifni, a few minutes' walk from the train station. Excellent topographic maps with scales starting at 1 cm to 20,000 m can be bought for about $2 each. Unfortunately, according to the clerks here, none of the maps can be ordered by mail nor bought from any other source in Morocco. A few French and British map dealers occasionally stock some of the maps: McCarta, 122 Kings Cross Road, WC1 London, and West Col Productions, Goring, Reading, Berkshire, England. This office is open daily from 8:30 to 11 A.M. and 2:30 to 5:30 P.M., except Fridays 8:30 to 11 A.M. and 3 to 5 P.M.

Hotels

Several reasonably priced hotels are within walking distance of the train station. A few of these are in the medina, which means that they are quite cheap, but often lacking in cleanliness and comfort. The Hotel Marrakesh on Rue Sbahi is a favorite among travelers—less than $3 per person in tiny rooms with clean bathrooms. The best hotel in the medina is the two-star Hotel Darna, which is on Boulevard Laalou just past the Bab El Alou gate.

In the new city, there are several choices in each star category. The four-star Hotel Chellah (tel. 640-52 or 640-57), 2 Rue d'Ifni, is a centrally located tourist-class hotel about 1 1/2 blocks from the Grand Mosque. Most of the rooms were recently renovated and upgraded. Singles and doubles are about US $28 and $36.50, respectively. The Hotel Splendide at 8 Rue Ghaza, a block-long street between Avenue Mohammed V and Avenue Allal Ben Abdallah, has clean, but not really splendid, rooms with showers. Toilets, however, are down the hall. Singles and doubles with shower are about $9 to $12, respectively. Nearby is the two-star Hotel de la Paix, with somewhat nicer rooms at about the same prices. Across Avenue Mohammed V at 1 Zankat Hims is the two-star Hotel Gaulois with clean, inexpensive rooms. A more upscale hotel is the three-star Hotel Balima, which has a popular café and restaurant in front. It used to be one of the most elegant hotels in Rabat and was popular with Morocco's elite until the late 1950s. Today its elegance has almost completely faded, but its rooms are comfortable and reasonably priced and the café is a great place for watching people. For a full list of Rabat's twenty-three hotels, ask at the Syndicat or the ONMT reception desk.

There's a youth hostel at No. 34 Boulevard Misr just outside the medina walls about a block north of Bab El Had and Boulevard Hassan II. Nothing fancy, but it is the cheapest bed in town—less than $2 per night with a youth hostel card, which is available at the hostel.

Camping is possible at a municipal campground across the river from Rabat near the Salé "beach." Facilities include toilets, a small shop, and cold showers. The charge per person is less than $1 per night. Take Bus 6 from Boulevard Hassan II and Avenue Allal Ben Abdallah to Salé's Bab Bou Haja and follow the signs to the campground.

Restaurants and Cafés

The new city and medina offer a fair selection of restaurants, cafés, and food stands. The Café/Restaurant & Pâtisserie Karima, 3 Rue Hemss, just off Avenue Mohammed, offers a good introduction to the *tajine* (pronounced *tah-jeen*), one of the staples of Moroccan cuisine (see the food section). For about $3.25 to $4, you can get a tasty chicken or lamb tajine mildly spiced and garnished with almonds, prunes, or raisins. The waiter puts a bottle of mineral water on the table, but you don't have to accept it. The Restaurant Mounalisa, which is in a passageway just off Avenue Mohammed V, also serves tajines, but they occasionally run out of meat. I didn't know that until my beef tajine arrived with lots of carrots, tomatoes, and "meaty tasting" bones, but no meat. This fixed-priced tajine "*marocaine*" was about US $3.50 and included bread, an omelette, yogurt, and tea. The Hotel Balima Café is a good people-watching hangout for both Moroccans and foreigners, popular particularly for its large outdoor tree-shaded area. I will remember the café for the strange man who invited himself to my table, sat down across from me, but promptly got up when I told him I didn't want him there. He sat at an adjoining table and scowled at me for about a half an hour while I drank coffee and wrote postcards. The Hotel Balima is on Avenue Mohammed V across from the parliament building. For a decent fixed-price lunch or dinner (from US $3 to $4) with a bottle of Moroccan wine, try the Grand Hotel Restaurant de Rabat at 19 Rue Patrice Lumumba. Depending on your tastes, this could be your first and last glass of Moroccan wine. The restaurant Les Fouquet at 285 Avenue Mohammed V is an upscale place that offers a sumptuous Moroccan feast, as well as several Spanish-style dishes such as paella, for reasonable prices.

For an especially unusual culinary experience, try the Chinese-Vietnamese restaurant on the second floor of an Avenue Mohammed V building around the corner from the Hotel Splendide.

The extent of French influence in Rabat is particularly noticeable in the numerous French-style cafés on and around Avenue Mohammed V. Most of the cafés are similar to the Ceupucine Pâtisserie & Glacier at 345 Avenue Mohammed V, which serves fresh croissants and *pain au chocolat* (chocolate-filled croissants). Expect to pay about 50 cents for a decent cup of Moroccan-style (strong) French coffee and a pastry.

Getting Things Done and Shopping

Money

Foreign currency and traveler's checks can be exchanged in a small room next to Banc Marocaine on Avenue Mohammed V around the corner from the Hotel Splendide from 8 A.M. to 8 P.M. Monday through Friday and Saturday and Sunday from 10 A.M. to 2 P.M. and 4 P.M. to 8 P.M. There are other banks and exchange offices along Avenue Allal Ben Abdallah, as well as at the train station.

American Express has an office in Rabat, but it's inconveniently located a few kilometers south of downtown at the Rabat Hilton, which is at the end of Avenue Omar Ibn Khattab.

Post and Telephone Offices

The telephone office and poste restante (general delivery) desk are in the old post office building, which is across the street from the new post office building. Collect calls can be made and poste restante mail picked up at the far end of the counter. You'll see the small cabinet where the mail is kept. This office never closes except on special holidays, such as on Throne Day, March 3.

Shopping

Souvenirs. There are a few shops along Avenue Mohammed V that sell traditional Moroccan-style handicrafts. The prices seem reasonable because Rabat isn't as popular a tourist destination as Marrakesh and Fez. Across the river, Salé has a few traditional souks where you can buy typical Moroccan jewelry, carpets, baskets (in the souk *kissaria*, or covered market) and brasswork.

Bookstores and Newsstands. Rabat has some of the best bookstores and newsstands in Morocco. The American Bookstore at Rue Tanja and

Nut and Basket shop, Rabat Medina. *Photo by Scott Wayne.*

Rue Patrice Lumumba offers the best selection of English-language books and periodicals, including a great collection of books about Morocco and Islam. You can find most of Paul Bowles's novels and translations here. Along Avenue Mohammed V in the vicinity of the train station are a few other *librairies* or bookstores that sell some books in English. Good newsstands can also be found on Avenue Mohammed V and in the train station.

Things to See

The Medina

Rabat's medina isn't as fascinating and labyrinthine as the medinas of Fez and Marrakesh, but if this is your first visit to an old walled city, then this is a good introduction. The easiest way to begin exploring the medina is to walk up Avenue Mohammed V, across Boulevard Hassan II and through the wall to Rue Mohammed V. On your left as you enter the medina is a basic market for food and household goods along with several food stalls. On your right about a block over is the fourteenth-century Grand Mosque, which was originally built by the Merenid dynasty, but most of the structure was built much later. Walk toward the mosque and follow Rue Souika. This is one of the principal shopping streets in the medina; it becomes Rue Souk Es Sebt as it cuts through the heart of the medina and skirts the edge of the *mellah*, or old Jewish quarter, which is the poorest part of the medina. The Jewish population has vanished and, except for the remnants of about seventeen synagogues, there's really nothing of great interest in this now-squalid quarter.

As you approach Bab El Bahr at the end of the Rue Souk Es Sebt, the mellah will be on your right. Turn left up Rue des Consuls, which is before the end of Rue Souk Es Sebt, and you'll immediately notice the different architectural styles. In the nineteenth century, this was the only part of Rabat where European consulates were allowed. They built distinctively grander, more ornate European-style houses, several of which are still well maintained. Rue des Consuls continues along the edge of the medina passing a small museum that seems to be closed more often than it's open and ending at the Kasbah des Oudaïas.

The Kasbah des Oudaïas is a well-preserved part of the original city of Ribat El Fatih. It sits on a beautiful promontory overlooking the ocean and the mouth of the Oued Bou Regreg river. You can start exploring the kasbah by either first visiting the palace museum complex and the Andalusian gardens, which will be on your immediate right if you have just walked up Rue des Consuls, or continuing straight on to the Bab Oudaïa gateway.

You can't and shouldn't miss seeing the gateway because by all accounts it is one of the most beautiful gates in Morocco. Yacub El Mansur built the gate in the late twelfth century as the entrance to what was then the town center. Today, the kasbah quarter is an interesting village-like quarter that is, despite the warnings of the hustlers and would-be guides clustered around the gate, quite easy and safe for exploring on your own. The most direct route through the kasbah is to walk the main—and really only, thoroughfare—Rue Djemā'a—from one end to the other, a distance of about 500 feet (150 m). Rue Djemā'a passes the eleventh-century mosque for which it's named and ends at a terrace known as the Platform, which during the seventeenth century was a principal cannon emplacement for the pirates. The commanding view of the ocean and river makes a great photo, so bring your camera.

Backtrack along Rue Djemā'a to the narrow zig-zagging street of Rue Gazzo and follow it down to your left to the palace complex and the Café Mauré ("Moorish café"). The Café is set on a terrace overlooking the river and is a wonderful place to relax over a glass of mint tea and a piece of baklava or other sweet traditional pastry.

The palace complex is separated from the café by a wall, but there's a small entrance nearby. The complex includes a seventeenth-century palace built by Sultan Moulay Ismail that now houses the Museum of Moroccan Arts. Displayed in the palace's various reception rooms are collections of traditional jewelry and costumes, several types of which are still worn in the countryside.

The New City

Aside from walking along the Almohad walls that extend south of the medina into the New City and examining the Bab Rouah gate, the only sights worth visiting in the New City are the Archaeological Museum and the Chellah Necropolis.

Almohad Sultan Yacub El Mansur built most of the walls and *babs* or gates around the medina and into what is now the New City in the late twelfth century. The Bab Rouah was and still is one of the most impressive parts of the wall, second only to the Bab Oudaï in the kasbah.

From the Bab Rouah, walk along Avenue Yacub El Mansur (also spelled Yacoub El Mansour) to Bab Zaer and the Necropolis of Chellah at the end of the street. The Chellah resembles a medina with its high, towered walls and ramparts, but it has been uninhabited since the mid-twelfth century. By the mid-fourteenth century, the Chellah was a necropolis with a royal sanctuary that included a mosque, a *zaouia* (marabout or saint's tomb), and several royal tombs. The mosque was completed by the Merenid Sultan Abou Youssef in the late thirteenth century after his predecessor Abou El Hassan had conquered North Africa as far east as present-day Tunis and went on a building spree that included most of the walls and gates of the Chellah. Today, the sanctuary is the most intact portion of the Chellah, thus the only part really worth visiting. Most of the sanctuary structures are in ruins; however, it is possible to discern their past grandeur and functions.

The Archaeological Museum

Rabat's Archaeological Museum is just south of the Place Hassan II and across from the Hotel Chellah. It's worth visiting to get an idea of some of Morocco's principal archeological sites. The museum's collections are small, but they do include an impressive assortment of Roman, Carthaginian, and Phoenician relics, such as bronze and marble busts, ancient coins, and various tools. Admission is about US $0.40. Hours are daily except Tuesdays from 8:30 A.M. to noon and 2:30 to 6 P.M.

Salé

Just across the Oued Bou Regreg river from Rabat, Salé is the more traditional of the two cities. Most of Salé is composed of small, narrow passageways, traditional souks, and Islamic monuments, all in a compact area surrounded by crenellated ramparts and walls. It's difficult to get lost here, so just start at Bab Mrisa, which is across from the Salé bus terminal, wander around and find the following sights:

The Kissaria—center of Salé souks—is found among these streets: Rue Bab El Khabaz for cloth and weaving, Rue Haddadin for metalwork, and Rue Kechachin for wood and stone crafts.

The Medressa of Salé's Grand Mosque was built by Abou Hassan at about the same time as most of the Chellah (see above). It was used as a school of Islamic studies and included small rooms for the students. As with similar *medressas* in Fez (the Bou Inania), this one is decorated with intricate stucco and wood carvings on its walls. Non-Muslims are permitted to visit this recently renovated structure, but not the Grand Mosque. Try to get the guard to open the door to the roof—there's a great view of Rabat across the river.

You can get to Salé by bus, boat, taxi or, of course, foot. Buses 6 and 12 leave Rabat from Boulevard Hassan II and drop you off at a lot or "terminal" near Bab Mrisa and Bab Fes. Boats depart frequently from a landing just below Rabat's mellah and only charge about a dirham for the crossing near to Salé's beach area and campground. It's about a 10-minute walk from the landing to Salé's walls. By foot, you would have to go farther up river to the Hassan II bridge and walk across to Bab Mrisa at the southern corner of the Salé medina.

TANGIER

With a population of more than 300,000, Tangier is Morocco's biggest city north of the Rif mountains. It is also one of the country's most visited cities, because a steady flow of ferries and hydrofoils connect it to Europe just across the narrow straits of Gibraltar. This strategic location and proximity to Europe have made it a uniquely internationalized Moroccan city with a checkered history that included numerous conquerors and patrons.

As early as 146 B.C., Tangier was a relatively large and important town; back then it was known as Tingis, the principal town of Mauretania Tingitana, which was one of several loose kingdoms established during the decline of the Carthaginian Empire. By the third century A.D. it was the capital of what had become the Roman province of Mauretania Tingitana. However, that lasted only until about the sixth century when Vandals from Central Europe established a kingdom along most of the central coastal region of North Africa. Mauretania Tingitana remained semiautonomous and politically detached from this region until the late seventh and early eighth centuries when waves of Arab armies crossed and conquered North Africa in the name of Islam. Tangier became a strategic staging point for the Islamic conquest of Spain and a small portion of southern France in the eighth century.

The Rif mountain Berber tribes of Morocco were also converted to Islam, but rather than cooperate with their new conquerors they wrested control of Tangier from them in A.D. 740. As the arabized and Islamized Berber tribes and confederations of Morocco increased in strength and numbers, Tangier was the strategic prize of many intertribal and interdynasty rivalries over at least the next five centuries—the Idrissids in the late eighth century, the Umayyad emirate of Cordova, Spain, in the early tenth, the Fatimids of Tunis in the mid-tenth, the Almoravids in the eleventh, the Almohads in the twelfth, and the Hafsids in the thirteenth.

By the fifteenth century, Tangier was again the object of European interests; first of the Portuguese and then alternately over the next few centuries also of Spanish, English, and Moroccan Alawite claims and interests. Rival European claims on Tangier intensified in the nineteenth century and precipitated a few diplomatic and military skirmishes among the French, Spanish, English, and German leaders of the late nineteenth and early twentieth centuries. Apparently, the only way to appease such a multinational array of interests in Tangier was to accord the city and its immediate surroundings special international status. In 1923, Tangier was declared an international zone and placed under multinational administration, which was its status until national independence in 1956.

Under multinational administration, Tangier was a semiautonomous entity detached economically and politically from the rest of Morocco. Its tax-free, duty-free port status attracted several international financial institutions and businesses. As a city long accustomed to many cultures, Tangier also acquired a reputation as a tolerant, free-spirited city where "anything goes." Writers and gays found a haven here, especially in the 1950s. Gay bars and brothels flourished. After independence, however, the latter were closed, the multinational administration dismantled, and the tax advantages eliminated.

Today, Tangier is a popular destination for hundreds of thousands of vacationers of many nationalities coming from or through Spain and France. This large influx of foreign tourists, however, has spawned a small army of multilingual Moroccan hustlers and unofficial "guides." If you arrive by ferry or hydrofoil, it's almost impossible to avoid being approached by one of this army's persistent foot soldiers. The ferry terminal seems to be this group's favorite hangout, but the medina is also popular. Don't believe anything these guys say (in six or seven languages), just head straight for a taxi, or at least pretend to know where you are going. Most importantly, maintain your sense of humor, and disregard the age-old maxim "First impressions are lasting ones." Also, even though these prospective guides can be as irritating as a fly in your ear, they are merely trying to earn a living in a country with an unemployment rate that's usually at least 20 percent.

Arrival and Departure

By Train

Tangier has two train stations both conveniently located on the same main line. On the quay adjacent to the ferry terminal is the Port

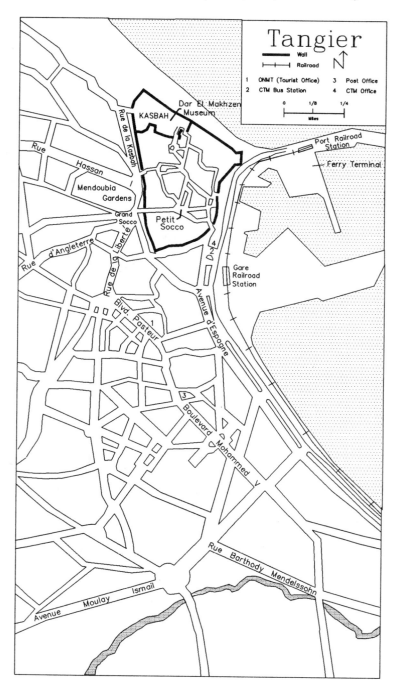

Tangier

- Wall
- Railroad

1 ONMT (Tourist Office)   3 Post Office
2 CTM Bus Station   4 CTM Office

0   1/8   1/4
Miles

KASBAH · Dar El Makhzen Museum

Rue de la Kasbah

Rue Hassan

Mendoubia Gardens

Grand Socco

Rue d'Angleterre

Rue de la Liberté

Petit Socco

Blvd. Pasteur

Avenue d'Espagne

Gare Railroad Station

Port Railroad Station

Ferry Terminal

Boulevard Mohammed V

Rue Barthody Mendelssohn

Avenue Moulay Ismail

terminal, which is the end of the line. The other station is the Town (referred to as Gare or Ville) terminal, which is on Avenue d'Espagne, just south of the CTM bus station and the medina. All but a few trains arrive at and depart from both terminals. Check the latest "Horaire des Trains" (train schedule) for the most recent schedules; it's available at both terminals for 1 DH (approximately $0.13).

There are several trains daily in both directions. From Tangier Ville or Gare terminal, there are direct first-class "express" trains to Rabat-Salé, Mohammedia, and Casablanca (Port terminal) at 7:22 A.M. and 4:10 P.M. There's also a nonexpress train that departs at 11:15 P.M. from the Port terminal and continues all the way to Marrakesh arriving at 8:45 A.M. after stops at Rabat, Casablanca (Voyageurs terminal), and several other cities.

There are also trains to and from Meknes, Fez, and Oujda, but be wary of the schedules because a few require train changes at Sidi Slimane or Sidi Kacem, which are junction towns south of the Rif mountains.

By Bus

Located on Avenue d'Espagne just outside the entrance to the Petit Socco part of the medina, the CTM bus terminal is the biggest and busiest of the seven terminals in the city. The other six terminals are operated by smaller, private bus companies and can be found nearby. There are two CTM buses daily to Fez (8 hours), Meknes (7 hours), Rabat (5 hours), and twelve to Tetouan (1 1/2 hours); other companies also serve these destinations.

By Grand Taxi

Grand taxis congregate near the CTM terminal. The majority go to Tetouan, but there are also a few usually available for more distant destinations, such as Laraiche.

By Plane

Tangier's international airport is about 15 km (9 miles) outside the city. An hourly bus runs between the airport and the Grand Socco square. There are direct flights between Tangier and the following foreign and domestic cities: Agadir, Amsterdam, Barcelona, Brussels, Casablanca, Düsseldorf, Fez, Frankfurt, Geneva, Lisbon, London, Lyon, Madrid, Marseilles, Paris, and Vienna.

By Sea

Ferries and hydrofoils arrive at and depart from separate terminals on the same quay in Tangier. There are many runs between Tangier and several European Mediterranean cities, with the most frequent service in the summer months. The following is approximate schedule information:

By Hydrofoil. You can travel on the *h.f. Aladin* or the *h.f. Scheherezade* (Transtour company). Hydrofoils leave from Tarifa (less than half an hour, three times daily), and Algeciras (1 hour, once daily) in Spain and from Gibraltar (1 hour, once daily). Since this is the fastest way to cross by sea, the hydrofoils tend to be crowded, especially in the summer. They do not run in rough seas, though.

By Ferry. Ferries are run by Compania Transmediterranea, Isnasa Line, Limadet Ferry, the Bland Line, Compagnie Marocaine de Navigation, and Comanav. Ferry departures are more numerous and frequent, but take longer than the hydrofoils. There are ferry crossings from Algeciras (2 1/2 hours) and Gibraltar to Tangier (2 hours, Wednesdays and Fridays); and from Sète, France, a twice-weekly 14-hour trip.

By Catamaran. There's also daily catamaran service between Gibraltar and Tangier on the Gibline. Additional information was unavailable at the time of writing because it was relatively new.

If you don't have advance reservations, then taking one of the car ferries from Algeciras to Tangier is the easiest way to go. There are at least two ferries daily to Tangier at 12:30 and 8 P.M. between November 1 and March 31; three daily at 9 A.M. and 1 and 6 P.M. between April 1 and June 14; and sometimes as many five or six daily the rest of the year. One-way fares are about $26 (Class A) and $21 (Class B). Bicycles and motorcycles cost an extra $19.50.

The Gibraltar ferries are operated by the Bland Line, which has its offices in the Cloister Building, Gibraltar; tel. 79-200. The boats run on Wednesdays and Fridays, departing Gibraltar at 6 P.M. and arriving Tangier at 8 P.M. Write to the company for more information.

One of the twice weekly ferries from Sète, France is operated by Comanav, SNCM, 12 Rue de Godot de Mauroy, Paris (tel. 2666-6019). The other is operated by the Compagnie Marocaine de Navagation. If you can get them, reservations are essential.

Getting Around

Orientation

Tangier is divided into two parts—the European-built Ville Nouvelle and the Medina. The Ville Nouvelle is crisscrossed by several major streets and avenues that intersect, as in Europe, in open areas known as *places* (squares or plazas).

From the CTM bus terminal at the southeast corner of the Medina and the western side of the port, Avenue d'Espagne runs along the waterfront and becomes Avenue des Forces Armées Royales just after the Hotel Rif. Most of the latter part is tree lined and along the beach, which makes a short, but pleasant walk.

The focal point for the Ville Nouvelle, however, is inland and due south of the Medina a few blocks—Place de France. Several French-style cafés are on the square and the surrounding streets. Heading southeast from the square is the Boulevard Pasteur with a few hotels, the tourism offices, American Express (at No. 54 in the Voyages Schwarz office), and the post office. Going north from the square is the Rue de la Liberté, which leads to the Medina, the Mendoubia Gardens, and another major square—Le Grand Socco. Continuing across the Grand Socco with the gardens on your left, there's an entrance through the wall to the Medina and Rue Es Siaghin ("Silversmith's Street") on your right. You can either enter here and walk straight to the Petit Socco, one of the Medina's principal squares, or walk just outside the Medina along Rue d'Italie and Rue de la Kasbah to Place du Tabor, the entrance to the Kasbah portion of the Medina.

First Things First

Information

The Moroccan National Tourism Office (ONMT) is at 29 Boulevard Pasteur. The English-speaking staff can be helpful in arranging accommodations. Obtain a copy of the latest "Guide des Hotels" for a full listing. They also have most of the ONMT brochures and maps for the rest of Morocco. Hours: 8 A.M. to 2 P.M. Monday to Saturday.

If you don't find what you need at the ONMT office, try the Syndicat d'Initiative (chamber of commerce), also on Boulevard Pasteur, about a block away toward the Grand Socco.

Guides

Frankly, there is not much reason to hire a guide—official or unofficial—in Tangier. Initially, you may want a guide to steer you out of the arrival chaos at the port terminals and toward a hotel, but beyond that it's unnecessary. The Medina is relatively compact and not as confusing as other medinas. The Ville Nouvelle is well laid out and easy to visit on your own.

Forewarning! To reiterate what I mentioned above—Tangier is notorious for its persistent would-be guides and hustlers. Don't believe their stories about what is good, bad, possible, impossible, cheap, or expensive.

Hotels

Tangier has a good selection of hotels ranging from the beautiful five-star Hotel El Minzah to the one-star Hotel El Muniria, which was a popular writers' hangout in the 1950s. There's enough variety of hotels on Boulevard Pasteur, Rue de la Liberté and Avenue des Forces Armées Royales, as well as on side streets just off these streets, that you can just shop around and see which one you like best. The Muniria on Rue Magellan south of Rue de la Plage about a block in from Avenue d'Espagne is simple, but with lots of character and a popular bar—a traveler's favorite.

There are also several pension-style hotels in the Medina around the Petit Socco, but only the one-star Hotel Continental on Rue Dar El Baroud seemed noteworthy—complete with a great view and a grand piano in the hall.

Restaurants and Cafés

Shop around on Boulevard Pasteur and surrounding side streets for Franco-Moroccan cuisine and along the beachfront for Spanish-style fish restaurants. The Hammadi restaurant on Rue d'Italie is highly recommended by Moroccans and expatriates for its excellent, albeit relatively pricey, Moroccan food. The Café-Restaurant Detroit is also recommended for its meals, café atmosphere, and Moorish decor à la "Rolling Stones."

Getting Things Done and Shopping

Consulates

The U.S. Consulate (tel. 359-04) is at 29 Rue El Achouak Chemin des Amoureux; Great Britain at 52 Rue d'Angleterre; France at Place de France; Spain at 85 Rue Sidi Boabid; and West Germany at 47 Avenue Hassan II.

Money

There are several banks on Boulevard Pasteur and on its continuation, Boulevard Mohammed V. American Express is also on Boulevard Pasteur at No. 54 in the Voyages Schwarz office.

Post and Telephone Office

The main post and telephone office (postes, télégraphes, et téléphones, or PTT) is at 33 Boulevard Mohammed V. The postal section is open from 8:30 A.M. to 12 noon Monday to Saturday, and the telephone section is open 24 hours.

Bookstores

English-language periodicals can be found in the shops along the Boulevard Pasteur. For books, particularly Paul Bowles's works, try the Librairie des Colonnes at 54 Boulevard Pasteur (same building as the American Express office).

Things to See

The main sights of interest in Tangier are in the Medina, the older walled part of the city. Start at the Grand Socco, which was the city's largest market square. The Mendoubia Gardens along the northern side of the Grand Socco are worth a quick visit before crossing to the Rue Es Siaghin entrance to the Medina.

The Rue Es Siaghin ("Silversmiths' Street") used to be the Medina's main street and center of the silver jewelry market, but today most of the shops and stalls sell clothing and produce. The mellah or Jewish quarter was also concentrated here; however, after independence, most of the city's Jewish residents left. This street ends at the Petit Socco—an area made legendary in Paul Bowles's stories and once renowned for its back-alley brothels.

From the northern side of the Petit Socco, follow Rue des Chrétiens through the Medina as it veers to the left and becomes Rue Ben Raisouli. This street leads into an open area with a short street on the northern side that leads to the Place de la Kasbah and the entrance to the Dar El

Makhzen museum. The museum houses a superb collection of traditional handicrafts and well-preserved antiques. The buildings served as a palace from the seventeenth century (for Moulay Ismail) up to 1912 when the French forced Sultan Moulay Hafid into an early retirement. It's open daily except Thursdays from 9:30 A.M. to 12 noon and from 3 to 6 P.M. The Dar El Makhzen is really the only part of the Kasbah complex worth visiting because most of the rest of the structure has suffered from numerous attacks through the centuries.

CHAPTER 6

Marrakesh

Marrakesh is a city of many faces, a city that epitomizes past and present Morocco. In the distance beyond the Haouz plain where Marrakesh sits, the snow-capped peaks of the Atlas mountains rise like an immense shimmering fairy tale land of castles and towers. In the city, the fairy tale is acted out in the Medina, the original city of Marrakesh, with its medieval markets, craftspeople, narrow winding streets and alleyways, and crenellated ramparts and red walls. Outside the Medina is Gueliz, the "new" city of Marrakesh founded by the French in the early part of this century. It was intended as a base for their colonial offices and purposely located outside the Medina in order to limit their intrusions on the local traditions. However, as the Moroccan economy developed, changes in both parts of the city became inevitable, particularly in the human faces of Marrakesh.

Since its establishment as a capital city around the beginning of Almoravid rule in about 1062, Marrakesh has always attracted many people from the surrounding countryside and mountains. However, more than any of the other three "imperial" (past or present capital) Moroccan cities—Rabat, Fez, and Meknes—Marrakesh has been and continues to be mostly a Berber, rather than Arab, metropolis.

It was founded first as a military outpost by Abu Bekr, leader of the Berber tribe of Sanhajis. As the Sanhajis adopted the teachings of a Moroccan philosopher named Ibn Yasin, they became known as the "people of the *ribat*," the *al-murabitun*, or, in rough transliteration, the Almoravids. Under Abu Bekr's cousin, Youssef ben Tachfin, the outpost became a *ksour* or fortified town, and a good base and capital from which Tachfin and his son, Ali Ben Youssef, could expand both the city and the Almoravid empire. By the end of the century, the Almoravid empire stretched from Spain in the north to Algiers in the east and the Senegal river in the south. Marrakesh reaped the benefits of this growth.

The city became more fortified, more permanent, as a variety of religious and public works projects were completed. The foundation for an intricate network of underground water channels was laid, which solved the city's water shortage and continues to provide it with water.

100

The city's first extensive gardens were planted, and a palace and mosque were constructed. If it hadn't been challenged by a rival Berber tribe in the mid-twelfth century, the Almoravid dynasty probably would have continued this expansion.

However, by 1146 the Masmouda tribe had taken Marrakesh and established itself under Abd El Moumin as the Almohad dynasty. He was succeeded in 1163 by Abu Yuqub Youssef, who expanded the city's walls and ramparts by using "pisé"—a red, concrete-like substance of lime and gravel that originated in Spain. Greater expansion occurred under his successor, Yacoub Al Mansur, whose architectural accomplishments in Marrakesh included palaces, a hospital, a mosque, and more gardens. Great architecture, though, wasn't enough to prevent the city from again being sacked, this time by the Merenids in the 1220s.

The Merenids became the third Berber dynasty to rule Morocco, but they weren't able to seize control of Marrakesh until 1271, by which time they had already made Rabat their capital. Unlike their predecessors, they shared power with the marabouts or mystic holy men of the countryside, and thus splintered their authority, which eventually caused their demise first in Spain and then Morocco.

The Saadians, who claimed direct descent from the Prophet's family, rose to power after the Merenids and once again made Marrakesh a capital city. With tribute and ransom for prisoners gained from the Portuguese defeat in the Battle of Three Kings and other victories, Sultan Ahmed Al Mansur (1578–1603) built one of the city's most lasting monuments—the Saadian tombs—and the El Badi Palace, of which only ruins remain. The tombs were expanded during the succeeding Alawite dynasty.

Under the Alawite dynasty, which has ruled Morocco since the late seventeenth century, Marrakesh became a bigger city, but Meknes became the capital. Marrakesh also became run down and squalid, mostly out of neglect because the Alawites had to contend with great internal strife among Morocco's various tribes. By the nineteenth century, they also had to contend with European colonial interests, both political and economic, in Morocco. Marrakesh figured greatly in French plans when the country was made a protectorate in 1912.

From 1912 to 1925, Morocco was governed by the French resident general Marshal Louis Lyautey. He ruled according to three main precepts, "pacify, preserve, and centralize": Pacify the tribes, attempt to preserve their traditions, and centralize authority. These policies increased the power of the pasha of Marrakesh, Thami El Glaoui, from one of the three predominant Atlas mountain Berber families, perhaps as a counterbalance to their rivals, the Alawites. The Medina was cleaned up and Gueliz, the "new" part of town, was constructed. Slave sales and beheadings were stopped.

Today, both the Medina and Gueliz are thriving commercial centers of a different kind. Tourism and industry have helped to make Marrakesh a prominent economic center, thus a source of increased employment. As drought and lower commodity prices blighted the countryside and mountains, people emigrated in droves to Marrakesh and to other cities to search for work. Unfortunately, there haven't been enough jobs for everyone—unemployment and underemployment are rife. Also, shantytowns have begun popping up just outside the walls because of overcrowding in the Medina and shortages of low-income housing in Gueliz.

For travelers, this explosive influx of people from all over Morocco has made Marrakesh somewhat of an interesting showcase of traditional rural life and a fascinating source of urban "adventures." As you explore the city, particularly the Djemā'a El Fna part of the Medina, keep in mind this recent influx and the lack of employment because you will undoubtably be approached by peddlers, prospective guides, con artists, snake charmers, water bearers, jugglers, and many others.

ARRIVAL, DEPARTURE, AND GETTING AROUND

Whether you arrive by plane, train, bus, or grand taxi, once you are in the city, it's easy to learn how to get around. Marrakesh is divided into two parts—Gueliz and the Medina. Surrounded by miles of chalky red walls made from *tabia* or *pisé*, the Medina is the traditional heart of Marrakesh. Like the walls, parts of the Medina date back to the founding of Marrakesh in the twelfth century and still offer a view into a past that is practically nonexistent in Gueliz, the new part of town.

Relative to the Medina, Gueliz is new because much of it was built this century by the French colonial government and by French-inspired Moroccans. Aside from numerous French-style cafés, the most notice-able French influence, however, is in the street layout. Like Paris but on a smaller scale, wide, tree-lined streets were laid out in a hub-and-spoke pattern with two main "hubs" and numerous "spokes" of varying widths.

From the hub on Place de la Liberté, just outside Bab Larissa, the principal western gate into the Medina, Avenue Mohammed V (also known as a boulevard in some books and brochures) cuts through Gueliz on one side and into the Medina on the other. Most services of interest to travelers, such as banks, tourist offices, post and telephone offices, car rental and travel agencies, American Express, small grocery stores, and a few slick curio shops are on or just off Mohammed V.

The other important hub on Mohammed V is Place du 16 Novembre, from which Avenue des Nations Unies goes northeast to Bab Doukkala and the bus terminal, and Avenue Hassan II heads west to the train station.

Getting around the narrow, twisting passages and fragrant souks of the Medina is an adventure that requires enough explanation to merit a separate section later in this chapter. In summary, the Djemā'a El Fna is the best place to begin exploring the mysteries of the Medina. If you don't stick to the main thoroughfares, though, you will probably get lost in a sticky web of alleys and passages.

First find the Café des France on the Djemā'a El Fna and walk north away from the Djemā'a and across a lot that is usually full of donkeys, camels, and vegetable sellers. Continue north through the farthest passages on your left and into the Medina. The passage widens and becomes the covered street Rue Souk Smarine, which has been the principal market area for cloth and clothing.

To get into Marrakesh from the airport, 5 km southwest of the city, you can either take a petit taxi for an amount that depends on your haggling skills or Bus 11, which runs about every half hour. The bus deposits you right in the heart of old Marrakesh at Square de'Foucauld, which is at the edge of the Djemā'a El Fna. If you have not already arranged accommodations and are looking for a good, inexpensive hotel, this is a great place to start.

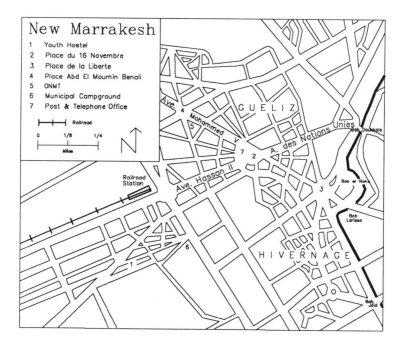

New Marrakesh

1 Youth Hostel
2 Place du 16 Novembre
3 Place de la Liberte
4 Place Abd El Moumin Benali
5 ONMT
6 Municipal Campground
7 Post & Telephone Office

Railroad

0   1/8   1/4
Miles

From the bus terminal, just outside the Medina gate of Bab Doukkala, you can either walk to the Djemā'a (about 25 minutes, a long walk in blistery summer heat), take a petit taxi from in front of the terminal, or hop on Bus 3 or 8.

From the train station, it is about a 10- to 15-minute walk to the ONMT office (tourist office) at Place Abd El Moumin Benali. The International Youth Hostel and Municipal Campground are within easy walking distance (see map and section above). There are also plenty of taxis and, on the opposite side of the street, buses into Gueliz and the Medina. *Warning*: Be prepared to confront a hungry hoard of taxi drivers as you enter the arrival hall. They will insist on carrying your bags right to the biggest, most expensive taxis rather than to the smaller, cheaper petit taxis. The clamor of taxi drivers and hustlers squawking and squeaking like scratched records—"Hello, hello, I take you to the kasbah," "Come taxi with me," and "You need hotel, you need guide" makes your ears ring and head spin. Dash through the hoard, swat away any hustlers still whistling and whispering in your ears, and get to the front of the terminal where the chaos is less and taxi fares are lower.

The faster, air-conditioned *"rapide"* trains run to and from Marrakesh (the railway terminus) according to the following schedule:

Departure Times	Arrival Times
9.08 A.M.	5.16 A.M.
2.15 P.M.	12.43 P.M.
6.41 P.M.	3.13 P.M.
	10.17 P.M.

The train with sleeper cars arrives in and departs from Marrakesh at 8:54 A.M. and 7:40 P.M. Reservations are recommended.

Grand taxis, the six-passenger Peugeots and Mercedes that shuttle between towns and cities, are in a lot near Bab Er Robb, one of the Medina's principal southern gates, either coming from or going to Asni and the Ourika valley. For other destinations, the taxis are either in the Djemā'a El Fna, at Bab Doukaala near the bus terminal, or at Bab Er Raha, just north of Bab Larissa and the Hotel de Ville.

The most romantic way of getting around Marrakesh is by *calèche* or horse-drawn carriages. These exist only here in Marrakesh and are a popular form of transportation, not only for tourists but also for locals because they often cost about the same as petit taxis. They can take up to five people, but if you are a couple looking for a bit of Marrakesh romance, hire a calèche for a sunset ride around the Medina walls and through the garden areas adjacent to the palaces. The easiest place to arrange a calèche is in the Medina at Square de Foucauld (see map), but be sure to haggle and set a price before you leave.

Bicycles are also a popular way of getting around Marrakesh, particularly for travelers, but I recommend them only for touring outside the Medina and the main streets of Gueliz. Many Moroccan drivers seem to be of the "push accelerator to floor and then look for obstacles" school of driving where the quick swerve apparently overrules the steady-handed pass. Even "drivers" of donkey carts and horse-drawn carriages are adept at quickly swerving within inches of obstacles such as bicyclists, so ride defensively and try to be aware of what is coming up behind you. For some suggested routes, see below. Bicycles can be rented from several agencies along Avenue Mohammed V in Gueliz and from a few agencies near the Grand Hotel Tazi (see map).

Marrakesh is a great place to rent a car because there are many agencies for you to choose from and there are several one-day to one-week trips worth doing from the city into the countryside. Most of these trips, which will be described later in this chapter, can be done without a car, but then you have to rely on buses and taxis and you may not see as much of the country. Get a group of four together, and split the cost. The average price for three days in a Renault 4 GTL was about $150, including taxes and insurance, thus $37.50 per person.

Your hotel can help you find an agency or just shop around on Avenue Mohammed V. I rented a car from Mabrouk Auto Location (tel. 332-04), next to the Hotel Marrakesh near Place de la Liberté, and was pleased. Abhir El Houcine, the agency's Berber owner, speaks English and is quite helpful and friendly. The only drawback was that the car could not be returned to another city.

Avis, Hertz, and Budget all have offices at the airport and on Avenue Mohammed V at Nos. 137, 154, and 213 and tel. 337-27, 346-80, and 346-04, respectively. Their daily and three-day rates for a Renault 4, the most inexpensive, were comparable, averaging about $22 per day plus $0.23 per km plus 19 percent tax plus insurance, or three days for about $165 and 19 percent tax but with unlimited mileage. Reservations for all three agencies can be made in North America and Europe.

FIRST THINGS FIRST

Tourist information

For basic tourist information, including maps of Marrakesh and other cities, and official guides to the souks or markets in the Medina, visit one of two types of tourist information offices here. The ONMT (Office National Marocaine du Tourisme), which is a branch of the national tourism office, and the Syndicat d'Initiative, which is equivalent to a chamber of commerce, are both in Gueliz on Avenue Mohammed V. ONMT is at Place Abd El Moumin Benali, and the Syndicat is at No. 170 on the opposite side of the street going toward the Medina. Hours are 8:30-12 and 3-6 daily, but the Syndicat is closed Saturday afternoons and Sundays.

For the latest trek and travel information, local guides and travelers are often one of the best sources. Berber mountain guides and a variety of travelers and adventure-seekers often gather to eat and/or stay at the Hotel Ali (see below). Adventure travel groups such as the British-based Sherpa Expeditions, Guerba Expeditions, and Encounter Overland use the Hotel de Foucauld (see below) as their Marrakesh base and can sometimes be helpful sources of information about trekking and overland travel conditions. Other adventure travel groups, particularly those from Spain, France, Italy, and Switzerland, often stay at the Grand Hotel Tazi (see below) and can be an equally good source of travel information. Hard-core backpackers and travelers-on-the-cheap who are often walking encyclopedias of travel tips can also be found at the municipal campground and the youth hostel (see below).

Specific information about High Atlas mountain treks can sometimes be obtained, albeit with some difficulty, from the Club Alpin Français, Boite Postale 888, Marrakesh. Reservations for camping spaces and beds at their mountain refuges can be made in writing, but if you want a reply, be sure to include International Reply Coupons (available at most post offices).

Trekking information may also be available from specialized tour operators, such as Atlas Sahara Treks, which is run by a knowledgeable trekker named Bernard Fabry. Keep in mind, however, that Fabry is in business to sell trips and not to dispense information. If you want to arrange a special trek, he can be contacted at 72 Rue de la Liberté, tel. 4-337-57.

Accommodations Information

Both tourist information offices can help arrange accommodations by calling any of the hotels listed in ONMT's "Guide des Hotels." The guide is fairly comprehensive, with thirty-nine hotels ranging from "one-star B," the lowest classification, to "five-star luxury," the highest listed and described by symbols. Generally, but not always, the lower the classification the lower the room rates and the fewer amenities available.

Most budget accommodations in Marrakesh are in the Medina on or near the Djemā'a El Fna, which for most travelers is the place to stay. Unless you need to be near the train station or are staying at the International Youth Hostel, there is little reason to stay in Gueliz, the relatively new section of town outside the Medina walls, which is too far removed from the colorful, bustling action of the Djemā'a El Fna.

At the top of the list is the palatial Moorish-style La Mamounia Hotel, built in 1923 and renovated in 1986 with plenty of marble, silk, brass, and cedar. Its 179 rooms and 49 suites start at about $181 per night for a double room and are surrounded by sumptuous gardens of lilac, hibiscus, and orange trees. Not surprisingly, the hotel was a favorite of Sir Winston Churchill in the 1940s. Also, they are careful about whom they allow through the front door. I found this out when guards grabbed me as I went through the door in my hiking boots; apparently topsiders (a lightweight casual leather shoe) are OK, but not hiking boots. For more information about the hotel, read an excellent article about it in the June 21, 1987, edition of the *New York Times*. For reservations in North America, call "Leading Hotels of the World" at 1-800-223-6800. Even if you do not stay here, have a comparatively pricey drink or cup of tea on the terrace so you can then tour the finely manicured grounds.

There are several hotels in the four- and five-star range, most of which are outside the Medina, that are less luxurious and more inexpensive, but still quite comfortable. Two of these, the Hotel Es-Saadi (tel. 320-11, telex 720-42) and the P.L.M. Hotel Toubkal (tel. 329-72, telex 729-80), are particularly well situated amidst the garden suburb of the Hivernage, a few blocks south of Place de la Liberté and just outside Bab Jdid, one of the Medina's western gates.

The 367-room Hotel Le Marrakech (tel. 343-72, telex 720-67) at Place de la Liberté is also well situated and could probably be considered one of the better large tourist hotels. It has typical tourist-class amenities, such as tennis courts, swimming pool, and night club, as well as comfortable rooms, but the main restaurant seemed large enough for everyone in the hotel. As with most of the hotels in its class, it tends to cater to many tour groups.

There is also a Club Méditerranée in Marrakesh; it is hidden behind trees and high walls at the edge of the Djemā'a El Fna. In typical Club Med fashion, once you pass through the entrance, a single wooden door marked by only one small Club Med sign, you leave behind the poverty, dirt, and pleas of street urchins and would-be guides and enter a glittery, brocaded world of smartly attired guests and scantily clad "hostesses." It is worth visiting, if only to feel the immediate contrast of two different worlds and to get some idea, perhaps, of a European interpretation of the king's palaces.

My personal preferences are the smaller hotels near the Djemā'a El Fna, which have far fewer amenities, less comfort, and smaller groups, but lots of character and are still quite adequate for recuperating from or preparing yourself for a trek into the Atlas mountains. However, none have swimming pools, so if you seek a cool pool for recuperation, you may want to look beyond the following hotels.

The Bennani family dominates the hotel business near the Square de Foucauld, just off the Djemā'a El Fna, with three popular hotels, each owned by a Bennani brother: the Hotel Ali, the Grand Hotel Tazi, and the Hotel de Foucauld. The family also owns hotels in Casablanca.

Among the three, my favorite is the Hotel Ali (tel. 449-79), which is on Rue Moulay Ismail only about 50 m, (160 ft) from the Djemā'a El Fna. It is owned and managed by Farouk Bennani, a Canadian-educated Moroccan economist, and opened only in 1987, the newest of the three hotels. A ground-floor restaurant with low tables and colorful brocaded cushions serves a variety of meat and chicken tajines for very reasonable prices—only about $5 for a full meal (see below). Most of the rooms have telephones and bathrooms with hot showers. At only about $10 to $15 per night for a double, it tends to be quite popular among backpackers, students, and small adventure travel groups. Several Berber mountain guides, such as Aït El Kadi Brahim, head of the Atlas mountain village of Douar Aroumd (near Mount Toubkal), congregate here to organize groups for mountain treks. Farouk Bennani speaks fluent English and can put you in touch with the guides.

The Hotel de Foucauld (tel. 254-99), across from Square de Foucauld on Rue El Mouahidine, is similar to the Ali in both room rates and standards, but the restaurant tends to have higher prices then Ali's. Groups from Encounter Overland, Guerba Expeditions, and Sherpa Expeditions often stay here en route to or from Trans-Africa, -Sahara, or -Morocco trips and Atlas mountain treks. You will know they have arrived if you see their well-marked Land-Rovers and tanklike overland vehicles across the street. Usually, you cannot join any of these groups without having made advance reservations, but the participants and group leaders can be good sources of travel information.

The Grand Hotel Tazi (tel. 221-52), at the corner of Rue de Bab Agnaou and Avenue Hoummam El Ftouak about three blocks from the Foucauld (away from the Djemā'a El Fna), is slightly more comfortable than the other two Bennani hotels and thus costs more. The additional cost, though, has not discouraged various European adventure travel groups from staying here, thus making it a good source of travel information. If you have ever seen the film *Ishtar*, starring Dustin Hoffman and Warren Beatty, you will recognize the Tazi as the hotel where Hoffman and Beatty stayed and made their Morocco "singing" (squawking?) debut.

There are many other hotels, especially in the "no-star" to "two-star B" range, around the Djemā'a El Fna and on nearby streets south of the Djemā'a such as Rue Zitoun El Kedim and Rue El Mouahidine. On the Djemā'a, these include the "one-star A" Hotel CTM, which has been both praised and condemned by travelers, the "no-star" Hotel Oukaïmeden that a few travelers reportedly liked, and the bustling Hotel du Café de France attached to the Djemā'a's most famous café. For others you might look on the small side streets off Rue Zitoun El Kedim and Rue El Mouahidine.

The Auberge de Jeunesse or Youth Hostel (tel. 32831) is in Gueliz, conveniently located near the train station, but about a 25-minute walk from the Djemā'a El Fna. As you leave the train station, the street in front is Avenue Hassan II. Turn right on Hassan II and then left on the first street. Follow this street past Rue Ibn El Qadi to Rue Mohammed El Hansali, where you will turn left. The hostel is on your right. Depending on the exchange rate, a bed for one night in this reasonably well maintained hostel is about $1 to $2.

The Municipal Campground is also near the train station. As you leave the station turn left on Hassan II and then right on Avenue de France at Place de L'Empereur Haile Selassie. The campground is about two long blocks down on your right. Aside from being the cheapest "place" to stay and a good place to meet travelers and possibly arrange rides, there are really no reasons to stay here. Although it is relatively secure, some travelers have reported losing belongings here. And, anyway, who wants to camp in a city? You are not saving much money, and you don't have to stay here to meet people—a visit is possible.

Guides

Hire a guide in Marrakesh to lead you through the souks (markets) and maze of passageways near the Djemā'a El Fna (at least the first time) and, most importantly, to fend off the annoying advances of other guides and hustlers. As you will quickly discover, there are official and unofficial guides, both of whom can be useful or useless and unnecessary for shopping.

Official guides have shiny brass badges like sheriff deputies, usually speak impeccable English as well as several other languages, and can be arranged for "official" government-set rates at the tourist office and most hotels. They generally offer a good introduction to the Medina, the only area in Marrakesh where you need them, for about $8 per group for a half-day.

Unofficial guides come in all shapes, sizes, and ages and often call themselves "your friend" or "a student who wants to practice speaking English." According to Moroccan law, unless they have been government certified, they can't legally call themselves guides, although some may be equally or even better qualified than official guides. However, not all would-be friends are necessarily unofficial guides in disguise. Deciding who is who and distinguishing truth from fiction will sometimes be a true test of your ability to interpret human nature, but don't be surprised if you occasionally flunk.

Boys are sometimes the best unofficial guides because they usually don't overtalk, successfully ward off prospective guides, and often know some of the Medina's off-the-beaten-track sites. They also aren't usually adept at trying to sell you the moon or lure you into a carpet shop. Most likely, these "guides" will find you in the Djemā'a El Fna when you are between the pythons and the acrobats (see section on Djemā'a El Fna below).

Restaurants, Cafés, and Food Stands

Marrakesh abounds with restaurants, French-style cafés, and food stands. Several of the city's finer, thus more expensive, restaurants are found in Gueliz, the newer part of town. One of the best for traditional Moroccan cuisine is the Restaurant Marocaine Dar Tagine (tel. 46044) at Place Abd El Moumin Benali across from the Café Renaissance. A full meal that includes various breads, appetizers, a big tajine stew, a second entrée, dessert, and mint tea is more than enough for two and costs about $15.

Downstairs and next to the restaurant entrance is the Pâtisserie & Boulangerie Dar Tagine ("Pastry Shop & Bakery..."), which must be one of the world's greatest Moroccan pastry shops and bakeries. If you can walk out of there without buying or at least sampling something, then your willpower is superhuman or your sense of smell is amiss. It is a virtual museum of culinary delights that smell and taste as good as they look—almond cookies, cheese breads, minipizzas, chocolate-filled croissants, baklava dripping with honey, and croissant-like *kab el ghazal* ("gazelle horns") stuffed with a crushed almond filling and rolled in powdered sugar. Although most of the goods wouldn't endure a long trek, stock up here for at least the beginning of your trip into the countryside.

Around the corner from the Dar Tagine establishments are several other decent restaurants, including the French-style Grand Café de l'Atlas Restaurant on Avenue Mohammed V, where two can eat a tomato salad and shish kebab for about $5.

On the Djemā'a El Fna, most travelers sample or are tempted to sample the various grilled chicken, beef, lamb, fish, and boiled vegetable dishes served by a legion of food stands set up almost every day at sunset. You probably won't find more inexpensive cooked food in Marrakesh, but you may also be exposing your innards to a temporary invasion of nasty microbes. This gastronomic adventure is worthwhile if you think you can handle it. As a general rule, avoid raw vegetables and eat only those foods that have been well cooked (see health section in Part I, especially the information on diarrhea and dysentery).

Along the edges of the Djemā'a El Fna and on nearby streets are several good restaurants with prices not much higher than the food stands. The restaurant at the Hotel Ali, only 50 m (160 ft) from the Djemā'a on Rue Moulay Ismail, is an increasingly popular travelers' choice. The cutesy Moorish decor, comically big cushions, and low tables are almost a study in Moroccan *Thousand and One Nights* kitsch. However, I swallowed my cynicism after a taste of one of the Ali's special tajines, (try the chicken and prunes) and began to enjoy the surroundings. A full meal including soup, a tajine, bread, dessert, and tea costs about $5.

Other restaurants in the area include the Hotel-Restaurant Foucauld, which is similar to the Hotel Ali Restaurant in both decor and menu but with a larger French salon-like ambience and higher prices. The Café-Restaurant Oriental, 33 Rue de Bab Agnaou just of the Djemā'a is a good inexpensive choice with basic Moroccan fare such as tajines and brochettes. The Café-Restaurant-Hotel de France on the Djemā'a El Fna is known more for its café terrace views of the Djemā'a than its meals. Have a drink on the terrace, sit back, and watch the action below.

Food for Treks and Trips

Marrakesh is a convenient place to fill your pack with staples and bottled purified water for treks and trips to the mountains and western edge of the Sahara desert. There are small grocery stores, open-air markets, and produce stands in both Gueliz and the Medina. In Gueliz, grocery stores and a daily morning open-air market on Avenue Mohammed V between Place du 16 Novembre and Place Abd El Moumin Benali sell various canned meats and juices, crackers, La Vache qui rit (Laughing Cow) cheese, toilet paper, bread, corn flakes (if you're desperate), fruit, vegetables, and other goods convenient for a picnic or off-the-beaten-track trek.

Similar items are available at Medina stores and fruit and vegetable stands on or near the Djemā'a El Fna and daily open-air markets such as the Thursday Market (yes, it is daily) at Bab El Khemis (gate of the Thursday Market), one of the northern gates.

With persistence and patience, you can also search the souk for bins of basic staples such as beans, nuts, and noodles.

Getting Things Done and Shopping

Money Exchange

Foreign currency and traveler's checks can be exchanged at banks, bank exchange *guichets* or pay desks, the exchange window at the bus station, and at most hotels. Exchange money and checks at hotels only as a last resort, because they usually offer the lowest rates and, unlike the banks, also charge a commission. Banks and *guichets* can be found around and near the Djemā'a El Fna and on Avenue Mohammed V.

If you have an American Express Card, you can cash personal checks at the American Express office at Voyages Schwarz, Rue Mauritanie, second floor. The actual cash transactions are made at a bank around the corner, but you have to come here first for the appropriate papers. Also, don't expect to receive U.S. dollars: foreign checks are almost always automatically converted to Moroccan dirhams. Rue Mauritanie is a small street that intersects Avenue Mohammed V just across from the Syndicat d'Initiative (170 Avenue Mohammed V). Look for the barely noticeable American Express sign jutting out from a second-story window. Hours are Monday–Friday 9 A.M. to 12:30 P.M. and 3 to 4:30 P.M., although it often stays open to about 7 P.M. for mail pickup.

Photography Stores

On Avenue Mohammed V, you can find stores stocked with most types of film and some basic camera supplies. However, try to buy what you need before entering Morocco because Moroccan prices tend to be higher, and slide and transparency film is often unavailable. Film is also sold in the gift shops at most major hotels.

Post, Telegraph, and Telephone Office (PTT)

The main post and telephone office of Marrakesh is at Place du 16 Novembre in Gueliz. As you enter the large hall, veer to the counters on the left for postage and to the right for telephone calls. A long glass partition separates the telephone section from the postal section. Telephone calls, both international and domestic, must first be booked at the counter. Then you must wait until the operator at the counter finds an operator to place your call; that could take anywhere from 30 seconds to an hour, depending on the number of people waiting. Don't be timid about reminding the operator that you are still waiting. Collect calls are possible for a small fee. Hours are Monday–Saturday 8 A.M. to 2 P.M., but the telephone section sometimes stays open longer hours. The telephone office is supposed to be open 24 hours daily, but I didn't find this to be true.

Another PTT is on the Djemā'a El Fna a few doors down from the Hotel Ali, with the post office facing the Djemā'a and the telephone office in the basement (stairway entrance on the Rue Moulay Ismail). This branch tends to be somewhat less crowded than the main one, but you still have to elbow your way to the counter. Hours are the same as above.

Shopping and Bargaining

Shopping for traditional Moroccan handicrafts, clothing, and spices in the souks of the Medina is a major pastime and attraction of Marrakesh. Before venturing into the souks, however, visit the Ensemble Artisanal on Avenue Mohammed V between Bab Larissa and the 230-ft-high (252 ft, counting the tip of the spire) Koutoubia minaret for a good overall idea of what is available at the higher (than the souk) official prices. The Ensemble is also worth visiting to observe the artisans and apprentices at work producing many of the things you will see in the Ensemble shop and Medina souks: hand-painted ceramic tiles, loom-woven Berber carpets, leather shoes, brass and copper plates and bowls, silver jewelry, and tablecloths.

For other price checking try the high-priced leather stores and curio shops on Avenue Mohammed V in downtown Gueliz near the tourism offices (see above). The only advantages of shopping here are that these shops are not as crowded (if at all) as the souks and they seem to accept almost every credit card (although many shops in the souks now also accept cards).

Bargaining is the general rule for shopping in the souks, but even more importantly, never go shopping with a guide, *either* official or unofficial. Most guides are happy to bargain for you, but that means the price will probably not go as low as you like because the shopkeeper will include a commission for the guide.

There are no set rules on bargaining except that you are expected to reject the shopkeeper's first price, offer a much lower one, and then settle somewhere in the middle. Do not offer a price for something that you have no intention of possibly buying. And you should be prepared to pay the price you offer. Whatever you offer, expect the shopkeeper to laugh, scoff, say you are crazy, and tell you that he has twenty kids and business has been bad. Do not be intimidated by this into paying more than you think something is worth.

Carpets and Rugs are some of the most popular and beautiful, albeit expensive, souvenirs to bring home. In the Medina, carpet shops abound, just ask someone to show you the way. If you show any interest at all in seeing what carpets are available, be prepared for a lengthy display that begins with a small glass of mint tea and the most expensive carpet and ends with the most inexpensive, unless of course you liked a more expensive one. Almost always, though, there's an impressive pile of carpets stacked before you. Careful bargaining is in order when buying a carpet because prices, although government-regulated, vary according to quality and design. For a full description of the government carpet standards and approximate prices, see the Fez section.

Bookstores and Newsstands. Aside from a few hotel gift shops, I was not able to find any bookstores in Marrakesh with a good stock of English-language books. However, there are newsstands on Avenue Mohammed V in Gueliz that sell some books, British newspapers, *Newsweek*, and *Time*.

Camping Supplies. I was not able to locate a store in Marrakesh that specializes in camping supplies and gear, so you should bring your own major items from home. Tents, backpacks, camp stoves, backpackers' dehydrated foods, appropriate cookware, good sunscreen and insect repellent are difficult, if not impossible, to obtain here.

Propane and butane gas refills and canisters and kerosene for stoves are usually available at hardware stores just off Avenue Mohammed V and near the youth hostel and municipal campground.

Dry and canned foods including powdered milk, most toiletries, flashlight and radio batteries, rope, nylon cord, matches and most other basic camping essentials are available in small grocery stores on and just off Avenue Mohammed V and in the Medina souks. Almost all necessary first-aid items can be obtained at pharmacies near the Djemā'a El Fna and on Avenue Mohammed V.

THINGS TO SEE

Before leaving Marrakesh for the desert, the mountains or other parts of the countryside, there are several sights that you shouldn't miss, such as the Djemā'a El Fna, the souks, and at least one of the city's extensive gardens.

Koutoubia Mosque and Minaret

Visible from miles around, the 252-foot-high Koutoubia minaret is not only one of the tallest structures in Marrakesh, but also one of the city's oldest. It was built starting around 1150, not long after the Almohad conquest of the Almoravids, and completed during the reign of Sultan Yacoub Al Mansur (1184–1199). Many of the architectural features that originated with this minaret have since been used in other structures. For example, at about the middle of the southeast side of the minaret, there's a set of small arches; a similar set can be seen in a few of the gates later built by the Almohads. It was named Koutoubia, which means "booksellers," because the lot at the base of the minaret was once full of booksellers' stalls. The mosque and minaret are inside the medina just off Avenue Mohammed V and before the Djemā'a El Fna.

Djemā'a El Fna

The Djemā'a El Fna is the central square of the medina in Marrakesh, a place that pulsates with the traditional sights, sounds, and smells of Morocco, a perfect place to begin a tour of Marrakesh. It's as close to a bona fide medievalism as you'll probably ever see—magic, witchcraft, spells, potions, scribes, jugglers, snake charmers, storytellers, dentists

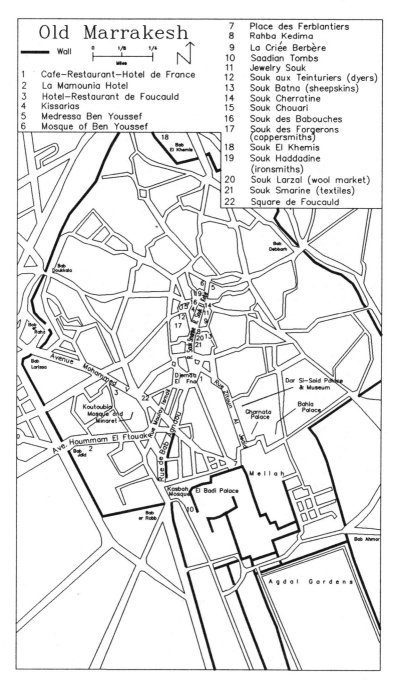

Old Marrakesh

━━━ Wall

0   1/8   1/4
Miles

1 Cafe—Restaurant—Hotel de France
2 La Mamounia Hotel
3 Hotel—Restaurant de Foucauld
4 Kissarias
5 Medressa Ben Youssef
6 Mosque of Ben Youssef

7 Place des Ferblantiers
8 Rahba Kedima
9 La Criée Berbère
10 Saadian Tombs
11 Jewelry Souk
12 Souk aux Teinturiers (dyers)
13 Souk Batna (sheepskins)
14 Souk Cherratine
15 Souk Chouari
16 Souk des Babouches
17 Souk des Forgerons (coppersmiths)
18 Souk El Khemis
19 Souk Haddadine (ironsmiths)
20 Souk Larzal (wool market)
21 Souk Smarine (textiles)
22 Square de Foucauld

Bab El Khemis
Bab Debbarh
Bab Doukkala
Bab Raha
Bab Larissa
Avenue Mohammed V
Ave. Hoummam El Ftouak
Bab Jdid
Koutoubia Mosque and Minaret
Djemaa El Fna
Souk Smarine Rue de Souk
Rue Zitoun Al Jedid
Rue de Bab Agnaou
Rue Bab Moulay Ismail
Dar Si—Said Palace & Museum
Bahia Palace
Charnata Palace
Mellah
Kasbah Mosque
El Badi Palace
Bab er Robb
Bab Ahmar
Agdal Gardens

whose sole equipment is a pair of crude pliers, makeshift food stalls, thieves, and pickpockets all abound. All this attracts quite a number of tourists and also Moroccans, many of whom come from the countryside solely for the entertainment and services of the Djemā'a.

At sunset, which is usually the best time to see the performers, I visited the Djemā'a for the first time. Ignoring the calls of the peanut and orange vendors who line one edge of this sprawling open area, I walked toward the center to watch a man with a cobra sway and twist to the ghostly wail of his partner's flute.

A little boy stood at my side whispering in French, "*Monsieur, il y a des voleurs partout*" ("Sir, there are thieves everywhere").

"Thieves?" I asked.

"Yes, sir, the thieves are everywhere," he said, waving his arm slowly and pointing to the crowds around the square. With wide eyes, he nodded and continued, "So I will be your friend, sir, and no more thieves and you can take many photographs." I immediately checked my book bag for open pockets and razor slashes (a tactic sometimes used when standing in a crowd or slow-moving line) because maybe he had seen something happen, but there was neither.

"That's not necessary," I insisted, and walked away, but he followed me for the next half hour whispering, "but the thieves, monsieur, the thieves…" After avoiding the slithery advances of the fangless cobra and its owner, I lost the boy somewhere between the acrobatic monkeys and the contortionist herbalists.

To demonstrate the powers of the contorted roots, potions, and piles of herbs and desiccated lizards spread on a blanket before them, some of the herbalists show off their contortionist talents. One man, for instance, pulled his foot up behind his head, propped himself up on his hands, and grabbed a chart with the toes of his free foot that seemed to show photos of a man before and after he had ingested a lizard potion. The "before" photo showed the man with ghastly open sores, and the "after" without. I would not have inferred from the photos that dried lizards had curative powers if the man had not neatly arranged his lizards in one pile, small corked bottles of potion in the next, and continually pointed from his chart to the piles.

The herbalists are almost always in the Djemā'a El Fna, especially in the afternoons, and have probably been coming here for the many centuries that the Djemā'a has existed. No one is certain exactly when, though, the Djemā'a was first established as an "assembly" area, which is one definition of its name, for the herbalists and assorted others. It was also known as the "assembly of the dead" because until almost the end of the last century this was where the sultan had criminals, rebels, and misfits executed, usually by decapitation. The Jews of Marrakesh were given the unsavory task of pickling a week's worth of heads in *mellah* or salt (thus the origin of the name *mellah* for Jewish quarters in Morocco) and then displaying them on stakes around the Djemā'a. Fortunately, those "sights" are long gone and more savory ones have replaced them.

In the evening, wander over to the food stalls and sample some of the cheapest cooked food in Marrakesh. As I mentioned earlier, however, this eating adventure is only worthwhile if you think your innards can handle the probable temporary invasion of nasty microbes. At the very least, have a look at the stalls if only to tease your nose with a variety of odors and aromas and to watch a constant parade of characters from all over Morocco and the rest of the world.

The Medina

The Medina is the older, walled-off portion of Marrakesh, the original city, parts of which date back to the founding of Marrakesh in the late eleventh century. The red mud walls surrounding the city were first erected in 1126 and have been rebuilt and extended many times since. Several palaces and mosques were also built at about the same time to serve the needs of the expanding empire of Almoravid leader Ali Ben Youssef. Until the early part of this century, palaces rose and crumbled with each new dynasty.

First find the Café de France on the Djemā'a El Fna and walk north away from the Djemā'a and across a lot that is usually full of donkeys, vegetable sellers, and occasionally camels. Continue north through the farthest passage on your left and into the Medina. The passage widens and becomes the covered street Rue Souk Smarine, which has been the principal market area for cloth and clothing, but in recent years a variety of tourist souvenir shops and carpet shops have begun opening. Some of the more interesting, less touristic shops and stalls are past Rue El Ksour, which dead-ends on Smarine from the left.

As you continue along Rue Souk Smarine, keep looking to your right until you see the passageway that leads to a small square called the Rahba Kedima. If you have reached the point where the "street" forks into two, you have gone too far, so backtrack. The shops, stalls, and passageways around and just off the Rahba are home to an array of old souks and workshops, which seem arranged haphazardly, but when referring to the tourist office map the logic of the arrangement is somewhat clearer.

On the right, or south side of the Rahba is the Souk Larzal or wool market, then the Souk Btana or sheepskin market, and the herbal medicine stalls with shelves full of ampules and bottles and bins of gnarled roots and leaves. If you definitely want to get yourself lost in the medina, then continue east through the end of the Rahba or south just after the Souk Larzal. Otherwise, go north or left from the corner of the

Rahba into an adjoining square full of carpets called La Criée Berbère, which until as recently as 1912 when the French began their "protectorate" occupation of Marrakesh was the thrice-weekly slave market. Today, the Criée is the center of Marrakesh's thriving carpet and rug business. If you want a demonstration of the types of carpets available, this is the place to come.

Walk around the square and leave through the passageway at the northeast corner that leads to Rue Souk El Kebir, the right side of the fork from Rue Souk Smarine. This street continues past the jewelry souk and then to the Kissarias, a set of small, covered passageways off to the left that used to be considered the essence of the medina souks. Today, most of the shops seem to sell various household goods such as blankets and plastic bowls.

The area to the north (northwest and northeast) of the Kissarias, however, is a much more traditional souk area, thus far more interesting because the methods used to produce many of the objects here have probably not changed much in centuries. Follow the map to find your way around. The souks in this area include the following:

- Souk Cherratine—leatherwork, including sandals, cushions, and wallets
- Souk des Babouches—slippers
- Souk Haddadine—ironwork and other metalwork
- Souk Chouari—carpentry and woodwork
- Souk aux Teinturiers—wool dyers
- Souk des Forgerons—coppersmiths

The other main sights in this part of the medina are the Medressa Ben Youssef, the tanneries near Bab Debbarh, and the Souk El Khemis at Bab El Khemis.

The Medressa Ben Youssef is across from the Mosque of Ben Youssef and just north of the leather souk. It was first built in the fourteenth century under the Merenid dynasty of Sultan Abu El Hassan as an Islamic school and "dormitory" for about 800 students, but the name and much of what stands today dates back to sixteenth-century Saadian rule and was recently renovated. The sixteenth-century reconstruction of the medressa was heavily influenced by Muslim Spanish architects who had settled in Morocco after the fall of Muslim Spain (Granada) in 1492. Ornate designs in wood and stucco similar to those found on some buildings in Granada still cover the walls. Be sure to visit, if possible, the tiny students' quarters upstairs, which surround a series of small open courtyards. Roaming through the quarters and peeking through the lattice screen windows, it's not difficult to imagine how the medressa probably once looked. Hours are daily 8 A.M. to noon and 3 to 7 P.M.

From the northern corner of the Medressa Ben Youssef, walk about fifteen minutes due east along Rue Amesfah, which after Place du Moukef becomes Rue de Bab Debbarh, the "street" to the old city gate of Bab Debbarh and the tanneries.

The tanneries are worth visiting to see the traditional method of preparing animal skins for the craftsmen in the souks. An age-old process is used whereby the skins are soaked first in certain vats and then transferred to a row of dark, dank rooms where men and boys yank out the fur, and stretch and beat the skins. From there the skins go into more vats for cleaning and dyeing and, finally, drying on terraces overlooking the vats. The best overall view of the vats is from the terraces or from atop Bab Debbarh.

The entrance to the tanneries is a short side street on the right just before the gate. You'll know that you are in the area when the hustlers descend on you, which they will most likely do unless you are already with a guide. By the way, you don't need a guide to enter the tanneries, despite what anyone tells you, so be polite and firm with the would-be guides if you don't want any of them. Also, photographs are permitted; however, exercise discretion and be prepared for loud (probably justified) protests from the tannery workers. If you are wondering about the protest, then consider this: Would you want your photo taken, if you, like the workers, were covered with ghoulish green gook from groveling in the curing vats with slimy animal skins? Probably not. Cigarettes, money, or other inducements help keep the peace and prevent something horrible from happening such as getting thrown into one of the vats—which smell, incidentally, as awful as they look. Lastly, try not to wear your best shoes and be careful where you step, because the narrow paths between the vats can get muddy and slippery.

The next places worth visiting are Bab El Khemis and the daily Souk El Khemis or Thursday Market. From Bab Debbarh, turn left and walk northwest along or next to Route des Ramparts for about twenty minutes to Bab El Khemis, which is the one with a single entry. Bab Kechich, a smaller, double-entry gate is just before Khemis. The Thursday Market is about 1,300 feet north of the gate. It is more traditional than markets near the Djemā'a El Fna because most things for sale here are for the locals.

The Lower Medina

The Lower Medina is that part of the Medina south of the Djemā'a El Fna, a part that is known more for its palaces, tombs, and remnants of a once-thriving Jewish quarter called the Mellah, than for its spicy, colorful souks.

The El Badi Palace and Saadian Tombs

The Saadians ruled Morocco from the mid-sixteenth century to the mid-seventeenth as the first truly Arab dynasty since the Idrissid dynasty of the ninth and tenth centuries. The Saadians were some of the most respected religious leaders in Morocco because they were *sharifs*, or direct descendants of the Prophet Mohammed's family. They rose to power gradually in the sixteenth century as the power and influence of the short-lived Berber dynasty of the Wattasids completely disintegrated. The Saadians united northern and southern Morocco and established Marrakesh as their capital. In keeping with their religiosity, perhaps, they first built the Kasbah Mosque and, in 1557, the first elaborately decorated tomb for a member of the royal household. They didn't build an actual "government center" or palace—the El Badi Palace—until after the pivotal Battle of the Three Kings in 1578 when the Portuguese were chased from Morocco by Sultan Ahmed Al Mansur (1578-1603).

Ahmed Al Mansur was the richest, cruelest, most powerful Saadian sultan, so it's not surprising that most of the structures of the richly decorated Saadian tombs can be attributed to his architects. Consisting of two main mausoleums, the tombs were built behind the Kasbah Mosque in a small palm garden surrounded by high walls. As you enter through the passageway adjacent to the mosque, the three rooms of the first and most lavish mausoleum are on your left.

This mausoleum was constructed for Al Mansur and completed before his death in 1603. The first room was originally only for prayer, but after the demise of the Saadian dynasty in the late seventeenth century other Saadian princes and Marrakeshis were buried in the floor here. Each of the inscribed marble slabs and tiles that compose the floor is the top of a tomb, the most recent being that of Sultan Moulay Yazid, who died in 1792. Al Mansur's tomb is in the center of the domed second room.

The second mausoleum also comprises three similarly decorated rooms and was intended, at first, only for Mohammed Esh Sheikh, the founder of the Saadian dynasty, and Lalla Messaouda, Ahmed Al Mansur's mother. However, other Saadians have since been entombed there. A total of sixty-six royal Saadians lie in both mausoleums. More than a hundred other royal and prominent people are entombed beneath marble slabs spread around the court and garden.

The Saadian tombs are most easily found by starting from the Djemā'a El Fna and following Rue de Bab Agnaou to a small square at the gate of Bab Er Robb. Turn left at Bab Agnaou, which is immediately before Bab Er Robb, and you'll see the Kasbah Mosque just ahead of you. Facing the mosque, the passageway entrance to the tombs is on your right, the south side. Hours are 8 A.M. to noon and 3 to 7 P.M. daily except

Fridays when it is closed. A guide isn't mandatory, but can be helpful in explaining certain architectural details.

El Badi Palace

The ruins of the El Badi Palace are near the mosque and the tombs. Follow the map and/or ask the way to Place des Ferblantiers, which was once known as the Place du Mellah, the heart of the old, but now barely distinguishable Jewish quarter. Hours are daily 9 A.M. to noon and 2:30 to 5:30 P.M.

Although the palace was plundered by Sultan Moulay Ismail in the late seventeenth century, there are still remnants of its past splendor. The palace was built by Al Mansur, mostly with the tribute and ransom paid to him by the Portuguese after their defeat in the Battle of the Three Kings (1578). Additional wealth was acquired by Al Mansur's conquest of Timbuktu and its gold mines in western Sudan. Some of this wealth found its way to the palace in the form of beautiful gardens and pools, a great fifty-columned hall and Italian marble fixtures and decorations, all of which exists today and serves as the site for the spectacular annual Folklore Festival in late May and early June.

The Folklore Festival is a big event that attracts traditional musicians and dancers from all over Morocco. The shows start every day at sunset for about two weeks and are preceded daily by the celebrated fantasia—a colorful, thundering display of Berber horsemen galloping and firing guns in the air.

The Mellah

Returning to the Place des Ferblantiers (previously Place du Mellah), you begin to enter the Mellah, which was once the Jewish quarter. It is now overwhelmingly Muslim because most of the Jews left after independence, but remnants of their once-thriving community remain. There are still a few synagogues, an old Jewish cemetery, and Jewish hostels just off Place des Ferblantiers. You'll know by the narrower streets and taller houses that you have entered the quarter.

The Jews of Marrakesh, many of whom were descendants of Jews expelled from Spain in 1492, were confined to the Mellah from 1558 when it was established by the sultan until the French Protectorate in the early years of this century. They were permitted to leave the Mellah, but forbidden to wear shoes when outside its walls. Despite their confinement, Jews came to dominate several businesses in Marrakesh—jewelry, tailoring, banking, and the sugar trade—all of which could be conducted from within the quarter.

The Bahia Palace

After wandering around the Mellah, return to the Place des Ferblantiers and follow Rue Zitoun Al Jedid north to the PTT (post office) with your back to the Place des Ferblantiers and the Badi Palace, Rue Zitoun Al Jedid will be on your right. Follow the signs to the Gharnata Palace (Palais Gharnata), which isn't really a palace now, but a sappy touristic restaurant. The "real" palace—the Bahia Palace—faces the Gharnata. Hours are 9:30 A.M. to noon and 2:30 to 5:30 P.M.

The large courtyards, halls, apartments, and harem quarters all make the Bahia Palace seem quite fitting for a king or sultan, but they were built and occupied—in the late nineteenth century—by neither. Sultan Moulay Hassan's chamberlain, a former slave named Bou Ahmed, had the palace built for himself after Hassan's death in 1894. Hassan died while on an expedition in the then-hostile Tadla region of Morocco. Bou Ahmed hid his death from all but Hassan's personal slaves until he could proclaim as sultan Hassan's 14-year-old son, Moulay Abd Al Aziz, seven days later. The secret of Hassan's death was kept, in part, because Bou Ahmed feared reprisals from the surrounding tribes if they knew that the sultan had died. Also, with a child ruler as sultan rather than Hassan's older son Moulay Mohammed, Bou Ahmed could appoint himself a Grand Vizier. He pushed Hassan's viziers out of power, built the Bahia Palace, and controlled the court until his death in 1900 from cholera, in an epidemic.

After Bou Ahmed's death, the slaves, women, and courtiers of the palace went on a feeding frenzy, grabbing everything of value in the palace and leaving only the building. Moulay Abd Al Aziz, totally ill prepared for ruling a country, had suddenly become sultan. Descriptions abound about the folly of his weak reign over Morocco. See the history section in Chapter 4.

The Dar Si-Saïd Palace and Museum

Built by a brother of Bou Ahmed's, the Dar Si-Saïd didn't seem to suffer the same plundering fate as the Bahia and is thus better preserved. Today, it is home to a beautiful little Museum of Regional Art that gives a good overview of traditional crafts. The collections include High Atlas wood carvings from the eighteenth and nineteenth centuries, silver jewelry from southern Berber tribes and, seemingly out of place here, fair swings used up to the 1940s. The easiest way to find the Dar Si-Saïd is to return to Rue Zitoun Al Jedid, turn right, walk north, and turn right again across from a mosque. Hours are 9:30 A.M. to noon and 2:30 to 5:30 P.M.

To return to the Djemā'a El Fna, continue walking north on Rue

Zitoun Al Jedid and veer left on to Rue des Banques, which enters the Djemā'a at the Café de France. If you haven't yet had a drink on the café's terrace, then now is as good a time as any. The view overlooking the Djemā'a is one of the best, so bring your camera and, if you have one, a zoom or telephoto lens.

Agdal Gardens

By bicycle, foot, or horse-drawn carriage (calèche), make your way to the Agdal gardens and its pools, about four miles south of the Djemā'a and just beyond the gate Bab Ahmar. Most of the gardens were laid out in the nineteenth century with scores of olive trees and orchards of oranges, lemons, pomegranates, figs, and apricots. The biggest pool, and most popular destination in the gardens, is the Sahraj El Hana, located about 1 1/2 miles into the gardens. Although this and six other smaller pools look quite refreshing, the water isn't good for swimming because it is often stagnant and dirty.

CHAPTER 7

Near Marrakesh: The High Atlas Mountains and Valleys

On a clear day in Marrakesh, you can see the towering, snow-capped peaks of the High Atlas mountains looming like a great shimmering wall in the distance. The image is alluring and magnetic, with an attraction that few can resist. If you resist the temptation for even a day trip into these mountains and the surrounding Berber villages, then you will miss one of Morocco's highlights.

The High Atlas mountain range forms a wide backbone about 720 km (446 miles) in length from the edge of the Sous plain in southern Morocco northeast to Jebel Ayachi and the southern edge of the Middle Atlas range. Among the peaks in this range is Africa's seventh highest—Jebel (Mount) Toubkal at 4,167 m, or 13,671 ft—and at least 22 of North Africa's highest peaks (all more than 3,003 m, or 9,852 ft). There are five principal routes into the mountains, but only the following four are directly accessible from Marrakesh; the fifth route runs between Ouarzazate and Er-Rachidia and is described in Chapter 8:

- Along Road S501 to the Tizi-n-Test pass with a detour to Imlil—the principal base for several hikes to and around North Africa's highest peak, Jebel Toubkal (4,167 m or 13,671 ft)
- Along Road S513 to the Ourika Valley and the ski slopes of Oukaïmeden
- Along Highway P31 over the Tizi-n-Tichka pass to Ouarzazate with a detour to Telouet
- Along Highway P23 to Road S508 and Azilal with a detour to Demnate

Transportation for the main segments of all four routes is readily available from Marrakesh by bus, grand taxi, and—for more intrepid travelers—hitchhiking. For trips to Aremd, the Ourika valley, and Oukaïmeden maybe you should seriously consider getting a group of four together and renting a car for a few days. A car would obviously allow you to tour the countryside at your own pace and stop whenever and wherever you wish.

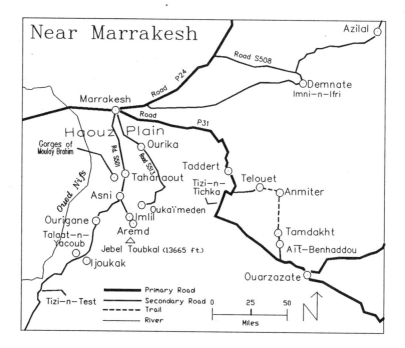

Near Marrakesh

Azilal

Road S508

Road P24

Demnate
Imni−n−Ifri

Marrakesh

Road

Haouz Plain   P31

Gorges of
Moulay Brahim

Rd. S501

Road S513

Ourika

Taddert

Tahanaout

Tizi−n−
Tichka

Telouet

Anmiter

Oued N'fis

Asni

Oukaïmeden

Ourigane

Imlil

Talaat−n−
Yacoub

Aremd

Tamdakht

Jebel Toubkal (13665 ft.)

Aït−Benhaddou

Ijoukak

Ouarzazate

Tizi−n−Test

——— Primary Road
——— Secondary Road
- - - - Trail
——— River

0   25   50

Miles

However, if you are planning hikes, mule treks, or horseback trips—Jebel Toubkal National Park and other nearby destinations from Imlil (very popular in the summer), to or around Telouet, along the Ourika valley, or from Oukaïmeden toward Imlil—then you may want to just get to the base point as quickly as possible either by public transportation or by arranging transportation and/or a Berber mountain guide in Marrakesh. The most expeditious option, although not necessarily most economic, is to join an organized tour, a few of which will be described later.

ROAD S501: TAHANOUT, ASNI, IMLIL HIKES, AND THE TIZI-N-TEST PASS

Road S501 begins at Bab Er Robb, which is one of the principal southern gates of Marrakesh's Medina and the location for many buses and grand taxis to towns and villages along this road. Although sights along the main road can be interesting, particularly the traditional Berber markets in Tahanout and Asni, the most interesting trips and treks are away from the main road and accessible only by rough dirt roads and mule trails.

Getting to Tahanout or Asni is easy by bus or grand taxi from Bab Er Robb, especially in the morning when departures are most frequent. Between Marrakesh and Tahanout, the first major town on Road S501, is the Haouz plain, a wide swath of some of the most fertile land in

Morocco. Tahanout is about 32 km (20 miles) from Marrakesh and is a major regional farming and market center with a great weekly open market.

Every Tuesday morning, a large lot on the northern outskirts of town becomes the Souk Tahanout as makeshift stalls are erected and colorful blankets are spread out to display and sell everything from soap powder to powdered milk, grain, chickens, and vegetables. Since this is probably a fairly "typical" Berber souk, it has become a popular stop for tourists to ogle outdoor Berber barbers and butchers and, perhaps, buy souvenirs such as curved daggers, crude jewelry, and Berber *kilim* or tapestries. And wherever there are tourists, there are water bearers—men in frilly hats and patchwork vests attached to masses of shiny equipment that resemble a cross between a Scottish bagpipe and an Italian espresso machine. It's all mostly for photogenic effect, though, because they seem to spend most of their time chasing camera-toting tourists rather than selling water.

Leaving the market and heading south, the road passes between the mud-brick houses and shops of the village, small buildings that almost seem to have popped up from the ground around them. At strategic points along the 15-km (9 1/2-mile) road to Asni in and beyond the village, particularly along sharp curves, young men rush toward you with grapefruit-sized chunks of sparkling cobalt crystals. Instinctively, from experience in much more troubled spots of the world, I ducked down with my arms over my head waiting for the impact of rock on windshield. But it didn't happen—these rocks were meant for sale to tourists, and were not being slung by terrorists.

Less than a mile (1 km) before reaching Asni is the 4-km road to the seldom-visited Moulay Brahim gorges, a quiet place for a picnic and a short hike. You can drive up the dirt road to the gorges or hike from Asni and back easily the same day. The two maps that I used for this region— "La Carte Routière" (Paris: Éditions Marcus, 1987) and "Oukaïmeden-Toubkal—Feuille NH-29-XXIII-1" (Rabat: Division de la Carte, 1972)— are both misleading, the former because it shows the gorges in the wrong location and the latter because the gorges aren't even indicated. If for some reason the road to the gorges is no longer signposted (the sign was becoming hard to read), then ask locals for directions (*"la piste pour les Gorges de Moulay Brahim"*). Part of the confusion on the maps may lie in the fact that the road to the gorges seems to backtrack and run parallel to the main road.

Asni is a village that is known mostly for its Saturday market. Although some things are sometimes available at the mountain village of Imlil, Asni is really the last place to buy food and bottled water before heading into the mountains. The shopkeepers here seem to know that— their prices for most staples, including fruit and canned juices produced locally, are higher than in Marrakesh. If you plan to stock up here, then try to arrive the night before or early on Saturday and shop in the souk, where prices tend to be more reasonable and negotiable than in the shops. It's also easier to get to Imlil on Saturdays, the principal village near the base of Mount Toubkal, because the bus runs more frequently than during the week.

Actually, during the week, the "bus" is a blue minibus called a *camion* that doesn't depart the Asni marketplace until it has about twenty passengers. Other options for getting to Imlil are to hire a taxi for the 17-km (10 1/2-mile) trip, hitchhike, or hike (see below for more information).

If you decide to spend the night in Asni, there's a youth hostel (Auberge de Jeunesse) signposted near the marketplace and a three-star hotel-restaurant, the Grand Hotel du Toubkal, just outside the village and past the road to Imlil. The hostel is modest, but pleasant, and well situated near a stream and among a clump of trees.

The hotel is also in a good location with its dining room, bar, and several of its rooms facing Mount Toubkal. On warm days you can eat on the terrace next to the dining room, but don't be surprised if you hear some strange noises emanating from the side of the building. For amusement, the owner has assembled a caged menagerie there that includes wild boar, monkeys, and birds. For humans, the hotel has 19 rooms, 12 of which have private bathrooms and cost about $15 to $20 per person; a meal from the restaurant's *"menu touristique"* is about $7.

To Imlil and Beyond

Just past the Grand Hotel du Toubkal is the 17-km (10 1/2-mile) road to Imlil, which is paved for the first few miles and then graded dirt and gravel the rest of the way with occasional bumpy, potholed portions. However you choose to travel—by vehicle, foot, or bicycle—this road is a dramatic way to enter the Atlas mountains. As it rises gradually toward Imlil, the road hugs the edge of the Oued Rhirhaia river valley and passes several small Berber settlements. During most of the trip, which takes at least a half hour by car or bus, Mount Toubkal looms like an illusory white castle at the end of the valley. Hiking and bicycling (preferably by mountain bike) are easily feasible because the approximate elevation gain is gradual as the road goes from 1,165 m (3,822 ft) at Asni to 1,650 m (5,413 ft) at Imlil. That amounts to an average gain of 28 1/2 m (94 ft) per km (6/10 mile):

Approximate Distance	Approximate Gain
km 0 to km 5	76 m (250 ft)
km 5 to km 11	193 m (633 ft)
km 11 to km 17	216 m (709 ft)

Depending on road and weather conditions, the weight of your equipment, and your photo-taking proclivity, this hike from Asni to Imlil should take about two to four hours.

If you get to Imlil too late to begin trekking and you don't have a tent, then you can either stay at the Refuge d'Imlil or negotiate for a room with a family in or just outside the village. The Refuge is a small two-story building with thirty-eight bunkbeds, Turkish toilets, showers, and a kitchen, all established by the Club Alpin Français de Casablanca (the French Alpine Club of Casablanca). The club charges members about $1.25, nonmembers $2.50 per night. The gas stove in the kitchen can be rented for about $0.50 per hour. Reservations are advised for both staying in and camping next to the refuge during the summer because the trek to Mount Toubkal is popular. According to signs at the refuge, they can be obtained by writing to the Club Alpin Français, Boite Postale 888, Marrakesh.

Planning Your Treks

Trekking information is available in Imlil at the Refuge and from local shopkeepers and guides. A bulletin board at the Refuge briefly describes some of the trails in the area and includes information about "official" rates for hiring guides, donkeys, and horses. Some of the rates cited were much lower than rates quoted by locals, probably because locals expected bargaining.

The following map shows some of the popular hiking trails from Imlil.

The hikes are described in greater detail below, but here's a brief rundown of what is possible and how long each takes:

- **Ascent of Mount Toubkal**—approximately nine hours from Imlil, with rooms available for overnight stops at Aremd (one hour from Imlil), Sidi Chamharouch (three hours from Imlil), and Neltner (six hours from Imlil).
- **Lake Ifni extension from Neltner**—approximately 4 1/2 hours (one way) with lots of switchbacks on descent to the lake; camp overnight.
- **Imlil to Oukaïmeden via Tacheddîrt**—approximately 7 hours (or 5 if daily truck from Imlil to Tacheddîrt is taken) with a Club Alpin refuge available at Tacheddîrt (3-hour walk from Imlil).
- **Circuit from Imlil to Tacheddîrt, Azib Likemt, Azib Tifni, Sidi Chamharouch, and back to Imlil**—a challenging mountainous circuit that takes approximately 18 hours of walking (if by truck to Tacheddîrt, then two hours less), which can be done probably in a minimum of four days; rooms are available at Likemt (4 hours from Tacheddîrt), Tifni (3 hours from Likemt), and Sidi Chamharouch (5 hours from Tifni).

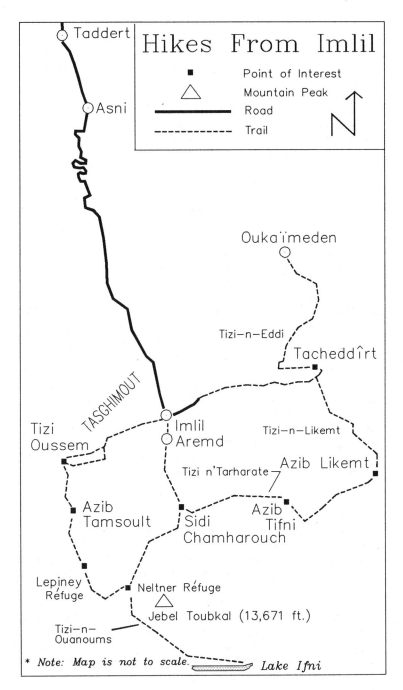

Hikes From Imlil

■ Point of Interest
△ Mountain Peak
▬▬ Road
- - - - - - Trail

Taddert

Asni

Oukaïmeden

Tizi–n–Eddi

Tacheddîrt

TASGHIMOUT

Imlil
Aremd

Tizi
Oussem

Tizi–n–Likemt

Azib Likemt

Tizi n'Tarharate

Azib
Tamsoult

Sidi
Chamharouch

Azib
Tifni

Lepiney
Réfuge

Neltner Réfuge

△
Jebel Toubkal (13,671 ft.)

Tizi–n–
Ouanoums

Note: Map is not to scale.

Lake Ifni

- **Circuit from Imlil to Tizi Oussem, Lepiney Refuge, Neltner Refuge, Sidi Chamharouch, and back to Imlil**—approximately 21 hours of walking, which can probably be done in four to five days; rooms available at all points. The most difficult stretch is a rocky 5 to 6 hours between Lepiney and Neltner.

These times could all be reduced, of course, if a horse or donkey were carrying your gear. Each can be rented next to the Imlil Club Alpin refuge for about $8 per day depending on availability and your bargaining skills.

Most of these hikes are possible only in the summer from about June to September, unless you are properly equipped and experienced to trek through the snow that usually blankets much of this area the rest of the year. Depending on conditions, trekking in the snow can require special skis, a "seal skin" *peau de phoque* (no longer a real seal skin) for ascents, and (recommended) a local guide.

Guides are readily and anxiously available to lead you up the various trails in the area, but they aren't absolutely necessary for most of the summer hikes because the trails are frequently used by local inhabitants, thus relatively easy to follow. Topographical maps indicating most of the trails are available at scales of 1:50,000 ("Toubqal [Toubkal]"—No. NH 29 XXIII 1A) and 1:100,000 ("Oukaïmeden-Toubkal"—No. NH 29 XXIII 1) in Rabat from the Direction de la Conservation Foncière et des Travaux Topographiques (Division de la Carte) at 31 Avenue Hassan I for about $3 per sheet. Occasionally, they are also available for sale or at least reference at the Club Alpin refuge in Imlil. Be forewarned, however, that the 1:100,000 map is somewhat outdated and incomplete, and some of the trails aren't marked. The 1:50,000 is also somewhat outdated, but more trail and topographic information is indicated. The basic trail map shown above tries to fill in some of the information gaps, but it shouldn't be used for wandering off the trails.

Imlil to Mount Toubkal

From Imlil (spelled "Imelil" on the 1:50,000 map), the trail to the village of Aremd and beyond to Mount Toubkal starts as Imlil's main street, which is really nothing more than an inclined dirt path that passes through the village, turns left across a stream, and then winds around to the trailhead.

It takes about ten to fifteen minutes to reach the trailhead, which is the beginning of a series of long switchbacks that rise above the stream. For a beautiful view and photograph, look down at the stream and over the tree line to the bright green terraces of the small hillside farms surrounding Imlil and the neighboring Berber village of Targa Imoula.

The trail and switchbacks are steep and rocky with an elevation gain of more than 200 m (656 ft) in less than 1 km, but after about forty minutes (with a donkey carrying the gear), the trail levels off and passes between the mud-walled houses of the village of Aremd (also known as Aroumd or Around on some maps). Usually, a noisy group of children appears and pleads for "*stylos*" (pronounced *stee-lo*, which means "pen" in French) and "dirhams" (Moroccan currency) before leading you through the village and down a short, but steep path of mud and manure. The path runs into another trail, to the left it goes to the house of the village leader—Aït El Kadi Brahim—and the rest of the village and to the right into the valley and up toward Mount Toubkal.

Aït El Kadi Brahim's boyish frame and kangaroo gait belie his age, which he says, is "something over 60." As a government-certified High Atlas guide, he still leads groups of foreigners on mountain treks all year and in all weather conditions. I watched him one morning on the terrace of his mud-walled "ksar"-style house as he waxed his skis and sharpened an ice axe for a trek to the snowy summit of Mount Toubkal. Behind him the bright blue sky and white peaks were fading to a menacing gray as he tugged a wool cap over his ears and tightened the laces on his Nike shoes. He said goodbye to his family and then hurried down the path to catch up with a group of Austrians who wanted to hike up Toubkal and then ski down.

The Kadi, as he prefers to be called, finds most of his clients at the Hotel Ali in Marrakesh, which is where I met him, and enthusiastically invites people to visit his village. He arranges accommodations at the relatively new guesthouse in the valley below Aremd, in his house or in a neighbor's house.

As with most of the houses in the area, the Kadi's house resembles a small medieval fortress with thick mud walls, log beams separating each floor, and crude wooden window shutters. On the ground level in front is a muddy pen for garbage and animals and a heavy wooden door to a storeroom for grain and walnuts and, in a dark corner, a pit latrine. Uneven steps cut into the side of the house lead from the pen to the entrance. Just inside to the right is a low doorway to the kitchen that's partially covered by a sheer, ragged cloth. I could see two or three women sitting on their haunches in mud puddles around a gas lamp, a one-burner stove, and a large bubbling pot. As they whispered and stirred the pot, the burning glow of the lamp partially lit their faces and cast dancing shadows on the walls. It was how I imagined the three witches in Shakespeare's *Macbeth* as they chanted, "Double, double, toil and trouble;/Fire burn, and cauldron bubble." As I discovered later, however, they were making couscous for me and the other guests, hardly the ghoulish stew that I vividly imagined.

Guests stay upstairs in the only room on the third floor, a room with man-sized bags of walnuts on one side, straw mats and cushions on the floor, and a window looking out on a terrace and Mount Toubkal. The view through the window, especially in the morning when Toubkal and its neighboring peaks are illuminated by the rising sun, is breathtaking. The cushions make adequate beds, but you need a sleeping bag or blankets because the Kadi has only enough for his family. I counted nine family members, all of whom shared the same room across from the kitchen, but there may have been others hidden beneath the stack of blankets.

Although the Kadi didn't ask for any money, the four of us who spent the night here paid about $5 each. A stay in the guesthouse probably would have cost slightly more because hot showers and actual beds are available.

The Kadi can be contacted through the Hotel Ali or by writing to him at the following address: Guide du Haut Atlas, Douar Aroumd—Imlil Poste Asni, Marrakesh. He speaks some English, but I'm not sure if he's able to read it. If he can't, there are people in Imlil who can translate for him.

Aremd to Mount Toubkal

From Aremd, the first stop on the way to Mount Toubkal is Sidi Chamharouch, which is reached after about two hours of hiking the well-marked (red dots on some rocks) trail that runs along the east side of the Mizane river valley. This part of the trail is about 5 km (3 miles) long with a few switchbacks and a gradual elevation gain from approximately 1,900 m (6,330 ft) to 2,310 m (7,540 ft) at Sidi Chamharouch. Rooms and a few basic staples are available here, but more in the summer than in the winter. If you started hiking fairly early, you should be able to easily continue on to the Neltner refuge.

The rest of the trail to Neltner is straightforward and relatively easy because it parallels the Mizane river, but it does have a significant elevation gain from 2,310 m (7,540 ft) at Sidi Chamharouch to about 3,106 m (10,200 ft) at Neltner. It takes about three hours to hike this 6-km (4-mile) portion of the trail. Most of the elevation gain occurs in the first few hundred meters of switchbacks following Sidi Chamharouch. The refuge marks the end of the trail and is similar to the one in Imlil. It costs about $3 per night and is open all year. The refuge is a good place to meet hikers returning from the summit and thus to get the latest information on trail conditions.

There are three main trails or approaches to the summit: from the south, north, and west. Taking about three hours up and two down, the southern approach is easiest, most direct, and thus most popular. Although the trail doesn't really require a guide, you should at least consult people at the refuge for directions on following it, because there are a few misleading sidetracks. Also, you may have to take precautions for altitude sickness—the hike goes from 3,106 m (10,200 ft) at Neltner to 4,167 m (13,671 ft) at the summit. Aspirin and swallowing hard are the most obvious ways to prevent altitude sickness, but if you start feeling nauseous and ready to vomit, then descend immediately. Lastly, be careful of scree—the loose stones and rocky debris that cover part of the trail—because it can make parts of the hike seem like walking on a treadmill or climbing a sand dune.

Lake Ifni Extension

After your "assault" on Toubkal, if you still have the strength and inclination, you can do the four-hour, 8-km hike to Lake Ifni. Follow the main trail that heads south from Neltner and turn left after about 1 km on to another trail. Numerous switchbacks and loose rocky conditions on this second portion made it difficult to precisely measure the time and distance. The time required for some hikers could easily be longer, especially if you aren't used to scrambling through scree. The hike becomes increasingly challenging as the trail reaches the end of the Mizane river valley and climbs through a series of pebbly switchbacks to the summit of Tizi-n-Ouanoums at 3,664 m (12,021 ft). From here the trail descends in a tortuously steep and rocky zig-zag passing a small waterfall on your left about 200 m until the lake is almost in sight. The trail splits and follows opposite shores of the lake; you can take either trail.

The lake is a pleasant, isolated place to relax, camp, and fish for a day or two, with a few usually vacant huts that you can use. Camping is also possible along the lakeshore away from the huge heaps of shattered rock that surround it. All in all, Lake Ifni is really only a good hiking destination for dedicated hikers, not for novices just out for some stony sightseeing.

Imlil to Oukaïmeden via Tacheddîrt

The hike from Imlil to Oukaïmeden is possible in one day (seven hours) but you should start early because it could take from five to seven hours of mostly uphill walking. The first 8 km (5 miles), however, can be done by riding the daily 10 A.M. truck from Imlil, thus cutting about two hours off your total travel time. The donkey "piste" between Imlil and Tacheddîrt was recently widened to make the village more accessible, although not many tourists seem to be venturing there yet. If you decide to walk this stretch, the elevation gain is gradual—from 1,650 m (5,413 ft) to 2,291 m (7,516 ft) at Tacheddîrt—although there are a few sharp switchbacks along the way. With its Club Alpin refuge hut, the village makes a good overnight stop, but you must bring your own food.

From Tacheddîrt, it's about an 8-km (5-mile), 3 1/2-hour hike to Oukaïmeden along an old donkey trail. The first part of the trail can be somewhat confusing, because it isn't clearly marked on the main maps (1:100,000 and 1:50,000) and veers west before heading north, so you should ask for directions. However, once you are on the northbound portion, the trail is fairly straightforward as it climbs toward the summit of Tizi-nou Eddi at 2,960 m (9,711 ft), which is approximately the halfway point. From there the trail follows a depression called the Assif n'Aït Irene and then descends slightly to the small ski "resort" town of Oukaïmeden where accommodations, food, and transportation to the Ourika valley and Marrakesh are available.

Tacheddîrt–Azib Likemt–Azib Tifni–Sidi Chamharouch–Imlil

Another possible route from Imlil via Tacheddîrt is to veer south from Tacheddîrt on a rough 5-km (3-mile) donkey trail to the summit of Tizi-n-Likemt, which is about 3,600 m (11,811 ft). After the summit, the trail has fewer switchbacks and then descends for about 3 1/2 km (2 miles) to Azib Likemt, a hamlet of a few stone huts at about 2,568 m (8,425 ft). It takes about four hours to reach this point from Tacheddîrt, so you may want to spend the night here in one of the huts. The next portion of the trail heads west and gradually climbs about 4 km (2 1/2 miles), three hours, to the hamlet of Azib Tifni, which is at an elevation of about 2,820 m (9,252 ft). Between Likemt and Tifni, the trail is unmarked on the 1:100,000 map and marked with numerous trails on the 1:50,000 map, so directions from locals or maybe even a guide would be helpful, if not essential. From Azib Tifni to Sidi Chamharouch, the trail is a challenging 5 km (3 miles), five hours, that veers northwest first and then southwest to the summit of Tizi-n-Tarharate (3,456 m). The 1:50,000 seems to be accurate on this portion. As mentioned earlier, rooms are available at Sidi Chamharouch, which is about a three-hour hike from Imlil (two hours from Aremd). If you want to do this hike, gather as much information as possible about the trail conditions before you begin and be prepared for some strenuous hiking.

Imlil—Tizi Oussem—Lepiney—Neltner—Sidi Chamharouch

This circuit involves approximately 21 hours of challenging hiking and could probably be done in about four to five days. The first stretch from Imlil to Tizi Oussem rises to an elevation of about 2,664 m (8,740 ft) along the edge of the Tasghimout (also known as "Tasserimoute") ridge, descends first to Tizi Mzik at 2,489 m (8,166 ft) and then to Tizi Oussem at an elevation of about 1,800 m (5,905 ft). The trail splits after the summit of Tizi Mzik; follow the branch on the right. This first-stretch hike to Tizi Oussem is approximately 6 km (4 miles) and takes about four hours. Rooms are available in the village, so spending a night here is a reasonable possibility.

The next stretch is shorter—approximately 5 km (3 miles)—but involves about five hours of more arduous hiking, the most challenging part being the switchbacks after Azib Tamsoult. A small refuge is available at Azib Tamsoult. From Azib Tamsoult to the Lepiney hut, the trail parallels the river or riverbed Assif n'Ouarzane almost all the way to the hut, except for one portion of switchbacks near the waterfall of Irhoulidene, which is about 1 km north of Lepiney. The Lepiney refuge is at an elevation of approximately 3,600 m (11,811 ft).

Beyond Lepiney to Neltner is the most difficult stretch of the hike—a rocky set of switchbacks that takes about five to six hours to traverse. Before leaving Lepiney, get as much information as possible on this part of the trail because it is unmarked on the 1:100,000 map and inadequately marked on the 1:50,000 version. Only experienced hikers should consider doing this stretch.

Back to Road S501—To Tizi-n-Test Pass

From Asni, Road S501 meanders south-southwest through pine forests through the Berber villages of Ouirgane (63 1/2 km, or 40 miles from Marrakesh), Ijoukak (96 km, or 60 miles), Talaat n'Yakoub (99 km, or 61 miles), Tin Mal or Tinmel (104 1/2 km, or 65 miles) and Idni (118 km, or 73 miles) before reaching the summit of the Tizi-n-Test pass (136 1/2 km, or 85 miles) at 2,100 m (6,890 ft). After the pass, the road descends into the Sous plain, passing through the crenellated city of Taroudannt (266 km, or 140 miles) and ending at the beach hotel city of Agadir (306 km, or 190 miles); these cities are described in the "Deep South" section.

The village of Ouirgane is known mainly for its two hotel-restaurants—the Hotel Residence La Roseraie and the Auberge Au Sanglier Qui Fume—either of which is a good overnight or lunch and dinner stop, and the fact that it roughly marks entry into the gorges of the Oued Nfis. The four-star Roseraie is the larger and more deluxe of the two, with 30 rooms (all with showers or bathtubs), tennis courts, a swimming pool, a sauna, and an excellent restaurant. The two-star Sanglier (its full name means "the smoking boar") is an old country inn-style place with a restaurant that is as good as the Roseraie's, but its seventeen rooms are smaller and simpler.

The French blasted a road through the gorges in the 1920s along a course roughly parallel to the Oued Nfis river. Completion of the road was significant because it opened up this previously isolated area to the rest of the country and facilitated a closer relationship between the French Protectorate government and the Goundafi family, one of three predominant families or so-called Lords of the Atlas in southern Morocco. Cooperation with the French enabled the Goundafi *qa'ids* to dominate the Oued Nfis valley, the Tizi-n-Test pass, and part of the Sous plain. Their principal kasbah, and thus power base, was at the village Talaat n'Yakoub about 35 1/2 km (22 miles) down the road from Ouirgane; part of the kasbah can still be visited.

Between Ouirgane and Talaat n'Yakoub is the village of Ijoukak, which is noteworthy mostly for a possible hiking trail or *piste* southeastward along the Assif n'Aït Ahmed river and the Asserhdoun n'Irhzifen tributary. The topographic map titled "Tizi n' Test—1.2" (scale 1:100,000) could be helpful for this hike; it's available in Rabat from the map office (see below for address). The trail turns northward at the village of El Merhzen, 8 km (5 miles) from the beginning of the trail, and then follows the tributary. If you do this hike, please send us details.

Back to the main road, the turnoff for the village of Talaat n'Yacoub is about 3 km (2 miles) from Ijoukak and then another 1 1/2 km (1 mile) along a piste to reach the kasbah. Although Tinmel, which is a few kilometers down the road, was the site of significant religious and political changes in Morocco, it was at Talaat n'Yacoub in the mid-nineteenth century that Goundafi power was truly consolidated.

By the 1850s, a schoolmaster named Si Ahmed-n-Aït Lhassen had deftly maneuvered himself into power over the region by taking the kasbah of Tagoundaft, a mountaintop stronghold a few kilometers down the main road. By 1860 he had consolidated his control over the valley's 50,000 inhabitants by constructing a kasbah at Talaat n'Yacoub. Sultan Hassan I, who liked to think that he dominated the entire country, felt threatened by Si Ahmed's rise to power, so in 1875 he sent in government troops to destroy most of the region's buildings, including the kasbah at Talaat n'Yacoub. In exchange for Si Ahmed's future cooperation, however, the sultan appointed him qa'id—the government's official representative—of the valley.

After his death in 1885, Si Ahmed was succeeded by his son Si Tayyeb, who rebuilt the kasbah at Talaat n'Yacoub, expanded the Goundafi domain into the Sous plain, and acquired a reputation as a gracious host and gentleman. The kasbah was not built as an impregnable fortress, like most kasbahs, but as a palatial residence for Si Tayyeb and the more than 1,500 members of his entourage, which included an army of servants and slaves and a harem of about four hundred women. The kasbah's lack of defensive structures such as towers and ramparts and its vulnerable location in a low-lying plain as opposed to a mountaintop are perhaps indicative of Si Tayyeb's confidence in his control of the region.

Today the kasbah is crumbling and unoccupied, but you can still visit part of the main building and see some of its intricate decorations, such as carved walnut ceilings and arched window frames. Although the Goundafi family is now based in Casablanca, they continue to maintain a "summer" kasbah adjacent to the old one. Returning to the main road, on the left side atop a 1,317-m (4,346-ft) hill just after the turnoff is the Agadir n'Gouj, a fortress constructed in 1907. It is no longer inhabited and can't be visited.

Continuing along the road about 3 km (2 miles) from the Talaat junction is the turnoff for the 2 km (1 1/4-mile) road to the ruins of the Mosque of Tinmel. At a second junction 2 km farther up the main road is the turnoff for the 1-km (6/10-mile) road that also leads to the mosque.

The mosque was erected in the mid-twelfth century by the self-proclaimed Sultan Abd Al Moumin in honor of his predecessor Ibn Tumart, the founder of the Almohad dynasty. Tumart was a devout Muslim who, on his return from Mecca, denounced the religious and moral laxity of the reigning Almoravid dynasty. He was particularly concerned with the mix of pagan folk religion and Islam that many Berber tribes practiced. Tumart also objected to art, music, wine, and well-dressed unveiled women—all of which he believed was the result of Almoravid rule and contrary to Islam. To gain support for his Islamic orthodoxy, Tumart took advantage of a political rift between the poorly organized Berber confederation of the Masmoudas and the Almoravids by introducing a traditional Islamic government structure to the Masmoudas. The structure was simple—a hierarchical theocracy with him at the head as the Mahdi or "Directed One" of Islam, and a traditional Berber assembly of tribal leaders that supposedly checked his authority. This structure was the foundation of his Almohad movement, which derived its name from the Arabic words for "those united in the oneness of God" and was based at Tinmel.

At first, not all the tribes in the confederation joined Tumart and his movement, but those that didn't were eventually "persuaded" by brute military force and, according to one of the first journalists to write about Morocco—Budgett Meakin—by "numerous ingenuous tricks." In his book, The Moorish Empire (London: Swan Sonnenschein, 1899), Meakin recounted one of Tumart's (the Mahdi's) typical tricks:

> After a battle with the Lamtûna in which he was defeated with serious loss, the Mahdi went at night to some of his surviving followers and buried them alive, with only a hole through which to breathe, inducing them to submit to this process by the promise that if they would inform any who made inquiry that they were enjoying in Paradise the rewards of death in conflict with the infidels, he would disinter them, and allot them important posts. Returning

to his disheartened supporters, Ibn Tumart remarked upon the good fortune of those who had fallen in battle, adding that if any had doubts they should go and ask the dead themselves....They went to the grave-sides and shouted, "O dead Companions, tell us what you have received from God Most High." One can imagine their surprise when gladsome voices from the very earth assured them of a present state of bliss....Ibn Tumart's cause was revived, but as really dead men tell no tales, return of fortune was denied to his accomplices, whose breathing holes the Mahdi filled up after lighting fire over them.

Despite their brutal methods, however, it wasn't until 1147 (seventeen years after Tumart's death) that the Almohads were able to totally subdue the Almoravid tribes by conquering their capital Marrakesh.

In 1153 Abd El Moumin built a fortified mosque at Tinmel to protect the village that had become his center of power and to venerate Tumart, who was still considered the spiritual leader and founder of the dynasty. Most of the mosque was destroyed in 1276 by the Merenid conquest, but enough is still discernible to get some idea of the interior of a typical Almohad mosque; this is the only one in Morocco open to non-Muslims. For a great view of the surrounding area, you can climb the stairs of the minaret.

The main road continues climbing through the Oued Nfis valley toward the Tizi-n-Test pass and 5 km (3 miles) from Tinmel it reaches a junction for the road and donkey trail to the kasbah of Tagoundaft. Some historians argue that the inability of government troops to attack and destroy this kasbah in 1875 was what prompted Sultan Hassan to make Si Ahmed, one of the Lords of the Atlas, his qa'id or official representative in the area. The now-dilapidated, uninhabited kasbah is strategically located atop a 1,600-m (5,250-ft) hill that is accessible only by way of a precariously narrow donkey trail. If you do this trek, let us know how it was.

A more visited and, perhaps, more interesting destination is the hamlet of Idni, which is about 8 1/2 km (5 1/4 miles) up the road. Idni is the last bus stop before the Tizi-n-Test summit and a good takeoff point for short hikes around the area. The Hotel Alpina, owned and managed by a French woman named Madame Gipolu, is the only place to stay and eat here. The rooms are basic and comfortable, but lack water and electricity. Madame Gipolu provides great meals and plenty of candles, both of which help you forget the lack of other amenities.

The Tizi-n-Test pass is at 2,120 m (6,955 ft) and lies 18 1/2 km farther up the road. The bus leaves you off at a café-restaurant just after the pass, which offers a great view of the Sous plain toward Taroudannt.

THE OURIKA VALLEY AND OUKAÏMEDEN

The road up into the mountains surrounding Oukaïmeden, one of only two ski resorts in Morocco, starts near the beginning of the Ourika valley. The roads to Oukaïmeden and into the valley are both paved, but parts of the latter were recently severely damaged by flooding.

After passing the road to Oukaïmeden, the valley road passes a few small restaurants. The first one you'll see is the Auberge Le Marquis at Arhbalou, which, despite its fancy name, is not recommended. Their meals are measly, overpriced, and, from personal experience, possibly a cause of diarrhea and stomach cramps.

Farther down the road, the multistory Hotel Amnougour (tel. 28-30) is a much better place to have a meal or spend the night. It is beautifully situated, hanging from the edge of a cliff with spectacular views of the river valley below. In the summer, the hotel is usually packed with Moroccan and foreign tourists, but in the winter and spring there are often more employees than guests. Most of the rooms are carpeted, with one twin bed and one double, a bathtub, and a wall heater, and cost about $25.

The four-star Hotel Ourika (tel. 339-93) at Km 42 in the valley is also fairly good, with doubles for about $25 and singles for $20 in the low season and $29 and $23 in the high season (summer). Breakfast is $2.75 and lunch $10.

On Thursday mornings, visit the souk or open-air market across from Le Marquis. With its numerous stalls of fruits, vegetables, spices, pots, pans, and utensils, it's not really any different from most other Moroccan souks. However, it was the first souk that I visited where the butchers and their "victims" were out in the open, thus making it impossible for blood-and-guts-squeamish visitors to avoid seeing the multicolor gore. At first I was a bit taken aback to see cow heads displayed on the stall tables, but that proved to be nothing compared to watching the butchers pick up the heads, place their mouths on the cows' mouths, and then blow furiously as if trying to inflate a thick balloon. (This procedure loosens the skin from the skull.)

From Arhbalou, the road meanders through the valley, following the Oued Ourika river past several villages and settlements. In late 1986 and early 1987, heavy rains caused the river to overflow its banks and flood the valley, wreaking much destruction on several buildings in certain villages. Most of the year, however, the valley is a favorite refuge from Marrakesh. It's a great picnic spot and, at several points, a good hiking area, but you'll need a guide to show you the way up the surrounding cliff trails. Although it is outdated, a map titled "Marrakech Sud—7.8," which is available from the map office in Rabat, could be helpful in negotiating the trails.

At Oukaïmeden—if there's enough snow, of course—there are several skiing options: chair lifts, rope pulls, and bar lifts, up inclines and hillsides of various heights and angles. When I was there in late February, the snow was already thinning quickly and the skiing at higher, steeper levels was mostly on thin ice and frozen mud, a dangerous condition especially for novice skiers. At lower levels, the skiing was slow, wet, and mushy.

All equipment, even including caps and gloves, can usually be rented near the ticket booth for negotiable prices, but some of it, particularly the boots and bindings, is antiquated and quite dangerous.

My boots were old leather ones with shoelaces that couldn't keep the flaps closed, so they had to be wrapped around my feet with duct tape. The bindings were useless, a fact I didn't discover until I fell trying to ski down a steep, icy incline and the skis stayed on rather than pop off as they should have. I ended up inching my way down, half by sliding on my rear end and half by waddling sideways.

By the end of this session of Moroccan skiing, despite the dangers, I must admit that I really did have a good time. However, be forewarned—their rental equipment is generally bad and snow conditions reputedly more often bad than good, all of which adds up to risky skiing.

Lift tickets cost from $3.25 for ten times up the bar lifts to $5.75 for five times up in the big chairs.

Rooms and meals can be had at the French-managed, ski lodge-style Chez Juju hotel for $15 per person in a four-bunk bedroom with breakfast and dinner included. Higher prices and slightly better amenities can be found at the Hotel Imlil, which is behind the Juju; they charge $145 for two to four people, including dinner and breakfast and a whopping 25 percent tax (skiing is definitely a luxury in Morocco). Or you could always go back down to the Ourika valley.

FROM MARRAKESH TO OUARZAZATE

The 204-km (126 1/2-mile) road from Marrakesh to Ouarzazate first goes east across the fertile Haouz plain and then, after about 60 km, it reaches the village of Aït-Barka and begins the twisting journey into the mountains. The scenery is probably spectacular, but if you are traveling by bus (as I was), you will most likely have your face pressed to the window watching as the bus careens around blind curves and takes you to the edge of the precipice and deep, dark ravines. My stomach knotted up when I saw the rusty skeletons of several cars, trucks, and buses over the edge. I wondered how well the bus driver knew the road and if he really knew what he was doing when he jerked the bus to within inches of the cliff on the right to miss colliding with on-coming traffic. The drive becomes even more terrifying in the winter when snow and ice cover the road, particularly along the stark and forbidding Tizi-n-Tichka pass at

2,260 m (7,415 ft). If weather conditions, however, are too forbidding, the road is temporarily closed.

Before reaching the pass, the bus usually stops at the mountain village of Taddert, which is only 19 km (12 miles) past Aït-Barka. The distance seems much greater because of the numerous steep, sharp curves on the road and the gear-grinding pace of the bus. By the time the bus reaches Taddert, you're ready for a break.

Both sides of the road through Taddert are lined with small shops and stands selling chunks of sparkling quartz, cobalt, amethyst, and several other minerals gathered from the region. There are also a few small grocery stores where you can buy snacks and some staples such as bread, canned fish, and bottled water. Hot, steaming tajine stews and lamb shish kebabs can be bought from the grills in front of a few stores.

At one ramshackle little shop, the shopkeeper, a young man in three layers of brown and white wool robes, asked me to help him relocate his stand to "Ameereeca." "I want to go to Ameereeca. Can I have this store in Ameereeca?" he asked with a sheepish grin. I said, "Sure, anything is possible in America," and shrugged. We both knew that this great American credo was the stuff of unobtainable dreams for some, if not most people. Sure, anything is possible—especially if you have a way to finance your dream, but his "finances" came from sales of crackers and chewing gum. By local standards, he was probably doing quite well—he had his own business on a busy road.

After another 18 km (11 miles) of harrowing curves, the Tizi-n-Tichka pass is reached at an elevation of 2,260 m (7,415 ft). The pass itself isn't particularly scenic, except for about two months each year when snow covers the ground. The rest of the year, the pass is a drab, brown-green dotted with a few mangy bushes and plants. There's no reason to stop here, but about 2 km (1 1/4 miles) farther is the junction for the 21-km (13-mile) dirt road to the village of Telouet, which was once the heart of the Glaoui empire, and that is worth exploring if you have the time.

The village is accessible by foot if you're an energetic hiker or by taxi from the village Igherm-n-Ougdal, which is about 10 km (6 miles) past Tizi-n-Tichka. From Telouet, the road briefly heads north and then east past the short road to a salt mine that was once the source of the Glaoui's wealth. The village of Anmiter lies about 4 km (2 1/2 miles) beyond the mine about the end of the Assif Ounila (also known as Wounila and Aounila) river valley. A rougher dirt road or trail goes south following the river for about 25 km (15 1/2 miles) to Tamdakht, where the Ounila flows into the Assif Mellah (also known as the Marghene) river and a 6-km (4-mile) chain of kasbahs stretching to Aït-Benhaddou begins. From Aït-Benhaddou it's only another 6 to 7 km (4 1/2 miles) to the main Ouarzazate road.

According to a French family who drove this road in a Land-Rover in late February, it takes about three hours to drive from Telouet to Aït-Benhaddou. They said that the road was beautiful, but quite steep and narrow in some sections and often partially blocked by boulders and large rocks.

In the mid-nineteenth century, most inhabitants of the villages and hamlets in this region were of the Glaoui family or, since it numbered many thousands, tribe (also known as Glaoua). This tribe, in turn, was distantly related to and indirectly controlled by the qa'id of a larger southern tribe, which was an unsettling situation for the Glaoui, because they were thus forced to share the healthy profits of their salt mines with this distant qa'id. In the area around Telouet, however, nominal leadership of the Glaoui was exercised by Si Mohammed Ben Hammou, who unsuccessfully tried to unite the Glaoui in the 1850s. He failed to unite them in battle, but did succeed through political maneuvering in having the sultan appoint him as qa'id over the region and its people. That also meant control of the salt mines and taxation of camel caravans, both of which were sources of great wealth. Qa'id Si Mohammed Ben Hammou, who died in 1888, had thereby established the foundation of what was to become an empire under his sons Madani, born in 1866, and T'hami, born in 1879.

Birth of the Glaoui empire could be said to have occurred in the fall of 1893 when Sultan Moulay Hassan and his beleaguered army arrived in Telouet on their return to Marrakesh. Hassan had taken his army on an ill-planned expedition to the desert region of Tafilelt. They hadn't brought enough food and water for themselves and the camels, mules, and horses, so many were dying along the way. By the time they reached the hills below Telouet, snow had begun to fall and some of the soldiers were resorting to cannibalism. Madani welcomed the sultan and his entourage to Telouet with the necessary flourishes of protocol, including the following recitation that was reported by journalist Walter Harris in the early 1900s:

> Lord of all, be pleased to rest with us a while; Lord of all, accept our humble homage; Lord of all, be pleased to offer what little your slave can offer; Lord of all, be gracious, and with your illustrious presence lighten the darkness of my kasbah; Lord of all, bestow the favour that I may feed your harka [retinue]; Lord of all, bestow your blessing upon my will to be your slave; Lord of all, tell me how I may serve you.

Madani and his brother then proceeded to treat the sultan to a long, lavish banquet that included roast sheep, huge tajines of chicken and pigeon, and mounds of couscous. After several days of feasting, the sultan reciprocated Madani's hospitality by making him his *khalifa* or personal representative with authority over all tribes in the region from the High Atlas mountains to the Sahara. His authority was reenforced by the sultan's gift of arms and ammunition including a 77-mm Krupp canon, the only "modern" cannon among the southern tribes. This gave the Glaoui brothers and their ever-expanding kasbah at Telouet an aspect of invincibility.

In his book, *The Kasbahs of Southern Morocco* (London: Faber & Faber, 1969, pp. 52–53), Rom Landau aptly summarized the subsequent rise of the Glaoui brothers from their base at Telouet:

> The brothers Madani and T'hami were the only Glaoui who attained real wealth and power. In the 1890s, they supported the Sultan Moulay Hassan, then his son Moulay Hafid, Sultan between 1908 and 1912; finally, they made common cause with the invading French. Madani, evidently an outstanding personality, became War Minister and then Prime Minister (Grand Vizier). When he died, in July 1918, he left 64 children, 36 of them sons. Yet he bequeathed his power and his fortune to none of them, but to his younger brother T'hami, whose leadership of the Glaoui family was legalized by General Lyautey, France's first Resident General in Morocco. According to authoritative sources, he added to his own harem of ninety-six, fifty-four from Madani's. He also strengthened his position with the imperial palace by marrying one of Madani's widows....
>
> T'hami el Glaoui followed the ancient ways of Berber chieftains, in attacking unwelcome neighbors, sequestering their lands and women, and proving himself a warrior as brave as he was ruthless. In the course of his tribal ventures he accumulated large fortunes; yet he seemed usually to be out of funds, and it was the French who came to his rescue time after time. He became a "grand seigneur," a collector of beautiful things, and an avid builder of kasbas....His most famous visitor, one who often enjoyed his hospitality and who repeatedly entertained him in his own English home, was Winston Churchill.

After Sultan Moulay Hafid's rise to power in late 1908, the Glaoui brothers followed the sultan to Marrakesh. For Madani's military cooperation and political intrigue in bringing him to power, the sultan rewarded him with first the post of war minister and then that of grand vizier, which amounted to being in charge of all administrative affairs in Morocco. Madani made his brother T'hami pasha of Marrakesh and his son-in-law Si Hammou Qa'id of Telouet and of most of the rest of the south.

Granting Si Hammou control over the south proved to be a mistake for Madani and T'hami. Until his death in 1934, Si Hammou prevented first Madani and then T'hami and the French Protectorate government from dominating the south. In fact, because of mutual dislike between the French and Hammou, the road from Marrakesh to Ouarzazate was built over the more difficult Tizi-n-Tichka pass rather than through Telouet, an easier route. Hammou was partially untouchable because he had expanded mining operations near Telouet and thus greatly increased his personal wealth and, consequently, power. The kasbah at Telouet was his base and in its crude, chaotic architectural style reflected both the man and his so-called miniempire.

By all accounts Hammou was a vulgar guy, and his kasbah was a hodgepodge of high walls and crudely constructed buildings. If a total lack of design could be called a style, then that describes Hammou's kasbah. It was so bad that after Hammou's death, T'hami's son Brahim, who was educated in France and appointed qa'id of Telouet, built a new kasbah on the hill above Hammou's.

According to Rom Landau, who visited Brahim's kasbah in 1949, Brahim succeeded in making his kasbah "the most luxurious mountain palace of the age." Mosaics covered the floors of the entire complex of buildings, halls, and courtyards. Many of the walls were decorated with carved arabesque designs and colorful hand-painted tiles. Intricately woven carpets were spread and hung everywhere. After independence in 1956 and the Glaoui family's fall from power and grace for supporting the French Protectorate, Qa'id Brahim was banished to France and the kasbah was abandoned.

Today the kasbah is still uninhabited and neglected. It would cost too much to renovate and maintain the complex, and also it represents a black period of Moroccan history. It is possible, however, to visit part of the kasbah, which is definitely a worthwhile excursion to get some idea of the tremendous wealth and power the Glaoui family once possessed. The first kasbah is in complete ruins at the base of the hill to Brahim's kasbah. Climb the hill and pound hard on the kasbah's double-door entrance. Eventually, the caretaker will appear to lead you through a few of the kasbah's buildings and halls. Most of the carved walls and ceilings and mosaic decorations are still visible, but the paint has all but peeled away and holes have begun appearing in the walls.

From Telouet, the main road briefly heads north and then east past a short road to one of the Glaoui's principal salt mines. The village of Anmiter lies about 4 km (2 1/2 miles) beyond the mine at about the end of the Assif Ounila river valley. The elevation gain along this route is less than 100 m (328 ft), so this hike is quite manageable.

It's also possible to hike the remaining 31 km (19 1/2 miles) along the Assif Mellah (also known as the Marghene) river valley to a 6-km (4-mile) chain of kasbahs that leads to the village of Aït-Benhaddou. It's an easy route to follow because most of the road or track runs parallel to the river. It should take you about one and a half to two days to walk from Anmiter to Aït-Benhaddou.

Before the French built the road over the Tizi-n-Tichka pass, Aït-Benhaddou was an important village on the trading route between Marrakesh and Ouarzazate. As testimony to its economic and political importance, many kasbahs were built over the centuries, so that by the 1930s when the village was in decline because of the road, it was still a veritable village of well-preserved kasbahs. Somehow word spread outside of Morocco about this village of beautiful high-walled, crenellated kasbahs and Hollywood movie producers in search of typical "medieval" and "Arab" settings began arriving. By now, several movies have been made at Aït-Benhaddou, including *Lawrence of Arabia* and *Jesus of Nazareth*. *Romancing the Stone* was made at the kasbah in nearby Ouarzazate.

Getting to Aït Benhaddou from Ouarzazate is easier than from Telouet, but still challenging if you don't have a car or haven't hired a taxi. A man (or a woman with another person, preferably a man) can try hitchhiking, which is no problem from Ouarzazate to the Aït-Benhaddou road 22 km (13 1/2 miles) away; however, it could be a problem from there to Aït-Benhaddou, which is about 6 to 7 km (4 1/2 miles) up the road. Only about six families live in Aït-Benhaddou today, so there isn't much traffic on the road. Unless you feel like hiking, try to arrange a ride all the way to the village from Ouarzazate.

After the Telouet junction near the Tizi-n-Tichka pass, the rest of the route is mostly like the previous stretch. However, now you are descending toward Ouarzazate and the edge of the Sahara and there seem to be far fewer sharp curves and precarious cliffs.

FROM MARRAKESH TO THE NORTHWEST FACE OF THE HIGH ATLAS MOUNTAINS

The fourth route from Marrakesh into the High Atlas mountains goes northwest out of the city along Highway P24. After 53 km (33 miles) it reaches the town of Tamelelt El Kedima; a few kilometers further is the junction for Road S508 to Demnate (pronounced *dem-na-tay*). From Tamelelt, it is about 60 km (37 miles) to Demnate. An alternate paved, but less traveled, route to Demnate from Marrakesh is along a secondary road that goes via Sidi Rahal. The latter is more interesting, particularly on Friday when one of the largest outdoor markets in the region is held here. Buses from Marrakesh follow both routes.

Sidi Rahal is named for a fifteenth-century marabout or saint whose legendary mythical powers included an ability to float himself and others through the air and tame potentially devastating streams. During the summer, a week-long moussem or religious and social celebration is held to venerate Sidi Rahal. The date varies so you may want to get more information from tourist offices in Marrakesh, Azilal, or branch offices overseas.

The walled town of Demnate is also noted for its market, which occurs every Sunday just outside the walls and ramparts. Until the nineteenth century, it was known for having a sizeable Jewish population, but most of the Jews were eventually forced to seek refuge in Marrakesh. Today, aside from the Sunday market, it's also worth stopping in Demnate for any of several annual moussems held in the summer and early fall. One of the largest is held two weeks after the Aïd El Kebir; the date varies according to the lunar calendar, but over the next few years it will be between late May and mid-July. The Aïd El Kebir commemorates Abraham's obedience to Allah in sacrificing his son Isaac and is celebrated by each household with the ritual slaughter of a sheep. The following is an approximate schedule of moussems in Demnate and vicinity provided by the Azilal tourist office:

Moussems	Location	Time of Year
Moussem Imin Tizgui	Aït Chitachen plain near Demnate	First week in August
Moussem Sidi Boulkhalf	Douar Aït Toutline near Demnate	Second week in August
Moussem Sidi Hicham	Douar Aït Toutline near Demnate	Third week in August
Moussem Sidi Bou Ali	Douar Iwariden near Demnate	Third week in August
Moussem Sidi Benaâmer	Douar Iwariden near Demnate	Fourth week in August
Moussem Aït Bou-Aïssa	Douar Iwariden near Demnate	Last week in August
Moussem El Hadi Ben Aïssa and Sidi Ali Ben Hamdouch	Demnate	End of September

Lastly, in the Demnate area there's also a worthwhile 13-km (8-mile) round-trip day hike from town to a natural stone arch and group of beautiful springs. In town, ask people to direct you outside the walls to the trail for Imni n'Ifri, which means "the mouth of the river." If you're really serious about hiking, though, continue on to Azilal for adventurous forays into the mountains.

On the way to Azilal, 70 km (43 1/2 miles) away, you may want to visit the spectacular Cascades d'Ouzoud (waterfalls) and Oued El Abid gorges if you have your own car. The junction for the 16-km (10-mile) dirt road (No. 1811) to these falls is about 42 km (26 miles) from Demnate and 28 km (17 miles) from Azilal. If you don't have a car, then hire a grand taxi from Azilal. Supposedly there's a bus three times daily in the summer, the best and most practical time to visit, but I wasn't able to get what I thought was reliable information about it.

The falls are part of the Oued El Abid river, which flows from the Bin El Ouidane lake. They are created as the river pours over two tiers of rocks and into small pools and rivulets. A forest of pine trees and Barbary apes and well-marked trails surround the falls and make an excellent place for photography and camping. There are two "official" campsites open from about March to September, both of which are beautifully situated near the falls. One of the campsites also doubles as a restaurant, café, and basic hotel. A variety of short hikes along the river and into a nearby valley are also easily possible, but be careful when walking near the falls and around the observation point. It gets dangerously slippery here—visitors have been known to slide over the edge.

AZILAL

Azilal is a growing town in the high foothills of the Atlas mountains; it serves as the main administrative and military center for the region. It has also become the focus of a unique effort to enhance tourism in Morocco. The effort is spearheaded by the local tourism office and an organization called Azourki Expéditions Randonnées.

The tourism office is on the main avenue through town on the second floor of a small, well-marked building. If you are coming from Beni Mellal and Bin El Ouidane lake, then the office is on your left before you reach the market square and unmarked bus depot. According to Redouane Belkhouya, deputy delegate for tourism in Azilal, the office's main objectives are to promote "cultural" tourism in the High Atlas mountains and valleys near Azilal. They are attempting to introduce small groups of foreign visitors to Berber culture by arranging visits with families in remote mountain villages. Belkhouya explains that by not building large hotels and bringing in large groups to the region, the potential for a negative environmental and cultural impact is minimized.

At the same time, however, local inhabitants will presumably benefit economically by the extra income brought by tourism. The key issue is how much tourism is too much for the region.

Belkhouya and other people I spoke with in Azilal often mentioned the coastal beach resort city of Agadir as an example of what they don't want to happen in their region. Agadir is a city of hotels and large tour groups mostly oriented to beach vacations. If it weren't for tourist camel rentals on the beach, occasional traditional dance presentations, and fantastic weather most of the year, this city could be almost anywhere in the world. It is definitely not the place to come if you want to learn about Moroccan history and culture; it's purposely detached from both in order to relate better to foreign tourism.

The people in Azilal also seem to want to cater to foreign tourism, but not by overhauling or negatively affecting their land and culture. Undoubtedly, as the number of foreign visitors to the region increases, the local Berbers will be affected or influenced in some way. It will be a challenge for the tourist office and Azourki Expéditions Randonnées, the principal travel company here, to simultaneously reap the benefits and minimize the potentially negative impact of increased tourism.

Azourki Expéditions Randonnées is a travel company that specializes in "mountain tourism" such as backpacking and hiking trips, ski expeditions, and mountain bike trips. They offer a variety of standard itineraries, mostly in the High Atlas mountains near Azilal, but also in the lesser ranges and massifs of Jebel Saghro, Siroua, and the Anti-Atlas. The company is run by Ahmed Outeglaout and a team of mountain guides, all of whom are Berbers from nearby villages who were sent to the French Alps for professional mountain guide training at a school called the Centre de Formation aux Métiers de la Montagne, or CFAMM (Training Center for Mountaineering). Not surprisingly, several U.S. and European adventure travel companies work with Azourki in arranging their trips.

Outeglaout founded Azourki Expéditions Randonnées in 1984 after he and his fellow guides returned from their Moroccan government-sponsored training program in the French Alps. Since then he seems to have developed a well-organized company offering trips at a variety of skill levels. The trips described below depart from Outeglaout's village in the valley of Aït Bougmez, where he has stored enough camping supplies for eighty people including forty two-person Canadian tents and a kitchen tent. Although foreign visitors often stay with Berber families here, there's also a small hotel with showers, several hostel-style rooms for four to five people, a terrace, and a dining room.

The itineraries described below could be done on your own, directly with Azourki or indirectly by going through one of several foreign adventure travel companies. If you don't have the time, patience, and knowledge of French necessary to negotiate and arrange a trip on your own, however, then I recommend that you contact any of the companies listed after the itinerary descriptions. It's also possible to contact Outeglaout directly (mail from the United States to Azilal and vice versa takes approximately 10 days each way). Outeglaout and his staff don't know much English, but the tourist office can translate for them. Even if you want to do an independent trip, it's a good idea to first talk or write to Outeglaout or any of his guides for information and travel tips about the region. A few of their tips and suggestions are included with the itinerary descriptions. They are quite friendly and willing to help, but remember that they are a business, not a travel information service. There address is Azourki Expéditions Randonnées, Boulevard Mohammed V, Azilal, Morocco; tel. 048-83-32, telex 74088M.

Practical Information for the Azilal Region

Buses

Daily buses from Marrakesh to Azilal depart at 8:30 A.M. and 3:30 P.M. and, in the opposite direction, at 6:30 A.M. and 2 P.M. (approximately a 3 1/2-hour trip); all go via Demnate. Buses to and from Beni Mellal start and end their journeys at Demnate several times daily (approximately US $2 and 2 1/2 hours from Azilal).

Grand Taxis

The fastest way to go to Afourer and Beni Mellal is by grand taxi. If you're lucky, the taxi is going all the way to Beni Mellal, but usually they only go as far as Afourer, where you have to change taxis. The same applies in the opposite direction. Grand taxis also run frequently to Demnate and to Aït Mohammed.

The only hotel in Azilal worth mentioning is the Hotel Telnout, which doubles as a Shell service station at the edge of town on the road to Bin El Ouidane. The rooms are comfortable, but without toilets, heating, and (often) hot water. Above the rooms is a café that sometimes functions as a restaurant. The bus to and from Beni Mellal stops in front of the hotel.

Trekking from Azilal

Information and Tips

Most of the following information and comments are edited and rewritten translations of Ahmed Outeglaout's statements and advice

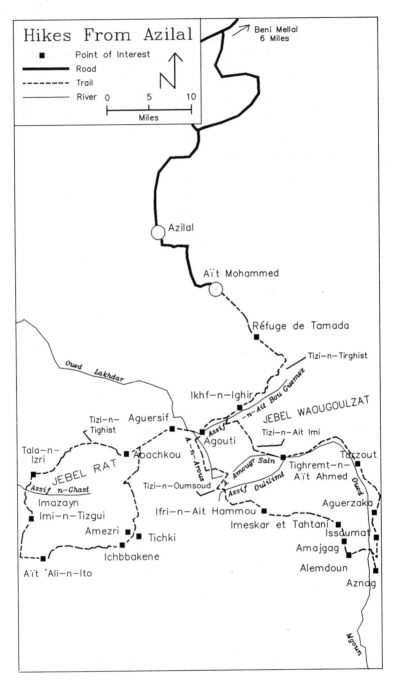

Hikes From Azilal

- ■ Point of Interest
- —— Road
- ------ Trail
- —— River

0   5   10
Miles

N

Beni Mellal
6 Miles

Azilal

Aït Mohammed

Réfuge de Tamada

Tizi–n–Tirghist

Oued Lakhdar

Ikhf–n–Ighir

A. –n–Aït Bou Guemez

JEBEL WAOUGOULZAT

Tizi–n–
Tighist

Aguersif

Assif

Tizi–n–Ait Imi

Agouti

A.–n–Arous

Tala–n–
Izri

Abachkou

JEBEL RAT

Tizi–n–Oumsoud

A. Amougr Salm

Assif Oukiliml

Tighremt–n–
Aït Ahmed

Tazout

Assif n–Ghast

Oued

Imazayn

Ifri–n–Ait Hammou

Aguerzaka

Imi–n–Tizgui

Imeskar et Tahtani

Amezri

Tichki

Issdumat

Ichbbakene

Amajgag

Aït 'Ali–n–Ito

Alemdoun

Aznag

Mgoun

concerning trekking in the High Atlas mountains near Azilal. His comments, in turn, are derived from his coursework at the professional mountain guide school in the French Alps and his own experiences growing up in the mountains. At the risk of seeming somewhat redundant, I have included parts of this section in other parts of the book because the topics covered—personal safety and respect for the people and environment—deserve repeated emphasis.

In structuring his trips, Outeglaout has tried to adhere to the Berber belief that human beings and nature share a very fragile, living community and that nature is to be respected rather than conquered and tamed if that community is to be perpetuated. As Outeglaout takes you into the "community" of Berbers in the isolated villages of the High Atlas Mountains, you'll see that Berbers take this idea of human beings and nature very seriously. As you visit the Berbers, respect their ways and try as best you can to understand their traditional life style and customs.

When hiking one of the itineraries described below, the following tips are strongly recommended for both men and women:

- Shorts, bathing suits, and low-cut necklines shock the inhabitants, so respect their modesty and local customs—cover up when passing through Berber villages or other inhabited places.
- Be discreet in photographing local people. Taking a photo is acceptable as long as you ask. If refused, don't insist. If you promise to send photos, take addresses, and make good on your promises; it will be a marvelous gift.
- Be economical in your use of firewood, because it is a precious commodity. The local women walk for many hours in the mountains to gather bundles of sticks for firewood.
- Don't discard cans, bottles, and other nonbiodegradable materials. Burn all paper refuse, including toilet paper.
- You may be invited to eat with a Berber family. The host will probably not request compensation for the meal, but it is customary to offer about 40 to 50 dirhams per person. Inquire beforehand at the tourist office for the current customary rate. Compensation is not expected when invited to tea.
- Helpful map terms:

aghbalou	spring
azibs	shepherds' huts, often used for overnight stays on treks
igherm	fortress-like collective granary, usually for several villages
ighil	elongated summit
ighir	rocky shoulder

jebel	mountain
tighremt	solidly built house usually belonging to a local notable
tizi	mountain pass

When to Go and What to Bring

All year, whatever the season, hiking in the High Atlas mountains can be challenging even for experienced hikers. If you plan to do any extended hikes, you should at least be in good shape and well equipped. Although the weather in the mountains can turn nasty any time of year, your equipment needs will partially depend on the altitude at which you'll be hiking. For example, a ski expedition at higher altitudes requires special ski equipment and clothing. Whatever the altitude, though, if you're on one of Outeglaout's trips or any other company's, you will need at least the following (beyond the most obvious items like toiletries and a first-aid kit):

- Rain gear
- Warm sleeping bag
- Warm clothing
- Thermal underwear
- Canteen or water container
- Good tough walking shoes
- Lightweight tennis shoes for crossing streams and creeks

Although mules are used to carry your baggage and equipment, it is strongly recommended that your baggage not exceed 12 kg (28 1/2 pounds).

Most of the hikes in the High Atlas mountains are only practicable between April and October. Trails on the northern slopes, however, are sometimes blocked by chunks of glacier ice as late as the end of May. Hikes into the Mgoun gorges are feasible between June and November; southern approaches to these gorges from Skoura and Kelaat d'Mgoun are described in the southern Morocco section. In August and September, hikes through any gorges are sometimes risky because of violent afternoon storms that cause temporary flooding, so it's better to complete as much of your hiking as possible in the morning and then get to high ground above the gorges in the afternoon.

During the rest of the year, treks into the High Atlas mountains are possible, but primarily for experienced skiers with the appropriate equipment because most of the high-elevation trails are covered with snow. If you have the equipment and experience, these trips are highly recommended, albeit challenging and risky, adventures.

According to Brian Favreau, a ski equipment specialist with the "outdoor sporting specialists" L. L. Bean, the type of equipment best suited for this type of ski trip is a telemark ski set that includes specially adapted skis with "climbing skins," made with a grooved plastic or polyurethane or a mohair base attached to the skis for increased traction, thus allowing you to scale slopes more easily. Most of the time, the skis are a bit wider than cross-country skis and longer than downhill skis, but they are still suitable for both types of skiing. The ski boots are more similar to hiking boots with heels that aren't bound to the skis and, therefore, permit your heels to come off the skis. Special cable bindings are sometimes added for more lateral stability. Clothing should not be cotton but polypropylene, wool, or other typical ski clothing. Special backpacks with outside loops for carrying your skis when hiking and compression straps for attaching other equipment are also useful; North Face and Lowe travel gear companies manufacture this type of equipment. Another very useful piece of equipment is adjustable ski poles that allow you to adjust pole length according to the type of skiing you'll be doing. Other equipment that is often recommended for ski expeditions includes an ice axe and crampons. For more information from L. L. Bean in the United States and Canada, call 800-341-4341, ext. 3100.

Topographical maps of the region are available from the map office in Rabat (see introductory section for the address). The recommended maps (scale 1:100,000) include

Zawyat Ahançal	Feuille NH-29-XXIV-4
Skoura	Feuille NH-29-XXIV-1
Azilal	Feuille NH-29-XXIV-3
Qalaa't Mgouna	Feuille NH-29-XXIV-2 (same area as Kelaat d'Mgoun)
Imichil	Feuille NI-30-I-1
Demnate	Feuille NH-29-XXIII-4

Maps of part of this region are also available at a scale of 1:50,000.

Trip Descriptions and Suggested Itineraries

The first trip described below takes you into the heart of the Central High Atlas mountains through valleys, Berber villages, and gorges, into caves, atop summits, and across plateaus. Parts of this trip, particularly the ascents of the summits and ridges, can be strenuous.

Itinerary 1

Day 1. Arrive Marrakesh and spend the day touring the city.

Day 2. Depart by Land-Rover for Azilal and the village of Aït

Mohammed (20 km, or 12 1/2 miles from Azilal). The secondary road to Aït Mohammed is paved and passes through a series of austere brown hills covered with white and gray chunks of basalt and small patches of greenery. When the hills aren't shrouded in fog, just beyond them the peaks are visible. At a few points on the road, the hillsides are blanketed with various sizes of rock and resemble the ruins of an ancient city. Farther on just before Aït Mohammed, a spring pops from the top edge of a cliff and pours toward the road in a weblike fall.

Aït Mohammed is a village on its way to becoming a town and a regional market center. On Saturdays the village comes alive as Berbers from surrounding villages set up the weekly souk with their sheep, cattle, mules, and produce. Many people arrive the night before and sleep with their animals in special stalls at the souk for 5 dirhams (DH) per person, 2.50 DH per cow, 5 DH per mule, and 1 DH per sheep.

The Land-Rovers continue past Aït Mohammed along 7 km (4 1/3 miles) of paved road and then approximately another 40 km (28 miles) along a winding piste, or rough mountain road, to the valley of Aït Bougmez. The road rises to an elevation of about 2,629 m (8,625 ft) at the Tizi-n-Tirghist pass and then descends to about 1,800 m (5,906 ft) in the valley.

Walking or riding mules along this road takes about six to eight hours for extremely well-acclimated Berbers, so ten hours might be a reasonable estimate for others. If you want to walk it in two days, possible overnight points are the Refuge de Tamda about 15 km (9 miles) from Aït Mohammed or one of the villages along the Assif Aït Hkim, a ridge that stretches for about 15 km from the beginning of the Aït Bougmez valley toward the Tirghist pass.

Accommodations are arranged with a Berber family in one of the villages in the valley. Sometimes a sheep is slaughtered and a traditional meal is prepared for the group.

Day 3. Mules are readied and loaded with equipment and baggage. The hike proceeds through the narrowing valley of Aït Bougmez to the village of Agouti and then southward along the Assif-n-Arous, where a campsite is set up at an altitude of about 2,300 m (7,646 ft). Cool weather expected.

Day 4. From Assif-n-Arous, the trail crosses part of the Tarkeddid plateau and skirts the edge of the valley of Tessaout. Sometimes shepherds from the valley are seen grazing their sheep here. Off to the side of the plateau, the peaks of Mgoun massif form an impressive picture. Camp is set up at 2,850 m (9,350 ft). Cool weather expected.

Day 5. A gradual climb through the Tizi-n-Oumsoud pass and then toward the 4,068-m (11,346-ft) summit of the Mgoun subrange. Once over the summit, the campsite is set up at the entrance to a series of small gorges and near the caves of Ifri-n-Aït Hammou at 2,400 m (7,874 ft). Cool weather expected.

Day 6. A short descent into the valley of Aït Ahmed, an area renowned for traditional wheat cultivation with basic implements that probably haven't changed in centuries. The people in this region seem even more untouched by the outside world than other villages encountered so far. Camping at Imeskar et Tahtani at 2,000 m (6,562 ft) near gorges and wooded areas.

Day 7. From Imeskar, the countryside begins to change dramatically as the hike proceeds along the Assif-n-Imeskar to the hamlet of Amajgag and a vast, well-cultivated plain. The fortress-like appearance of red multistory kasbahs in the area attests to the permanence of its residents and prosperity of the fields. The trail continues through the hamlet of Alemdoun, a few small gorges and a veritable forest of pink laurels before reaching the Oued Mgoun river valley. The villages in this region are some of the most picturesque in the High Atlas mountains. Camping at 1,600 m (5,250 ft).

Day 8. At this point, you can either continue south through the river valley to the town of Kelaat d'Mgoun on the main road or north along the road from Aznag to Issoumat (the latter route should be with a guide). From Issoumat the trail veers away from the river again, crosses the Tizi-n-Mademt pass and heads into the hamlet of Aguerzaka, which is about 1,800 m (5,905 ft) and usually the campsite.

Day 9. The trail follows the river through gorges barely wide enough for the baggage-laden mules. At some points the equipment on the mules scrapes the sides of the gorges. This is challenging hiking. At the tiny hamlet of Tarzout, a Berber tea-serving ceremony is demonstrated and the mule handlers sacrifice a sheep or goat for the evening meal. Camping is at about 1,870 m (6,135 ft) near Tarzout.

Day 10. From the campsite, the trail continues following the river as it heads northwest and then turns west and southwest. On this stretch the trail borders the long massif Waougoulzat and passes through a string of Berber villages. The terrain is hilly, but well cultivated as terraced fields above and behind several villages. The hamlet of Taskalia at about 2,100 m (6,890 ft) is the last camping site in the Assif Mgoun.

Day 11. A relatively easy day of hiking along the river of the Assif Mgoun and through several villages and settlements to the hamlet of Tighremt-n-Aït Ahmed where the rivers of the Assif Amougr Saln and the Assif Oulilimt meet the Assif Mgoun. Camping here with local shepherds at an altitude of 2,200 m (7,218 ft).

Day 12. This final day of hiking involves a short trek along the Assif Amougr Saln river and then northwestward over the Tizi-n-Aït Imi pass (2,905 m, or 9,531 ft). After the pass, the trail goes through a sharp series of descending switchbacks and then straightens as it enters the valley of Aït Bougmez. Accommodations are with Berber families.

Day 13. Return to Marrakesh.

Supplemental Information

Because this hike involves approximately five to six hours of daily walking, you should be in good shape. On the ninth and eleventh days, half-day rest stops are scheduled or, for avid hikers, short solo hikes are possible. On the ninth day, the solo hike can also be done by mule.

During the hike, food will include fresh fruit and vegetables, some canned foods imported from France, and goat or lamb meat bought locally. Hot meals will be served in the evenings, picnics or salads in the afternoons, and basic instant food and drink in the mornings.

Itinerary 2

This hike is similar to the one above, but it is about three days shorter and has fewer steep ascents. Compared to the first hike, this one is more "cultural" in that learning about the region's Berber inhabitants is emphasized more than is exploring the surrounding terrain.

Day 1. After participants arrive by Land-Rover from Marrakesh and spend the previous night in the valley of Aït Bougmez with families in the village of Ikhf-n-Ighir, the mules are readied and the caravan is formed. The group proceeds through the Aït Bougmez and toward the valley of Aït Bouli passing a tributary of the river Oued Lakhdar and several elaborate mud-walled kasbahs of various stories. Camping is in the valley of Aït Bouli beside the river Oued Lakhdar at Aguersif.

Day 2. From Aguersif the group enters a deep, green valley where the kasbahs are perched precipitously along the edges of terraced fields. The trail continues somewhat flatly through the village of Abachkou and then steepens as it approaches the foot of the Tizi-n-Tighist pass at about 2,100 m (6,890 ft). The campsite is set up just above the stream at this point.

Day 3. Ascent of Tizi-n-Tighist pass (2,389 m, or 7,838 ft) and then approach the east slope of the Jebel Rat through a forest of juniper. A climb to the summit at 3,781 m (12,405 ft) is possible from this slope. The camp is at Tala-n-Izri.

Day 4. The trail descends to the village of Tarbat-n-Tirsal, where the red-earth kasbahs and surrounding mountains make a particularly striking picture. From there it's a relatively short, easy hike south to the hamlet of Imazayn along the Assif-n-Ghasf at 2,100 m (6,890 ft), which is this evening's campsite.

Day 5. From Imazayn the trail climbs through a relatively low mountain pass and then descends to Imi-n-Tizgui, the Assif Tissili, and the big river Oued Tessaout. The camp is set up next to the river near the hamlet of Aït Ali-n-Ito, which is at 1,825 m (5,988 ft).

Day 6. The trail continues west along the river past a variety of kasbahs and other smaller mud-walled buildings to the village of Ichbbakene. The village is beautifully situated alongside the Tessaout river, with lush green fields all around and the mountains forming a magnificent backdrop—a perfect place to camp.

Day 7. The trail continues climbing up the Oued Tessaout toward its source after passing through the villages of Amezri and Tichki. The camp is set up between the gorges of Tessaout at 2,483 m (8,146 ft).

Day 8. The Tizi-n-Rouguelt pass (2,900 m/9,514 ft) is crossed en route to the Tarkeddid plateau (2,800 m/9,186 ft). An optional ascent of the Ighil Mgoun is possible in the afternoon or very early the following day if the weather is good, but this is only recommended for experienced hikers.

Day 9. A somewhat strenuous hike through the Tizi-n-Oughri pass at 3,900 m (12,795 ft) and then a descent toward the Assif Arous and the village of Agouti, where you will spend the last night of the hike.

Variations

There are several variations of these two main itineraries with both shorter and longer, easier and more difficult trips and treks offered by a variety of companies, including Ahmed Outeglaout's Azourki Expéditions Randonnées. Many of the arrangements in the High Atlas mountains are made by Outeglaout's group.

One of the most interesting set of trips is offered by Cross Cultural Adventures, a Virginia-based company run by Piotr Kostrzewski, a former Peace Corps volunteer in Morocco. Kostrzewski's easiest trip is a fifteen-day Land-Rover tour through the High Atlas and part of the Middle Atlas mountains. The itinerary includes a two-day visit to Marrakesh, a drive through the Dadés gorge and over a 10,000-foot (3,048-m) pass to the famous Imilchil Betrothal Fair (described later), two to three days in the valley of Aït Bougmez staying with Berber families and participating in a *méchoui* (roast lamb) feast, a drive-through visit to the cedar forests and lakes of the Middle Atlas mountains, and a one-and-a-half-day visit to Fez.

More challenging trips include a fourteen-day Mgoun Mountain Trek in mid-June with almost ten full days of trekking, and a fourteen-day Tessawt Cultural Trek. The itineraries are quite similar to the two Azourki trips described above, but the latter also includes festivities at the house of the chief of Aït Ali-n-Ito and a visit by Land-Rover to the once-grand kasbah of the Glaoui family in Telouet (see Telouet section). Some of the elevation gains are steep on the Mgoun trip and may only be manageable for well-experienced trekkers. Both trips, however can be done by mule.

For less experienced hikers and those seeking a "cultural" adventure, a series of day hikes and home stays with Berber families in the Aït Bougmez valley is planned for late June and early July. Approximately half the trip includes visits to Marrakesh and the medieval Portuguese fortress in the coastal fishing town of Essaouira.

Home stays with Berber families from a week to a month can also be arranged between June and September. You will stay with an English-speaking student who will introduce you to the ways of life of his or her family and tribe.

Cross Cultural Adventures can be reached at P.O. Box 3285, Arlington, Virginia 22203; tel. 703-204-2717.

Several other companies offer similar hiking trips, but most of them don't include home stays with Berber families. Overseas Adventure Travel (6 Bigelow Street, Cambridge, Massachusetts 02139; tel. 617-876-0533 and 800-221-0814) offers an eight-day trek through the High Atlas mountains near the Mgoun summits between May and October. REI Adventures (P.O. Box 8090, Berkeley, California 94707-8090; tel. 415-526-4005, 800-624-2236 (in California) and 800-622-2236 (outside California)) offers a 10-day trek that seems quite similar to one of Ahmed's; the land cost of just over $1,000 seems reasonable. Forum Travel International (91 Gregory Lane, Pleasant Hill, California 94523; tel. 415-671-2900 and 415-946-1500) offers two 15-day treks similar to Ahmed's and a 22-day trek along the entire spine of the Atlas mountains. Forum is run by a man named Dr. Nicholas Hetzer, who once served in North Africa with the French Foreign Legion and is now considered a veritable expert on northwestern Africa (mainly Morocco and Algeria).

When evaluating the trips offered by these companies, I suggest that you try to contact past participants for their opinions and descriptions. Overseas Adventure Travel insists on this practice, and the others should be able to arrange it.

Imilchil

The village of Imilchil is nestled in the heart of the High Atlas mountains alongside the twin lakes of Tislit and Isli, both of which are great camp sites. The grand event here is the annual marriage market of the Aït Haddidou tribe in September, which used to be isolated from the throes of mass tourism, but that has now changed. A bevy of tour buses and Land-Rovers invades the area with scores of eager foreign travelers who ogle the brides and grooms-to-be as they ogle each other. Immense goatskin tents are erected and serve as temporary accommodations and "restaurants" and "cafés."

It is possible to get to Imilchil on your own, but it's an arduous, time-consuming journey. The main approaches are from Kasba Tadla northeast of Imilchil and Tinerhir to the southeast. The first legs of each approach can be done either by bus or grand taxi. From Kasba Tadla, you can go as far as the villages of Naour and Arhbala, but after that you must begin hoping and hitching for souk truck rides to Imilchil. During the marriage fair, this shouldn't be a problem because there's a fairly steady stream of traffic. From Tinerhir, it's easy to get as far as Tamtatouche by grand taxi or often souk truck. However, the rest of the trip, like the second leg from Kasba Tadla, requires hoping and hitching for unpredictable truck rides to any of the four principal villages before Imilchil— Aït Hani, Toumiline, Agoudal, and Bouzmou. It is not unheard of to have to spend as many as four days waiting for a ride and then, once a truck finally does arrive, to have to stand in the back for several hours like a sardine with mud-covered sheep.

Cross Cultural Adventures offers Land-Rover trips to the fair as part of a fourteen-day tour. The itinerary includes visits to Marrakesh and Fez and follows the tortuously twisting Dadés gorge route to Imilchil. After the fair, the Land-Rovers proceed to the Aït Bougmez valley described above in previous itineraries for a home stay with a Berber family and an easy day-hike around the valley.

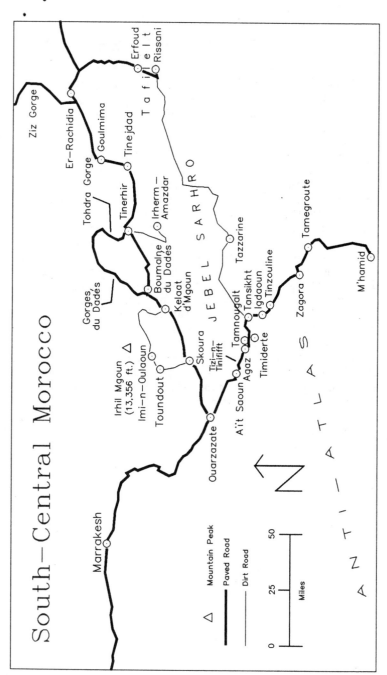

South–Central Morocco

Ziz Gorge

Erfoud
Rissani

Er–Rachidia

Goulmima

Tinejdad

Tohdra Gorge

Tinerhir

Irherm –
Amazdar

Tafilelt

JEBEL SARHRO

Tazzarine

Tamegroute

Gorges
du Dades

Boumalne
du Dades

Kelaat
d'Mgoun

Tansikht

Tinzouline

Zagora

M'hamid

Irhil Mgoun
(13,356 ft.) △

Imi–n–Oulaoun

Toundout

Skoura

Tizi–n–
Tinififft

Tamnougalt

Igdaoun

Timiderte

Aït Saoun

Agaz

Ouarzazate

Marrakesh

ANTI–ATLAS

N

△   Mountain Peak

━━ Paved Road

── Dirt Road

Miles

0   25   50

CHAPTER 8

The South: Along the Desert Spine
of the High Atlas Mountains and
Side Trips to the Gorges

Over the High Atlas mountains south of Marrakesh is the land of kasbahs, the harsh, hot edge of the vast Sahara. For centuries, Berbers, Arabs, and Jews have eked out a living in this region as farmers, nomads, and artisans wherever there was water from rivers, streams, and springs. Most of the Jews have left for other parts of Morocco and other countries, but the water still flows from snow-capped Atlas peaks through the sharply cut Dadés and Tohdra gorges and lushly verdant river valleys, palmeries, and oases. In the well-cultivated Drâa and Dadés river valleys, hundreds, perhaps thousands, of earth-colored kasbahs stand as they probably have for centuries, with crenellated ramparts, towers, and courtyards. Less than a hundred years ago, kasbahs had to be built like fortresses to protect the inhabitants from rival tribes, but today the principal threats are drought and overpopulation, neither of which, of course, is deterred by a strong kasbah.

A long drought that ended in 1986 ravaged the region by decreasing the amount of both cultivable land and grazing areas for cattle and sheep. The U.S. government sent wheat and other staples to prevent famine, and the Moroccan army has launched a massive "reforestation" campaign to forestall further denudation of the land. As you drive along the road between Ouarzazate and Kelaat d'Mgoun you'll see the results of the army's efforts—thousands of eucalyptus saplings planted alongside the road.

For travelers, both the towns and the countryside offer plenty of opportunities for adventures by foot and by bus or car. Ouarzazate, the region's largest town, is a major administrative center and crossroads for routes along the Dadés and Drâa river valleys and along the edge of the Jebel Sarhro range and the Anti-Atlas mountains near the Jebel Sirwa range. Ouarzazate is a convenient departure point for hikes in the Dadés

161

and Tohdra gorges and the Sirwa and Sarhro ranges. The road from Ouarzazate to Zagora is a fascinating path through villages and towns of kasbahs, oases, and palmeries. Zagora was once the last major settlement along the ancient camel caravan route to Timbuktu, but today that route is seldom, if ever, traveled. Camels are still plentiful here, so if you have been anxious to play Lawrence of Arabia and traipse around the edge of the Sahara on a camel for a few hours or a few days, now is your chance.

OUARZAZATE

Ouarzazate is a relatively new desert town 204 km (126 1/2 miles) from Marrakesh. The nearby kasbah and fortresses of Taourirt existed as a major power center of the Glaoui family (see Telouet section) long before the town was constructed by the French in 1928. They built a main street that supposedly has changed very little over the years, a set of buildings for government offices, and a red-orange Foreign Legion fort on a hill overlooking the town and the kasbah. After World War II, Hollywood discovered Ouarzazate and made it a popular shooting location for films needing stereotypical Arab desert scenes with mud-walled kasbahs and lots of burnoosed extras in flowing robes. As noted earlier, *Romancing the Stone* (starring Michael Douglas) was filmed at the Taourirt kasbah, and *Lawrence of Arabia* and *Jesus of Nazareth* were filmed nearby.

Arrival and Departure

Ouarzazate has an "international" airport about 2 km (1 1/4 miles) northeast of downtown, with direct flights to and from Agadir, Casablanca, Marrakesh (on Royal Air Inter), and a single international flight—weekly to and from Paris, France (on Air France).

Buses arrive at and depart from two dirt lots, one on the main street near the post office and the other about two blocks up (in the opposite direction from the post office) and one block off the street. The first lot is for all CTM buses, and the other is for more inexpensive, shoddier lines and grand taxis. Taking one of the latter buses could be for you, as it was for me, a memorable cultural experience.

The ticket office for the second lot is a small, dark room at the back of a ramshackle café. I bought a ticket for the 3:30 P.M. bus to Zagora and settled into a crude metal chair fashioned from tubing. Across the table was the only other foreigner around, an Irishman in his mid-20s named Patrick, who described himself as a "bloke," but I had to ask him three times where he was from and what he called himself because his accent was so thick, heavy, and clipped. For some reason, perhaps out of boredom in waiting for the bus, he was keen to tell me about his life.

"I've been woorkin' in the poobs in Germany getting drunk, sleepin' til four in the afternoon," he said. "This life gets to ya, mahn, ya know sleepin' drinkin' all the time, so I 'ad enough, so I told the boss 'hey I just bought a cheap ticket to Morocco, so I'm going for a month.' What could 'e say?"

For a moment, Patrick paused and looked up from the table. He stopped drumming his fingers just long enough to cram two sticks of bubble gum in his mouth and offer me one. The drumming began again and in a now slushier drawl, he continued his story.

"Not much. So I said goodbye to the kid. Yeah, I got a two-year-old."

"What's your wife doing? Is she working?"

"Naw, she's not my wife. And she 'as been on the dole for five years. I been on myself for two and a 'af."

"But weren't you working?"

"Yeah, yeah, but yah know what I mean? Yah know, under the table," he said putting his hands under the table and grinning. "But, hey I put in me 'ours at the bahr. The system got me money, so I'm taking some of it back."

A beat-up bus squealed into the lot trailing a cloud of dust and diesel smoke. People poured out the doors, and a few even squeezed out through the windows as packages and bundles were tossed on and off the roof. We found seats in the middle and watched out the window as a man in a long brown robe with voluminous sleeves heaved a box to the roof. The box was tied with twine, bursting at the seams with straw and seeping a sticky yellowish substance. Some of the substance landed on the man's forehead and dripped down his left eye and cheek and over his chin, but he didn't seem to notice. He boarded the bus with an armful of egg cartons, which he pushed into the luggage rack above, and then wiped his face with a sleeve and settled into a seat two rows behind us. An old woman sat across from him with a loud, clucking chicken whose legs were tied, presumably so it wouldn't run around under her seat. A bigger woman whose hands, forehead, and chin were painted with intricate, rust-colored henna tattoos and whose body seemed shrouded in several layers of black gowns filled two seats across from us.

The bus began to move as if it were in pain, groaning and grinding up hills in second gear and then sighing as it coasted down in neutral. Dust whistled through the windows, coating everyone with a fine layer whenever the bus coasted. None of the windows that were open could be closed. And the ones that were closed were covered with dirt, thus making it almost impossible to see anything outside.

Patrick was quiet for a while, but then he nudged me and said matter-of-factly, "Ya know, I've traveled a bit, but this is a first."

"What's a first? What do you mean?" I asked because I didn't think that he was talking about being on a dying bus.

"Look to me right and at our big friend, and you tell me if she's doin' what I think she's doing."

I glanced over at her and saw a skinned orange on her lap. Big chunks of orange peel were crammed up her nostrils. She kept the peel up her nose for almost the entire four hours of the trip. Later, I asked Moroccan friends if this was a local practice; they said no, it was probably just to keep the dust out of her nose.

Meanwhile, the egg man, the man two rows behind her with the egg cartons, had brought out a long thin pipe and was puffing slowly, carefully, and filling the bus with clouds of sweet-smelling smoke. His eyes were squinted and droopy, and his lips were drawn together in a sheepish little smile. Whenever I looked back at him, he was always smiling, always staring straight ahead, totally oblivious to everything including the chicken that squawked all the way to Zagora.

This bus to Zagora is usually late because it's often delayed coming out of Agadir 337 km (209 miles) to the west on the coast. If the bus arrives in Ouarzazate too late, the trip to Zagora is occasionally delayed until the following morning. The trip takes about four hours in a bus that can't go beyond second gear; it could take even longer. The fare is about $2.75.

Buses to Skoura, Kelaat d'Mgoun, Boumalne du Dadès (three hours), and Tinerhir (four hours) are supposed to depart at 6 and 10 A.M. and 12 P.M. There's also a 4 A.M. "express" bus to Boumalne. Fares range from about $1 to $3. Buses also run more than once daily to Marrakesh and Taroudannt. Check the CTM lot near the post office for these destinations.

Grand taxis service some of the same destinations as the buses, but usually for a few more dirhams. They depart from the second bus lot when the drivers have finished their tea and think that they have enough passengers to fill the car.

First Things First

The tourist information office is on the main street—Avenue Mohammed V—at a fork in the road just past the post office. The staff can help with information about souk (market) days, accommodations, and schedules for buses and moussems (festivals of the saints). They are open from Monday to Friday 7:30 A.M. to 2 P.M., but closed on the weekends.

Although official guides can be arranged at the tourist office, I don't think you really need one here. However, don't be surprised if you are approached by a Moroccan "friend" who just wants to "practice English." Based on stories from travelers and confirmed by my interview with a "friend," my version of the usual story goes something like this: A young

Moroccan, usually in his late teens or twenties, approaches, smiles, and tells you he wants to be your friend and practice his English or French. He insists that he's not a guide and doesn't want any money. OK, so far he sounds legitimate. You walk and talk for a while and then finally he says something like "You know, since you are such nice people, I'm going to take you to a village that tourists can't visit. You can see how the people live, and perhaps we will even spend a night there." Inevitably, the village happens to specialize in hand-woven traditional carpets. By the time you are taken to the carpet "factory," you have gotten a magnanimous helping of hospitality, so you will probably want to buy a carpet or two, which, of course, you have been told can be sold for much less here than in the town. Two groups of travelers I met had bought carpets and later found exactly the same ones in the Marrakesh medina for at most half the price.

Finding a place to stay should be as easy as finding an unofficial guide. In the past few years, Ouarzazate has gone through a spate of hotel construction and now has several hotels including a 60-room Club Méditerranée (tel. 22-83 and 26-50) and the 70-room five-star deluxe Hotel Riad Salam (tel. 22-06)—with their brown walls and geometric designs, both resemble modernistic kasbahs. On a less grandiose scale, there are three four-star hotels: the 110-room Hotel Tichka Salam, the 106-room Hotel Azghor, and the 60-room Hotel Zat. All these seem to cater mostly to tour groups and visiting movie companies.

On a much more modest scale, there are three hotels: the Hotel Atlas, the Hotel Royal, and the Hotel la Gazelle. The Atlas is on Rue de Marché near the market square and the grand taxi lot (see above) and is recommended more for its low prices—about $5 to $10 for a room—than for its comforts and amenities (or lack of). The Royal is centrally located at 24 Avenue Mohammed V next to the Café Dmitri and, at about $5 for a clean, comfortable room with big windows, it is considered a good deal. My personal favorite is the two-star Hotel la Gazelle, which is about 1 1/2 km (1 mile) from the center of town on the road to Agadir. It has been owned and managed by the same French couple since the 1940s and includes a small swimming pool and cool garden courtyard, which is a great relief if you're here when it's hot. There's also a restaurant dining room that serves various French-Moroccan dishes that seem to be popular with expatriates, particularly film crews.

During my visit, the Gazelle's proprietors told me that yet another film crew had just arrived that morning. So when a great gold Cadillac convertible driven by a heavy-set man with a bushy gray beard and a flower-festooned fedora rolled into La Gazelle's dirt lot, I assumed that both were a part of a movie set. I was wrong.

The man was Jean Pierre Batard, *a chef de village* for Club Méditerranée, a French chain of exclusive club resorts located in exotic locales around the world, including Ouarzazate. Batard told me that he had always wanted a big gold Cadillac Eldorado, a convertible with white-walled tires and preferably California license plates. When he found the one he wanted while vacationing in Florida, he bought it and shipped it to his home town of Toulon, France. From there he eventually drove to Morocco for a six-month vacation of Club Med-hopping. By the time he had arrived at Ouarzazate's Club Med, he had logged more than 5,000 kilometers just in Morocco.

I wanted photographs of Batard and his Cadillac in front of a kasbah. So off we went, down the main street of Ouarzazate, with the top down, air conditioner blasting, and me sliding around on the soft leather seat. Everyone smiled as we glided through town to one of several old kasbahs. We parked, and Batard posed beside his car like a man quite used to having his photo taken. I reached the end of my roll, so we climbed back in and Batard lightly stepped on the gas. With the air conditioner cranked up to a steady hum and the wind whistling past, we sailed back down the road to the Gazelle.

Camping is possible at two places in and near town. The closest is the Camping Municipal, which is about 2 1/2 km (1 1/2 miles) from the center of town on the road to Skoura and Boumalne. It has a swimming pool, cold showers, and a small restaurant. They charge about $0.50 per person, $0.25 per vehicle, and $0.30 per tent. The other campground sites are just outside of town beyond the usually dry riverbed on the road to Zagora. More information about these follows, in the section "En Route to Zagora."

Restaurants and Cafés

Aside from the restaurant at la Gazelle and other hotels in town, there are only about three or four others, all of them centrally located near the CTM bus lot. One of the most popular, and perhaps most interesting, is the Café/Restaurant Dmitri next to the Hotel Royal. Supposedly, it hasn't changed in about forty years, which is when Dmitri, the Greek owner, first arrived in Ouarzazate. With waiters in red and white "Johnny Walker" smocks, walls decorated with black-framed flower prints and pen and ink drawings of pottery and houses, and a grumbling Dmitri hanging on the bar counter, it is unlike most restaurants in Morocco. The "menu of the day" is a full meal for $5 that includes a beef tajine, carrots, peas, bread, dessert, and tea. Breakfast is usually generous and considered a reasonable deal.

Getting Things Done

Foreign currency and travelers' checks can be exchanged at the major hotels or at the bank near the post office. The international telephone office and post office are in the same building on Avenue Mohammed V (the main street) and open from about 8:30 A.M. to noon and from 2:30 P.M. to 6 P.M.

The small grocery store across from Dmitri's is a good place to stock up on a few staples, canned goods, and bottled water. It's also one of the few places in the immediate area with a telephone.

Postcards, paper, a few basic toiletries, and occasionally foreign newspapers and magazines are available at the hotel gift shops.

Things to See and Do

Ouarzazate doesn't have an abundance of sights and activities for tourists and travelers, but, if you are walking, at least a day could easily be spent here. The major sights in the area are the *ksour* (plural of *ksar*), which are the complexes of multistory, fortress-like, mud structures that you see throughout the southern Morocco countryside and in the Atlas mountains. A *kasbah* is the palace or central building of a ksar.

The ksar of Taourirt is closest to town and thus most visited by tourists; it is about a thirty-minute walk from the post office on the road to Skoura and Boumalne. In addition to being a main location for filming *Romancing the Stone*, it's also a museum and the town's cultural center. However, the building is made of mud and is susceptible to gradual melting and crumbling in the rain, which is what has been happening the past few years. In 1988, the structure had to be closed to visitors because of unusually heavy rains, but it was due to reopen once the walls were patched or, in some cases, rebuilt. With its traditional crenellated ramparts and imposing towers, arch-framed windows, and geometric patterns on the walls, the outside of the structure alone is still worth seeing.

The kasbah was one of several erected or adapted from previous structures by the Glaoui family (see Telouet section) in the early 1900s and was meant to protect the principal southern trading routes—mainly in a symbolic sense, though, because the most serious threats to these routes were greatly diminished by the French. At one time, Taourirt was considered Morocco's largest kasbah, housing as many as 1,500 people, including members of the Glaoui family and their retinue of slaves, servants, beggars, shepherds, Jewish moneylenders and tailors, musicians, and laborers.

While you are at Taourirt, you may want to stop by the handicrafts cooperative across the road where local crafts such as the smooth wool Ouzgita carpets are displayed. Everything on display is for sale, usually at government-fixed prices. The coop is open Monday through Friday from 8:30 A.M. to noon and 1 P.M. to 6 P.M., and Saturday from 8:30 A.M. to noon.

EN ROUTE TO ZAGORA

Just outside of Ouarzazate, the road to Zagora crosses the usually dry narrow Oued Ouarzazate (riverbed) and passes through small palm groves and the villages of Douar Tabounte and Douar Tigemmi-n-Lajdid, where basic campgrounds can be found near the roadside. The campgrounds are well situated in the *palmerie* near a couple of restaurants and cafés and seem to be quite popular with foreign travelers who have their own Land-Rovers. The villages are about 1.7 km (1 mile) from the southern edge of Ouarzazate and another 3⁄4 km (1⁄2 mile) from the Ouarzazate CTM bus terminal. When the weather is good, not too hot, the walk from the bus station to the campgrounds and beyond through the villages is a flat easy hike, although the portion before reaching the villages is not particularly interesting. Otherwise, local taxis are available to take you there.

After passing between the village kasbahs and the surrounding palmeries, the road heads southeast into a rough, rocky landscape that is generally known as the Aït Ouarzazate. At about 8 km from the villages, the road begins to gradually rise through the Aït and then more steeply into the foothills of the Jebel Sarhro, the highest range in the Anti-Atlas mountains.

The Jebel Sarhro range is a massif of volcanic lunarlike plateaus and peaks more than 100 km (62 miles) long. It is not as explored and well known as the other ranges because it is prohibitively hot and dry most of the year, but it is no less interesting and offers some great hiking opportunities. If you are really keen to trek around here away from the main dirt roads, though, you should either arrange for an experienced guide or join one of a handful of adventure travel groups described later in this chapter and in other parts of this book.

Despite its generally inhospitable climate and terrain, the Jebel Sarhro region has been home to a tough, resilient Berber tribe known as the Aït Atta. These seminomadic people weren't subjugated by the French colonial army until the early 1930s, although they numbered only a few hundred families. One of the last major battles of the French conquest of Morocco occurred at Bougafer in the heart of the Jebel Sarhro, a place that is no longer indicated on contemporary Moroccan maps. If you are trying to locate it on the "Morocco Carte Routière" (Éditions Marcus, Paris), it is supposed to be north-northeast of the settlement of Timerzif.

By February 1933, most of the Aït Atta tribe had retreated from French forces to a formidable natural fortress at Bougafer. Over 5,000 men, women, and children and 25,000 head of cattle, sheep, goats, donkeys, and camels were hidden among the steep walls, cliffs, and rocky slopes of Bougafer, with about 2,000 rifles and plenty of stones ready for the French attack. Against this seemingly meager defense, the French expected an easy victory and launched the attack on February 21, 1933. However, the Aït Atta resistance proved tougher than the French had anticipated.

It took the French fifty-two days, 80,000 French soldiers, forty-four planes, and a continual aerial and artillery bombardment to force the Aït Atta to surrender. By the end of the battle, over 1,000 Frenchmen and 1,200 Ait Atta had been killed or wounded.

Today, the quasi-capital of the Aït Atta is at Ighrem Amerdar (indicated on the map as "Irherm Amazdar") due south of Tinerhir, which is where local chieftains congregate to resolve tribal disputes. An Aït Atta qa'id appointed by the king is installed at Ikniounn southeast of Ighrem Amerdar.

Inevitably, the Aït Atta have had to change their lifestyle from being mainly nomadic to more permanent settlements. That hasn't meant, however, that they have had to give up their primarily pastoral livelihood. Instead, they divide their time between their ksour or houses and goatskin and camel-hair tents; sometimes they set up their tents right outside their houses. The woman are unveiled, dress in traditional patterned gowns, and wear wide black shawls with bright, multicolored fringes, which often double as head scarves. The men wear basic wool gowns with hoods—fairly standard dress for most of Morocco.

To explore this region Azourki Expéditions Randonnées, run by Ahmed Outeglaout (see Azilal section), organizes Land-Rover and hiking trips. Recently, it offered a fifteen-day hike from Agdz in the Drâa valley to Jebel Bougafer (now known as a *jebel*, or mountain, rather than a settlement). The trail crosses canyons and plateaus and passes through the villages and settlements of the Ait Atta. This hike is done only in the winter.

Atlas Sahara Treks, a Marrakesh-based company run by a Frenchman named Bernard Fabry, also offers hikes through the Jebel Sarhro— a 7- and a 12-day hike, each with about five to six hours of walking daily. Azouki Expéditions Randonnées assists them with these trips. Atlas Sahara Treks is at 72 Rue de la Liberté (tel. 337-57) and attempts to run these trips between October 15 and April 30.

If you don't venture too far off the main roads, you could probably arrange to tour the area on your own. A main departure point is at Tansikht in the Drâa valley 98 km (61 miles) from Ouarzazate and 96 km (59 1/2 miles) from Zagora, which is easy to reach from either town by bus, grand taxi, or even hitchhiking. From Tansikht, there are occasional buses, grand taxis, and souk trucks across the Jebel Sarhro to Tazzarine 73 km (45 miles) away where an overnight stay is possible at the village café-hotel. Transportation can also be arranged all the way to Rissani in the Tafilelt region 164 km (102 miles) to the northeast. Supposedly, you can also get a ride from Zagora to Tazzarine, but in 1988 that road was partially washed out and not being driven much. Hiking is possible, of course, along any of the stretches between Tansikht and Rissani, but get updated information about local conditions from the tourist office in Ouarzazate or, if you speak French, from villages and settlements along the way.

Continuing along the road to Zagora, the hamlet of Aït Saoun is passed about 40 km (25 miles) from Ouarzazate and approximately marks the beginning of the 1,660-m (5,466-ft) Tizi-n-Tinififft pass, but the actual pass is 4 km (2 1/2 miles) farther down the road. The lush green palmeries of the Drâa valley begin about 24 km (15 miles) beyond at the town of Agdz, but don't bother stopping here unless you want to buy a traditional carpet or rug or need basic staples for a trip through the Jebel Sarhro. Thursday is the market day, which is also a good day to hitch truck rides, because of the frequent traffic through the town. If at all possible, arrange for a ride to Zagora that permits you to make stops along the way because after Agdz a dramatic congregation of ksour stretches almost the entire length of the valley. The various architectural styles, ornamental designs, and traditional gowns worn by the women are reflective of the cultural mix of Arabs, Berbers, Jews, and Harratines (blacks descended from Sudanese slaves brought into Morocco) that has settled the valley. To really get a full picture of the structures, however, you need to get a few kilometers off the main road, particularly at Tamnougalt, Timiderte, Igdaoun, and Tinzouline.

In his book, *The Kasbahs of Southern Morocco* (London: Faber & Faber, 1969), Rom Landau aptly describes a way of life in the kasbahs that continues, at least in part, today:

> [The kasbahs] were not built for "gracious living", in the European sense of the term, not meant to endure for posterity. It must be remembered that, unlike the average urban home, the kasba was not a European-type domicile. During much of the year the men would spend their days in the oasis, working the land, and taking their afternoon siesta in the shade of a tree or a wall. Regular meals were not always taken for granted, and might consist of some bread, a handful of dates and a couple of tomatoes. Some charcoal and a pot for the brewing of mint tea were always carried to, or kept at, the place of work. A house was the refuge for the night and shelter for the women and the little children and animals. There was no time and no tradition for the two sexes to mix in social life, the sort of life that would call for the amenities and the beauty of a comfortable home....
>
> The people had no furniture, no need for it, no money

for buying it. One low table for meals might be thought useful enough to make its acquisition worth while. Cupboards and chests would have served no purpose, for the people had little to store away. If they had a spare garment, this would be left lying about or would be hung on a nail in the wall. Chairs were unthought of, for everyone was used to sitting on a mat or on the ground.

ZAGORA

Zagora is the biggest and most economically important town in the Drâa valley. At 164 km (102 miles) from Ouarzazate, it approximately marks the terminus of the valley's long swath of palmeries and oases and the beginning of the edge of the Sahara. Historically, this has been a strategic point, first and foremost for the gold and slave trade that flowed between here and Timbuktu and other parts of Africa, and in the 1970s and 1980s as a supply depot for the battles in the western Sahara between the Morocco and the Polisario front (which called for independence of the western Sahara). A hand-painted sign at the arched entrance to the town indicates that it's only 52 days to Timbuktu by camel.

Unless you are keen on experiencing some of the most intense dry desert heat in the world, don't come here in the summer. It's not unusual for temperatures to go higher than 52°C (125°F) and no lower than 43°C (110°F) even at night. With regularly high temperatures and extremely low humidity, conditions are ideal for quick dehydration, so be careful.

Arrival and Departure

Buses and grand taxis gather in a lot adjacent to the marketplace at the north end of town on Avenue Mohammed V, the town's main street. There are at least three buses daily to Ouarzazate, one of which usually continues all the way to Marrakesh. Grand taxis also go to Ouarzazate, as well as deeper into the desert to M'hamid. Since M'hamid was, and might still be, a military zone, you may need permission and a guide before venturing there.

First Things First

For information about the region and permission, if necessary at the time, to travel to M'hamid, go to the administrative offices at the Cercle de Zagora, which is on Avenue Mohammed V at the southern end of town. Guides and camel excursions can usually be arranged through this office, but don't be duped into thinking that you are being charged "official" nonnegotiable prices. For the latest information about camel excursions and other forms of travel in the region, you might try chatting with travelers at the Hotel de la Palmerie across the street from the administrative offices.

Hotels

The Hotel de la Palmerie is a budget traveler's haven, with good, clean rooms for about $4 to $10 and space on the terrace for about $1. Closer to the center on Avenue Mohammed V is the even cheaper Hotel des Amis, with rooms slightly less comfortable than the Palmerie and a café/restaurant. Another low budget hotel is the Hotel Vallée du Drâa, which is also on Mohammed V. At the other end of the scale is the cool, marble-floored pseudo-kasbah called the Hotel Tinsouline with a palm-shaded courtyard and swimming pool and very comfortable rooms. Singles cost about $30.

Camping is possible at campgrounds about 3 to 4 km (2 to 2 1/2 miles) from downtown near the village of Amezrou. To get there, continue past the Cercle de Zagora administrative office on the road to M'hamid and cross the river to the edge of Amezrou on the opposite bank. You should see the signs first for the Camping d'Amezrou site and then, farther down the road, the Camping Montagne site. Both are quite well situated in the beautifully lush Amezrou palmery and are good bases from which to make short day hikes around the village and palmery and trek up to the nearby summit of Jebel Zagora.

Getting Things Done and Shopping

Foreign currency and travelers' checks can be exchanged at the Hotel Tinsouline or at banks along Avenue Mohammed V. The post office and telephone are in the same building also on Avenue Mohammed V.

Basic staples, fruits, vegetables, and occasionally local handicrafts and souvenirs can be bought at the souk held on Wednesdays and Sundays in a big dirt lot next to the bus terminus lot. With its many stalls of fruits and vegetables and assortment of butchers, it's a fairly typical souk; however, often there's also a group of Tuareg women here bedecked in silver jewelry, black robes, and veils with bright multicolored trim, trying to sell clothing and jewelry.

Food and a few toiletries can be bought at small grocery stores along Mohammed V and on a parallel street near the Hotel Tinsouline.

Things to See and Do

Aside from the souk, there is nothing else in town to see. The most interesting sights are south of town in and near the villages of Amezrou,

Tamegroute, and Tinfou. As mentioned above, Amezrou is where the area's two "official" campgrounds are located and is the center of a wonderful palmery that produces some of the best dates in Morocco. There's also an old Jewish kasbah here that's no longer inhabited by Jews, but it does, at least, give some idea of the once-flourishing Jewish community in the area. The kasbah is on the main road just past the turnoff for the road to Jebel Zagora.

The hike to the summit of Jebel Zagora is about 5 km (3 miles) round trip from the main road turnoff. The summit resembles a foreboding pile of brown pancakes stacked as if intentionally just outside of Amezrou. It's a good half-day to full-day hike depending on how long you want to linger on the summit savoring the great views of the palmery and encroaching sand dunes. The remnants of a few walls of the Saadian dynasty's (sixteenth-century) first fortress can still be seen along the edges of the summit.

After passing through Amezrou, the road enters a stony *wadi* (gully or wash) and then a stark, treeless plain. At about 20 km (12 1/2 miles), from Zagora is Tamegroute, a village of sand dunes, palm trees, numerous kasbahs, and the once-notable *zaouia* (saintly brotherhood) of the Nassiriya.

The origins of the brotherhood can be traced to a twelfth-century scholar named Ahmed Ali Ansari At-Tamegroute, who founded a religious center and school here. The brotherhood became famous in the seventeenth century under the tutelage and teachings of Sidi Mohammed Ibn Nasir who expanded the library and the center's role in local agricultural activities and arbitration of disputes.

The library was one of the first, if not the only, libraries in the region. Until this century, it was also one of the most significant in Morocco. It housed many of the original works of Islamic scholars such as Ibn Khaldun, but the most important of them have been transferred to official collections in Rabat. The library, which can be visited today, still holds an impressive collection of books and manuscripts, including hand-printed Korans.

At the heart of the complex is the ornately designed inner sanctuary where the founder of the brotherhood is entombed and venerated as a marabout, or saint. A moussem is celebrated here every year around or on November 8–10. The practice of maraboutism or saint worship is generally anathema to Islam, but Islam in Morocco has historically been a unique integration of Qur'ānic strictures and local Berber culture, of belief in one God and reverence for many marabouts through pilgrimages to shrines and celebrations of moussems.

Continuing along the road to M'hamid, just past Tamegroute an imposing horseshoe of mountains appears on the horizon and sand dunes dotted with palms begin getting closer to the road. After a few more kilometers, a low brown structure between the dunes and the road seems to pop up from the earth. It's almost impossible to discern that this is the "Auberge Repos des Dunes" or the "Auberge de Repos au Sable à Tinfou" (literally, "The Inn of Rest in the Sand at Tinfou") or anything other than a huge block of clay until you have turned into its "camel lot."

With a row of rooms on one side and a set of larger rooms surrounding the courtyard on the other, the auberge resembles a cross between an old Spanish mission and a Moroccan kasbah or ksour. Berber rugs and abstract paintings done by the owners of the auberge grace the inner and outer walls of the rooms around the courtyard. Next to these buildings is the "cool" swimming pool advertised on a sign in front—a pea-soup affair that could easily have been the setting for a monster movie, maybe *Creature from the Green Lagoon* or something similarly green and gooey.

Fortunately, perhaps, I wasn't here for the pool, but for a ride on one of the screaming, gurgling dromedaries "parked" with eight others in the camel lot. I and eight other travelers were supposed to ride across the Sahara to a clump of palm trees, have mint tea and lunch, and then plod through a village and back into the desert to camp "under the stars." Since I was the last to arrive and claim a camel, or rather dromedary, I got the last one in the group. His owner, Yusuf, called him a "*chameau sauvage*" ("savage camel") because the camel's bloody nose had been pierced for a ring and reins just that morning and he was screaming and flailing about in pain. I called him Clyde and wondered how I was supposed to ride a dromedary that seemed to hate the world—and could you blame him?

Yusuf was optimistic. He made a clucking sound with his mouth, yanked on the reins to get Clyde to kneel on all fours, and had me climb into the saddle. Once I was seated, he made some other sounds, pulled the reins a certain way, and got Clyde to first raise his hindquarters. Suddenly, I was lurched forward and trying to lean back to keep from tumbling off and onto Clyde's head. More clucking, and Clyde's front legs straightened. I clung to the saddle to keep from rolling off and over Clyde's rear. One more cluck-cluck and Clyde finally stood, but he was not a happy dromedary. He was spewing, dribbling, and uttering a deep throaty gurgle that made him sound like he was being strangled.

Under an ominous sky of gray and black, the other dromedaries rose, each loaded with heavy cargo, human and otherwise, including tents, pots, pans, and mattresses for our Sahara sojourn. The others were tied together in groups of two or three with each group led by a camel handler, but since mine was the "*sauvage*" he was left unattached and given his own handler.

Clyde didn't seem to be in much of a mood for crossing the Sahara that morning. He plodded and groaned, occasionally turning his head to scream at me. The handler yelled what were probably Berber curses to get him to keep up with the caravan; however, this only seemed to make him slower and more stubborn. We had been away from the inn only ten minutes, but the sky was getting darker and the wind stronger. The first raindrops fell and washed away Clyde's stubbornness.

Rain in the Sahara was something that neither I nor Clyde expected. He screamed, spit, and tugged frantically at his rope reins. The handler yelled back and tugged harder, too hard. The rope fell out of the nose ring. Clyde screamed again. I hollered for the rope, but it was too late—Clyde and I headed into the Sahara. The handler "rescued" us, but I decided that walking in front of and leading Clyde was far preferable to depending on him to get us through the rain.

The rain produced dramatic rainbows over the desert, soaked us and our equipment, and made muck of the sand dunes and mud of the fields. Despite the muck, mud, and downpour, though, our Berber camel handlers still halted the caravan to serve us mint tea and a mixed salad of tomatoes, olives, sardines, and tuna. We had to return to the mud-walled auberge, which had somehow resisted this region's first major rainstorm in seven years without leaks or cracks. Some of us spent the night on cushions behind thick doors with medieval wooden locks, listening to BBC broadcasts of *Romeo and Juliet* and to news on Radio Moscow.

Background Information and Tips for Riding Camels

My legs ached from not being limber enough to sit on a camel. To better prepare yourself for this leg-widening experience, do some deep knee bends to limber up before climbing on. Once on top, you can try sitting with both legs hanging over one side or both perched up on the camel's neck; however, that also becomes uncomfortable for both you and the camel.

Expect your nose to twitch from being assaulted by the noxious stink from the camel's mouth. You'll want to cram a pack of breath mints or a tube of toothpaste in its mouth, but obviously that isn't going to work. Like giraffes and sheep, camels are hoofed ruminant mammals with three or four stomach chambers. Chewed food is partially digested in the first stomach and then returned to the mouth as cud for a second chewing. Except for wearing a gas mask—an extreme measure—there's not much you can do about the cud, so get used to it.

Don't make clucking or clicking sounds, unless instructed by your camel handler. Camels are trained to react to certain sounds, particularly clucks and clicks, but there doesn't seem to be a uniform system of training among camel trainers and handlers, so a cluck may make one camel stand and another sit. You will also probably hear the handler say "*zeet, zeet,*" which means "go."

Piotr Kostrzewski and his company Cross Cultural Adventures organized this camel trip, which was a departure from the other adventure trips described in this book. He can be contacted at Cross Cultural Adventures, Box 3285, Arlington, VA 22203; tel. 703-204-2717; telex 440283 ACI UI.

You can also try getting to Tinfou on your own, but transportation and rent-a-camels aren't always assured. I hitchhiked from Tinfou to Zagora, but I had to run down the road after the car and that was the only car in an hour. From Zagora, transportation, including hitchhiking opportunities, is much easier to arrange.

ALONG THE DESERT SPINE

Going east from Ouarzazate, the road runs roughly parallel to the Dadés river, but you don't see much of it. When you can see the river, it resembles a thin blue ribbon as it cuts through the surrounding parched rock-strewn plain. Despite the water, though, it isn't until about 30 km (19 miles) from Ouarzazate that the river begins to transform this dry black-red volcanic land into flowering oases of fields and palmeries. The first major town and set of oases along this route is Skoura, which is renowned for its kasbahs and fields of roses. In the spring, you can see the roses in bloom on both sides of the road as you continue on to Kelaat d'Mgoun. This town is a good departure point for excursions into the Atlas mountains, particularly to the peak of Irhil Mgoun. The next town is Boumalne du Dadés, which is the principal jumpoff point for trips into the Dadés gorge and, to a lesser extent, into the Jebel Sarhro range. After Boumalne, the river veers north through the gorge and the road passes through 53 km (33 miles) of more harsh and inhospitable land before reaching Tinerhir, a good base for exploring the Tohdra gorge and, for much more adventurous travelers, deeper into the High Atlas mountains. Beyond Tinerhir, the main road again passes through wasteland and then reaches the oasis villages or towns of Tinejdad and Goulmima. Finally, you reach Er-Rachidia, a city similar to Ouarzazate that serves as a crossroads for the road south to the Tafilelt oasis towns of Erfoud and Rissani, north through the Ziz gorge and the Middle Atlas mountains to Fez, and east to Figuig and the Algerian border.

SKOURA

Skoura is a town of kasbahs and fields of roses about 30 km (19 miles) from Ouarzazate. With four rivers meeting here—the Oued Madri, the Oued Bou Jhila, the Oued Hajjaj, and the Oued Dadés—and irrigating the land around the town, the region is literally overflowing with kasbahs and lush fields. The town itself isn't anything special—a regional administrative center and a market square for the weekly souk. Nearby, however, there are several interesting kasbahs worth visiting. The ones usually open to visitors include the Dar Lahsoune and the Dar Toundout—both formerly for the Glaoui family (see Telouet section)—and the Dar Aït Haddou and the Dar Aït Sidi El Mati.

If you are arriving by bus or grand taxi, you will most likely be dropped off at the market square. Usually, as soon as you step into the square, you will be besieged by boys wanting to serve as your guide for the kasbahs. Negotiate a price with one of them for a tour; it would be difficult for you to find the kasbahs on your own.

With their crenellated towers, ramparts, and intricate designs, the kasbahs resemble impressive medieval castles. For the Glaoui family, the Dar Toundout kasbah was, in fact, supposed to be one of their several bastions of power and was built to resemble the fortified kasbah of Telouet. The other three kasbahs were similarly constructed (and repeatedly damaged in war and rebuilt), but they have belonged to various other families.

If you need to stay in Skoura, you can negotiate for a room through or with your guide's family.

KELAAT D'MGOUN

About 50 km (31 miles) down the road from Skoura is the smaller oasis town of Kelaat d'Mgoun, which is best known for converting the pink roses of the region's plantations into attar, or rosewater. Most of the rosewater is processed and bottled in a French-built factory in town. Bottles of attar are, of course, sold by local shops. Don't be surprised if you get sprayed with attar as you enter the shops; that's a common sales tactic here. Here the phrase "to come out smelling like a rose" should be taken literally! In early June (check with tourist office for an exact date), a rose festival is held here to celebrate the year's rose harvest—lots of food, music, dancing, and villagers in traditional dress.

The town is also a departure point for excursions into the Atlas mountains, particularly to the peak of Irhil Mgoun. A dirt road heads north from the center of town and approximately follows the Oued Mgoun river for about 18 km (11 miles) into the High Atlas mountains as far as the base of Jebel Guersif (1,847 m, or 6,060 ft) and the hamlet of Aït Saïd. You can easily do this stretch on your own, but to go beyond that to higher elevations, you should either hire a guide or join an organized group.

One of the most challenging adventure trips from Skoura and, occasionally, from Kelaat d'Mgoun is organized by Azourki Expéditions Randonnées of Azilil, Morocco, a group mentioned earlier in the High Atlas mountain section. It is a ski expedition trip, which is probably beyond the abilities of most travelers, but it is included here as an example of what is possible from Skoura. Shorter (or even longer), less challenging hikes and ski treks can also be arranged by Azourki.

The following is a condensed version of their 12-day itinerary from Skoura:

Day 1. Arrive in Marrakesh.

Day 2. Early departure in minibus or Land-Rover for the Tizi-n-Tichka pass, Ouarzazate, and then Skoura. From Skoura, you are taken 80 km (50 miles) into the High Atlas mountains to Imi-n-Oulawn and the Assif of Imi-n-Oulawn (also spelled Imi-n-Oulaoun) where a team of Berbers has already set up camp for the group. The team includes mule handlers, guides, and cooks from the valley of Aït Bougmez.

Day 3. The climb toward Azilal begins along one of two paths:
a. Northwest through the Tizi-n-Oulawn pass and then northeast to the hamlet of Tichki.
b. Northeast through Assaka to Azib Tagoulzit at about 2,800 m (9,200 ft).

The choice of route depends on weather conditions, but each takes approximately 5 1/2 hours of walking and passes through several beautiful valleys.

Day 4. Climb to the "balcony" of Tiferdiym at 3,978 m (13,051 ft) and then on to the principal summit of Mgoun at 4,071 m (13,356 ft). The camp is set up at Tiferdiym or, if necessary, at 2,800 m (9,200 ft) on the Tarkeddid plateau. To facilitate the climb and allow for skiing this day and the next, the equipment is transported by the porters.

Day 5. Climb to the summit of Jebel Tarkeddid at 3,400 m (11,155 ft), and descend by ski to Azib Arous at 2,000 m (6,562 ft). From here you can reascend 600 m (1,969 ft) in about 2 1/2 hours, or another 800 m (2,625 ft) in two more hours, for more skiing. The special ski "skins" for reascents and added traction are essential here.

Day 6. Descent from the valley of Assif Arous to the valley of Aït Bougmez and pass through several beautiful villages of multistory kasbahs. A campsite or home stay with local Berber families is arranged in the valley, at the village of Ikhf-n-Ighir.

Day 7. Ascent from the valley of Aït Bougmez through the Assif-n-Rbat to the foot of the Jebel Waougoulzat. The camp is set up near the Azib-n-Rbat at 2,300 m (7,546 ft) after about 4 1/4 hours of walking.

Day 8. Climb to the summit of Tagafayt at 3,729 m (12,234 ft) and return to Azib-n-Rbat—a 3 1/2-hour trip. Descend to the Lake of Izourar and camp at 2,526 m (8,287 ft).

Day 9. Ascent from the lake to the summit of Jebel Azourki at 3,682 m (12,080 ft) in about five hours and then ski down to the Assif Tamda (also referred to as the Agoudal-n-Tamda). The night is spent at a refuge there.

Day 10. From the Assif Tamda, it's a two-hour hike to the road and Land-Rovers for the return to Marrakesh, where the night is spent at a hotel.

Day 11. Free day in Marrakesh. Hotel.

Day 12. Return flight.

The following supplemental information for the Azourki ski trips is also relevant to other trips in the High Atlas mountains:

The 12-day itinerary described above can be done by experienced hikers and skiers who are familiar with ski treks and the use of special ski traction skins. Most days of this trip involve approximately five to seven hours of walking and an average daily elevation gain of 1,200 m (3,937 ft). The snow conditions are similar to the Swiss and French Alps, but the temperatures are generally lower here.

Nights are quite cool with temperatures often as low as -6°C (21°F) and sometimes even -10°C (14°F). During the day, temperatures can reach as high as 16°C (61°F).

The basic equipment needed includes a very warm sleeping bag, backpack, gloves, hat or cap, sunglasses, waterproof garments, warm underwear, a heavy sweater, a flashlight, and special ski equipment. The latter is described in the High Atlas section. As a general rule, travel with the bare essentials, to keep the weight of your equipment down.

This trip or similar versions is usually possible in February or March.

BOUMALNE DU DADÉS

The town of Boumalne du Dadés is about 22 km (14 miles) from Kelaat d'Mgoun. Between the two towns, the road runs parallel to the Dadés river and passes through a score of kasbah villages and rich green fields. Boumalne is beautifully situated at the junction for the road into the Dadés gorge. To the north loom the peaks of the High Atlas mountains, and to the south, the peaks and foothills of the Jebel Sarhro range. Excursions to the gorge and into both ranges can be organized in Boumalne.

The town itself isn't particularly interesting. There's a small kasbah near the center that the French Protectorate government once used as a prison for political "undesirables" and criminals. If you have to stay here, there's only one hotel—the four-star Hotel El Madayeq, which is on a hill overlooking town. It caters mostly to tour groups that pass through for visits to the gorge. Otherwise you can stay in one of the overpriced rooms at the Café-Restaurant Bougafr near the market square, but it would be more interesting and inexpensive to venture up the Dadés gorge and either camp or stay at one of the hotels described in the next section.

Buses, grand taxis, and occasionally souk trucks gather in or near the market square next to the Café-Restaurant Bougafr. The Ouarzazate-to-Er-Rachidia (and vice versa) bus stops here. There's also a daily 2 P.M. bus to the Dadés gorge village of Msemrir 47 km (29 miles) away. Grand taxis service the same routes, but one usually doesn't depart until the driver thinks he has enough passengers. I once waited almost two hours in the rain for a taxi to Tinerhir to fill up; the wait was longer than the ride.

THE DADES GORGE

As soon as you leave the main road and head toward the gorge, you enter a beautiful valley of mud-brick kasbahs and ksour villages, lush palmeries, and well-tended fields. The traditional fortress-like architecture and contrasting shades of green and brown make a dramatic picture. After about 2 km (1 1/4 miles) you'll pass an old Glaoui family kasbah (see the Telouet section about the Glaoui family) and, after another 3 km (2 miles), the group of kasbahs known as the ksour of Aït Arbi. Twenty minutes' drive into the valley, craggy limestone towers appear just off the road and approximately mark the actual beginning of the gorge. The valley narrows here, the road becomes more serpentine and the scenery more spectacular. You'll want to stop for photographs at the viewpoints along the way, something difficult to do if you don't have your own transportation or aren't with a group.

Not surprisingly, some of the best viewpoints are strategically occupied by dagger salesmen and tourist trinket hawkers. At the first such stop, I watched one of these dagger men welcome a U.S. guide with a big kiss on the cheek. The man was adorned with several layers of ropes, gaudy chains, and crude medallions. The guide then said to his group, "This is a good picture spot. Don't look at daggers, and don't kiss anyone." Sound advice: the kiss was, according to the guide, merely intended to give the effect that he and the dagger man were long-lost buddies, which wasn't true. If daggers, flashy jewelry and a cheeky buss weren't enough to prove the "sincere" friendliness of the hawkers, then they would offer everyone, as they did this time, mint tea and almonds.

At 40 minutes' drive and 23 km (14 miles) from the main road, the gorge road becomes a piste or bumpy dirt road and crosses the Dadés river. Just past the crossing is the Auberge des Gorges Dadés, a hotel and

Todhra Gorge, Morocco. *Photo by Scott Wayne.*

restaurant. The auberge offers simple rooms and meals and is a good base for taking short hikes around the valley and into the first part of the gorge. The rooms have sinks and electricity and cost about $6.25 for twin beds and $5 for a double. Camping in the yard next to the auberge costs about $0.50 per person, including access to showers and bathrooms.

The road climbs past the auberge and then along the side of the gorge. The river seems to flow faster and closer to the road here. The valley is greener and more densely packed with poplar and almond trees. About 3 km (2 miles) from the auberge, the "official" entrance to the gorge is marked with a sign. The Café du Peuplier and the Café, Restaurant & Hotel Kasbah de la Valleé are about 50 m (165 ft) past the entrance and quite well situated as bases for treks up into the gorge. Supposedly camping is possible alongside the hotel and river. The road ascends the sheer cliff walls of the gorge through a series of precariously sharp switchbacks. The view from above of the gorge and valley is spectacular and definitely worth the hike (if you don't have transportation). For hard-core rough-and-ready travelers with their own transport or the time and patience to hitch rides, the road continues all the way up to Imilchil (see Imilchil section) via the village of Msemrir or, going east from Msemrir, to the villages of Tamtatouchte and Aït Hani, which are along the piste that heads through the Todhra gorges, and then through the gorges themselves. A group organized by Cross Cultural Adventures occasionally attempts this circuit in the spring in a minivan, but recent heavy rains had made the road impossible to traverse without a high-clearance four-wheel drive. I saw one vehicle coming from the gorge that had easily driven the muddy road, but it resembled a cross between a tank and a motor home. A more direct route through the Tohdra gorges is from the town of Tinerhir.

TINERHIR

The town of Tinerhir is about 53 km (33 miles) from Boumalne du Dadés and, perhaps, a more interesting base from which to explore the surrounding countryside, particularly the valley and the gorges. Surrounded by a wonderful palmery and oasis, Tinerhir is both a regional administrative and agricultural center. After passing through oases at either end of the town, you'll arrive at the Plaza Principal where the main shops, hotels, cafés, restaurants, and bus and grand taxi lots are located.

You can stock up on staples such as cheese, bottled water, crackers, jam, bread, and eggs at the small grocery stores around the square. Otherwise head for the restaurant at the Hotel Salam where a great meal of tajine, vegetables, and melon costs about $4. The Café-Restaurant Gazelle d'Or also serves tajine as well as couscous, for about the same prices. There are also good restaurants at the Hotel Todra (sic) and the

Hotel Sargho. For accommodations, the Salam is adequate, not fancy, for a night—about $5 for a simple, comfortable room with a shower. The two-star Hotel Todra has good, clean singles and doubles for prices ranging from $8.25 and $10, to $10 and $13, respectively. There's also the four-star Hotel Sargho, which has the only swimming pool in town, possibly an important amenity during blistering summers. Other more scenic and adventurous accommodations and campsites are available in the Tohdra gorges.

Getting to the gorges or elsewhere can be arranged by bus, grand taxi or, occasionally, Berber trucks (the cheapest way into the gorges) from the Plaza Principal. There are two daily CTM buses to Er-Rachidia (3 hours) and three to Ouarzazate (5 hours), both of which make stops at major points along the way.

Hiking from Tinerhir to the mouth of the gorges is a fairly easy and very scenic 15-km (9-mile) day hike, although there are a few steep portions. Less than 1 km from town, a road heads through the wide green valley that precedes the gorges. Some of the most beautiful kasbahs and ksours in Morocco are found here surrounded by a grand oasis of date palms and terraced fields of almond and olive trees. You could wander for hours amongst the kasbahs and then head back to town or continue on to the mouth.

There are three hotel-restaurants and a campsite in or near the mouth of the gorges. The first one you'll see is the Café-Restaurant Hotel El Mansour at the end of the paved road, which is usually as far as the grand taxis will take you. Doubles are about $5, but you could also sleep in your sleeping bag on the front terrace for less than $1. The standard meal served at the restaurant is a good deal at about $3. Less than a kilometer (about a 10-minute walk) further into the gorge are the other two hotels—the Hotel-Restaurant Yasmina and the Hotel des Rocheurs, both adjacent to each other alongside the river at one of the narrowest points in the gorges. Their location between the sheer orange cliffs of the gorges is reason enough to stay here. The Hotel des Rocheurs has double rooms for about $5 and also allows you to sleep on its terrace—a wonderful option in the summer—for a negotiable price. The Hotel Yasmina has clean, simple, but comfortable rooms—about $5 for one person and $6.50 for two. In the summer you can sleep on the terrace or on cushions in a large "salon" for less than $1. Of the three hotels, most travelers agreed that the Yasmina had the best food.

As with the routes from Boumalne du Dadés, it is also possible to go through the Tohdra gorges along a bad piste to Tamtatouchte and then westward to Msemrir and through the Dadés gorge. However, for the stretch between Tamtatouchte and Msemrir, transport is rare, so you really should have your own rugged vehicle or hitch a ride with someone who has. An easier route transport-wise is to continue from Tamtatouchte to Ait Hani, Agoudal, Bouzmou, and Imilchil. This route is described in the Imilchil section.

FROM TINERHIR TO ER-RACHIDIA

The road east from Tinerhir crosses 79 km (50 miles) of flat, dry terrain to the small oasis town of Tinejdad. The bus to Er-Rachidia stops in front of the post office here for about 30 minutes, which is convenient if you have some mail to send. The only other reason to get off the bus here is if you wish to somehow arrange transportation east-southeast across an oasis strip to Erfoud. There aren't any buses and rarely any grand taxis, so you'll have to arrange a taxi yourself or try hitchhiking. If you seem to be getting stuck here, then get a bus or taxi to Goulmima.

GOULMIMA

Goulmima is an oasis of 78,000 (includes surrounding valley) about 24 km (15 miles) from Tinejdad, 146 km (90 1/2 miles) from Erfoud, and 58 km (36 miles) from Er-Rachidia. Unless you have the time to visit the well-preserved and still inhabited kasbahs and ksours here, then this wouldn't be an easy or worthwhile stop for most travelers. The kasbahs and ksours are hidden from the main road by a 16-km (10-mile) maze of date palm groves, fava bean fields, olive trees, and mysteriously sticky alfalfa paddies. I stopped in Goulmima to visit a friend, Natasha Haugnes, who was teaching English at the local lycée (local high school) for the U.S. Peace Corps. She showed me around the town and a few of the kasbahs and invited me to speak to her English classes. Although writing about this is a deviation from the usual travel book material, it's worth recounting just to give you some insight into the seldom-reported, but tremendously beneficial, work of the Peace Corps, the life of one of its U.S. participants, and life in this fairly typical rural Moroccan city.

Morocco began hosting Peace Corps volunteers in 1963. According to a report by the Peace Corps office in Rabat, Morocco, "more than 2,000 volunteers have assisted in national development and [in advancing] cross-cultural understanding between our nations. Peace Corps cross-cultural goals are often overlooked. They are to promote a better understanding of Americans by Moroccans and a better understanding of Moroccans by Americans. The Minister of Economic Affairs...said that public and private sector officials know the benefits of friendship and cooperation with Americans in America. He said that these officials want more people of Morocco to know and to appreciate Americans and that Peace Corps volunteers in general and, in particular, in Morocco's high schools represent America well."

In 1988, there were 150 Peace Corps volunteers assigned to a variety of projects in the fields of education, agriculture, village water supply, parks development, endangered species protection, education of the handicapped, and rural health education. According to the Peace Corps report, the volunteers receive "11 weeks of full-time training in Morocco in the Arabic language, Morocco's culture and their technical specialty prior to their swearing-in. They receive an average of $270 per month for living costs plus $200 per month in a U.S. account which they can draw down at the end of their volunteer service or in case of an emergency during their service."

Some of the projects they worked on included

- English-language instruction at seven Moroccan universities
- Protection of endangered species such as the bald ibis, Dorcas gazelle, Barbary sheep, and Barbary panther through work at six reserves
- Installation or repair of village water systems
- Rehabilitative education by working with handicapped youth and on-the-job training for Moroccan counterparts
- Development of a Moroccan sign-language system
- Afforestation projects in semiarid regions of the country

Several volunteers are, like Natasha, teaching English at lycées throughout Morocco. She lives alone in a rented house in town that's big enough for at least a family of four. There's nothing really noteworthy about the place except that there is no hot water and that most of the building is surrounded by a high mud-brick wall; these features are fairly typical of other houses in the area. Hot baths are available in the traditional-style *hammam* or bathhouse across the path from her house. The high walls seem more appropriate for a fortress or prison and are, perhaps, a vestige of the days when houses really had to be built like defensive fortifications to protect the inhabitants from rival families or tribes. Whatever their reason today, though, I had to squelch my curiosity and resist the temptation to try peeking over the walls of Natasha's neighbors.

After having learned quite a lot of Moroccan Arabic and the local Berber dialect, Natasha seems to have assimilated to many of the customs and traditions as much as someone who describes herself as an "earth bean" could. Actually, it was her blonde, very Californian sister who coined the description because Natasha eats wheat germ and garbanzo beans, but Natasha seems to have adopted the nickname. If "earthiness" means being "down-to-earth," sincere, and disinclined to fill one's life with frills, then I guess Natasha really is an "earth bean."

Recently, she wrote to say that she "love[s] the town and people here more than ever. I am finally able to appreciate and accept the generosity of people here as unconditional generosity. Coming from a place where friendships are much more earned than they are here, I guess I was a little suspicious and defensive at all the invitations from people I felt I hardly knew last year. I was often afraid they wanted something from me. But they demand nothing which, paradoxically, makes me share my relative wealth much more readily....I have been spending lots of time with families—playing with the kids, making couscous for hours on end with the women, and drinking lots of tea. I feel so comfortable in this setting now that it is sometimes a bit of a shock when I catch a glimpse of myself in a window or mirror and realize how different I still look from everybody else."

One afternoon, she visited the family of one of her students and "witnessed a really unforgettable moment." The family has asked to remain anonymous. "The mother [of the family] was telling about how she had had to go to the bank and sign for something, but she didn't know how to write her name. We were telling her it is never too late to learn, so a couple of the kids got a notebook and a pen and tried to teach their Mom how to write her name....She tried really hard to form the letters, and took the whole lesson in very good humor, but finally gave up, stating that she didn't know how to write, but did know how to grind flour, make bread, mend clothes, etc."

The woman's 20-year old son does know how to write—in Arabic, Berber, French, and English! Like his family, he also requested anonymity, but I will call him Mohammed. He was in Natasha's English class and fairly similar to his classmates in linguistic background, but much better in ability. For most of the students, Berber is their language from birth, written Arabic is learned in Qur'ānic school at a young age, colloquial Moroccan Arabic is the lingua franca, French is learned in school at an early age, and English is studied in high school. I spoke to a group of second-year students in English about my travels through Morocco and then asked for questions. The first questions were quite general—What do you think of Moroccans? and so on—but then Mohammed livened things up by asking specific questions about poverty and world political events. I was more interested in hearing Mohammed and his classmates speak than in hearing myself, so I kept my responses short and tried to ask questions about their lives. Mohammed said that he wanted to be a journalist. Most of the others weren't sure what they wanted to be, so I challenged them to write and tell me their dreams and aspirations. Three students, including Mohammed, responded. Mohammed has written me several times, and another student, whom I will call Ahmed, has written me twice.

Their letters present a brief, but telling description of their life, interests, and aspirations. The letters aren't political, but Mohammed and Ahmed both insisted on anonymity. With their permission, I include a few excerpts from their letters.

From Mohammed:

> Everybody has a wish, but they must work for it. In my life, I wish I was a journalist because this work…would help me to write many things about people who are poor or haven't any house … about man or woman who is hungry.…I will write against technology which often goes wrong and about other disasters because they can kill everyone in our gorgeous land.
>
> When I think, especially about my last years of my life in my town where I grew up, I feel glad to be able to read and write.…[My] mother is illiterate. So she couldn't help to learn or understand my lessons during my first years in primary school at all. However, she always told me to be busy with my studies, if I wanted to dodge problems in my future life.…I also needed my father (he wasn't illiterate) for his help to explain the lessons to me which I thought were difficult. Alas, I lost my father when I was twelve years old.…My aspiration: reading, writing, to be busy with my studies almost daily, in order to help my brother, sisters, friends and anyone how to be on the right track and, especially, to get back happy days for my family after my father's death.
>
> In my small town of Goulmima, people are ready to invite everyone to their houses even if they don't have any idea about him, his life, temper or family. If one person invites a man or woman to his house for lunch or dinner, he must prepare for him a good meal. What a meal! Meat and vegetables! It's necessary for the meal to be excellent, even if he doesn't have enough money to buy all that, he should borrow some money from his friends or others.

From Ahmed:

> In our society, there are several restrictions on what women can do. Firstly, as they are Moslems, they must respect the laws that the God imposed on them in the Koran. Secondly, women can't go outside their houses unless their husbands authorize it. If they go outside their houses without authorization from the men, the angels will insult them until they go back to their houses. Finally, the Koran maintains that women have got two times to go out of their houses: the first time is when they get married and they want to go to the groom's house and the second time is when they die and the man takes her to the grave.

In my opinion, I agree that women can't go out to work, because they cause several problems for men. They begin to imitate American women or European women, so they begin to forget the laws of our God.

I haven't had any luck in love because one time I was in love with a girl and I ran. I don't understand why I run with love: Is it shy[ness]? Is it fear? I don't know, but I think that it is the laws of our society.

It's three years ago that I followed one girl. She was very beautiful. I sent her letters and received answers....I felt that I needed her: "I love her" but I couldn't meet her. In the end I decided to meet her. We had to agree on the appointment. In the road, when I meet her. I felt my heart beat very fast. It seemed to me that it wanted to jump out of my chest. It was the first time that I went to meet the girl and to stay with her.

On arriving, I saw her sitting on the grassy place. She appeared to me as a beautiful red flower. She looked at me and her look pricked my heart. I greeted her and I sat near her, but I didn't know what to do. I was very embarrassed. I was like a soldier who lost his way in the desert and a bird which lost its wing. One hour later, I saw my father coming past. I was very ashamed and I put my head down until he passed and went far away from us. The girl asked me "Why are you so very ashamed? I think you have never frequented the girls." I couldn't answer her and I couldn't tell her about my love. In the evening, I entered our house and found my father. He asked me about the girl. As I couldn't answer him, he hit me with his left hand and cried "People in our tribe don't like to frequent the girls, it is banned forever." But it's not right, love is indispensable for life.

Before I left Goulmima, Natasha took me to Frank (not his real name) and Embarek's house—both were high school English teachers. Frank was also with the Peace Corps, but he hadn't adapted or wished to adapt as well as Natasha. He was a clean-cut chain-smoking drama major from Illinois. Like many expatriates I've met who are working or studying in exotic locales, Frank had brought a few things from home—a jar of caviar, gabardine pants, and an airmail subscription to *Vanity Fair*. He also had a nervous little dog with sharp teeth that he had found in the streets of Goulmima. I generally like dogs, but this one was schizophrenic. One moment it was sitting quietly next to me on the couch, and the next it was trying to sink its teeth into my forearm. Fortunately, my jacket prevented its teeth from getting through to my arm. After I stopped shaking and the color returned to my face, Frank told me that the dog was a bit wild because everyone in town threw stones at both him and the dog whenever they were out for a walk. He was the only person in town with a pet dog.

One more noteworthy aside about Frank: I witnessed the day that *Vanity Fair* arrived at his high school mail drop. He tore off the brown wrapping and dashed from person to person showing off photo pages of the latest Pierre Cardin suits and trendy New York bistros. The Moroccans who saw the magazines scratched their heads and frowned, but Frank, flushed with excitement, was hurriedly flipping through the pages and saying, "Wow, look at this" and "Check this out" and "Isn't this great?"

My gut reaction was "*Vanity Fair* in the Sahara, he's got to be kidding!" But this was Frank. Frank was American and *Vanity Fair* was a slice, albeit a thin slice of Americana. If anything, the differences between Frank, who had left his heart somewhere near Chicago, and Natasha, who was absorbed with Morocco and Moroccans, aptly symbolized the diversity of Americans and U.S. culture. That was and still is, perhaps, one of the most important missions of the Peace Corps and its volunteers throughout the world.

After *Vanity Fair* in the Sahara, I headed for the grand taxi lot, which is down a side street about one block off the main street. This side street intersects the main street at the intercity bus station and cafés. A man in the front seat of a crowded taxi for Er-Rachidia insisted on giving his seat to me and squeezing into the back. The driver tied his door shut with a piece of string and off we went through 58 km (36 miles) of desert to Er-Rachidia.

CHAPTER 9

The Deep South of Morocco

In this book, the deep south of Morocco is an area south of the High Atlas mountains and the Ouarzazate-Zagora stretch described in Chapter 7. It encompasses an area almost as big as the regions to the north. Unfortunately, it isn't within the scope of this book to describe all the possible adventures in this region. Because of space and time restrictions, only the following highlight destinations have been covered:

- Agadir
- Cascades des Imouzzer des Ida Outanane
- Taroudannt
- Tafraoute
- Goulimine

The area south of Goulimine was, until recently, mostly off limits to travelers because of the western Sahara war between Morocco and the Polisario front guerrillas. Before 1975, the Moroccan border extended as far as 537 km (333 miles) south of Agadir to Tarfaya, and the area south of Tarfaya was a Spanish colony called the Spanish Sahara. King Hassan II of Morocco forced a Spanish withdrawal from the area in 1975 by organizing the Green March. More than 300,000 Moroccan civilians were bussed to the border and marched across to reassert Morocco's historical claim on the region. The Spanish withdrew, and an independence movement called the Polisario front was formed by Saharawi rebels to fight Morocco's claim on the territory. The Moroccans seem to have won the fight, in part, by constructing a 3-m (10-ft)- high berm or rampart of stone and sand that extends from the Zini mountains westward almost 1,613 km (1,000 miles) to Dakhla. The wall itself is a veritable fortress of gun emplacements and radar, and beyond it the ground bristles with mines and electronic sensors.

In an effort to normalize the region and integrate it with the rest of Morocco, the Moroccan government has been pouring in millions of

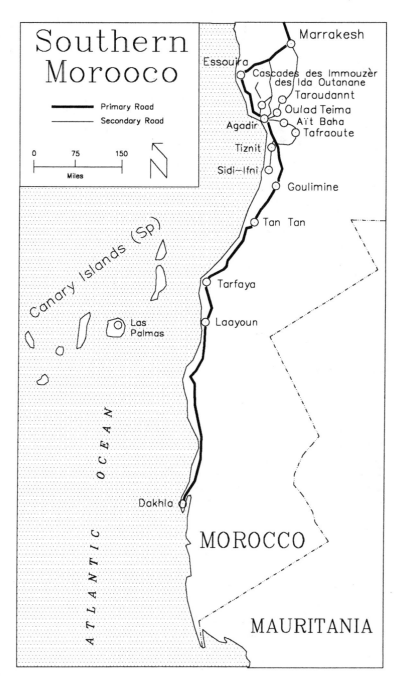

Southern
Morooco

▬▬▬ Primary Road
——— Secondary Road

0   75   150
|_____|
Miles

Marrakesh

Essouira

Cascades des Immouzèr
des Ida Outanane

Taroudannt

Oulad Teima

Aït Baha

Agadir

Tafraoute

Tiznit

Sidi-Ifni

Goulimine

Tan Tan

Canary Islands (Sp)

Tarfaya

Las
Palmas

Laayoun

A T L A N T I C   O C E A N

Dakhla

MOROCCO

MAURITANIA

dollars to develop the towns and phosphate mines of the western Sahara. Laayoun has become a commercial center with new public facilities, including schools, a hospital, a multimillion-dollar port, an airport, and roads as well as two 5-star hotels, and a handicrafts center. Farther south at Dakhla, similar developments are being completed. You can travel as far as Laayoun and, if the region remains calm, all the way to Dakhla, but don't expect much from either place because both are still essentially administrative centers and military bases.

AGADIR

The present Agadir was built over the ruins of an earthquake-ravaged Agadir in 1960. Except for a few traces of an old kasbah on a hill overlooking the city, nothing of the city's history as a medieval trading center and port remains. If it were not for camel rides on the beach, the new Agadir could be almost any beach resort city in the world. Most of the city was designed to cater to tourism and thus seems like a virtual city of hotels and touristy restaurants. After Marrakesh with its snake charmers and Berber storytellers or the kasbahs of the countryside, Agadir seems quite un-Moroccan and, unless you are here for fun in the sun or a foray to one of Morocco's best English-and-American bookstores, not very interesting.

Arrival and Departure

By Air

Almost all year, the airport is bustling with direct flights to and from Europe, Casablanca, Dakhla, Laayoun, Tangier, Marrakesh, Ouarzazate, Tan Tan, and Las Palmas in the Canary Islands. Many of the flights from Europe are inexpensive charters full of package tourists, but you may be able to just book the flight rather than the whole package. The airport is about 4 km (2 1/2 miles) from town on the way to Agadir's sister city—Inezgane. Buses depart every hour and grand taxis whenever they are full, from Place Salam in Agadir.

By Bus

The bus situation in Agadir can be somewhat confusing because there are actually three terminals or stations—the main one is in central Agadir at Place Lachen Tamri, a small city bus terminal is at Place Salam and a chaotic intercity terminal is in the sister city of Inezgane. Most CTM and private-line intercity buses from northern destinations arrive at (and depart from on return trips) the Place Lachen Tamri terminal.

Around the corner from this terminal on the side street of Rue de Sidi Abdallah Hadj is the Autobus Immouzer office for buses to the waterfalls near Immouzer des Ida Outanane north of Agadir. Southern destination buses—for Goulimine, Taroudannt, and Tafraoute—depart from both Place Lachen Tamri and a long, dusty lot in Inezgane. To get to Inezgane, which is a few kilometers south of Agadir, take a city bus from the Place Salam station or get a taxi. Ask the tourist office staff or reception clerks at any of the bigger hotels in Agadir for help in sorting out this mess. Or just head for the Place Lachen Tamri terminal and take your chances.

By Grand Taxi

Similar advice applies to grand taxis, which depart from the same locales as the buses. For grand taxis to the airport and Inezgane, go to Place Salam. For grand taxis to Taroudannt, you have to change taxis at Oulad Teima/Quarante-Quatre, which is about one-third of the way to Taroudannt. Be forewarned: Changing taxis at Oulad Teima isn't always easy. When I was there, people were chasing taxis through the lot and then fighting each other for the seats.

Getting Around by Taxi

Learn to tell the difference between a city taxi and a grand taxi because the difference in fares for the same trip is tremendous. City taxis are smaller than grand taxis and charge much less. Don't be duped by the grand taxi drivers into thinking that they are regular city taxis, and vice versa by the city taxi drivers, or they will take not only you, but also your wallet, for a ride. If in doubt, ask the driver before hopping in.

First Things First

Information

The ONMT tourist information office is at Block A, Avenue Sidi Mohammed, in the shopping mall near the post office; it's open Monday to Saturday from 9 A.M. to noon and 4 to 6 P.M. The Syndicat d'Initiative is on Avenue Mohammed V at Avenue General Ketani, but it didn't seem to be very helpful with information about the area.

Hotels

Agadir is a virtual city of hotels with over fifty establishments of every type, standard, and price other than a youth hostel. Take your pick, but try to make reservations before you arrive, especially in July and

August, when even the seediest places seem to fill up. If you arrive without reservations, then the best approach is to first head for the tourist office, pick up a copy of its hotel guide, and have the staff call a few places for you or just start walking. Almost every street around the ONMT tourist office has at least one hotel. Some of the cheapest, but also the seediest, hotels are found around Place Lachen Tamri near the CTM bus station. The Hotel Bahia on Rue Ibn Toumert near Place Lachen Tamri is often recommended by travelers. Some of the most expensive hotels are, of course, found on the beach.

Camping is another possibility at the well-maintained official campground on Avenue Mohammed V at the northern end of the beach. As with most other establishments in the city, it tends to get quite crowded in the summer.

Restaurants and Cafés

The majority of restaurants and cafés cater to the packaged-holiday tourists, but competition keeps prices fairly moderate, though still higher than other cities. Try the restaurants on the side streets near Place Lachen Tamri for inexpensive fare and multilingual menus. The Place des Orangiers has a few other inexpensive restaurants and cafés. Menus at most of the restaurants in both squares seemed similar in prices and offerings, so don't spend a lot of time looking.

Getting Things Done and Shopping

Money. Foreign currency and travelers' checks can be exchanged at any of the banks along the Avenue des Forces Armeés Royales or along Avenue Mohammed V. After hours, go to the exchange windows at any of the big hotels. American Express has an office in Agadir at Voyages Schwarz near Boulevard Hassan II and the local marketplace. Emergency cash refunds are available during office hours—Monday to Friday from 9 A.M. to noon and 3 P.M. to 6 P.M.

Post and Telephone Office. The main post and telephone office is centrally located at the end of Avenue Sidi Mohammed and across from Place du Marché. Postal services are open Monday to Friday from 9 A.M. to noon and 3 to 6 P.M. and Saturday 9 A.M. to noon; telephone service is open 24 hours.

Shopping. Souvenir shopping is possible in Agadir, but this is predominantly a tourist resort, so don't plan on finding the best prices here. However, if you're short on time, you can find most of the main crafts souvenirs in Agadir's shops: that is, traditional carpets, bright yellow *babouche* slippers, and copper kettles. Unfortunately, with the number of tourists usually in town it's more of a seller's than a buyer's market, so do your best in bargaining.

Books. There are three bookstores in Agadir that sell books, magazines, and newspapers in English—the Debit Pilote bookstore on Avenue Hassan II, La Drugstore at Avenue Sidi Mohammed and Avenue Hassan II, and the Crown English Bookshop in the relatively new shopping mall. Of the three, the Crown English Bookshop seems to offer the best and most up-to-date selection of books and periodicals. This is definitely the place to come for stocking up on all sorts of books, including novels and books about Morocco. The shop is owned and run by the Bacons, a friendly American couple from California. It is in Immeuble (Building) A on the second floor at No. 8.

Things to See

The only sight or place to visit in Agadir other than the beach is the old kasbah perched atop a hill about 4 km (2 1/2 miles) from town. Most of the ancient medina quarter and Portuguese-built fortress that composed the kasbah were wiped out in the 1960 earthquake. Today, only part of the ramparts remain, but the beautiful view of Agadir makes it worth visiting if you can get a ride here. You could also take a city bus (Nos. 12, 13, or 14) to the port and then follow the signs to the kasbah.

NEAR AGADIR

About 9 km (5 1/2 miles) north of Agadir is the turnoff for the narrow paved road through "Paradise Valley" and the Tamrahrt gorge to Imouzzer des Ida Outanane. Two Autobus Imouzzer buses make the daily trip between Agadir and Imouzzer in about an hour from a "station" around the corner from the main terminal at Place Lachen Tamri. It's a trip definitely worth doing, not only to see the town and waterfalls, but also for great day hikes and camping by the stream. If you don't want to camp, the three-star Auberge des Cascades is highly recommended for its beautiful layout and location in the mountains amid lush gardens and olive groves.

Thursday is souk day in Imouzzer, the most interesting time to visit because members of the Ida-Outanane Berber tribes arrive from surrounding villages to buy and sell livestock, food staples, and various household goods.

Otherwise, during the rest of the week, the main attraction in the area is the set of waterfalls about 5 km (3 miles) from town. To get there, you can either hitch a ride with other travelers or walk down from the town along a pleasant road. Spring is the best time to visit—the winter snows in the mountains are melting. By the summer, most of the falls have vanished and dried up. However, you can swim in a wonderfully cool pool there even when the falls have practically vanished. There's a restaurant near the falls that serves decent food, but, unfortunately, they seem to have seen too many package tours from Agadir, so their prices are often inflated.

TAROUDANNT

Situated in the heart of the Souss valley between the High Atlas mountains to the north and the Anti-Atlas mountains to the south, Taroudannt has long been an important market center for the region. Most of the city is wrapped in crenellated pink-orange walls and ramparts, imperial vestiges of the city's role as capital of the Saadian dynasty in the sixteenth century. Its capital status makes the city one of Morocco's six imperial cities—the other five being Rabat, Casablanca, Meknes, Fez, and Marrakesh.

Taroudannt is a great place to get an idea about how life may have been in medieval Morocco. With its walls, age-old souks and comparative lack of tourist trappings and traps (such as in Agadir and Marrakesh), traditional life in the city seems well preserved, almost untouched by modernity. Fortunately, walls and traditional souks have not yet been enough to attract the package-tour hordes and pesky would-be guides and hustlers, so you're free to wander around the city mostly without being hurried, harried, and hassled.

Arrival and Departure

By Bus

Buses arrive at and depart from Taroudannt's two principal squares—Place Tamaklate and Place Assarag. All CTM buses use a small lot at Place Tamaklate, while SATAS buses use a lot at Place Assarag in the heart of the city near the entrance to the souks. Both companies have frequent departures for Agadir and Marrakesh, including a 5 A.M. bus to Marrakesh that traverses the Tizi-n-Test pass.

By Grand Taxis

Grand taxis depart from Place Tamaklate, but they only service local towns and villages as far as Oulad Teima.

First Things First

Hotels

For a relatively small city, Taroudannt offers a good selection of hotels ranging from deluxe and expensive to seedy and cheap. At the top of the list is the five-star Hotel La Gazelle d'Or, built in the 1930s by painter-architect Baron Jean Pellenc to serve as his hunting lodge. In the 1960s he converted it into a deluxe hotel with twenty bungalows and a cool, lush garden of flowers, bamboo, and bougainvillea. Today its facilities include a swimming pool, tennis courts, a bar, and a restaurant that requires men to wear ties and coats. The four-star Hotel Palais Salam is almost as luxurious and easily as beautiful as the Gazelle. Located just inside the walls next to the kasbah quarter, the Salam was once a pasha's minipalace. The most inexpensive rooms are in the older part of the hotel, while a new wing has more expensive modern kasbah-style rooms and suites. On a much more modest, but equally interesting, scale is the one-star Hotel Taroudannt on Place Assarag, a few doors down from the bus lot. It has been owned and run by an elderly French woman for at least the last forty years and still has the only beer in the medina. Reputedly, this was a popular French Foreign Legion hangout during the last years of the French Protectorate. The rooms are simply furnished, clean, and cheap; hot water is available on request from the bartender. In the cheap unclassified—possibly seedy—category, try the hotels near Place Assarag—the Hotel Mantega and the Hotel les Oliviers as well as several others in the area.

Restaurants and Cafés

The restaurants at the Gazelle and the Salam are, not surprisingly, the best and most expensive in town. The restaurant at the Hotel Taroudannt offers a good, fairly priced *menu touristique* that seems to change everyday. Across the square is the Restaurant de la Place, an inexpensive place with meals of *harira* and tajines that are popular with budget travelers. A couple other places worth checking out include the Boulangerie-Pâtisserie Tamaklate on Place Tamaklate for a breakfast of coffee and croissants and the Restaurant Nada at the edge of the walls for a great meat tajine.

Getting Things Done and Shopping

Money

Foreign currency and travelers' checks can be exchanged at banks in Place Assarag or after hours at the Gazelle or the Salam hotels.

Post and Telephone Office

The main post and telephone office is on Place Assarag.

Shopping and Things to See

For shopping, head for the souks, Taroudannt's main attractions. Start from Place Assarag and just wander through the passageways. The souk here is hardly as labyrinthine as the Marrakesh souk, so you won't get lost. It is much less touristy than souks in Marrakesh and Fez because most of the shops and stalls cater to locals from the town and surrounding countryside. In one courtyard, people gather to buy and sell huge burlap bags of grain; usually many of the bags are open, with their contents in big golden piles spread on the ground. Other parts of the souk specialize in dates, with some stalls offering as many as 35 varieties, and natural toiletries such as musk made from gazelle glands. However, this is also one of the best souks for fair prices on traditional handicrafts such as carpets, colorful kaftans, leather goods such as handbags, belts, and wallets and the ubiquitous *babouche* or bright yellow slipper. Thursday and Sunday are the market days, thus the best and busiest days to come.

TAFRAOUTE

Nestled in the Ameln valley (Almond valley) among the slopes of the Anti-Atlas mountains, Tafraoute is a French-created town that's worth visiting mostly for the day hikes that are possible through the surrounding villages in the valley. The town itself doesn't hold much attraction except on Wednesdays, when its weekly souk is held, and in mid-February when the Almond Festival celebrates the blossoming of the almond trees. A few tour buses come up from Agadir on Wednesdays, and the town is packed with tourists during the festival, but the rest of the time, it is practically deserted.

There are only four hotels in Tafraoute, all of which are found near the main square and bus station. The best in town is the four-star Hotel des Amandiers, with 60 rooms, air conditioning, a restaurant-bar, and swimming pool. The other three are unclassified: the Hotel Salama, which was the best of the three until it burnt down (supposedly being rebuilt); the Hotel/Restaurant Tanger, the cheapest for both rooms and meals; and the Hotel Redouane. Aside from the hotel restaurants, there's also the Restaurant Etoile du Sud set under a large velvet tent à la *One Thousand and One Nights*; they serve a very filling meal for under $5.

Also on the main square are the town's principal services: the post and telephone office and the bank (for changing money). For after-hours exchange, you can try the Hotel des Amandiers.

Beyond the town, the real adventures begin in the countryside. A good starting point for day hikes through the Ameln valley is the village of Oumesnat about 7 1/2 km (almost 5 miles) from Tafraoute. You'll have to hitch a ride in the direction of Aït Baha and Agadir and ask to be dropped at the village. From Oumesnat, begin roaming through the villages and settlements in the valley toward Aït Taleb about three to four hours' walk away. If you wish to camp in the valley, ask the locals at the nearest village for permission; there usually isn't a problem.

A shorter hike is possible from town about 3 km south to the village of Agard Oudad. Its chief attraction is a unique granite formation just above the village that has been dubbed Le Chapeau du Napoleon (Napoleon's Hat). Even stranger are the rocks about 1 1/2 km (1 mile) from "*le chapeau*" that were painted in bright colors by a Belgian painter; you won't miss them.

Getting to Tafraoute isn't as simple as it first seems because the direct 112-km (70-mile) route between Agadir and Tafraoute is usually impassible and rarely serviced by public transportation. This was supposed to change soon, which would make the trip much quicker. For now, you have to first travel to Tiznit and then change to a bus or Land-Rover taxi for Tafraoute, thus a total of 185 km (115 miles). Unfortunately, service from Tiznit is somewhat erratic and unpredictable, so you may be in for a long wait.

GOULIMINE

The only reasons to visit Goulimine, which is 186 km (115 miles) south of Agadir, are the Saturday morning camel market and an annual religious festival (ask the Agadir tourist office for information). The market is 1 km from town on the road to Tan Tan; try to get there by 6 A.M., well before the tour buses arrive from Agadir and just as the trucks unload their cargoes of adult and baby camels. The adjacent vegetable and meat market is quite colorful and pungent, definitely worth seeing and smelling.

If you decide to spend the night here, there are only two budget hotels, both unclassified, and a two-star hotel. The two, the Hotel la Jeunesse and the Hotel l'Ere Nouvelle are both on Avenue Mohammed, the town's main street. Neither has hot water, but both are quite cheap—less than $3 for a night except on Friday nights when the prices are sometimes inflated. The third place is the Hotel Salam on the road to Tan Tan and the camel market and easily the best in town.

There is also a campground in a slightly wooded area about 1 1/2 km (1 mile) from Place Hassan II; signs lead the way. If you have transportation, camping is also possible a few kilometers from town at the oasis village of Abbaynou in a walled-in enclosure adjacent to some hot springs. However, the campground is sometimes crammed with recreational vehicles from Europe that don't leave much space for tents. Despite the hot springs, this isn't a pleasant option.

CHAPTER 10

Fez

Fez is three cities in one—the French-built Ville Nouvelle, Fez El Jdid or New Fez, and Fez El B'ali or Old Fez. Fez El B'ali is the ancient heart of Fez and, perhaps, one of the best examples you will ever see of a medieval Arab city. Parts of Fez El B'ali date back to the city's founding by Moulay Idriss I and his son, Idriss II in the late eighth and early ninth century. Fez El Jdid was founded in the mid-thirteenth century first as a huge royal enclosure for the city's conquerors, the Merenids. Later, part of it became a refuge for Fez's Jewish population and was known as "the mellah," but few, if any, Jews remain. The Ville Nouvelle (or, literally, "New City") was built by the French in this century for government buildings and other modern structures such as the train station. Today, it is still the modern center of town, but almost all major government business is conducted in Rabat.

Until the French arrived, Fez dominated the political, economic, and cultural life of Morocco alternately with Marrakesh since its founding as a city in the late eighth century. Before his death by poisoning in A.D. 793, Moulay Idriss I established the foundation of an Arab empire at Volubilis, which is near Fez, and then moved on to what was then the village of Fez. Refugees from the Abbassid empire in the east had begun settling in the Fez area. Idriss was anxious to gain their support in consolidating his power against neighboring rival kingdoms and Berber tribes. His son, Idriss II, succeeded him and attempted to expand the empire from Fez.

Idriss II was abetted in his empire building by an additional influx of refugees in the early ninth century, this time from Kairouan in Tunisia and the Andalusian kingdom of Cordoba, Spain. Walled quarters, the remnants of which form Fez El B'ali today, were erected in Fez to accommodate the refugees. Idriss II treated the rest of his sporadically expanding empire as divisively as he treated his new-found capital at Fez. He attempted to consolidate his kingdom against threats from the Omayyad Emirs of Cordoba, the Shi'ite Fatimids of Ifriquiya, the

200

Kharidjites, and various Berber tribes by cooperating with western Berber tribes. This cooperation meant that he had to cede parts of his kingdom to the Berbers, but he was still able to establish enough stability for his successors to make Fez one of the Arab world's predominant centers of Islamic religion and culture. The Kairouine University was founded in the tenth century and remains one of the most important Islamic universities in the Arab world.

Fez's role as a political center, however, was eclipsed in the mid-eleventh century when the Berber dynasties of first the Almoravids and then the Almohads established a stronger base at Marrakesh. They were followed by the Merenids, who conquered Fez in 1248 and began building much of what you see today in Fez El Jdid and Fez El B'ali.

The Merenids created Fez El Jdid just outside the walls of Fez El B'ali to serve as a huge royal compound. In Fez El B'ali, they also built a series of *fondouks*—multistory buildings built around courtyards to accommodate traders and their animals—and expanded the Kairouine mosque. The city remained as a capital of Morocco until about the sixteenth century, when the Saadians came to power in Marrakesh and isolated the region as much as possible from European cultural influences.

Fez experienced another heyday when the Alawite dynasty briefly made it their capital in the mid-seventeenth century. When Moulay Ismail, however, came to power in 1672, he decided to move the capital to Meknes. According to Budgett Meakin in his 1899 book *The Moorish Empire*, Ismail announced his decision by sending "ten thousand heads, including those of women and children slain in his rival's camp, to adorn the walls of Fez and...caused the bodies of prisoners of war to be interwoven with rushes to form a bridge whereby the victorious army might cross a river. Thus commenced the horrors of that regime."

Meakin described these "horrors" in great detail in his book. He wrote, "As his rule of life....Most of his murders were committed on Fridays, as in fulfillment of divine decrees, under the influence of the other world, and the many hundreds who died by his hand were taught to believe that such a death ensured admission to paradise, for which his pardon, often granted after the victim's death, was held to be ample passport....So fond was he of shedding blood himself, that he would lop off the head of the nearest attendant to try the edge of a new sword or hatchet, and when a French ambassador was in his presence he slew a number of slaves by way of amusement; in reply to the envoy's remonstrances he declared, 'King Louis rules men, I rule brutes.' "

After Ismail died in 1727, all Morocco fell into anarchy. Fez was repeatedly pillaged and besieged so much that at one point its inhabitants were all forced to retreat to the surrounding hills. Instability reigned in Fez throughout the rest of the century and well into the nineteenth century, until the rule of Moulay Hassan III was forced on the city in the

1870s. In the early part of this century, French rule was instituted in Fez. Under the French Resident General Lyautey, most government functions were moved to Rabat and a new city (*La Ville Nouvelle*) was constructed adjacent to Fez El Jdid for the French and their administration of the city. Part of Lyautey's plan included the restoration and preservation of Fez El B'ali, the effects of which can be seen today in the quarter's well-preserved medieval streets and buildings. With the return of independence in 1956, Rabat was maintained as the country's capital and about 17,000 Fassi ("of Fez") Jews left the Fez mellah for Israel, France, and Casablanca. Arab wars with Israel in 1948 and 1956 had made conditions for Jews in Morocco seem unsafe.

Today, almost half of the city's 500,000 inhabitants reside in the relatively compact area of Fez el B'ali. Since the departure of most of the Jews in the 1950s, Fez El Jdid has become somewhat overrun with migrants from the countryside. For a sense of the mix of traditional country and city life, some travelers opt for rooms in some of the basic hotels in these parts of town. For running water, more comfort, but much less character, there are also many hotels in the Ville Nouvelle. The Hotel Palais Jamaï is the one notable exception in Fez El B'ali; it will be described later in this chapter.

ARRIVAL AND DEPARTURE

By Train

The Fez train station is in the Ville Nouvelle at the end of Boulevard Chenguit, which is about a 10-minute walk from the center of town. All east-bound passenger trains end their trips at the border town of Oujda, although the tracks continue all the way across Algeria to Tunis as part of the once-thriving Trans-Mahgrebian railway. In 1988, after several years of embittered relations between Morocco and Algeria had closed the border, the railway was revived for cargo trains. Passenger train service was also expected to be restarted soon. For now, there are four trains daily to Taza and Oujda that take about 2 1/2 and six hours maximum.

In the opposite direction, approximately seven trains daily go to Meknes in about 45 minutes; six of those trains continue on to Sidi Kacem (2 1/2 hours), Kenitra (3 1/2 hours), Salé (four hours), Rabat (4 1/4 hours), and Casablanca (six hours). Of these six trains, three go all the way through to Marrakesh in about 11 1/2 hours.

By Bus

Traveling by bus to and from Fez can be confusing because there are four intercity bus stations or lots. The CTM station is on Boulevard

Mohammed V between Avenue Mohammed Es Slaoui and Avenue
Youssef Bin Tachfine. CTM buses for Meknes, Casablanca, Rabat,
Tangier, Chaouen, Ouezzane, Oujda, and Marrakesh use this terminal.
Nearby on the same street is the Laghzani terminal for private-line buses
to Azrou and Sefrou. Private-line buses for Taza and Oujda use a terminal
lot at Bab Ftouh near the eastern end of Fez El B'ali. Buses for all other
destinations—including Imouzzer, Ifrane, Midelt, and Er-Rachidia—are
found at the Bab Boujeloud-Place El Baghdadi terminal lot, which is
between Bab El Mahrouk and Bab Boujeloud.

The following chart helps clarify which buses go where and how
often, and how much time their trips take.

Destination	Number per Day	Trip Duration (hours)	Terminus
Azrou	5	3 1/2	Laghzani
Beni Mellal	3	8 1/2	CTM
Casablanca	8	7	CTM
Chaouen	2	7	CTM
Er-Rachidia	3	8 1/2	Bab Boujeloud
Ifrane	5	1	Bab Boujeloud
Imouzzer	5	1	Bab Boujeloud
Laraiche	2	6 1/2	CTM
Marrakesh (via Beni Mellal)	3	11	CTM
Meknes	9	1	CTM
Midelt	3	5 1/2	Bab Boujeloud
Oujda			CTM and Bab Ftouh
Rabat	6	5 1/2	CTM
Sefrou	3	1 1/2	Laghzani
Tangier	2	8	CTM
Taza	3	2 1/2	CTM and Bab Ftouh

By Grand Taxi

Arrival and departure points for grand taxis are as numerous as for
buses. The most frequent grand taxi departures, thus shorter waits for the
taxis to fill up with passengers, are for Meknes from Place des Alaouites
at the northern end of Boulevard Moulay Youssef in Fez El Jdid. For

Sefrou, go to Place de l'Atlas, which is a few blocks southeast of the CTM station (south of Boulevard Mohammed V and then left on Avenue Youssef Ben Tachfine). For Taza, leave from Bab Ftouh. There are also grand taxis to Ifrane and Imouzzer, but I am not sure about their arrival and departure point.

By Plane

The Fez airport is about 12 km (7 1/2 miles) from central Fez (Ville Nouvelle). There are nonstop flights between Fez and Marrakesh, Casablanca, Er-Rachidia, Lyon (France), Marseille, Paris, and Tangier. To get to the airport, take City Bus 16 from Place Mohammed V or arrange for a grand taxi.

GETTING AROUND

The best way to see the city is to walk through the Ville Nouvelle, Fez El Jdid, and Fez El B'ali, but if you have a limited amount of time, you may want to take a city bus or petit taxi between the Ville Nouvelle and Fez El Jdid or Fez El B'ali. Taxis are cheap and plentiful and can usually be flagged down from just about anywhere in the Ville Nouvelle. There are also a few taxi stands spread around the Ville Nouvelle. Fares are usually determined by a meter, but sometimes you have to do a bit of haggling.

Some of the most convenient city bus routes include the following:

No. 19 From the train station to Place des Alaouites at the southwestern end of Fez El Jdid.

No. 9 From Place Mohammed V, just north of the CTM and Laghzani bus terminals and in front of the Syndicat d'Initiative (where official guides can be arranged), to Place de la Résistance (tourist office), Place de l'Istiqlal and the Dar Batha museum a short distance from Bab Boujeloud and Fez El B'ali.

No. 10 Place des Alaouites to Bab Guissa, which is just next to the luxurious Hotel Palais Jamaï and within easy walking distance of the Merenid Tombs on the hill overlooking the city.

No. 18 Place de la Résistance (Ville Nouvelle in front of the tourist office) to Bab Ftouh via Rsif Mosque in Fez El B'ali.

Orientation

Fez is divided into three parts—the newest part called the Ville Nouvelle, Fez El Jdid, and the ancient heart of the city, Fez El B'ali. The

New Fez

Railroad Station

Avenue des Almondes

Avenue des Forces Armées Royal

Avenue

B. Chenguit

A. de France

Boulevard Mohammed

Mohammed Es Slaoui

5

6

4

7

1

7

Avenue Hassan

A. Mohammed

A. Youssef Bin Tachfine

Rue Moulay Slimane

2

3

Oued Fez

|├──┼──┤ Railroad

1 Youth Hostel
2 Camping Moulay Slimane
3 CTM Station
4 Main Post Office
5 ONMT (Tourist Office)
6 Place de la Résistance
7 Syndicat d'Initiative and
  Place Mohammed V

0   1/8   1/4

Miles

Ville Nouvelle is organized along somewhat typical Parisian-style plans with hublike roundabouts called "places" that are intersected by wide, tree-lined boulevards and avenues. The widest street of the city is Avenue Hassan II with the main post and telephone office, the ONMT tourist office, banks, and a few hotels and restaurants located along it. Several of the city's other hotels and services, such as the bus and train stations, are just off Hassan II or on one of its secondary intersecting avenues and boulevards. Hassan II intersects Place de la Résistance and splits into two branches—Boulevard Moulay Youssef on the left, which ends in Place des Alaouites at the southern end of Fez El Jdid, and Avenue de la Liberté, which skirts the edge of Fez El Jdid and leads to side streets that head into Fez El B'ali.

At Place des Alaouites, the walls of the Royal Palace can be seen on your left and the small streets leading into the mellah on your right. The biggest of these streets—La Grande Rue des Merenides—starts at about mid-way in the Place and zigzags through the once-thriving Jewish mellah or neighborhood of Fez El Jdid to Bab Smarine and the Grande Rue de Fez El Jdid. This latter street cuts straight through Fez El Jdid to Avenue des Français, which then goes directly to Bab Boujeloud, the main entrance to Fez El B'ali. Navigating through Fez El B'ali could take days and require a guide at first, but a self-guided tour is described later in this chapter.

FIRST THINGS FIRST

Information

There are two main official sources of tourist information—the Office National du Tourisme Marocaine (ONMT) and the Moroccan equivalent of the Chamber of Commerce (Syndicat d'Initiative). ONMT is in a convenient location at Place de la Résistance and is open daily (except Sunday) from 8 A.M. to 12 P.M. and 2 to 6 P.M. (except Saturday). Some of the staff speak English and can be quite helpful with finding a place to stay and getting around the city. The official city map lacks many details, but it is useful for visiting the highlights.

The Syndicat d'Initiative is at Place Mohammed V and can also provide some information about Fez. However, the main reason to visit this office is to arrange an official guide. Although the rates will probably change, they are officially set for half-day and full-day tours for any size group. In 1988 the rates were about $6 for a full-day tour.

Other sources for travel information might be travelers at the Youth Hostel (18 Mohammed El Hansali) or the campground (Rue Moulay Slimane). The campground can also be a good place to find rides to destinations outside the city.

Guides

You can get around Fez on your own, but you may miss many of the lesser known sites of Fez El B'ali. You may also be subjecting yourself to a seemingly endless stream of encounters with males of almost every age who seek to tap you as a tourist resource. In other words, would-be unofficial guides. As much as you may want to stay warm and open to these guys and also enjoy the sites on our own, this can be difficult. You will most likely become—as I did— tired of having to constantly say "thanks, but no thanks" to offers to show you around. Frankly, it's better and easier just to hire a guide. Unofficial guides will quickly find you (see below) and charge you very negotiable rates. Official, government-approved guides can be arranged at the Syndicat d'Initiative and at most major hotels; their rates are set by the government.

My first day in Fez, I was determined to set out on my own without the rambling chatter of a guide; however, that didn't last long. As I walked down Avenue Hassan II, two teenagers tried convincing me that I really needed a guide for the medina. "Hello, hello. Where you from? Français? English? American? You need guide for medina."

I said, "No, it's not necessary" and they said, "Yes, yes, you need guide. You get lost in medina. Very bad."

Back and forth it went—yes, no, yes, no. They were beginning to seem like irritable little flies buzzing in my ear. Since swatting them away wasn't possible, I hopped a taxi, figuring that I would leave them back on the street. Wrong! A tiny horn beeped just outside my back seat window. Hell, there they were again, this time on a Moped waving, grinning, and tooting that damn little horn all the way to the Merenid Tombs on a small hill above Fez El B'ali.

Once I was out of the taxi, a man in a *djellaba* approached, flashed a shiny brass badge, and said in English, "I'm an official guide." He turned to the would-be moped guides, muttered some harsh words, and they quickly left.

"I will be your guide. You need a guide," the djellaba guide announced with a big, toothy smile.

I said, "No, thank you. I want to see the area on my own today."

"Well, I can show you the way," he insisted. I politely, but firmly said no and walked away, fortunately without the guide.

I walked along the ridge toward a luxury hotel and the remnants of the Merenid Tombs, relieved to finally have the chance to do some exploring alone. My relief from would-be guides was short-lived, though, because within minutes of the last episode, a boy of about 12 or 13 approached me from behind and tugged on my sleeve. He was very fair-skinned, with light brown hair, and could easily have been mistaken for a European. He was at my side saying, "Bonjour, monsieur, I only want to talk with you. My name is Yusuf. I'm not a guide."

My reply was snide: "If all you want to do is talk, then talk. All I want to do is walk. So you keep talking, and I'll keep walking."

Yusuf followed me up the hill and talked about the ancient walls and streets of the great old walled city spread below us. My curiosity was piqued, but I told him that an official guide would be leading me around the next day.

"Where?" he asked.

"The tanneries," which I had read was where animal skins are cleaned, cured, and dried in a process that probably hasn't changed in centuries.

"Ah, monsieur, the tanneries are just through that gate," he said, pointing to an arched gateway below.

We walked down the hill toward the gateway. On the one hand, I didn't want him as a guide. On the other hand, I did want to see the tanneries. Also, I noticed that since he had started walking with me, I hadn't been approached by any more prospective guides. We entered the medina and walked swiftly through a series of narrow alleys and passageways. I lost track of the corners we had turned and landmarks we had passed. We were in an ever-narrowing, dizzying maze that seemed to have neither end nor beginning. I had heard that getting foreigners lost in the medina and then demanding more money to be shown the way out was a common tactic. However, Yusuf did take me to the tanneries and also through a dark, unmarked tunnel to an ancient medina house. After showing me a few more sights around the medina, we got a bus back to the Ville Nouvelle. He never asked for money, but I gave him a few dirham notes and said goodbye.

Back on Avenue Hassan II, I was walking toward the Fez train station, yet I wasn't certain which street would be the shortest. I didn't want to pull out my map and attract the attention of would–be guides. However, the moment I stopped walking to consider which of two streets to follow, a short, bald man approached.

He asked me in English, "What is this please? What is this in English?" He opened his palm and gingerly unwrapped a small piece of wire from tissue paper.

I said, "It looks like a paper clip," but he didn't understand me. So I said, "It's a wire," and he still didn't seem to understand.

"Write for me, please," he asked and then meekly suggested, "Let's sit down, and you tell me about this."

"Sorry, I don't have time. I have to go to the train station." I was sure he wanted to talk about more than paper clips.

I was still looking for the way to the train station when another man approached and asked me in English, "Where you go?"

"I don't know," I said.

Tanneries, Fez Medina, Fez, Morocco. Photo by Scott Wayne.

"Where you want to go?" he asked.

"I really don't know," I replied.

The man smiled, unsure if I was serious and asked, "How you not know where you want to go?"

"I forgot," I said. "That's it. I really forgot where I wanted to go."

He tapped a forefinger on the side of his head and said, "I think you need doctor" and then walked away shaking his head.

Hotels

Fez has a variety of hotels, albeit not as many as Marrakesh. At the top of the list, the five-star deluxe Hotel Palais Jamaï is easily on a par with the Mamounia of Marrakesh. Located at the edge of the medina just inside Bab Guissa, it was originally built toward the end of the eighteenth century as a pleasure palace for the local vizier. Many of the rooms, service buildings, and grounds are decorated with intricate, hand-painted Islamic tiles, antiques (inside only), traditional Moroccan and Berber carpets, and carefully carved stucco walls. The single and double rooms start at about $85 per night. If you don't plan to stay here, try to have dinner (about $20) in one of the hotel's resplendent salons or at least have a look around the public areas. Reservations for the hotel are necessary most of the year and can be made in the United States through Leading Hotels of the World (tel. 800-223-1230).

Although not quite as plush as the Jamaï, the Hotel de Fes (tel. 250-02 and 230-56) and the Hotel Merinides (tel. 452-25 and 452-29) are both five-star hotels. The Fes is a fairly modern establishment with traditional decor; it's located at Place Ahmed El Mansour—the intersection of Avenue Hassan II and Avenue des F.A.R. The Merinides is in a prize location on the hill adjacent to the Merenid Tombs and thus offers some of the best views in the city.

On a much less grand scale is the four-star Hotel Volubilis (tel. 211-25) on Avenue Allal ben Abdallah across from the Hotel de Fes. Its facilities include a swimming pool, restaurant, and night club. The Hotel Salam-Zalagh on Rue Mohammed Diouri is a four-star hotel that belongs to the well-maintained Salam hotel chain and has facilities and amenities that are almost at a five-star level. The Hotel Sofia at 3 Rue du Pakistan offers similar amenities, but isn't quite at the same level.

On a lower level, yet still clean and comfortable, are several three- and two-star hotels. The Hotel de la Paix at 44 Avenue Hassan II is a great choice for modest-budget travelers. The Hotel Lamdaghri at 10 Avenue Hassan II Rue No. 3 is inexpensive, basic, and clean, but the bathrooms could use some work; a double is about $13. If budget is your main concern, then head for the one-star Hotel C.T.M. on Rue Ksar El Kebir or the Youth Hostel at 18 Boulevard Mohammed El Hansali (about four blocks northeast of the Syndicat d'Initiative).

Some of the other budget hotels often mentioned and sometimes recommended by travelers include the one-star Hotel Central, at 50 Rue Nador just off Avenue Mohammed V and one block south of Place Mohammed V, and the Hotel Jeanne d'Arc at 36 Avenue Mohammed Es Slaoui.

All these hotels, except for the Jamaï and the Merenides, are in the Ville Nouvelle. There are also a few low-budget hotels in Fez El Jdid and Fez El B'ali that are more interesting than the Ville Nouvelle hotels, but lack even a modicum of the same amenities. In Fez El Jdid, the Hotel du Parc and Hotel du Croissant are both basic $2.50-a -night hotels on the Grande Rue de Fez El Jdid; the latter is at Bab Smarine and the former near the intersection with Avenue des Français. In Fez El B'ali, most of the budget hotels are clustered near the Bab Boujeloud. The Hotel du Jardin Public is in an alley just before the Bab Boujeloud with clean, very basic rooms and Turkish-style toilets. The Hotel Kaskade is just inside the gate, with similar rooms, cold showers, and—its chief benefit—a rooftop terrace. Next door on Rue Serrajine is the Hotel Mauritania, but it has not been recommended.

Camping is possible at the Camping Moulay Slimane, which is in a pleasant wooded area on Rue Moulay Slimane about a block off Avenue Allal Ben Abdallah. In addition to decent campsites, there are also hot showers, a café-bar, and a swimming pool. The main negative to staying here, though, is having to maneuver past a phalanx of would-be guides and fast-talking hustlers that seems to have become a permanent fixture at the entrance. To get here, walk southwest on Avenue Hassan II, across Place Ahmed El Mansour and past the Hotel de Fes on your right and the Hotel Volubilis on your left. Turn left on the first street just after the Hotel Volubilis and then right on the next street, which is Rue Moulay Slimane. The campground is a short distance down the street on the left side.

Restaurants and Cafés

Most of Fez's best restaurants and cafés are in the Ville Nouvelle. Boulevard Mohammed V and the side streets just off the Boulevard have a great concentration of restaurants. On one such street off to the left as you walk up Mohammed V from Hassan II—Rue Kaïd Ahmed—the Restaurant Chamonix at No.5 and the Casse-Croute Belkhaiat at No.41 are both recommended. The former specializes in grilled lamb and tomatoes, and the latter serves good couscous for about $2.50 per person. For a more substantial meal in a semiromantic setting, try the Restaurant Roi de la Bière at 59 Boulevard Mohammed V, about a block up the street from Rue Kaïd Ahmed (going away from Hassan II) on the right side. It serves a very filling three-course meal for about $3.50 and offers a full selection of Moroccan wines. There are several other restaurants in the area; walk around and check out the menus. Also on Boulevard Mohammed V at No. 81, try the Boulangerie Pâtisserie Epi d'Or for a breakfast of croissants or other pastries and coffee; they offer a great selection of pastries.

If you think that your stomach has been properly initiated, you might want to try some of the simpler restaurants in Fez El B'ali near the Bab Boujeloud such as the Restaurant des Jeunes at 16 Rue Sejjarine. A full meal that includes souplike harira, a tajine, and a few other dishes for about $3. Many of the places in this area don't have specific menus with standard prices, so it's a good idea to ask the prices before you order. For a more upscale restaurant with a menu, but somewhat touristy and pricey, try the Restaurant Dar Saada or at least just stop by for a visit. It's housed in a beautiful renovated palace at 21 Rue Attarine, a wonderful location in the medina.

Getting Things Done and Shopping

Money

Foreign currency and travelers checks can be exchanged at any of the banks on Boulevard Mohammed V. VISA card advances can be arranged at Crédit du Maroc on Mohammed V. After hours, try the exchange windows at major hotels such as the Hotel Palais Jamaï or the Hotel de Fes.

Photography

Film is usually available in the gift shops of major hotels, but any other photographic supplies in Fez could be difficult. I'm sure that in a city as large as Fez, there must be a photo store, but I wasn't able to find it.

Post, Telegraph, and Telephone Office

The main post, telegraph, and telephone office (PTT) is at the corner of Avenue Hassan II and Boulevard Mohammed V. Winter hours are 8.30 A.M. to 12 P.M. and 2.30 to 6 P.M.; summer hours are 8 A.M. to 2 P.M. The telephone office is open until 9 P.M.

Shopping

Fez is a souvenir shopper's dream. The shops and stalls in the alleyways of the medina (Fez El B'ali), which is the scene of most souvenir hunting, are overflowing with traditional Moroccan crafts and kitsch. If you think that the competition between shops selling the same things

Coppersmith in Fez Medina, Fez, Morocco. *Photo by Scott Wayne.*

somehow brings down prices, you're wrong. Despite the abundance of yellow slippers, brass lamps, scented cedar boxes, red leather wallets, and assorted other items, it's more a seller's than a buyer's market. You may find one of the best selections of crafts in Morocco here, but you can probably get better prices elsewhere. Be prepared to bargain furiously, but be prepared for guffaws, however low the prices you offer, and don't be surprised if the shopkeeper shoves you out the door. They don't need your business—there are plenty of suckers who will buy from them.

At some point during your visit to the medina, you will undoubtedly visit a carpet "factory." They are more like mini department stores for traditional carpets than factories or workshops. Usually, the presence of a single working loom makes it a "factory." Teenage girls are usually the weavers.

Carpets are one of the most popular, but also costliest, souvenirs to take home from Morocco. The Bet Nijjarin, a fourteenth-century house, is now the Cooperative of Moroccan Carpets. Before being recently converted into a cooperative by its owners, the house was owned by the wealthy Glina family. On the death of Mr. Glina, however, his four wives—two of whom lived upstairs and two down—decided to make the conversion. Carpets as small as doormats and big enough for a 9- by 12-foot room are stacked from the floor to the ceiling of each room. The largest rooms are reserved for presentations of the carpets, usually done while sipping complimentary mint tea served in small glasses. Naturally, they want you to buy one, but if you only want to look, then let them know before they begin showing you the full range of carpets available. The salesmen are cunning, so be prepared to fend off their persistent advances. The salesmen explained that there are basically four styles of carpets:

- Berber carpets are hand-woven wool carpets with no dyes and minimal designs; each of Morocco's more than thirty-five tribes has its own particular design. The carpet is inauthentic if you can pull the knots out—a sure sign that it was machine-made. The lack of intricate and colorful geometric designs doesn't make this style a favorite, but their authenticity makes them more expensive than the others.
- Arab carpets are half cotton, half wool, with an intricate design in the center that is often made to allow alignment with the *mihrab* of a mosque—the pulpit-like structure showing the direction of Mecca, which all Muslims must face in prayer. The area around the design is usually devoid of decoration. By Moroccan law, an "Arab" carpet must have 225,000 knots per square meter.
- Fez carpets are the local high-quality specialty. It takes as much as a year and a half to weave a 9- by 12-foot Fassi ("of Fez") carpet with the requisite 365,000 wool knots per square meter; prices average about $2,500.
- Old Style carpets have far fewer knots and are not as tightly woven as the Arab and Fassi carpets.

The main government criteria for evaluation and certification of carpets are

- Number of knots per square meter—the higher the number, the higher the quality.

- Wool from live sheep is of higher quality.
- More complex and beautiful designs make a carpet higher in value.
- Natural dyes are a sign of high quality: poppies for red, mint for green, henna for yellow, and indigo for blue.

If a carpet doesn't have an official government certification on the back, then you can't be sure of its quality. From best to basic, these are the four official quality levels: *extra superior*, *superior*, *moyenne* (average), and *courante* (ordinary).

In addition to the styles described above, there are also the following five, each of which is available in at least three out of four quality levels and priced accordingly (approximate prices):

Styles	Extra	Superior	Moyenne	Courante
Moderne	$156.00	$113.00	$87.50	$62.50
Rabat		$113.00	$87.50	$62.50
Gene Rabat		$ 94.00	$75.00	$62.50
Mid-Atlas		$ 62.50	$44.00	$31.25
Haouz		$ 62.50	$ 50.00	$37.50
(100% cotton)				

Bookstores. There are two bookstores in the Ville Nouvelle that offer a good selection of English and American books: the Librairie du Centre at 60 Boulevard Mohammed V and the Librairie de l'Oasis at 68 Avenue Hassan II. Gift shops at a few of the major hotels also usually stock a few foreign books and magazines.

THINGS TO SEE

Fez El B'ali

The most fascinating sights of Fez are found in Fez El B'ali, commonly known as "the medina" or "old city." Although the medina really isn't as confusing as guides and hustlers make it out to be, you may want to hire an official or unofficial guide to show you the way and keep other prospective guides at bay. A guide can also take you to some of the many sights that aren't normally visited by tourists and described in guide-books.

My guide, Yusuf, whom I described above, took me through a confusing maze of alleys to tanneries that are seldom visited by tourists. The route we followed was so circuitous that I couldn't begin to tell you how to find them.

We ducked through an ancient doorway and into a dark foyer. As my eyes adjusted to the dark, I saw two sets of white smiling teeth and then

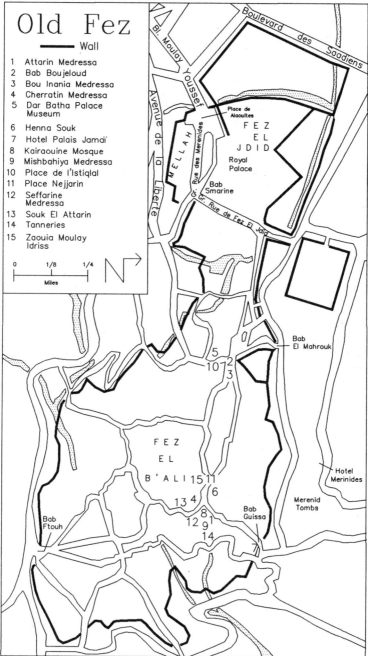

Old Fez

— Wall

1 Attarin Medressa
2 Bab Boujeloud
3 Bou Inania Medressa
4 Cherratin Medressa
5 Dar Batha Palace Museum
6 Henna Souk
7 Hotel Palais Jamaï
8 Kairaouine Mosque
9 Mishbahiya Medressa
10 Place de l'Istiqlal
11 Place Nejjarin
12 Seffarine Medressa
13 Souk El Attarin
14 Tanneries
15 Zaouia Moulay Idriss

0   1/8   1/4
Miles

Bl. Moulay Youssef

Avenue de la Liberté

Boulevard des Saadiens

Place de Alaouites

MELLAH

Rue des Merenides

FEZ EL JDID

Royal Palace

Bab Smarine

Gr. Rue de Fez El Jdid

Bab El Mahrouk

FEZ EL B'ALI

Hotel Merinides

Merenid Tombs

Bab Ftouh

Bab Guissa

Hotel Palais Jamaï

gradually the teenaged faces that belonged to each set. For a moment, I shuddered and my stomach tightened as I wondered if I had been led here to be robbed. I had heard rumors about the mysterious dangers of the medina, and now my imagination was running at full speed. Yusuf greeted the boys and continued around a corner into a sunny courtyard of vats dug into the ground. A heavy, suffocating odor rose from the murky green liquid in each vat. As we tip-toed across the slippery stepping-stones that formed narrow walkways between the vats, Yusuf pointed to a vat and told me about a "Hollandaise" who had fallen into that one. We stepped over a stone conduit that fed a fast stream of water toward a big, round metal drum in the corner of the courtyard. A man in a wet, ragged shirt was stuffing skins through a hatch in the drum and then turning it with a great crank on the side. We ducked into another doorway and mounted a dark stone staircase to a row of dank, dirty rooms that looked down on the courtyard. Each room was packed from floor to ceiling with animal skins at different stages of the curing process. Half hidden by a heap of skin scraps and sawdust, another stone stairway led to the roof where the skins were being dyed yellow or blue and laid in the sun to dry. After drying, the skins are softened and taken to the souks to be sold to artisans. Our next stop was the Talaa Kebira, one of the main thoroughfares and the starting point for most tours of the medina.

Actually, one of the best places to start a tour of the medina is at the chromatic tiled gate of Bab Boujeloud, one of its principal entrances. City buses and some private-line intercity buses conveniently stop nearby at the Place Baghdadi, so it's easy to get here from both Fez El Jdid and the Ville Nouvelle. City buses are also available a few minute's walk to the southeast at Place de l'Istiqlal in front of the Dar Batha museum.

If you have the time, visit the Museum of Moroccan Arts & Crafts at the Dar Batha before heading into the medina. This restored palace is a stunning showcase for one of the best collections of traditional Moroccan craftsmanship in Morocco. One room contains a beautiful collection of Middle Atlas Arab and Berber carpets. Other collections include carved wooden furniture, wall sections, and decorations that are all remarkable in their intricacy. The museum is open daily (except Tuesdays) from 9 A.M. to 11:30 A.M. and 3 P.M. to 6 P.M. Admission is free.

From the museum, walk north to the Talaa Kebira and turn right. If you see the Hotel Amrani on your left, then you have turned too soon. Once you are on Talaa Kebira, look on your right for the entrance to the Bou Inania medressa (place of study and lodging), one of the most beautiful and well-preserved Merenid-era buildings you'll see in the medina. It was built as a medressa for students of Islam by the Sultan Abou Inan during his rule from 1351 to 1358. Most of the beautiful tile and stucco work, as well as intricately carved cedar panels, are original. Much of this artwork adorns the domed entrance foyer, big central courtyard, and two prayer hall wings. Stairways lead from each wing to the monastery-like cells that comprised the students' quarters and to the roof. If you can go to the roof, bring your camera because the view of the medina is fairly good from there. The medressa is open daily (except Friday morning) from 8 A.M. to 5 P.M. Admission is free, but you're expected to give the guard a dirham tip.

Across from the medressa is a water clock that was also built by Sultan Abou Inan. Most of the clock is still intact—thirteen windows, each with a brass bowl beneath it that supposedly caught a weight that was pushed out each window every hour. The clock is no longer functioning, and no one is certain how it once really worked.

Continuing along the Talaa Kebira, there's a large fondouk (inn for traders) on the left that was also once a prison. Today, it serves as a "garage" for mules and horses and as a storage area. The Talaa begins to rise over the crest of a hill; at the top, it changes its name to Rue Ech Cherabliyyin ("Street of the Slipper Makers") as it enters an area of leather craftsmen and shops. The yellow and white slippers you will see piled on the tables here are a Fez specialty called *babouches* . At the foot of the hill, the street enters an area called the Souk El Attarin (spice sellers market), which extends as far as the northeast corner of the Kairouine mosque straight ahead.

The Attarin Souk and its many small alleys and passageways compose the heart of the medina, an area replete with markets, medressas, and monuments. It's a perfect place to wander and explore the medina's variety of sights, sounds, and smells. Rather than try to lead you through this relatively compact area, here are the major recommended sights:

- **The Henna Souk.** A few stalls selling henna and various traditional cosmetics such as kohl and antimony as well as several materials reputedly used for casting magical spells and warding off evil curses.
- **Place Nejjarin.** In and around this square are carpenters hammering and chiseling away at cords of wood and metal-workers pounding and shaping hunks of metal into household goods and tourist souvenirs.
- **Dar Saada Restaurant.** An upscale, touristy, and pricey restaurant housed in a beautiful renovated palace that's worth at least just a look around.
- **Zaouia Moulay Idriss.** Moulay Idriss II, recognized as the founder of Fez, is entombed and enshrined here. The inside is open only to Muslims who come here to pay respects to the now-saintly spirit of Moulay Idriss. Through one of the zaouia's wide, open entrances, you can look in and see the tomb and, usually, several devotees praying with lit candles and pieces of incense. Many of the devotees are women who flock here for good luck with childbirth. It's customary to buy chunks of sandalwood and long green and white candles

A street in Fez Medina, Fez, Morocco. *Photo by Scott Wayne.*

striped with gold foil from the shops and stalls just outside the shrine. There are also small shops nearby that sell pink, green, and brown chunks of *nougah* or nougat because it's considered good luck to give this to children after visiting the shrine. The wooden barriers set across the surrounding alleyways block the passage of horses and mules, but they were also originally meant to mark the boundaries of the zaouia beyond which non-Muslims weren't permitted to go until the French took over in 1911.

- **The Attarin Medressa.** Built in 1325 by the Sultan Abou Said, it's one of the oldest Merenid medressas in Fez. As with the Bou Inania medressa, the stucco and wood carving here are magnificent, particularly around the inner courtyard. Again, if it's possible to climb the stairs to the students' quarters and the roof, bring your camera for photos of the view of the Kairouine mosque and the surrounding medina. The medressa served as student housing for the Kairouine university until as recently as the 1950s.

- **The medressas of Mishbahiya, Seffarine and Cherratin.** All are located around the Kairouine mosque and can be visited, although they aren't as complete and well maintained as the Bou Inania and the Attarin.

- **The Kairouine mosque.** The most imposing building in the medina and largest mosque in Morocco. It can't be visited by non-Muslims, though. Originally founded in A.D. 857, significant additions were made by the caliph of Cordova in the tenth century and by Sultan Abd er Rahman in the twelfth century. The complex was designed to accommodate as many as 20,000 worshipers. As you walk around the building, you can get a fairly good idea of the mosque's immensity through its open gates and doors.

- **The Tanneries.** Some of the city's biggest tanneries are not far from the Kairouine mosque. Go from the southeast corner of the mosque north-northeastward approximately following the river, but not crossing it. You'll pass the street leading to the Bein el Moudoun bridge, but continue straight ahead to the tanneries.

- **The Hotel Palais Jamaï.** At the northern side of the medina; see the hotel section for more information.

Fez El Jdid

Going to or from Fez El B'ali, you may want to make a quick visit to Fez El Jdid. From Bab Boujeloud, you can walk straight down Avenue des Français to Grande Rue de Fez El Jdid and one of entrances to Fez El Jdid in about 10 minutes. On your left, you will pass the Boujeloud gardens, which are worth a brief visit if the Avenue des Français entrance is open. The Grande Rue isn't renowned for any historical sights, but it does offer

Interior of a medressa in the Fez Medina, Fez, Morocco.
Photo by Scott Wayne.

a glimpse at a daily medina that's generally unaffected by foreign tourism, unlike life in parts of Fez El B'ali.

At the end of the Grande Rue, turn right on to the Grande Rue des Merenides and you will be entering the mellah, which was once a thriving Jewish ghetto. Nothing Jewish really remains except for the buildings of two small synagogues, neither of which functions as a synagogue today, and a Jewish cemetery along the edge of Fez El Jdid. Some of the houses that were built here in the eighteenth and nineteenth centuries are more non-Arab than distinctly Jewish, with their cramped façades and fancy ironwork.

NEAR FEZ

Fez is a good base from which to head south to explore part of the Middle Atlas mountains. The most straightforward route into the mountains, yet seldom explored by travelers, is the 61-km (38-mile) paved road through Imouzzer du Kandar, Ifrane, and Azrou. Some of the best hikes in the Middle Atlas mountains start in these towns, but they still pall in comparison to the possible hikes in the High Atlas mountains. Ifrane is popular as a base for day trips to the ski slopes of nearby Mischliffen. The crossroads city of Azrou offers ample opportunities for day hikes and trips through the surrounding cedar forests and to springs and waterfalls. From Azrou the road continues another 82 km (51 miles) to Khenifra, but there really aren't any worthwhile stops and nearby sidetrips along this stretch.

Imouzzer du Kandar

There's not much to the town of Imouzzer du Kandar—a small Monday souk, a main street and central square, a few inexpensive hotels and restaurants, and a municipal swimming pool. The biggest influx of travelers comes in July for the Fête des Pommes or harvest festival. The rest of the year, most visitors who stop here are on their way to picnics, paddle boats, and fishing at Dayet Aaoua, which is about 9 km (5 1/2 miles) south of town just off the road to Ifrane. If you don't have a car, you'll have to hitch a ride, take the Ifrane bus, or walk along the road. The two-star Chalet du Lac hotel has rooms and a restaurant along the lake, but you can also camp on just about any of the pleasant, grassy spots along the lakefront. For those with rugged cars, a dirt road around the lake marks the beginning of a 70-km (43-mile) route to other lakes in the region.

Another possible one- to two-day hike from town is the 10-km (6-mile) one-way trek to the 1,768-m (5,800-ft) summit of Jebel Abad. From Imouzzer, ask for directions to the piste to Sefrou, which starts

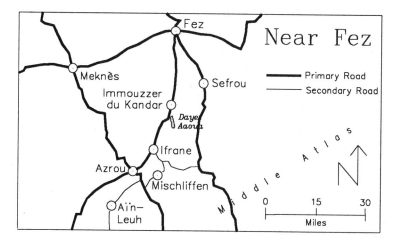

Near Fez

Fez
Meknès
Immouzzer du Kandar
Sefrou
Daye Aaoua
Ifrane
Azrou
Mischliffen
Aïn-Leuh

■■■■ Primary Road
──── Secondary Road

Middle Atlas

N

0   15   30
Miles

about 6 km (4 miles) out of town, and follow that to a gravelly trail on your left. The trail leads to the summit. A small stone pillar marks the highest point of the summit.

Back in town, you can stay at the three-star Hotel Royal, which is the best place in Imouzzer; it has forty-two rooms, all with heating, and some with balconies (the preferred ones to have). There's also a good restaurant and bar. For lower room rates and fewer amenities, but still comfortable, try the one-star Hotel des Truites, which also has a restaurant and bar. To hit bottom in quality and price, try the no-star Hotel du Centre conveniently located next to the bus station.

To get to Imouzzer from Fez, there are five buses daily for the 1-hour trip and frequent grand taxi departures. Most of the buses continue on to Ifrane and Azrou, but to go further—as to Khenifra—you'll have to change at Azrou.

Ifrane

The town of Ifrane is a surreal French Alpine creation 61 km (38 miles) from Fez. It was built in 1929 for the French administrators of Morocco. Today, its luxury chalets are inhabited by Moroccan government ministries and wealthy Moroccans; even King Hassan II has a chalet here—the Royal Hunting Lodge—which is visible across the valley from the main part of town. There's really nothing distinctly Moroccan about the place, thus it's not exactly a popular destination for foreign travelers. Between January and March, most visitors come here for the ski slopes at the nearby resort of Mischliffen. Before getting a taxi from town to the Mischliffen lodge and restaurant, you can rent ski equipment from the Café-Restaurant Chamonix.

Other services available in town include a Syndicat d'Initiative that offers basic information about the area and map of the town; it's near the Mobil station. The post and telephone office is across from the station. All three offices are open in the winter from 8 A.M. to noon and 2 to 6 P.M. and in the summer from 8 A.M. to noon and 4 to 6 P.M. Buses to Azrou, Imouzzer, and Fez depart from a lot next to the post office—a direct bus to Fez departs at 5:30 and 8 A.M. For money exchange, try the Hotel Mischliffen.

Although Ifrane isn't popular with foreign tourists, Moroccans flock here and fill the few hotels in town. Finding a room can sometimes be difficult. The most inexpensive place to stay, if it has reopened, is the youth hostel and then next in price is the one-star Hotel Tilleuls. Next in price is the three-star Hotel Perce-Neige with twenty-three rooms, all with telephones and heating, a restaurant, and a bar. The three-star Grand Hotel on Rue de la Poste, with thirty rooms, a restaurant and bar, and even a hair salon , is another possibility. At the top of the scale is the five-star Hotel Mischliffen with ninety-five rooms, all with telephones and heating, a restaurant and bar, a nightclub, and a swimming pool. Supposedly rooms can also be rented from private families in town, but that is something you would have to arrange on your own. The last option is camping, which is really only possible in the summer, unless, of course, you have the appropriate equipment for cold-weather camping. However, even in the summer, you'll have to make reservations for a space in the campground—tel. 6156—because it can get quite full.

Aside from skiing at Mischliffen, the only other thing to do from or in Ifrane is to hike 4 km (2 1/2 miles) out of town along the road to Ozouyia to the Cascades d'Ifrane. I was unable to make this trip, so if you manage to see the falls, please write us with the details.

A last note about skiing: As with skiing at Oukaïmeden in the High Atlas mountains, equipment and slope conditions aren't always—if ever—great. After sliding down an Oukaïmeden slope on my rear and nearly breaking my legs because of antiquated bindings, I decided against testing the Mischliffen slopes. Safety can't be emphasized enough when skiing in Morocco.

Azrou

Azrou is at a crossroads 17 km (10 1/2 miles) south of Ifrane with well-paved roads leading to Fez, Meknes, Khenifra, and Midelt. It's a convenient stop between these cities and worth an overnight stay if you want to visit the Tuesday souk and Cooperative Artisanale in town and the surrounding hills and Oum er Rbia falls just outside of town.

The Tuesday souk is an interesting spectacle because it's the principal regional trading center for the Berbers from the surrounding villages. Many of them come here to buy and sell food, clothing, and household supplies as well as a few handicrafts, including carpets and cedar wood carvings. The souk is across the valley from the town and usually starts before sunrise: just follow the crowds.

For a better selection of handicrafts—at prices lower than just about anywhere else in Morocco—visit the Cooperative Artisanal or, as it's also called, the Ensemble Artisanal downhill from the main square, Place Hassan II. At the cooperative, you can get a good idea of what crafts are made locally and even watch some of the weavers and carpenters at work. Although some of the finished products are for sale, better prices can be found at the souk and a few touristy shops in town.

After visiting the market and cooperative, head for the hills and down to the river. If the weather is good, you can spend a pleasant day wandering through the cedar forests on the hills and then go fishing at the river. Camping may be possible at the river.

Outside of town, the chief attraction is the Oum er Rbia falls near the village of Aïn Leuh 30 kms (19 miles) due south of Azrou. Once you've made it to Aïn Leuh, you can either hitch a ride, hire a taxi, or, if you're feeling particularly energetic, walk the 33-km (20 1/2 mile) forested trail to the bridge over the falls. From the bridge it's about a fifteen-minute walk to the actual falls—a spectacle of more than 30 waterfalls spilling and spraying over the edge of a high cliff. The trail continues winding through the mountains all the way to Khenifra about 30 km (19 miles) further.

Back in town, there are a few hotels and a youth hostel, but don't expect anything on a grand scale. The best is the one-star Hotel des Cedres at Place Mohammed V; balconies are its chief amenity. The unrated Hotel Beausejour is slightly more basic, but also has clean rooms with balconies for about $3 to $4. The Hotel Ziz is near Place Mohammed V and has also been recommended. The youth hostel is in a quiet, isolated location about 2 km (1 mile) from town and not really worth the hike, because the hotels charge about the same for a night.

Transportation to and from Azrou is easy, with over seven daily buses to Fez (stopping en route at Ifrane and Imouzzer); four to Meknes; three to Khenifra, Kasba Tadla, Beni Mellal, and Marrakesh; and five to Midelt and Er-Rachidia.

PART THREE

⁂

Algeria

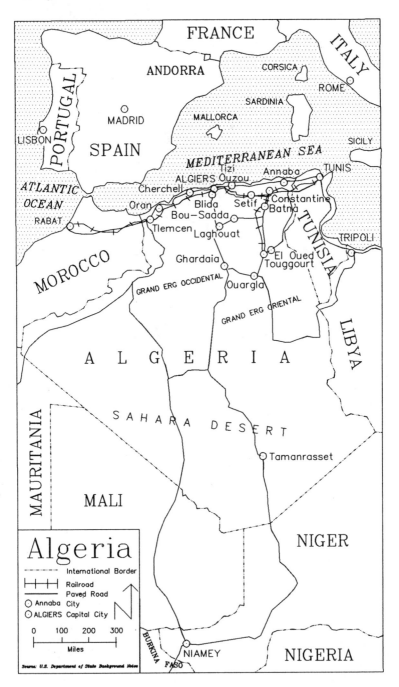

Algeria

International Border
Railroad
Paved Road
◯ Annaba City
◯ ALGIERS Capital City

0   100   200   300
Miles

Source: U.S. Department of State Background Notes

Chapter 11

Algeria

Name:	Democratic and Popular Republic of Algeria (Al Jumhiriyya Al Jaza'iriyya Al Dimuqratiyya Ash Shabiyya)
Political status:	Socialist government with one legislative house
Capital:	Algiers
Population:	23.84 million (U.N. statistics, 1989)
Land area:	2,381,741 square kilometers (919,595 square miles)
Language:	Arabic (official), French (widely spoken), various Berber dialects
Currency:	Dinar (DA); DA 1 = 100 centimes
Urban population:	49 percent
Rural:	51 percent
Doubling time for population:	22 years
Ethnic composition (percentage):	Arab, 82.6; Berber, 17; French, 0.1; Other, 0.3
Religious affiliation (percentage):	Sunni Muslim, 99.1; Roman Catholic, 0.5; Other, 0.3;
Major cities:	Algiers, 1,483,000; Oran, 590,000; Constantine, 438,000; Annaba, 310,000; Batna, 182,000

When Arab conquerors first entered Algeria in the late seventh century A.D., they called it *jazirat al maghreb*—literally, "island of the west." For them the fertile heartland of the region—a relatively narrow expanse of land across the north—was an island between the Mediterranean Sea and a "sea of sand" that came to be called the Sahara. Although the country is now predominantly Arab and Muslim, it is still culturally diverse, with a large population of Berbers, the original inhabitants, in several parts of the country. Unlike its Maghrebian neighbors Morocco and Tunisia, Algeria was a full-fledged French colony with over a million settlers. This legacy deeply affected all parts of Algerian society and precipitated a long, bloody fight for independence. Many of the country's challenges today can be traced to its struggle to create a modern Arab, rather than French, state and nation. For foreigners who are unfamiliar with the growing pangs of an evolving nation-state, a visit to Algeria can be quite an insightful experience.

For travelers, Algeria is still a comparatively virgin place to visit. Mass tourism has not yet discovered Algeria's well-preserved Roman ruins, beautiful unspoiled stretches of coastline, Atlas mountains replete with streams, lakes, and forests, and a Sahara desert that is much more than immense shifting sand dunes and veiled men on camels. Adventuring in Algeria is as diverse as its land and sites, but it lacks the sophisticated facilities and easy access of Morocco and Tunisia, where tourism has been a well-developed economic sector for several years. The Algerian government is quickly working to change this through various projects. In the meantime, you can still tour the countryside, ski and trek in the mountains, wander through the Sahara with a camel and a "Blue Man," or wander the old Mozabite streets of Ghardaïa—either on your own, with some patience and perseverance, or on an organized tour.

THE NATURAL ENVIRONMENT

Physical Characteristics

Algeria's geographic position at approximately the center of North Africa makes it a Mediterranean, African, and Middle Eastern country. Composed of a total area of 2,381,741 sq. km and sharing 6,000 km of borders with Tunisia, Libya, Niger, Mali, Mauritania, and Morocco, Algeria is a diverse combination of people, culture, and land.

With 1,200 km of Mediterranean coast, a variety of Mediterranean invaders and influences have had relatively easy entry into Algeria throughout its history—Phoenicians, Carthaginians, Romans, exiled Jews, Vandals, Byzantines, Arabs, Ottoman Turks, and French colonists and rulers.

Generally, these invaders settled in the coastal plains and foothills just north of the Tellien Atlas mountain ranges, a region known as the Tell. Except for the French, most of the invaders rarely ventured into and beyond the mountains. Even today most of the population and major cities are concentrated in the Tell.

The Tellien Atlas mountains form a great swathlike barrier across northern Algeria. Starting from the west just south of Tlemcen, this range is an extension of the Atlas mountains of Morocco and is known as the subrange of Monts de Tlemcen. Jebel Dar Sheikh, which is southwest of Tlemcen, stands at an altitude of 1,616 m (5,302 ft) as the highest peak in this subrange.

Farther to the east-northeast is a wider subrange with foothills and other lower portions that extend all the way to the coastline—the Massif de l'Ouarsenis. At the northeastern edge of this massif, another subrange begins—the Atlas de Blida mountains, named for the city of Blida, which lies at its base. One of the highest points in these mountains is the ski resort of Chréa at an altitude of 1,492 m (4,895 ft). The area around Chréa is considered a national park.

Between Blida and Algiers, a distance of approximately 40 to 50 km depending on which roads you follow, is the Mitidja plain, one of the most fertile agricultural areas in Algeria, thus a center of development throughout Algeria's history.

One of the most significant subranges of the Tellien Atlas mountains is the Grande Kabylie. Actually, the Grande Kabylie mountains are probably substantial enough in their own right to be considered a separate range. The Grand Kabylie range roughly encompasses the area from Bejaïa west through Tizi Ouzou to the Atlas de Blida mountains and south to the edge of the High Plateaus. During the independence struggle, the mountainous terrain, numerous valleys, and traditionally fierce independence of its people—the Kabyle Berbers—proved to be a major obstacle to French efforts to completely colonize Algeria. The Grande Kabylie mountains are also known for the beautiful snow-covered peaks of its southern subrange—the Djurdjura massif. The two highest peaks of this region are Ras Timedouine (2,305 m/7,562 ft) and Lalla Khedidja (2,308 m/7,572 ft).

As with Chréa, this mountainous area of gorges, lakes, and high plateaus is also considered a national park. From the main settlement of Tikjda at an altitude of 1,475 m (4,839 ft), there is easy access to ski runs in the winter and hiking trails, mountain-climbing "paths" and caves (for spelunking or cave exploration), weather conditions permitting, the rest of the year.

From the eastern edge of the Grande Kabylie mountains, the Atlas Tellien mountains are broken into several smaller subranges. Foremost among these are the Petite Kabylie mountains with spectacular cliffs and foothills right up to the coastline forming an area called the Corniche Kabyle that easily rivals the natural beauty of California's renowned Big Sur coast.

South of Constantine and detached from the Tellien Atlas mountains is the Aurès mountain range. Traditionally, the Aurès mountains have been the home and stronghold of the Chaouïa Berbers. During the French period, this area proved to be one of the most difficult for them to subdue. The mountains offered a nearly impregnable set of natural fortresses for the Berbers. The El Kantara pass through the Aurès mountains, however, was a major transit point to the High Plateaus and Sahara desert and thus considered worthy, perhaps, of many bloody battles.

The High Plateaus comprise a broad area beginning south of and

Grand Erg Oriental, The Sahara, Algeria. *Photo by Scott Wayne.*

running almost parallel to the Tellien Atlas mountains. For the most part, it's a fairly desolate area where esparto grass, known locally as *alfa*, is about the only prevalent form of life. However, a large portion of these grasslands are used for cattle grazing. This is a good prelude to the Sahara, which really begins further south beyond yet another range of mountains.

These "Sahara" mountains are generally known as the Saharan Atlas range, although they consist of a few subranges. The most notable subrange is called Les Monts des Ouled Naïl, named for its main inhabitants—the Ouled Naïl tribe. The women of this tribe are renowned for their distinctive silver jewelry and facial decorations.

Beyond these mountains is the Sahara, a vast region that comprises more than 85 percent of the total area of Algeria—one of the world's biggest deserts. The Arabs call it an "ocean without water" ("*bahr bila maa*") because parts of it resemble a huge sea of sand with vast shifting dunes known locally as *ergs*.

Actually, the dunes comprise only about 20 percent of the Sahara's total surface. They are concentrated in three parts of the Sahara: to the east just south of Ghardaïa-Ouargla-Hassi Messaoud is the Grand Erg Oriental; to the west of Ghardaïa and north of Timimoun is the Grand Erg Occidental; and in the southwest are the most isolated ergs—Erg Chech, Erg Er Raoul, and Erg Iguidi.

The rest of the Sahara is a varied landscape that includes *hamadas* (rock-strewn areas usually devoid of plant life), *tassilis* (rocky plateaus), *regs* (similar to hamadas, but broader expanses of land), and *gueltas* (ponds created by underground springs and streams and occasional rain). There are also mountain ranges and deep canyons such as the Hoggar (around Tamanrasset; also called the Ahaggar) with peaks as high as 2,908 m, or 9,541 ft (Tahat) that are occasionally snow-capped, the Tassili du Hoggar (south of Tamanrasset), Tefedest range (north of Tamanrasset), and the Tassili-n-Ajjer (north of Djanet; a region mostly of deep canyons but also a few peaks).

The Hoggar mountains form a massif of several geological parts with an average altitude of about 762 m (2,500 ft). One of the principal mountain chains of this massif is the Atakor, a lunar-like landscape of ancient volcanoes and jagged peaks. Towering well above the other peaks at an altitude of 2,585 m (8,481 ft) is Assekrem, site of Father Charles de Foucauld's reclusive "hermitage," which was built in 1905.

The Tassili du Hoggar is a set of relatively high sedimentary rock plateaus that begins approximately 300 km south of Tamanrasset and extends to the Niger border. The plateaus are characterized by enormous fingers of sculpted rock, all in a variety of shapes ranging from sharp pinnacles to squatty mushroomlike formations. Great sand dunes fill the spaces in between.

The Tefedest region is a granite massif beginning 300 km north of Tamanrasset that is about 130 km (81 miles) and 20 km (12 1/2 miles) wide. Some of its peaks average as high as 1,524 m (5,000 ft), with one peak—the Garet El Djenoun—reaching an altitude of 2,327 m (7,635 ft).

Algeria's climate varies dramatically from region to region. Along the coastal plains and lowlands, an area at approximately the same latitude as southern California (give or take a few degrees), the climate is essentially Mediterranean, with moderate temperatures and rainfall. In the Tell, summer temperatures average about 21° to 24° C (70° to 75° F) and in the winter 10° to 12° C (50° to 54° F). It can rain as much as 67 cm (about 27 in) per year in this region, but mostly between September and May.

Rainfall can often be even heavier in the Tellien Atlas mountains during these months. Freezing temperatures and even snow aren't uncommon at higher altitudes. In fact, on the highest peaks such as Ras Timedouine (2,305 m, or 7,562 ft) and Lalla Khedidja (2,308 m, or 7,572 ft) there is snow almost all year.

The Tellien Atlas mountains, however, catch most of the precipitation and thus prevent much rain from reaching the High Plateaus and the Sahara. Winter temperatures in these latter regions are often just above freezing, particularly at night. At higher elevations such as in the

Hoggar mountains, freezing temperatures are common with occasional rain and even light snow possible.

In most of the Sahara, though, rain is quite rare, with some parts receiving none at all for several years. Summer temperatures are some of the highest in the world—occasionally over 120° F. Winter temperatures at lower elevations of the Sahara can also be intolerably hot. Although Sahara travel in the summer is not recommended, you must also exercise caution in the winter.

Flora and Fauna

Algeria's flora and fauna vary from region to region. In the lowlands and on the coastal plains north of the Tellien Atlas and Saharan Atlas mountains, the land is primarily used for farming. In the Tellien Atlas mountain ranges, there's a great variety of flora and fauna. Even in the Sahara, which is stereotypically regarded as a vast wasteland, there are plants and animals, much more than I imagined but much less than what existed thousands of years ago.

Along the coastal plains the only truly indigenous plant remaining after hundreds, perhaps thousands of years of cultivation and human intervention is the grapevine. However, even that has long since been farmed. Not surprisingly, most animal life has been pushed into the Tellien Atlas mountains by rapid population growth along the plains.

In the mountains, the most prevalent flora are forests of cedar and cork, particularly at lower elevations. At higher and wetter elevations, Aleppo pine, cork oak, and evergreens are common. In the area around Chréa, zeen and holm oaks are common. Similar oaks, as well as mastic trees, heath trees and shrubs, and holly, olive, and pine trees, can be seen in the Chiffa gorges near Chréa.

Farther to the west, at Theniet El Had in the Ouarsenis massif, an entire national park is dedicated to protecting the cedars of the region— the National Park of Cedars of Theniet El Had.

Aside from protecting the flora of certain regions by declaring them national parks, the Algerian government has also initiated several reforestation projects. One of its more successful projects has been at the National Park of Belezma, which is situated about 7 km northwest of Batna in the Belezma mountains. The park was created in 1984 by the Ministry of Waterworks, the Environment and Forests for the conservation and restoration of the flora and fauna of this region. It's especially known for extensive cedar groves that have been restored in the last two decades, after being napalmed by the French during the revolution. The Belezma region was a nationalist bastion during the revolution. Several bloody battles were waged in the Belezma woods and around the peaks of Djebels (Mounts) Chellala, Touggourt, and Boumerzoug in the park and Djebels Refaa and Mestaoua just outside the park.

Other prominent trees founds in the northern mountainous regions of Algeria include the black pine, thugas (a cypress-like tree), and various species of maples.

Animals in this region include:

Birds	Green woodpecker, blackbird, chickadee, Bonelli eagle, partridge, magpie, hawk owl, royal eagle, falcon, skylark, quail, dove, turtledove, wood pigeon
Mammals	Hare, Barbary ape and monkeys, *Felis caracal*, wild cat, serval, wild boar, jackal, fox, mongoose, striped hyena, ibex, partridge, and various reptiles and frogs.

On the High Plateaus and pre-Sahara regions between the Tellien and Saharan Atlas mountains, the drier climate and thinner soils support far less flora and fauna. The most prevalent types of vegetation are drought-resistant shrubs and grasses such as esparto grass. In the mid-1970s the Algerian government began a massive reforestation program to help control erosion and expansion of the Sahara in this region. The main objective was to create a *barrage vert* ("green dam or barrier") along a 1,500-km-long (930-mile) ridgeline of the Sahara Atlas from Morocco to Tunisia. The line was supposed to be 20 km wide (12 1/2 miles) and consist mostly of Aleppo pine. So far only part of the barrage vert has been planted.

In the Sahara, which comprises more than 80 percent of Algeria, thorny acacia trees are common throughout the region, but especially near *gueltas* (ponds) in canyon areas. The Tassili-n-Ajjer canyon area is renowned for its 1,000-year-old cypresses; in fact, a valley there has been dubbed the Valley of the Cypresses. Other plants found in the Sahara include a pealike plant called *fabaceae*, fig and olive trees, tamarisk trees, and doum and date palms.

Animals in the Sahara include camels (actually called *dromedaries*), of course, the fennec (see the Morocco section), various mouselike rodents, maned sheep, and the Mendes antelope. In the gueltas, it's not unusual to see fish, toads, and frogs. The Sahara is also sometimes blighted with locusts; a massive infestation in 1988 threatened to destroy hundreds of thousands of acres of crops.

Numerous cave paintings and wall engravings left by the Sahara's inhabitants thousands of years ago attest to a very different Sahara. Water was once abundant throughout the region with geologic and fossil evidence showing that part of this immense dry area was once a huge lake or even possibly an inland sea surrounded by a tropical forest and well-watered savannah. Human beings left paintings depicting great hunting expeditions for a wide variety of animals and herding of cattle. Other paintings show that elephant, leopard, cheetah, and many types of gazelle once roamed the Sahara. Although most of these species, except for elephant, can still be seen in Algeria, they are considered endangered.

HISTORY

As with most other parts of North Africa, archeological evidence suggests that Algeria experienced substantial periods of Mesolithic (Middle Stone Age) and Neolithic (New Stone Age) culture. The most graphic signs of both periods are colorfully brilliant rock paintings in the Tassili-n-Ajjer mountains deep in the southeastern corner of Algeria (see "Djanet and Surroundings"). These paintings show that the Sahara region was once an area of lush vegetation and abundant animal life.

The Mesolithic period was marked by the diversification of stone tools and the appearance of the bow and arrow, which increased our ability to hunt more effectively. The Neolithic period saw the development of agriculture and more sophisticated stone tools and detailed rock paintings. It's impossible to assign specific years to each period because there was some overlap from one period to the next. However, the Mesolithic period is estimated to have begun around 35,000 B.C., lasting until about 6,000 B.C. The Neolithic period lasted until approximately 4000 B.C. when inhabitants especially in the south were forced to migrate due to climatic changes that desiccated the region.

By 2000 B.C., a composite group of people now called Berbers had begun to settle throughout North Africa. The precise origins of Berbers are uncertain, because racially they are a mix of central European and southwest Asian. Linguistically, their present-day dialects seem to have southwest Asian roots. Language is still the most definitive, albeit still somewhat vague, cultural characteristic of the Berbers.

Being mainly an agricultural and pastoral people, the Berbers tended to settle away from the coast on the plains and low-lying slopes of the Atlas mountain ranges. With little, if any, coastal resistance from the Berbers, Phoenicians were able to easily establish a string of trading posts along the North African Mediterranean coast, starting in about 1000 B.C. One such post, the trading settlement of Carthage near present-day Tunis, grew to become the predominant power in North Africa by the fifth century B.C. However, less than two centuries later they were defeated in the Punic Wars by the rapidly expanding Roman Empire.

The power and authority of both empires was also challenged in North Africa by the unification of various Berber tribes into two loosely organized kingdoms or confederations—Numidia and Mauretania. The former kingdom roughly corresponded to present-day northeast Algeria and Tunisia, while the latter corresponded to west-central Algeria and part of Morocco. Neither the Carthaginians nor the Romans were able to completely subdue the Berber kingdoms. However, the Roman Empire under Julius Caesar was able to make a large part of Numidia an official province of the empire. One of the results of this was the establishment of extensive Roman cities at places such as Timgad (near Batna) and Djemila (near Sétif). By the fourth century A.D., Roman North Africa extended southward as far as the edge of the Sahara, just over the Aurès mountains.

The Romans were followed in the fifth century by the Vandals, a Germanic tribe that had crossed through Spain. Their exploitative rule lasted just over a century and was supplanted by the Byzantine armies of General Belisarius. Byzantine rule also lasted only about a century and was replaced by Arabs and Islamic rule.

By the early eighth century, the Arabs were in control of most of North Africa. The Berbers had been converted to Islam, but they retained many of their traditional folk beliefs and values, many of which are still practiced or followed (see the section on Berbers). The use of Arabic by the Berbers in Algeria spread slowly and really didn't occur in the countryside until about the eleventh century. Over the next two centuries, the histories of Algeria and Morocco were mostly one and the same. The Berber dynasties of first the Almoravids and then the Almohads ruled most of northern Morocco and Algeria. The Almohad dynasty is often regarded as the first imperial Maghreb state, the foundation of the present kingdom of Morocco. Since both dynasties were based in Morocco, see the Morocco history section for more information.

The Almohads were followed by other weaker Berber dynasties. The Zayanid dynasty loosely ruled western and central Algeria from its capital at Tlemcen. However, they were greatly dependent on the Merenids in Morocco and on the Hafsids, who controlled Tunisia and eastern Algeria. All three dynasties were weakened by Arab defeats in Spain because the door was thereby pried open to direct European, especially Spanish, attacks on North Africa.

By the fifteenth century, the Spanish had established fortified enclaves at Oran, Algiers, and other points along the coast. A century later, the Spanish were sharing power with various bands of Mediterranean pirates, the most notorious of whom was "Redbeard," also known as Barbarossa or Khair El Din. He fought and plundered his way into Algiers and became the local military commander. His authority over the inhabitants, however, was somewhat tenuous, so he turned to the Ottoman Empire for military support. The Ottoman sultan sent troops and appointed Redbeard his *beylerbey* or local commander-in-chief. The sultan regarded Algiers as a good base from which to control North Africa and threaten Charles V of Spain and the rest of the Hapsburg Empire. Redbeard successfully fulfilled his role and established a durable, but politically unstable, Ottoman regency in Algeria.

In the late sixteenth century, long after Redbeard's death, the Ottoman sultan created a ceremonial representative called a *bashaw* to rule or at least represent the regency for him. The bashaw, in turn, ruled through the *aga*, the local commander of Turkish troops in Algeria, and his *Divan*, or council of officers.

A century later, a group of pirates booted both the bashaw and aga out of power and, instead, appointed a *dey* to head the government. The dey was required to rule through both the Divan and the pirates. Algeria was then divided into three provinces or *beyliks*, each extending southward to the edge of the Sahara and governed by a dey-appointed *bey*. Although the dey was supposedly the head of government, real power rested with the military, thus the Divan and its troops, and the pirates. The dey proved to be no more than an expendable figurehead. Between 1671 and 1830, of the twenty-nine deys who ruled, fourteen were assassinated.

The regency proved to be no more than a political-military machine supporting piracy and Turkish troops. It didn't create a unified Algeria because significant authority was rarely, if ever, asserted south of the coastal plains in the Kabylie mountains and beyond. Small, autonomous Berber city-states were permitted to flourish.

On the coast, the pirates continued to control Algerian commerce as well as much of the shipping throughout the Mediterranean until the early 1800s. European naval commerce was forced to pay tribute in order to be able to conduct business in Algeria and many other parts of the Mediterranean. By the 1790s, U.S. ships were also making trading forays into the Mediterranean, but ships and sailors were frequently seized because tribute hadn't been paid. In 1797, the U.S. government signed a treaty with the dey of Algiers that promised payment of $10 million in tribute over twelve years. This was about 20 percent of the U.S. government's annual revenue in 1800. The tribute was discontinued in 1815 by the threatening force of ten U.S. war vessels harbored in the Bay of Algiers.

By 1815, the dey was also having problems with most of Europe, especially France. Most of Europe was demanding that the dey end piracy and slavery, the mainstays of Ottoman suzerainty in Algeria. The French refused to pay a bill for 8 million francs worth of Algerian wheat that had been purchased in the 1790s until piracy and slavery were eliminated. In 1827, the dey summoned the French consul in Algiers, argued with him over the wheat bill, and smacked him with a fly swatter. Legend has it that the fly swatter precipitated a three-year French naval blockade and then the invasion of Algiers.

The French first moved quickly to grab all land that had been owned by the dey and his beys, even before Algeria was annexed to France as a colony in 1834. Land owned by religious bodies, tribes, and individuals was all expropriated. In addition, loosely defined plots of land that were inherited from one generation to the next were also expropriated. The French governor general in Algiers, Bertrand Clauzel, established a company to acquire for, sell to, and settle with European farmers. In about a decade, there were more than 100,000 European colonists settled in northern Algeria.

Although the French were firmly in control of most of northern Algeria, they did encounter some tribal opposition to their rule. The most notable resistance came from a holy man named Abd Al-Qādir (also variously spelled Al Kader, Al-Kadir, or Al Qader) who rallied from his capital at Tlemcen. By the late 1830s, he was leading continuous attacks on French settlements in Algeria. The French responded with Foreign Legionnaires and more than 100,000 soldiers, who conducted a *razzia* in which entire villages and their fields, farms, orchards, and ranches were destroyed. Abd Al-Qādir was forced to surrender by 1847, but he is still considered the first hero of Algerian independence.

Less than a year after Abd Al-Qādir surrendered, a revolution in France created the Second Republic. Algeria was divided into three *départements* (administrative units equivalent to provinces) and more politically integrated with France. French law became the norm over Islamic law. Algeria remained, however, divided politically and socially in three parts—the French military, the colonists (*colons*) and Algerian Muslims.

Throughout the 132 years of French rule in Algeria, the Algerians were the majority of the population, but they were blatantly discriminated against in every part of the society and economy. Algerians paid 70 percent of the direct taxes levied on the departements, but earned only 20 percent of the total income. Out of a population of 4 million Algerian Muslims in the early 1900s, only 50,000 were eligible to vote in elections. Traditional Muslim schools had declined because the French had expropriated the land that once supported these schools. A system of French schools was installed throughout Algeria that rarely included study of Arabic and Arab culture. Yet World War I service in Europe introduced many Algerian men to concepts of freedom, democracy, self-determination, and prosperity that they had been denied by French bureaucrats, soldiers, and colons in Algeria.

Under these circumstances, it was hardly surprising that an independence and nationalist movement began to evolve after World War I. In the late 1920s and 1930s, various movements arose emphasizing socialist ideals and the Islamic-Arab character of Algeria. By 1936, the French government conceded full political rights to certain members of Algeria's educated elite. This was insufficient, but further progress was hampered by World War II.

British and American troops landed in Algeria on November 8,

1942, under the command of Lieutenant General Dwight D. Eisenhower. First, they snuffed out the French and colon resistance orchestrated by the collaborationist Vichy regime in France. Then they proceeded eastward across North Africa in an offensive against German forces. Earlier, the British had fought a fierce battle at El Alamein in Egypt and began to push German forces westward. By May 1943, North Africa was clear of Axis forces. The war ended in 1945.

After the war, the Algerian independence movement heated up. The French government attempted to accommodate the various factions of the movement, but then they were faced with opposition from colons and their military allies. In response to the opposition, the Revolutionary Committee of Unity and Action (CRUA) was formed in 1952. Its members are considered the founders of the Algerian revolution—Ben Bella, Aït Ahmed, Mohammed Boudiaf, Belkacem Krim, Larbi Ben M'Hidi, Mourad Didouche, Moustafa Ben Boulaïd, and Mohammed Khider. As you travel around Algeria, you will see many streets and squares named after these men. By 1954, CRUA was officially known as the FLN (the National Liberation Front) and their still-fledgling military forces the ALN (the National Liberation Army). On November 1, 1954, the FLN launched widespread guerrilla attacks throughout Algeria. The war had begun.

The war lasted eight years with the principal battles being waged between FLN/ALN and the French government. In the process, the FLN also had to subdue resistance from splinter independence movements, which resulted in thousands of Algerian deaths, in both Algeria and France. The colons organized unofficial vigilante groups against the FLN in response to increased kidnappings and what amounted to urban terrorism. In 1956 there were at least 800 incidents of violence each month in the cities. This prompted the French government to commit over 400,000 troops to Algeria, including several units of Foreign Legionnaires. Ironically, about 170,000 of these troops were Muslim Algerians.

French military tactics subdued most of the terrorism, but they did little to appease the FLN. Villages suspected of aiding and abetting the ALN were bombed. Approximately 2 million Algerians were resettled in military camps. Search and destroy missions often destroyed more than just ALN targets. The ALN seemed to be losing the war at home, so they began conducting acts of terrorism in France. The FLN also waged a public relations campaign in France by presenting graphic examples of French brutality in Algeria. Public opinion in France and throughout the world was swayed in favor of granting Algeria independence.

President Charles de Gaulle, head of the French government, was also convinced that at the very least Algeria should be granted the possibility of self-determination. This declaration immediately precipitated a violent reaction among colons and some army units in Algeria. Both groups began fighting against the French government and the FLN. The FLN was still fighting to subdue its more radical elements. The colons' radicalism caused de Gaulle to completely abandon support for them. By 1962 all the infighting and battles were beginning to wane, and colons had begun leaving Algeria. In June 1962 more than 350,000 colons, the majority of whom were born in Algeria, left the country; this continued the rest of the year. De Gaulle proclaimed Algeria independent on July 3, 1962, although the official Algerian date is considered July 5 because that is exactly 132 years to the day that the French entered Algeria.

Independent Algeria

No one is exactly certain how many people died because of the war. Estimates range from 300,000 to a million and possibly even higher. Whatever the number, independent Algeria was socially and economically in shambles. Most of the economic infrastructure had been destroyed, severely damaged, or disrupted—factories., farms, shops, roads, the transportation system—nothing was untouched by the war. In addition, the departure of the colons, who made up most of the country's educated population, produced drastic shortages of everyone from doctors and engineers to teachers and managers.

On top of all this, a power struggle among the various factions of the FLN almost prevented the rapid formation of a government. Ahmed Ben Bella, with the support of Houari Boumediene, who was commander of the ALN, eventually became the first prime minister and also secretary general of the FLN and president of the republic. Ben Bella's consolidation of power was challenged by FLN factionalism and revolts in the Kabylie mountains against the government. He was also confronted by a brief, but bitter, border dispute with Morocco concerning a common undefined frontier in the Sahara.

Ben Bella's solution to this worsening state of affairs was to consolidate economic control in the hands of the state. In other words, confiscate all businesses and property potentially worth anything at all to the government. Bureaucracies were created to control virtually all sectors of the economy, including, most significantly, an evolving petrochemical industry, which became known as SONATRACH (Société Nationale de Transport et de Commercialisation des Hydrocarbures). Each sector was supposed to run itself according to socialist-style systems of worker self-management whereby the workers directly participated in managing each enterprise. This system was a horrendous failure that worsened an already deteriorating economy and led to Ben Bella's overthrow by Boumediene in a bloodless coup. As you travel around Algeria, you will rarely, if ever, see Ben Bella's name on street signs.

Boumediene immediately dissolved the National Assembly and suspended the 1964 constitution. As defense minister he had already established stable relations with the Algerian military, but his power base outside the military was practically nonexistent. He extended his base somewhat by pursuing more pragmatic economic policies than his predecessor.

Boumediene's main policy goal was economic self-sufficiency. To achieve this, he believed that Algeria first needed to have an export-oriented heavy industry sector and greatly expanded educational system. However, to finance both areas, he heavily relied on the development of and capital generated by the hydrocarbon sector, particularly natural gas. In doing so, he ignored the agricultural sector, which was where more than half the population made their living. Consequently, an increasing amount of hydrocarbon revenues had to be spent on food imports—one-third by the mid-1970s. This, in turn, prompted increased migration from the countryside to the cities, where housing shortages and poor living conditions were exacerbated. Boumediene died in 1978 before he was able to fully implement the corrective provisions of the 1976 constitution that he helped draft.

Chadli Benjedid was appointed president by the Central Commit-tee of the FLN. He was formally elected on February 7, 1979, and reelected in 1984 and 1988. The main thrust of his policies has been the liberalization and decentralization of the economy away from the central state control and excessive dependence on the hydrocarbon sector. He also began to make concessions to Berber culture by reinstituting Berber studies programs at Algerian universities.

In the economy, the effects of Benjedid's policies will most likely require several years before significant gains are realized. The following is a summary of the current economic situation and trends prepared by the U.S. Embassy in Algiers for the U.S. Department of Commerce:

> The hydrocarbon sector is of critical importance to the Algerian economy, representing over 98 percent of the country's hard currency earnings. It accounts for a far larger proportion of GDP than indicated by its 22 percent share in the national accounts, which are denominated in over-valued dinars. The over 40 percent drop in this sector's earnings since the beginning of 1986 has forced the Algerian government to slash expenditures and take a series of other austerity measures. While up-to-date economic statistics for Algeria are almost impossible to obtain, it is certain that most growth indicators are now considerably below their 1985 levels. Estimated real GDP growth in 1986 was

around 2 percent, less than one-half its 1985 level. Industrial production and the hydrocarbon sector saw declines in their rates of growth. Agriculture, which accounts for about 8 percent of GDP and which grew by an impressive 30 percent in 1985, was up only 6 percent in 1986. Farm output will probably fall significantly during 1987, because of severe drought in the West.

Based on an average of $17 a barrel, nominal GDP in 1987 is expected to grow at the rate of 2.2 percent, according to the FLN Party magazine. The magazine predicted that nonhydrocarbon industrial production will stay near its 1986 growth rate of 5.4 percent. The construction and service sectors will face further declines. Because the overvalued dinar exaggerates the value of local production, Algeria's GDP figures are inflated. For example, a locally-produced small television sells for the equivalent of $350, but reportedly export models will retail in France for about $150. In the United States a similar television set would cost $60 to $80 dollars. Such examples could be produced for almost all Algerian manufactured goods. Further, nonsubsidized food products sell at many times the prices prevailing in Europe and neighboring Morocco and Tunisia, when calculated at the official exchange rate.

The government's slogan in 1986, the first year of the downturn, was "self-reliance." In 1987, it has become "autonomy for enterprises." A third policy, with great potential importance, is the granting of greater financial and managerial autonomy to state-owned enterprises, which account for 80 percent of the country's GDP....

The government has actually forced some public enterprises mainly in the construction sector to close their doors and has sanctioned layoffs of personnel in limited cases. (American Embassy, Algiers, Algeria, "Foreign Economic Trends and Their Implications for the United States—Algeria," prepared for the U.S. Department of Commerce, International Trade Association, International Marketing Information Series, September 1987, pp. 3–4)

The government's attempts to diversify the Algerian economy away from overdependence on hydrocarbon industries has brought some increases in agricultural output (6.4 percent in 1987) and tourism. However, most increases have been outpaced by inflation, rapid population growth, urbanization, and drastic housing shortages.

Tourism receipts are still minuscule and constitute approximately 0.5 percent of the total gross domestic product (US $51,360 million). The government is increasingly funding tourism-related projects because hard currency brought in by tourists is a potentially valuable resource for overcoming the country's foreign debt problems. However, Algeria doesn't produce the resources necessary to construct an infrastructure strong enough to support increased tourism. In addition, import controls hamper efforts to bolster this because the necessary materials can only be imported at higher cost.

In 1987 coffee and tea suffered because of import controls. To save hard currency, the government ceased imports of coffee and tea for six months. An election was held during this period, and rather than vote for a candidate many people cast write-in votes for coffee.

The currency is gradually being devalued because compared to most hard currencies, it has been greatly overvalued. Its overvaluation was yet another way to keep as much hard currency in the country as possible.

On the foreign policy front, one of Benjedid's most significant actions has been the gradual restoration of full relations with Morocco. Throughout the 1970s and early 1980s, the Algerian government was an ardent supporter of the Polisario independence movement in the western Sahara. The Moroccan government, however, claimed the region as part of Morocco after the withdrawal of the Spanish colonial administration in the mid-1970s. Morocco annexed the western Sahara, which immediately precipitated a war with the Algerian-backed Polisario forces. Today, Morocco is entrenched in the western Sahara, Polisario forces have been pushed almost into oblivion, and Algerian support has waned. The border between Algeria and Morocco is now easy to cross, and the Trans-Maghrebian passenger train service was reactivated. In 1988, serious discussions began among the governments of Morocco, Algeria, and Tunisia to consider a Maghrebian Common Market.

POPULATION, PEOPLE, AND CULTURE

Population

Algeria's population is estimated to be approximately the same as Morocco's—23 to 24 million—and even growing at about the same annual rate—3.1 percent for Algeria and 3.3 percent for Morocco. Over 90 percent of the population lives along the Mediterranean coast on 12 percent of the land. Almost half of this group now lives in urban areas, mainly the Algiers area (estimated population of over 3 million), Oran (600,000), Constantine (450,000), and Annaba (325,000). About half the total population is under age 18.

Since independence, economic problems in Algeria have spawned massive emigration to France. At least 800,000 Algerians now live throughout France, many of them are Kabyles from poor, depressed villages in the Kabylie mountains.

People and Culture

Algerians are overwhelmingly Muslim, of Arab, Berber, or mixed Arab-Berber stock. Arabs make up approximately 80 percent of the population while the remainder are Berbers. The major Berber groups are the Kabyles of the Kabylie mountains, the Chaouias of the Aurès mountains (near Batna), the M'Zab (also known as Mozabites) of the area in and around Ghardaïa, and the Tuareg (the "Blue Men" of the Sahara).

The main factors distinguishing the Berbers from Arabs are mostly linguistic differences. In areas such as the Tell where Arabs predominate, Arab and Berber lifestyles are similar. Recent Berber migrants to this region still tend to continue speaking one or another of their traditional dialects.

Adherence to tradition is especially stronger and more pronounced among the Kabyles, the largest of the Berber-speaking groups in Algeria. Their relative isolation from Arab society and their tight-knit, independent village communities in the Kabylie mountains enabled them to maintain group solidarity. This solidarity proved to be a thorny challenge for the French; bloody guerrilla warfare was often waged during the revolution.

It has also proven to be a contentious issue for the Algerian government, which has tried since independence to create a distinct Algerian nationality and identity (see below). For the Kabyles, this has meant Arabization and an official deemphasis of Kabyle language and culture, something that has occasionally stirred the Kabyles to violent protests. In the mid-1980s, the situation had been somewhat defused by the creation of Kabyle departments at Algerian universities and the opening of Kabyle-language radio stations.

The Tuareg have been much less affected than the Kabyles by changes in Algerian society and attempts to create a national identity and ethos. Tuareg "centers" are in and around the towns of Tamanrasset and Djanet, deep in the heart of the Sahara and well away from the Tell, Algeria's northern heartland. The men still wear blue-dyed cotton robes and veils, thus the nicknames "Blue Men" and "Veiled Men" of the Sahara. Women are increasingly wearing veils in town, perhaps out of increased deference to Islamic tradition.

The Tuareg were traditionally nomadic camel and cattle herders and often hired to protect trans-Sahara trading caravans. However, Algeria's march to modernity has all but phased out both vocations and prompted the Tuareg to become more sedentary. Although camels are still prevalent, pickup trucks and Land-Rovers are becoming equally common, particularly as many Tuareg begin working in tourism. Sahara tourism is the fastest-growing "industry" for this region.

Who Is an Algerian?

Since independence, Algeria has attempted to create a new, or some would say renewed, sense of national identity. During 132 years of French economic and political domination in Algeria, there was also cultural imperialism. Everything was controlled by the French including, most importantly, education. The traditional mesh of Arab, Berber, and Muslim culture was relegated to second-class status by colonial rulers who generally regarded the French way as superior. Consequently, an apartheid-like system evolved under which Algerians educated in Algeria had fewer rights than the French and French-educated Algerians.

In education, the French language and culture were taught over Arabic and Arab culture. In fact, Arabic was rarely taught in the schools, especially at the universities. To succeed in Algeria, an Algerian had to speak French and adapt to French culture.

After independence, subservience to and dependence on French society was scorned. At first, Algerian nationality seemed to be determined by a rejection of everything French. However, after 132 years—many generations—of Frenchification, it proved to be quite impractical to change everything overnight.

To have a truly independent Algerian political system, Arabic had to be rehabilitated as the language of government, which meant that a new education system had to be developed. And to have an independent economy, the Algerian government nationalized, centralized, and assumed full control of almost all industries, including agriculture.

The Algerian government aspired to be a Soviet-style "cradle to grave" welfare state system whereby the state controls or directs most of the country's institutions, industries, and businesses—all supposedly for the benefit of the people. However, preservation of the system—all in the name of helping the people and fostering an Algerian nationality—became the overriding goals. Consequently, inefficient businesses and industries were kept open and running, and incompetent employees and managers were not fired.

Today, Algeria is still dealing with the problems of nation building. A centralized economy and overnight arabization have been traded for gradual privatization of the economy and gradual arabization. The French language continues to be widely used in business and government.

National and Religious Holidays

National Holidays

The following holidays have national recognition:

January 1	New Year's Day
May 1	Labor Day
June 19	Celebration of the Revolutionary Reparation (Fête du Redressement Revolutionaire)
July 5	Independence Day
November 1	Anniversary of the Outbreak of the Revolution (Fête du Declenchement de la Revolution)

Religious Holidays

Algeria's religious holidays and festivals are predominantly Islamic and correspond to similar celebrations in Morocco and Tunisia. These are celebrated at varying times each year because dates are determined by the Islamic lunar calendar (see introductory chapter):

Ras al Sana
New Year's Day, celebrated on 1 Moharram (July 13,1991; July 2, 1992; June 21, 1993).

El Mawlid Ennabawi
Birthday of the Prophet Mohammed; celebrated on 12 Rabei El Awal (September 21, 1991; September 12, 1992; August 30, 1993).

Ramadan
The ninth month of the Islamic calendar, Ramadan is considered the fourth of Islam's five fundamental pillars of faith. For the entire month, faithful Muslims fast from dawn to sunset in order to gain strength against evil spirits. No food or water are allowed until sunset. The *feteer,* or breaking of the fast, occurs the moment the sun has set. This is not followed as closely in Algeria as in other predominantly Islamic countries. The starting date of Ramadan slips back 10 to 12 days each year. For the next few years Ramadan starts on March 17, 1991; March 5, 1992; and February 23, 1993.

Idul Fitr
The end of Ramadan fasting. The celebration lasts from 1 to 3 Shawal (April 16–18, 1991; April 4–6, 1992; March 25–27, 1993).

Idul Adhah
The time for Muslims to fulfill the fifth pillar of Islam, the *haj*

or pilgrimage to Mecca. Every Muslim is supposed to make the *haj* at least once in his or her lifetime. This special period for making the *haj* lasts from 10 to 13 Zuu'l Hagga (June 23–26, 1991; June 11–14, 1992; June 1–4, 1993).

Language

Arabic is the official language of Algeria, but French and various Berber dialects are also widely spoken. Arabic is the mother tongue for a majority of the population.

Three types of Arabic are used in Algeria: Koranic or classical written Arabic, modern literary written Arabic, and spoken Algerian Arabic. Literary Arabic is used throughout the Middle East in literature and the media in both spoken and written forms. Spoken Algerian Arabic is an informal dialect that includes words derived or borrowed directly from French and Berber dialects. It differs, consequently, from Moroccan and other colloquial dialects.

The Berber dialects that can be distinguished in Algeria correspond to existing ethnic groups, although certain groups such as the Tuareg use more than one dialect. These include Kabyle, Chaouia, Mozabite, and Tamshek (Tuareg dialect). Except for an ancient script called *tifinagh*, which is still used by the Tuareg, these dialects aren't written.

For travelers, Arabic isn't essential for touring the country; however, at least a few words could be helpful. Knowledge of French isn't absolutely essential, but it also could be quite helpful. Following are a few words and phrases of Algerian Arabic that will help you get around; you will see a few similarities to Moroccan Arabic:

Pronunciation notes: In the following examples, the letter *x* is pronounced as a throaty "ch" or "kch" sound.

Greetings

Hello. (Peace on you.)	*la bahs* or *salaam alakekoom*
Hello *or* How do you do?	*osh xchubarak*
Hello. (*response*)	*la bahs hamdililah*
Pleased to meet you.	*maht-sha-raf*
How are you?	
(*to a man*)	*wahsh-rahk*
(*to a woman*)	*wahsh-rah-kee*
(*to a group*)	*wahsh-rah-koom*
Good morning.	*sabah il xeer*
Good morning. (*response*)	*sabah il nuur*
Good night.	
(*to a man*)	*tissbah ala xeer*

(to a woman)	*tissbahee ala xeer*
(to a group)	*tissbahoo ala xeer*
Goodbye.	*bislamma*

General Expressions

Yes	*naam*
No	*la*
Please	
(to a man)	*minfadlee*
(to a woman)	*minfadlee-kee*
Thank you.	*sah-hate* and *shukerahn*
You are welcome.	
(to a man)	*mah-rah-bik*
(to a woman)	*marh-hah-ba-bik*
(to a group)	*marh-hah-ba-bee-koom*
Excuse me.	
(to a man)	*ehs-mah-lee*
(to a woman)	*ehs-mah-laya*
(to a group)	*ehs-mah-hoo-nah*
good	*meh-leh*
bad	*mashee-meh-leh*
How much?	*shah-hahl?*
How many?	*shah-hahl?*
What do you want?	
(to a man)	*wahs-tah-hahb*
(to a woman)	*wahs-tah-hah-bee*
(to a group)	*wahs-tah-hah-bu*
I, me	*ana*
you (masculine)	*enta*
you (feminine)	*entee*
you (plural)	*entuma*
he, him	*howa*
she	*hee-yah*
we, us	*hehna*
they, them	*homa*
my wife	*marh-tee*
my husband	*rahg-lee*
my sister	*ukhtee*
my brother	*khoo-yah*
I am	*ana*
a student (m)	*talab*
a student (f)	*taleeba*
American (m)	*mehr-ree-kahnee*
American (f)	*mehr-ree-kahniyya*
British (m)	*ni-glee-zee*

British (f)	ni-glee-zay-yah
Australian (m)	australhee
Australian (f)	australhiyya
Canadian (m)	canadee
Canadian (f)	canadiyya
I speak .	nah-dar
French	ghow-ou-ree
German	al-mahn-nee
I didn't understand.	mah-fah-hem-tiksh
I understand.	ana fah-hem
What does this mean?	wahsh-hahb-ee-kool?
We need an interpreter.	lazim-ellnah-moo-tar-jim
Do you speak English?	
(to a man)	tah-dahr lin-glee-zee-ah?
(to a woman)	tah-dree lin-glee-zee-ah?
Does anyone speak English?	shkoon yih-hah-dar lin-glee-zee-ah?

Finding Your Way Around

here	hen-nay-yah
there	leh-hee-kah
right	yah-mean
left	lee-yah-seer
straight ahead	qi-bell-lah
at the corner	ill-leh-qayyah
Where?	wheen?
Where is ?	wayn
the police station	dar iss-shurta
the men's room	mir-hahd ir-reh-jel
the women's room	mir-hahd il nee saher
the train station	mah-hattit il qattar
the bus station	mah-hattit il el moo-sah-fah-reen
the airport	mah-tar
Give me a ticket.	ah-tee-nee bee-tah-kah
What bus goes to	shkoon lee-roo-hah

In the Hotel

hotel	foon-duke
Do you have a room?	andak bate?
a double room?	bate leh-zoorg?
I want a room (m)	breet bate or andkoom bate
vacant room	andkoom bate fahr-rah

with double bed	*ma'ah bunk kebir*
with shower	*ma'ah douche*
with hot water	*bil mahs skhoon*
cheap	*reh-chaysh*
cheaper	*reh-chaysh ala hadee*

Miscellaneous Essentials

customs	*dee-wah-nah*
post office	*boosta*
I want to send this by	*heh-bate neh-baht-hah*
air mail	*par avion*
soap	*sah-boon*
toilet paper	*papier hygienique*
I am busy. (*literally*, "Leave me in peace.")	*hah-lee-nee tranquil.*
OK	*sah-hah*
thief	*sah-rahq*

Numbers

Numbers	Pronunciation	Numbers	Pronunciation
0	*sefar*	30	*talateen*
1	*wahid*	40	*arba'aeen*
2	*juje*	50	*khamseen*
3	*talata*	60	*sitt-teen*
4	*arba'a*	70	*saba'aeen*
5	*khamsa*	80	*taman-nee-yen*
6	*setta*	90	*sane*
7	*seba'a*	100	*meyah*
8	*temaniya*	101	*mayyah-wi-wahid*
9	*sa'ode*	110	*mayyah-wi-ashara*
10	*ashara*	1000	*alf*
11	*hidash*	2000	*alfane*
12	*itnash*	3000	*talat-talaf*
13	*talatash*	4000	*arba'a-talaf*
14	*arba'atash*	5000	*khamas-talaf*
15	*khammahstahsh*		
16	*sittahsh*		
17	*saba'atahsh*		
18	*tamantahsh*		
19	*tissa'atahsh*		
20	*ayshreen*		
21	*wahi-wi-ayshreen*		
22	*itnane-wi-ayshreen*		

THE TRAVELER IN ALGERIA

Information

ONAT (Office National de l'Animation de la Promotion et de l'Information Touristique) is the government tourist office. Official guides can usually be arranged through some of the ONAT offices.

Algiers
The main national office at 25 Rue Khelifa Boukhalfa (tel. 61-80-82) has a helpful English-speaking staff and extensive written materials, particularly about ONAT excursions around the country. Other offices in Algiers are at 2 Rue Didouche Mourad (tel. 63-10-66), 5 Boulevard Ben Boulaid (tel. 64-15-50), Hotel El Aurassi (tel. 64-82-52), Hotel El-Djazair (tel. 60-10-00), Raid El Feth, in a shopping mall (tel. 66-66-11), and the airport (tel. 75-33-67).

Annaba
1 Rue Tarik Ibn Ziad (tel. 82-58-86)

Batna
14 Allée Ben Boulaid (tel. 55-93-45)

Bejaïa
31 Rue Ahmed Ougana (tel. 92-80-01)

Biskra
Rue Gamri (tel. 71-28-18)

Blida
21 Avenue Amara Youcef (tel. 49-83-39)

Constantine
6 Rue Zaabana (tel. 94-39-54)

Djanet
Place du Marché (tel. 73-50-24)

El Oued
17 Boulevard Talbi Larbi Guemoud (tel. 72-81-17)

Ghardaïa
2 Boulevard Emir Abdelkader (tel. 89-17-51)

Oran
10 Boulevard Emir Abdelkader (tel. 39-16-11);
Antenne es Senia (airport) (tel. 38-74-81)

Sidi bel Abbes
12 Rue Bendida

Skikda
1 Rue Rezki Kahal (tel. 95-69-14)

Tlemcen
15 Boulevard de l'Indépendence (tel. 20-88-01)

Tizi-Ouzou
   3 Rue Larbi ben M'hidi (tel. 40-27-11)
Tamanrasset
   Boulevard Emir Abdelkader (tel. 73-41-17)
Timimoun
   Hotel Gourara (tel. 23-44-41)

Information about travel in Algeria should be obtained from Algerian embassies overseas or direct from the main ONAT office at 25 Rue Khelifa Boukhalfa. Algeria maintains an embassy in the United States at 2118 Kalorama Road NW, Washington, DC 20008.

In Algeria, another possible, albeit unlikely, source of information in English for travelers is the French-language daily newspaper *Horaison*. It's a popular youth-oriented paper that usually includes one or two pages in English. Although the information is not usually travel related, you can usually glean something about what's happening in Algeria.

Maps

The most accurate up-to-date maps of Algeria are published by Michelin. Map 953 covers all of Northwest Africa and Map 172 covers just Algeria and Tunisia. Although No. 953 includes the areas around Tamanrasset and Djanet and No. 172 does not, there really isn't enough detail for No. 953 to serve as more than just a general reference.

Michelin also publishes a special map of Algeria and some surrounding areas for the Paris-Dakar road race. The map is an extract of Michelin Map 953 and shows the route of the race including a fair amount of detail. In 1988 it was published with the Thierry Sabine Organisation, one of the race organizers.

There are other maps such as the Swiss company Hallwag's map of Algeria-Tunisia and the Hungarian company Cartographia's map of Algeria, but neither company is noted for updating its maps as often as Michelin.

The Astrolabe Company of France publishes a map of the Sahara region including southern Algeria. However, the scale is 1 cm to 20 km.

Topographic maps dating from before independence were compiled by the Paris-based Institut Géographique National; a few may still be available. I would be dubious of their accuracy, though.

Detailed maps of the Sahara at a scale of 1 cm to 2 km are available from Därr Expeditionsservice GmbH, Theresienstrasse 66, 8000 Munich, West Germany (tel. 089-28-20-32). They carry sets of sheets that cover the following routes:

- **In-Salah to Tamanrasset** (also Oued Djaret, Aïn Tidjoubar, Arak, Ifetesne, Tesnou, In Eker, and Assekrem)

- **Tamanrasset to Djanet** (also Assekrem, Tazrouk, In Sakane, Serenout, and Zaoutallaz)
- **Djanet to Illizi** (also Zaoutallaz and Iherir Dider)
- **Amguid to In-Salah** (also Kranguet El Hadid, Aïn Tidjoubar, and Ers Um El Lil)
- **Amguid to Zaouia El Kahla** (also Bordj Omar Driss and Ta-n-Elak)
- **Tamanrasset to Amguid**
- **Amguid to Illizi**

In the United States, some of the Algeria maps mentioned above may be obtained at Pacific Travelers Supply, 529 State Street, Santa Barbara, California 93101 (tel. 805-963-4438).

Money and Banks

On arriving in Algeria, all foreigners, except residents, must change an amount equivalent to 1,000 DA into Algerian dinars at official bank rates. This money may be changed either at the relevant bank or customs counters at your point of arrival. You will be handed a receipt that you must keep throughout your stay. Occasionally you will be asked for the receipt at customs on departure from the country.

Exemptions to this exchange regulation include students and tourists arriving in Algeria either in groups or as individuals who come as part of an organized tour.

For independent travelers, this regulation can prove to be quite costly because the official exchange rate of approximately 6.5 dinars to US $1 is overvalued by as much as 300 percent. The black market rate, a rate that is usually determined by the typical market forces of supply and demand, can often be as much as 30 dinars to US $1. At that rate, prices for goods and services seem more realistic. It will, therefore, be quite tempting to change money on the black market, but exercise caution. The government isn't fond of black market currency exchanges because less dollars are being exchanged for more dinars compared to official exchanges.

Algerian banks are government controlled. The main bank is the Banque Centrale d'Algerie (Central Bank of Algeria) and runs exchange counters at Algeria's international airports and most other ports of entry. Beware—they will only exchange foreign currency for dinars and not vice versa, so don't exchange more than you think that you may need.

Money and travelers' checks can also be exchanged at most major hotels throughout Algeria.

A few more money facts:

- American Express cards are accepted at most major hotels and a

few restaurants. There are no American Express offices in Algeria.
- To buy airline tickets in Algeria, you must pay in foreign currency either with cash, travelers' checks, or a credit card.

Costs, Accommodations, and Food

The overvalued dinar (see above) makes Algeria overpriced at official exchange rates. For example, at a small pizzeria in downtown Algiers I paid US $7 for an individual pizza and a soda. If I were in New York savoring a thick-crusted pizza with the works piled on, then US $7 may make sense, but not in downtown Algiers, where the crust was thin and the works were meager.

Accommodations will also seem similarly overpriced for a developing country. But, if you're used to paying ridiculous rates at U.S. motels, then Algerian hotel rates will hardly shock you.

The following chart shows official "hotel tariffs" in dinars per person per day.

Room type	Two Stars	Three Stars	Four Stars	Five Stars
Double room	66	75	100	213
Single	105	120	160	340
with full board	190	262	319	450
with half board	135	179	221	400

More inexpensive accommodations are available at small private hotels and youth hostels. Algeria has a network of hostels throughout the country. The main office for the Algerian Youth Hostel Association is at 26 Rue Ahmed Ouaked Dely-Ibrahim, Algiers (tel. 78-55-45).

There are youth hostels at

Aïn Defla
Auberge de Jeunes Tenes, Route de Cherchell, tel. 43-72-35, 20 beds
Batna
Auberge de Jeunes Saïdi Rachid, Route des Abattoirs, tel. 55-38-07, 10 beds
Bejaïa
Auberge de Jeunes de Bejaïa, Rue des Frères Soumani, tel. 92-29-08, 12 beds
Biskra
Auberge de Jeunes d'El Kantara, tel. 87-32-80, 50 beds
Bou-Saada
Auberge de Jeunes Boussada, BP 190, Bou-Saada, tel. 54-49-45, 20 beds

El Oued
> Auberge de Jeunes Er-Rhimel, tel. 72-85-86, 30 beds

Ghardaïa
> Auberge de Jeunes Emir Abdelkader, BP 85, Ghardaïa, tel. 89-44-03, 38 beds

Jijel
> Auberge de Jeunes Bounab Rachid, Rue des Frères Khacha, tel. 96-42-47, 20 beds

Laghouat
> Auberge de Emir Khaled, tel. 72-39-80, 40 beds

Oran
> Auberge de Jeunes, 13 Rue Gascon, tel. 35-02-45, 50 beds

Skikda
> Auberge de Jeunes Mohamed Namous, tel. 74-34-00, 20 beds

Tamanrasset
> Auberge de Jeunes El Hoggar, tel. 73-40-47, 50 beds

Tipaza
> Auberge de Jeunes Nedjm El Djamil, Camp de Jeunes de Zeralda, tel. 81-21-12, 20 beds

Tlemcen
> Auberge de Jeunes Sidi Chaker, Tlemcen, tel. 20-32-26, 20 beds

Touggourt
> Auberge de Jeunes Emir Khaled, Rue Emir Abdelkader, tel. 67-47-07, 30 beds

Camping

Camping is another inexpensive option for touring Algeria. There are official campgrounds throughout the country. Theoretically, it is possible to camp on any public land, including beaches, as long as the local authorities have been informed and have approved your campsite. On the other hand, you could just take your chances that no one complains about your choice of campsite.

There are several official campgrounds on the beach, including the following which are open all year:

Collo
> At a site 5 km (3 miles) east of Collo called Ouled Maazouz, which is near the beach and not far from the National Route. There are 120 spaces on an area of about 3 hectares.

Tichy
> Situated 12 km (7 1/2 miles) east of Bejaïa, it's well isolated from the noises of the town and the road. There are 180 spaces.

Tipaza   Located at the foot of Mount Chenoua 70 km (43 1/2 miles) from Algiers and just a few meters from the beach. There are 120 spaces. There are several campgrounds in the Tipaza area.

Cherchell
Near Cherchell at a place called Oued Bellah, which is 7 km (4 miles) from town, this campground is situated just across from the sea and between two small hills. There are 160 spaces.

Aïn El Turk
Situated 15 km (9 miles) west of Oran on the Corniche at a charming site surrounded by palm trees; 140 spaces.

Biskra
Situated near town in a palmerie; 50 spaces.

El Goléa
Situated at the edge of town near a palmerie; 50 spaces.

Algerian Cuisine

Algerian cuisine is a composite of regional dishes that have been influenced by traditional Moroccan, Spanish, French, Italian, and Turkish (among others) foods, drinks, and spices. The following is a short guide to Algerian specialities and Algerian versions of North African specialities:

Bourek
A cigar-shaped puff pastry stuffed with meat, onions, and fried eggs; an Algiers-area specialty.

Chakchouka
Peppers and tomatoes simmered in a sauce of garlic, onion, red peppers, and olive oil. In certain regions, one or two eggs are also added. This dish is found from Egypt to Morocco.

Chorba
A smooth delicious soup prepared by cooking mutton, vegetables, herbs, spices, and tomatoes in a low-temperature oven for several hours. Just before it is fully cooked, *maktfah* (hand rolled vermicelli) or *frik* (cornmeal) is added.

Couscous
Undoubtedly the best-known North African specialty. It consists of semolina grains mixed with water and a bit of oil. The mixture is then run through a sieve, rolled by hand, and steamed in a "couscousier" with various vegetables—cabbage, turnips, carrots, squash, eggplant, tomatoes, chick peas, onions—and meat (beef, mutton, or chicken) added to the bottom before the couscous is poured in. The complete dish is served hot with a vegetable sauce.
Variations consist of beans and peas replacing the sauce, or

adding raisins and sugar. The taste is further enhanced by adding some milk (*leben*).

Crepe Farci

Crêpes stuffed with meat or fowl (occasionally pigeon). This dish originates in Fez, Morocco.

Dolma

Various vegetables stuffed with meat and pungent spices and then cooked in butter.

Fruit

One of the most renowned fruits in Algeria is the deglet nour date, nicknamed the "fruit of the light." Although there are several other types of dates in Algeria, the deglet nour is the most common. It accounts for about 20 percent of Algeria's total date output. Various citrus fruits are also widely cultivated, especially several varieties of oranges.

Kebab

Roasted lamb and potatoes cooked in a parsley and onion sauce. Many versions of this exist throughout the Middle East and North Africa.

Kebda Mchermla

Liver stew; it's not one of my favorites, but it does seem to be popular in Algeria.

Lham Lahlou

Mutton cooked together with dry prunes or butter and cinnamon and scented with orange blossoms.

Méchoui

Preparation of the méchoui is somewhat of a ceremony. A sheep is slaughtered and roasted for several hours on a spit over a bed of hot coals. It is constantly basted with butter to give it a golden color. When cooked, the sheep is taken from the spit and presented to the guests on a coffee tray. You are then expected to tear off the most succulent pieces of meat with your fingers.

Mint tea

Preparing mint tea is also somewhat of a ceremony in Algeria. Traditionally, the tea and mint leaves are carefully chosen before being plunked into a silver teapot. Hot water and heaps of sugar are added to the pot, and then the tea is poured back and forth between pots until it is sufficiently frothy and tasty. It is served very hot in small, finely decorated glasses.

Pastries

Algerian cakes generally contain copious amounts of semolina, almonds, dates, and honey. These cakes are particularly popular during Ramadan celebrations. The best known are *baklawa* (a flaky almond pastry dripping with honey), *makrout* (date or almond "lozenges"), *samsa* (a triangular pastry stuffed with with an almond-honey mash), *cornes de gazelles*, *khatayef* (balls of noodles stuffed with almond paste), *benidlet, grionach, hrissa,* and *mhencha*.

Soups

Algerian soups are delicious and could easily sustain you for the duration of your stay in the country. A few of the more popular soups, aside from *chorba*, include the mainstay of chicken soup with vermicelli noodles, spicy garlic soup, shrimp soup, and wild thyme soup. There are also various vegetable purée soups that are worth sampling.

Vegetables dishes

Marinated vegetables are popular as hors d'oeuvres—eggplants or carrots in vinegar, sweet pepper and tomato salads, and sweet peppers in olive oil. Cooked vegetable dishes include baked artichoke stew, potato fritters in sauce, stuffed squash, and white bean ragout.

Other common dishes

include fish prepared in as many ways as there are fish, tajine (a beef, veal, chicken, or fish stew cooked in a clay pot over charcoal), lamb in steamed milk, caraway meatballs, beef with stuffed dates, beef with prunes, mutton with raisins, stuffed mutton tripe and sheep's head.

Wines

Western Algeria in the coastal and mountain regions has long been renowned for its vineyards and wine making. Some of the more popular wines include Cuvée du Président (red wine), Nadim (red), Khayyam (red and rosé), Montagne des Lions (red and rosé), Dahroussa (red and rosé), La Treille-Muscat (dessert wine), and La Treille-Grenade (dessert wine).

Where to Go

Algeria is the second largest country in Africa; almost one-third the size of the continental United States. In such an immense country, two to three weeks is an ideal amount of time to get a fair overview of its three main regions—the northern coastal plains and mountains, the High Plateaus and central Algeria, and the Sahara. Conceivably, you can get a brief idea of the country in one week, but you would have quite a hectic trip and most likely not have much time, if any, to pursue any adventures.

If you plan to tour Algeria independently, you should have a very flexible itinerary and definitely intend on spending more than a week in the country.

ONAT, the government tourism organization, offers several itineraries covering almost all Algeria. A few of these are described below to give you an idea of what they offer and what you might be able to do on your own:

There are several one- to three-day tours from main departure points around Algeria:

From Algiers	and the other departure points listed below, one or two of the following sets of destinations can be done in one to three days—a city tour, the Mitidja plains between the Blida Atlas mountains and Algiers, Zaccar and the Chiffa gorges (the monkey gorge), Tipaza and Cherchell (extensive Roman ruins), the Kabylie mountains, Bou-Saada and the High Plateaus.
From Oran	Oran City tour, Bou Hanifia, Tlemcen, and Ghazaouet.
From Annaba	Annaba city tour, Seraidi, Skikda, El Kala, and Constantine.
From Ghardaïa	Ghardaïa city tour, Beni Isguen, El Atteuf, Metlili, Zelfana, and Berriane.

Note: Trips from Tamanrasset and Djanet require four-wheel-drive vehicles.

From Tamanrasset	town tour, Assekrem and Abalessa.
From Djanet	Erg Admer, Tegharghart, Issendilene, and Jabbaren (the two latter places are prime sites for viewing ancient cave paintings).

The Itineraries

Roman Algeria
Nine days (northern Algeria and part of the High Plateaus):

Day 1. Arrival in Algiers.

Day 2. Visit to Tipaza and Cherchell (ancient ruins and museum in both places), the tomb of Queen Selena, wife of Juba II. Return to Algiers for overnight.

Day 3. Algiers-Sétif: Visit to Gorges of Lakhdaria en route; afternoon excursion to the Djemila Roman ruins. Overnight in Sétif.

Day 4. Sétif-Batna: Travel via the Chotts region, tour the town and Roman ruins at Timgad. Overnight in Batna.

Day 5. Batna-Guelma-Annaba: En route visit the "Medracen"

(Berber Mausoleum), town of Guelma, and nearby ruins of an amphitheater, and ruins near the town of Annaba.

Day 6. Early-morning departure for Constantine. Visit the kasbah, the Ben Badis mosque and museum, the ancient Roman city of Tiddis, and other ruins in the vicinity.

Day 7. Constantine-Sétif-Tichy: Travel via Sétif and the gorges of Kherrta. Afternoon visit to the Jijel Corniche and caves.

Day 8. Tichy-Bejaïa-Yakouren-Tizi Ouzou-Algiers: tour of Bejaïa, Akfadou National Park, quick visit to Tizi Ouzou.

Day 9. Departure.

Saharan Oases

Eight days (High Plateaus and northern Sahara):

Day 1. Arrival in Algiers.

Day 2. Algiers-Bou-Saada: Afternoon visit to El Hamel and a small waterfall near town.

Day 3. Bou-Saada-Biskra-El Oued: Stops at Chaiba, Tolga, M'Chouneche Oasis, Chott El Melghir. Visit the Sahara museum in El Oued and the great sand dunes just outside of town.

Day 4. El Oued-Touggourt: Visit El Oued market and en route to Touggourt the *gots* (small, sheltered oases) and the Bedouin "hotel." After lunch, visit the fortresses of Temacine and Temalhat, the crafts center, and kings' tombs.

Day 5. Touggourt-Ouargla-Ghardaïa: Visit the Saharan Museum and old part of Ouargla, including the "desert rose" market. Afternoon visit to the holy town of Beni-Isguen and free time roaming around Ghardaïa.

Day 6. Ghardaïa-Laghouat-Bou-Saada: Guided tour of Ghardaïa and markets. After lunch depart for Bou-Saada, stopping en route at Berriane and Laghouat.

Day 7. Bou-Saada-Algiers: Afternoon visit to the Algiers kasbah.

Day 8. Departure.

Discovering Algeria

Sixteen days (the grand tour, northern Algeria, High Plateaus, northern Sahara). This tour is a combination of the above tours with

additional stops farther west of Tipaza—Chlef, Oran, Tlemcen. Aïn
Ouarka, Bechar, Taghit, Beni Abbes, Oasis of Kerkaz, Timimoun, El
Goléa, Ghardaïa, Beni Isguen, El Atteuf, Ourgla, Touggourt, El Oued,
Biskra, Batna, Constantine, Tichy, and Bejaïa are also visited. This is
definitely an overdose trip.

A variety of specialized itineraries are offered for the Sahara starting
from either Tamanrasset or Djanet. These trips tend to be much more
adventure oriented than the ones mentioned above.

From Tamanrasset

The Hoggar. Eight days (Land-Rover and some walking):

Day 1. Arrival in Algiers.
Day 2. Algiers-Tamanrasset flight. After lunch, assembly of
        the expedition into small groups for trip over the
        massif of Atakor to the Pic of the Iharem (previously
        known as Laperine), the neolithic tomb of Aderni in
        the Wadi Mezoulit, rock carvings, and gueltas. Arrival
        at the refuge of Assekrem in the late afternoon.
Day 3. Assekrem-Hirafok-Ideles: Set out through the gueltas
        along a piste to the Targui village of Hirafok, which
        has rock engravings and abundant vegetation. Visit
        rock paintings and other carvings in the area, then on
        to Assekrem, Wadi Zarzoura, Immaara, along the
        Wadi Irharrar to Ideles and back to Hirafok for dinner
        and camping.
Day 4. Ideles-Tazrouk: Taderaz mountain, the village of
        Tazrouk (hottest village in the Hoggar) and its lush
        oases; lunch at Wadi Azrou; afternoon exploration of
        the area around the campsite and near the sharp rocky
        peak of Aokasit. Camping.
Day 5. Tazrouk-Tahifet-Tamekrest: Drive via the Azrou pass
        and an impressive track through a wadi (riverbed).
        Arrive in Tahifet, a sprawling village in a valley,
        surrounded by a lush palmerie. Continue to Tamekrest
        and pitch camp at the base of the Cascade of Tamekrest
        ("the impassable one").
Day 6. Tamekrest-Tamanrasset: Across a piste to
        Tamanrasset, arrival late morning. Visit the hermit-
        age of Father de Foucauld. Free time in Tamanrasset.
Day 7. Tamanrasett-Algiers: Flight to Algiers and overnight
        in Algiers.
Day 8. Departure.

Tassili du Hoggar. Eight days (by Land-Rover):

Day 1.   Arrival in Algiers.

Day 2.   Algiers-Tamanrasset by air: Afternoon assembly of the expedition and departure for Assekrem. Trek across the first volcanic site overlooking the peak of Iharen, then stop for a visit to the Tahabort spring. After the visit to the Gueltas of Imlaoulaoulaouene and Afilale, late-afternoon arrival in Assekrem.

Day 3.   Assekrem-Igharghar: Early-morning return to Tamanrasset and departure for the massif of the Tassili du Hoggar. Most of the day is spent driving along the sand dunes, ergs, and wadis. Late-afternoon arrival in Igharghar to set up camp for the night.

Day 4.   Igharghar-Tagrera: Expedition to Tagrera through a spectacular landscape of peaks and needles and set up camp amid a prehistoric site that's rich in neolithic remains such as pounders, grinding wheels, stone tools, and rock carvings. Overnight at Tagrera.

Day 5.   Tagrera-Youf Haket: Follow a track along the Tassili Tin Meskor to see flagstones carved with Tifinagh (Targui script). Afternoon hike through a labyrinth of mineral oddities.

Day 6.   Youf Haket-Tamekrest: Depart the Tassili du Hoggar for a landscape of plains and wadis interspersed with mountains that link the two Tassilis. Picnic lunch in Wadi Tin Tarabine or Tadaouete. The landscapes of green wadis, or regs and canyons overlooking the Tamekrest cascades where water, rare in these parts, runs along a granite bed.

Day 7.   Tamekrest-Tamanrasset: Morning departure for Tamanrasset; afternoon free to visit the town, Father de Foucauld's bordj, the museum and market.

Day 8.   Tamanrasset, departure.

Hoggar by Camel. Six days:

Day 1.   Arrival in Tamanrasset; afternoon visit to the town.

Day 2.   Tamanrasset-Akar Akar: Assemble the caravan of camels, and start the trek across the volcanic massif of the Hoggar. Set up camp for the evening.

Day 3.   Akar-Akar to Afilal: Continue expedition to higher elevation.

Day 4.   Afilal-Oued Taramoute-Assekrem: En route, visit the rock carvings, and continue on to the Assekrem plateau. Spend night in the shelter.

Day 5. Assekrem-Tamanrasset: Visit the hermitage of Father de Foucauld and the sharp rocky peaks of Atakor. After lunch, return by four-wheel-drive Land-Rovers or Land-Cruisers to Tamanrasset; overnight in Tamanrasset.

Day 6. Tamanrasset, departure.

The Unusual Hoggar. Six days:

Day 1. Arrival in Tamanrasset; assemble the group and depart by Land-Cruiser for trip across the massif of Atakor. Overnight in the shelter at Assekrem.

Day 2. Assekrem-Hirafok-Ideles: En route, visit rock carvings and paintings.

Day 3. Ideles-Tazrouk: Cross Mount Taderaz through panoramic surroundings.

Day 4. Tazrouk-Tahifet-Tamekrest.

Day 5. Tamekrest-Tamanrasset: Visit town and museum.

Day 6. Tamanrasset, departure.

From Djanet

The Tassili-n-Ajjer. Eight days:

Day 1. Arrival in Algiers.

Day 2. Algiers-Djanet by plane; afternoon visit around the oasis.

Day 3. Djanet-Tamrit: To the edge of the Tassili range to prepare for a slow climb along a mountain track to the first plateau of the Akba Tafelalet. Continue to Tamrit where camp is set up next to a great cypress tree that's estimated to be more than two thousand years old. Afternoon visit to rock paintings.

Day 4. Tamrit-Sefar: Extraordinary landscape surrounds Sefar as well as rock paintings and carvings. Visit en route to In Itinen.

Day 5. Sefar-Tin Tazarift: Visit a "city" built of stone in the morning; after lunch, a two-hour trek to the sites of Tin Taferiest, the highest point of the trek. Camp at Tin Tazarift.

Day 6. Tin Tazarift-Tin Zoumaitok-Tamrit: Continue to Tamrit with a visit to Tin Zoumaitok and its famous fresco. Set up camp at Tamrit and walk around this mountainous area. Return via the valley of cypresses.

Day 7.   Tamrit-Djanet-Algiers: flight to Algiers.

Day 8.   Departure from Algiers.

Expedition through the Hoggar and Tassili-n-Ajjer (from Tamanrasset to Djanet). Six days (by Land-Rover):

Day 1.   Arrival in Tamanrasset in the afternoon.

Day 2.   Tamanrasset-Assekrem: Visit town in the morning and assemble the expedition for departure to Assekrem.

Day 3.   Assekrem-Ideles: Visit area and overnight in Ideles.

Day 4.   Ideles-Serouenout: Continuation of expedition across the Telertheba and Anahaf.

Day 5.   Serouenout-Djanet: Last leg of the expedition. Afternoon arrival in Djanet. Overnight at the Hotel Zeribas.

Day 6.   Morning transfer to airport.

Expedition across the Tassili-Tenere area. Seven days (by Land-Rover):

Day 1.   Arrival in Djanet, overnight.

Day 2.   Djanet-Gautier: Assemble group for Land-Rover trip, across Mounts Tiska and Gautier.

Day 3:   Mounts Gautier-Tisnar: Continue to panoramic site of the Erg Admer; camp overnight.

Day 4.   Tisnar-Dider-Iherir: Visit surroundings and rock carvings of Dider; camp overnight.

Day 5.   Iherir-Issendilene: Explore area en route to Issendilene.

Day 6.   Issendilene-Djanet.

Day 7.   Djanet, departure.

Expedition across the Tassili-n-Ajjer. Six days (by Land-Rover and foot):

Day 1.   Arrival in Djanet.

Day 2.   Djanet-Tamrit: Transfer in the morning to Land-Rovers for trip to mountainous region around the Tamrit plateau. Overnight stay in a tented village.

Day 3.   Tamrit-Sefar: Visit one of the Tassili's most important rock-carving sites.

Day 4.   Sefar-Tin Tazarift: Visit more rock carvings and paintings.

Day 5.   Tin Tazarift-Tin Zoumaitok-Tamrit: Visit to well-known frescoes at Tin Zoumaitok.

Day 6.   Tamrit-Djanet. Depart Djanet.

Side trips from the northern Algeria itineraries might include skiing at one of Algeria's ski runs—Chréa, Tikjda, and Tala Guilef.

Chréa is in the Atlas de Blida mountains above Blida and is accessible in a day trip from Algiers. Facilities include two 1,500-m ski runs, two rope pulls, and one 1,500-m-long chair lift.

Tikjda and Tala Guilef are in the Grand Kabylie mountains south of Tizi Ouzou. At Tikjda, there are two 1,800-m-long ski runs with two rope pulls and two 1,900-m-long ski runs with two chair lifts. Tala Guilef has one 1,800-m ski run, two rope pulls, one chair lift up to 2,000 m (6,562 ft.).

GETTING THERE

Visas and Permits

Four visa application forms must be completed, each hand-signed by the applicant. A passport photo should be attached to two of the forms and enclose a money order for $11.25 (check with the embassy for the latest figure because this varies with the exchange rate) payable to the Embassy of Algeria. Personal checks are not accepted.

Tourists are required to include a photocopy of their round-trip air tickets (this didn't seem to be strictly enforced).

Visas are valid from the date of issue and usually take about four days to process. For return of your passport, please include a self-addressed envelope with return postage and a certified notice attached. State on your application or cover letter whether you wish to have your passport returned by Federal Express.

The visa is void if you have obtained an Israeli or South African visa. The Algerian government does not recognize either government.

Nationals of the following countries are required to produce a valid passport, but aren't subject to visa regulations: Denmark, Spain, Finland, Italy, Ireland, Iceland, Norway, United Kingdom, Sweden, Switzerland, and Tunisia.

Other nationalities must obtain visas, but the regulations vary country to country. In the United States, begin the visa process well in advance of your departure because it can take as long as a month.

Customs Regulations

Import regulations apply mainly to tobacco, alcohol and jewelry. Each person is permitted to bring in a maximum of 200 cigarettes, 50 cigars, 1 liter of alcohol, and any personal jewelry under 100 grams. All gold, pearls, precious stones, and jewelry weighing more than 100 grams must be declared on arrival.

No restrictions apply to the temporary import of the following items as long as they are only for private use: personal effects, sports equipment and accessories, a tent and camping accessories, a standard camera and 10 rolls of film, a musical instrument, a radio receiver, a tape recorder, a typewriter, and a bicycle.

Bringing a car into Algeria requires various special papers. Inquire at an Algerian embassy for the latest details.

Prohibited items for import are: narcotics, books, films, tapes, and other objects "contrary to good moral habits and customs"; counterfeit books and publications; arms and war munitions.

By Air

From Europe

Several airlines fly between Algeria and Europe including Air Algerie, Air France, Aeroflot, Alitalia, Balkan, Iberia, LOT—Polish Airlines, Lufthansa, Sabena, SAS (Scandinavian Airlines System) and Swissair.

Air Algerie is the agent for all other companies not represented in Algeria. They fly to the following European cities: Athens, Barcelona, Belgrade, Berlin, Brussels, Bucharest, Frankfurt, Geneva, Lille (France), London, Lyon (France), Madrid, Malta, Marseilles, Moscow, Nice (France), Las Palmas (Canary Islands), Paris, Prague, Rome, Sofia (Bulgaria), Toulouse (France), Valetta (Malta), Vienna, and Zurich.

From Africa

EgyptAir, Royal Air Maroc, and Tunis Air all have frequent flights between Algeria and Egypt, Morocco, and Tunisia respectively. Air Algerie also flies to these countries, as well as the following: Angola, the Congo, Guinea-Bissau, Libya, Mali, Mauritania, Niger, and Senegal.

From the Middle East

Air Algerie has flights to Damascus, Jeddah, and Kuwait.

By Sea

Ferries and Other Ships

Travel between Algeria and Europe by ferry boat is possible through the Compagnie Nationale Algerienne de Navigation (CNAN) and the Enterprise Nationale de Transport Maritime de Voyageurs (ENTMV) in association with the Société Nationale Maritime de la Corse et de la Méditerranée (SNCM) and, indirectly, the Compagnie Generale Maritime (CGM). (Are you confused yet?)

In Algiers, the CNAN's main office is at 2 Quai d'Ajaccio, Nouvelle Gare-Maritime (tel. 61-14-78, telex 67099). According to SNCM brochures, they operate five "liners" of their own and are, supposedly, also able to make bookings for the three SNCM passenger ships that regularly run between Marseille and Algiers. However, according to Thomas Cook's International Timetable, ENTMV (not CNAN) operates six "car ferries"; the five liners aren't mentioned. By the time I figured out (or sort of) who operates which ships, I didn't have enough time to find out if CNAN really does operate five ships.

Of all the companies mentioned, SNCM seemed to have the largest and best organized boat transport to Algeria. Between January and May, they offer an average of one departure weekly from Marseille. The rest of the year, there are seven to nine departures monthly. The trip takes approximately 20 hours. The 12,000-ton ship *Liberté* and car ferry *Napoleon* are the most frequently used vessels. Tariffs in French francs (adult rates) for 1989 were as follows:

One way	1097 (couchette)/649 (seat)
Round trip	2000/1184

A 25 percent discount rate is available through some travel agents:

One way	843/515
Round trip	1686/1030

Cabin supplement rates were:

From November 1 to May 31,

Class	A	134	(single cabin with full bathroom)
	A2	69	(double cabin with full bathroom)
	A4	45	(four bed cabin with full bathroom)
	B2	45	(two bunk beds with shower and toilet)
	B4	27	(four bunk beds with shower and toilet)

From June 1 to October 31, for the same accommodations,

Class	A	270
	A2	179
	A4	89
	B2	89
	B4	54

SNCM maintains an office in Algiers called the Délégation Générale at 28 Boulevard Zighout Youcef (tel. 63-03-33, telex 67067). Other addresses are

In France: Marseille, CNAN, 29 Boulevard des Dames 13002; tel. 91-90-64-70; Paris, CNAN, 12 Rue Godot de Mauroy (Opera) 75009; tel. 01-42-66-60; Sète, CNAN 4 Quai d'Alger 34200; tel. 67-74-70-53 and telex 49-0545.

In Algeria: They also have offices or representatives in Annaba

(Cours de la Revolution; tel. 82-55-55), Batna (1 Avenue de la République; tel. 55-14-58), Bejaïa (Centre Commercial, Rue de la Liberté; tel. 92-03-60), Biskra (Avenue Ben Badis; tel. 71-38-10), Constantine (16 Rue Didouche Mourad; tel. 94-88-49), Oran (13 Boulevard Abane Ramdane; tel. 33-27-67), Sétif (Cité des 600 Logements, Bel Air; tel. 90-25-06), Skikda (10 Avenue Zighout Youcef; tel 95-64-73), Tizi-Ouzou (Cité du 20 Août, Rue Larbi Ben M'hidi; tel. 40-30-34), Tlemcen (Avenue du 1er Novembre, Gare Routière; tel. 20-42-50).

In Spain: Alicante, Agencia Romeu, Jorge Juan 6, P.O. Box 303; tel. 20-83-33; Las Palmas, Mallorca, Agencia Schembri, Plaza Lonja 2 y 4, P.O. Box 71; tel. 22-14-17 or 22-79-76.

By Land

Algeria can be entered overland from Morocco, Tunisia, Libya, Niger, and Mali. Daily train and bus connections are available between Tunisia and Algeria. Train service between Morocco and Algeria was reactivated in 1989. Taxis and occasional buses can get you from the Algerian border post to the Maghnia train and bus stations.

Overland travel is also possible, but much more difficult, from Niger and Mali. There are no public buses, so you will have to either join an organized tour or hitch a ride with overland vehicles or commercial trucks.

GETTING AROUND ALGERIA

By Air

Every major city and town in Algeria has an airport and is linked by Air Algerie to Algiers and sometimes other cities. Connections are as follows:

From Algiers:	Adrar, Annaba, Béchar, Bejaïa, Biskra, Bou-Saada, Constantine, Djanet, El Goléa, El Oued, Ghardaïa, Hassi-Messaoud, In-Amenas, In-Salah, Jijel, Mascara, Oran, Ouargla, Tamanrasset, Tebessa, Tindouf, Tlemcen, Touggourt
From Annaba:	Algiers, El Oued, Ghardaïa, Hassi-Messaoud, Oran
From Constantine:	Algiers, Ghardaïa, Oran, Ouargla, Tamanrasset, Tindouf
From Djanet:	Algiers, Ghardaïa, Illizi, Ouargla, Tamanrasset
From El Goléa:	Algiers, Ouargla, Tamanrasset

From El Oued:	Algiers and Annaba
From Ghardaïa:	Adrar, Algiers, Annaba, Béchar, Constantine, Djanet, In-Salah, Oran, Tamanrasset, Timimoun
From Hassi-Messaoud:	Algiers, Annaba, In-Amenas, Oran
From In-Amenas:	Algiers, Hassi-Messaoud, Oran, Ouargla
From In-Salah:	Algiers, Ghardaïa, Ouargla, Tamanrasset
From Oran:	Adrar, Algiers, Annaba, Béchar, Constantine, Ghardaïa, Hassi-Messaoud, In-Amenas, Ouargla, Tamanrasset, Tindouf
From Ouargla:	Algiers, Constantine, Djanet, El Goléa, Illizi, In-Amenas, In-Salah, Oran, Tamanrasset
From Tamanrasset:	Adrar, Algiers, Bordj-Badji-Mokhtar, Constantine, Djanet, El Goléa, Ghardaïa, Illizi, In-Salah, Oran, Ouargla

The following are sample round-trip air fares from Algiers to a few of these domestic destinations (U.S. dollar equivalents calculated at an average official exchange rate of 5 dinars to US$1):

Annaba	652,00 DA	($130.40)
Béchar	880,00 DA	($176.00)
Constantine	506,00 DA	($101.20)
Djanet	958,00 DA	($192.00)
El Oued	586,00 DA	($117.20)
Oran	586,00 DA	($117.20)
Tamanrasset	990,00 DA	($198.00)

By Bus

Every major city and town, as well as most smaller locales, are linked by one of the national bus companies. Under a government-controlled umbrella company known as EPTV (Enterprise Publique de Transport de Voyageurs, or Public Bus Travel Enterprise), there are five autonomous regional companies based in the following cities:

EPTVC	Rouiba
EPTVO	Oran
EPTVE	Constantine
EPTVSE	Ouargla
EPTVSO	Béchar

Buy tickets in advance because there are shortages of buses on some routes.

By Grand Taxi

Most cities and towns have intercity grand taxis that run between most major destinations. The rates are supposedly government-controlled, but be prepared to bargain.

By Train

The Algerian train system is fairly extensive and reasonably well maintained. The main lines are Algiers-Annaba via Sétif and Constantine; Algiers-Oran via Blida, Ech-Cheliff, Relizane, Mohammedia, Oued Tlelat; Algiers-Sétif (direct); Algiers-Tizi Ouzou (direct); Algiers-Tunis via Bouira, Sétif, Constantine, Annaba, Souk Ahras, and Ghardimaou (Tunisia); Oran-Tlemcen-Maghnia via Tlelat and Sidi Bel Abbes and Constantine-Touggourt via Batna and Biskra.

First- and second-class tickets are available on most lines, but don't expect much from first class. A first-class seat is basically the same as a second-class one except that in first you are in a reserved seat, while in the latter you're not.

The following are some sample fares and schedule information for a few of the above-mentioned routes:

1. Algiers-El Harrach-Blida (9 DA) -El Affroun-El Asnam-Relizane-Mohammedia-Oued Tlelat-Oran (84 DA)
2. Algiers-El Harrach-Thenia-Beni Mansour-Bejaïa (259 km, or 161 miles, 68 DA) -Sétif (308 km, or 191 miles, 82 DA)- El Gourzi-Constantine (463 km, or 287 miles, 125 DA) - Ramdane Djamal-Annaba (626 km, or 388 miles, 167 DA).

On the first route, there are trains to Oran at 6.55 A.M. (No. 1001), 12 noon (No. 1003), 5 P.M. (No. 1005), and 9 P.M. (No. 1008, sleeper cars available), all of which stop at Blida after approximately 50-60 minutes. There are also trains to Blida at 5.35 A.M. (No. 1021), 8.25 A.M. (No. 1023), 10 A.M. (No. 1025), 12.10 P.M. (No. 1027), 2.55 P.M. (No. 1029), 3.55 P.M. (No. 1031), 5.25 P.M. (No. 1051), 6.10 P.M. (No. 1033) and 6.55 P.M. (No. 1035).

On the second route, there's a "*rapide*" train to Annaba, at 7.30 P.M. (arrives 7.45 A.M., sleepers available). This is called the Trans-Maghrebian train because it continues all the way to Tunis. The Trans-Maghrebian also stops in Sétif (12.58 A.M.) and Constantine (3.17 A.M.). There are also trains to these cities at 7.30 A.M. (No. 1, *rapide*), 12.30 P.M. (No. AC, *rapide*), and 9.05 P.M. (No. 3). All these trains, except the Trans-Maghrebian and the No. 3, stop at Bejaïa; there are others to Bejaïa at

5.45 A.M. (No. 11), 8.35 A.M. (No. 13), 3.05 P.M. (No. 15) and 4.50 P.M. (No. 19).

A third, less traveled route is Algiers-El Harrach-Thenia-Tizi Ouzou (107 km, or 66 miles) at 6.35 A.M. (No. 31), 11.50 A.M. (No. 33) and 6.05 P.M. (No. 35). The trip takes approximately two hours.

By Car

Roads in Algeria are generally well marked and well maintained. However, many roads, especially south of the High Plateaus, can be quite dangerous if you and your vehicle aren't prepared. Through ONAT, the Algerian government publishes a list describing the conditions and equipment requirements of each road.

Car rental is possible in most major cities, but the prices can be extortionate because you must pay by credit card or with officially exchanged money. This isn't a practical option for touring the country. ONAT often acts as a car rental agent, so check with them for any possible package deals. They were offering a basic Fiat 75 for about 400 DA ($80) a day or a Land-Rover for over 1,000 DA ($200) a day.

It may be cheaper to bring a car into Algeria by ferry from Europe, but the fares and fees can be prohibitive. The ferries to Morocco or Tunisia may be more economical options. In 1989, the ferry system was rapidly improving, so prices were apt to change, perhaps for the better.

By Hitchhiking

Hitchhiking around Algeria is a possibility, but don't be surprised if you are asked to pay for your rides. It is generally safe for men, but women should not hitchhike around Algeria on their own.

By Animal

It is possible to rent camels, donkeys, or horses in small towns and villages. Bargaining is usually the rule because there aren't any set rates. Most camels for hire, though, are rented by organized groups.

CHAPTER 12

Algiers and the North

If Algiers were a person, it would probably be institutionalized for its schizophrenic mishmash of multiple personalities. Its varied character is the result of a ping-pong history in which the city was bounced from one conqueror to the next.

The Phoenicians were among the first to enter the game when they established a small trading post in approximately the same location as present-day downtown Algiers. With a set of small islands offshore acting as a breakwater, the location offered a naturally well protected, thus strategically valuable, harbor. Phoenician dominance of Mediterranean commerce eventually spawned the great Carthaginian Empire, which spread throughout most of North Africa to include Algiers. The Carthaginians were followed by the Romans, who called the city Icosium after destroying and rebuilding it. More destruction and reconstruction followed with invasions by Vandals, Byzantines, and Arabs, all of which eclipsed the city's heyday as a center of Mediterranean trade. Aside from bringing Islam to the city's inhabitants, the Arabs also gave the city its current Arabic name—El Djazaïr, "the Island"—so named for the important islands in its harbor. Rule by a Berber dynasty followed in the tenth century and by Spaniards in the sixteenth before the Ottoman Turks established a prosperous regency there in the seventeenth. One of the key reasons for the regency's prosperity was the Ottoman's support of piracy from the city. In return for varying amounts of the booty stolen from ships in the Mediterranean, the *dey* or Ottoman-appointed ruler of the regency offered a relatively safe haven for the pirates. Apparently, however, the city seemed to become safer for pirates than for its own rulers. The last two deys sequestered themselves behind the high walls and thick ramparts of the kasbah, parts of which still offer a commanding view of the city, albeit in far worse condition today than two centuries ago. When the French captured Algiers in 1830, they partially dismantled—or, as some historical evidence suggests, destroyed—the kasbah. The wealthiest, most beautiful parts of the kasbah were plundered by Napoleon III's soldiers with the tacit approval of Napoleon's officers.

This was regarded as a form of compensating and rewarding these otherwise ill-paid troops. Algiers became the administrative and military capital of their Algerian colony and was gradually transformed into a French-style city with a bayfront boulevard of vaulted arches, "places," or squares surrounded by cafés, and colonnaded government buildings. The Ottoman-era mosque of Ketchaoua was converted into a cathedral, and the dey's kasbah palace was laid to ruin.

During World War II, Algiers was important to the Allied war effort in North Africa. General Dwight D. Eisenhower established his North Africa headquarters in the Hotel El Djazaïr in Algiers and plotted his maneuvers against Rommel's panzer divisions from there. After the French government fell to the Germans, a provisional French capital was also temporarily established in Algiers during the war. Less than a decade later, Algiers was the scene of several bloody street battles as the struggle for independence from France heated up.

Today, after almost three decades of independence, Algiers is confronting a different set of struggles and challenges. One of its biggest struggles has been how to stem a rapidly growing population of rural migrants who come searching for a better livelihood. However, many have had to settle in *bidonvilles*, or shantytowns, because of housing shortages; unemployment has increased because jobs are unavailable. In October 1988, riots broke out in the streets of Algiers to protest government housing and economic policies. The government has promised significant changes and has thus far been able to maintain stability in the city. It has been attempting to expand beyond the city's chief economic role as Algeria's biggest port and, instead, create more labor-intensive industry.

For travelers, the events of October reaffirm the city's image as a bubbling cauldron of social problems, but this doesn't necessarily mean that Algiers is an unsafe place to visit. As in many big cities, these problems manifest themselves in an increased crime rate, but you probably won't notice this unless you wander off the beaten track into the poorer parts of the kasbah.

Today, Algiers is an adventurous place to visit, but more for wandering among its symbols of a nation in transition than for hiking through its parks and old historic quarters. As you walk its crowded main streets and pedestrian malls, there's a mystique about the people, a glaring sense of urgency, a certain frown of uneasiness. It's as difficult to decipher as it is to determine from the surrounding buildings whether this is an Arab country trying to shed its French past or a piece of France striving to be Arab. There are French-style bakeries with baguettes and sticky sweet baklawa displayed in the windows, outdoor cafes that serve French espresso and café *turc*, restaurants with white-coated waiters, Châteaubriand, couscous, and kebab. Overlooking all this are apartment

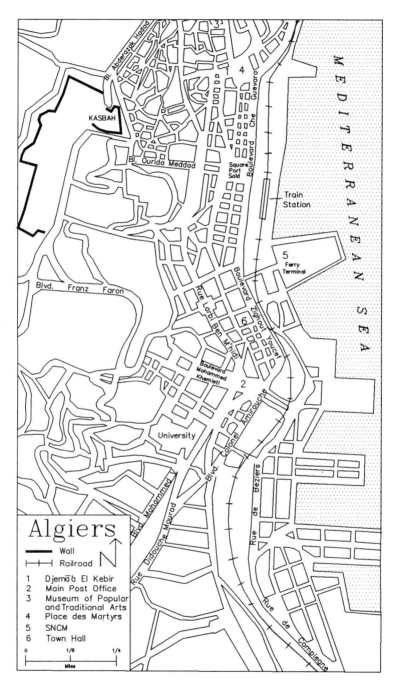

MEDITERRANEAN SEA

KASBAH

Bl. Abderazak Hadad

3

4

Boulevard Che Guevaro

Bl. Ourida Meddad

Square
Port
Said

Train
Station

5
Ferry
Terminal

Blvd. Franz Faron

Rue Larbi Ben M'hidi

Boulevard Zighout Youcef

6

Boulevard
Mohammed
Khemisti

2

University

Blvd. Colonel Amirouche

Rue de Beziers

Blvd. Mohammed V

Rue Didouche Mourad

Rue de Compiegne

Algiers

—— Wall

├─┼─┤ Railroad

N

1 Djemāa El Kebir
2 Main Post Office
3 Museum of Popular
  and Traditional Arts
4 Place des Martyrs
5 SNCM
6 Town Hall

0   1/8   1/4
├─────────┼─────────┤
        Miles

buildings with narrow, shuttered windows and wrought-iron balconies reminiscent of Marseilles or New Orleans. On surrounding hills are the steel and glass creations of contemporary Algeria—the Hotel Aurassi with signs and stature of Stalinistic proportions, a Palace of Culture with long halls and high windows, a towering monument to the martyrs of the independence struggle, and, in its shadow, the sparkling multilevel Riad el Feth mall.

ARRIVAL, DEPARTURE, AND GETTING AROUND

At first, the layout of Algiers seems confusing and illogical because a few of the major streets climb like undulating serpents from the bayfront port area up and over the slopes of the surrounding Sahel hills. If you are looking for a decent workout, then walk up one of these streets or the long, steep staircases that intersect many of them.

The central post office on Boulevard Mohammed Khemisti between Rue Larbi Ben M'hidi and Rue Assilah Hocine is a good starting point for exploring the city. From there, both of these streets are parallel and run north through the central business district. Rue Larbi Ben M'hidi curves eastward before ending at the Place Port Saïd city bus terminal. Rue Assilah Hocine follows a similar route one block closer to the bay, but it is known as Rue Abane Ramdane after it passes the Town Hall. Along the bay and parallel to both of these streets runs the arcaded Boulevard Zighout Youcef, one of the city's first major streets. It begins about one and a half blocks from the post office as an extension of a street that meanders south and west along the edge of the port. Going south from the post office area, this street is first known as Rue de Bapaume, then Rue de Beziers (location of one of the intercity bus terminals), Rue de Compiegne and finally the Route de l'Armée de Liberation Nationale, which is a highway that leads to the international airport.

Back on Boulevard Zighout Youcef, the street passes the waterfront Gare Maritime (main ferry and passenger ship terminal) and main train station. About one and a half blocks north of the train station (to the right as you exit), the boulevard ends at the Place Port Saïd. If you arrive at the station or the terminal at night and are looking for a taxi, you may have to cross the boulevard and climb the steep stairs on the other side to Rue Abane Ramdane.

From the north side of Place Port Saïd, the wide Boulevard Che Guevara leads to the city's other principal square (Place des Martyrs) and main mosque, the Djemā'a El Kebir (literally "the great" or "big" mosque). Going up the hill to your left are the labyrinthine streets of the old, run-down neighborhoods of the kasbah. To your immediate right is the fish market, which looks out on the admiralty's docks and a causeway-breakwater that connects the islets for which Algiers is named.

Going west and southwest from Hotel Albert 1er, which is about two blocks up Boulevard Mohammed Khemisti from the main post office, Rue de Pasteur becomes Rue El Khetabi and then Boulevard Mohammed V as it wanders into the hills. Rue Abdelkrim branches off from Rue El Khetabi and becomes Rue Didouche Mourad, which is where many of the airlines have their offices. About one block southeast of Rue Didouche Mourad is Rue Khelifa Boukhalfa, which is where ONAT (the government tourism organization) has its main offices.

Continuing along Rue Didouche Mourad, follow the street as it veers to the left (south) and past the Cathedral du Sacre Coeur (Cathedral of the Sacred Heart), a giant snail-like shell of a place situated on a slab overlooking a government gas station. Around the bend just past the cathedral is Parc de la Liberté (Liberty Park), which could just as well be named Liberated Lovers' Park because, according to locals, it is one of the few places in Algiers where lovers can meet. The park is alongside a hill and offers a shortcut to Avenue Franklin Roosevelt and the Bardo Museum. Streets branch off in all directions from here with the main southward thoroughfares heading for the Hydra area, a neighborhood favored by many countries for their embassies and official residences.

Arrival and Departure

By Air

Algiers's main airport—the Aeroport International Houari Boumediene—is located 19 km (12 miles) east of the city. All international arrivals and departures are through the international terminal, which is the larger of the two terminals at the airport. The domestic terminal is in a separate building adjacent to the international terminal.

There are ONAT desks (government tourism organization) in both terminals, but only the international terminal branch, which is just inside the departures entrance, seemed to be open. The staff was helpful, especially with hotel reservations; however, they lacked basic printed information such as city maps.

There are several money exchange counters near the entrance foyer where you can exchange currency and travelers' checks.

A bus to the Hotel Es-Safir in downtown Algiers departs about every thirty minutes from 6 A.M. to 6 P.M. in front of the international terminal. From the Hotel Es-Safir, the bus runs from 5:15 A.M. to 7:30 P.M.

Several international carriers fly to Algiers and maintain offices at the airport and in town. These include

Airline	Address	Telephone number
Air France	Place du Perou, Carrefour de l'Agha	63-16-10, 64-90-10
Aeroflot	7 Rue Malki Nassiba	60-56-61

Alitalia	7 Rue Hamani	64-68-50
Balkan	36 Rue Didouche Mourad	63-72-28
EgyptAir	4 Rue Didouche Mourad	63-05-05
Iberia	11 Rue Hamani	63-37-12
LOT (Polish Airlines)	12 Avenue Pasteur	64-00-75
Lufthansa	49 Rue Didouche Mourad	64-27-36
Sabena	61 Rue Larbi Ben M'hidi	63-32-14
SAS (Scandinavian Airlines Systems)	116 Rue Didouche Mourad	59-09-34
Swissair	19 Rue Didouche Mourad	63-33-67
Tunis Air	16 Rue Emir El Khattabi	63-26-14

Air Algerie is the agent for all other companies not represented in Algiers. It maintains offices throughout Algiers; the main booking office is at 1 Place Maurice Audin, tel. (64-24-28). Air Algerie regularly flies between Algiers and the following foreign cities: Athens, Bamako (Mali), Barcelona, Belgrade, Berlin, Bissau (Guinea-Bissau), Brazzaville, Brussels, Bucharest, Casablanca, Dakar (Senegal), Damascus, Frankfurt, Geneva, Jeddah, Kuwait, Lille (France), London, Luanda (Angola), Lyon (France), Madrid, Marseille, Moscow, Niamey, Nice (France), Nouakchott (Mauritania), Palma, Paris, Prague, Rome, Sofia (Bulgaria), Toulouse (France), Tripoli, Tunis, Valetta, Vienna, and Zurich. Some of these destinations are also served by international airports in other Algerian cities: Annaba, Constantine, Ghardaïa, Oran, Tebessa, and Tlemcen. These cities, as well as the following, have regularly scheduled flights to and from Algiers: Adrar, Béchar, Bejaïa, Biskra, Bordj-Badji-Mokhtar, Bou-Saada, Djanet, El Goléa, El Oued, Hassi Messaoud, Illizi, In-Amenas, In-Salah, Jijel, Mascara, Ouargla, Tamanrasset, Timimoun, Tindouf, and Touggourt.

By Bus

For the airport bus, see the preceding section.

There are frequent direct buses between Algiers and almost every major town and city in the country, except for the far flung towns of Tamanrasset and Adrar. A nationally owned company known by the acronym EPTVC (Enterprise Publique de Transport de Voyageurs du Centre), which roughly means "Public Bus Company for Travelers from the Center [of the country]"), maintains three *gares routiè*re or bus terminals. The newest and biggest terminal is at Rampe Fréderic Chassériau with service to and from the following destinations: Aïn Azel, Aïn Beïda, Aïn Kebira, Aïn Oulmène, Annaba, Arzew, Aïn Témouchet, Batna, Barika, Bordj Bou-Arréidj, Béchar, Béni Aziz, Biskra, Bougaâ, Bou-

Hanifia, Bou-Saada, Chelghoum Laïd, Constantine, El Eulma, El Milia, El Oued, El Bayadh, El Kala, Ferdjioua, Frenda, Ghardaïa, Gulema, Guenzet, Guerrara, Hassi Messaoud, Jijel, Khenchela, Laghouat, Mansouria, Mascara, Metlili, Mila, M'Sila, Mostaganem, Oum El Bouaghi, Oran, Oued Amizour, Ouenza, Ouargla, Relizane, Ras El Oued, Saïda, Sedrata, Sétif, Sidi Aïssa, Sidi Bel-Abbes, Sidi Khaled, Skikda, Sougheur, Souk Ahras, Taher, Tébessa, Touggourt, Texenna, Tiaret, Tizi Ouzou, Tlemcen, Tolga.

The terminal on Rue de Béziers services the following destinations: Sidi-Fredj, Chéraga, Zéralda, Bou-Ismaïl, Bou-Haroun, Koléa, Douéra, Saoula, Berard, Hadjout, Tipaza, Cherchell, and Ténés.

From the Tri-Postal terminal, the following destinations are served: Pins Maritimes (a renowned recreation area near Algiers), Bordj El Kiffan, Coco Plage (beach), Bordj El Bahri, Figuier, Boumerdés, Boufarik, Blida (access to Chréa).

The following is fare and schedule information for buses from Algiers:

Destination	Departure Times	Fare
Annaba	4.30 A.M., 10.15 A.M.	102 DA
Batna	5.30 A.M., 10 A.M., 12 noon, 3 P.M.	80 DA
Batna-Sétif	5.45 A.M., 10.30 A.M.	80 DA
Béchar	4.30 A.M., 5.30 A.M.	155 DA
Bejaïa	5 A.M., 7 A.M., 6 P.M.	48 DA
Beni Yenni	1 P.M.	21 DA
Biskra	5 A.M., 11 A.M., 3 P.M.	78 DA
Bou-Saada	5 A.M., 9 A.M., 12 noon, 2 P.M.	49 DA
Constantine	9 A.M., 11 A.M., 12 noon, 1 P.M., 2 P.M.	79 DA
Djelfa	5 P.M.	56 DA
El Oued	6 A.M.	98 DA
Ghardaïa	5.30 A.M., 6 A.M., 10.30 A.M., 6 P.M.	103 DA
Guelma	6 A.M., 8.15 A.M.	94 DA
Jijel	4.30 A.M., 9 A.M., 11 A.M., 2 P.M.	64 DA
Laghouat	6.45 A.M., 10 A.M., 12 noon	74 DA
Maghnia (Moroccan border)	2 P.M.	105 DA
Mostaganem	7.15 A.M., 10 A.M., 2 P.M.	57 DA
Oran	5.30 A.M., 9 A.M., 11.30 A.M., 3 P.M.	80 DA
Ouargla	7.30 P.M.	142 DA
Sétif	3 P.M., 5 P.M.	56 DA
Skikda	5.30 A.M., 9.30 A.M.	90 DA
Tiaret	6 A.M., 6.30 A.M., 11 A.M., 1 P.M.	62 DA
Tizi-Ouzou	6 A.M., 9 A.M., 1 P.M., 4.30 P.M., 6.15 P.M., 5.45 P.M.	18 DA

By Train

Algiers's main train station is on Boulevard Zighout Youcef next to the Gare Maritime (passenger and shipping terminal). For information about routes and fares, see the Getting Around Section in Chapter 11.

FIRST THINGS FIRST

Tourist Information

As mentioned in the introduction, ONAT—Office National Algerien de l'Animation de la Promotion et de l'Information Touristique (Algerian National Office of Promotion and Tourist Information)—is the principal source of tourist information about Algiers and surrounding areas. Although it has branch offices at various locations in the city, such as directly across from the Hotel Es-Safir, it's better to visit the main office at 25-27 Rue Khelifa Bou Khalfa, which is about a 10- to 15-minute walk southwest from the central post office. Walk down Rue El Khetabi and ask someone to show you the way to Rue Didouche Mourad; from there, ask for Rue Khelifa Bou Khalfa. The telephone numbers are 61-29-86 and 61-26-55. There is usually someone around who speaks some English. The main ground-floor office is closed on Thursday and Friday and open from about 9 A.M. to 5 P.M. the rest of the week. The office usually has a few brochures in English available that give an overview of Algiers and other parts of the country. Your best source of information here, however, will be the staff.

Other ONAT offices in Algiers are at

5 Boulevard Ben Boulaid:	tel. 64-15-50
2 Rue Didouche Mourad:	tel. 63-10-66
Hotel El Aurassi:	tel. 64-82-52
Hotel El Djazaïr:	tel. 60-10-00
Riad El Feth (shopping mall):	tel. 66-66-11
Airport:	tel. 75-33-67

Other Information

The U.S. Cultural Center (tel. 60-66-52 and 60-68-97), 8 Rue Ali Messaoud, Hydra, run by the U.S. Information Service, is mostly for Algerians interested in the United States. However, the center's library has a useful collection of books and materials in English about Algeria, which can be quite helpful to curious travelers. For the homesick or otherwise, they also occasionally present U.S. network news broadcasts and movies.

For information about the Tassili National Park around the southern Saharan town of Djanet, contact the ONPT (Office National du Parc du Tassili), Parc Zyriab; tel. 60-53-39.

Embassies

The following is a list of some of the foreign embassies and representatives in Algiers:

Australia
   12 Escalier Emile Marquis (Djenane El Malik), Hydra (tel. 60-19-65)
Austria
   Rue No. 02 Lot. No. 09 Les Vergers, Bir Mourad Raïs (tel. 56-29-09)
Belgium
   22 Chemin Youcef Tayebi, El Biar (tel. 78-57-12 and 78-64-46)
Republic of Burkina Fasso
   12 Boulevard Victor Hugo (tel. 61-38-97)
Republic of Burundi
   22 Lotissement du Carrefour, El Biar (tel. 79-48-78)
Cameroon
   60 Boulevard Colonel Bougara, El Biar (tel. 60-61-90 and 60-66-11)
Canada
   27 Bis. Rue des Frères Benhafid, Hydra (tel. 60-61-90 and 60-66-11)
Chad
   Cité D.N.C., Villa No. 18, Rue Kara Ahmed, Chemin du Kaddous, Hydra (tel. 60-66-37)
Republic of the Congo
   Lot. Cadat No. 179 Ben-Omar, Kouba (tel. 58-38-88)
Egypt (Interests Section)
   c/o 8 Chemin Gaddouche Abdelkader, Hydra (tel. 60-16-73). By publication time, this will probably be a full-fledged embassy, because of renewed relations between Algeria and Egypt.
Federal Republic of Germany
   165 Chemin Sfindja (tel. 63-48-27, 63-48-45 and -46)
France
   6 Rue Larbi Alik, Hydra (tel. 60-44-88 and 60-98-44)
Great Britain
   7 Chemin des Glycines (tel. 60-54-11)
Italy
   18 Rue Finalterie, El Biar (tel. 78-33-99 and 78-23-30)
Ivory Coast
   Immeuble le Bosquet Parc du Paradou, Hydra (tel. 60-24-82)

Mali
    Cité D.N.C. Villa No. 015, Chemin du Khaddous, Hydra
    (tel. 60-61-18 and 60-62-22)
Mauritania
    107 Lot. Baranes, Air de France, Bouzarea (tel. 79-21-39 and
    79-20-44)
Morocco (Interest Section)
    8 Rue des Cedres, El Mouradia (tel. 60-74-08). This is
    expected to become a full embassy soon because of renewed
    relations between Morocco and Algeria.
Netherlands
    23 Chemin Bachir El Ibrahimi, El Biar (tel. 78-28-28)
Niger
    54 Rue du Vercours, Air de France, Bouzarea (tel. 78-89-21)
Nigeria
    27 Bis Rue Blaise Pascal (tel. 60-65-00 and 60-60-50)
Senegal
    1 Rue Arago, El Mouradia (tel. 56-90-85)
Spain
    10 Rue Azil Ali (tel. 61-70-63 and 61-70-62)
Switzerland
    27 Boulevard Zighout Youcef, B.P. 482 (tel. 63-39-02)
Tunisia
    11 Rue du Bois de Boulogne, El Mouradia (tel. 60-15-67)
Turkey
    13 Chemin de la Rochelle, Boulevard Colonel Bougara, El
    Biar (tel. 60-12-57)
United States
    4 Chemin Sheikh El Ibrahimi, El Biar (tel. 60-11-86 and 60-
    18-28)

Accommodations

Algiers has a shortage of accommodations at all levels. The two best hotels in the city are the Hotel Aurassi and the Hotel El Djazaïr (formerly the St. George Hotel), both of which often tend to be filled with business travelers, international meeting participants, and European tour groups.

The Hotel Aurassi (tel. 64-82-52) is worth visiting just to see the symbolic product of an era when Algeria emphasized its international identity as a socialist "Democratic and Popular Republic." Everything about the place is big with a sort of bigness that reminded me of the intimidating Stalinistic edifices I visited in Moscow a few years ago. With over 400 rooms, it towers over the city from a commanding position on the Plateau des Tagarines and astride the steep Boulevard Franz Fanon.

It's a monolithic block of concrete, steel, and glass that resembles an airport terminal. The interior seems designed to make you feel like a flea in a land of giants. Signs behind the reception desks— "CAISSE...CONCIERGE...RECEPTION"—were big enough for even the most myopic to read. Just off the main lobby are the hotel's shops, most with dusty glass cases and yawning clerks reading newspapers. Bright yellow suede pants on a bald mannequin graced the window of a leather store. In the jewelry store, a pair of gold earrings worth probably no more than $35 in the United States was selling for $750. A plate of spaghetti and a sweet fizzy drink in the "Coffeeshop" cost approximately $8.

The Hotel El Djazaïr (tel. 60-87-77) is also worth visiting, if only to see a more traditional side of Algerian hotel architecture. It was built in 1889 as the St. George Hotel and incorporated the arches, mosaics (originally from Cherchell), and hand-painted tiles of a small castle that existed on these grounds centuries before. During World War II, General Dwight Eisenhower used the hotel as his headquarters for the U.S. Army's North Africa campaign. The hotel was renovated between 1978 and 1982 with a new wing added that increased the total number of beds from 250 to 600. It was renamed the Hotel El Djazaïr after renovation. The hotel is hidden amid two gardens on Avenue Souidani Boudjemâa near the Hydra district of Algiers; the Bardo Museum is just down the street toward downtown. A double room costs about 430 DA although special group rates are available through ONAT.

One level down in price from the Aurassi and the El Djazaïr is the Hotel Es-Safir (tel. 63-50-40), which is centrally located on Rue Abane Ramdane just down the street from the central post office. Although most of the hotel is decorated in an art deco style, with rococo plaster ceiling moldings and brocaded wallpaper, there's a sense of faded elegance about the place, dusty reminders of the French and France. A double costs 280 DA ($56). This hotel was formerly known as the Aletti and is also sometimes called L'Ambassadeur.

A more moderately priced hotel is the Albert 1er (tel. 63-00-20) at 5 Avenue Pasteur, which is quite well situated about a block from the central post office. It's clean and comfortable, but not really worth the $40 per night that they charge for a double. If you decide to stay here, check out a few rooms first. Try to avoid the rooms on the upper floors because the water pressure often isn't strong enough to reach their bathrooms. Also, a few toilets are missing seats (which is why they provide buckets of water).

Other centrally located hotels in approximately the same price range as the Albert include the Hotel des Etrangers (tel. 63-32-45, Rue Ali Boumendjel), the Hotel Central Touring (tel. 63-54-40, 9 Rue Abane Ramdane), the Hotel Djemila Palace (tel. 63-13-35, 1 Rue Louise de Bettignies), the Hotel Ifriquia (tel. 63-11-12, 11 Boulevard Ben Boulaïd) and the Hotel Oasis (tel. 63-06-20, 2 Rue Smain Kerrar).

There are a few hotels even lower in price, but their standards will also be lower. These include: the Hotel Terminus (2 Rue Rachid Kessentini), the Hotel Ziri (Pins Maritime, El Harrach), the Hotel Timgad (4 Rue Smaïn Kerrar), the Hotel Regina (27 Boulevard Boulaïd), the Hotel de Nice (4 Rue Garibaldi), the Hotel Victoria (6 Rue Hocine Tiah), the Hotel Arago (6 Rue Nafaâ Haffaf), the Hotel Es-Salem (2 Rue Omar l'Agha) and the Hotel Moderne (7 Rue de la Liberté).

Restaurants

Algiers has a good selection of restaurants, but the inflated value of the dinar makes even the most inexpensive places seem overpriced. For example, at the Pizzeria La Gondole in the Bois des Arcades/Riad El Feth, a simple cheese and tomato pizza for one costs about $8. At the excellent Restaurant Zeriab in the same locale, superb traditional Algerian cuisine is served at what may seem like exorbitant prices. Near downtown, especially on Rue Didouche Mourad, there are several restaurants serving everything from French and Italian to traditional Algerian cuisine. The Café Anglais, a favorite among local business people, is across the street from the Hotel Es-Safir and a few doors down from an ONAT branch office. Its 55 DA three-course lunch, including plenty of bread, soup, salad, main dish such as chicken or veal, and dessert is a good deal compared to other prices around town.

For traditional and French-style breads and pastries, try any of the bakeries found on almost every downtown street.

Getting Things Done

Money Exchange

Foreign travelers' checks and currency can be exchanged at Bureaux de Change at the airport, most major hotels, and banks located throughout the city.

Post and Telephone Office

The central post office and telephone office are adjacent to each other on Boulevard Mohammed Khemisti; they are two of the largest buildings, so you can't miss seeing them.

THINGS TO SEE AND DO

Algiers isn't renowned for its sights and adventurous activities. However, there are a few things worth seeing and doing.

ONAT, the government tourist office, offers a half-day city tour for 40 DA per person that includes visits to the Botanical Gardens, Martyr's Memorial, Riad El Feth (mall and artisans' village), a short walking tour of the Kasbah, the Ketchaoua Mosque, and the Museum of Popular and Traditional Arts. If you are keen to do a strenuous hilly walk through the city or catch a variety of buses and taxis, you could do this tour on your own in about a day (a very full day, though).

The Botanical Gardens are known as Le Jardin d'Essai and are located in the southern quarter of Diar El Mahçoul across from the Museum of Fine Arts. The gardens are an appealing place for a short, easy hike and a lazy afternoon picnic. The museum maintains a fair collection of contemporary Algerian painting and sculpture. Both the museum and gardens are at the foot of the hill or plateau where the Bois des Arcades complex (Riad El Feth, artisans' village, and Martyr's Memorial) is located. Nearby is a cable car that climbs through the trees to the Palais de la Culture (Palace of Culture).

The Bois des Arcades is also a wooded area, but its 146 hectares (350 acres) is dominated by the Riad El Feth (Victory Park) and the Martyr's Memorial (also known as the Sanctuary of the Martyr and the Makam Echadid Memorial).

The memorial comprises 92-m (302-ft) -high concrete slabs resembling the flickering parts of the eternal flame at the center of its base. The memorial was erected on the twentieth anniversary of Algeria's independence, to honor the martyrs of the independence struggle. There are elevators and stairs up to a room near the top that offers fantastic views of Algiers and its surrounding neighborhoods. At the base of the monument is the Djihad Museum with exhibits covering the Algerian resistance movement from the beginning of French colonization in 1830 to independence in 1962. Exhibits include photographs, personal objects belonging to Emir Abdelkader, significant documents, and arms used during various resistance battles. The museum is open every day except Saturday.

East of the memorial is the rest of the Bois des Arcades complex, most of which opened on November 1, 1984. The pulsating heart of the complex is a gleaming U.S.-style multilevel shopping mall. In most other countries, I wouldn't suggest a visit to a shopping mall as a possible miniadventure, but it's somewhat of an oddity in a country where shortages of consumer goods have been rife. Its location at the foot of the immense independence monument—a monument to Algeria's past struggles—is also odd. The mall itself stands as a sort of monument—a monument, perhaps, to Algeria's future.

The mall includes over 150 shops such as clothing stores, a one-hour photo-processing center, jewelry stores, a poster shop selling posters of Madonna for 35 DA ($7), a musical instrument shop and art galleries; 26 restaurants and cafés; a Socio-Cultural Center (Centre Socio-Culturel); a music club, a library, two movie theaters, a film library, an audio-visual center, a record library, exposition gallery, and a marionette theater.

Just outside the mall complex is the Museum of the National Popular Army and an artisans' village. During my visit, the museum was closed for renovation. The artisans' village is divided into two main galleries with a total of 26 minigalleries arranged somewhat like a traditional souk or market where you can watch the artisans work. In Gallerie A, the artisans do traditional wood paintings and sculptures, pottery, ceramics, bookbinding, cast brasswork, metal engravings, violin making, picture framing, wood carving, and illuminated calligraphy work. In Gallerie B, the crafts represented include silk weaving, traditional jewelry making, cabinetmaking, cloth embroidery, corduroy embroidery, leatherwork, slipper making, lacework, blanket weaving, and saddlemaking. Most of the artwork and handicrafts produced here is sold in the mall galleries.

Adjacent to the "village" are three restored villas housing a traditional-style café and restaurant and a music library with a good collection of traditional Algerian and Berber music. Nearby is a 600-seat outdoor theater.

The Palace of Culture is on a hill next to the Bois des Arcades complex. It's a relatively new convention center with long halls and high windows, another awesome monument to Algeria's future. Occasionally, one of the exhibit halls is used for cultural exhibitions, such as a display of traditional Berber costumes. The building also serves as home to the Ministry of Culture and Tourism—ONAT's parent. The easiest way to get to the palace from the Bois des Arcades is to walk down the hill from the Martyr's Memorial to the Museum of Fine Arts and take the cable car to a lot near the palace.

The Kasbah is the poorer, older, northern quarter of Algiers. Frankly, because of repeated battles in this area during the independence struggle and terrible overcrowding in recent years, the area has lost most of its "Old World" charm and become a vast slum. For a quick tour on your own, start at the Palais du Dey (Dey's Palace) fortress, which approximately marks the upper perimeter of the kasbah district, and follow the stairs down to Rue Abdelrahman Arbadji and Rue Amar Ali. Turn left when you get to the street and veer right toward the Place des Martyrs; if you're uncertain about directions, just ask the way to the Place des Martyrs and Djemā'a El Kebir.

About a block northwest of the Place des Martyrs are the Ketchaoua and Ali Bitchin mosques; the former is a restored Ottoman mosque. Between the two mosques is the Museum of Popular and Traditional

Arts, which was formerly the first French Hôtel de Ville (town hall) in Algiers and, before that, an Ottoman palace. Displays in the museum are similar to the works of the minigalleries in the Riad El Feth artisans' village.

The last main sight worth visiting in Algiers is the Zoological and Leisure Park of Algiers (Le Parc zoologique et des loisirs d'Alger) located southwest of downtown Algiers on 304 hectares (730 acres) of wooded land. It's large enough for a few short hikes through the woods.

NEAR ALGIERS

One of the most popular half-day or one-day side trips from Algiers is westward to Cherchell along what the Algerians call their Turquoise Coast. It's a beautiful drive and, if you wish, a walk or hike at certain points on the way, particularly along the beaches. Highlights include:

• **El Djemila** ("The Beautiful"), a small, sheltered fishing port 16 km (10 miles) from Algiers that is renowned for its seafood restaurants and fresh seafood market.

• **Le Club de Pins** (literally "Club of the Pine Trees"). The "club" is actually an international conference center with a Palace of Nations, several vacation villas and restaurants, and a very beautiful beach.

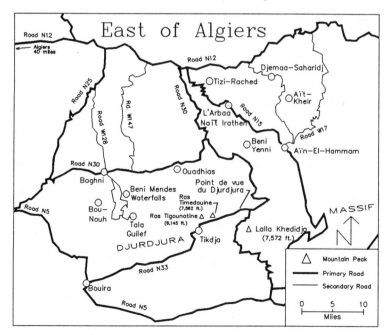

- **Sidi Fredj** (also known as Sidi Ferruch), a bayside resort complex located on a small peninsula about 26 km (16 miles) from Algiers. The complex is especially known for its boat harbor where you can rent sailboats and motorboats. There are also two main hotels: the Port Hotel with 94 rooms, each with a bathroom, telephone, and private balcony overlooking the sea; and the El Manar Hotel with 374 large, cozy rooms, each with a bathroom and telephone. There are restaurants and swimming pools at both hotels.

The Tourist Center, which is adjacent to the hotels, is a popular summer refuge with several shops and restaurants, including a good pizzeria and the Bistrot restaurant. Sailboats, motorboats, and pedal boats can be rented from the center.

- **Bou Ismaïl.** This small seaside village 45 km (28 miles) from Algiers has a pleasant Boulevard Front de Mer along the shore, a fish pond, an aquarium, and museum. It's also home to the Maritime Institute.

- **Berard**, a small village 54 km (33 miles) from Algiers that's known for its plane trees and easy access to the first-century tomb of the Mauretanian royal family. The tomb is an impressive stone structure 60 m (197 ft) in diameter and 40 m high (131 ft) with a beautiful panoramic view overlooking the Mitidja plain. It's surrounded by 60 Ionic columns and makes for a good, short hike up from the village. The road is well-marked, so you shouldn't have any problem finding it.

- **Tipaza**, a village 70 km (43 miles) from Algiers that's renowned for its Roman ruins. The Romans were preceded by Phoenicians, who established a trading outpost there beginning in the fifth century B.C. By the first century A.D., the Roman Empire had expanded to North Africa and made Tipaza part of the colony of Latium. During the fourth century, a rift between Byzantine Catholics and a heretical North Africa sect known as the Donatists resulted, according to legend, in the martyring of St. Salsa at Tipaza. By the end of the fifth century, bitter disputes between the two groups had destroyed most of the town. The actual modern-day village of Tipaza wasn't founded until 1857 as the French developed the area for wine making, which is probably why many of the principal structures of the original Roman village have been so well preserved. These structures or, in some instances, ruins include a relatively big cathedral with nine naves, a Roman forum, an assembly area, thermal baths, a theater, shops, and stone-slab streets with the remnants of an ancient underground sewer system visible through the cracks. The complex is beautifully situated amid a grove of olive trees, asphodels, and mastic trees that grow right to the edge of the sea. Albert Camus, author of *The Plague*, *The Stranger*, and several other existentialist novels, used to like wandering among the ruins. Most of the best-preserved artifacts from the complex have been transferred to a small building about two blocks away called the Museum of Tipaza (Museé de Tipaza).

The museum is only one room, but its collection of colorful mosaics salvaged from the archaeological site is magnificent.

If you want to spend the night in Tipaza, there are two hotel resort complexes, both of which tend to be full in the summer. The Tipaza-Matares hotel complex includes three hotels: the four-star Bay Hotel, located right on the beach with 100 rooms overlooking the sea; the three-star Residence Hotel with 352 rooms; and the three-star Bungalows, located at the edge of the beach.

The other complex is called the Tipaza Village; it has several restaurants and various sports facilities, as well as 600 beach bungalows.

• **Le Chenoua.** Just outside Tipaza is the Le Chenoua area, which is named for the 905-m (2,969-ft) -high Djebel Chenoua above the village. A 32-km (20-mile) side road (W109) branches off the main road and forms sort of a corniche as it curves around the mountain and along a small bay. Any of the sand and pebble beaches along the road that aren't occupied by clear plastic greenhouses are great little refuges for a picnic or one-night campsite. The greenhouses are seen throughout the northern coastal areas and are sometimes placed over entire fields for irrigation by condensation.

• **Cherchell.** A small maritime town about 100 km (62 miles) from Algiers surrounded by beautiful green hills. The Phoenicians arrived here in the fourth century B.C. and established a trading post and colony known as Iol. Later, under Juba II, it became Caesarea, capital of Mauretania Caesarea. The Romans arrived and expanded the city by building an amphitheater, aqueduct, thermal baths, fountains, and a wonderful seafront esplanade. Today, the city's ruins are barely discernible in what is now a city park along the esplanade. A few columns, statue fragments, and broken mosaics lie scattered on the grounds. The best-preserved artifacts have been transferred to the Cherchell Archaeological Museum adjacent to the park.

The museum houses a good collection of Roman statues, columns, and mosaics, among which are a well-preserved statue of Appolonia and a fairly complete mosaic representation of the Three Virgins. Most of the noses have been knocked off the statues.

There are two hotels near the museum—the Hotel Cesarée and the Hotel Les Messageries—both on Rue Abdelhak. Camping is also possible 28 km (17 miles) to the west of Cherchell at La Crique de Gouraya (Gouraya Cove) and to the east at Rocher Blanc (White Rock).

Since Cherchell is a popular resort town in the summer and tourist attraction all year, there are several restaurants. The following are often recommended by travelers: Le Méditeranée on Rue Abdelhak, Le Penalty on Rue Sidi Ali, El Marhaba on Rue de la Mosquée, L'Oasis on Place du Marché, La Vague on a small beach near the town, and Les Amis on Rue Sidi Ali.

Getting to all of these places from Algiers is possible by bus. City or local buses run to El Djemila, Le Club des Pins, and Sidi Fredj, while inter-city buses service the destinations farther afield.

To the east, the most popular excursions are to the following beaches and beach towns:

- **Bordj El Kiffan**, a small village 18 km (11 miles) from Algiers that is known for its excellent grilled seafood skewers.
- **Alger-Plage** (literally, "Algiers-Beach"), a stretch of beach about 27 km (18 miles) from Algiers that is known for its sailing and boating competitions.
- **Tamentefoust-La Marsa,** a port town 30 km (19 miles) from Algiers where it's possible to rent sailboats for short excursions in the area.
- **Aïn-Taya-Surcouf**, a beautiful stretch of beach about 35 km (22 miles) from Algiers that's situated at the foot of a spectacularly steep cliff.
- **Boumerdes**, an immense beach that's especially popular with various school groups throughout the year. The village is a good departure point for a drive along coastal road N24 or a hike along the beach to the seafront village of Le Figuier (5 km, or 3 miles) and nearby Cap Blanc.

FARTHER ALONG THE COAST

Bejaïa

The bustling port city of Bejaïa is the first major coastal city east of Algiers. Along the most direct route possible—inland via Tizi Ouzou and a sinuous, almost tortuous road through the Grand Kabylie mountains— Bejaïa is about 222 km (138 miles) from Algiers.

Although the mountains have long sheltered Bejaïa from the rest of the country, it has served as an important economic and political link between the Kabylie mountains and other parts of the Mediterranean throughout its history. Archaeological evidence in the form of sparse ruins suggests that Bejaïa was originally founded by a group of Roman military veterans who called it Saldae. The Bejaïa Berber tribe later staked a claim to the town and increased its prominence as a regional trading center. By the eleventh century, the Hammadid dynasty had made the town their capital and built several fortified strongholds to protect themselves. It gained importance as a fortified Hammadid capital in 1067.

Over the next few centuries, Bejaïa was a popular refuge for the Barbary pirates who preyed on Mediterranean shipping. The town was then known as Bougie because, according to local legends, it introduced the wax candle or *bougie* (French for "candle") to Europe. Its reputation as a pirate stronghold also attracted the military interests of various Mediterranean powers. The Spanish occupied the city from 1510 to 1555 after explorer Pedro Navarro conquered it in 1509. Then, the Ottoman Turks ruled the city with various pirate chieftains and Algiers-based deys and caused the city to decline in economic importance until the French arrived in 1833.

Bejaïa was well situated to become an important port and agricultural center under French tutelage. Located at the mouth of the Oued Soummam river, the narrow plains along both riverbanks leading into the city were, and still are, fertile agricultural areas. Although the valley receives approximately 102 cm (40 in) of rain annually, it is sheltered from cold winds by the Grand Kabylie range on the northwest and the Petit Kabylie range on the southeast, thus making it ideal for growing citrus fruits, olives, and grains.

To take full advantage of this fertile valley, most of the older part of town was built on the lower slope of Djebel Gouraya, the 660-m (2,165-ft) mountain overlooking the town and jutting cape peninsula of Cap Carbon. The French extended the town into the valley and along the main road to Algiers and, in the early 1900s, developed the harbor into a full-fledged port. Its port facilities greatly facilitated the export of key products and materials—olive oil, wine, phosphates, and iron ore. By 1959, oil and natural gas pipelines reached from the Sahara to Bejaïa, thus making the city one of the country's most important shipping outlets.

Bejaïa is more renowned for its beautiful location and hilly streets at the foot of Djebel Gouraya than for its historic sites. There are a few Roman ruins in town, but they are really no more than vestiges of the once-extensive ramparts. Fort Moussa (or Fort Barral, as it's also sometimes called), which was constructed by Pedro Navarro in the early sixteenth century, is worth visiting for a great view of the bay. There's also a small museum, but its hours are somewhat erratic.

For a miniadventure hike, follow the circuitous road behind the city and up Djebel Gouraya to the Pic des Singes (literally "Peak of the Monkeys"), which is named for the many monkeys in the area. At 430 m (1,411 ft) above the city, the peak offers a fantastic view of Bejaïa and the Soummam valley. Farther up the mountain at 660 m (2,165 ft) is the Fort du Gouraya, which is high enough for a good extended view beyond the city and well into both Kabylie ranges.

Back in town at the foot of Djebel Gouraya, a road leads west along a picturesque corniche to Cap Carbon. With a beautiful wooded area on one side and a steep cliff overhanging the sea on the other, this area is great for short hikes from town.

From Bejaïa to Jijel

The (57-mile)-92 km coastal road between Bejaïa and Jijel is the main reason many travelers visit this region. More than half of this stretch is called the Corniche Kabyle, which is where the road narrows and passes through a series of short tunnels as it skirts the edge of the sea.

Before you reach the Corniche, however, you'll pass through the resort village of Tichy (also Tichi) just outside of Bejaïa. Campgrounds and a few hotels are available in Tichy. The three-star Hotel Les Hammadites (tel. 92-66-80) with 150 rooms—several of which overlook the beach—is the biggest in the area and especially popular in the summer because of its beachfront location. Singles are 141 DA and doubles 192 DA.

Transportation between Bejaïa-Tichy and other destinations is readily available by bus and train (Bejaïa only). From Bejaïa, there are buses to Algiers at 5.30, 6.15, 7, and 9 A.M., all of which pass via Tizi Ouzou. Buses to Jijel via Tichy depart at 8.30 and 11 A.M., and at 12.30, 3, 4, and 6 P.M. From Jijel to Algiers via Tichy and Bejaïa, there are buses at 5.35, 7.15, and 9.10 A.M., and at 1.30 and 3.10 P.M. From Bejaïa to Sétif, there are buses every hour from 5 to 11 A.M. and then at 12.30, 2, 3, 4, and 6 P.M.

The train departs Bejaïa for Algiers at 5.35, 7.30, and 8.20 A.M. and at 1, 2.05, and 3.10 P.M.

At 33 km (21 miles) from Bejaïa is the mouth of the river Oued Agrioun and the junction with Road N6, the 76-km (47-mile) route to Sétif. This road cuts through the heart of the Petit Kabylie range and offers access to the Parc National Tizi N'Béchar, which is dominated by the 1,833-m (6,014-ft)-high peak of Djebel Babor. There are a few hiking trails in the park, but I was unable to obtain current information. Ask at the tourist office in Bejaïa before attempting to trek into the park.

Just beyond the N9 road junction on the road to Jijel, the first community you reach is Les Falaises ("the Cliffs"), which approximately marks the beginning of the most spectacular part of the Corniche Kabyle. From here to the fishing village of Ziama Mansouria, the road winds through tunnels cut in the cliffs right along the edge of the sea. On a sunny day, the water is every imaginable shade of blue and green.

From Ziama-Mansouria, a partially paved road—W137—leads into the forested foothills and lower slopes of the Petit Kabylie range. After about 10 km (6 miles), it reaches a large lake that was created by the

Merdj-ez-Erraguene dam and hydroelectric project. Beyond the lake, the road twists and turns and becomes quite rough as it climbs through a forest of cork trees, many of which have had their bark stripped for the cork. It's a beautiful 65-km (40-mile) route, but it takes at least two hours. The road returns to the coast at El Aouana, which is about 19 km (12 miles) from Jijel.

Jijel is a small fishing and shipping port at the edge of an immense forest of cork oaks, a wooded area known as the Bois des Oasis, and the "maritime" pine forests of Beni Caïd. Any of these areas are good for short hikes. There's also a decent beach a short distance from the port area where you can camp.

THE GRAND KABYLIE MOUNTAINS

The Grand Kabylie mountains are one of the main ranges of a wide swath of Atlas mountains that stretches from the middle of Morocco to western Tunisia. The Grand Kabylie range roughly encompasses the area from Bejaïa west through Tizi Ouzou to Blida and south to the edge of the High Plateaus. During the independence struggle, the mountainous terrain, numerous valleys, and traditionally fierce independence of its people— the Kabyle Berbers—proved a major obstacle to French efforts to completely colonize Algeria.

Tizi Ouzou is considered the capital of this region and principal city of the Kabyle Berbers. It is also a good base from which to explore the towns, villages, national parks, ski slopes, and mountains of the region.

The villages of the Grand Kabylie mountains are renowned for their traditional handicrafts. In Beni Yenni, the specialties are enameled silver jewelry decorated with coral, and wood furniture decorated with hand-carved geometric designs. Similar jewelry is also found at Boghni and Bouira. And similar furniture is found at Djemā'a-Saharidj, Tizi-Rached, and Aïn-El-Hammam. Pottery in age-old shapes and forms with black and red geometric motifs is the specialty of Aït-Kheir, Les Ouadias, and Bou-Nouh. Traditional weaving can be found at the villages of Aït-Hichem, Ouadhias, and Ouaghzene. Decorative and utilitarian palm frond basketry is the specialty of Dellys, Lakhdaria, and Ouadhias.

TIZI OUZOU

With a population of more than 100,000, Tizi Ouzou is the largest city in the Grand Kabylie mountains and has long been considered the capital of this region and the Kabyle Berbers. In recent years, Tizi Ouzou has been the center of a Kabyle Berber cultural movement, a protest movement against government arabization efforts.

Arabization programs were intended mostly to negate the overwhelming influence of French culture in Algeria. These programs were considered related to the government's economic development efforts, which were being attempted through the centralization and bureaucratization of policy making. The Kabyle Berbers suffered because their language—the main cultural characteristic distinguishing them from Arabs—was not recognized as an official national language. In the early 1980s, student demonstrations against the government resulted in some concessions for Kabyle culture: that is, the reinstatement of chairs and departments of Berber studies at the universities of Algiers and Tizi Ouzou. Today, Berber ethnicity is still an issue in Tizi Ouzou, but the city is also becoming known for its hotel and tourism personnel-training institute, one of the most prominent institutions of its kind in the country.

Arrival and Departure

There are three trains and numerous buses daily between Algiers and Tizi Ouzou. The trains depart Tizi at 5.12 and 10.25 A.M. and 4.30 P.M. for the 107-km (66-mile), approximately 2 1/2 -hour trip to Algiers; they stop at Thenia and El Harrach. From Algiers, there are trains at 6.35 and 11.50 A.M. and 6.05 P.M. Check the Algiers section for bus information.

First Things First

Tourist information

There is an Office Local du Tourisme that's supposedly open Saturday to Wednesday from 8 A.M. to 12 noon and 1 P.M. to 6 P.M. and Thursday 8 A.M. to 12 noon, but they seemed to have somewhat erratic hours because so few visitors stop by the office. The office is in the Maison de l'Artisanat, which is a collection of small shops that display and sell the handicrafts of the people who live in the Kabylie mountains located behind La Mairie (city hall or mayor's office). They didn't have much in the way of information about the region, but that was supposed to change.

Accommodations

Tizi Ouzou has several hotels of various categories. At the top of the list is the four-star Hotel Amraoua (tel. 40-85-46), which is a semideluxe affair beautifully situated atop a hill overlooking the city, with the Grand Kabylies as a spectacular backdrop. This is one of the best all-round hotels in Algeria—excellent service, modern carpeted rooms, most with balconies, a traditional-style restaurant that serves some of the best Algerian cuisine in the country, and a good collection of handicrafts from the mountains.

In town, there's the three-star Hotel Lalla-Khedidja on Rue Khodja Khaled with 40 rooms of varying quality; some are air-conditioned and have televisions. The manager is one of the most fastidious I have ever encountered. He will gratefully show you around the premises and explain exactly where children can sit in the garden during the summer. Singles are 100 DA and doubles 120 DA.

Other hotels in town include the Hotel Beloua at 16 Rue Larbi Ben M'hidi and the Hotel Andalous at 74 Rue Oubouzar.

For meals and food supplies, there are plenty of restaurants and shops in town.

TRIPS FROM TIZI OUZOU

Heart of the Grand Kabylie

The most popular route to follow from Tizi Ouzou is a circuit that begins on Road N12 going east out of town 7 km (4 miles) to N15. This road climbs into the mountains passing through several villages and viewpoints. After 20 very serpentine kilometers (12 1/2 miles), you reach the town of l'Arbaa Naït Irathen at 900 m (2,953 ft) where you can stock up on some basic staples such as bottled water, bread, canned food, and some fruit and vegetables. A big cherry festival is held here in June. Another 20 km beyond l'Arbaa is the town or village of Aïn El Hammam, which has become somewhat of an all-year resort.

Aïn El Hammam

Aïn El Hammam is renowned both for its status as a small vacation center and for its age-old production of traditional-style Kabylie tapestries. Views from the village of the beautiful, often snow-covered peaks of the Djurdjura massif, particularly the two highest—Ras Timedouine (2,305 m or 7,562 feet) and Lalla Khedidja (2,308 m or 7,572 feet)—are alluring and one of the village's principal attractions. You'll probably want to head farther into the mountains as soon as possible. However, if you're not rushed, you can spend a night at the only hotel in the village—the three-star Hotel Djurdjura (tel. 40-90-41) with 40 rooms and a restaurant. The hotel sits above the village at an altitude of about 1,300 m (4,265 ft) and serves as a good departure point for short hikes into the surrounding mountain foothills and slopes.

From Aïn El Hammam, you can either continue southward on N15 along the eastern edge of the Djurdjura massif or backtrack 2 km

(1 1/4 miles) to W17, a tortuous 20-km (12 1/2-mile) dirt road that passes through several small villages before exiting on N30. Road N30 begins about a kilometer closer to Tizi Ouzou than N15 and follows approximately a parallel southward route through the mountains. Most people traverse W17 from N15 as a short cut to N30 and as a way of reaching the picturesque village of Beni Yenni.

Beni Yenni is accessible via a very rough dirt road that goes north from the junction of W17 and N30 or a track that leads south from l'Arbaa Naït Irathen. Aside from its beautiful location, the village is also known for its jewelers, whose specialty is silver decorated with enamel and coral. They also specialize in wood furniture decorated with hand-carved geometric designs. If you wish to spend the night in Beni Yenni, there's one unclassified lodge called the Auberge Bracelet d'Argent (tel. 59 and 60 at Beni Yenni). It has 10 rooms, a restaurant and snack bar, and great views of the surrounding countryside.

After Beni Yenni, return to N30 and continue about another 18 km (11 miles) to the point where N30 splits to the left and N33 begins on the right. If you stay on N30, the first 12 km (7 1/2 miles) are on a dirt road that curves around the summit of Lalla Khedidja (2,308 m, or 7,572 ft) and through a pine and cedar forest. The road then steadily improves as it descends 16 km (10 miles) to a main national road N5. Following N33 instead leads you into the heart of the National Park of Djurdjura and one of Algeria's principal ski areas.

National Park of Djurdjura

The National Park of Djurdjura comprises a mountainous area of approximately 18,500 hectares (7,708 acres) cut by the numerous gorges, abysses, and vales that lie between lakes and high plateaus. In the higher mountains, those with elevations above 2,000 m (6,562 ft), there can be snow all year with as much as 150 cm (59 inches) in the winter. Although the snowfall can be comparatively heavy even at lower elevations, the recommended time to visit the park is between October and June. That doesn't mean it isn't worth visiting during the summer, but you will miss seeing the snow-covered peaks of the massif—a magical shimmering masterpiece of nature.

Flora in the park is a uniquely North African blend of African, Euro-Asiatic, and Mediterranean. Some of the most prominent trees include cedars, cork oak (a major source of cork), zeen oak, black pine, and various species of maples.

Animal life is also varied. The types inhabiting the park include Barbary ape, Bonelli eagle (*aigle de Bonelli*) nocturnal and diurnal birds of prey, *Felis caracal*, wild cat, serval, wild boar, jackal, fox, mongoose, striped hyena, hare, ibex, partridge, and various reptiles and frogs.

The village of Tikdja at 1,500 m (4,921 ft) is the main settlement in the park. It lies about 13 km (8 miles) from the Tizi-n-Kouilal pass (1,600 m or 5,249 ft), which is the junction with N30. If possible, you may want to hike along N33 from the pass to the village; this is quite a beautiful stretch of road, with cedar forests covering both sides and several peaks towering overhead. Proceed with caution during the winter, because this area often gets snowbound. There are two vista points en route at 2 1/2 km (1 1/2 miles) and 8 km (5 miles) from the pass—Point de vue du Djurdjura and Le Belvédère—that are great points for familiarizing yourself with the surrounding mountains.

The highest, most dramatic peaks lie on the right (north) side of the road. Just before Le Belvédère is the Gouffre peak (2,158 m, or 7,080 ft) and then after the viewpoint are the peaks of Akouker (2,148 m, or 7,047 ft), Ras Timedouine (2,305 m, or 7,562 ft) and, adjacent to Tikjda, Ras Tigounatine (1,873 m, or 6,145 ft). Tikdja is a good jumpoff point for hiking, climbing, and/or skiing the slopes of these peaks. Supposedly, there are also opportunities for some decent spelunking (cave exploring) but you will have to ask local inhabitants for details.

Skiing is possible from Tikdja because of direct access to two ski lifts for runs at 1,800 m (5,906 ft) and two chair lifts for runs at 1,900 m (6,234 ft). Equipment can be rented at the mountain sports "chalet" in the three-star Hotel Djurdjura, which lies on the southerly slopes of the massif.

For summer mountain climbing, experienced climbers are recommended to try any of several sites in the area, including the following: Ras Timedouine (2,305 m, or 7,562 ft), Akouker (2,148 m, or 7,047 ft), Ras Tigounatine (1,873 m, or 6,143 ft) and the Tizi-n-Kouilal pass (1,600 m, or 5,249 ft).

Some of the most popular summer hiking areas include the cedar forest of Aït Ouabane, the Tizi-n-Kouilal pass, and the Goulmine lake. Hiking to the lake requires at least two to three days; the trail begins at the foot of Ras Tigounatine right near the center of the village. Ask locals for directions to the trailhead. This hike is quite apt to change because a road was being constructed between Tala Guilef and Tikjda that would pass via the lake. Aït Ouabane is accessible via a track that begins in the village of Bou-Adenane, which is on N30 north of the Tizi-n-Kouilal pass. There may be another track or trail, so ask in Tikjda.

At an altitude of about 1,460 m (4,790 ft), the Hotel Djurdjura (tel. 52-72-70) is a great base for hiking in the summer and skiing in the winter. The hotel is located at the foot of Ras Tigounatine, surrounded by a beautiful forest of cedars, black pines, and chene verts (evergreen oaks and holm oaks). It's actually a hotel "complex" that includes 80 rooms with 171 beds (each room with a private bathroom), a youth hostel for students and young people, and restaurants.

BOGHNI

At the western edge of the Djurdjura massif and National Park is the ski area of Tala Guilef, which is accessible from the north via the town of Boghni. If you are coming from Tizi Ouzou, you can either take one of the paved, well-maintained "N" roads or hard-surface "W" roads south to Boghni. Although the "W" roads are more direct than the "N" roads, they may take just as long to traverse because of lower road quality.

The easternmost route begins about 6 km from Tizi Ouzou with N30. After 20 km in which the road follows the twists and turns of the river Oued Aïssi, N30 breaks into two branches, with the left side heading to the Tizi-n-Kouilal pass and Tikjda and the right side heading to Boghni, which is 27 km (17 miles) from this junction. Another way to reach Boghni is to travel westward 11 km along N12 to N25, which leads into W128 after 8 km (5 miles). W128 follows the river Oued Boghni 28 km (17 1/2 miles) to Boghni. Yet another secondary route to Boghni is to follow W147 south from Tizi Ouzou for 35 km (22 miles) to its intersection with N30 and then an additional 7 km (4 1/3 miles) west to Boghni.

From Boghni, the road climbs 19 km (12 miles) southward through cedar and oak forests to the ski center of Tala Guilef. In the winter, the last 14 km (9 miles) of this road tend to become snowbound. The center is at the foot of Djebel Heizder (2,164 m, or 7,100 ft) at an altitude of about 1,500 m (4,921 ft). It includes a main ski run at 1,800 m (5,905 ft) with two ski lifts and a chair lift (goes to 2,000 m, or 6,562 ft), the two-star Hotel El Arz, swimming pool, tennis courts, and a youth hostel.

In the summer, Tala Guilef is a good departure point for hikes into the surrounding forests, the Beni Mendes waterfalls (14 km or 9 miles, back up the road toward Boghni) and around Lake Goulmine. A road was being built from Tala Guilef to Lake Goulmine and all the way to Tikjda; it should be finished by the time this book is published, thus making it possible to easily traverse most of the National Park of Djurdjura.

The two-star Hotel El Arz (tel. 42-24-76) has 80 rooms, all with private bathrooms, a restaurant, a small ski school, and ski equipment rental facilities.

SMALLER ATLAS RANGES NEAR ALGIERS

Blida and the Atlas de Blida

Blida is a city of more than 200,000 at the foot of the Atlas de Blida mountains, which is a subrange of the Atlas mountains, and the edge of the Mitidja plain, one of the most fertile agricultural areas in Algeria. The town was founded in the sixteenth century by Andalusian refugees who created a system of canals to irrigate and cultivate the plain just outside of town. Less than 50 km (31 miles) from Algiers, Blida is the gateway or jumping-off point to the National Park of Chréa, which includes the ski center at Chréa, and the Chiffa gorges.

The National Park of Chréa

The National Park of Chréa comprises an area of 26,000 hectares (64,246 acres) in the western part of the Atlas de Blida mountains, which approximately begins as you ascend the 20-km (12 1/2-mile) road to the town and ski center of Chréa at an altitude of about 1,150 m (3,773 ft). In the winter, especially between December and February, temperatures are commonly below freezing and the roads snowed-in, but when the roads are clear Chréa becomes a popular ski resort. In the summer, the weather is hot and dry and often ideal for hikes into the surrounding mountains.

Flora and fauna in the park include zeen oak, holm oak, green woodpecker, blackbird, chickadee and hare.

Most of the park's facilities are concentrated in or around Chréa, including a research station of the National Institute of Forestry Research (reforestation programs), two 2-star hotels, one 3-star hotel, 438 public cottages, one campground with 20 two to three-person cabins, several restaurants, and mountain sports chalets where equipment can be rented. Tent camping is possible at the campground.

For skiing, there are two runs from 1,500 m (4,921 ft), two ski lifts and one chair lift up to 1,500 m.

The Chiffa Gorges

Returning to Blida and west on N4 and then south on N1 takes you through the Chiffa gorges, a great area for walking and seeing some of the indigenous vegetation, a veritable tapestry of mastic trees, heath shrubs and trees, holly, holm and cork oaks, and olive and pine trees. At one point in the gorge—Le Ruisseau des singes ("monkey stream")—Barbary apes and monkeys can be seen scaling the gorges and ravines. Ask at an ONAT office in Algiers for directions to the trailheads.

The Ouarsenis Massif

The Ouarsenis mountains lie south of Chréa and the Chiffa gorges and extend more than 200 km (124 miles) southwesterly in a slight crescent. Part of the massif includes the National Park of Cedars of Theniet El Had, which is accessible from the town of Theniet El Had.

Theniet El Had is on the southern slope of the Ouarsenis massif on national road N14, 58 km (36 miles) south of the city of Khemis Miliana.

Blida is 69 km (43 miles) and Algiers 110 km (68 miles) northeast of Khemis Miliana. The drive southward along N14 from Khemis Miliana is magnificent as the road cuts right through the heart of the Ouarsenis massif and the forests of Mattmattas and Oued Massine. The river Oued Rherga Massine runs approximately parallel to the road. The town is a pleasant place to stop before heading into the park, which is only about 3 km (2 miles) away.

The National Park of Cedars of Theniet El Had is relatively small—only 3,616 hectares (8,932 acres)—but it's a great introduction to the many trails that crisscross the Ouarsenis range. Follow dirt road W54 northwest out of town to the mountain hut at the Rond-Point des Cèdres, 14 km (9 miles) from town. In the winter, this area can be snowed in, but in the summer you can continue walking along the road all the way through the mountains. From the Rond-Point, which is approximately the center of the park, you can see an astonishing variety of trees, including several species of cedar and oak. Several animal species are indigenous to the park—the magpie, hawk owl, royal eagle, falcon, skylark, partridge, quail, dove, fox, and hare. Although the park is open all year, the best time to visit is between March and October.

Transportation

All the destinations described are accessible via public transportation, but be prepared to deal with a variety of bus and train schedules. For Blida, there are daily PTVC buses every 30 minutes from Algiers starting at 6 A.M. and ending at about 8 P.M.; it takes about 1 1/2 hours just to go 50 km (31 miles). A few of these buses continue to Chréa, otherwise transportation can be arranged in Blida. The trains to Oran stop in Blida; the trip takes about an hour. For the Chiffa gorges, if you don't have your own transportation, you can take the Algiers-Médea bus and hope that the driver stops in the gorges. The only other option is to try hitchhiking, which really shouldn't be difficult in this part of Algeria. (Women should not hitchhike alone; ideally, women should have a male companion.) For Theniet El Had, you'll have to rely on buses from Algiers to Khemis Miliana and then to Theniet; the Algiers-Oran also sometimes stops in Khemis.

SÉTIF

Sétif is a city of approximately 200,000 situated on a high plateau just south of the Petit Kabylie mountains, the eastern extension of the Grand Kabylie range. At an altitude of 1,096 m (3,596 ft), it is Algeria's highest provincial capital. Throughout its history, Sétif was considered rich and strategically valuable—rich for its black, fertile soil (sétif means "black" in a local Berber dialect) and valuable for its control of the region's water supply. It was also an important trading crossroads between eastern and western parts of the Maghreb. Not surprisingly, Romans, Vandals, Byzantines, Numidians, and various Berber tribes all passed through or settled in and around Sétif.

In the center of town, Romans and Byzantines left ruins that are still visible today, but an odd thing happened a few years ago after most of the artifacts were excavated and transferred to the local museum. An amusement park was erected over the excavation site and some of the ruins became part of the park—somewhere between the ferris wheel and the bumper cars. This is reason enough to pass through Sétif for a short visit. There's not much else to see in town, but it is a good base from which to visit the extensive Roman ruins at Djemila and the national park around Djebel Babor in the Petit Kabylie mountains.

Transportation

Sétif is still considered a major crossroads between eastern and western Algeria, so consequently, there are frequent buses between Sétif and Algiers, Bejaïa, and Constantine. Sétif is also on the Trans-Maghrebian train route, with five trains stopping en route to Algiers and four trains in the opposite direction. The "rapide" trains to Algiers depart at 3.45 and 9.24 A.M. and 1.49 P.M. and for Annaba-Tunis at 12.58 A.M. and 5.50 and 12.39 P.M. The train station is on Rue des Frères Mezaache (tel. 90-20-93).

First Things First

The post office is at Place du 8 Mai 1945. The telephone office is on Boulevard de l'ALN. The city tourism office is in the Cité Aïn Tebinet part of town.

Accommodations

There are several hotels in Sétif. The biggest and best is the four-star Hotel El Hidhab (tel. 90-40-43), which overlooks the amusement-park-cum-Roman-and-Byzantine-ruins. It has 68 clean, comfortable rooms with bathrooms, telephones, and air conditioning. Other hotels include the Hotel El-Raedh at 22 Rue des Frères Meslam, the Hotel Marhaba at 6 Rue des Frères Hebbache, the Grand Hotel at Avenue du 8 Mai 1945, the four-star Hotel Setifis (tel. 90-11-11) at 1 Avenue Saïd Boukhrissa, the Hotel La Paix at 9 Rue Ben Boualem, the two-star Hotel Mountazah (tel. 90-48-28) at 12 Avenue Ben Boulaid, the one-star Hotel Continental (tel. 90-56-16) at 12 Rue Haffad Abdelmadjid and the one-star Hotel Marhaba (tel. 90-56-16) at 6 Rue des Frères Habbache.

Things to See

Aside from roaming around the amusement park and visiting the old fortress wall and Roman columns, the only other "site" is the Regional Archaeological Museum (also known as the Museum of Sétif), which is adjacent to the Hotel El Hidab. Its exhibits cover regional history beginning with prehistoric times and including Numidian, Roman, Byzantine, and Islamic periods with samples of sculpture, eighteenth-century Turkish arms, Roman mosaics, and Islamic geometrical paintings and carvings.

NEAR SÉTIF

Djemila

In Arabic, *djemila* means "pretty" or "beautiful"—an apt description of the green hills surrounding the extensive Roman ruins now at Djemila. The Roman city that existed here was called Cuicul. Today, it is easy to imagine what a bustling city this once was—the streets are still paved with carefully placed flagstones and traces are visible of an ancient sewer system beneath the stones. Many of the ancient buildings lack only roofs, a ceremonial arch stands complete on a slight rise, and a third-century Christian basilica with a dome occupies part of the low-lying area. A beautiful set of mosaics from the basilica are now found in the Sétif museum.

La Kabylie des Babors

The main road heading north from Sétif is N9, which cuts through the Petit Kabylie mountains, the National Park of Tizi N'Béchar and the Chabet El Akra (Chasm of Death). Access to the park is approximately 42 km (26 miles) from Sétif at the Tizi N'Béchar pass. Just beyond the pass, on your right, looms the 1,833-m (6,014-ft)-high peak of Djebel Babor. There are a few hiking trails in the park, but I was unable to obtain current information. Ask at the tourist office in Sétif before attempting to trek into the park from the pass. Once over the pass, you will see the Ighil Emda dam and a small emerald-green lake created by the dam. Then, you will begin to enter the impressive 7-km (4-mile) Chasm of Death cut precariously over the eons by the Oued Agrioun river. After 76 long, tiring km (47 miles), the road intersects the coastal road to Bejaïa. This route was due to be greatly improved soon with the completion of a tunnel and new road.

CONSTANTINE

At its center, Constantine is a city built on a broad, sloping plateau that is split into two halves by deep, ominous gorges resembling severe earthquake faults. However, the gorges, which range in depth and width from about 152 to 305 m (500 to 1,000 ft) and 5 to 366 m (15 to 1,200 ft), are probably the result of the river below—the Oued Rhumel—not of earthquakes. These dramatic topographical features have made the city a beautiful and strategically valued prize throughout its history.

Archeological evidence found in caves carved along the sides of the gorges suggests that prehistoric humans settled here. The settlement became an important Phoenecian and Numidian town known as Cirta by the third century B.C. A century later, under the rule of King Micispa, the town was fast becoming the most prosperous in the region. Not surprisingly, it attracted the attention of Julius Caesar and his confederates, who established a settlement here that eventually became the capital of the Roman Empire's four North Africa colonies. By the fourth century A.D., the town had been destroyed in a war against Alexander the Great and rebuilt by Constantine the Great. The Vandals ignored it, but the Arabs conquered what was then known as Constantine in the seventh century and made it into a major commercial center. Its prosperous commerce attracted European traders in the Middle Ages who, in turn, attracted Ottoman Turkish rulers. Under Ottoman military rule, the city became a *beylik* (provincial capital of the Turkish regency) and was able to resist French rule until 1837. Constantine wasn't militarily significant again until the 1942 Allied North Africa campaign in Africa when U.S. forces made it an important command center.

Today, Constantine is considered the capital of eastern Algeria. Bridges, including the highest suspension bridge (the El-Kantara) in the world, now span the gorges. Streets, buildings and old quarters are a hodge-podge of old and new styles reflective of the city's varied history. The Romans built most of the old walls and kasbah fortresses still extant around the city. The major mosques—such as the eighteenth century mosques of Salah Bey and Sidi Lakhdar and the Souk El Ghezel mosque, which was converted into the Notre-Dame des Sept Douleurs Cathedral during French rule—were built during Ottoman days. There's also a Moorish-style palace built by the Ottomans in the late eighteenth century. Tree-lined streets and open plazas were originally laid out by the French.

One of the city's most prominent features, however, is the new, sparkling mosque and Islamic center at the University of Constantine. Built on a slight hill apart from the center, it towers over the city and is one of the world's biggest and highest mosques.

Arrival, Departure, and Getting Around

The major street in the city is Rue Didouche Mourad, which runs from northeast to southwest, cutting the city into two parts. To the east and southeast is the older quarter of the city with its Ottoman mosques, narrow lanes, and age-old shops and artisans. To the west of Rue Didouche Mourad are the Souk El Ghezel mosque, the palace of Ahmad Bey, and the Kasbah. Rue Didouche Mourad ends at Place du 1er Novembre, the heart of the city. The gorge and river cut along the eastern edge of the city before winding northwestward.

EPTVE buses run frequently between Constantine and Algiers, Annaba, Batna, Biskra, Collo, Djelfa, El Oued, Ghardaïa, Gulema, Hassi-Messaoud, Laghouat, Mila, Sétif, Skikda, Souk-Ahras, Tebessa, and Tunis (one bus daily at 5 A.M. for the nine-hour trip).

The train also passes through Constantine en route to Annaba at 3.17 A.M. on the Trans-Maghrebian route and, in the opposite direction, to Sétif, Bejaïa, and Algiers at 7.10 and 11.30 A.M., 8.40 P.M. and 12.53 A.M. These are all considered "rapide" trains.

First Things First

Tourist and Travel Information

ONAT has an office around the corner from the Hotel Cirta, but it didn't seem to have much information about the region.

Accommodations

The three-star Hotel Cirta (tel. 94-30-33) is the best hotel in town. Most of the ground floor, from the arched entrance to the huge dining room, is decorated with Moorish-style wall moldings, but the decorations have a sense of faded elegance about them. The rooms are also old and faded, but parts of the hotel are being renovated. Other hotels in the area include the Hotel Transat at 1 Avenue Aouati Mustapha and the Hotel El Oumara at 29 Rue Abane Ramdane. All three hotels have fairly good restaurants where you can get reasonably priced meals. Otherwise, just head for the restaurants and cafés on Rue Didouche Mourad.

A bank, post office, and telephone office can be found at Place 1er Novembre.

Things to See

Constantine's most popular sights are its gorges and bridges. For a great view of the gorges (or gorge, if you want to consider it all a single gorge), walk along Boulevard Zighout Youcef (once known as Boulevard de l'Abime) near the suspension bridge of El Kantara. Then cross the bridge and hike up the hill to the mini Arc de Triomphe monument to French and Algerian soldiers lost in the wars. From the monument, the view of the gorges and surrounding valley of Hamma Bouziane is spectacular. Don't expect the monument to be equally spectacular, because local kids have taken to using its walls as a pissoir and defacing the names carved into the marble.

The other major sight worth seeing is the Faculty of Superior Islamic Studies at the University of Constantine. More than $300 million were spent on the mosque and towering minarets, some of the largest and highest in the Islamic world.

East of Constantine

About 240 km (149 miles) northeast of Constantine and 87 km (54 miles) east of Annaba is the National Park of Kala. The park stretches westward from the town of Kala and comprises an area of 78,400 hectares (190,648 acres) along the coast. The park is best known for three long stretches of sandy beach and three lakes (two brackish and one fresh water) where more than 52 species of birds can be found. Hiking, climbing, and bicycling are all possible in the park. There's one three-star hotel—Le Mordjane —and various other hotels in the town of El Kala. For more information about the park and camping possibilities, write to Parc National de Kala, BP 73, El Kala, Algeria.

NORTHWESTERN ALGERIA

Tlemcen

I didn't visit the city of Tlemcem (also spelled Tilimsen after 1981), but after reading numerous accounts and descriptions, I wish I had. Perhaps more than any other city in Algeria, this city of 150,000-plus inhabitants only 60 km (37 miles) east of Oudja and the Moroccan border has managed to preserve much of its traditional heritage, particularly its medieval monuments. There are, however, also monuments or at least portions of monuments dating before the Middle Ages.

Tlemcen's temperate location at the foot of the Monts de Tlemcen and overlooking the fertile plains of Maghnia and Hennaya attracted a Roman settlement in the fourth century B.C., which was known as Pomaria ("Orchards"). A Berber settlement known as Agadir ("Escarpment") gradually replaced the predominantly Roman settlement. By the eleventh century A.D., Tlemcen was being volleyed back and forth between rival tribes and empires in present-day Morocco and Algeria. When the Almoravids merged the settlement with the nearby settlement of Tagrart in the eleventh century, they laid the foundation for the present city of Tlemcen.

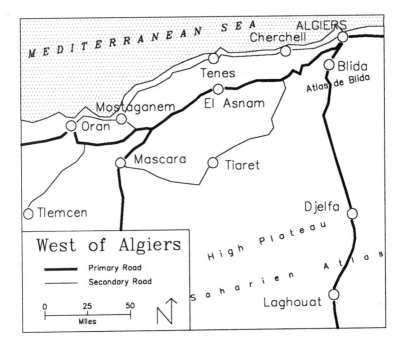

By the thirteenth century, the settlement had become a city called Tlemcen, a derivation of the Berber word for the area's natural springs, and was fast becoming a major trading and Islamic cultural center in the Maghreb. It also became a political capital of sorts as the chief city of the Abd-Al-Wadid dynasty. However, because of its proximity to Moroccan political centers, Tlemcen was repeatedly subject to dynastic rule originating in Morocco. This changed in 1559 when Ottoman Turks seized power and ruled until the French arrived in 1842. The French presence here eventually precipitated resistance to its rule and produced the first president of an independent Algeria—Ben Bella.

Today, Tlemcen is capital of the province of Tlemcen, an agricultural center concentrating on leather and textile products and a light industry center. With numerous well-preserved medieval buildings and narrow, winding streets with traditional-style shops around the city, there's no shortage of things to see:

> **The Mosque of Sidi bel Hassan.** Built in 1296, it now houses a museum.
> **The Mechouar** ("Citadel"). Now used by the military as barracks and a hospital.
> **The Sahrij** ("Great Basin"). A big, dry reservoir built in the fourteenth century.

The Grotto of Rabbi Ephraim Ben Israel Ankawa. In the fifteenth century, the rabbi led a fairly prosperous Jewish community in Tlemcen.

The Great Mosque. Built by the Almoravids in the twelfth century.

Ruins of the Marinid city of Mansura.

Bab El Kermadine. One of the principal vestiges of Tlemcen's medieval ramparts.

Museum of Classic and Moslem Antiquities.

Walks in and around Tlemcen

- Jardin de la pepiniere "The Nursery Garden"
- The picturesque village of El Eubbad
- The Sacred Woods of Sultan Sidi-Yaccoub. His tomb is located here.
- The Plateau of Lalla Setti, for a magnificent view of Tlemcen.
- The Grottoes of Beni Abd El Oued
- The *barrage* (dam) of Beni Bahdel
- The cork oak forests and mountain passes of Zerifète (1,212 m, or 3,976 ft) and Hafir (1,260 m, or 4,134 ft).

Transportation

Tlemcen is on the Trans-Maghrebian train route. All trains on this route originate in Oran. The schedule from Oran is as follows:

From	Departure Times		
	Train 1112	Train 1114	Train 1116
Oran	6.35 A.M.	12.35 A.M.	6.15 P.M.
Oued Tlelat	7.06 A.M.	1.06 P.M.	6.45 P.M.
Sidi bel Abbes	8.05 A.M.	2.05 P.M.	7.47 P.M.
Tlemcen	9.35 A.M.	3.32 P.M.	9.14 P.M.
Maghnia	10.59 A.M.	———	———

The schedule from Maghnia and Tlemcen is

	Train 1102	Train 1104	Train 1106
Maghnia	———	12.05 P.M.	———
Tlemcen	4.25 A.M.	1.27 P.M.	5.34 P.M.
Sidi bel Abbes	5.51 A.M.	2.55 P.M.	7.00 P.M.
Oued Tlelat	6.44 A.M.	3.50 P.M.	7.54 P.M.
Oran	7.12 A.M.	4.17 P.M.	8.20 P.M.

There are also buses between Tlemcen and major regional destinations—Maghnia, Oran, and Sidi bel Abbes.

ONAT has an office at 15 Boulevard de l'Indépendence in Tlemcen and at 52 Avenue du 1er Novembre in Maghnia.

ORAN

With a population of more than 700,000, Oran is Algeria's second largest city and port. Founded in A.D. 903 by Arabs who migrated from Andalusia in Spain, the city retained close links to Spain for at least the next 900 years. Although numerous tribes, dynasties, regencies, and empires controlled Oran throughout its history, 300 years of Spanish rule left the most visible mark on the city, especially in its architecture. Spanish rule over Oran began in 1509 with an expedition by explorer Pedro Navarro and ended in 1791 with a devastating earthquake that killed more than 2,000 people. Subsequent attacks by the Turkish *bey* (Ottoman-appointed provincial governor) of Mascara further weakened the beleaguered city. Charles IV of Spain, who was faced with the growing menace of Napoleonic France, was forced to cede Oran to the Dey (Ottoman boss of the beys) not long after the earthquake. The French attacked and conquered Oran in 1832 and ruled until Algerian independence.

Arrival, Departure, and Getting Around

Oran's main thoroughfares branch out from the Place du 1er Novembre, which is considered the city center. The City Hall, Municipal Theater, and main Air Algerie office are all found on the Place. Almost everything of interest in the city is reached by following one of the streets from the Place.

The train station is north of downtown Oran near the old port. There are trains to Algiers at 7 A.M. and at 12:15, 5:15 and 9:15 P.M. (not *"rapide"*). See the Tlemcen section for information about trains to Sidi bel Abbes, Tlemcen, and Maghnia.

There are several terminals for intercity buses. The following chart should help you determine which bus line and terminal:

Bus line name	Address and Telephone	Destinations Served
SOTAC Transport	Rue Dumont d'Urville, tel. 503-44-544-11	Aïn El Turk, El Ancor, Bou-Sfer, Andalouses, Cap Falcon, Boutlelis
TVRO	3 Rue Emir Abdelkader tel. 339-81-316-05	Arzew, Loumel, Valmy, Sidi bel Abbes, Aïn Franin

TRCFA	15 Boulevard Abderrahmane Mira	Tlemcen via Aïn Temouchant, Maghnia via Aïn Temouchent, Nemours, Nedroma, Bou-Hadjar, Sidi bel Abbes with connections for Bedeau and Tlemcen, Saïda, El Bayad, Mascara, Frenda, Trezel, Mostaganem, Cassaigne, Perregaux, and Mostaganem.
EPTVO	15 Boulevard Abderrahmane	Aïn Sefra, Algiers, Béchar, Beni-Saf, Bou-Hanifia, El Bayadh, Morocco Border, Ghardaïa, Ghazaouet, Mascara, Mecheria, Mostaganem, Saïda, Sidi bel Abbes, Sig, Tlemcen
EPTVO (different terminal from that given above)	Rue des Soeurs Benslimane	Aïn el Turk, Arzew, Boufatis, Bou-Sfer, Canastel, Cap Falcon, Kristel, Les Andalous, Mers El Kebir, Sig, Zahana

Various other bus companies have buses departing from a terminal at Boulevard Sheikh Abdelkader for Aflou, Ammi-Moussa, Bou-Hanifia, Ech-Chlef, Frenda, Ghriss, Mascara, Mohammedia, Mostaganem, Relizane, Sidi-Ali Hacham, Tiaret, Tighennif, and Tissemsilt.

From May to December, SNCM ferries run between Oran and Marseille (France). There's one ferry in May, two in June, July and August, three in September, five in October, four in November, and two in December. Fares (in French Francs) are FF 1,203 in a four-person cabin and FF 730 for a couchette one way, and FF 2,178 and 1,318 round trip. The SNCM office is at the Gare Maritime. Supposedly, there are also CNAN ferries between Oran and Séte (France) and Alicante (Spain), but I wasn't able to find information about these routes, except that they run only in the summer.

Getting around Oran is easy, thanks to an extensive city bus system. Following are the principal routes:

Bus No.	Route Description
1	Boulevard de la Soummam-Gambetta-Falaises (Cliffs)
2	Place 1er Novembre-Place Theus
3	Place 1er Novembre-Cimitière Tamzhouet
5	Place 1er Novembre-Planteurs (par St. Louis)
6	Choupot-Marine Nationale (trolley bus)
7	Place 1er Novembre-Eckmuhi
8	Place 1er Novembre-Cité Petit
11	Boulevard de la Soummam-Gambetta H.L.M.
12	Place 1er Novembre-Cité Jourdain
13	Gare Maritime-Cité Petit Lac (par Boulevard Zabana)
14	Place 1er Novembre-Saint Hubert
15	Place 1er Novembre-Planteurs (par Ravin Raz El Aïn)
17	Place 1er Novembre-Eckmuhl-Stade Montreal
19	Place 1er Novembre-National Cemetery
21	Boulevard de la Soummam-Gambetta-Courbet
22	Place 1er Novembre-Cité Dar Beida
23	Gare Maritime-Cité Petit Lac (par Boulevard de l'Indépendence)

First Things First

Hotels and Restaurants

The best hotel in Oran is the four-star Hotel Timgad (tel. 39-47-97) at 22 Boulevard Emir Abdelkader, with 200 rooms. The three-star Hotel Le Martinez is comparable and just down the street at 1 Boulevard Emir Abdelkader. Other hotels on the same street include the Hotel El Amir (tel. 39-16-72) at No. 34 and the Astoria Hotel at No. 31. Boulevard Emir Abdelkader starts at the northeastern corner of Place 1er Novembre and runs southeast through the city.

As you walk down Boulevard Emir Abdelkader, you will see Boulevard de la Soummam on your left; at No. 3 is the two-star Royal Hotel (tel. 39-31-44). A few blocks down, the next major street is Rue Mohammed Khemisti, where you'll find most of Oran's best restaurants, the central post office, and Place du Maghreb.

At 1 Place du Maghreb is the three-star Grand Hotel (tel. 39-01-81), which has over 100 rooms and is run by students from the local hotel school.

Continuing down Boulevard Emir Abdelkader, the next major street is Rue Larbi ben M'hidi. The two-star Windsor Hotel is at No. 1 and several good restaurants are nearby.

Getting Things Done

Money. Money and travelers' checks can be exchanged at the Hotel Timgad and other major hotels, as well as the Banque Central at the corner of Boulevard de la Soummam and Rue El Moungar.

Post and Telephone Offices. The central post and telephone offices are on Place du Maghreb and Rue Mohammed Khemisti, just up the street from Boulevard Emir Abdelkader.

Things to See

Near the center of town, the typical tourist itinerary has included a visit to Oran's kasbah or old quarter, which can be entered through the Spanish Gate (Porte d' Espagne) or the Caravansary Gate (Porte du Caravansérail), both ornately decorated Moorish-style gates. The Spanish-Moorish influence is visible throughout the kasbah in the narrow streets and passageways and red-tiled buildings. However, most of the kasbah is gradually being renovated and modernized, so it's beginning to lose much of its traditional Moorish character.

Other highlights in the city include the sixteenth-century Spanish Fort de Santa Cruz, which overlooks the city from the 400-m (1,312-ft) Murdjadjo plateau and clifftop. From downtown Oran, it's quite a good hike up to the fort. Bring your camera, because the view of Oran and the surrounding Sahel hills and marshes is spectacular.

If you want to do other walks around town, try any of the following:

- **Boulevard Front de Mer,** a long bayside promenade near the port
- **Parc Municipal,** a municipal park with a pleasant flower garden, artificial lakes, and a small zoo
- **Parc des Planteurs** (Park of the Planters), a forest of green oaks and pine trees located along the slope of the Murdjadjo plateau
- **Le Belvedere,** a great place for a panoramic view of Oran and surroundings

There are also two museums in Oran. The Museum of Oran is known for its painting collections and ethnographic displays, and the Demaeght Museum has exhibits covering the prehistory, ethnography, and archeology of the region, and a great collection of old photographs and prints of Oran.

CHAPTER 13

The High Plateaus, Aurès Mountains, and Middle Sahara

Just south of the various Tellien Atlas mountain ranges that approximately parallel the Mediterranean begins that infamous inland sea of sand known as the Sahara desert. It starts as an arid region of high plateaus known collectively as the Hauts Plateaux, or High Plateaus. There's nothing of great repute in this region other than the cities of Bou-Saada and Biskra, both of which are renowned for their lush date palmeries and status as gateways to the Sahara. Biskra is also known as a gateway northward to the Rhoufi gorges, the Aurès mountains, and the city of Batna. Heading south from Bou-Saada, you actually enter the Sahara after traversing various small ranges of the Saharan Atlas mountains, most notably the Monts du Zab (en route on N46 to Biskra) and the Monts des Ouled Naïl (en route on N1 to Laghouat and Ghardaïa). Ghardaïa is famous for its seven small cities, which are home to the Mozabite Berbers, members of the secretive Ibadite Islamic sect. From Biskra, you can follow part of the Paris-Dakar road race route along N3 and skirt the edge of the Grand Erg Oriental (a great shifting sea of sand dunes, some as big as mountains). Or you can drive through the Erg to the concentrated oasis Souf region in and around the city of El Oued. The road along the edge—N3—runs through Touggourt, a big oasis city of date palms, and continues on to Hassi Messaoud, Algeria's oil exploration center, and beyond deep into the Sahara. The sand dunes of the Grand Erg Oriental, the cities, oases, and gorges are the highlights for travelers in this region.

BOU-SAADA

Translated from Arabic, "Bou-Saada" means "city of happiness." Located 250 km (155 miles) south of Algiers, Bou-Saada is the closest major oasis to the capital. The city itself is a quaint place of old, arched streets, mosques, and a few interesting market stalls and artisan shops. For several centuries, it was a major trading post and supply point on the caravan route between the Mediterranean and West Africa.

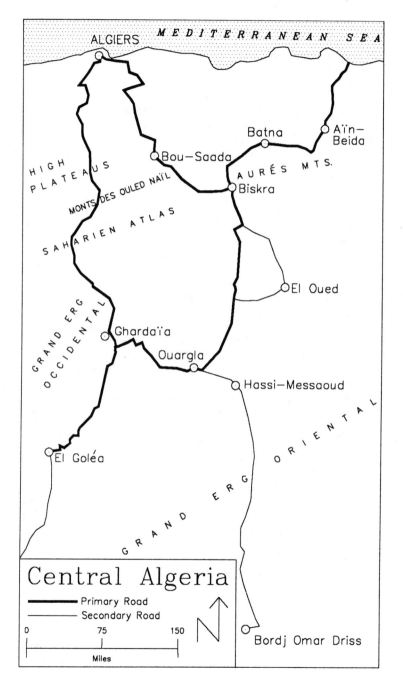

MEDITERRANEAN SEA

ALGIERS

Aïn–Beida

Batna

Bou–Saada

HIGH PLATEAUS

AURÉS MTS.

MONTS DES OULED NAÏL

Biskra

SAHARIEN ATLAS

El Oued

GRAND ERG OCCIDENTAL

Ghardaïa

Ouargla

Hassi–Messaoud

GRAND ERG ORIENTAL

El Goléa

GRAND ERG

Central Algeria

━━━ Primary Road
─── Secondary Road

0   75   150

Miles

Bordj Omar Driss

Bou-Saada's artisan shops include works in gold, pottery, weaving, and silk, particularly wood rugs woven with special knotted stitches. The artisans are also known for their long, tapering *bousaadi* knives. Occasionally, the city's main and sometimes only hotel—Hotel Le Caïd—presents art of a different form—the dance performances of the Ouled Naïl Berbers. This group has traditionally inhabited the mountains and foothills of the low-lying Monts des Ouled Naïl range south of Bou-Saada. Also south of the city, but only a few kilometers away, are the region's other main attractions—Moulin Ferraro and the Zaouia at El Hamel.

The Moulin Ferraro is a 50-year-old now-defunct wheat-grinding mill. It was built along the Oued Bou Saada, a river, usually no more than a stream, that runs past the Gobr El Oucif gorge where the mill is located and then through town. The mill is at a picturesque part of the gorge where there's a small waterfall and natural pool.

The beautiful zaouia or religious fraternity of Sidi Mohammed Ben Belkacem is located in the village of El Hamel about 13 km (8 miles) southwest of Bou-Saada. Founded in the mid-nineteenth century by Sidi Mohammed, the *zaouia's* members claimed direct descent from the Prophet, and thus preached the necessity of remaining purely Arab and not intermarrying with local tribes such as the Ouled Naïl people. The most impressive features of the structure are its main doorway, which is surrounded by a careful arrangement of blue glazed tiles, and a stunning whitewashed façade topped by six cupolas. The zaouia still functions as a Koranic school and mosque. You can visit as far as the center of the mosque's main hall, but be sure to remove your shoes before entering.

Back in town, you can stay at the four-star Hotel El Caïd or at a clean, but basic youth hostel. The Hotel El Caïd (tel. 54-43-97) attempts to recreate a sense of Saharan atmosphere with a ksar-style (mud fortress) architecture and a Bedouin tent complete with locals in the flowing robes of full desert dress and groomed camels in the small garden behind the hotel. This hotel is popular with tour groups.

The youth hostel is on the main road across from the hotel. Ask for the Auberge de Jeunesse, and people will show you the way. During vacation periods, the hostel is often full of school children.

There are frequent daily buses between Bou-Saada and several other cities, including Biskra and Algiers.

The Bou-Saada branch of the ONAT tourism office is on Rue Emir Abdel Kader.

BISKRA

Biskra (also spelled Beskra after 1981) is an oasis city surrounded by a sprawling set of lush date palmeries located south of the Aurès mountains, the Rhoufi gorges, and the city of Batna. Founded by the Carthaginians and later converted into a fortified town named Vescera by the Romans, its moderate dry climate (average temperature of 21°C, or 70°F) and plentiful water supply have long attracted visitors and settlers. Arabs arrived in the ninth century and made Biskra a prosperous commercial center. A few centuries later, it had become the capital of the semiautonomous Zab oasis region. The Turks arrived in 1552, but were booted out by the French who arrived in 1844, destroyed the age-old kasbah part of town and built Fort St. Germain in 1849. The Fort is now indistinguishable from the center of town.

Today, Biskra has a population of 139,000 with the majority concentrated on the right bank of the usually dry Oued Biskra riverbed. At the northern edge of the city is the Col de Sfa (Sfa mountain pass) and national road N3, one of the principal roads to Batna. The other road to Batna—N31—heads east and then veers north from town past the wonderfully lush palmerie and village of M'Chounèche, along the edge of the Rhoufi gorges, and through the Aurès mountains—a much more dramatic route than N3.

Biskra's specialty is the deglet nour date, a tasty golden date that is reputedly prized throughout the world. These dates, known popularly as doigts de lumière ("fingers of light"), are cultivated in and around Biskra, particularly at the neighboring oasis of Tolga. Figs and apricots are also specialties of this region. Biskra, Tolga, and other oases and palmeries in this region comprise the Zab oasis region, which approximately marks the beginning of a string of oases that extends southward 219 km (136 miles) along the edge of the Grand Erg Oriental to the city of Touggourt.

Arrival, Departure, and Getting Around

Biskra is an important crossroads transit point for transportation between northern and central Algeria. There are trains running between Constantine and Touggourt according to the following schedule:

Constantine to Biskra

Depart					
	Constantine	5.30	A.M.	6.10	P.M.
	El Ghourzi	6.07	A.M.	6.47	P.M.
	Batna	7.24	A.M.	8.04	P.M.
	Biskra	9.24	A.M.	10.11	P.M.

Biskra to Constantine

Depart					
	Biskra	5.25	A.M.	5.25	P.M.
	Batna	7.25	A.M.	7.30	P.M.
	El Ghourzi	7.26	A.M.	8.38	P.M.
	Constantine	9.12	A.M.	9.19	P.M.

Biskra to Touggourt

Depart					
	Biskra	4.20	P.M.	6.30	P.M.
	El Meghaier	6.31	P.M.	8.42	P.M.
	Djamā'a	7.30	P.M.	9.42	P.M.
	Touggourt	8.27	P.M.	10.39	P.M.

from Touggourt to Biskra

Depart					
	Touggourt	1.00	A.M.	6.15	A.M.
	Djamā'a	2.02	A.M.	7.17	A.M.
	El Meghaier	3.02	A.M.	8.17	A.M.
	Biskra	5.08	A.M.	10.23	A.M.

The main Biskra bus terminal is on the eastbound Route de Sidi Okba. The EPTVE bus company (tel. 71-42-55) runs frequent daily buses to the following cities: Algiers (five hours, departures at 5 A.M. and 1 and 9.30 P.M.), Batna, Bou-Saada, Constantine, El Oued (3 1/2 hours, departs at 1 P.M.), Ghardaïa (departures on VSE buses at 5.30 and 11 A.M.), Hassi Messaoud, In Amenas, Ouargla, Sétif, and Touggourt.

First Things First

The local branch of the ONAT tourism office (tel. 71-23-36) is on Rue Ghamri Hocine and Place Larbi Ben M'hidi across from a park of mimosa trees. The park is worth a quick visit, if only to inhale the sweet aromatic scents of these trees, especially in the spring when small, puffy, yellow flowers on the trees are in bloom.

Accommodations

The four-star Hotel les Zibans (Tel. 71-30-67) is Biskra's best and largest hotel. It's located adjacent to the Oued de Biskra riverbed at the edge of town. The hotel has a good restaurant and cafeteria, as well as a swimming pool.

Other hotels include the two-star Hotel Oasis (tel. 71-16-08) with a restaurant and cafeteria, the three-star Hotel Guendouz (tel. 71-57-69), the unclassified Hotel Chaoui (tel. 71-15-75), and Hotel Mansour (tel. 71-37-50).

There's also a 50-bed youth hostel (l'Auberge de Jeunesse Emir Abdelkader/tel. 71-32-22) on Boulevard Emir Abdelkader with kitchen facilities available. If you prefer to camp at the city's official campground, ask at the youth hostel for directions.

Getting Things Done

The post and telephone office is on Boulevard Emir Abdelkader. There are banks on Boulevard de la République, Place Larbi Ben M'hidi, and Boulevard Hakim Saadane.

Things to See and Do

There's not much to see or do in Biskra other than just wandering through the park at Place Larbi Ben M' hidi and nearby streets to check out the market stalls, particularly those specializing in the varieties of dates from the city's over two million date palms. Wandering through the palmeries, which encircle the city, also makes for a pleasant hike.

Another possible hike is through the palmerie and oasis village of Tolga, 42 km (26 miles) west of Biskra. There are buses to Tolga at 8 and 11.30 A.M. and at 4 and 7.15 P.M. and from Tolga to Biskra at 5.50 and 9.30 A.M., and 2.30 and 5.15 P.M. There are also local buses to Sidi-Okba and the village of M'Chounèche.

About 37 km (23 miles) northeast of Biskra is the equally verdant palmerie and village of M'Chounèche. The Oued El Abiod river flows through from the Aurès mountains nurturing the thousands of date palms and almond trees which compose the palmerie. About 23 km (14 miles) downriver is the artificial lake and dam of Foum El-Gherza. If you have a day or two and the water level isn't too high, hike upriver to the village of Bamiane (two hours) and the base of the Rhoufi gorges (approximately 34 km, or 21 miles; five hours). Bamiane is renowned for its goat-and-camel-hair blankets, which you will see displayed on the main road if you decide to take a detour from your hike. Continuing on to Rhoufi, you can camp in the gorges in an ancient "ghost town" village of crumbling stone and wood-beam huts and houses. Some parts of the gorges are still inhabited and being cultivated. The view from the Balcon de Rhoufi (literally "balcony," more commonly known as a viewpoint or vista point) overhanging the gorges is magnificent and well worth the climb up (or, if you haven't been hiking, the drive) from Biskra.

THROUGH THE AURÈS MOUNTAINS TO BATNA

If you have hiked from M'Chounèche to the Rhoufi gorges, you can continue hiking up the Oued Abiod river another 8 km (5 miles) to the village or settlement of Rassira, which is at a junction with the national road 31 and a mountain road. The latter heads north from Rassira and then east as it passes the farming village of T'Kout and skirts the northern edge of the Djebel Ahmar Khaddou mountains. After a distance of 15 km (9 miles) from Rassira, the road reaches the village of Aïn El Beïda. You can either head north from here through the forests of Beni-Imboul or south to the forests around the village of Djemina.

Continuing north along the Oued Abiod river, after about 8 km (5 miles) you begin to enter the Tighanimine chalk gorges, which are less impressive than the Rhoufi gorges, but still spectacular.

You don't have to hike through the gorges to see them because N31 follows the twists and turns of the Oued Abiod river as far as the village of Arris, which is 18 km (11 miles) from the main viewpoint for the Tighanimine gorges. Arris is a good place to see the variety of heavy, encrusted jewelry produced by the Chaouïa Berbers who inhabit the villages of the Aurès mountains. From Arris, the road meanders through the Djebel Ichmoul mountains and foothills and passes the W54 road junction, which is the road to the Roman ruins at Timgad. An additional 8 km (5 miles) along N31 is the junction for N88, another road to Timgad. The city of Batna, capital of the Aurès mountain region, is 15 km (9 miles) from this point.

BATNA

Batna is 101 km (63 miles) south of Constantine and 161 km (100 miles) north-northeast of Biskra on a fertile plain at the edge of the Aurès mountains to the south and the smaller Belezma mountain range to the west. As capital of the Aurès mountain region and the wilaya or province of Batna, it's well situated for excursions to the Roman ruins at Timgad and the surrounding mountains and foothills.

Batna is a relatively young city. It was founded by the French in 1844 as a military fort to protect the strategic El Kantara mountain pass to the southwest and to subdue Chaouïa resistance in the Aurès mountains. El Kantara was a major transit point on the trade route between Constantine and the Sahara. The actual city site was first called Nouvelle Lambese, moved slightly to the east in 1848 and then renamed Batna in 1849.

The original fort area is now attached to the city and still functions as a military center. In addition, Batna has become a major regional agricultural and forestry center. Today, this city of 200,000 inhabitants doesn't really have much in the way of tourist attractions. There is one particularly interesting "attraction" in town that is definitely not standard tourist fare, but still worth a visit—two Algerian friends and a pizzeria called Liverpizza (after Liverpool, in England) that belongs to one of them.

How, you may ask, can a pizzeria and two Algerians be considered an "attraction"? The answer is, because the circumstances of both the restaurant and the two friends can be considered, in a way, a reflection of the challenges and problems faced by a wide segment of Algerian society.

As with many Algerian men, the two Algerians, whose names are Mostefa Hamouda and Hocine Ben M'hidi, went abroad to study at universities in England and the United States, respectively. The Algerian government sponsored them and thousands of other students because it desperately needed well-educated engineers to build and maintain Algerian industry, especially those industries related to petroleum and natural gas production.

Mostefa studied electrical engineering in Liverpool, fell in love, and decided to stay and search for work. Engineering jobs were in short supply, so he ended up working in various restaurants, including a pizzeria and a Greek restaurant, where he waited on tables, sang Greek ditties, and told jokes. He also worked in a clothing business. After ten years, he had thoroughly learned both the clothing and restaurant businesses and decided to return to Batna to start a clothing import business and a pizzeria called Liverpizza.

Hocine spent eleven years in the United States at various universities and earned a Ph.D. in engineering. His uncle was Larbi Ben M'Hidi, who is considered one of the heroes of Algeria's independence struggle and founders of the independent republic. The name M'Hidi is instantly recognized by most Algerians. It seemed that every city, town, and village I visited had a street or square named after him. After eleven years in the United States, Hocine seems to be a blend of his uncle's revolutionary spirit and charismatic American moxie.

Over a slice of anchovy, olive, and tomato pizza and a can of Pepsi, Hocine told me and my wife, Shirley, a rapid-fire set of stories about his experiences in America. He tried to eat, drink, and do everything American, but his government scholarship only covered his studies and left little for adventuring through the country. So Hocine put on a double-breasted suit that his brother had sent him from Italy and went job hunting. Well, there weren't many jobs available for young Algerians on student visas. He scanned the classified ads and saw an opening for work at a service station. So he went there in his suit for the interview. The boss, a gruff New Yorker named Joe, saw him and grunted, "Yeah, whah d'ya want?" Hocine replied, "I want a job. I really need a job." Joe needed someone immediately, so Hocine took off his jacket and tie, rolled up his sleeves, and said, "OK, put me to work." Hocine had found his first job in America. He passed through many other jobs and experiences, including a stint as a member of a college fraternity, but after eleven years, he returned home to do his military service and to try to make Algeria the way he wants—"the best place on earth." Or, maybe, Hocine said, he'll just help Mostefa open a chain of Liverpizzas around Algeria. According to a recent letter from Mostefa, Hocine married in late 1989, grew a beard, and became a Muslim Fundamentalist.

Mostefa is trying valiantly to make Liverpizza a success. Everything in his small pizza restaurant, except the oven, had to be imported. The small green awning hanging over his storefront at 9 Avenue de la Republique stands out among the other storefronts on the street, which are mostly plain and dusty. Inside, everything seems carefully arranged— the tables, chairs, placemats, English-style prints on the walls, and so on. The biggest problem, Mostefa says, is getting good employees.

Since independence, many Algerians have scorned any sort of

service work because that is automatically associated with 132 years of Algerian subservience to the French. In addition, until recently, the Algerian government aspired to be a Soviet-style "cradle-to-grave" welfare state system. In this system, the state controls or directs most of the country's institutions, industries and businesses, all supposedly for the benefit of the people. However, preservation of the system—all in the name of helping the people—became the overriding goal. Consequently, inefficient businesses and industries were kept open and running and incompetent employees and managers not fired. In fact, as a general rule, it was difficult for any employees to be fired, regardless of their incompetence, absenteeism, or tardiness. State subsidies skyrocketed in order to sustain the system, more dinars were printed to use as subsidies, thus causing inflation and a depreciation in the value of the dinar.

Service-oriented businesses—both private and public, particularly hotels and restaurants, were definitely victims of this system. Employees naturally asked themselves why they should expend any undue effort to serve guests or clientele if they were going to receive the same salary and weren't going to be fired regardless of how hard or little they worked.

Mostefa is attempting to overcome this mentality among his employees by offering them small financial bonuses for good work. He hopes that by building a good team of employees, he'll be able to begin producing 150 pizzas a day, start Algeria's first home delivery pizza service, and open other Liverpizzas around the country.

Arrival, Departure, and Getting Around

Batna is on a major transit route between Constantine and Biskra with frequent buses and trains in both directions.

Trains to and from Batna run according to the following schedule:

Constantine to Batna

Depart	Constantine	5.30 A.M.	6.10 P.M.
	El Ghourzi	6.07 A.M.	6.47 P.M.
	Batna	7.24 A.M.	8.04 P.M.

Batna to Constantine

Depart	Batna	7.26 A.M.	7.30 P.M.
	El Ghourzi	8.31 A.M.	8.38 P.M.
	Constantine	9.12 A.M.	9.19 P.M.

Batna to Biskra

Depart	Batna	7.24 A.M.	8.04 P.M.
	Biskra	9.24 A.M.	10.11 P.M.

To continue on to Touggourt, you have to change trains; two trains depart at 4.20 P.M. and 6.30 P.M..

Biskra to Batna

Depart	Biskra	5.25 A.M.	5.25 P.M.
	Batna	7.26 A.M.	7.30 P.M.

First Things First

Tourist information

The local branch of ONAT has an office at 14 Allée Ben Boulaïd (tel. 55-93-45).

Accommodations

The best hotel in town is the modern four-star Hotel Chelia (tel.55-18-62) with clean, comfortable rooms each with a balcony and most with great views of the snow-capped peaks of the Aurès mountains.

Other hotels in town include the Hotel Karim (tel. 55-89-81) across from the Liverpizza restaurant. A single without bath costs 105 dinars, with bath 115, double without bath 140, with 155; triple 230; all prices include breakfast. There's also the two-star Hotel El Hayat (tel. 55-26-01), the Hotel Amin (tel. 55-24-04), the Hotel Essalem (tel. 55-97-69), and the Hotel Aurès (tel. 55-14-36).

Things to See and Do

Except for a Festival of Aurèsian Songs in March, Batna's sights and diversions are all outside the city. The sight that usually tops most travelers' lists is the ancient Roman city of Timgad.

Timgad

Located about 35 km southeast of Batna on a plateau in the Aurès foothills, Timgad was known as the ancient Roman city of Thamagudi. It was founded about A.D. 100 by the Roman emperor Trajan, first as a military base because of its strategic location. The base quickly became a city as inhabitants discovered that a variety of crops could be grown on the fertile land of the region. At its peak, the city contained a population of approximately 15,000 with cobblestone streets laid out in a grid fashion, a theater large enough for 4,000, a forum, and many tiled public baths. The walls of most of these structures are still quite intact and extend over a broad area.

Just outside the entrance to the ruins, there's a hotel, restaurant, and campground.

National Park of Belezma (Parc National de Belezma)

Situated about 7 km (4 1/3 miles) northwest of Batna in the Belezma mountains, the National Park of Belezma was created in 1984 by the

Ministry of Waterworks, the Environment and Forests for the conservation and restoration of the flora and fauna of this region. The park is especially known for its extensive cedar groves, which have been restored in the last two decades after being napalmed by the French during the revolution. The Belezma region was a nationalist bastion during the revolution. Several bloody battles were waged in the Belezma woods and around the peaks of Djebels Chellala, Tuggurt, and Boumerzoug in the park and Djebels Refaa and Mestaoua just outside the park.

Today, the animal population in the park has increased to include abundant numbers of hare, partridge, turtle dove, wood pigeons, wild boar, fox, and jackal. Some of the predominant plant life includes Aurèsian holly tree, Etruscan honeysuckle, and various orchids such as the very rare *Epipactis helleborine*.

MIDDLE SAHARA

The M'Zab Region

The M'Zab region is an area around and including the city of Ghardaïa that is predominantly inhabited by Mozabite Berbers, a secretive group that practices a uniquely puritanical form of Islam known as Ibadite Islam. They shun or reject decorative mosques, smoking, music, the notion of baraka or holiness and spirituality, saints and zaouias or religious fraternities. The Idabites were one of several sects that broke off from mainstream Islam in the mid-seventh century after a dispute between Ali, the son-in-law and cousin of the Prophet Mohammed, and Moawija, the governor of Syria. Today, details of their practices are still unknown because of the self-imposed seclusion of the Mozabite Berbers who constitute the majority of the Ibadites.

Ghardaïa is the biggest of a clump of seven adjacent cities and towns where approximately 300,000 Mozabites are concentrated. It's a mixed city of Arabs and Berbers, whereas the others are totally Mozabite and, except for Beni Isguen, closed to non-Mozabite visitors.

Ghardaïa

Ghardaïa was founded in the eleventh century around the holy cave of Ghar, which was revered for its invisible inhabitant—the female saint Daïa. Although Mozabites generally don't venerate saints, Mozabite women continue to respect the presence of Daïa. Six towns sprouted up around Ghardaïa, four of which are on or near hills in the immediate area: Melika, Beni Isguen, Ben Noura, and El Atteuf.

As with many Algerian cities, Ghardaïa is divided into two main sections: an old, traditional quarter with narrow streets and a cobble-stoned marketplace and a newer French-built side with wider streets, traffic lights, and fortress-like architecture. The old town center is the marketplace, which is surrounded by blue arches and small shops, some selling brightly colored woven rugs and wall hangings. From the square, narrow streets branch off into the old quarter and what was once a Jewish quarter. A short walk through this quarter is the highlight of a visit to Ghardaïa. Other possible walks are through Beni Isguen and one of several palmeries in the area; both options are described later.

Arrival, Departure, and Getting Around

Although Ghardaïa is a fairly populous city, it's compact and easy to find your way through its streets. If you are driving into the city, the main roads first skirt the edge of cliffs and offer a beautiful view below of the dry Oued M'Zab riverbed, Ghardaïa, and the surrounding hilltop Mozabite towns.

Arriving by bus or grand taxi deposits you near the heart of Ghardaïa. There are several daily bus arrivals and departures between Ghardaïa and other cities. Following is bus schedule information:

Departures for	Times	Fare	
Adrar	5 A.M.	DA 151.60	($30.32)
Algiers	5 A.M., 7 A.M., 10 A.M., 12 P.M.	DA 106.60	($21.32)
Batna	11 A.M.	DA 110.40	$22.08)
Berriane	10 A.M., 12 P.M., 4 P.M., 6 P.M.	DA 7.80	($1.56)
Biskra	5 A.M., 12 P.M.	DA 102.40	($20.48)
Constantine	6 A.M., 8 A.M.	DA 137.10	($27.42)
Goléa	3.30 P.M.	DA 47.50	($9.50)
In-Salah	6 A.M.	DA 119.90	($24.00)
Laghouat	3.50 P.M.	DA 34.65	($7.00)
Metlili	7.15 A.M., 11 A.M., 4.15 P.M.	DA 4.00	($0.80)
Oran	5 A.M., 7 A.M., 9 A.M.	DA 126.50	($25.30)
Timmimoun	8 A.M.	DA 114.70	($23.00)

Arrivals from	Times
Adrar	4 A.M.
Algiers	4 A.M., 2.30 P.M., 6.45 P.M.
Batna	3 A.M.
Berriane	7.30 A.M., 11.40 A.M., 3.40 P.M., 5 P.M.
Biskra	12.30 P.M., 7 P.M.
Constantine	5 A.M., 7 P.M.
Goléa	9 A.M.
In-Salah	3 A.M.
Laghouat	7.15 A.M.

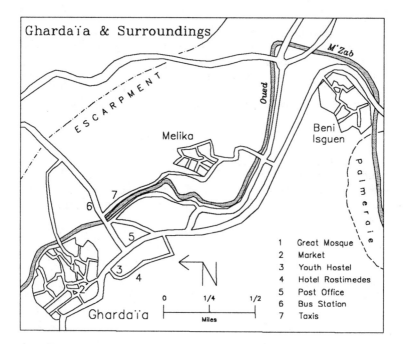

Ghardaïa & Surroundings

ESCARPMENT

Melika

Oued

M'Zab

Beni Isguen

Palmeraie

7
6
5
3   4
Ghardaïa

1   Great Mosque
2   Market
3   Youth Hostel
4   Hotel Rostimedes
5   Post Office
6   Bus Station
7   Taxis

0   1/4   1/2
Miles

Metlili	7 A.M., 10 A.M., 3 P.M.
Oran	4 A.M., 4.30 A.M., 5 P.M.
Timmimoun	2 A.M.

Baggage can be checked and securely left at the one-room station.

Grand taxis are in a lot across from the bus station. The majority go to Laghouat for about DA 50 ($10) where you can catch another to Djelfa for DA 30 ($6) and then from Djelfa to Algiers for DA 80 to 100 ($16 to $20). Other taxi routes include to Metlili (DA 15, or $3), Ouargla (DA 50, or $10), El Goléa, and Touggourt (DA 100, or $20). From Touggourt, there are connections to El Oued and then to Tunisia.

There is also frequent air service between Ghardaïa and other Algerian cities, including Adrar, Algiers, Annaba, Béchar, Constantine, Djanet, In-Salah, Oran, Tamanrasset, and Timmimoun. Warning: the flights to Djanet and Tamanrasset are often continuations of flights from Algiers, so they may be full when they arrive in Ghardaïa.

First Things First

Tourist and Travel Information. ONAT has a small branch information office at 2 Boulevard Emir Abdelkader (tel. 89-17-51), Ghardaïa's main street. However, they don't really have much information available about Ghardaïa and the M'Zab region.

The Syndicat d'Initiative at 12 Avenue 1er Novembre (tel. 89-26-01) has more information available. They can also help you find a room and a guide for the region. Hours are 8 A.M. to 12 noon and 3 to 9 P.M. except Fridays.

Accommodations. The Hotel Les Rostémides is the best one in town, thus making it—to its detriment—the most popular hotel with tour groups. During the winter and spring, it tends to be jammed with tourists, which somewhat spoils the hotel's pseudo-kasbah-like ambience. Facilities include a swimming pool, bar, and restaurant. A single with bath costs DA 141 ($28.20) or with shower DA 129 ($25.80); a double with bath DA 192 ($38.40) or with shower DA 177 ($35.40); all rates include breakfast.

There's also the three-star Hotel Le Rym, which really seems to deserve only one star because the rooms seem dingy, with worn carpeting or none at all. A few of the rooms have air conditioning and radiators. Including breakfast, a single with bath costs DA 141 ($28.20), a double with bath DA 192 ($38.40), a triple with shower DA 225 ($45.00), a single with shower DA 129 ($25.80), double with shower DA 177 ($35.40).

Another one in town is the Hotel Hanichi, which is a step above a youth hostel in comfort and cleanliness. It charges about DA 80 ($16) per person for a double.

The Hotel Izorane (tel. 09-89-15-60) is across from the Gendarmerie, with cool, basic rooms, some with showers and telephones. It charges about DA 120 ($24) for one person, DA 160 ($32) for two, DA 200 ($40) for three, all including breakfast. A restaurant is attached to the hotel.

Close to the bottom in quality and price is the Hotel, Café, Restaurant Atlantic, which has slightly smelly, dirty, overpriced rooms. It's near the main police station. A single is DA 35 ($7), double DA 80 ($16), and a triple DA 105 ($21). It was almost completely full of guests.

The youth hostel is next to the museum near the center of town and has been recently renovated. Dormitory-style with bunk beds.

There are two official campgrounds—one on the road to Beni Isguen and the other on the Algiers road.

Another option is to arrange a room in a beautiful multistory mud wall house in the palmerie. This can be done through Toufik Boughali of M'Zab Tours (tel. 09-89-00-02) at 73 Avenue du 1er Novembre. He built a magnificent house and renovated another in the palmerie, both of which can accommodate several guests. The newer house has a small, carefully tended garden with orange and palm trees and a common room that has a palm tree growing through the middle and out the roof. The other, which is equally impressive, dates back at least 200 years. It has 11 rooms, each with palm "wood" beams across the ceilings and around the door frames. This house has attracted the attention of French architects, one of whom has done a photo book featuring the house. The book is *Le M'Zab, une leçon d'architecture* by André Ravereau and published in 1981 by Sinblad, a Paris publisher (1 et 3 Rue Feutrier, 18eme Paris). In the summer, you can sleep on the terraces of either house.

Getting Things Done and Shopping

The post and telephone offices, banks, and main stores are all found on Avenue du 1er Novembre, the main street.

Things to See

In Ghardaïa, there's a small museum next to the youth hostel, but it was being renovated when I visited, so I can't tell you anything about it. If you happen to visit the museum, please tell us about it.

Standing on the main street with the youth hostel on your left, continue walking down Avenue du 1er Novembre until you reach the main marketplace or square. Try to arrive here in the morning when most of the stalls are set up. It's quite a colorful scene, with a variety of merchants in traditional robes hawking everything from Berber carpets and rugs to barrels of peanuts. From the square, follow any of the narrow side streets for a short walking tour of Ghardaïa's old quarters.

A more interesting daily market occurs at around 4 or 5 P.M. in the Mozabite town of Beni Isguen about 2 km (1 1/4 miles) from Ghardaïa's market square. Retrace your steps along Avenue du 1er Novembre, and follow it to the main gate of Beni Isguen. Just outside the gate before sunset, there's usually a group of musicians from Beni Isguen playing traditional tunes on a variety of goat skin drums and squeaky horns. Before passing through the gate, you're supposed to hire a local guide to take you around the town and to the Place du Marché for the daily market. As you enter the town, you are greeted by a big multilingual warning sign that says,

NO PHOTOS
NO IMMORAL BEHAVIOUR
NO CAMPING
NO SMOKING
NO LITTERING
NO DRINKING ANYTHING
NO EATING IN PUBLIC

These warnings have enabled the local Mozabite inhabitants to offer outsiders a glimpse of their puritanical lifestyle without sacrificing their traditions.

The town's narrow cobblestone streets and low-lying buildings are cleaner and better maintained than those outside its walls. In fact, certain parts of the walls have been so well preserved that UNESCO has declared them internationally protected historical monuments. The highest point on the main wall is the Bordj Boleila or "one-night tower." You are permitted to take photographs from inside and atop the tower, which is good because the top offers a commanding view of Beni Isguen and surrounding towns. After the tower, your guide will probably take you to the daily market and auction at the Place du Marché.

The Mozabites' reputation as shrewd merchants becomes especially evident in the main square where the market and auction are held. Actually, it is more an auction than a market. Local merchants and tourists sit around the perimeter of the square while several men in turbans or white peaked caps and blue smocks dash past them bearing everything from an electric Melita coffee grinder to a big plastic bag of squashed deglet nour dates. In high-pitched, staccato voices, they yell out the same price until someone buys the item or one of the five bosses sitting in the center of the square gestures for the price to come down or for the item to be dropped from the auction. Some items being sold are real schlock, such as a crudely carved wooden platter that sold for DA 600 ($120—at the official overvalued exchange rate). The auction occurs daily, except Fridays, between 5 and 7 P.M.

During the summer when the towns become unbearably hot, many people head for the cooler microclimate of nearby palmeries. The most prosperous Mozabite families often have second homes in the palmeries. Boughali Toufik of M'zab Tours (see above) can arrange tours and/or overnight stays in these homes, as well as four-wheel-drive tours farther afield into the desert and mountains surrounding the region. You can also walk through the palmeries on your own.

Some of Boughali's trips include a one-week Land-Rover circuit around the region for FF 1,200 to FF 1,650 ($200 to $275), trekking in the Chebka region FF 1,800 ($300, only between October 1 and May 1), a two-week tour of the M'Zab region for FF 2,400 to FF 3,000 ($400 to $500), Christmas in the dunes of the Sahara for FF 1,500 to FF 2,000 ($250 to $330), a 10-day tour of the M'Zab and Geurara regions for FF 2,250 to FF 2,800 ($375 to $466), and the Festival of Timmimoun at the end of October for FF 1,650 to FF 2,100 ($275 to $350).

Water supply in the palmeries is controlled by a system of canals. The width and height of each canal—the principal supply controls—are constructed according to the number of palms in that particular palmerie. Certain men in each set of palmeries have the task of determining how much water someone needs and therefore the necessary canal dimensions.

Ouargla

Located 165 km (102 miles) east of Ghardaïa, Ouargla is an oasis town along the western lip of a *sebkha* or Saharan depression. The town originated in the tenth century at Sedrata, about 14 km (9 miles) southwest of present-day Ouargla, although archeological evidence suggests that settlements existed at Sedrata as early as the eighth and ninth centuries. However, Sedrata was formally established in 901 as capital of the Ibadite Muslims, a heretical group that had split from mainstream Sunni Islam and was chased out of more hospitable climes to the north. Sunni Muslims led by the Hammadite leader El Mansour of Bejaïa arrived in 1072, razed the town, and forced the Ibadites to flee to the Ghardaïa area, where they remain today, but they are now known as Mozabites because they reside in the M'Zab region (see Ghardaïa section) The Ibadites were replaced by Berber and sub-Saharan African settlers, but by the sixteenth century the Turks took control and ruled until the late 1800s. In 1872, the French arrived, ejected the Turks, and built Fort Lutaud, where present-day Ouargla now stands.

Today the city is something of a boom town because of its proximity to the oil fields and natural gas reserves in and around the company town of Hassi Messaoud, which is about 85 km (53 miles) east of Ouargla.

The extensive oil and gas-related geologic surveys undertaken in the region have also unearthed another commodity—*rose du sable*, or, literally, "rose of the sand." The central marketplace in town is dominated by tables piled high with pink chunks of *rose du sable* crystals, which the merchants attempt to sell to tourists for outrageous prices. Behind these tables are other local souvenirs such as hand-woven thick-pile carpets and basketwork.

Ouargla's only other highlight is the Musée Saharien (Sahara Museum) with its decent collections of prehistoric artifacts, plants, stuffed animals, and geologic exhibits. The museum is closed on Thursday and Friday.

Another option is a walking tour of the palmerie that both comprises and surrounds Ouargla. There are over a million and a half palm trees.

Hassi Messaoud

Certain parts of the huge petrochemical complex at Hassi Messaoud, including a museum covering the history of the Algerian petrochemical industry, are open to the public during the day. If you can somehow arrange a visit at night, the burnoff flames from the refineries can be seen from many kilometers away. The flames cast an eerie, surreal, orange and yellow glow on the landscape. In a sense, they are specters, haunting images of a burning future.

The Souf and Oued R'hir Regions

Traditionally, Ouargla has been a principal gateway eastward to the Grand Erg Oriental, an immense area of sand dunes. The northern part of this area is dominated by two oasis regions: the Souf oases around the town of El Oued and the Oued R'hir oases strung from north to south along a now-dry riverbed that approximately ends at Touggourt.

Touggourt

Touggourt is at the southern end of the Oued R'hir string of oases and about 161 km (100 miles) north of Ouargla. It was once an important crossroads for trans-Sahara trade caravans and contributed to this trade with dates gathered from its extensive palmerie. Touggourt was also once the seat of a dynasty of kings known as the Ouled Djellab. Several of these kings are entombed under a large dome in an ancient cemetery near Touggourt.

Today Touggourt is a flourishing agricultural town, thanks in part to artesian wells that created a bigger water supply for irrigation. In addition to dates, various cereals and vegetables are now also harvested, and livestock are raised for meat, wool, and leather.

As with many Saharan towns, the older ksar quarter comprises narrow covered alleyways with bright white archways, winding streets, and low-lying clay-and-stone buildings. This part of town is dominated by a mosque with a high minaret that offers a great panoramic view of the area.

The best hotel in town is the three-star Hotel Oasis (tel. 62-42-60), a kasbah-like place with arched windows and doorways and palm trees around the swimming pool. It's run by a fastidious manager whose apparent ability to easily hire and fire his employees causes them to literally tremble when they are around him. In the hotel restaurant, a waiter served me dinner while the manager hovered nearby. The poor waiter was sweating profusely, and his hands were shaking as he tried to carefully serve each dish.

The other main hotel in town is the Hotel de la Paix near the market square with no-frills singles for DA 30 ($6), doubles DA 60 ($12), and triples DA 90 ($18). The rooms have concrete floors with simple metal frame beds.

You may also want to check out the Hotel Central and, next door, the Hotel des Dunes.

About 5 km (3 miles) outside of town on the road to El Oued is the Hotel Bedouin. A sign outside says "Welcome to Bedouin Hotel." This hotel is actually a big Bedouin-style tent that tends to get somewhat ravaged by sandstorms. You can stay in the tent for DA 15 ($3) or camp outside for DA 5 ($1). Meals are available for DA 40 ($8).

There's nothing specific to see in town other than the "camel market" and the palmerie. Unfortunately, the camel market has become quite small and is now confined to a pen that's big enough for only about ten camels. When I visited the market, there were only five camels hobbling around the pen. The market is situated next to a produce and meat market just off the road to El Oued.

Other sights worth seeing in the area are outside of Touggourt. On the road to El Oued, you will see the magnificent sand dunes that comprise most of the Grand Erg Oriental and a few roadside stands selling rose du sable crystals, woven baskets, crude jewelry, fennecs (desert foxes—see Morocco section), and an occasional camel. Heading south from Touggourt, after about 13 km (8 miles) you reach the town of Temacine, which is renowned for its mud-brick and palm-trunk houses built into age-old ramparts. About a mile further is the town of Tamelhat with the elaborately decorated mosque and mausoleum of Sidi El Hadj Ali that is a favorite local pilgrimage point. Brides visit here to pay respects to Sidi El Hadj before they get married.

El Oued

El Oued and surrounding villages form a unique group of oases called the Souf region. Unlike most oases, though, there are plenty of sand dunes, but few palm trees. In the immediate vicinity of the city, however, these dunes are man-made. Over the centuries, the inhabitants have dug immense craters and planted the palm trees at the bottom so that the roots would be closer to subterranean streams. Most of these basins have been replaced by more sophisticated methods.

Another unique feature of El Oued is its architecture style, which has earned it the nickname "city of a thousand cupolas." Every roof in El Oued is topped by at least one dome or rounded vault as a way of refracting intense summer heat. Just less than a century ago, these domes attracted the attention of an intrepid Sahara explorer and novelist named Isabelle Eberhardt.

At the age of 22, Isabelle Eberhardt, daughter of a Russian general and a Baltic baroness, set out on horseback on a journey through the Sahara. She dressed as a male Arab, called herself Si Mahmoud, converted to Islam, and married a Muslim. By 1900, she had adopted the Algerian fight against French colonialism, a tact that earned her the reputation of being anti-French. She spent over a year in El Oued. In 1904, at the age of 27 or 28, she was swept off the front porch of her house in Aïn Sefra by a flash flood.

CHAPTER 14

The Deep South of Algeria

The Deep South of Algeria is the Sahara, one of the world's biggest deserts. The Arabs call it an "Ocean Without Water," (*bahr bila maa*), a veritable sea of sand with vast shifting dunes. For eons, the vastness and desolation of this dry sea have not, however, deterred a variety of explorers, adventurers, traders and conquerors from crossing, settling, and conquering it.

The Sahara can be crossed, partially settled, and almost conquered only because it is more than just a vacuous sea of sand. In fact, the infamous dunes or *ergs*, as they're known in Algeria, compose only about 20 percent of its total surface, half of which is being continually shifted and reshaped by the wind. The rest of the Sahara is a varied landscape that includes *hamadas* (rock-strewn areas usually devoid of plant life), *tassilis* (rocky plateaus), *regs* (similar to hamadas, but broader expanses of land), and *gueltas* (pools created by underground springs and streams and occasional rain). Above and between these parts of the Sahara lie mountains high enough for snow, extinct volcanoes, plains pocked with moonlike craters, canyons, gullies, dry riverbeds, and sand, endless streams of sand always flowing, always silent. The silence is broken by the whistle and whoosh of the wind and the chirp or squawk of an occasional bird.

Several thousand years ago, the Sahara was wet and humid and abuzz with wildlife. It was a veritable tropical rainforest supporting an animal kingdom that included hippos, lions, crocodiles, zebras, giraffes, and hundreds of other species now found only thousands of kilometers further south. Human beings were attracted here, often settling in caves that they would decorate with rock carvings and bright paintings depicting the once extensive flora and fauna of the Sahara. Thousands of these decorations can still be seen in the caves and canyons of the Tassili-n-Ajjer region near Djanet.

Today, life in the Sahara is concentrated in and around the towns of Djanet (in the southeast near the Libyan border) and Tamanrasset

331

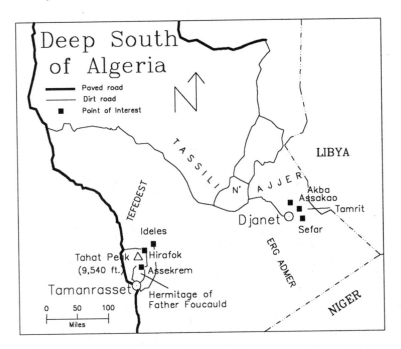

(south-central Algeria). Both are principal congregation points for the various Tuareg tribes of the Sahara and departure points for trips into the surrounding regions. I was able to visit Djanet and participate on a one-week hike and camel trek through the Tassili-n-Ajjer region north of town with a Paris-based travel company called Terres d'Aventure. However, I was unable to visit Tamanrasset, although I tried four times. My efforts are representative of the difficulties and challenges you must occasionally face when traveling in the Sahara.

The chief problem was a lack of sufficient advance planning, but incidents such as a sandstorm that grounded the plane and riots in Algiers that closed the airport were also factors. For the Tamanrasset section and general tips about traveling around the Sahara, I turned to a California-based Sahara expert, Dr. Nicolas D. Hetzer, who operates a unique travel company venture—Forum Travel International—in Pleasant Hill (northern California) that conducts numerous trips to all parts of the Sahara, including even the Libyan portion.

THE NATURAL ENVIRONMENT

Before visiting the Sahara, my preconceived notions about its topography were stereotypical ones, shaped by childhood cartoon depictions of Foreign Legion outposts and vast, endless sand dunes stretching over an area as wide as the United States. As I quickly discovered, though, while flying over the Sahara from Ghardaïa, my preconceptions were really misconceptions. The outposts have long since vanished, and the dunes or ergs, as they're known in Algeria, comprise only about 20 percent of an area that is actually larger then the contiguous United States and Alaska combined.

Through the window I saw a lunar landscape of dark, foreboding shapes—immense mounds of rock, sharp pillars, and craggy mountains punctuated by craters and rock-strewn depressions. Images of an ancient past and a cataclysmic future came to mind. Below me was the world as I had imagined it would be or might have been not long after the fires of creation and destruction had subsided.

Around Tamanrasset, the land is a mountainous region of black volcanic rock known as the Hoggar (also Ahaggar). Local Tuareg nomads dubbed the mountains of the Hoggar "the garden of hell," perhaps because it is still easy to imagine the violent volcanic upheaval that created this land over two million years ago. These haunting black mountains include peaks such as Tahat (2,908 m, or 9,541 ft) and Assekrem (2,585 m, or 8,481 ft), both high enough occasionally to be capped white with snow. Even Tamanrasset at an elevation of 1,372 m (4,500 ft) sometimes receives a bit of snow.

Around Djanet the prominent topographical features are deep, narrow canyons and dark craterlike depressions that often bear comparison to the moon. The canyons comprise part of a region called the Tassili-n-Ajjer. Nestled within many of the canyons are gueltas—pools of water—sometimes stretching for hundreds of meters and surrounded by surprisingly dense vegetation. To the west is an immense area of sand dunes known as the Admer Erg.

THE PEOPLE AND CULTURE

The original inhabitants of much of the Sahara are the traditionally nomadic Tuareg people. They are nicknamed the "Blue Men of the Desert" for the blue *tougoulmust* or veils that most of the men used to wear. The blue veils were so commonly worn that the dye would eventually rub off, giving their skin a slightly bluish hue. Today, however, other colors are also worn. Many of the men also wear a *takuba* (sword slung over the shoulder), a sharp dagger on the left forearm, and an "Agadez Cross" called a *tasagalt*. At an average height of 6 feet, the Tuareg men and their traditional accoutrements present a proud, impressive image of invulnerability and independence. It is no wonder that they call themselves Imuhar or Imarjen, which translated from their local language of Tamahak (also Tamashek) means "the free ones, the independent ones."

In the eleventh century as Islam spread across North Africa, the Arabs began calling them Tuareg, a word derived from the Arabic word *tarek*, which means something like "abandoned" or "the abandoned by God." With the Arab influx, the Tuareg were pushed south into the isolated mountainous regions of the Hoggar (near Tamanrasset), the Aïr (in northern Niger near Agadez), and the Tassili-n-Ajjer (around Djanet).

Although some intermarriage over the years with Arabs and black Africans proves that they weren't totally "abandoned" the Tuareg are a distinctly tall, slim people. Caucasian features among some of the Tuareg is considered possible proof of ancestral links to Vandals and Crusaders.

Despite intermarriage, the Tuareg have been comparatively isolated from many of the changes in North African society. This has enabled them to retain much of their traditional culture. Most notable is their ancient language of Tamahak, which is still spoken, albeit in eight closely related dialects, by the 300,000 or so Tuaregs who inhabit the southern Sahara and Sahel regions. The language has a twenty-five-character alphabet derived from the ancient Libyan language of Tifinar. A French monk named de Foucauld lived among the Tuareg of the Hoggar in the early 1900s and compiled the first dictionary of Tamahak.

In recent years, Arab influence and extended periods of drought have put much pressure on the Tuareg to change their ways, and to become sedentary, thus less pastoral. For a society that equates social prestige and economic survival with the ownership of livestock—particularly camels, cattle, donkeys, goats, and sheep—this would be a drastic change that is bound to affect everything from the status of women to types of transport, dwellings, and diet.

Traditionally, the status of women in Tuareg society is quite elevated, more so in a sense than Arab women. Most Tuareg are strictly monogamous, thus the husband-wife relationship is basically equal, unlike Arab society, wherein a Muslim man is traditionally permitted to have up to four wives and the women do not have the same degree of freedom. Tuareg women have property rights and often own more than their husbands. They have also contributed considerably toward the preservation of tradition in Tuareg society by maintaining and developing—among other things—highly developed forms of poetry and music (they play the one-stringed *imzad*). In addition, Tuareg women seldom wear veils.

Camels have long been the preferred mode of Tuareg transport in the Sahara. It is an increasingly common sight to see Tuareg men in Toyota Land Cruisers and other vehicles tooling through the streets and hamadas (rocky plains) in and around Tamanrasset and Djanet. However, camels haven't been completely replaced; in fact, they are almost always "parked" or tethered in town or near the Tuaregs' skillfully crafted leather and camel-hair tents. Camels are also a source of milk and meat, but the latter is less commonly eaten. Rather, the Tuareg seem to prefer a diet of butter and cheese made from sheep, goat, or cow's milk, as well as wheat and barley, millet, wild berries, roots, and some fruit and vegetables—the sort of diet you might expect among a predominantly pastoral people.

Another key aspect of this "diet" is tea, which the Tuareg seem to be able to prepare in small, but potent doses almost anywhere in the Sahara. Tea is so important to the Tuareg that its preparation has been elevated nearly to the status of a ritual. This ritual is described in greater detail in the Djanet section.

TRAVEL IN THE SAHARA

Arrival, Departure, and Getting Around the Sahara

By Air

Most travelers arrive and depart Tamanrasset and Djanet—the main Sahara trip departure points—by Air Algerie, which is the only carrier serving these destinations. Although there are frequent flights between Algiers, Ghardaïa, Djanet, Tamanrasset, and In Guezzem (on the Niger border), individual reservations are often difficult to arrange in advance on your own, particularly from the United States, where Air Algerie does not have an office.

I attempted to make reservations through the American Express ENVOY travel service in the United States. They sent telexes for me direct to Air Algerie in Algiers requesting reservations for return flights to Djanet and Tamanrasset; they were told that all flights to both destinations were fully booked. On arrival in Algiers, I learned that the flights weren't booked and that individual reservation requests from abroad were often routinely denied. One reason for this may be that they are trying to reserve as many seats as possible for organized groups, which occasionally add on new participants not long before their departure dates. This is especially common between November and April, which is the high season for visiting the Sahara because temperatures are moderate, even quite cool or cold in some parts.

Buying a ticket for the Sahara is, of course, possible from Air Algerie offices throughout Algeria. If flights are fully booked, however, for the periods you wish to travel, your only alternative is to sign up for an ONAT trip. ONAT is the Algerian government tourism organization and thus seems to have priority over foreign tour groups for flights on Air Algerie, the government-owned airline.

All this should not necessarily discourage you from trying to book flights on your own to the Sahara, unless, of course, you don't have much time and want more of a guarantee of getting there. I met a Japanese couple in Djanet who spoke almost no English or French and had somehow gotten a flight there during the high season. On arrival in Djanet, they were also able to get themselves onto a one-week Land-Rover tour of the region. Yet my attempts to catch a flight to Tamanrasset even with the intervention of the central ONAT office were thwarted once by a sandstorm and other times by mechanical problems and overbooking.

By Bus

Buses in the Deep Sahara service only the central route as far south as Tamanrasset. SNTV, one of Algeria's national bus companies, has a station in Tamanrasset. There is no public bus transportation to and from Djanet.

By Truck

Tamanrasset is a major Trans-Africa transit point for commercial trucks carrying goods between West Africa and Algerian ports on the Mediterranean coast. With some haggling over dinars and dollars, it should be easy to arrange a ride to and from Tamanrasset going north or south. Unless you are on a tour or have your own transportation, the only way to continue south from Tamanrasset into Niger (through the In Guezzem border post) is by truck.

Trucks also run along the eastern route through Hassi-Messaoud (a major petrochemical center southeast of Ouargla), Bordj Messaouda (near the Algeria-Tunisia-Libya border junction), In Amenas, Illizi, and Djanet. Occasionally trucks run between Djanet and Tamanrasset, but they run erratically and thus can't be depended on as a possible source of transport.

By Bicycle

You have to be a dedicated and gutsy bicyclist to want to ride across the Sahara. During my travels through Africa, I have met a few hardy souls who have accomplished this seemingly insane feat. In Malawi, I met a brother and sister from Holland who claimed to have crossed the Sahara by bike. And in Zimbabwe a tired British electrical engineer told me about having to push his bike through sandy stretches of Sahara roads.

A saner approach to bicycling in the Sahara is to sign up for a mountain bike trip now offered by a few tour operators. Trips offered by Forum Travel International and Terres d'Aventure (a Paris-based adventure travel company) include Tamanrasset and surroundings. For physically fit travelers who have some mountain biking experience, there's a fifteen-day (twelve days of actual riding) trip in the Hoggar mountains three times a year. The bikes are provided, although you could probably bring your own. Equipment and supplies are transported by vehicle. The itinerary begins in Tamanrasset and includes the following destinations, some of which can be located only on colonial-era maps: Tandjet, Tileline, Tassakint, Tiggatine, Ideles, Hirafok, Issakkarassene, Assekrem, Taessa, and Ikarhagane.

By Other Vehicle

Traveling the Sahara by Land-Rover or other vehicle is costly if you have to rent and potentially risky if you use your own. Renting a four-wheel-drive vehicle is expensive in Tamanrasset, although you could probably split the cost with three or four other travelers. Rentals are unavailable in Djanet.

The majority of travelers touring the Sahara with their own vehicles are, not surprisingly, Europeans. In Djanet I saw a wide variety of vehicles—motorcycles, jeeps, tanklike buses, Land-Rovers, and four-wheel-drive Peugeot wagons. For these vehicles and others crossing the Sahara, the Algerian government tourism authorities have issued precise guidelines and equipment lists. The following is a summary:

1. Private vehicles crossing the Sahara should be equipped with the following:
   - Special desert tires known as "Sahara specials"
   - An oil filter specially designed to prevent damage to the engine from sand
   - Reinforced springs and shock absorbers to limit risks of a puncture or broken spring, or of the vehicle getting stuck in the sand
2. Other highly recommended items include:
   - Perforated metal sheets for use as sand tracks
   - Short-handled shovels
   - Heavy-duty jacks
   - Spare car parts, oil filters, fan belts, spark plugs, springs, and tires
   - An air pump
   - A comprehensive repair kit
   - Adequate supplies of oil, gasoline, and water
3. Personal supplies or at least group supplies should include:
   - Emergency supply of victuals for two days and a sufficient supply for the journey
   - Ten liters of drinking water per person
   - A first-aid kit—tourniquet, scalpel, pair of scissors, sterilized sticking plaster, mercurochrome, hydrogen peroxide, antibiotic cream, antitetanus vaccine, anti-scorpion venom serum, anti-snake-bite serum, painkillers, two crepe bandages, three elastic

bandages, four ordinary bandages, a bottle of aspirin, hemo-
static and antibiotic ampules, a 5-cc syringe, a mirror or white
sheet for signaling, a compass, and two smoke bombs—one red,
one black.

4. Personal items for protection against the climate:
   - Sunscreen and moisturizing cream for your face
   - Antichapping stick for your lips
   - Mint or lemon lozenges for sore throats caused by the excessive
     dryness and dust
   - A *cheche* (pronounced "shesh") or scarflike veil for protection
     against harsh winds and sand storms; available in Djanet and
     Tamanrasset
   - Sunglasses with adequate ultraviolet protection
   - A wide-brimmed sun hat
   - Woolen clothes, blankets, and a sleeping bag for cool nighttime
     temperatures

General Sahara Driving Tips

- It is advisable when on a Saharan track for the load not to exceed four
  passengers per touring car (such as a Peugeot sedan) and five passengers per four-wheel-drive vehicle.
- In the event of a breakdown or if you get lost, do not under any
  circumstances stray far from your vehicle.
- If you find yourself in a sandstorm, stop the vehicle with the rear end
  facing the wind to ensure that your engine stays in working order. To
  avoid getting stuck in the sand, deflate your tires for travel on sand.
- For your own safety, it is advisable not to travel in the deep south
  between the first of June and the fifteenth of September because of
  high temperatures (usually 100 or more degrees Fahrenheit) and
  frequent blinding sandstorms.
- Drinking water and petrol are available only in the main oases. A
  special Michelin map issued for the Paris-Dakar race indicates the
  locations of wells and other sources of water in the Sahara.
- Water and petrol are unavailable on the 398-km (247-mile) road
  between Tamanrasset and In Guezzam on the Niger border. South of
  In Guezzam the next available source is a few kilometers away on the
  Niger side at Assamakka.

The government has also classified almost every road and track in the
Sahara by degree of risk; this is determined by road conditions and
amount of traffic. There are three categories of roads and tracks:

- **Class A.** Not risky
- **Class B.** Safety measures are essential. Owner-operators of all

vehicles who want to travel these roads must first apply for permission from the administrative offices of the local *wilaya* or *daïra*. The vehicles must meet certain equipment standards.

- **Subclass 1.** Roads that are frequently traveled and regularly maintained, but not necessarily paved. Vehicles can travel alone on these roads.
- **Subclass 2.** Roads that aren't traveled as frequently and not maintained. Caravans of at least two vehicles are required on these roads.

- **Class C.** All vehicle traffic on these roads is forbidden because of dangerous conditions. Although vehicles are forbidden in these areas, certain tour operators, such as the Paris-based Terres d'Aventure and local operators such as Tim Beur in Djanet, arrange Land-Rover, camel, and foot expeditions on and around these roads.

Road Numbers (corresponding to Michelin map road numbers)	**Route**
Class A Roads	
RN1	Laghouat-El Goléa-In-Salah-Tamanrasset
RN49	Ghardaïa-Ouargla
RN3	Ouargla-Touggourt
RN16	Touggourt-El Oued (toward Tunisia)
RN3	Ouargla-Hassi Messaoud-Bel Guebbour-Tin Fouye-Ohanet-In Amenas
RN48	El Oued-Stile
RN6	Béchar-Abadla-Adrar
RN6/RN51/RN1	Adrar-Timmimoun-El Goléa
RN50	Béchar-Abadla-Tindouf
Class B Roads	
Subclass 1	
RN52	In-Salah-Aoulef-Reggane
RN6	Adrar-Reggane
RN54	Hassi-Bel Guebbour-Bordj Omar Idriss
RN3	El Abed Larache-Illizi-Djanet
Subclass 2	
RN6	Reggane-Bordj Mokhtar (toward Gao, Mali)
RN1	Tamanrasset-In Amguel
RN55	Ideles-Zaouatallaz
RN3	Illizi-In Amenas
RN53	Fort Thiriet-Ghadames (Libya)
RN54	Bordj Omar Idriss-Amguide-In Ekker
RN55	Zaouatallaz-Ideles-In Amguel

| RN3 | Zaouatallaz-Djanet |
| RN1 | Tamanrasset-In Guezzam (toward Agadez, Niger) |

Class C Tracks—All Traffic Forbidden

Touggourt-Ghardaïa via Guerrara-Guerrara (an adequate alternate route is available)
Laghouat-Stile-Djanet-Chad border
Tamanrasset-Tin Zaoutene
Tamanrasset-Bordj Mokhtar
All other tracks and roads not mentioned above.

Do not take the preceding travel advice from the Algerian government as the final word on touring the Sahara by vehicle. Entire books have been written about driving in the Sahara. Unfortunately nothing in English has recently been written. The best books are in German: *Trans Sahara (Reise Know-How)* and *Durch Afrika*, both by a veteran traveler and explorer, Klaus Därr. The Därr family lives in Munich and also runs one of the world's best expedition services and travel supply stores—Därr's Travel Shop (Theresienstrasse 66, 8000 Munich 2; tel. 089-28-20-32).

Before setting out on your own for destinations described in any books, check with local authorities about the latest conditions and precautions.

By Foot and Camel

The best way to tour the Sahara is by foot with a camel carrying your equipment. It is not unheard of for an adventurous traveler to attempt this on his or her own, but these are the rare souls who have the time and wherewithal to sacrifice themselves to the pursuit of potentially perilous goals. For less adventurous, saner, and perhaps otherwise independent travelers, this may be the time for opting to join an organized group tour. There are several European companies offering a variety of Land-Rover, camel, and walking tours of the Sahara, but in the United States I know of only two companies—Forum Travel International and Turtle Tours.

Forum is run by a Sahara expert named Dr. Nicolas Hetzer who has long been in the business of arranging unique trips to the Sahara and other lesser-explored regions of the world such as Greenland and Namibia. He offers a wide range of Sahara trips, several of which are arranged in conjunction with two French companies that are the foremost operators in this region—Terres d'Aventure and Deserts. Most of the trips begin in Djanet or Tamanrasset after a flight via Algiers from Paris. They usually include camping under stars and a fair amount of

Road sign in the Algerian Sahara. *Photo by Scott Wayne.*

walking with camels carrying baggage and supplies. Their most special trips focus on particular interests germane to the Sahara. For example, in the regions of Tadrart, Tassili du Hoggar, and Tagrera El Ghessour, there are astronomy trips led by an astronomist who brings along telescopes and star maps. There are "prehistory" trips that focus on the ancient cave paintings and engravings of the Hoggar mountains and Tassili-n-Ajjer plateaus (near Djanet). The Deserts company also offers trips with an emphasis on regional geology, music, and storytelling. All these trips are accompanied by specialists in their respective fields. Forum is the U.S. representative for both companies. Contact them for more information by writing or calling: Forum Travel International, 91 Gregory Lane, No. 21, Pleasant Hill, California 94523; tel. 415-671-2900 or 946-1500.

Turtle Tours is run by Irma Turtle, a former Manhattan advertising executive, who fell in love with the Sahara, quit her job, and began taking people there starting in 1985. She offers four Sahara itineraries including a grand "overland" tour by foot and Land-Rover; a short camel caravan; and a prehistory trip in the Tassili-n-Ajjer region. She can be contacted at Turtle Tours, Inc., 9446 Quail Trail, Box No. 1147, Carefree, Arizona 85377.

Last-Minute Tips for Sahara Travel

Equipment and Supplies. The following is a *partial* list of things recommended for travel in the Sahara, a few of which are quite obvious:

- A travel bag such as a duffel bag (a backpack with a frame is too unwieldy to pack on a camel)
- A small pillow
- Some aluminum foil
- A parka or anorak
- A heavy and light sweater
- Cotton shirts
- Shorts
- Sunblock lotion
- Chapstick
- Moisturizer
- Toilet paper
- Handiwipes or something similar
- Plastic bags
- Sunglasses with adequate ultraviolet protection
- Flashlight
- Pocketknife
- A plastic canteen
- Dried fruit and biscuits
- Vitamins
- Personal medical kit
- Photocopies of essential pages from your passport
- Battery-powered razor

See the general introductory chapters for a more complete list.

Camel and Fly Tips. Don't walk too closely behind a camel. Camels are quite capable of defecating and urinating while walking. Moreover, if you're on a camel caravan, when you're nestled in your sleeping bag at night get used to hearing rustling bushes, crunching like someone stepping on a bag of tortilla chips, and enough spitting and lip smacking to almost force you into burying your head in the sand. Welcome to a camel feeding session! Believe it or not, after a couple of nights you can get used to it.

The Sahara is full of flies that seem to take intense pleasure in swarming around your head, clinging to your glasses, and crawling across your face. There's not much you can do except just continually swishing them away. Fortunately, they sleep or at least stop attacking at night and don't pursue you again until sunrise.

TAMANRASSET AND SURROUNDINGS

In the heart of the Sahara, Tamanrasset—or Tam, as it's commonly known—is the capital of the Great South—Le Grand Sud, as the French called it when they conquered this region with the help of the infamous Foreign Legion. Tam is the main administrative hub of the region and seat of the Amenokal, supreme chief of the Kel Rela Tuaregs. It has also become a magnet or crossroads of sorts attracting a variety of peoples from throughout Africa—Arabs, Berbers (Tuaregs are considered Berbers), and Sudanese blacks, mainly immigrants from Mali and Niger, and the ubiquitous Mozabites from the Ghardaïa who seem to run most of the trading activities.

Although the cultural mix makes Tam a fascinating place for people watching and learning more about some of the cultures of Africa, Tam is really a divided town. It's separated roughly in half—two worlds living side by side, without much understanding of and for each other—the "insiders" and "those from the north." Many of these people are refugees from black Africa, taxing already scarce resources.

Water is high on the list of scarce resources. It's a precious commodity and often rare and rationed. Despite its relatively high altitude of 4,500 feet and low maximum temperature of 35°C, Tam generally has a desertlike climate, with dry periods sometimes lasting several years. Although there is occasional rain and even light snow (very rare though), don't conjure up images of crystalline swimming pools and don't always expect showers to run. Tam's water comes from deep wells and an ancient, ingenious system of *foggaras* (a subterranean system of channeling ground water), but these must be replenished by water from the nearby Hoggar mountains and by infrequent rain showers. One can also always try to swim in one of the lovely waterholes (*gueltas*) at Imlaoulaoulene or Afilal (if the military hasn't declared it off limits) or even go to the valley of Issakkarassene, about 70 km from Tam, via the Assekrem circuit, where the gueltas can extend for several kilometers. The gueltas are often hemmed in by bushes and reeds and inhabited (believe it or not) by small fish. The water level of these gueltas, however, can get quite low, especially in the summer.

Aside from water and bountiful natural beauty, Tam and its surroundings have practically no exploitable resources or any that have yet been discovered. Consequently, unlike the central Sahara area around Hassi Messaoud, where extensive petrochemical facilities have been developed, the Great South has not yet been developed and industrialized. Tam has, therefore, managed to retain much of its traditional character and, with some exceptions, most of the people have kept their cultural identity under the age-old hierarchy of tribe and clan.

The Tuareg were the first settlers in this region, which they called

Tamenghest. Their settlements were and still are small and often temporary because of their traditionally nomadic nature. They're found scattered around Tam and throughout the Hoggar mountains. Many Tuareg men, dressed in long robes and burnooselike scarves over their heads and faces, come into town daily to go to the market and to small cafés for mint tea and the latest gossip. Tuareg women aren't seen on the streets as much as in past years—perhaps traditional Arab mores about the role of women are taking hold here, namely that a woman's role centers around maintaining the household. A man's role traditionally is to provide the resources for maintenance. These traditional roles aren't strictly enforced. It's more a matter of what is considered socially acceptable and unacceptable.

First Things First

Formalities

Tam is considered a border town, so immigration and customs formalities must be taken care of here for people traveling to and from Niger and Mali. Additional formalities are also often necessary when you reach the actual borders. Travelers who are en route to or from Djanet must register. All registration and immigration formalities are completed at the *wilaya*—literally "state"—office, the local administrative authority or prefecture. Customs formalities are done at the nearby customs office.

Tourists and Travel Information

ONAT, the Algerian government tourist office, has an office in Tam. As with several travel agencies in town, it organizes group trips into the surrounding areas at competitive prices. It usually has enough four-wheel-drive vehicles and camping equipment on hand to run most trips. However, you can't be absolutely assured of getting on a trip, because a minimum number of participants is required and this varies according to the trip. In addition, if you arrive a day or so after a trip has departed, you could be stuck in Tam for a few days, which isn't an appealing option when you are anxious to explore the surrounding region.

Another possibility for getting out of Tam and into the Sahara is to "hitch" a ride with one of the many private overland vehicles visiting the area from Europe. Occasionally someone may need or want another person for a trip. Be wary, though, of linking up with a group of inexperienced, ill-prepared travelers—travel in the Sahara is risky. If the group plans to venture beyond the well-trodden route of the Assekrem circuit (described below), then a local guide should be accompanying them.

Several foreign travel companies offer organized excursions to the areas around Tam. Foremost among these companies is the Paris-based Terres d'Aventure, (16 Rue Saint-Victor, 75005 Paris; tel. 01-43299450) which has been offering trips into the Sahara by foot, camel, Land-Rover, and now even mountain bike for several years. For non-Francophone travelers, however, these trips can pose a slight problem because the participants are overwhelmingly French, so there could be a minor language barrier. In the United States, a company called Forum Travel International (91 Gregory Lane, Suite 21, Pleasant Hill, California 94523; tel. 415-671-2900 and 415-946-1500) works with Terres in organizing "internationalized" groups for these trips.

Forum also represents another Paris-based company called Deserts, which was founded by Jean Didier, a long-time Sahara explorer who used to work with Terres d'Aventure. Through Deserts, Forum offers North American travelers a broad range of trips from Tamanrasset, a few of which are described below.

Aside from Forum Travel International, only one other travel company in the United States offers trips through Tamanrasset and surroundings—Turtle Tours, Inc. (9446 Quail Trail, Box No. 1147, Carefree, Arizona 85377). As mentioned earlier, it's a small company founded in 1985 by a former Manhattan advertising executive named Irma Turtle. She offers four itineraries for the central Sahara, two of which include the Tamanrasset area.

Accommodations

There are several somewhat rustic inns and two main hotels—the centrally located Hotel Tine Hinane and the slightly out-of-town and more expensive Hotel Tahat. And then there is, a few hundred yards further down the road to Adriane, the Zeribas Camping, which is similar to the Zeribas in Djanet—concrete-floored huts, usually with two beds and a single, bare lightbulb. The Hotel Tahat is popular with ONAT groups, so reservations are sometimes necessary. The Zeribas is used by most of the travel companies, including Terres and Deserts, and by many of the independent travelers. This is a great place to meet people and get information about trips around the area.

Food

With inhabitants from all over West, Central, and North Africa, Tam has a colorful souk (market) where locals like to meet, buy, sell, and trade goods and gossip. Vegetables, fruit (usually from the North), eggs cheese, milk, and canned goods can usually be found there.

In town, there's also a small supermarket, a butcher, and a baker (open as long as supplies last, which is often not very long).

Foreign-organized groups usually bring in many of their staples direct from Europe. The arrival of a Terres group resembles a small military expedition with compact, carefully labeled canvas bundles, each containing precisely measured quantities of victuals for the trip.

Restaurants and Cafés

Tam has an abundance of cafés and thus tea, but not restaurants. There are restaurants at the Zeribas and the two main hotels. The fearless can also eat couscous and chorba (a national staple served here as a delicious noodle soup) at one of the small "hole-in-the wall" joints in town.

Getting Things Done and Things to Buy

In the center of town, there's a bank (open Saturday to Wednesday from 9 A.M. to 4 P.M.) post office, hospital and pharmacy, a movie house, a gas station (often out of gas), the Air Algerie office, the SNTV bus station, a police station, and several car repair shops and garages.

The souk (market) is the best place to go for Tuareg handicrafts, but their quality is often not the best: jewelry, leather goods, carpets, trinkets, and various other souvenirs. You may want to take home a *takuba* (traditional Tuareg sword), a *tasagalt* (the famous Agadez Cross of the Tuareg), or perhaps some other object related to daily Tuareg life.

Things to See and Possible Itineraries

In Tamanrasset

Tam doesn't have much to offer in the way of actual tourist "attractions." There's one museum called the Museum of the Hoggar (also known as the Sahara Museum) which contains displays of typical Tuareg clothing and accoutrements such as swords and daggers. In the spring there's a yearly Hoggar-Fest where the area's various ethnic groups assemble to show off their traditional costumes, dances, and handicrafts. Every January there's a trade mass, a similar festival, but with participants from most of Algeria's neighboring countries.

Around Tamanrasset

One of the most popular local excursions is a trip to the Hoggar highlands along a route that includes a great representative sampling of typical Saharan topography. Conceivably, this area can be visited in a one-night, two-day trip, but three or four days would be more ideal. This is the most likely area for visiting independently in small groups or, for the most intrepid, individually. It's possible to walk through the mountains following a circuitous route and returning to Tamanrasset, although this may take at least a week and you should have adequate supplies and information.

As with most of the travel companies operating in this area, including Tamanrasset-based agencies, Forum Travel International offers a typical trip. Dr. Nicolas Hetzer, director of Forum, provided the following description of one of his itineraries:

> From Tam we head due north (by Land-Rover) and soon reach the small nomad settlement of Adriane where the making of leather and metal handicrafts can be watched from close up. Following the track toward the Iharen peak landmark (also known as Pic Lapperine) after about seven miles we get to a track leading to the Cahpouis source (five miles) where water reserves can be replenished. This is really a worthwhile little detour for the lovely landscape at the foot of the Adrar Hoggaren mountains and the presence of water. The slowly bubbling source itself is now housed in a little building, and you may have to pay some small amount for the water (unless you spend the night at the auberge). Unfortunately, the effects of vandalism and poor maintenance are also much in evidence.
>
> A couple of miles further down the road we reach the cutoff to one of the really grand experiences in the Sahara: the gueltas of Imelaoulaoulene. Unless there has been a period of prolonged drought, we will find a series of little lagoons and waterfalls, hemmed in by trees and bushes, where a rocky barrier—formed after a volcanic eruption eons ago—has impeded the free flow of one of the *oueds* (seasonally dry creeks), creating the falls. Water in the Sahara is always a joyful, nearly mystical experience!
>
> We continue north among beautiful vistas, leaving the Ahounahamt massif to our left and reaching a cutoff to the little Tuareg settlement of Ezernene (about two miles off the main track). En route, right and left, we find an occasional *adebni*—a megalithic round-grave. There are also many rock paintings and engravings to be found (watch out for snakes among the rocks), particularly in Akar-Akar mountain area, which legend says was once the abode of a powerful giant who piled up the huge granite blocks in the region. After descending into a little valley where more rock art can be admired—some at least 8,000

years old—we reach a cutoff to the gueltas of Afilale, which stretch out for miles: blue water surrounded by green vegetation in the midst of black basalt rocks, an invitation to take a dip (if the military has not taken over the place).

Steep grades on the winding track (up to 25 percent) finally lead us to the Assekrem (about three miles after the cutoff to Hirafok, Ideles and Djanet), where some of the most spectacular sunrises and sunsets can be witnessed. There is a hut (operated by the Tam tourist office) where one can spend the night and even find food at times (actually, most of the time it is a good idea to bring food not only for yourself but also some extra for the Fathers who live there, as a friendly gesture). There is no water, but there is a campground.

The sunrise and sunset is even more impressive from the hermitage of Father Foucauld, reached in about 30 minutes of uphill walking, and rock drawings can be seen by hiking even further. A few monks from Father Foucauld's order live up there and say mass every morning in the small, simple chapel built in this telluric wilderness—a wonderful testimony to the faith and endurance of these people, the "little brothers of Foucauld."

Father de Foucauld—revered as a saint by the locals...and murdered by a band of fanatic Senoussi Muslims in 1916—was right when he said that "up here, I am as close to God as I can get." In winter it can get quite cold up here and it may even snow, so take warm clothing.

Returning to Tam we curve down steeply along magnificent vistas, with the Aouknet on our left (rock drawings) and "the most beautiful mountain of the Hoggar," the Tahat (at 10,000 feet also the highest) on our right. A lovely series of gueltas can also be visited—partly by car and partly on foot—past the little village of Ilamane, where some Tuareg families eke out a living in tents and little reed huts, among a vegetation quite dense for this area. There is also some wildlife, such as jerboas (jumping mice), gerbils, agamas, marmots, fennecs (desert fox), perhaps mouflons, and even a very rare cheetah can be seen at times. Further down is the red granitic Taessa region and then we head toward the village of Terhenanet, inhabited by Rali Tuaregs who will offer their leather and jewelry handicrafts for sale.

Past some craters of extinguished volcanoes we reach the Oued Otoul with its few gardens, where more rock

engravings can be seen. The whole area is mountainous
with steep grades and washed-out tracks after the sporadic
rains which can come down with a lot of force. We cross the
savannah-like Ehara plains before hitting the sandy desert
again on the last miles leading back to Tam.

The Hoggar highlands is a massif composed of several geological parts
with an average altitude of about 762 m (2,500 ft). One of the principal
mountain chains of this massif is the Atakor, a lunar landscape of ancient
volcanoes and jagged peaks. Towering well above the other peaks at an
altitude of 2,585 m (8,481 ft) is Assekrem, site of Father Charles de
Foucauld's reclusive "hermitage."

Father Charles de Foucauld built the hermitage in 1905 where, in
solitude and poverty, he compiled a Tuareg language grammar and
dictionary. He was murdered in 1916 by a fanatic Muslim, not by the
local inhabitants, who revered him. A memorial column was erected in
Tamanrasset near the spot where he was murdered.

On other itineraries that include Tamanrasset, Otoul and Abalessa,
which are within a 100-km radius of Tam, are also sometimes visited.
Otoul is a picturesque site at the dry riverbed of the Oued Otoul where
gigantic black crags form phantasmal shapes and images. There are also
some prehistoric cave paintings and engravings here.

Abalessa is an oasis about 100 km west of Tamanrasset that is
remarkable mostly for the unexpected presence of the ruins of a castle
that was supposedly erected by the Romans. It was discovered in 1925 at
the same time as a cache of ancient funerary furniture, lamps, vases, all
of which was believed to have been left by Tin-Hinan, the first queen of
the Kel Rela Tuareg. These items are now in the Bardo Museum in
Algiers.

In addition to the Assekrem Circuit described above, there are
itineraries offered by Forum and other companies that incorporate the
following regions and/or routes or variations of them usually beginning
in Tamanrasset:

- **The Tassili du Hoggar,** a set of sedimentary rock plateaus that begins
  approximately 300 km south of Tamanrasset and extends to the Niger
  border. The plateaus are characterized by enormous fingers of
  sculptured rock, all in a variety of shapes ranging from sharp pinnacles
  to squatty mushroomlike formations. Great sand dunes fill the spaces
  in between. For centuries this region was frequently traversed by
  camel caravans bearing salt, cloth, and spices. Deserts offers a
  nineteen-day camel expedition through this region, and Terres
  d'Aventure offers three ten- to twenty-day walking tours. Itineraries
  of both companies include El Ghessour, where the rock formations

are especially dramatic and have often been compared to intricate castles of stone. Contact Forum Travel International for more information.

- **Tefedest**, a granite massif beginning 300 km north of Tamanrasset that is about 130 km long and 20 km wide. Its peaks, some almost as high as 5,000 feet, tower over rock-strewn valleys, immense dunes, oueds (riverbeds) covered with tamarisk and acacia trees and gueltas (natural pools). Toward the northern end of the massif is the 7,635-foot-high Garet El Djenoun—Mountain of the Genies, an area that has numerous sites of ancient cave paintings and engravings. Both Terre and Desert trips in this region are considered easy walks, accessible to most travelers in good shape.

- **Tamanrasset-Hirafok-Ideles-Zaouatallaz-Djanet**. The first portion of this route has been dubbed "route of the gueltas" because of the numerous beautiful natural pools and underground springs along the way. Between Hirafok and Ideles, you pass the Jebel Teddraz and a marvelous oasis at its base in which the inhabitants are famous for their traditional songs and dances. Just a few kilometers out of Hirafok there are also some cave paintings and engravings. The track continues east-northeast across the northern edge of the Hoggar mountains, and skirts the southern limits of the Adrar massif and the Tassili-n-Ajjer plateau region before turning south to Djanet. The first legs of this route—as far as Ideles—are incorporated into Terres and Deserts Hoggar trips. The Adrar and Tassili-n-Ajjer portions are included in Djanet-based Tassili-n-Ajjer trips with both companies. Turtle Tours offers the entire route overland via four-wheel-drive vehicles; the trip takes approximately four or five days.

DJANET AND SURROUNDINGS

At the southeast corner of Algeria, not far from the Libyan border, and seemingly at the edge of the world is the beautiful oasis town of Djanet. Like Tamanrasset, it has become something of a tourist center with many group trips departing into the surrounding plateaus and chasms of the Tassili-n-Ajjer region. However, Djanet is much more isolated than Tam because the only public transport into the area is by Air Algerie. An unpaved partially improved road links Djanet to Illizi, the closest main settlement—about 434 km to the north. Tracks link it to Tamanrasset, which is about 750 km to the west.

I flew into Djanet with a Terres d'Aventure group for a journey into the oases and canyons of the Tassili-n-Ajjer. As we approached the town, the plane banked in a wide semicircle, showing us a long, bright pocket of green through the windows. After hundreds of miles of yellow, black, and brown Sahara, the greenery seemed out of place here, almost as if it had been poured into a canyon from the heavens.

On the ground, a bus, two rows of Land-Rovers and their Tuareg drivers, several swathed in long burnooses and robes with daggers at their sides, waited for us in front of the "terminal." The terminal was nothing more than a single trailerlike building with two rooms—one for arrivals and the other for departures. The "baggage claim" section became the back of a tractor that pulled up next to the Land-Rovers. We grabbed our bags and boarded the bus to go into town.

The marvels of the Sahara were immediately apparent. On both sides of the bus, great cathedrals of rock towered over dunes dotted with tiny splotches of green. I expected a Sahara desert, a land desolate and devoid of all life, but plants were sprouting from every dune and crevice. Later, I learned that it had recently rained, a very rare occurrence that had resurrected plants long dormant and filled the canyon gueltas— natural pools. All heads were turned to the window in awe; nobody said a word until we rumbled into town.

First Things First

Formalities

Most travelers are registered with the police through the hotels, campground, or tour operators.

If you have your own vehicle and are planning to tour the region, you will need permission to enter the National Park of the Tassili-n-Ajjer and also an official local guide is sometimes required. The authorities will check out your supplies and vehicle to be sure that you are sufficiently equipped. Abdel Hak Bouafia, assistant director of the local ONAT office, speaks excellent English and can assist you with the approval procedures and paperwork. Boufia is also probably one of the best sources of travel information in town.

Travel Information

ONAT, the government tourist office, has an office in Djanet. Its official address is Boite Postale 44, Djanet, Algeria 33100; telex number 42014. If you wish to contact this office, the telex seems to be more efficient than the mail, but Boufia, the assistant director, did claim to have received my letters.

ONAT is one of the principal tour operators in Djanet. It offers several trips into the surrounding region, a few of which are made often in conjunction with foreign tour operators such as Turtle Tours. ONAT's trips tend to be much shorter and cheaper than foreign-organized trips. There are trips by foot, often with camels carrying the baggage, of three to eight days; and vehicle excursions of up to two days. Vehicle circuits include Iherir, Amadror, Tehoudaine, Tassili, and Jebbaren. Circuits by foot, with camels or support vehicles, include Issendilene, Tadrart, Tadret, Le Tenere, and the crossing to Tamanrasset.

Another principal tour organizer here is Tim Beur Agence Djanet, which is owned by Hamou Dahou, a dashing fellow who dresses up in full Tuareg regalia—a long, flowing robe and burnoose, mirrored sunglasses (somewhat of a fad here), and a dagger at his side—to greet new arrivals. He's not someone you can easily forget.

Hamou has a couple of Toyota Land Cruisers (a PJ45 and an FJ60) and a team of camels and herders, all of which he uses to run trips for several foreign travel companies, including Terres d'Aventure. Although he does offer individual trips arranged through his Djanet office, this is more likely in late spring or early fall when European groups aren't arriving in droves. His address is Tim Beur, Boite Postale 27, Djanet.

It is possible to just show up in Djanet and get on a trip even in the middle of the high season. I met a Japanese couple who arrived without bookings. They spoke no French at all and just a little English, but they somehow managed to get themselves booked on a trip.

There are a few other agencies in town, but they all seem to offer approximately the same trips.

- The Agence de Voyages Admer, Boite Postale 19, Tin Khatma, Djanet, Wilaya d'Illizi, Algeria; tel. 73-52-78. Offers various hiking, Land-Rover, and camel trips.
- The Sefar Agence Touristique, Boite Postale 4, 33100 Djanet, Wilaya d'Illizi; tel. 73-54-13, telex 42021 DZ SEFAR. The usual trips; all equipment and supplies are provided.

Accommodations

There are only two places to stay in Djanet—the Hotel Zeribas and the Auberge ONAT. The Zeribas is where almost everyone stays except perhaps travellers who are participating on prearranged ONAT trips. They have 50 concrete-floored huts each with two simple frame beds that tend to droop, and walls that shake when occupants in an adjoining hut open and close their door. The huts are arranged around a small garden where extra travelers usually end up camping—this happens quite often during the high season.

There are showers, but don't get your hopes up. They consist of five concrete stalls each with open pipe spigots jutting from the wall and a dirty piece of plastic sheeting that is a dismal excuse for a shower curtain. Each stall often floods, and the whole room turns swampy. My last night in Djanet I used Stall 5 at the end. As I left the room, my last fleeting image of this place was an enormous white rear end suddenly popping through the plastic in Stall 3. I side-stepped it (I didn't check on its gender) and headed straight for the door.

There's also a cafeteria where meals are simple, usually consisting of whatever food is available that day. While I was there, that meant salad and couscous for lunch, soup and couscous with a chunk of meat and a few vegetables thrown in for dinner. Breakfast is even sparser—bread, jam, and tea. Each meal, even breakfast, costs 100 dinars (which at the current official rate of exchange meant the absurd amount of approximately $20 per meal). It was overpriced even at the approximate black market rate of 20 dinars to $1. This is a true case of charging whatever the market will bear.

Between the cafeteria and the huts is a small dirt lot surrounded by palm trees and crammed with Land-Rovers and overland trucks, most of them privately owned. Every day the lot becomes an open-air garage and adventure center as travelers scramble around each vehicle preparing it for a journey deeper into the Sahara. One particularly interesting vehicle was a behemoth Mercedes-Benz truck-bus equipped with couchettes for twenty passengers, two huge truck tires under the front cab and eight behind them, and a full field kitchen beneath a collapsible tent in back. According to the driver, it gets an abominable 80 km per 50 liters of diesel fuel in the desert and 100 km on the road.

Rates at the Zeribas are as overpriced as the meals: a single room is 80 dinars, and a double is 100 dinars.

The Auberge ONAT is perched atop a hill near the center of town. It has more comfortable rooms than the Zeribas; some even have private showers. Rates are 110 dinars for a single and 120 dinars for a double. Reservations are recommended, especially during the high season.

At the time of writing, other hotels were being constructed in town and just outside (on the road to the airport).

Another source of food in Djanet is the town souk (market) just around the corner from the Zeribas. There's usually some fresh produce available, as well as a few canned goods and other basic staples, but prices are quite high.

Getting Things Done and Things to Buy

In the center of town, there is a post office, bank, Air Algerie office, the ONAT office, travel agencies, and a few government offices.

There's not much to buy in Djanet in the way of tourist souvenirs. Near the entrance to the Zeribas and in the souk, you'll see Tuaregs— both men and women—selling jewelry and *cheches* (the long scarves worn by Tuareg men). The latter are quite useful for traveling in the desert.

Things to See and Possible Itineraries

In Djanet

There are no sights in Djanet and not much to do other than climb the hill to the Auberge ONAT for a great view of the area and walk among the houses in town and around the oasis.

I headed for one of the outdoor cafés near the center of town for a good vantage point to do some people watching. Actually, I should say "Tuareg watching" because those are the people I really wanted to see. In their long, flowing robes and loose-fitting wraparound veils or burnooses, the Tuareg men and women (in town many of the Tuareg women are also veiled, often more completely than the men) are an impressive sight. Through their veils, the women's eyes have a mysteriously piercing allure, an almost hypnotic gaze.

In the café I struck up a conversation with a severely pock-marked Algerian man from Algiers. He had asked for a cigarette, which I didn't have, and then, as he sat down across the table from me, asked if he could join me. To avoid that brief uncomfortable period of silence in which you try to get a notion of who this person is, I quickly asked him one question, "Where are you from?" and within minutes he had given me a summary of his life. He was a construction worker who had worked in Europe, mostly Italy, for ten years, was happily married with one child and another on the way. Grim-faced and teary-eyed, he told me that his wife and child died in an accident. He seemed on the verge of breaking down and crying, so I asked him why he was in Djanet. "Construction," he said, "but there aren't any more jobs here, so I'll go someplace else. I don't know where. Maybe I'll cross the border into Libya just to visit. Maybe I'll continue on to Egypt." I didn't have the heart to tell him that I didn't think he could enter Libya from there nor, at the time, cross the Libyan border into Egypt. There was nothing more to ask, so I said goodbye and wished him good luck.

Around the corner from the café, the sonorous wails of Arabic music were emanating from the town "stadium." The townspeople were celebrating a local festival and had set up several small booths for games and food. One stall was selling biscuits and honey-coated cakes, while another had two tables, each with a small roulette wheel. Tuareg men swathed in blue hovered over the tables and tossed 1-dinar coins onto a piece of cardboard that was divided with hand-drawn lines into numbered spaces. At another table, a heavy-set man was hunched over a bubbling cauldron and ladling chunks of brown meat on to pieces of long French bread. Other games at this Tuareg carnival in the Sahara included a man with a BB-pellet rifle selling shots at a small target in a box and a hawker with a "ghetto blaster" full of disco music was challenging men to knock down stacks of empty juice cans. The prizes were—you guessed it—full cans of juice. There was also a mobile library and bookstore—a truck with a piggyback shipping container full of shelves of books in French and Arabic. The bookmobile was packed with Tuareg and Arab men.

Around Djanet

Most of the trips passing through Djanet head for a spectacular region north of town known as the Tassili-n-Ajjer—the Plateau of Chasms. However, it is much more than this. The plateau is actually a set of plateaus, cut into chasms, deep canyons, and crevasses by eons of erosion and volcanic eruption. As you walk through this geological wonderland, it's easy to imagine a visit to another planet or to regard each canyon and cliff as a mystical gate to another culture. In a sense, though, the plateau really is a repository of secrets and insights into bygone cultures.

Hidden in caves and etched on cliff walls of the Tassili-n-Ajjer are thousands of ancient rock paintings and carvings that show life in the Sahara thousands of years ago. Some of the paintings can be traced as far back as 7,000 B.C. and depict this part of the Sahara as teeming with animal and plant life. There were giraffes, elephants, hippos, crocodiles, cattle, and various birds here. Of course, human beings are also depicted—as hunters, dancers, bakers, even sailors with their boats, among other things. These depictions form the world's largest open-air museum of life and offer us a colorful window to our ancient past.

Unfortunately, this "museum" might also be a foreboding sign of our future. Today, the landscape is desolate and harsh, a region comparatively devoid of life. Although human beings and a few other species continue to eke out a living here, the paintings show that life in the Sahara was much more plentiful thousands of years ago. One of the main explanations for this drastic transformation has been environmental factors. Dramatic climatic changes through the years caused increased desertification. Several plant and animal species were unable to adapt to a warmer, drier environment, so they vanished from this region. As deforestation of the world's forests continues and air pollution worsens, the "greenhouse effect" also worsens and the world's deserts, particularly the Sahara, which is the largest, are spreading into population centers.

The Algerian government has recognized the need to preserve the prehistoric art and delicate environment of the Tassili-n-Ajjer. So it has made 100,000 hectares (250,000 acres) of this region a protected area—the National Park of Tassili. Travelers are required to carry out all waste material that can't be burnt and are not supposed to swim in the gueltas. These rules were constantly in force during the Terres d'Aventure trip I participated on with a group of French travelers.

The Oases and Canyons of the Tassili-n-Ajjer

Into the heart of the Tassili-n-Ajjer—that's where this 13-day walking tour was supposed to take us. I was the only American in the group; the rest were all French from a variety of backgrounds.

The first member of the group I met was Chantal, a shy nurse from eastern France. I asked her why she had chosen this trip. She replied in a somewhat frightening tone, "For the silence and solitude of the desert, to reflect on my life." She said that she hiked from the North Rim of the Grand Canyon to the bottom and then returned to Los Angeles by mountain bike—all by herself.

Next to Chantal was a short, stocky computer professor from Paris who spoke with the lightning speed of a computer processor. She was on the trip because it was something she had wanted to do for a long time.

Most of the other members of the group had similarly simple reasons for selecting this trip. They included a 59-year-old egg farmer from southern France, a pharmacist, a 50-year-old electrical engineer, an administrator for Shell Oil, and a pediatrician.

Leading the group was a deeply tanned French woman named Sylvie who had been living among the Tuareg for several years. She spoke the local Tuareg dialect and communicated easily with the camel herders who took care of the camels and equipment. The Tuareg called her Tabbarat. Throughout the trip, she was reserved and not at all prone to reveal much about herself.

After a night in the Zeribas, Land-Rovers took us 40 minutes beyond the paved road in town to the Adjereo valley where our camels and their three herders—Snousi, Ouchah, and Sahnny—had congregated. We helped pack up the camels, and then Sylvie handed us each a bright orange meal bowl and spoon, which we placed in our day bags.

The trek began with puzzling words of advice from Sylvie—"People walking towards the back [near the end of the line] will have less of a chance of stepping on something strange." I discovered what she meant after lunch when I made the stinky and nearly mushy mistake of walking behind one of the camels.

We walked up the dry riverbed of a canyon with steep cliffs on either side that seemed gradually to close in on us. After about an hour, we stopped in the shade of an acacia tree for a granola bar break. Then more walking until noon when we arrived at a small canyon, where we waited for the camels to bring our ready-made lunch of lentil salad with carrots, onions, and hard-boiled eggs, French bread, oranges, and cheese. After lunch the Tuareg napped for about an hour and then made tea.

Tea making is a ritual among the Tuareg. They first boil two to three teapotsful water and tea leaves together in a kettle, and then three big teaspoons of sugar are added to the pot so that it's almost half tea and half sugar. It boils for a minute or so before being poured several times back and forth between a big cup and the pot until the taste is right. Finally, the tea is poured into tiny glasses and offered to everyone in the group. They did this three times, thus giving us all quite a sufficient sugar and caffeine high.

By 4.40 P.M. the caravan was again loaded up and ready to continue. We walked for just over an hour and arrived at our campsite—a plain at the base of a cliff—just before sunset. I staked out a clear area of soft sand with a low rock that was perfect as a headrest. Under a bright, shimmering moon, Sylvie dished out vegetable soup, mashed potatoes, and sliced beef with sauce.

I climbed into my sleeping bag at about 10 and stared into the sky. I imagined that the man in the moon was smiling and that echoes of "Twinkle, twinkle, little star" were bouncing off the cliff. Soon another sound became apparent and continued all night—camels chomping on shrubs about 10 feet away from me. My imagination turned from smiling moons and twinkling stars to hungry camels stepping on me in the middle of the night. I woke up several times in the night and each time the sky was different. By 2 A.M. the moon had set and the sky was a masterpiece of stars, a virtual tapestry of bright, flickering pieces of the universe.

I closed my eyes with this vision imprinted on my mind and when I next opened them it was 6 A.M. The stars were gone. The sky was gray-blue and rapidly becoming bluer as the sun crept over the edge of the cliff. I crawled out of my sleeping bag, rolled it up, and packed my bag. Sylvie was already awake and starting the fire to boil water. Breakfast was simple—a variety of dry stuff such as powdered milk, hot chocolate, tea, coffee, and instant oatmeal, all of which just needed to be mixed with water.

Day 2 of hiking led us to the gueltas of Tajisat, green ponds surrounded with plants and a few stubby trees. Water and lush plant life in the middle of an otherwise dry, desolate region was something that I had heard existed in the Sahara, but didn't really believe until I actually saw it. We walked around the gueltas, then turned up toward a narrow canyon and gingerly climbed a stairway of rocks and pebbles. No one spoke during the climb. All I could hear was my own hard breathing and the grinding crunch of rocks beneath my boots. Sometimes I let beads of perspiration drip off my brow, through my sunglasses, over the tip of my nose, and down to my tongue. This occasionally helped keep my mind off the hypnotic crunch-crunch that each step created.

For the next three days we continued hiking through canyons and around gueltas. We averaged about 15 to 20 miles a day. One day our hike included an ascent of Akba Assakao, a hot, steep climb that offered a spectacular view of the Tassili-n-Ajjer and the immense dunes of Erg Admer once you reached the summit. Other points visited en route included the cliffs of Imaradjelli, the canyon of Talahouahouat, the small natural amphitheater of Ouan Bendar, the sandy plain of Allouf, the summit of Adrar Adjelaho, the Essendilene Oued, and the Tililine plain. Throughout the trip, there were also several caves and cliff walls with paintings and engravings showing life as it once was in this region.

On my fifth and last night with the group, the Tuareg camel herders made *galeta*, a traditional bread that is baked beneath coals in the sand. It is made from a mix of semolina and wheat that is kneaded together with water and salt. The bread was good dipped in soup or used to scoop up meat and vegetables, but alone it was practically tasteless.

At about midnight when only the camels weren't trying to sleep, a Toyota Land Cruiser roared into the camp. The next morning this was my ride back into town. I assumed that we were probably close to the main road back to town and that a track led from the camp to the road. I was quite wrong. We were about 35 miles from the road, and there was no track whatsoever. Hosseine, the Tuareg driver, seemed dressed for the return trip. He was cloaked in traditional Tuareg blue with a big burnoose, mirrored sunglasses, and a "shock-resistant" Seiko watch. There were no road signs and no roads. We roared through riverbeds, up steep stony embankments, and over sand dunes. The Land Cruiser went where I never imagined any vehicle, even a tank, could go. While shifting in and out of four-wheel drive, Hosseine explained that he knew the cliffs and rocks of the terrain like someone can know the streets and buildings of a city. After about an hour, we reached the main road back to Djanet. I stared out the window in utter amazement at the cliffs and canyons we had just left.

Other Trips near Djanet

Terres d'Aventure and Deserts offer other trips in this region through their U. S. representative, Forum Travel International, 91 Gregory Lane No. 21, Pleasant Hill, California 94523; tel. 415-671-2900 and 415-946-1500. One of their more popular trips concentrates on visits to the ancient paintings of the Tassili-n-Ajjer region. Terre's nine-day trip includes some of the most beautiful and most accessible paintings in the Tassili-n-Ajjer National Park:

- **Tamrit.** Located near the Tamrit riverbed and a group of ancient cypress tress, the red ochre paintings here depict cattle and hunters pursuing a group of antelope.
- **Tin Tazarift.** A citadel of rock with several walls of paintings from various eras that depict a lush, green Sahara. They show ancient human beings, elephants, antelope, hunters with bows and arrows, and herds of cattle.

- **Sefar.** One of the main sites of ancient paintings and engravings in Tassili-n-Ajjer. They number in the hundreds, possibly thousands, and include a variety of scenes—cattle, fish, gazelles, antelope, hunters, and other people.
- **Jabbaren.** As many as 5,000 figures are depicted on a variety of frescoes that represent various styles and epochs. They are similar in grandeur and detail to those at Sefar, thus one of the most beautiful sites of prehistoric art.

Another set of trips centers on Tadrart, a region 200 km (124 miles) south of Djanet near Libya and Niger. The landscape is dramatically different from the Hoggar and the Tassili-n-Ajjer—huge red sand dunes and black rocks are its distinguishing features. This region is only accessible on a guided tour. Both Terre and Desert offer trips into the Tadrart, including special trips emphasizing astronomy.

PART FOUR

❦

Tunisia

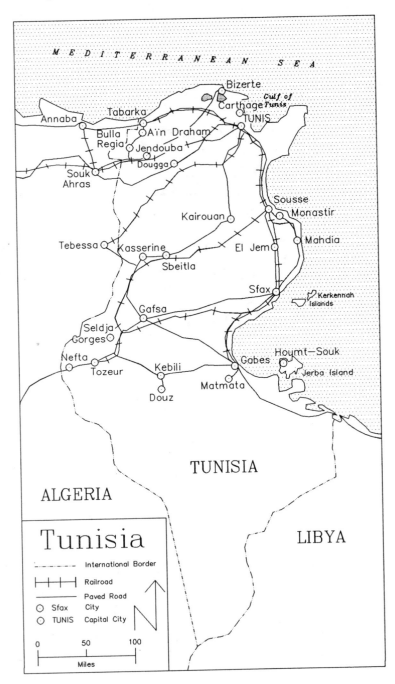

MEDITERRANEAN SEA

Bizerte
Gulf of
Carthage Tunis
TUNIS

Annaba
Tabarka
Bulla
Regia
Aïn Draham
Jendouba
Dougga
Souk
Ahras

Sousse
Monastir

Kairouan

Tebessa
Kasserine
Sbeitla
El Jem
Mahdia

Sfax
Kerkennah
Islands

Gafsa

Seldja
Gorges
Nefta
Tozeur
Kebili
Gabes
Houmt–Souk
Jerba Island

Douz
Matmata

TUNISIA

ALGERIA

LIBYA

Tunisia

- - - International Border
├┼┼┤ Railroad
──── Paved Road
○ Sfax   City
◎ TUNIS   Capital City

0   50   100

Miles

CHAPTER 15

Tunisia

Name:	Republic of Tunisia (al Jumhiriyya at Tunisiyya)
Political status:	Multiparty republic with one legislative house
Capital:	Tunis
Population:	7.81 million (U.N. statistics, 1989)
Land Area:	164,149 square kilometers (63,378 square miles)
Languages:	Arabic (official), French (widely spoken), and Berber dialects
Currency:	Dinar (D), D 1.00 = 1,000 millimes

Tunisia is the smallest of the Maghrebian nations of North Africa in both geography and population. Although its history is one of intense, long-term contact with almost all the peoples of the Mediterranean, Tunisia is a predominantly Arab Muslim country. Unlike Morocco and Algeria, its principal minority—Berber—is an increasingly negligible group, thus making Tunisia one of the least culturally diverse countries of the Maghreb.

From independence until late 1987, Tunisia was ruled and shaped by Habib Bourguiba. He put the country on a fast track of modernization that required the abandonment or loosening of many traditional social strictures. Islam was targeted as a social constraint, particularly in regards to women. Bourguiba sought to relegate Islam to a purely secular, adjunct role in mainstream Tunisian society. The power and influence of Islam prevented, however, the complete liberalization and modernization that he envisioned.

One result of Bourguiba's strategies was to open Tunisia to mass tourism, especially along its eastern coast and in the desert oases. Tourists now have easy access to most of Tunisia, which means that there are few, if any, places of interest that have been untouched by an almost daily onslaught of tour buses and Land-Rover caravans. This is fine if your main objective for visiting Tunisia is fun in the sun at a beach resort, or lounging by the pool after a ride on a camel named Lawrence of Arabia.

363

Tunisia does have wonderful beaches and tame camels. Unfortunately, there are relatively few options for adventure travel, thus fewer ways to get off the beaten track away from perfectly packaged and commercialized tours. These few options are described in the following pages.

THE NATURAL ENVIRONMENT

Physical Characteristics

Located almost in the center of North Africa between Algeria on the west and Libya on the southeast, Tunisia is a relatively small country of 164,149 square km (63,378 square miles) that is about the size of Missouri. It has a 1,600-km (1,000-mile) coastline on the Mediterranean Sea, renowned for beautiful beaches and clear water. At its closest point to Europe, Tunisia lies 144 km (90 miles) across the Strait of Sicily from Italy.

Topographically, Tunisia can be divided into four regions: north, central, east central, and south. The north is the fertile agricultural heartland of the country with well-watered arable land. At the core of this region between the Kroumirie and Mogod mountains on the north and the Tunisian Dorsale mountains on the south is the Medjerda river valley. Since the time of ancient Rome, this has been the principal grain-producing area of Tunisia. The Medjerda river, Tunisia's main tributary, flows from southwest to northeast and empties into the Gulf of Tunis.

The Kroumirie mountains stretch from Tabarka south to Fernana with foothills leading from there down to Jendouba and the Medjerda valley. Aïn Draham, along the flank of Jebel Bir (highest peak in the range at 1,014 m, or 3,327 feet) is the main town in the area and occasionally has snow in the winter. Rainfall here can be as much as 40 inches annually.

The Mogods are a coastal range northwest of Tabarka with peaks at an average elevation of 400 to 500 m (1,312 to 1,640 ft).

South of the Medjerda valley, the Dorsale range extends from the southwest to the northeast as a continuation of the Atlas mountains that stretch from Morocco. Jebel Zaghouan (1,295 m, or 4,249 ft) and Jebel Chambi (1,544 m, or 5,066 ft) are two of the highest peaks in this range, as well as in Tunisia.

South of the Dorsale range, semiarid steppes comprise the central region, which accounts for one-third of Tunisia's total area. Gradually, as you travel south, this region melds with the Sahara and becomes practically uninhabitable. Anyway, with only 6 to 16 inches of rain per year, it is usually too dry to sustain anything other than grazing. Some of Tunisia's principal phosphate deposits are found in this area.

The eastern portion of this central region is called the Sahel (not the same as the Sahel of north-central Africa) and is known for its olive groves and pastures. This region includes the Kerkennah islands off the coast of Sfax and Jerba island east of Gabés. Winters are mild with moderate rainfall and summers tend to be hot and dry, often because of the siroccos that blow up from the south.

A hot, dry climate characterizes the south, beginning approximately with the huge salt-lake depressions around Tozeur. The only life in this region is in and around the oasis towns of Tozeur, Nefta, and Kebili. Rainfall here is rare, usually less than 4 inches annually in Tozeur. Beyond these places is the Sahara desert, which is almost totally void of people and vegetation.

Flora and Fauna

For obvious reasons, there isn't a great variety of indigenous flora and fauna in and around the heavily settled northern and central valleys and plains. In the north, Lake Ichkeul is a world-renowned bird reserve, with over 300 species counted. The Kroumirie mountains are known for their forests, albeit increasingly deforested, of cork oak and pine and large numbers of wild boar (beware!). At higher elevations in these and the Dorsale mountains, you can find forests of red juniper.

The central steppes are populated with some small game, such as fox and rabbit, and are covered with esparto grass similar to the High Plateaus of Algeria.

In the Sahel region, most of the land has been cleared for settlement and cultivation. Olive groves are common here.

Except for date palms, fig trees, banana plants, and a few other types of flora in and around the oases, the south is devoid of vegetation. A few animals, such as the fennec (see Morocco section), do manage to survive. The once prevalent desert gazelle is rapidly disappearing. Locusts, the scourge of farmers throughout North Africa, occasionally spread north from the south.

Throughout Tunisia, scorpions and poisonous snakes such as horned vipers and cobras can be found.

HISTORY

Archeological evidence suggests that some of Tunisia's earliest settlers arrived during a time when neolithic culture prevailed along much of the Mediterranean coast of North Africa.

Stone tools such as hand axes found in coastal regions have been traced back as far as 50,000 years. The most significant prehistory discoveries, however, are more recent. Finely cut stone blades and arrows uncovered near the coastal city of Gafsa have been dated back to about

8,000 years. At that time, much of the Sahara desert, including the part that now composes most of the southern half of the country, was a verdant savanna replete with game. Hunters and herders were common throughout this region until about 4,000 B.C., when the Sahara began to desiccate. As these people migrated from across the Sahara northward to the mountains and plains of present-day Algeria and Tunisia, they mingled with Berbers. Historians are uncertain about the origins of Berbers, but their unique dialects—traces of which can still be found in small pockets of southern Tunisia—somewhat resemble languages of southwestern Asia.

In Tunisia, the Berbers eventually mixed with Phoenician traders who had begun establishing a string of coastal trading posts across North Africa by the twelfth century B.C. By 814 B.C. one of these posts in the area just north of present-day Tunis had become a full-fledged Phoenician or Punic colony and a growing regional power in its own right—Carthage.

Carthage's growing strength and power in the region was largely based on its predominance as a maritime power and ability to significantly influence the Berber tribes on the inland plains. The Berbers were gradually assimilated into Carthaginian society and culture, thus freeing the Carthaginians to expand their colony into an empire that stretched across North Africa from eastern Libya (known then as Cyrenaica) to northwestern Morocco, most of southeastern Spain, and substantial parts of Sardinia, Corsica, and Sicily.

In the third century B.C., Carthage attempted to expand further into Italy, but they were up against the emerging power of Rome. A war that became known later as one of the Punic Wars erupted between Rome and Carthage from 264 to 241 B.C. Carthage was defeated and forced to cede Sicily and Sardinia to Rome.

A Carthaginian general named Hannibal wanted, however, to avenge the defeat and recoup the empire's losses. In 218 B.C. he led an army of 40,000 from Spain over the French Alps and into Italy with an expedition of elephants. Although he was never able to capture Rome, he did manage to remain in Italy for sixteen years. By 202 B.C. Rome had begun challenging Carthaginian forces in central Tunisia, so Hannibal was forced to return home. He was immediately engaged in war with the Roman general Scipio and forced to surrender at the battle of Zama, thus ending the second Punic War.

Although Carthage's power in North Africa had all but vanished, Rome was worried that the still-healthy city of Carthage would someday rise again to challenge the Roman Empire. Rome declared war—the third Punic War—after Carthage had organized forces to defend itself against the invading army of Berber king Masinissa. Carthage surrendered to the Romans in 146 B.C. and was completely sacked. The Romans salted the ground so that crops could not again be grown there.

The North Afrcian portion of the Carthaginian empire was divided into three provinces—Mauretania Tingitana, Mauretania Caesariensia, and Proconsular Africa—which were the precursors to Morocco, Algeria, and Tunisia, respectively. For 400 years, Proconsular Africa was a prosperous, relatively secure Roman colony that became known as the bread basket of the Roman empire. Extensive, well-organized towns and cities with public baths, forums, paved streets, and many other amenities were established throughout Tunisia.

Roman power in Proconsular Africa began to ebb somewhat when Christianity was introduced in the beginning of the second century A.D. About a century later, most of Roman North Africa had been converted, including even several Berber tribes. Many of the Berbers, however, established sects such as Donatism, in part as a way to protest Roman control, thus as a vehicle of political expression.

The rise of Donatism across North Africa prompted Saint Augustine, an influential bishop in Mauretania Caesariensia, to distinguish between the church and the Roman state. He wrote *The City of God* to show that discontinued Roman authority should not impair adherence to church doctrines. Therefore, even if Rome fell, as it was about to do in North Africa, the church should survive.

Roman authority in North Africa, particularly Proconsular Africa, was toppled in A.D. 429 when Vandals, a Germanic tribe, crossed from Spain. The Vandals ruled from Carthage and were able by 455 to also conquer Rome. Their rule was short-lived, though, because by 533 the Byzantine general Belisarius had reconquered North Africa for the Roman Empire. However, the old Roman empire, thus a central Roman authority, was gone.

After about a century and a half of disparate Byzantine rule, Arab armies from Arabia brought Islam to Tunisia. In 670, the city of Kairouan was established as a military base. Carthage, 150 km to the north, endured Arab attacks until it fell in 693. Within fifty years, all North Africa and much of Spain had been conquered.

The Berbers readily converted to Islam, as they had with Christianity and Judaism, but again heretical sects emerged perhaps as a form of protest. However, this time the sects were Islamic rather than Christian. This spawned a move toward greater autonomy for North Africa away from the Damascus-based Abbassid caliphate.

During the ninth century, the Aghlabid dynasty rose in Tunisia and dominated eastern Algeria as far as the Kabylie mountains, much of the Libyan coast and Sicily. They also temporarily held Sardinia and parts of southern Italy. Their period of rule witnessed the transformation of Kairouan into a holy city and major center of Maghrebian intellectual and religious life; it still retains this status.

Over the next seven centuries, control over North Africa was juggled from dynasty to dynasty, ruler to ruler—Cairo-based Fatimids in the tenth century, Hilalian nomadic raiders in the eleventh, Normans and Almohads in the twelfth, and the Tunisia-based Hafsids in the thirteenth. The latter lasted for more than 300 years, until they were weakened first by piracy and then by Ottoman Turkish armies.

The Ottomans took control of Tunisia as one of three North African "regencies"; the other two were based in Algiers and Tripoli. The Ottoman sultan delegated rule over Tunisia to a *pasha*, or governor, who was appointed for a one-year term. The pasha, in turn, was assisted by forty companies of Anatolian soldiers with each company led by a *dey*. The deys eventually wrested power from the pasha and appointed one of the deys as pasha. By the late seventeenth century, this arrangement allowed Tunisia a certain degree of autonomy from Ottoman political and economic affairs.

By the 1830s when the French annexed Algeria, Tunisia was a relatively stable regime ruled by Ahmed Bey, a Husseinid dynasty ruler. He wanted to avoid foreign intervention, so he abolished slavery and abandoned support for piracy—both issues had previously been pretexts for intervention. However, that later proved insufficient.

The Tunisian elite believed that to truly maintain independence, Tunisia had to modernize its government and economy. This challenge posed a dilemma for the elite, because they essentially sought to emulate French and Turkish ways without French and Turkish intervention. A constitution was drawn up in 1861 that established a more efficient administration including, most importantly, tax collection. Emphasis on the latter function spawned government corruption and disenchantment, especially in the countryside, with "modern" government.

Seven years later the country was bankrupt and over half a million of its estimated population of 1.6 million perished in an 1868 cholera epidemic and famine. By 1871 Tunisia was again forced to accept Ottoman suzerainty or rather too weak to refuse it. This was partially the result of a British political maneuver to prop up the Ottomans as a bulwark against the expansion of Russian influence in the Mediterranean. In return, Turkey granted Great Britain a lease on Cyprus. At the Congress of Berlin in 1878, the French were "given" Tunisia in exchange for their acceptance of the British in Cyprus. However, it wasn't until 1881 that the French found an excuse to occupy Tunisia.

On the pretext of hunting down rebellious Algerians, over 40,000 French troops crossed the border into Tunisia. By 1883 a French "protectorate" had been established, thus putting the French in control of most aspects of the country. The French in Tunisia, unlike in Algeria, didn't attempt to Frenchify everything and everyone and encourage permanent French settlement. Instead, agricultural development for exports to European markets was emphasized. An infrastructure was established—schools, roads, railroads, port facilities, and so forth. The French, however, benefited more than the Tunisians because the system was designed to secure French investment interests.

Over the next several years, French control of the political system and economy was consolidated. This included French ownership of approximately one-fifth of Tunisia's best agricultural land. Not surprisingly, as French authority in Tunisia grew, a Tunisian nationalist movement evolved.

The movement was founded mainly by a new French-educated elite who sought, at first, to emulate French political ideals. A complete break with France was not advocated even when the movement became a full-fledged political party—the Destourian Party—in 1920.

The Destourian Party was basically unable, though, to achieve significant political concessions from the French. By 1933 the French had had enough of the party's demonstrations and strikes, so they disbanded it.

A year later, a Neo-Destourian Party was formed by Habib Bourguiba and other party activists. They called for an end to the protectorate. Unlike its predecessor, the Neo-Destourian Party looked beyond the urban elite for support. They organized party cells throughout the country, thus forming a broad base of mass support. Progress toward independence was temporarily thwarted by the outbreak of World War II.

Tunisia became a significant player in the North African theater of the war. After France fell in 1940, Tunisia was occupied by Axis forces, mainly German. In 1942 Allied forces led by Lieutenant General Dwight D. Eisenhower landed in Morocco and Algeria and immediately headed for Tunisia.

Battles waged between Allied and Axis forces in Tunisia from mid-November 1942 to May 7, 1943. U.S., British, Free French, and New Zealand troops fought against German forces that included fourteen armored divisions of Rommel's infamous Afrika Korps and 40,000 German and Italian troops. This marked the end of Axis operations in North Africa.

After the war, Bourguiba again rallied for independence. A new government was formed in 1950 with a Tunisian cabinet majority for the first time. Bourguiba wanted a fully Tunisian government without French involvement, but the French refused to make any major reforms. Several terrorist incidents against the French authorities in Tunisia occurred in retaliation, and in turn the French arrested all nationalist leaders. From 1952 to 1954 there were many terrorist and counterterrorist incidents until Bourguiba was released from prison to begin negotiating for independence. Finally on March 20, 1956, Tunisia became an independent state, and within five days Bourguiba was elected president.

Independent Tunisia

From independence until November 7, 1987, Bourguiba was the guiding force that shaped his country. He was regarded as the "father of Tunisia" and therefore had great popular support for most of his postindependence plans. Unlike Algeria and, to some extent, Morocco, Tunisia did not have an identity crisis. It did not have to arabize and create a Tunisian bureaucracy from scratch. Aside from the typical economic divisions of urban and rural Tunisians, most of the population was (and still is) Arab. Tunisians also had a history of close contact with Western values and culture. All this abetted Bourguiba as he pursued plans for a secular, democratic state freed from the traditional social and political constraints of Islam.

Bourguiba believed that certain aspects of traditional Islam were hindering economic development. So he legalized birth control and abortion and banned polygamy, to control population growth. He modernized the education system and made free schooling available for all Tunisians, including at the university level.

On the political front, a democratic constitution was drawn up that provided a bill of rights to protect individual rights and freedoms and specified the separation of the executive, legislative, and judicial branches of government. There were two "catches," though—only one political party would be permitted and the president could basically do whatever he wanted.

In practice, the Destourian Party, which was renamed the Destourian Socialist Party in 1964, became the vehicle of change in the Tunisian political system. It was guided, of course, by the executive branch, thus Bourguiba. Political dissent was allowed, but only through the confined channels of the party. The system emphasized unity, and dissent outside of a united party was considered unpatriotic. To further squelch potential opposition, Bourguiba did not play the role of a secluded potentate, but was often explaining his policies to the people and requesting their feedback. By 1975 Bourguiba had had the national legislature declare him president for life. A full-fledged, paternalistic, authoritarian government was in power.

On the economic front, a strong centralized government initially crippled the Tunisian economy. Socialist policies of collectivizing agriculture and nationalizing foreign-owned enterprises and property caused civil unrest and disrupted most agricultural production. However, in the 1970s, according to a U.S. State Department background report on Tunisia:

> Prudent economic management, higher prices for phosphates and oil, growing revenues from tourism resulted in a much brighter economic picture....Despite its small

resource base, Tunisia has succeeded in attracting foreign investment in labor-intensive, export industries. It has also received considerable amounts of aid from Europe, the United States, and, more recently, from other Arab states, such as Saudi Arabia and Kuwait.

Apparently, the economic picture in the 1970s wasn't quite bright enough for many Tunisians, because opposition movements began forming. By 1981 the government was pressured into opening up elections to opposition parties. Islamic groups were excluded, though, because Bourguiba was against having religion used for political purposes.

At about the same time, the Tunisian economy began experiencing a severe downturn. World oil and phosphate prices were down, so revenue was down. A drought in 1982 killed agricultural production, and this contributed to an overall economic growth rate of zero. A worldwide recession led to a drop in tourism. By 1986 the government was forced to implement a series of austerity measures including a currency devaluation, commodity price increases, deregulation of foreign investment, relaxation of import restrictions, and lowering of tariffs.

About a year later on November 7, Prime Minister Ben Ali decided that serious political changes were also necessary. According to a panel of physicians, Bourguiba had become "incapable of fulfilling the duties of the presidency." So Ben Ali assumed control of the government and immediately set out to loosen the reins of power. He declared that a pluralistic, democratic system of government was what Tunisia required to function as a truly free and democratic republic.

POPULATION, PEOPLE, AND CULTURE

Tunisia's population is over 8 million, which is approximately double what it was at independence in 1956, and growing at an estimated annual rate of 2.5 percent. At that rate, it should double again in twenty-eight years. Almost 53 percent of the population lives in cities and towns, while the rest is in the countryside. In addition, more than 40 percent is under the age of 15—that's an especially troubling statistic for a country with an estimated unemployment-underemployment rate of 50 percent. Another significant statistic to consider is that about 300,000 Tunisians live in foreign countries, the majority in France.

Tunis is the biggest city, with over 600,000 inhabitants, followed by Sfax, 232,000; Ariana, 99,000; Bizerte, 95,000; Jerba Island, 93,000; and Gabés 93,000.

Tunisians are overwhelmingly Arab (98.2 percent); only 1.2 percent of the population, mostly inhabitants of the extreme south, identify themselves as pure Berbers. The rest are French (0.2 percent), Italian

(0.1 percent) or other nationalities. About 99.4 percent of the population is Sunni Muslim, while the rest are Christian (0.3 percent), Jewish (0.1 percent) and various other affiliations (0.2 percent).

Tunisian Jews numbered almost 100,000 before the Arab-Israeli wars and Tunisian independence. Today, the population numbers about 5,000 with 1,200 residing on Jerba Island, 2,500 in Tunis, and the rest in other communities around the country. The Jerba Island community claims to have one of the oldest Jewish communities outside Israel. After Passover every year, its main synagogue is a popular pilgrimage destination.

Holidays and Festivals

National Holidays

Most government offices and businesses are closed on the following holidays:

January 1	New Year's Day
January 18	Anniversary of the Revolution
March 20	Independence Day
April 9	Martyr's Day
May 1	Labor Day
June 1,2	National Day
July 25	Republic Day
August 3	Bourguiba's birthday (with Bourguiba now an ex-president, this is no longer celebrated as widely)
August 13	Women's Day
September 3	Anniversary of the Destourian Socialist Party
October 15	Evacuation of Bizerte

Religious Holidays

Tunisia's religious holidays and festivals are predominantly Islamic and correspond to similar celebrations in Algeria and Morocco. These are celebrated at varying times each year because dates are determined by the Islamic lunar calendar (see Chapter 1):

Birthday of the Prophet Mohammed, celebrated on 12 Rabei El Awal.

Ramadan. The ninth month of the Islamic calendar, Ramadan is considered the fourth of Islam's five fundamental pillars of faith. For the entire month, faithful Muslims fast from dawn to sunset in order to gain strength against evil spirits. No food and water are allowed until sunset. The *feteer* or breaking of the fast occurs the moment the sun has set. In the early 1960s, Bourguiba attempted to ban Ramadan fasting as part of his secularization program, but he was met with numerous strong protests and forced to back down.

Aieed es Seghir. The end of Ramadan fasting. The celebration lasts from 1 to 3 Shawal (April 16-18, 1991; April 4-6, 1992; March 25-27, 1993).

The starting date of Ramadan slips back 10 to 12 days each year. For the next few years, Ramadan starts on

> March 17, 1991
> March 5, 1992
> February 23, 1993

Festivals

Tunisia has a variety of festivals throughout the year, but most are held in the summer months. The following lists some of the more popular celebrations:

January

> **Douz.** The Sahara Festival, a folkloric celebration featuring camel races and rabbit-hunting demonstrations.

March

> **Menzel Bou Zelfa.** Orange Day, a fair and festival celebrating the orange orchards of Menzel; oranges are one of the region's main agricultural products. Held last week in March or first week in April.

March-April

> **Nabeul.** Festival of Orange Blossoms. Art exhibits, sports competitions including a Cap Bon bicycle race, fantasia (horse and camel races), and a commerce fair.

April

> **Tataouine.** Festival of Tataouine.
> **Nefta.** Popular Festival of Nefta. Camel races, folkloric presentations, and parades.

May-June

> **Beja.** International Festival of Dougga. Internationally renowned performances of classical plays presented in the Roman theater of Dougga.

June

> **El Haouaria.** Hawk Day or Falcon Festival. Hawking/falconry demonstrations and traditional dance and music performances. It's usually held the first week in June or last week in May. El Haouaria is near Cap Bon.
> **Testour.** Festival of Malouf Music.

July-August
> **Tunis-Carthage.** Carthage Festival, an annual festival of music, theater, dance, and folklore.
>
> **Hammamet.** International Festival of Hammamet, an annual festival of music, theater, dance, and folklore.
>
> **Tabarka.** International Festival of Tabarka, an annual festival of avant-garde music, theater, dance, and folklore.
>
> **Houmt-Souk, Jerba Island.** Ulysses Festival of Houmt-Souk, an annual festival of local traditional music and dance.

July
> **Kelibia.** Amateur Film Festival, held every two years.
>
> **Kerkennah Islands.** Siren Festival, a wedding festival celebrating traditional wedding customs and folklore.

August
> **Sousse.** Aoussou Festival, musical entertainment, folkloric presentations and parades.
>
> **Sidi Bou Saïd.** Festival of the Kharja, a religious celebration.

September
> **Grombalia.** Wine Festival. Performances by various folkloric groups.

October
> **Carthage.** International Film Festival. This mini-Cannes film festival is held every two years and presents mainly Third World films, particularly Arab and African films.

December
> **Tozeur.** Festival of the Tozeur Oases. Camel races, folkloric presentations, and parades.

Language

Arabic is the official language, but French is still commonly used in government, education, and business. Four types of Arabic are used in Tunisia:

> **Classical.** Essentially Qur'ānic Arabic exactly as it appears in the Qur'ān and used mainly for religious purposes.
>
> **Modern standard Arabic.** Simplified classical Arabic used in print and broadcasting media.
>
> **Intermediary.** A mixture of colloquial and modern standard that is written and seems to be more commonly used in professional and government circles than modern standard. Basically, this is the written form of colloquial Tunisian Arabic.

Colloquial. Colloquial Arabic comprises many dialects from throughout Tunisia, although all are basically similar. One particularly interesting and common dialect is called Franco-Arabic, a blend of French and Arabic.

Pronunciation notes: In the following examples, the letter *x* is pronounced as a throaty "ch" or "kch" sound. The "@" sounds like "ine" but it's formed at the back of your throat by tightening your larnyx.

Greetings

Hello. (Peace on you)	*ahslemma*
Hello *or* How do you do?	*ahslemma shnia hawellak*
Hello. *(response)*	*la behs hamdililah* or *savah hamdililah*
Pleased to meet you.	*sha-rafna-beek*
How are you?	
(to a man)	*shnia hawellak*
(to a woman)	*shnia hawellik*
(to a group)	*shnia hawellkoom*
Good morning.	*sabah il xeer*
Good morning. *(response)*	*inharak a@sad liyiyam*
Good night.	
(to a man)	*tissbah ala xeer*
(to a woman)	*tissbahee ala xeer*
(to a group)	*tissb'hoo ala xeer*
Goodbye.	*bislamma* or *maasalamma*

General Expressions

Yes	*i@n-nam*
No	*la*
Please	
(to a man)	*minfadlak*
(to a woman)	*minfadlee-kee*
Thank you.	*shukerahn* or *merci*
You are welcome.	*li-afoo*
Excuse me.	
(to a man)	*sah-mah-nee*
(to a woman)	*sah-mah-nee-yah*
(to a group)	*sem-hoo-nee*
good	*beh-hee*
bad	*moosh-beh-hee*
How much?	*qadesh?*
How many?	*qadesh?*

What do you want?
(to a man)	wah-stah-heb
(to a woman)	wah-stah-hebee
(to a group)	wah-stah-heh-bu
I, me	ana
you (masculine)	enta
you (feminine)	entee
you (plural)	entuma
he, him	howa
she	hee-yah
we, us	ahna
they, them	homa
my wife	marh-tee
my husband	rahj-lee
my sister	ukhtee
my brother	khoo-yah
I am	ana
a student (m)	talab or tilmeez
a student (f)	taleeba or tilmeeza
American (m)	mehr-ree-kahn
American (f)	mehr-ree-kahniyya
British (m)	in-glee-zee
British (f)	in-glee-zay-yah
Australian (m)	australhee
Australian (f)	australhiyya
Canadian (m)	canahdien
Canadian (f)	canahdieniyya
I speak	ana itkalim
French	sooree
German	al-mahn-nee
I didn't understand.	ana mah-fah-hem-titsh
I understand.	ana fah-hemtak
What does this mean?	shnoo-ah-ha-tha
We need an interpreter.	ilzema moo-tar-jah

Do you speak English?
(to a man)	titkalim bil ingleeziyya
(to a woman)	titkelmee bil ingleeziyya
Does anyone speak English?	hamash wahid titkelim bil ingleeziyya

Finding Your Way Around
here	hen-nah or hoonee
there	radee
right	ee-yah-yimean
left	ee-sah

straight ahead	*qudam*
at the corner	*fi shooqa*
Where?	*wheen?*
Where is ?	
the police station	*markaz iss-shurta*
the men's room	*meh-hahd*
the women's room	*meh-hahd*
the train station	*lahn-gar*
the bus station	*mah-hattit el otobees*
the airport	*mah-tar*
Give me a ticket.	*ah-tee-nee teeskrah*
What bus goes to ?	*wheen lotobees emta@*

In the Hotel

hotel	*loteel*
Do you have a room?	*andak bate?*
a double room	*bate dooble*
I want a room (m)	*mehabe bate* or
	andkoom bate
vacant room	*andak bate fer-rah*
with double bed	*fee-hah ferj dooble*
with shower	*fee-hah douche*
with hot water	*fee-hah mahs-skhoo*
cheap	*reh-xisah*
cheaper	*arxas*

Miscellaneous Essentials

customs	*dee-wah-nah*
post office	*boosta*
I want to send this by	*ithebna ha-tha*
air mail	*par avion* or *bit ty-yara*
soap	*sah-boon*
toilet paper	*papier hygienique* or *papier*
	toilette
I am busy.	*ana mahshrule*
OK	*beh-hee* or *sah-vah*
thief	*ser-rahq*

Numbers

Numbers	Pronunciation	Numbers	Pronunciation
0	*sfer*	30	*telateen*
1	*wahid*	40	*arba'een*
2	*itnane*	50	*khamseen*
3	*talata*	60	*sitt-teen*

4	arba'a	70	saba'aeen
5	khamsa	80	thahman-neen
6	setta	90	tissa'een
7	saba'a	100	meeyah
8	tamaniya	101	meeyah-wahid
9	tissa'a	110	meeyah-wi-ashara
10	ashra		
11	hidesh	1,000	alf
12	atnash	2,000	alfane
13	thlatash	3,000	talat-talef
14	arba'atash	4,000	arba'a-talef
15	khummahstahsh	5,000	khamas-talef
16	sottahsh		
17	saba'atahsh		
18	thamantahsh		
19	tissa'atahsh		
20	ayshreen		
21	wahda-ayshreen		
22	itnane-wi-ayshreen		

THE TRAVELER IN TUNISIA

Information

Tunisia has one of the best organized government tourist information departments in North Africa—the Tunisian National Tourist Office or Office National du Tourisme Tunisien (ONTT). Its main office at 1 Avenue Mohammed, Tunis (tel. 341077) and branch office around the country are usually well staffed and well stocked with current information, especially rates for everything from youth hostels to luxury hotels and transportation schedules.

In addition to ONTT offices, there are also regional and local information offices, some of which are basically equivalent to chambers of commerce. Information offices can be found at the following locales in Tunisia:

Aïn Draham: Centre ville (tel. 08-47115)
Bizerte: 60 Avenue Habib Bourguiba (tel. 02-32558) and 1 Rue de Constantinople (tel. 02-32897 and 02-32703)
Douz: Place de la République (tel. PTT 10) and Rue Farhat Hached (tel. PTT 10-51)
Gafsa: Place des Piscines (tel. 06-21644)
Gabés: Place de la Libération (tel. 05-70254)

Hammamet: Avenue Habib Bourguiba (tel. 02-80423)
Jerba: Houmt-Souk (main office, tel. 05-50016 and 05-50581) and Midoun (tel. 05-57320)
Kairouan: Avenue Habib Bourguiba, Porte des Martyrs (tel. 07-20452)
Monastir: Quartier Chraga (tel. 03-61960)
Nabeul: Avenue Taieb Mehiri (tel. 02-86737)
Nefta: Avenue Habib Bourguiba (tel. 06-57184)
Port Kantaoui: (tel. 03-22231)
Sfax: Place de l'Indépendence (tel. 04-24606)
Sousse: 1 Avenue Habib Bourguiba (tel. 03-25157 and 03-25158) and Place Farhat Hached (tel. 03-20431)
Tabarka: 32 Avenue Habib Bourguiba (tel. 08-44491)
Teboursouk: Centre ville (tel. PTT 10-50)
Tozeur: Avenue Aboul Kacem Chebbi (tel. 06-50503) and Place Ibn Châabat
Tunis: 1 Avenue Moncef Bey (tel. 256957), Tunis regional office
Zarzis: Route des Hotels (tel. 05-80445)

Overseas Branches

There are ONTT offices in the following countries:

Austria
    Vienna. (Wien). Tunesisches Fremdenverkehrsamt, Landesgerichstr. 22, 1010 Wien (tel. 48-39-44)
Belgium
    Brussels. (Bruxelles). Bureau du Tourisme Tunisien, Galerie Ravenstein 60, 1000 Bruxelles (tel. 511-2893 and 513-5078)
France
    Paris. Office National du Tourisme Tunisien, 32 Avenue de l'Opera 75002 Paris (tel. 742-7267)
    Lyon. Office National due Tourisme Tunisien, 12 Rue de Seze, 69002 Lyon
Great Britain
    London. Tunisian National Tourist Office, 7A Stafford Street, London W1 (tel. 01-499-2234 and 629-0858)
Holland
    Amsterdam. Tunesisch Nationaal Verkeersbureau, Leidsestraat 61, 1017 Amsterdam (tel. 020-22-49-71 and 22-49-72)
Italy
    Milano. Ente Nazionale Tunisino Per il Turismo, 10 Via Baracchini, 20123 Milano (tel. 871-214 and 871-126)

Saudi Arabia
    Jeddah. Tunisian Tourism Office, Post Box 12582, Jeddah 21414 (tel. 6534612)
Spain
    Madrid. Office del Turismo Tunecino, Torre de Madrid 4-1, Madrid 13 (tel. 2481435)
Sweden
    Stockholm. Tunisiska Statens Turistbyra, Smalandsgatan 11, 11146, Stockholm (tel. 20-67-73 and 20-57-73)
Switzerland
    Zurich. Tunesisches Fremdenverkehrsburo, Bahnhofstrasse 69, 8001 Zurich (2114830)
West Germany
    Frankfurt-am-Main. Fremdenverkehrsamt Tunesien, Am Hauptbahnhof 6, 6000 Frankfurt (tel. 23-18-91 and 23-18-92)
    Dusseldorf. Fremdenverkehrsamt Tunesien, Graf Adolf Strasse 100, 4000 Dusseldorf (tel. 35-94-14)

The ONTT has several useful publications available in English that cover almost every major site and most tourist-related facilities in the country. The most informative ones include a small practical guide full of addresses and basic information and a hotel guide with current information on accommodations throughout Tunisia. They also have information available about some of the possible adventures and activities possible in Tunisia: diving and snorkeling, oasis camel trips, Land-Rover expeditions, gliding, and muleback trips.

Information about these activities can also be obtained from any of the numerous travel agencies and bureaus throughout Tunisia.

The main drawback, however, about adventuring in Tunisia is that most of the opportunities have become highly commercialized and touristic. Most operations, including the oasis camel herders such as in Tozeur and desert "safaris" to Matmata and beyond, now cater to mass tourism. Consequently, it is difficult to really get off the beaten track and away from the packed tour buses and air-conditioned desert safari Land-Rovers. It's even difficult to find a hiking trail, albeit not impossible though, that hasn't been discovered by tour groups.

With travel in Tunisia predominantly touristic and adventure opportunities far fewer than in Morocco and Algeria, my coverage is more limited. Tunisia has many beach resorts and several oasis resorts, but a visit to any of them, other than the one or two beach complexes with diving centers and oases with camel lots, is hardly an adventure.

Maps

Detailed maps of Tunisia and most major cities and towns are available at ONTT offices (see preceding section for addresses). Unfortunately, as far as I know topographic maps are unavailable. You may find them at the Institut Géographique in Paris or the Royal Geographical Society in London. If you do manage to track down topographic and trail maps, please let us know how you obtained them.

One of the most accurate, up-to-date maps of Tunisia is published by Michelin. Map No. 953 covers all Northwest Africa and No. 172 just Algeria and Tunisia. No. 953 includes all Tunisia from north to south, and it's a good general reference, but insufficient as a detailed topographic map.

Money and Banks

The dinar (D) is the official monetary unit and is divided into 1,000 millimes. It's illegal to import or export Tunisian dinars, so you can't buy any of this currency prior to arrival. There are no restrictions on the amount of foreign currency or travelers' checks you may bring into the country.

The dinar exchange rate floats with some control against most other currencies. Consequently, there is no black market for currency exchange.

Currency and travelers' checks can be exchanged at banks and *bureaux de change* (foreign exchange offices) throughout the country. All airports and many hotels also have *bureaux de change* that you'll probably end up using because bank hours tend to be somewhat erratic. Winter hours are Monday to Thursday 8 to 11 A.M. and 2 to 4.15 P.M.; Friday 8 to 11 A.M. and 1.30 to 3.15 P.M. Summer hours are Monday to Friday 8 to 11 A.M. Ramadan hours are Monday to Friday 8 to 11.30 A.M. and 1 to 2.30 P.M.

Reconverting extra dinars to foreign currency can be done on departure only up to 30 percent of the sum initially converted into dinars. Furthermore, you can't reconvert more than D 100. To prove how much you have exchanged, you must save your exchange receipts.

Pricing in Tunisia can occasionally be confusing because prices are sometimes expressed only in millimes. For example, D 2 1/2 might be indicated as 2,500 millimes or D 2,5. VISA and American Express cards can be used in Tunisia for purchases, some accommodations and meals, and cash advances. American Express cash advances, however, are difficult, if not impossible, to obtain at banks and American Express offices outside Tunis. VISA cash advances are possible at banks in major tourist centers.

American Express offices in Tunisia are operated through Carthage

Tours. The main Carthage Tours office is in Tunis at 59 Avenue Habib Bourguiba (tel. 01-254304).

Costs, Accommodations, and Food

Tunisia can be a very inexpensive country for travelers as long as you're willing to sacrifice some comfort and amenities. Accommodations range from camping (often as little as 500 millimes), youth hostels (D 1,5), unclassified hotels (anywhere from D 1,5) and classified hotels. All classified and some unclassified hotels, vacation villages, family pensions, and "apartment-hotels" are regularly monitored by the government tourism authorities and given a one- to four-star rating. The very best establishments, such as the Tunis Hilton, are given a four-star deluxe rating. Results of the government inspections are published in a useful annual hotel guide, which can be obtained in advance by contacting an ONTT office or the cultural attaché of a Tunisian embassy.

Hotel rates approximately correspond to the star ratings:

One star	D 12 to D 25
Two stars	D 15 to D 30
Three stars	D 25 to D 45
Four stars	D 35 to D 50
Deluxe	D 50+

Keep in mind that, as with most countries, prices in Tunisia are subject to inflation and currency exchange fluctuations. Consider these prices as a relative, rather than absolute, guide to hotel rates. Other factors that influence rates include location, season, single supplements, and the view, particularly along the east coast and on Jerba Island. For example, a single room with a sea view during the high season (summer) will cost more than the same room in the winter.

Youth hostels and "centers" are one of the cheapest ways to go, but they often cater to noisy youth groups and sports teams. Camping is sometimes possible at some of the hostels-centers. The following is a list of these centers:

Location	Number of beds	Telephone Number
Aïn Draham	120	08-47-087
Aïn Soltan	200	—
Béja	60	08-50-621
Borj Cédria		01-206026
Bizerte	120	02-31-608
Chebba	70	—
Dermèch	110	01-275762
Gafsa	56	06-10-268

Gabés	200	05-20-171
Ghardimaou	120	—
Kairouan	92	07-20-309
Kasserine	90	—
Kéliba	40	02-96-105
Le Kef	78	08-20-307
Nabeul	56	02-85-547
Menzel Temime	50	—
Monastir	64	03-61-216
Radés	54	01-295631
Rimel	50	—
Sfax	133	04-23-207
Sousse	130	03-23-269
Zarzis	40	—

Official Campgrounds include

Douz	Grad Camp Site, Zaafrane Camp Site, Nouaeil Camp Site, Paradis Camp Site
Gabés	Youth Center (Centre de Jeunesse)
Hammam Plage	Le Moulin Bleu
Hammamet	L'Ideal Camping
Jerba	Sidi Ali Camp Site
Nabeul	L'Auberge des Jasmins
Tozeur	Le Belvedere Camp Site
Zarzis	Sonia Camping & Caravan Grounds

There are also many unofficial campgrounds around the country, especially at Tozeur. Many hotels and hostels will often allow you to camp on their grounds.

Food and Drink

As with accommodations, food and drink in Tunisia can be relatively inexpensive. The most inexpensive sources are the weekly open-air markets held in almost every city, town, and village. Market days are important for many Tunisian communities and vary from place to place. Although most Tunisian tourist offices can tell you the latest market days, here are some of the more prominent ones:

| **Friday** | Jebeniana, Jemmal, Ksour Essaf, Mahdia, Mateur, Midoun, Nabeul, Oueslatia, Sfax, Tabarka, Testour, Thala, Zarzis |
| **Saturday** | Ben Gardane, El Alia, El Fahs, Thibar |

Sunday	El Jem, Enfidha, Hammam, Ksar Hellal, Sousse, Fernana
Monday	Aïn Draham, Chebba, Houmt Souk, Kairouan, Maharés, Mareth, Makthar, Tataouine
Tuesday	Béja, El Haleb, Ghardimaou, Haffouz, Kasserine, Krib, Menzel Témime, Souk Essebt
Wednesday	Jendouba, Moknine, Nefta, Sbeitla, Sers
Thursday	Bou Salem, Douz, Gafsa, Jerba, Menzel Bouzelfa, Siliana, Teboursouk

For cross reference, here's a list by city or town:

Aïn Draham	Monday	**Ksour Essaf**	Friday
Béja	Tuesday	**Maharés**	Monday
Ben Gardane	Saturday	**Mahdia**	Friday
Bou Salem	Thursday	**Makthar**	Monday
Chebba	Monday	**Mareth**	Monday
Douz	Thursday	**Mateur**	Friday
El Alia	Saturday	**Menzel Témime**	Tuesday
El Fahs	Saturday	**Menzel Bouzelfa**	Thursday
El Haleb	Tuesday	**Midoun**	Friday
El Jem	Sunday	**Moknine**	Wednesday
Enfidha	Sunday	**Nabeul**	Friday
Fernana	Sunday	**Nefta**	Wednesday
Gafsa	Thursday	**Oueslatia**	Friday
Ghardimaou	Tuesday	**Sbeitla**	Wednesday
Haffouz	Tuesday	**Sers**	Wednesday
Hammam	Sunday	**Sfax**	Friday
Houmt-Souk	Monday	**Siliana**	Thursday
Jebeniana	Friday	**Souk Essebt**	Tuesday
Jemmal	Friday	**Sousse**	Sunday
Jendouba	Wednesday	**Tabarka**	Friday
Jerba	Thursday	**Tataouine**	Monday
Kairouan	Monday	**Teboursouk**	Thursday
Kasserine	Tuesday	**Testour**	Friday
Krib	Tuesday	**Thala**	Friday
Ksar Hellal	Sunday	**Thibar**	Saturday
		Zarzis	Friday

Tunisia has three types of eating establishments:

- **French-style restaurants,** which serve meals of several courses, sometimes with wine; common mostly in Tunis and tourist centers.
- **Gargottes,** simple restaurants that serve simpler versions of French-style restaurants concentrating on meat, chicken, fish, and vegetable dishes.

- **Rotisseries,** serving mainly fried vegetable and egg dishes, usually open until about 9 P.M., although in Tunis they tend to stay open longer. The food is laid out behind the counter so you can just point to what you want.

Here are some descriptions of common Tunisian dishes:

- **Soups and Starters**
    Salade mechouia, mixed vegetable salad.
    Brik à l'oeuf, deep fried flaky pastry stuffed with egg, vegetables, and sometimes meat or tuna.
    Chorba, spicy, oily soup; often considered a mainstay.
    Harissa, spicy, diplike concoction of dried peppers mashed with olive oil, garlic, and various spices and usually served with olives at the beginning of a meal. Don't drink water with it, or you'll have diarrhea the rest of the day.
    Shakshuka, fried concoction of tomatoes, egg, peppers, and onions.
    Ojja, shakshuka with more egg.
- **Main Dishes**
    Couscous. Couscous is undoubtedly the best known North African specialty. It's made of semolina grains mixed with water and a bit of oil. The mixture is then run through a sieve, rolled by hand, and steamed in a "couscousier" with various vegetables—cabbage, turnips, carrots, squash, eggplant, tomatoes, chick peas (garbanzo beans), onions—and meat (beef, mutton, or chicken) added to the bottom before the couscous is poured in. The complete dish is served hot with a vegetable sauce.
    Variations consist of beans and peas in place of the sauce, or a sweet version with raisins and sugar. The taste is further enhanced by adding some milk or *"leben"*.
    Casse croute, a chunk of French Bread stuffed with vegetables, olives, oil, and sausage, tuna, or egg.
- **Fish and Shellfish**

Clovisses	clams
Crevettes	shrimp
Homard	lobster
Loup de mer	perch
Merou	grouper
Moules	mussels
Mulet	mullet
Rouget	red mullet
Thon	tuna

- **Meat Dishes**

Kefteji	meatballs
Méchoui	roast meat, often lamb
Merguez	spicy sausages
Mermez	stewed lamb
Poulet rotîî	roast chicken
Poulet haricot	chicken with beans
Tajine	vegetable, chicken, or meat stew similar to the traditional tajine of Morocco

- **Fruits and Desserts**

Baklava	flaky pastry dripping with honey and stuffed with nuts
Dattes	dates
Figues	figs
Grenade	pomegranate
Halva	sweet sesame seed cake with a chalky texture
Loukoum	Turkish delight
Makrouf	stringy wheat biscuit
Mesfuf	sweet couscous with grapes
Millefeuille	French cream puff
Pastèque	watermelon
Raisins	grapes

- **Drinks and Other Food-Related Items and Words**

Addition	bill or check
Bière	beer
Bouteille	bottle
Café (au lait, turc)	coffee (with milk, Turkish)
Eau	water
Fromage	cheese
Oeufs	eggs
Pain/kchoubs	bread
Sel	salt
Thé (noir, vert, au menthe)	tea (black, green, with mint)
Verre	glass
Vin	wine

Where to Go

Tunisia is a relatively small, compact country with an efficient transportation system, so it's possible to visit most of the tourist sites and a few off-the-beaten-track locales in one or two weeks or a series of short trips from Tunis. Unfortunately, unique adventures that have not been overcommercialized are practically nonexistent.

Just to give you some idea of travel times, a fast-paced two-week grand tour could follow this itinerary:

Day 1.	Arrive Tunis.
Day 2.	Day trip to Cap Bon; return to Tunis.
Day 3.	Visit Tunis and Carthage.
Day 4.	Day trip to Bulla Regia and Dougga Roman ruins; return to Tunis.
Day 5.	Visit Zaghouan and Monastir; overnight in Monastir.
Day 6.	Day trip to coliseum at El Jem and old walled city of Sousse; return to Monastir.
Day 7.	Tour Monastir, Kairouan, and Sbeitla; overnight in Sbeitla.
Day 8.	Travel through the Kasserine pass to Gafsa, oasis towns of Tozeur and Nefta; overnight in Nefta.
Day 9.	Nefta.
Day 10.	Visit oases near Nefta.
Day 11.	Cross the Chott El Djerid salt flats to Matmata and Jerba Island; overnight on Jerba.
Day 12.	Organized day trip from Jerba to deep south—Berber villages of Ksar Haddada and Chenini.
Day 13.	Visit Jerba Island; overnight on Jerba.
Day 14.	Return to Tunis for departure.

Some variations on this itinerary could include

- A three- to five-day loop from Tunis via Bizerte, Lake Ichkeul (great bird-watching territory), Tabarka, and then south through the Kroumirie mountains to Aïn Draham. From there, two half-day hikes are possible. Visit Aïn Draham, and then continue to the Roman ruins at Bulla Regia and Djendouba for transportation back to Tunis.
- Take the train straight from Tunis to Tozeur (when it's operating, it takes 9 1/2 hours), and visit the oases in the region around Tozeur and Nefta. A variety of day hikes or camel treks through the oases is possible from either town. You can also backtrack to Metlaoui (on the rail line) and head west to visit the Seldja gorges and the oases of Tamerza and Mides. You should plan on at least three days to visit this area.

GETTING THERE

Visas and Permits

U.S. citizens and West Germans do not need visas for stays up to four months; British, Canadian, Swedish, and Norwegian citizens for three

months. Citizens of New Zealand and Netherlands must obtain a visa in
advance from a Tunisian consulate.

An international vaccination certificate is required for travelers
coming from a yellow fever and/or cholera risk area.

Customs Formalities

The following items may be imported duty free into Tunisia:

- Used personal effects
- Three liters of alcohol
- 400 cigarettes or 100 cigars or 500 grams of tobacco
- Gift items up to total value of D 10

Any amount of foreign currency may be imported, but if you are a
nonresident and intend to take out of the country an unspent balance of
foreign currency to the value of D 500 or more, you are required to make
a currency declaration at the Customs Office on entry. You will be given
a certificate that must be presented to the Customs Office at your point
of departure. I have not heard of this ever being enforced. However, the
customs authorities could legally confiscate any currency over D 500 that
you haven't declared.

It is forbidden to import any of following items into Tunisia:

> Tunisian dinars
> Weapons other than hunting arms
> Explosives
> Drugs other than prescription drugs
> Immoral or obscene publications and illustrations
> Infringed literature
> Any product or article liable to endanger public safety, health,
> or morality

What the customs authorities mean by "obscenity" and "infringed
literature" is uncertain. I assume that the latter means anything defamatory
of Tunisia and Tunisians.

According to the customs authorities, the following items may be
temporarily imported:

> Two cameras and 20 rolls of film
> A movie camera and 20 rolls of film
> A portable radio
> Sports equipment
> A musical instrument
> A pair of binoculars
> A portable typewriter
> A small tape recorder

Camping gear
Two baby carriages
A bicycle

By Air

From Europe

There are flights to Tunis from Amsterdam, Athens, Barcelona, Belgrade, Berlin, Bilbao (Spain), Bologna (Italy), Brussels, Budapest, Copenhagen, Düsseldorf, Frankfurt, Geneva, Gothenburg (Sweden), Hamburg, Helsinki (via Brussels), Lille (France), Ljubjana (Yugoslavia), London, Lyon (France), Madrid, Málaga, Malta, Manchester, Marseilles, Milan, Moscow, Munich, Nice (France), Oslo, Palermo (Italy), Paris, Prague, Rome, Salzburg, Seville (Spain), Sofia, Strasbourg (France), Toulouse (France), Turin (Italy), Valencia (Spain), Vienna, Warsaw, Zürich.

The national carriers of almost every country mentioned above fly to Tunis: KLM, Royal Dutch Airlines; Iberia (Spain); Alitalia (Italy); Air France; Sabena (Belgium); Lufthansa; Swissair; Aeroflot; Czechoslovak Airlines; Balkan-Bulgarian Airlines; LOT, Polish Airlines; Interflug; and Malev, Hungarian Airlines.

Tunis Air also flies to most of the European destinations mentioned above. Tunisavia runs the flight between Tunisia and Malta in an old, noisy prop plane. It's an unusual flight because most of the passengers are foreign residents of Tunisia who are merely taking it to facilitate renewal of their four-month visas.

From Africa

There are flights to Tunis from Algiers, Cairo, Casablanca, Constantine (Algeria), Dakar, and Tripoli on Tunis Air, Air Algerie, EgyptAir, Royal Air Maroc, Saudia, Tunisavia, Libyan Arab Airlines, and Kuwait Airways.

From the Middle East

To Tunis from Abu Dhabi, Amman (Jordan), Baghdad, Beirut, Damascus, Dubai, Istanbul, Jeddah, Kuwait, Larnaca, and Riyadh on Royal Jordanian, Iraqi Airways, Middle East Airlines, Syrian Arab Airlines, Turkish Airlines, and Saudia and Kuwait Airways.

From the Rest of the World

There are no direct flights from North, Central, or South America and Asia other than Bombay. Most connections are via Frankfurt, Brussels, or Amsterdam.

By Sea

There are regular crossings linking Tunisia and Europe (mainly Italy and France) that offer a short but delightful cruise across the Mediterranean.

The ferry boats are run jointly by the Tunisian Navigation Company and the Société Nationale Maritime de la Corse et de la Méditerranée (SNCM). Between January and May, they offer an average of two to three departures weekly from Marseilles. In June, departures increase to three or four weekly; in July, August, and September, almost every day. For the rest of the year, there are only about four or five departures monthly. The trip takes approximately twenty-two hours. The 12,000-ton ship *Liberté* and car ferries *Napoleon*, *Habib*, and *Tarek* are the most frequently used vessels. The latest tariffs can be obtained by writing to SNCM offices and representatives in Europe or the Tunisian Navigation Company in Tunis.

- **In France:**
  Marseilles: 61 Boulevard des Dames 13002 (tel. 91-56-62-05, Metro Joliette; information tel. 91-56-62-05, reservations tel. 91-56-80-20)
  Paris: 12 Rue Godot de Mauroy (Metro Madeleine) 75009 (tel. 01-42-66-60-19, information and reservations tel. 01-42-66-67-98)
  Bordeaux: 4 Rue du Château-Trompette 33000 (tel. 56-44-46-07)
  Lyon: 3 Rue Président-Carnot, Cédex 02, 69226 (tel. 78-42-22-70, information and reservations tel. 78-37-84-84)
- **In Great Britain:**
  London: Continental Shipping and Travel Ltd., 179 Piccadilly, London W1V9DB (tel. 01-491-4968)
- **In Spain:**
  Barcelona: NAVETRANS S.A., 44 Rambla de Cataluna 08007 (tel. 216-0350)

Crossing	Times
Marseilles-Tunis	21 to 24 hours
Genoa-Tunis	21 to 24 hours
Naples-Tunis	21 to 24 hours
Palermo-Tunis	12 hours

In Tunisia, information is available from Tunisian Shipping Company, 5 Rue Dag Hammarskjold (tel. 24-29-99) *or* 122 Rue de Yugoslavie *or* SNCM, 47 Avenue Farhat Hached, Tunis (tel. 24-28-01). SNCM offers a variety of special package deals from France that include accommodations on self-guided driving tours through the country.

By Land

The only practicable land crossings for most travelers are from Algeria. The daily train between Algiers and Tunis, which is known as the Trans-Maghrebian, is the most convenient way to cross. Otherwise, buses and taxis are usually available at the border crossings.

GETTING AROUND TUNISIA

It is easy and relatively inexpensive to get around Tunisia by public transportation or private car. For the more adventurous traveler, bicycling, motorcycling, and hitchhiking are also possibilities.

By Air

Tunis Air flies from Tunis to Jerba Island, Sfax, and Tozeur (and vice versa). The Jerba Island and Tozeur flights are often full of tourists on package tours. Both flights are a quick and inexpensive (less than US $25 one way) way to cross the country.

By Bus

Tunisia has a national bus company known as the Société Nationale de Transport, or SNT, and several regional bus companies with some overlapping routes. The SNT runs buses in and around Tunis and from Tunis daily to almost every town and city in the country. The regional companies operate local buses and usually also offer services to Tunis. In many towns, it's not unusual to find separate bus stations for each company. Bigger towns sometimes have a central bus station with all relevant companies represented.

By Louage

The fastest intercity mode of transport is the *louage* or shared taxi. Usually these are seven- or eight-passenger Peugeot sedans, but the drivers often depart when they have at least five passengers. They charge officially set rates that are a bit higher than buses along the same routes. On the more popular routes, there may be more potential passengers than available seats, which means a mad dash for the car when it pulls into the lot. This experience will give new meaning to the maxims "Survival of the fittest" and "First come, first served."

Finding the louage stations in a certain town can sometimes be tricky. They may be near a garage, at a street corner or across from one of the bus stations. In addition, stations for different destinations may be at different locations and may consist of only an unmarked dirt lot.

By Train

Tunisia has a train system with routes to several principal tourist destinations. From Tunis there are lines to Bizerte, Algeria, Kalah Kasbah in central Tunisia, and along the coast to Gabés (with a northern spur to Hammamet and Nabeul) via Sousse, El Jem, and Sfax. The coastal line also splits off between Gabés and Sfax and turns westward to Gafsa, Metlaoui, and Tozeur, but at the time of writing this was closed for reconstruction. Another line, which splits from Metlaoui and goes to Redeyef, was also closed for reconstruction. The coastal lines are the most popular, especially in the summer, so reservations or advance ticket purchases are often necessary.

The Algeria line is part of the Trans-Maghrebian railway that goes from Tunis to Annaba, Constantine, Algiers, and Morocco.

By Car

It is possible to bring a car into Tunisia either overland from Algeria or by ferry from Europe or rent a car from an agency in the country.

To enter with a private car, you must have proof of ownership, a valid driver's license (preferable an international one), your *triptyque*, or gray card, and a green insurance card. If Tunisia is not listed on your green card, a 2-, 7- or 21-day policy may be purchased at the Customs Office at your point of entry. For further information, contact the National Automobile Club (NACT), 29 Avenue Habib Bourguiba, Tunis (tel. 24-39-21).

Hertz, Avis, Europcar, Africar, and Cartha Rent are the main car rental agencies operating in Tunisia.

Hertz rates for a four-passenger manual transmission subcompact such as a Fiat Inno or VW Polo are $24 per day plus $0.23 per kilometer plus a 17 percent tax plus a $2.30 stamp tax. The three-day rate with unlimited mileage is $167, and the seven-day rate is $335. A refueling charge is assessed if the car is returned without a full tank of gas.

Avis rates for a four-passenger Renault or Citroën minivan are $246 plus a 17 percent tax for a five- to seven-day rental with unlimited mileage; $144 plus 17 percent tax for a three-day rental with unlimited mileage; or $13 per day plus $0.14 per kilometer plus 17 percent tax.

For driving into the Sahara beyond the town of Medenine, you must first inform the National Guard Post in Medenine or the Saharan Center in Gabés of your plans. All Sahara travel must be done in a convoy of vehicles with four-wheel-drive capabilities. If you plan to venture off the paved roads, then your vehicle should be equipped as it would be for Algerian Sahara travel (see that section for further information).

By Hitchhiking

If you are male and have the time and patience, hitchhiking can be a decent means of getting around. Women should not hitch alone in Tunisia (potentially dangerous). Peugeot 404 pickups often make it their business to pick up foreigners and locals, but you are expected to pay. Watch what your fellow passengers are paying before you hand over any money.

THINGS TO BUY

A good selection of handicrafts is available at tourist souvenir shops and markets throughout the country. Some haggling over prices is necessary, but that may occasionally be difficult because many of the visiting tourists seem prone to accepting the first prices.

Some of the more popular items include hand-woven or hand knotted carpets. Carpet quality is monitored by the National Handicrafts Office, and each carpet is given an official rating. There are carpet museums in Kairouan and Gabés and shops in several government-run hotels, including the National Handicrafts Office carpet center on Avenue Habib Bourguiba.

There are two types of thick-pile carpets:

- *Guetifa carpet*, a colorfully decorated Berber carpet with twisted strands from 3 to 5 cm in length.
- *Kairouan carpet*, a hand-knotted carpet produced in Kairouan that is thinner and less detailed than the Guetifa carpet.

A smaller, somewhat less decorative carpet known as the *mergoum* carpet is also popular. Mergoums range from a loose macramé style (produced mainly in El Jem, Boussada, Tataouine, and Thibar) and wall hanging (Gabés, Matmata, Kebili, Douz, and Gafsa) to the Klim-style mix of wool and taffeta (Oudref, Jerba, and Sbeitla).

Consult the handicrafts booklet produced by ONTT for further information about carpets.

Leather goods such as wallets and handbags.
Red coral jewelry from the Coral Coast (Tabarka area).
Olive-wood sculptures.
Hand-embroidered linen.
Pottery: Nabeul is an especially renowned center for producing glazed old-Berber-style pottery.

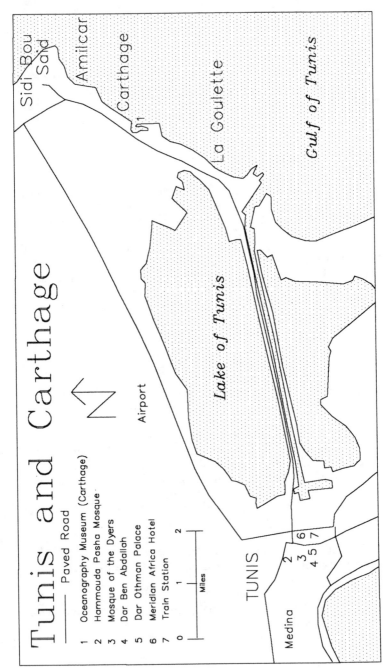

Chapter 16

Tunis and Carthage

— Paved Road

1 Oceanography Museum (Carthage)
2 Hammouda Pasha Mosque
3 Mosque of the Dyers
4 Dar Ben Abdallah
5 Dar Othman Palace
6 Meridian Africa Hotel
7 Train Station

N

Airport

0   1   2
Miles

Sidi Bou Said

Amilcar

Carthage

La Goulette

Gulf of Tunis

Lake of Tunis

TUNIS

Medina

Tunis and Carthage

During the ninth century, Tunis briefly became the capital of the Aghlabid dynasty, but then the Fatimids moved the capital to Mahdia. After the Hilalians sacked Kairouan in 1057, a new dynasty known as the Hafsids arose and made Tunis a capital once again. Beginning in the thirteenth century, their rule ushered in two centuries of prosperity for Tunis. It became a major trading center for the central Mediterranean, which enabled the Hafsids to initiate a building frenzy. Palaces, Muslim schools, and mosques popped up throughout the area that is now known as the Medina.

By the sixteenth century, this prosperous city began to attract the attention and imperialist designs of the Ottoman Empire, which had begun seizing control of much of the Mediterranean. The Ottomans retained Tunis until being muscled out by French imperialist interests in the late nineteenth century.

The French developed a new city of Tunis outside the walls of the Medina after first draining a swampy extension of the Lake of Tunis. The lake or swampy area reached the eastern edge of the medina occupying much of what is now Avenue Habib Bourguiba. Today, the medina is still the old heart of the city, but most of the population (about one-tenth of Tunisia's total), and the core of Tunisia's businesses and industries are in new and greater Tunis.

PHYSICAL DESCRIPTION AND ORIENTATION

Most points of interest for travelers are in a fairly compact area along the eastern edge of the Lake of Tunis. A main point of reference on the eastern shore is the TGM station. The TGM is a light railway that connects the eastern Tunis suburbs of La Goulette, Carthage, Amilcar, Sidi Bou Saïd and La Marsa with central Tunis via a causeway across the Lake of Tunis.

The TGM station marks the eastern end of Avenue Habib Bourguiba, which runs from east to west through the heart of central Tunis. Two blocks south of the station are the docks and warehouses of the Port of

Tunis. Heading west, one of the first main intersections is the Place de l'Afrique; the tourist office and tourism ministry offices are located here. Along the rest of the avenue are several hotels, restaurants, banks, and exchange bureaus, the French Embassy, and the American Cultural Center. Beyond the latter, Avenue Bourguiba becomes Avenue de France for three blocks before it ends at the Place de la Victoire and the British Embassy, which approximately mark the eastern entrance to the Medina.

The central post, telegraph, and telephone (PTT) office, train station, and food market are about two blocks south of the French Embassy.

Buses to almost every destination in and around Tunis can be caught on Avenue Bourguiba or from Place de Barcelone in front of the train station. *Louages* (intercity taxis) are also usually located near the train station.

Beyond central Tunis and the Medina, the main points of interest are the Bardo Museum and the Belvedere Park and Zoo. The Bardo is easily reached by bus from Avenue Bourguiba and the northern end of the Medina—Bab Souika; it's due west of the Medina. Belvedere is about a twenty-minute walk north of Bab Souika, but it's also easily accessible by bus. The area around the Belvedere is home to many foreign embassies.

GETTING THERE, AWAY, AND AROUND

By Air

The airport is about 5 km (15- to 20-minute drive) north of town. Bus 35 connects Avenue Bourguiba to the airport, but it stops running just after sunset. Taxis are plentiful, though, and fares are usually regulated by meters. In 1989 fares seemed to average about D 4.

All of the airlines listed in the introductory section fly to Tunis, and most have ticket offices on or near Avenue Bourguiba.

By Bus

Intercity bus terminals are located at Boulevard Hedi Saïdi and Bab Saadoun (for northern destinations such as Tabarka, Jendoub, and Beja) and the junction of Rue Sidi El Bechir and Avenue de Carthage a few blocks south of the train station (for the rest of the country). There are buses from Tunis to:

Destination	Departures	Duration (hours)	Distance (km)	Fare (D)
Aïn Draham	5.15 A.M. 6.45 A.M., 3 P.M.	4 1/2	205	3,50

Destination	Departures	Duration (hours)	Distance (km)	Fare (D)
Annaba (Algeria)	7 A.M.	5 1/2	320	5
Ben Ghardane	8.40 P.M.	9 1/2	563	10
Bizerte	5 A.M. and hourly to 8 P.M.	2 1/2	100	
Constantine	6 A.M.	9	470	7
Douz	9 P.M.	9 1/2	567	9
Fahs	7.30 A.M., 2.30 P.M., 9.30 P.M.	1	62	1
Gabés	5 A.M., 7 P.M., 8 P.M., 8.30 P.M.	7	416	
Gafsa	4.30 A.M., 5 A.M., 7 A.M., 9 A.M., 1 P.M., 3 P.M., 4.30 P.M., 9 P.M.	7	425	6,50
Hammamet	9.45 A.M., 4.30 P.M.	1 1/2	66	1,50
Jerba	5 A.M., 6.30 A.M., 8 P.M.	9	520	10
Jerissa	5 A.M., 10 A.M.	5	226	4
Kairouan	6 A.M., 7 A.M., 8 A.M., 9 A.M., 10 A.M., 3 P.M., 4.30 P.M.	3 1/2	160	3
Kallaat Snam	8 A.M.	5 1/2	265	4
Kasserine	8 A.M.	5 1/2	283	4, 25
Kelibia	6 A.M.	3 1/2	133	2
Le Kef	5 A.M., 7 A.M., 10 A.M.	4	172	3
Mahdia	6.30 A.M. 3.30 P.M.	4 1/2	200	3,25
Makhtar	6 A.M., 1 P.M.	4	174	3,25
Medenine	5 A.M., 6.30 A.M., 7 P.M., 8 P.M., 9.15 P.M.	9	483	
Metlaoui	4.30 A.M., 7 A.M., 9 A.M., 1 P.M., 3 P.M., 4.30 P.M.	7 1/2	467	7
Monastir	6.30 A.M., 1.30 P.M.	3	162	
Nabeul	2.30 P.M., 7.30 P.M.	1 1/2	65	1,50

Nefta	7 A.M., 11 A.M.	8 1/2	492	7
Sakiet Youssef	11 A.M.	5	214	3,50
Sbeitla	4.30 A.M., 5 A.M., 8 A.M., 1 P.M.	3	268	4,25
Sfax	5 A.M., 7 P.M., 8 P.M., 8.30 P.M.	4 1/2	282	
Sidi Bouzid	7.30 A.M.	3 1/2	298	4,50
Sousse	5 A.M., 6.30 A.M., 12.30 P.M., 7 P.M., 8 P.M., 8.30 P.M., 9 P.M.	2 1/2	149	2,50
Tabarka	6.15 A.M., 10 A.M.	4	175	3
Tataouine	7 P.M.	10 1/2	600	7
Teboursouk	8 A.M., 4.30 P.M.	2 1/2	101	2
Thala	7 A.M.	5 1/2	246	4
Tozeur	7 A.M., 9 A.M., 1 P.M., 3 P.M., 4.30 P.M., 9 P.M.	8	469	8
Tripoli (Libya)	5 A.M.	16 1/2	765	17
Zaghouan	6 A.M., 5 P.M.	1 1/2	57	1
Zarzis	6.30 A.M., 8.30 P.M.		550	9

City bus stations for Tunis and surroundings are at Jardin Thameur (near the junction of Avenue de Paris and Rue de Londres), Place Barcelone (in front of the train station), and Jardin Belhaouane. There's also a small station on the left side of Avenue Bourguiba as you exit the TGM station; just follow the crowd. Some of the main routes are

No. 1	Around the Medina with stops at each of the major *babs* or gates.
No. 5	Avenue Bourguiba to Belvedere Park
No. 20	Jardin Thameur to La Marsa (on coast just north of Sidi Bou Saïd and Carthage)
Nos. 21 and 26	Place Barcelone to Mornag
No. 27	Jardin Thameur to Raouad
No. 35	Avenue Bourguiba to the airport
No. 38	Avenue Bourguiba to Beledevere Park
No. 40	Marsa to Raouad
No. 44	Jardin Belhaouane to Kalaat El Andalous
No. 50	Between the north and south intercity bus terminals

By Train

From Tunis, there are the following train lines:

- **The Trans-Maghrebian.** Tunis-Djeieda-Tebourba-Beja-Mastouta-Jendouba-Ghardimaou (border)-Annaba (Algeria); there's a daily overnight express to Annaba that departs at 5.28 P.M. and arrives at 9.40 A.M. This train continues all the way to Algiers.

- **Tunis to Bizerte and Tabarka.** There are four trains daily to Bizerte, but for Tabarka you have to change trains in Mateur (64 km from Tunis).

- **Tunis to Kalaâ Kasbah.** Tunis-Fahs-Gafour-Dehmani-Kalaâ Kasbah; three departures daily for the four- to five-hour trip.

- **Tunis to Nabeul, Sfax, and Gabés.** There are three trains daily all the way to Gabés; they also stop en route at Sousse, El Jem, Sfax, and Maharés (for changing to Tozeur line when it's operating). Trains to Nabeul also usually stop at Hammamet and Bir Bou Rekba. There are also several trains daily that serve only the Bir Bou Rekba-Hammamet-Nabeul route.

By Louage

Unfortunately, the louage congregation points for various destinations are dispersed throughout the city. First, check with the tourist office for the latest locations. For most destinations, you can find louages near the train station, particularly on or near Avenue de la Gare. You can also find louages along the edge of the Medina at Bab Souika and Bab Djedid.

By Car

Most of the agencies mentioned in the introductory section have offices along Avenue Bourguiba, including Hertz and Europcar near Place de l'Afrique.

By Ferry

Ferries dock at La Goulette port, which is northeast across the Lake of Tunis causeway from Tunis and on the TGM (urban train) route. In Tunis, tickets for the ferries to France can be bought at NAVITOUR (8 Rue d'Alger; tel. 24-95-00), the Tunisian Shipping Company (5 Rue Dag Hammarskjold; tel. 24-29-99) and SNCM (47 Avenue Farhat Hached; tel. 24-28-01). For ferries to Italy (specifically Sicily), go to Tirrenia Navigazione (tel. 24-27-75). See the introductory section for additional information about ferry crossings.

FIRST THINGS FIRST

Tourism information and facilities are readily available in Tunis.

Tourist and Travel Information

The main office of the Tunisian National Tourist Office (ONTT) is in the tourism ministry building at Place de l'Afrique and Avenue Bourguiba. They usually offer a good selection of printed information about Tunis and Tunisia and seem to be able to answer most questions. Ask for their "Practical Guide" and "Tunisia Hotel Guide." Hours are from 8.30 A.M. to noon and 3 to 6 P.M. from September to May, and from 7.30 A.M. to 1.30 P.M. the rest of the year.

Accommodations

Tunis has a good selection of hotels for all budgets, most of which are concentrated in the downtown area or near Avenue Bourguiba and the Medina. Generally, the cheapest and dirtiest hotels can be found in the Medina.

In the grid of streets between the train station and Avenue Bourguiba and west from Rue de Grèce there are several reasonable unclassified, one- and two-star hotels. One inexpensive favorite is the Hotel Capitole at 60 Avenue Bourguiba, with clean, comfortable rooms for about US$8.

Also on Avenue Bourguiba, but at the other end of the budget spectrum are the Meridien Africa Hotel and the International Tunisia Hotel. At 21 stories, the Africa Hotel is the tallest building in downtown Tunis, a fact that prompted the government to limit future structures to much lower heights, to avoid producing a city of skyscrapers. For travelers, the newsstand just off the lobby is a great source of English-language newspapers and magazines. The rooms are deluxe with full amenities at $80 for a single and $100 for a double. The International isn't quite as deluxe, but the rooms are equally well appointed; rates are $65 for a single and $75 for a double.

Other recommended hotels in this area include the one-star Metropole at 3 Rue de Grèce, the two-star Carlton at 31 Avenue Bourguiba, the one-star Transatlantique at 106 Rue de Yougoslavie, the appropriately named three-star Hotel Majestic at 36 Avenue de Paris, and the two-star Maison Dorée at 6 Rue de Hollande.

The Medina hotels tend to be simple, not often clean, and not recommended for women traveling alone. The Hotel Medina at Place de la Victoire is an exception, although it is considered unclassified by the ONTT.

Consult the hotel guide published by ONTT for additional listings and just walk around central Tunis.

Food

As with hotels, most restaurants and cafés are concentrated on Avenue Bourguiba and nearby side streets. Rotisseries where you can buy cheap Tunisian takeaway food are found on every street. French-style Tunisian restaurants with fixed menus are almost as common. Most restaurants and rotisseries post their prices outside. A few of the recommended restaurants include Le Palais at 8 Avenue de Carthage, Le Grille on Avenue Bourguiba at Place de l'Afrique and the Erriadh at 98 Rue de Yougoslavie.

For fruit and vegetables, try the huge food market at Rue Charles de Gaulle and Rue d'Espagne (across from the main post office) or the stands in the Medina souks or markets.

Getting Things Done and Shopping

Money Exchange

Banks and money exchange kiosks are found throughout Tunis, but the ones with the longest hours are on Avenue Bourguiba and side streets and at the airport. Hotel cashiers at the Africa, and International hotels will exchange money and travelers' checks.

American Express has a representative office in Carthage Tours at 39 and 59 Avenue Bourguiba. Travelers' checks can be bought, but not cashed here. Hours are 9 A.M. to 5 P.M.

Post and telephone office (PTT)

The main PTT is on Rue Charles de Gaulle; the poste restante is located here. The telephone section is open 24 hours and has pay telephones you can use to make direct overseas calls.

Embassies and Consulates

Tunisia maintains good relations with most countries and is, therefore, able to host a number of foreign embassies and consulates.

Algeria
   136 Avenue de la Liberté (tel. 28-00-82)
Canada
   3 Rue Didon (tel. 28-65-77)
Egypt
   16 Rue Essayouti, El Menzah (tel. 23-00-04)
France
   Place de l'Indépendence (tel. 24-57-00) (where Avenue Bourguiba becomes Avenue de France)

Great Britain
> 5 Place de la Victoire (tel. 24-51-00) (at the end of Avenue
> de France and the Porte de France entrance to the Medina)

Morocco
> 39 Rue 1er Juin (tel. 28-80-63)

Netherlands.
> 6 Rue Meycen (tel. 28-74-55)

United States
> 144 Avenue de la Liberté (tel. 23-25-66) (the USIA cultural
> center and library are on Avenue de France across from the
> French embassy)

West Germany
> 18 Avenue Challaye (tel. 28-12-46/28-12-55)

Shopping

Tunis shops offer a good selection of traditional handicrafts. For an overview of what is available, visit the ONA (National Organization of Crafts) at the corner of Avenue de Carthage and Avenue Bourguiba. Prices are high compared to what you may find in the Medina shops and in other Tunisian cities and towns, but at least you can get an idea here of what is available and what is considered high quality.

In the Medina, be prepared for haggling over prices if you're interested in buying something. Also be prepared for a few hassles whether you want to buy or not. The hassles and haggling are an intrinsic part of visiting and shopping in the Medina.

THINGS TO SEE

Tunis is divided somewhat like an island and its surrounding sea. The "island" is the Medina, the foundation of Tunis with its old buildings and mosques and narrow streets and alleyways. The "sea" is Tunis outside the Medina walls, most of which was constructed in the last two centuries. For travelers, the main points of interest are in the Medina and across the Lake of Tunis in Carthage.

In "new" Tunis—the areas outside the Medina—the only sights worth visiting are the Bardo Museum and Belvedere Park. The Bardo Museum is northwest of the Medina and central Tunis at Place de l'Assemblée Constitutionelle (junction of seven major avenues). In a former nineteenth-century Ottoman palace adjacent to the National Assembly building, the museum houses one of the world's finest collections of Roman mosaics. The mosaics are a colorful record of bourgeois life in the Roman Empire, with many depicting the decadent leisure activities of the upper class. Other exhibits cover earlier periods of Tunisian history, including the Punic and early Christian times.

To get to the museum, take Bus 3 from Avenue Bourguiba or Nos. 4, 16, 23, 30, or 42 from the Jardin Thameur bus terminal. Hours are 9.30 A.M. to 4.30 P.M. daily, closed on Mondays.

North of central Tunis and the Medina is Belvedere Park, which is a pleasant nearby escape from the city that is as large as the Medina. Aside from just roaming around the park, you can also visit the Museum of Modern Art and Cinema and the zoo. The museum cinema is one of the sites for the internationally renowned Carthage Festival. Unfortunately, though, the museum has a relatively meager collection of modern art exhibits. The zoo is fairly well maintained and worth a visit if you wish to see a few of the animals that can now rarely, if ever, be seen roaming the "wilds" of Tunisia.

The Medina—Walking Tours

As the old, original part of Tunis, the Medina offers a picture of Tunisia's past, albeit somewhat tarnished by the modernity that has crept in from "new" Tunis. Narrow streets and cramped alleyways, traditional *souks* (markets) for cloth, perfume, and jewelry, intricately decorated mosques and schools dating from the ninth century—all this describes the Medina. In the central part of the Medina, however, shops selling every imaginable sort of traditional Tunisian kitsch to hordes of tourists have taken over. Many of the shops are concentrated on and around Rue Jamā'a Zitouna, a principal thoroughfare leading from Place de la Victoire straight to the Great Mosque at the heart of the Medina.

Starting from Place de la Victoire, walk up Rue Jamā'a Zitouna to the Great Mosque, closing your ears to the persistent tourist hawkers along the way. On your left at No. 14 is a church built in 1662, one of the first in the city. Rue Jamā'a ends at the Great Mosque.

Known as the Great Mosque of Zitouna ("olives"), this immense mosque was one of the first major buildings in Tunis when it was built by the Aghlabid dynasty in the ninth century. Although the mosque has undergone numerous changes through the years, most of the present structure can be traced to the Aghlabids. About a century after its founding, the mosque also became an important university, particularly for theology and the promulgation of Islam. The university endured until the 1960s, when its study programs were incorporated with the University of Tunis. The mosque can be visited every morning except Fridays from 8 A.M. to noon.

As you leave the Great Mosque, turn right on Souk des Librairies and then right again on Souk de la Laine, which is along the side of the mosque. This street along the length of the mosque was once a flourishing wool market, but little remains today.

From the upper left corner of the Great Mosque, continue on Souk de la Laine as it crosses Souk des Femmes and ends at Souk des Orfèvres (goldsmiths). Turn left and then left again to watch the goldsmiths hammer and bend the gold into jewelry. Weave through the alleys back to Souk des Femmes and you'll also pass a small cotton market.

Back on Souk des Femmes, turn left and cross Souk de la Laine. You should now be along the north side of the Great Mosque on Souk des Etoffes (cloth and fabric). After checking out the red- and green-columned cloth stalls, backtrack to Souk Sekkajine (the last passageway before Souk de la Laine), turn right and follow this to Souk El Berka.

The Souk El Berka was once the marketplace for Tunis's thriving slave market. Slaves were brought here from throughout the Mediterranean and North Africa, often to be sold as labor for pirate galleys.

Along Souk El Berka on the left is the early seventeenth-century Mosque of Youssef Dey. Its most distinguishing feature is an octagonal minaret adopted form Turkish designs, a sign that Ottoman rule had begun in Tunisia. Across from the mosque is the Dar El Bey, which was once a royal guesthouse and is now the Prime Minister's office. At this point, Souk El Berka becomes Souk El Bey, a pleasant arcaded market area that parallels the Dar El Bey.

Turn right on Souk des Chechias, an interesting market area that has until recently specialized in producing wool *chechias* (traditional Tunisian skull caps). This passageway deadends at Rue Sidi Ben Arous and the Zaouia of Sidi Ben Arous. Zaouias are the houses of Islamic orders founded to perpetuate the teachings of a spiritual leader such as fourteenth-century Sufi teacher Sidi Ben Arous. His zaouia was built in 1437, many years after his death. Heading left from Souk des Chechias, you'll see the seventeenth-century Hammouda Pasha Mosque on the right. Built in the same era as the Youssef Dey Mosque, it incorporates a few similar architectural features—Italian marble and an octagonal minaret.

At this point, if you continue past the mosque and along Rue Sidi Ben Arous, the street becomes Rue du Pasha and enters the northern part of the Medina.

Follow Rue du Pasha as far as Rue Sidi Ibrahim and turn right. You'll see the Zaouia Sidi Ibrahim on the left. This zaouia, or Islamic order, was founded in the nineteenth century to perpetuate the teachings of eighteenth-century Islamic scholar Sidi Ibrahim. From there, continue along Rue Sidi Ibrahim as it becomes Rue El Mestiri and turn left on Rue Sidi Mehrez. The Mosque of Sidi Mehrez begun by Mohammed Bey in 1692 stands on the left as an impressive example of typical Ottoman Islamic architecture. Its minaret remained unfinished until the 1970s because a myth had evolved that whoever finished the mosque would die. Continuing past the mosque, Rue Sidi Mehrez leads into Place Bab Souika, a popular café area.

An Alternate Medina Tour

Starting from Place de la Victoire, follow Rue Jamā'a Zitouna as far as Rue Sidi Ali Azouz, which will be on the left. After a few minutes walk, you'll see the Zaouia Sidi Ali Azouz at No. 7, built in the nineteenth century to promulgate the ideas of this seventeenth-century religious leader. Continuing along this street, it becomes Rue des Teinturiers (Street of the Dyers), although the only dyeing done today is for the tourist trade. One of the most prominent features of this street is the early eighteenth-century Mosque of the Dyers with seventeenth-century octagonal minaret and hand-painted Turkish tiles. Rue Sidi Kassem intersects Rue des Teinturiers at this point. Turn left on Rue Sidi Kassem, and the Dar Othman palace stands on the right. You can't miss it because a beautiful doorway marks the main entrance. The palace was built by Othman Dey, who ruled here between 1594 and 1610.

Backtrack along Sidi Kassem, and cross Rue des Teinturiers to the arched entrance of the Dar Ben Abdallah. The Dar is a well-preserved eighteenth-century palace that has been converted into the Museum of Traditional Heritage of Tunis. Most of the exhibits are items representing daily life in the eighteenth century—clothing, rifles, engravings, a few paintings, and so on.

Returning to Rue des Teinturiers, turn right and follow it to Bab Jazira. From there you can either go right along the periphery of the Medina to Place de la Kasbah or left and return to "new" Tunis.

NEAR TUNIS: CARTHAGE

Carthage was once a powerful city-state with an empire that stretched across North Africa from Tunis to the Atlantic coast of present-day Morocco. Founded by Phoenician traders in 814 B.C., it became a thorn in the side of the growing Roman Empire. The Romans eventually destroyed the city and left a few scattered remnants. Today, these remnants are crammed between the luxurious villas of what is now a posh Tunis suburb, all of which is a far cry from the grandeur of the Carthaginian Empire.

After the Romans destroyed Carthage in 146 B.C., Roman philosopher and poet Virgil wrote the *Aeneid*, an epic 12-book poem recounting the founding of Carthage and the rise of Rome. Apparently the power of Carthage in the Mediterranean was so great that its establishment had to be mythologized by Virgil. According to the *Aeneid*, Princess Dido of Tyre (soon to be called Queen) fled her brother, Pygmalion, the King of Tyre, and landed at Carthage. She proceeeded to claim the land based on what she could encircle in ox hide. Thus Carthage was founded. As she directed construction of the city, Aeneas, a mythical hero of Troy, was shipwrecked on the shores of Carthage. The gods had instructed Aeneas to found a new city for them in Italy (Rome) after the Greeks had conquered Troy. Dido took him in, and they fell in love. Their love story, however, was soon overshadowed by Aeneas's divine mission to Rome. Dido committed suicide when Aeneas abandoned her, and Carthage began a gradual decline. The story was more fiction than fact, and meant more as an allegory of Roman history, particularly the career of Augustus.

According to archeological evidence, Phoenician traders began establishing a permanent settlement at Carthage in the seventh or eighth century B.C. An ideal site was selected on a peninsula of low hills with the well-guarded Lake of Tunis on one side and the Gulf of Tunis on the other. A fortress or acropolis and a set of Punic dwellings were erected on Byrsa hill, one of the most prominent points on the peninsula. Today, Byrsa is the site of the extensive ruins of these structures and the Carthage Museum.

From Byrsa the city spread along the coast and eventually included two protected ports (now lagoons next to the Oceanography Museum), an aqueduct system, thermal baths (the ruins adjacent to the Presidential Palace), and various small temples. As the city of Carthage grew, so did the navy and empire of Carthage. With its naval supremacy Carthage dominated Mediterranean trade routes, thus threatening the rising power of the Roman Empire. By the mid-third century B.C., both empires were engaged in a century-long series of wars that ended in 146 B.C. with the sacking of Carthage.

Julius Caesar returned in 46 B.C. to establish a Roman colony at Carthage. He was followed by Augustus, who made Carthage the prosperous capital of the Roman province of Africa. It continued to thrive until the Roman Empire was attacked by Goths at the beginning of the fourth century A.D. and began to fall. Carthage declined as it was juggled from the Byzantines to the Vandals and then the Arabs in 698 A.D. By the time of Arab rule, most of Carthage was in ruins.

Today, most of the ruins of Carthage that can be visited date from the Roman period. They are easily accessible from the TGM (urban train) Carthage stations, with all but a few sites less than a 10-minute walk away.

Starting from the Carthage-Byrsa station, on the right are the lagoons that were once the main Punic ports, the heart of Carthaginian power. Between the ports is the Oceanographic Museum, with a sad collection of dusty stuffed birds and fish in dirty tanks. Next to the museum is the Tophet, or sanctuary, where Carthaginian children were brought by their parents to be ritually sacrificed to the gods Baal and Tanit.

Return to the road next to the TGM station and walk north to a path that begins on the left side of the Carthage Dermech TGM station.

Follow it up to Byrsa hill where the Carthage Museum and ruins of the original Carthaginian acropolis are located. The museum's exhibits offer a good overview of life during the heyday of Carthage. Scattered ruins of the acropolis and Punic quarters are in the garden around the museum. Additional information about Carthage, including a map, is available at the museum.

Walk down the opposite side of the hill and turn left at the road junction. Follow this road straight through a major intersection to the ruins of a Roman amphitheater. The Romans often used this arena for executions of Christian rebels (or, rather, Christians whom they believed to be rebels). Across the road are the Malga cisterns and a part of the ancient Roman aqueduct, all of which were a major element of Carthage's water supply. Unfortunately, most of this has been built over, and thus some imagination is required to conjure up an image of what was once here.

Follow the road from the cisterns back towards the TGM line. On the left you'll see an impressive theater that has been restored for the Carthage Festival. Continuing down the road, cross the TGM tracks to the ruins of the Antonine Baths, one of the best and biggest examples of Roman baths in North Africa. Paved passageways and a few columns and walls remain, but really not much else. Again, unfortunately, you'll have to use your imagination to envision these ruined structures as the beautiful baths they were over a thousand years ago.

CHAPTER 17

Adventures in Tunisia

Compared to hiking through the High Atlas mountains of Morocco or trekking in the Algerian Sahara, adventures in Tunisia are tame. Some of the possible adventures include

- Bird watching and hiking around Lake Ichkeul near Bizerte
- Scuba diving and snorkeling in the Mediterranean (from Tabarka) and in the Gulf of Tunis (from Port El Kantaoui)
- A bicycle tour of Jerba Island
- A tour of the Djerid oases

BIRD WATCHING AT LAKE ICHKEUL

Lake Ichkeul is southwest of Bizerte and adjacent to the town of Menzel Bourguiba. In the late 1980s, this lake region became a national park for the protection of over 300 species of birds that inhabit its 50-km (31-mile) shoreline. Lake Ichkeul has the unusual distinction of having salt water in the summer and fresh water in the winter, a factor that attracts a unique combination of birds here. However, the government was attempting to build a dike that would prevent the summer influx of salt water.

On the south shore of the lake is Mount Ichkeul, a 511-m (1,676 1/2-ft) summit that can be easily hiked in an hour or two. On the north side of the summit (facing the lake), a small bird museum was constructed here in 1988 with the assistance of Prince Philip of Britain and the World Wildlife Fund.

The summit and lakeshore are also inhabited by 300 buffaloes, descendents of a couple that Abraham Lincoln sent to Tunisia as a gift.

British ornithologists have compiled a comprehensive list of birds that inhabit Lake Ichkeul and other parts of Tunisia. The number of species (more than 300) at Ichkeul far outnumbers any other area in

408

Tunisia. Some of these species include various types of warbler, redstart, finch, sparrow, gull, tern, lark, pipit, heron, egret, eagle, plover, and sandpiper. If you're a fan of bird watching, this is the place to come. To get to the lake and museum from Bizerte, you can get off the bus or taxi from Bizerte at the road junction. From there it's an easy 10 km (just over 6 miles) walk to the museum. Another option is to take the train from Bizerte and get off at Tinja, the northeastern corner of the lake, and then hitchhike or try to hire a taxi to get you around to the road junction.

SCUBA DIVING AND SNORKELING

Tunisia has well-equipped diving centers in Tabarka on the northwest Mediterranean coast and Port El Kantaoui just north of Sousse.

Port El Kantaoui is a modern tourism complex that is an almost fully self-contained beach resort. It's part of a string of resorts that stretches south for several miles along the coast as far as Monastir. Except for its stark white Andalusian-style arches and shops of traditional woven carpets and copper plates, this complex could be in any other country with a beautiful coastline. The dive center, of course, offers a good selection of rental equipment, diving courses, and boat trips.

To get to Port El Kantaoui from Sousse, you can either take a taxi or the miniature tourist train that makes frequent runs between Sousse and the port. Accommodations are plentiful in Sousse and Port El Kantaoui, but the latter caters to European tourists on package deals.

The Sousse medina is worth visiting for a few hours. The Medina was the original city of Sousse and still has several monuments that date back several centuries. At the northeastern corner, just inside the wall from Place Farhat Hached, is a ninth-century *ribat*, or fortress tower, although it is really a collection of towers rather than a single one. Across from the Ribat is Sousse's ninth-century Great Mosque, which can be visited daily from 8 A.M. to 12 noon except Fridays. A small museum is at the opposite corner of the Medina, in the Khalef Tower. Most of the exhibits are mosaics salvaged from nearby Christian catacombs.

Compared to Sousse and Port El Kantaoui, Tabarka has been passed over for massive tourist development. This is probably due, in part, to the lack of great beaches and historical monuments. Other than cool, quiet isolation and diving, the town's other attractions are few—a medieval castle atop a hill overlooking town, and red coral. The castle was built in the mid-sixteenth century by a Turkish pirate named Barbarossa, who relinquished it to Charles V of Spain in 1541, who in turn sold it to a Genoese family. You can't visit the now-abandoned castle, but it is an impressive sight.

Diving for bright red coral has long been a favorite pastime or, for some, avocation among many of Tabarka's inhabitants. For several centuries, local artisans have crafted the coral into beaded necklaces, earrings, and other jewelry. Shops along Avenue Bourguiba sell the finished products. The Yachting Club of Tabarka has been training many of the coral divers. They also provide general diving instruction through the small diving center attached to the club. Unfortunately, the courses are almost always in French. Some diving equipment can be rented here, and boats are usually available for dive trips.

BICYCLE TOUR OF JERBA ISLAND

Jerba Island, off the southern coast of Tunisia east of Gabés, is a great place for a one- or two-day bicycle tour. The Carthaginians were the first settlers on Jerba, although a Greek legend had evolved before their settlement that this island was the mythical Land of the Lotus Eaters. A substantial population of Jews settled on the island, about 1,500 of whom remain today, thus comprising one of the oldest Jewish communities outside Israel. Romans and various other groups followed the Carthaginians. Today, the island has been invaded by massive waves of package-deal tourists, many of whom arrive on direct charter flights from Europe.

Houmt-Souk, the main town on the island, is the best place to start

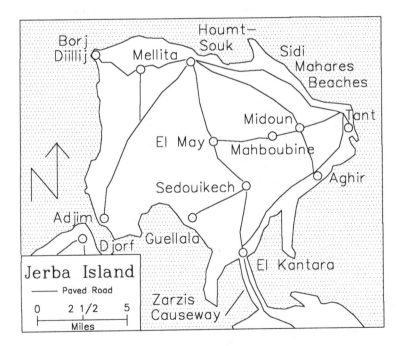

a tour. Bicycles and mopeds can be rented from any of several shops and garages in town or almost any of the hotels on the island. Ride north on Rue Tai'eb Mehiri to the Borj El Kebir ("big fort") on the waterfront at the end of the street. Foundations of the Borj date back to 1289 when Aragonese King Roger de Loira constructed the first fort here. Philip II of Spain unsuccessfully laid siege to the fort when it was occupied by pirates and Ottomans in the early sixteenth century. Hundreds of his soldiers were massacred inside the fort after their fleet was destroyed. Most of the fort lay in ruin until excavation and restoration work was recently begun.

From the fort, return to the main road—Avenue de la République—and turn left. Follow this road as it skirts some of the best beaches and biggest tourist complexes in Tunisia to the turnoff for Midoun. If you're not planning to return to Houmt-Souk for the night, there are campgrounds on the beach near Tanit. There's not much of interest in Midoun, so continue on toward Mahboubine, El May, and then right on the road back to Houmt-Souk. Turn left on the road to Er Riadh and follow the signs to the synagogue of El Ghriba.

The present synagogue was built in 1920 over a place where a sacred stone fell from heaven. This was interpreted as a sign that a synagogue should be constructed at that spot. Every year after Passover this synagogue is a place of pilgrimage for thousands of Jews. From the synagogue, you can return to Houmt-Souk.

To get to Houmt-Souk, there are frequent louages (collective taxis) and buses via the Djorf-Adjim ferry from Tunis, Gabés, and Sfax; and via the Zarzis causeway from Zarzis, Ben Ghardane, Medenine, and Tataouine. There are also popular daily flights between Houmt-Souk and Tunis.

Visit the tourist office in Houmt-Souk for accommodations information. There are many options ranging from hostel-style rooms to luxury hotels.

TOUR OF MATMATA AND THE DJERID OASES

The paths to adventures in Matmata and the Djerid oases have been well trodden by group tours, usually caravans of Land-Rovers with cushioned seats, air conditioning, and quadraphonic stereo music. If you're short on time, then these tours are convenient and perhaps worthwhile to give you at least some idea of the Tunisian portion of the Sahara. However, be prepared for cultural experiences and contact with Tunisian traditions that are as packaged as the tour you're on.

Matmata is a favorite destination of both Land-Rover and coach tours. Almost daily this village of a few hundred Berbers, many of whom live in caves just off courtyards dug beneath the ground, are overwhelmed and outnumbered by a tourist onslaught. These troglodyte dwellings are a sensible way for local inhabitants to keep cool in the dry, blistering desert heat. Several of the dwellings have been converted into restaurants, hotels, and souvenir shops. Many of the residential caves are open to sightseers—for a price, of course. It's still worth visiting Matmata for a glimpse at this unique subterranean lifestyle and to witness the transformation of the villagers as the tourists arrive.

They come in droves, for lunch in a cave and perhaps a tour of an "actual" underground home. Often the tour passes through the underground bar where the stellar bar scene of *Star Wars* was filmed. Not surprisingly, the villagers go into a feeding frenzy when the caravan of usually over twenty tour buses rumbles into the village. Tourists represent financial salvation for many of the villagers. Try to get here before lunch, thus before most of the tour buses, so you can visit a few of the caves with at least some tranquility.

There are seven buses daily from Gabés to Matmata. Some local transportation (buses and taxis) exists to villages near Matmata—Tamezret, Haddej, and Toujane—but for destinations farther afield you must return to Gabés (unless, of course, you're with a tour).

WEST TO TOZEUR—THE DJERID

From Gabés (and Jerba), Land-Rover tours follow a desert circuit through a phosphate-rich region known as the Djerid. Two routes cross Djerid from Gabés—Highway GP16 direct to Tozeur and GP15 through Gafsa and Metlaoui. GP15, the more interesting route, passes through the hot springs town of El Hamma (open for public bathing) and then 88 km (54 1/2 miles) across the desert to Kebili.

Kebili is a small oasis town that was once an important center for Nefzaoua Berbers. Today, there's not much of interest for travelers other than ways to depart as quickly as possible for Douz (27 km, or 17 miles, to the south) or Tozeur (96 km, or 59 1/2 miles, to the northwest).

Douz is another favorite destination for the Land-Rover tours, especially toward the end of January when the Festival of the Sahara is held. Although it is still the center for some 15,000 or so Mrazig Berber nomads, government efforts to settle these people and an annual influx of about 100,000 tourists have taken a toll on the local culture and traditions. As with Matmata, the packaged tours have spawned packaged culture. Consequently, the camel lot camels and owners, who all seem to think they are Lawrence of Arabia, are of course ready and waiting to take you for "adventures" in the oases. In the evening, musicians and dancers bedecked in traditional costumes are ready to entertain you.

From Douz you can return to Kebili and continue on to Tozeur. There are buses to Tozeur from Kebili at 8.45 A.M. and 3 P.M. And there's also a bus from Douz via Kebili that goes to Tozeur. After Kebili the Land-

Rovers and buses cross the Chott el Djerid, a vast salt lake that is deceptively depicted on maps as an ordinary lake, but it's dry most of the year.

TOZEUR

Since its establishment as a major southern trading post for the Romans in the second century A.D., Tozeur has been one of the most important commercial centers of southern Tunisia and the Djerid. Today, the town hosts a continual influx of tourists, some of whom arrive direct from Europe on charter flights.

Tozeur's main attractions include a restored old quarter with structures that date back to the fourteenth century. One particularly interesting building is the tomb of Sidi Bou Aïssa, which has been converted into a small museum of "popular art." Actually, its exhibits are more along the lines of traditional artifacts than contemporary or "popular art"—two big medieval doors that once belonged to a local house, an old silk wedding dress, manuscripts, statues, and some pottery.

Also in town is the Zoo du Desert Tijani, the better of two zoos in the area. For 1 dinar you get a guided "grand tour" through a small, but memorable menagerie. First, there's a raven and monkey peacefully sharing the same cage. Then there's a temperamental bear that growls at every passer-by and claws menacingly at his chain-link fence cage. Next to him (or her—it's hard to tell on a furry bear) in an enclosure surrounded by a flimsy waist-high fence is the star of the zoo—Hercules the lion.

If you've ever wanted to hug a lion and live to tell about it, now is your chance. Hercules is either truly friendly or truly drugged, but he's definitely not detoothed, a fact that is all too apparent when he yawns on cue. I hugged Hercules and got a close look at his palm-sized incisors. At that moment I thought of a story I once heard in Nairobi from a former safari guide. He was sleeping in his tent in the bush and had carelessly left the flaps unzipped. In the early morning, he was visited by a hungry lion that began to casually chomp on his foot and calf. The man yelled and the lion chomped a bit harder, so he grabbed his long-lensed camera and whacked the lion on the head. The lion scampered out of the tent. I know that this story may sound far-fetched, but the guide showed me scars on his foot that looked like big tooth marks.

I looked again at Hercules, but couldn't imagine this lion, which seemed to resemble the good-hearted lion in the *Wizard of Oz*, chomping on anything other than hamburger, so I gave him another hug and hopped over the fence.

Nearby is a lion named *Musique* that is renowned for his moaning talents. He moans in unison with the guide. What a duo! Then there's

Ali Baba the alcoholic camel, that can suck down a shot of whiskey and Fanta orange drink from either a glass or a bottle before you can count to three. Among the other creatures, there's also Margaret the scorpion, Anna Marie the horned viper, and Rambo III the ticklish desert lizard that fancies breakfast snakes.

Last, but not least, is Tozeur's camel lot, which is in front of Le Petit Prince Restaurant about half a block past the Hotel Oasis. The camels and their owners are, of course, eager to take you for rides through the surrounding oasis of date palms, banana plants, and fig trees. This is as good a place as any to have your proverbial adventure, albeit totally staged, with a camel. Or, if you prefer, just start walking. You can't really get lost.

Accommodations from cheap to expensive are available in Tozeur, but reservations are recommended most of the year for middle- and upper-level hotels. The bigger hotels, especially along Abdelkacem Chebbi, are often full of tour groups.

Getting to and from Tozeur shouldn't be a problem. There are daily louages (collective taxis), a diesel train to Metlaoui, and three buses to Tunis, El Oued (Algeria), and other destinations.

From Metlaoui, a few Land-Rover tours and independent travelers continue on to Tamerza and Mides, oasis villages about 50 km (31 miles) to the west. Tamerza's highlights are two waterfalls—one cold and the other hot (warmed by sun during the day)—along the edge of the oasis. The hotel just above one of the waterfalls may have reopened by the time you read this; otherwise there are numerous unofficial campsites in small clearings amid the date and fig groves of the oasis.

An excellent 6 km (4-mile) day hike is possible from Tamerza to the neighboring oasis village of Mides. A popular route is to hike across the desert to Mides in the morning and return in the afternoon following a stream as it cuts through a small canyon. If you don't feel like hiking, donkeys can be hired in Tamerza.

Last few words of advice: If you plan to camp, bring mosquito repellent.

PART FIVE

ॐ

The Maltese Islands

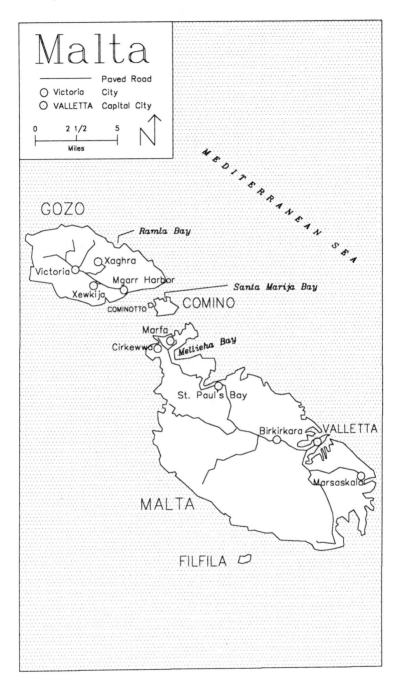

CHAPTER 18

The Maltese Islands

Name:	Repubblika ta' Malta (Republic of Malta)
Political Status:	Unitary multiparty republic with one legislative house
Capital:	Valletta
Population:	0.35 million (U.N. statistics, 1989)
Land area:	316 square kilometers (122 square miles)
Languages	Maltese, English, and Italian
Currency:	Maltese lira (Lm); Lm 1 = 100 cents (c)
Major cities	
(population):	Birkirkara, 20,300; Qormi, 18,413; Hamrun, 13,651; Sliema, 13,650; and Valletta, 9,263
Religious	
affiliation:	Roman Catholicism

At first, it probably seems odd to include the Maltese islands in a book that concentrates on Morocco, Algeria, and Tunisia. Although the islands are closer to Sicily than North Africa, the Arabs did influence the people and culture. The Arabs ruled and settled here for more than two centuries before Roger the Norman of Sicily initiated the gradual process in 1090 of re-Christianizing the Maltese. Malta became a tiny, little-known (albeit significant out of proportion to its size) bridge or link between Europe and North Africa. Consequently, more than any other Mediterranean people, perhaps, the Maltese are a reflection of their history. Through the centuries, they have been a people who has adopted aspects of various Mediterranean cultures and created what seems to be a distinct and resilient Maltese cultural identity.

As a land of adventures it doesn't have an abundance of activities to offer, but as a land where the past and present so clearly mesh Malta has a surprising abundance of history from prehistoric to present. The following section introduces you to some of the fascinating history and places of the Maltese islands.

417

NATURAL ENVIRONMENT

The Maltese islands are a set of limestone-based islands 93 km (58 miles) south of Sicily, 290 km (180 miles) east of Tunisia, and 350 km (220 miles) north of Libya, with a total area of 122 square miles. At a maximum length of 27 km (17 miles) and width of 14 km (9 miles), Malta is the largest of the islands, followed by Gozo, which is 14 km (9 miles) and 7 km (4 1/2 miles) respectively, and the uninhabited island of Comino (2 1/2 square km) and islets of Cominotto and Filfla.

Malta has 136 km (84 miles) of coastline, and Gozo 43 km (27 miles), punctuated by numerous rocky coves, small harbors and bays, and steep cliffs. There are no mountains, lakes, or rivers on any of the islands. Malta mainly consists of a series of low hills and terraced fields that gently rise toward the southwestern half of the island and the highest point—a hill that is 253 m (829 ft) above sea level. Gozo has similar topography, with a few sets of hills that rise toward the 244-m (800-ft) mark.

The land on both islands, as well as the smaller ones, appears stark and infecund (60 percent of it is) because surface layers are mostly hard limestone. Beneath this are layers of softer rock such as greensand, blue clay, and globigerina limestone. Gozo has more surface layers of blue clay, thus making it comparatively more fertile than Malta. Globigerina limestone is quarried on Malta and used throughout the islands for construction.

The Maltese islands have a typical two-season Mediterranean climate—cool, occasionally cold between November and March, and warm or hot the rest of the year. Most of the rainfall is in the winter (a monthly average of more than 100 mm, or 4 inches); almost no rain between June and August. Temperatures follow a similar pattern, with average winter temperatures of 12°C (54°F) and summer 25° to 30°C (77° to 86°F). It's not unusual for winter temperatures to briefly dip below freezing and cause some frost. In the summer, droughtlike conditions are occasionally exacerbated by sciroccos—hot, dry winds that blast north out of the Sahara and across the Mediterranean.

HISTORY

Malta's history prior to the arrival of Abbassid Arab conquerors in the ninth century A.D. figures prominently in most histories of the islands. Archeologists and historians have divided Malta's prehistory into three periods, based on evidence uncovered at various sites on the islands:

Neolithic   5000 to 3750 B.C.
Copper Age 3750 to 2200 B.C.
Bronze Age 2000 to 800 B.C.

During the Neolithic period, Malta's first inhabitants sailed across from Sicily and established small farming communities similar to what existed in Sicily and other parts of the Mediterranean. Bright red pottery is one of the chief archeological finds of this period. As the communities became more permanent, the pottery became more decorative and ornamental.

Small temple complexes, the remains of which are a key source of knowledge about prehistoric human beings in Malta, appeared toward the end of the Copper Age. This period is also notable for the construction of extensive collective burial sites in rock-cut tombs, particularly a set at Xemxija overlooking St. Paul's Bay. Layouts of the tombs and temples and artifacts found in them suggest the existence of a fairly sophisticated religion or set of religious cults. A priestly caste, animal sacrifices, and healing ceremonies were all parts of the temple complexes. Despite the name of this period—the Copper Age—copper or any other metal tools dating to this time have not yet been found in Malta.

Metal tools were used, however, during the Bronze period, a period dominated by the warlike Tarxien Cemetery people. A large cremation cemetery uncovered at Tarxien is the only vestige of this Bronze Age people's civilization. Archeologists found the ruins of small, rudimentary structures, many simple metal tools and burial objects such as urns, clay figures, and jewelry. They inhabited the Maltese islands until about 1450 B.C. when another Bronze Age group—the Borg Nadur people—invaded the islands, probably from Sicily, and built several fortified villages. Malta's prehistoric periods ended in about 800 B.C. with the rising cultural influence of Phoenician traders, who had begun visiting the islands in about 1000 B.C.

Phoenicians were supplanted by Carthaginians who colonized the islands in the seventh and eighth centuries B.C. Temples such as the one excavated at Tas Silg near Marsaxlokk were erected. By the fourth century B.C., the Roman Empire had begun to expand into southern Italy and threaten the Carthaginian presence in Malta. Carthage lost Malta to the Romans in the First Punic War (262 to 242 B.C.), but won it back a few years later. In the Second Punic War (218 to 201 B.C.), Rome reclaimed Malta and used it as a base from which to launch incursions into North Africa. During the Third Punic War (149 to 146 B.C.), Rome finally conquered and destroyed the city and thus the empire of Carthage.

Despite Roman rule over Malta from about 218 B.C. to the fifth century A.D., the Maltese were never fully romanized. They had been influenced by Christianity, which supposedly arrived on their shores in A.D. 60 with the shipwreck of St. Paul the Apostle. Their language retained what linguists believe were Phoenician-Semitic roots, thus a distinctly non-Latin, non-Roman character. Economically, the Maltese did adapt to the ways of the Roman Empire and prospered as an exporter of various agricultural products and textiles. Malta is still renowned for producing high-quality textiles.

By the fifth century A.D., Roman power over Malta and the rest of the Mediterranean had begun to wane. As the Roman Empire receded, Vandals, Byzantines (sixth to ninth centuries A.D.), and Arabs (in A.D. 870) followed; the latter remained for several centuries and greatly influenced Maltese culture, particularly the language. Today, the majority of place names are still of Arab origin, and many words and phrases bear some resemblance to Arabic.

Arab influence began to abate around 1090 when Roger the Norman, king of Sicily, conquered Malta. However, the population remained Muslim even after a subsequent invasion and conquest in 1127 by Roger II. Toward the end of the thirteenth century, though, a Catholic community was able to install itself in Malta. A cathedral was built at Mdina. In the fourteenth and fifteenth centuries, various Catholic orders established themselves in Malta—the Franciscans, Carmelites, and Dominicans. More than 400 churches were constructed during this period.

At the same time, the number of villages decreased in Malta, a trend that historian Brian Blouet attributes in his book, *The Story of Malta* (Valletta, Malta: Progress Press, 1987), to increased insecurity from war and pirate raids in the Mediterranean. He asserts that with fewer villages to defend, the Maltese were more secure. Another discernible trend is an increased Europeanization of the population as more Italians and Spaniards emigrated to Malta.

By 1530 a group that was to earn a significant place in Maltese history also arrived—the Knights of the Order of St. John of Jerusalem. Originally, the Knights' purpose was to maintain a hospital for Christian pilgrims to Jerusalem, but the order became militarized as the Crusades heated up. Muslim invaders pushed it out of Jerusalem and westward, first to Cyprus and then Rhodes. In 1523 the Ottoman Turks forced it out of Rhodes, so a few years later it settled in Malta, after being invited there by Charles V.

The Knights were a well-organized multinational order ruled by a grand master and council of knights. The Knights were divided into eight *langues* (languages) based on their regions of origin: Aragon, Auvergne, Castile, Provence, England, France, Germany, and Italy. The English *langue* disappeared with the Reformation. An *auberge* or residence was built for each *langue*; a few of these are still inhabited today. The Knights also fortified Valletta, the Grand Harbor, and surrounding areas; they expected a Turkish invasion someday.

That day came in 1551 when a Turkish fleet invaded and overwhelmed most of the islands' defenses. Gozo was almost completely depopulated and destroyed; most of Malta also suffered. Overall, the losses of both Malta and Gozo prompted the Knights to build stronger forts, most notably the star-shaped Fort St. Elmo, the Forts of St. Angelo and St. Michael, and the fortified towns of Birgu and Senglea (adjacent to what was eventually called Valletta). Although the Turks had left for raids on Tripoli, the Knights expected them to eventually return.

In early 1565, the Knights learned of an impending Turkish attack. Fearing a massive Turkish invasion, many of the islands' inhabitants departed for Sicily.

On May 18, 1565, a Turkish armada arrived off Malta and landed an army of several thousand soldiers. After more than a month and at least 8,000 Turkish dead, they captured the Fort of St. Elmo; the Christians had lost 1,500, including 130 knights. Despite greater numbers of Turkish soldiers and a few key breaches of the walls of the remaining forts and fortified towns, Grand Master Valette (for whom Valletta is named) was able to successfully rally his knights and soldiers. By the end of the summer, the losses had demoralized the Turks and Mediterranean storms were threatening the armada, so they were forced to abandon Malta and return home.

The Knights regarded the "Siege of Malta" as a turning point in the wars against the expansion of Islam and the Ottoman Empire. It was feared that if Malta fell to the Turks, then the rest of Europe would be threatened. Whether the Turks really would have been capable of expanding further is debatable because the rise of European navies from the late sixteenth century onward was gradually encroaching on Turkish spheres of influence.

For Malta, however, defeat of the Turks was definitely a turning point. The Knights remained in Malta and embarked on a relatively rapid process of development. Valletta was founded as the capital city and chief fortress of the Knights. New towns and fortresses were built throughout the islands during the rest of that century and through most of the seventeenth century, mostly in anticipation of another Turkish invasion. The Turks did attempt an invasion in 1614, but it failed. With peace and stability, Malta became a flourishing trade center and its population increased.

By the end of the seventeenth century, the Knights had become something of an anachronism in Malta. Its influence beyond certain commercial affairs in the islands was limited; militarily, it was practically defunct by 1720. In Europe it was weakened by upheavals such as the French Revolution, which resulted in the confiscation of all of the order's properties and holdings in France.

Napoleon arrived in Malta on June 9, 1798, with his army and navy, en route to Egypt. He encountered little resistance and gave the Knights three days to leave the islands. Although Napoleon left a garrison of 4,000 men in Malta while he continued on to Egypt, he lost the islands to the British after his army and navy were defeated by Admiral Nelson in the Battle of the Nile.

Malta became a crown colony of the British Empire after the French were booted out in 1800. With the opening of the Suez Canal and expansion of the British Empire, Malta also became and remained an important naval base until 1979.

During World War II, Malta's value as a naval and air base was one of the factors that made it a prime Axis target for sea and air attacks. In April 1942, more than 16,000 tons of Axis bombs were dropped on the island. Axis forces were never able, however, to take the islands. By June 1943, Allied offensive actions in Europe and North Africa had ended Axis threats to Malta.

Postwar Malta required massive British reconstruction aid, part of which included the maintenance of British forces on Malta. The British government recommended that Malta diversify its economy so that it could be less economically dependent on the military for employment. Agriculture, small industry, and tourism were to be encouraged.

Political changes were also part of the development program. Internal self-government was granted and universal suffrage instituted in 1947. On September 21, 1964, Malta was granted full independence as a member of the British Commonwealth, which it retains today. The Nationalist and Labor parties became the political parties in the country.

The Nationalist Party governed from 1962 to 1971 and emphasized diversification of the economy. The Labor Party won the general election in 1971 and also sought to diversify the economy, so that Malta would not have to depend on the presence of a foreign military base (British and NATO) for economic survival. Under the Labor Party, some businesses were nationalized, a factor that may have contributed to ending their 16-year period of rule in 1987.

On May 9, 1987, the Nationalist Party was again voted into power, this time mainly on a platform of neutrality in foreign affairs, stronger law and order, and economic liberalization.

Both Labor and Nationalist administrations emphasized three economic sectors: industry (mainly textiles), agriculture, and tourism. In the 1980s, tourism skyrocketed, with almost a million foreign visitors expected during the last years of the decade—that's almost three times the population of the country.

POPULATION, PEOPLE, AND CULTURE

Population

Malta and Gozo have a population of 343,334 crammed into a scant 122 square miles (316 square km), thus more than 2,800 people per square mile. That makes the Maltese islands one of the most densely populated countries in the world. The population is expected to increase to 353,000 by 1990 and 370,000 by the year 2000.

The largest towns in the country include Valletta (9,263) and the adjoining communities of Birkirkara (20,300), Qormi (18,413), Hamrun (13,651), and Sliema (13,650). The island of Gozo has a total population of 25,112. Comino is inhabited by one family.

Relatively slow economic development in Malta has prompted the emigration of many Maltese to Australia, Great Britain, the United States, and Canada. Over 300,000 Maltese are estimated to have emigrated—almost as much as the total remaining population of the country.

People and Culture

The Maltese are a composite people who physically resemble most other peoples of the Mediterranean—Italians, Greeks, Spanish and others. Since they are predominantly Roman Catholic, culturally they are probably more similar to Italians than any other culture or nationality. This is particularly apparent in their Catholic-oriented *festas*, or religious festivals, and the preponderance of Italian-style classical and baroque architecture. In general, however, the Maltese are distinguished from European culture by their language, a Semitic language with Arabic roots that is the only one written in Latin script.

National and Religious Holidays

Some of the most colorful days to visit Malta are the holidays, especially

January 1
    New Year's Day.
February 10
    Feast of St. Paul's Shipwreck. St. Paul the Apostle's shipwreck on Malta in A.D.. 60 is regarded as the year Christianity was introduced to the Maltese. St Paul is venerated by some Maltese as "Father" of the nation.
February 12 to 16
    Carnival Days. The Maltese equivalent of Mardi Gras, Carnival is celebrated with parades of floats and people in costume. The main events are held in Valletta and Victoria (Gozo), but there are festivities held throughout the country.
February 21
    The Malta International Marathon.
March 19
    St. Joseph's Day. A feast day celebrated in Rabat in central Malta.

Late March/Early April
    Holy Week celebrations:
        Maundy Thursday. Evening religious celebrations
        commemorating the institution of the Holy Eucharist.
        Parishioners pay homage to the Blessed Sacrament at
        specially decorated altars set up in each church throughout
        the country.
        Good Friday. In fourteen towns and villages church
        services followed by pageants or parades of people in biblical
        costume re-enacting Old Testament scenes. Nine life-sized
        statues from scenes depicting the passion and death of Jesus
        Christ are carried through the streets.
        Easter Sunday. Early morning processions with the
        statue of the Risen Christ are held in various towns and
        villages. It is customary for Maltese children to have their
        figolla blessed by the "Risen Christ" during the procession.
        The *figolla* is a special Easter sweet—a pastry filled with
        marzipan and decorated with colored icing. It's often made
        in the shape of a lamb or a basket.
May 1
        Workers' Day. Feast of St. Joseph the Worker (equivalent of
        May Day in many other countries).
June 29
        Imnarja (or **Mnarja**). Feast of St Peter and St. Paul. This is
        one of the biggest festivals of the year in Malta. Tradition-
        ally, it is a harvest festival centered around the wooded park
        of Buskett near Mdina and celebrated with folk music
        competitions and a fried rabbit picnic. Horse and donkey
        races are also held.
May to September
        The Festi Season. Each town and village has a patron saint,
        whom they commemorate for five days each year with a huge
        feast, church services, marching bands, and fireworks.
        Streets, homes, and churches are specially decorated. The
        climax of each *festa*, usually on a Sunday, is a procession with
        a life-sized statue of the saint carried through the streets.
June to September
        The Valletta Yacht Club organizes a series of regattas
        throughout the summer and into the beginning of the fall.
July 11
        Arts Festival. A fortnight of cultural activities at San Anton
        Gardens.
August 15
        The Assumption. Also known as the Santa Marija feast, it is

celebrated annually at Attard, Dingli, Ghaxaq, Gudja, Mgarr, Mosta, Mqabba, and Qrendi in Malta; and at Victoria in Gozo.

September 8

Our Lady of Victories. A commemoration of the lifting of the three great sieges of Maltese history—1565 against the Turks, 1800 against the French, and 1943 against the Axis powers. A regatta is held in the Grand Harbor.

September 21

Independence Day. Celebration of independence from Great Britain.

December 8

The Immaculate Conception. A feast day celebrated at Cospicua.

December 13

Republic Day. The day Malta was declared a republic in 1974.

December 25

Christmas Day.

THE TRAVELER IN MALTA

Information

Tourist Offices

The National Tourism Organization (NTO) is the principal tourism organization and source of tourism-related information in Malta. Their main office (tel. 22-44-44 and 22-82-82) is on Harper Lane in Floriana, which is adjacent to Valletta. Other NTO offices in Malta are at 1 City Gate Arcade, Valletta (tel. 22-77-47) and Mgarr Harbour, Gozo (tel. 55-33-43).

There are also NTO offices in the following countries:

France
Office de Tourisme de Malte, 82 Rue Vaneau, Paris 75007 (tel. 549-1533).

West Germany
Fremdenverkehrsamt Malta, Schillerstrasse 30-40, D-6000 Frankfurt-am-Main 1 (tel. 28-58-90).

United Kingdom
Malta National Tourist Office, College House, 2nd floor, Suite 207, Wrights Lane, Kensington, London W8 5SH (tel. 938-1140).

In other countries, NTO information can be obtained from Maltese embassies and consulates:

Australia
Malta High Commission, 261, La Perouse Street, Red Hill, Canberra A.C.T. 2603 (tel. 95-15-86 and 95-16-45). Consulate, Mirvae Trust Building, 185 Elizabeth Street, Suite 713, Sydney, New South Wales 2000 (tel. 264-2874).

Canada
Malta Consulate, 3323 Dundas Street West, Toronto, Ontario (tel. 416-767-4902).

Italy
Embassy of Malta, 12, Lungotevere Marzio 00186 Rome (tel. 65-99-47).

Switzerland
Malta Consulate, 2, Parc Chateau Banquet 1202 Geneva (tel. 31-05-08).

United States
Malta Consulate, 249 East Street, New York, NY 10016 (212-725-2345). Embassy of Malta, 2017 Connecticut Avenue N.W., Washington, D.C. 20008 (tel. 202-462-3611).

The NTO publishes and distributes a variety of printed materials about Malta. Its comprehensive lists of hotels, tourist complexes, guesthouses, self-catering apartments, holiday flats, and villas are especially useful. These lists provide basic information on virtually every form of accommodation in Malta, Gozo, and Comino.

A pocket-sized biweekly publication called *What's On in Malta and Gozo* is a great source of information about all tourist-related activities, places, and things of interest in Malta and Gozo. It's published by the Publications Division of Promotion Services Ltd. and is available at most bookstores, newsstands, and hotel gift shops in Malta for 15 cents (Maltese).

Maps

An excellent map of Malta and Gozo at a scale of 1 cm to 460 m is published by Intermap (Enschede, The Netherlands) and distributed throughout the islands by Miller Distributors, Ltd., of Valletta. In addition to the main map of the islands, there are smaller maps covering bus routes and car ferry lines, historical sites, and individual town plans of Sliema, Valletta, Victoria, Mdina, and St. Paul's Bay.

A good map of Valletta with 68 map points indicated is published by the Mid-Med Bank and distributed for free at most branches.

A few basic maps are also included in the publication *What's On in Malta and Gozo* (see above).

Books

The Maltese islands, especially their history, have been covered in many books, but most of these were published in Great Britain and Malta and can be difficult to find in North America. The best selections of books on Malta and Gozo can be found in the islands' several bookstores.

There are almost no books, other than a few outdated guidebooks, that offer general introductions to the islands. The *Malta Blue Guide*, edited by Peter McGregor Eadie (London: Ernest Benn Limited,1979 and New York: Rand McNally & Company,1979) is a fair introduction to Malta and Gozo. It emphasizes details of most of the islands' historical sites. Christopher Kinimonth's *The Travellers' Guide to Malta & Gozo* (London: Jonathan Cape, 1981) is similarly organized, but it also offers more than 10 possible routes that can be followed by bus or car (or even by foot).

For a general history of Malta, *The Story of Malta*, by Brian Blouet (Valletta, Malta: Progress Press Company, 1987), is a good overview beginning from about 5000 B.C. up to 1979. About half the book covers the medieval period and Malta under the Knights of the Order of St. John, including a fairly lengthy section on the Great Siege of Malta in 1565. Unlike most writers on the siege, Blouet attempts to more closely examine the Turkish side of the battles.

Malta's prehistoric periods are described in greater detail in *The Prehistoric Antiquities of the Maltese Islands*, by J. D. Evans (London: Athlone Press, 1971).

For the medieval period, consult *Approaches to Medieval Malta* by Anthony Luttrell (London: The British School at Rome, 1975). Another good source is *Medieval Malta: Studies on Malta Before the Knights*, a series of studies edited by Luttrell in 1975.

The Knights of the Order of St. John and the Great Siege of Malta have been examined in many books. One of the most readable, albeit definitely slanted in favor of the Knights, is Ernle Bradford's *The Great Siege: Malta 1565* (London: Penguin Books, 1976).

Although not obtainable outside of Malta, the best source of information about life in Malta after the Great Siege and under the rule of the Knights is the official archives of the Order of St. John. The catalogue alone to these archives is seventeen volumes thick; both catalogue and archives are held by the National Library in Valletta. Unfortunately, there doesn't seem to be much available today that covers only this period of Maltese history; again, refer to Blouet's *The Story of Malta*.

For the British period, there are a variety of mostly British-based studies and articles on specific topics, but no general surveys or reviews of the British presence in Malta. Most of these studies are primarily of academic interest—*Maltese Legal History, Malta 1813–1914: A Study in Constitutional and Strategic Development*, and other political histories.

The National Library of Malta on Old Treasury Street in Valletta (tel. 22-65-85) is the country's biggest public library and repository of anything and everything related to the Maltese islands. Between October 1 and June 15, the library is open Monday, Tuesday, Thursday, and Friday from 8.15 A.M. to 1 P.M. and 1.45 to 5.45 P.M.; Saturday from 8.15 A.M. to 1.15 P.M. The rest of the year it's open the same days from 8.15 A.M. to 1.15 P.M.

Contemporary statistical information and listings covering everything from "Malta dairy products" and the Malta Blood Bank to "Notable Dates in Maltese History" and "Early Maltese Priests in Australia" are packed into *The Malta Year Book*, which is published annually by De La Salle Brothers Publications, St. Benild's School, Sliema, Malta.

Foreign Embassies, Consulates, and High Commissions

The following are some of the diplomatic missions in Malta:

- Commonwealth of Australia—High Commission, Airways House, Gaiety Lane (tel. 33-82-01)
- Great Britain—High Commission, 7 St. Anne Street, Floriana (tel. 23-31-34)
- Embassy of France, Villa Seminia, 12 Sir Temi Zammit Street, Ta'Xbiex (tel. 33-11-07)
- Embassy of the Federal Republic of Germany, Il-Pjazzetta Building, Entrance B, 1st floor, Tower Road, Sliema (tel. 33-65-31)
- Embassy of Italy, 5 Vilhena Street, Floriana (tel. 23-31-57)
- Sovereign Military Hospitaller Order of St. John of Jerusalem, of Rhodes and of Malta, St. John's Cavalier, Valletta (tel. 22-36-70)
- Embassy of the Republic of Tunisia, Villa "La Grotte Aux Pigeons," Qormi Road, Attard (tel. 49-88-53)

Money and Banks

Foreign currency, travelers' checks, and in some cases postal checks can be exchanged or cashed at most branches of Malta's two main banks—the Mid-Med Bank and the Bank of Valletta. Both banks have 24-hour, seven days a week, foreign exchange bureaus at the Luqa international airport.

The Bank of Valletta has two foreign exchange bureaus that operate after hours—in Valletta on Republic Street Monday to Saturday in the afternoons; and in Sliema on the Strand the same days, but 3 to 6 P.M. in the winter and 4 to 7 P.M. in the summer.

Exchange services are offered the same hours and days in the summer at the following branches: South Street, Valletta; Tagliaferro Centre, Sliema; Birzebbugia; Bugibba; Mellieha; St. Paul's Bay; and St. Julian's.

Service is available in Gozo at Victoria It-Tokk all year Monday through Saturday from 10 A.M. to 12.30 P.M. and, in the summer, from 3 to 6 P.M.

Foreign exchange services, including cash advances from VISA, MasterCard, Excess, and Eurocheque, are available at all other Bank of Valletta branches throughout the country during normal banking hours, which are

From October 1 to June 14
Monday to Friday, 8.30 A.M. to 12.30 P.M.
Saturday, 8.30 A.M. to noon

From June 15 to September 30
Monday to Friday, 8 A.M. to noon
Saturday, 8 A.M. to 11.30 A.M.

Branches and representative agencies of both banks are in almost every community in Malta. The above hours are for both banks.

The Mid-Med Bank special foreign exchange bureaus are located in most of the same communities and open approximately the same hours as the Bank of Valletta bureaus.

American Express has financial (foreign exchange), travel, and mail services available through A.& V. Brockdorff, Ltd., at 14 Zachary Street in Valletta (tel. 23-21-41).

Postal and Telephone Services

The main post office is housed in the Auberge d'Italie on Merchants Street in Valletta and is open in the winter (October 1 to June 15) Monday to Saturday 8 A.M. to 6.30 P.M.; the rest of the year the same days from 7.30 A.M. to 6 P.M. Branch offices located throughout the country are open all year round Monday to Saturday from 7.30 A.M. to 12.45 P.M. Smaller post offices located in several villages in Malta and Gozo are open Monday to Friday from 8 A.M. to 1 P.M. and 4 to 6 P.M. and Saturday 8 A.M. to 1 P.M. all year.

In my personal experience, mail between Malta and the United States can take two or more weeks.

Malta has an efficient telephone system that is well connected to international lines. Overseas calls can be made easily from private lines or public telephone offices. The main office is in St. Julian's and is open twenty-four hours a day. The airport office is open daily, including Sundays and public holidays from 7 A.M. to 7 P.M. There are branch offices in Valletta, Sliema, Qawra, Gozo, and Marsalforn (police station).

Costs, Accommodations, and Food

The cost of a visit to Malta is at the low end, budget-wise, of European tourism, especially if you come on one of the many package deals offered from Great Britain, France, and West Germany. Without factoring in air or ferry fares, a safe estimate would be about $20 per day for budget travelers. If you wish to stay in youth hostels or plan to split expenses with other travelers, this figure could be even lower.

For a country that is smaller than West Berlin or Rhode Island (the smallest U.S. state), the Maltese islands have a remarkable variety of accommodations. According to the National Tourism Organization, the following types of tourist accommodations are available:

Hotels	Number of establishments	Number of beds
Deluxe	5	1,396
First Class A	13	4,499
First Class B	11	2,835
Second Class A	27	3,240
Second Class B	33	2,219
Third Class	27	1,298
Fourth Class	7	246
Unclassified	1	408
Tourist Complexes		
First Class	13	5,377
Second Class	13	3,169
Third Class	18	2,710
Unclassified	1	255
Guesthouses		
First Class	24	551
Second Class	38	767
Hostels	3	180
Self-Catering		8,311

For the most current information available on accommodations in

Malta, contact the National Tourism Organization or a Maltese Consulate for a copy of the NTO's comprehensive accommodation lists.

Food and Drink

Most food served in Maltese restaurants is a combination of British and Italian. Obtaining typical Maltese dishes, however, can be difficult. These usually include the following:

Bragioli, a deep-fried dish of bacon, eggs, onions, and breadcrumbs wrapped in thin slices of steak.

Gbejna, goat cheese. A popular version made in Gozo and known as Gozitan pepper cheese is worth trying; it's a sharp, dry cheese covered with pepper, quite pungent.

Minestra, a thick minestrone-like vegetable soup that is also sometimes made with pork and beans and called *kawlata*.

Prinjolata, a decadent concoction of sponge cakes, cream, almonds, chocolate, and cherries that's popular during Carnival.

Timpana, somewhat equivalent to baked macaroni, but containing a greater mix of ingredients and a flaky pastry-like casing. It can be filled with a combination of ricotta cheese, eggplant, eggs, onions, tomato sauce, and/or meat.

Torta tal-Lampuka. The lampuka fish is commonly found in Maltese waters and specially prepared by first frying and then baking the fish in a pastry casing filled with onions, olives, tomatoes, and parsley.

Most soft drinks are available in Malta; one of the most popular ones is the locally produced Kinnie, a bittersweet orange drink. Malta also produces several types of beer, including Cisk Lager, and a good variety of wines. The Gozitan wines are supposedly stronger than the wines of Malta.

Getting There

Visas

Visas are unnecessary for citizens of the United States, most European countries and Commonwealth countries, including Great Britain, Canada, and Australia.

By Air

Air Malta flies between Malta and Amsterdam, Brussels, Cairo,

Catania (Sicily), Copenhagen, Frankfurt, Geneva, London, Lyon (France), Munich, Palermo (Sicily), Paris, Rome, Tripoli (Libya), and Zürich.

Other airlines operating in Malta include

Aeroflot	Conakry (Guinea), Dakar (Senegal), and Moscow
Air Europe Limited	London and Manchester
Alitalia	Palermo (Sicily) and Rome
Austrian Airlines	Vienna
Balkan Bulgarian Airlines	Harare (Zimbabwe), Lagos (Nigeria), and Sofia (Bulgaria)
British Islands Airways PLC	London and Manchester
Czechoslovak Airlines	Luxembourg and Prague
Libyan Arab Airlines	Tripoli
Lufthansa	Frankfurt
Monarch Airlines	London
Swissair	Zürich
Tunisavia	Sfax and Tunis

Package deals and discount charter flights to Malta are offered in much of Western Europe, especially in Great Britain, which sends over half a million tourists to the Maltese islands every year.

By Sea

Although most of Malta's visitors don't arrive by sea, there are regular ferry connections with Sicily and Naples on Tirrenia Lines. From Naples, a boat departs every Thursday at 8.30 P.M. and arrives in Valletta at 9.30 P.M. Friday; one-way fares range from $175 with private bath to $135 without bath (plus $14 tax). From Sicily boats depart Catania and Syracuse on Tuesday, Friday and Sunday at 1 P.M. and 4.30 P.M. respectively and arrive in Valletta at 9.30 P.M.; one-way fare is about $70 (plus $14 tax).

Hydrofoil service is available between Sicily and Malta, but the latest schedule and fare information was unavailable at the time of writing.

In the United States, for bookings and further information, contact Extra Value Travel, 683 South Collier Boulevard, Marco Island, Florida 33937 (tel. 813-394-3384). In Naples, contact Tirrenia Navigazione, Rione Sirignano No. 2, P. O. Box 438, 80121, Naples, Italy (tel. 081-72-01-11).

Getting Around the Maltese Islands

By Bus

Malta and Gozo have an extensive bus system to almost all parts of the islands. All Malta buses begin and end their journeys in Valletta at the City Gate around the Triton Fountain. They run every 5 to 30 minutes until 9.30 P.M. (to the smaller villages) and 11 P.M. (to the larger towns). Information on the latest bus route listings and schedule changes are posted at the gate.

Buses on Gozo begin and end their journeys in the main square in Victoria, the capital city. Almost every village on the island is covered by the bus service.

By Car

Renting a car in Malta isn't really necessary, because buses run frequently throughout the islands. However, there are several agencies, including Avis, Budget, Hertz, and various European agencies. Shop around because rates can vary from agency to agency.

Avis has six offices in Malta, including an office in Msida at 50 Msida Sea Front (tel. 62-66-40) and in St. Julian's at the Hilton (tel. 33-68-04). Their most inexpensive car is similar to a Ford Fiesta and rents for Lm 11 ($30) per day with unlimited miles.

Budget has an office in Marsa on Zimelli Street in the Mexico Building (tel. 62-71-11). They rent a Ford Fiesta or similar car for a daily rate of Lm 7.50 ($21) for one to two days, Lm 6.25 ($17.50) daily for three to six days, and $142.85 for a week.

Hertz has offices on Gozo at the Calypso Hotel, at the airport, and in Gzira at the United Garage on Gzira Road. The telephone number 31-46-37 is the same for all three offices. They rent an Opel Corsa with unlimited mileage for Lm 7 ($20) per day.

By Taxi

Taxis are available 24 hours a day at government-set rates determined by meters. No squabbling over fares is necessary.

By Boat

There are several ferries daily from Cirkewwa and Marfa at the northern tip of Malta to Mgarr in Gozo. Buses 45 and 48 run from the City Gate in Valletta to these departure points. The trip across the channel to Gozo takes about an hour. Another car ferry runs less frequently (usually only once daily) from the Sa Maison landing in Marsamxett Harbor between Valletta and the neighboring community of Msida.

The Comino Hotel on Comino island offers daily boat service between Cirkewwa (Malta), Comino, and Mgarr (Gozo) several times daily starting at 6:30 A.M. from Gozo and running first to Comino and then Cirkewwa. Return fares start at Lm 1 and Lm 1.50 (after 6 P.M.).

Various boat companies offer day cruises around the islands from the Sliema Marina. Captain Morgan's Cruises has grand boat tours around the islands, or just to Comino, that often include lunch.

ADVENTURES IN MALTA

Malta is one of the world's most densely populated countries, which means there is little space, if any, for getting off the beaten track. There are really no places and activities in the Maltese islands that could really be considered adventurous compared to, for example, exploring the Sahara in Algeria or riding in a camel caravan in Morocco. However, there are a few activities and places that are considered at least miniadventures.

The farthest off the beaten track you can get in Malta is underwater—by scuba diving or snorkeling. Equipment, lessons, and dive trips can be arranged at any of several water sports centers located on Malta, Gozo, and Comino.

The dive center at the Comino Hotel on Comino island is extremely popular during the high season (summer); it's not unusual for the hotel and dive center to be booked up almost a year in advance. If you have brought your own equipment, a few dive sites around Comino island are accessible from the shore: the Blue Lagoon, San Niklaw bay, and Santa Marija bay; these are, perhaps, the best sites in the country.

Gozo's prime diving sites are accessible from the bays along its northern coast. The Calypso Diving Centre at Marsalforn can give you information about the sites and arrange for equipment rental and transportation.

Other water sports centers on the islands include

- The Banis Water Sports Facilities, 12 Spinola Beach, St. Julian's (near the Cavalieri Hotel; tel. 33-98-31)
- The Beach Haven, Xemxija Hill, St. Paul's Bay (tel. 47-36-82)
- The Bonett Diving Centre, 55 Tower Road, Sliema (tel. 33-89-38)
- Borg Ski School, Golden Bay (tel. 47-25-98)
- Divewise Services Ltd. c/o Dragonara Palace, St Julian's (tel. 33-64-41)
- Dive Systems, 48 Gzira Road, Gzira (tel. 31-71-37)

- Il-Fekruna Water Sports Centre, Shipwreck Promenade, Xemxija, St. Paul's Bay (tel. 47-30-02 and 33-19-17)
- Maltaqua Diving School, Mosta Road, St. Paul's Bay (tel. 47-18-73)
- Mellieha Bay Hotel, Water Sports Centre, Mellieha Bay (tel. 47-38-41)
- Mel Divers, c/o Melovan Galea, Seabank Complex, Mellieha Bay (tel. 47-31-16)
- Ramla Bay Hotel, Water Sports Centre, Ramla Bay (tel. 47-35-21)
- Luzzu Restaurant, Water Sports Centre, Qawra (tel. 47-39-25)
- Jerma Palace Hotel, Marsaskala, (tel. 82-32-22)

Sailing and windsurfing are possible from most of these centers. Travelers fond of walking and hiking can follow any of several footpaths and secondary roads that crisscross Malta and Gozo between villages and towns. The map of the Maltese islands published by Intermap (Enschede, The Netherlands, 1985) indicates most of the paths, roads, and topographical features of the country. To get away from Malta's population centers, head for the hillier southern half of the country. A good portion of relatively isolated countryside is accessible by foot west of Rabat.

Many walks or self-guided tours are also possible through the historical quarters of several towns and villages, parts of which have maintained basically the same architecture since the sixteenth and seventeenth centuries.

VALLETTA

Valletta is the usual starting point for most visits to the Maltese islands. Founded by Grand Master La Vallette in 1566 just after the Great Siege against the Turks in 1565, this beautiful walled capital city juts out on a promontory between the Grand Harbor and Marsamxett Harbor. It's one of the greatest existing examples of a late medieval fortified city because many of the old architectural styles have been maintained in the city's buildings, walls, and gardens.

Aside from just walking the city's streets, several of which are partially sets of steep stone steps, and enjoying the picturesque views of the harbors, the chief sights are as follows.

Mediterranean Conference Center—The Malta Experience. A relatively new international conference center at Merchant and North streets that was built over the ruins of the Hospital of the Knights, the reason for coming here is to see an audiovisual show called "The Malta Experience." Although this 45-minute show is a glorified picture of Maltese history that is too perfectly suited for tour groups, it is a good basic introduction to the people and history of Malta. You can either

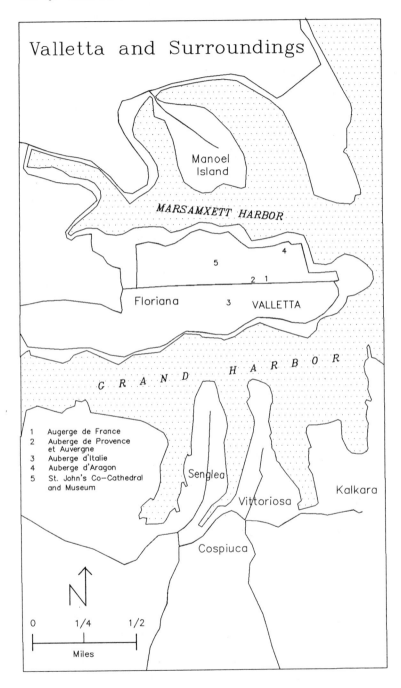

Valletta and Surroundings

Manoel Island

MARSAMXETT HARBOR

4

5

2 1

Floriana   3   VALLETTA

GRAND HARBOR

1 Auberge de France
2 Auberge de Provence
   et Auvergne
3 Auberge d'Italie
4 Auberge d'Aragon
5 St. John's Co—Cathedral
   and Museum

Senglea

Vittoriosa   Kalkara

Cospiuca

N

0   1/4   1/2

Miles

walk (15 minutes) or take Bus 98 from the City Gate bus terminus. Shows are Monday to Friday hourly from 11 A.M. to 3 P.M. and Saturday at 11 A.M. and noon.

The War Museum. Follow the map to the War Museum, which is housed in part of Fort St. Elmo. The Fort earned an important place in Maltese history when it successfully withstood the brunt of Turkish attacks in the Great Siege of 1565. It was renovated, fortified, and expanded several times since then. The museum houses relics from Malta's second "siege"—Axis bombardments of the country during World War II. Over 16,000 tons of bombs were dropped on Malta during the war. Hours are October 10 to June 14 Monday to Sunday 8.30 A.M. to 1 P.M. and 2 to 4 P.M., June 15 to September 30 Monday to Sunday 8.30 A.M. to 1.30 P.M.

Manoel Theater. Built in 1732 on Old Theatre Street between Old Bakery and Old Mint streets, this is one of Europe's oldest functioning theaters. The theater is decorated with a paneled ceiling and a spectacular crystal chandelier surrounded by forty-five gilded seating boxes. A variety of performances are presented here—recitals, orchestral concerts, ballet, opera, and plays—by local and internationally renowned performers and groups. These have included Yehudi Menuhin, Segovia, Rostropovitch, Ashkenazy, the Berlin State Opera Ballet, and the Bolshoi Ballet. Guided tours are held Monday to Friday at 10.30 and 11.30 A.M.

Palace of the Grand Masters and Armory. Built in 1569 by Eustachio del Monte, nephew of the Grand Master, the palace is a beautiful example of late sixteenth- and seventeenth-century architecture. Although it was raided by Napoleon on his way to Egypt, many of the paintings and suits of armor remain to this day. The central corridor is decorated with a well-preserved painted ceiling. Guided tours are offered of the palace's various rooms, including the state apartments. The palace also houses the Maltese House of Representatives. Hours are Monday to Saturday from 9 A.M. to 1 P.M. It's in the heart of Valletta on St. George's Square across from the Italian and Libyan cultural centers.

The Malta Library. Next to the Palace of the Grand Master on Republic Square, the Malta Library is the principal repository of documents, books and records on everything related to Maltese history. There are over 10,000 manuscripts and 300,000 books, including documents signed by Henry VIII in which he declared himself head of the Church of England. Hours are Monday to Friday 8 A.M. to 1 P.M. and 2 to 5.45 P.M., Saturday 8 A.M. to 1.15 P.M., closed Wednesdays.

St. John's Co-Cathedral and Museum. Continuing southwest on Republic Street, the next notable sight is St. John's Co-Cathedral and Museum, which is on Great Siege Square. Constructed by architect G. Cassar between 1573 and 1577, this was the most important cathedral in Malta for the Order of the Knights of St. John. Until the knights were expelled from Malta in 1798, almost every Grand Master embellished some aspect of the cathedral before his death and entombment here. All knights who were promoted by the order were also required to add something to the cathedral.

On the outside façade, some of the most noteworthy features include an eight-pointed Maltese Cross and a three-faced clock. The cross is the symbol of the Knights of St. John of Jerusalem. The three faces of the clock show the hour, the day of the month, and the day of the week.

Inside, the cathedral consists of a single nave with six chapels and bays on each side. Along the nave walls were Flemish tapestries portraying scenes from paintings by Poussin and Rubens, which are in the church museum every month except June, when they are hung in the church. The stone vaults were painted in the seventeenth century by Mattia Preti, who decorated many of Malta's churches, with eighteen scenes from the life of St. John the Baptist.

Each of the chapels was reserved for a *langue* of the order. The knights were grouped according to their region of origin, thus *langue* or literally language.

As you enter from the front, one of the most important bays is the third on the right, which is also called the Oratory of St. John. Caravaggio painted 'The Beheading of St. John," which sits above the altar in the oratory (now part of the cathedral museum); this is considered by some Maltese as the most important painting in the country. This bay is also the entrance to the church museum.

The crypt is worth visiting; it contains the lavishly decorated tombs of the first twelve grand masters (except for Didier de Saint Jaille).

Another impressive feature that you'll notice the moment you enter the church is the floor. Over 400 slabs, each composed of colorful marble pieces, were laid in honor of the knights. The pieces have been arranged in pictures that include angels, musical instruments, coats-of-arms, skeletons, and crowns.

Hours are Monday to Saturday 9 A.M. to 1 P.M. and 3 to 5.30 P.M. and Sunday 9 A.M. to 1.30 P.M.

National Museum of Archaeology. Housed in the former Auberge de Provence building on Republic Street, the museum has an extensive collection of relics dating from Malta's prehistoric to Roman periods. The prehistoric collections show the development of different pottery styles among Malta's first settlers. Pottery has been one of the main sources of knowledge about Malta's early history. Tools and various sculptures are also exhibited. Hours are 8.15 A.M. to 5 P.M. between October 1 and June 15 and 7.45 A.M. to 2 P.M. the rest of the year.

National Museum of Fine Arts. The National Museum of Fine Arts is in a historic building known as the Admiralty House. It contains paintings from the fourteenth century to the present, including works by Mattia Preti, Antoine de Favray, and Antonio Sciortino. There are also exhibits illustrating the various roles of the Knights of the Order of St. John—ship models, silver pieces for the hospitals (patients were once served meals on silver plates), church vestments, suits of armor, and coins of the order. Hours are 8.15 A.M. to 5 P.M. between October 1 and June 15 and 7.45 A.M. to 2 P.M. the rest of the year.

Upper Barracca Gardens. Located at the southwestern corner of Valletta, the gardens overlook the Grand Harbor and offer an impressive view of the Three Cities across the harbor. The gardens were created by an eighteenth-century knight as a gift to Valletta and a retreat for knightly strolls.

AROUND VALLETTA

Adjacent to and heading inland from Valletta is the suburb of Floriana. When Italian military engineer Paolo Floriani originally designed and constructed it, Floriana was meant to protect Valletta from attack by land. Its walls and related fortifications were never put to the test.

Today, Floriana's architectural highlights include the two-towered St. Publius church built in the eighteenth century and named for Malta's first bishop, and the Porte des Bombs—literally Gate of the Bombs—a stately double arched entrance on the western side of the suburb.

The Three Cities—Vittoriosa, Senglea, and Cospicua

Across the Grand Harbor from Valletta and Floriana is a set of suburbs or neighborhoods known collectively as the "three cities." Historically, Malta's dockyards and dry-docks have been concentrated along the shores of Dockyard Creek on the parallel peninsulas of Vittoriosa and Senglea. Cospicua is between these two peninsulas at the end of Dockyard Creek and has long been a popular residential area for the dockworkers. Of the three, Vittoriosa survived the battles and bombings of Malta with the least damage, so there's more to see.

Buses from Valletta can leave you at Vittoriosa Square, which is a good starting point from which to visit the area. On one side of the square is the small Church of St. Joseph and its interior Chapel of St. Catherine, which is noteworthy mainly for its knightly relics—a hat and sword that belonged to Jean de la Vallette, the grand master who defended Malta against the Turks in the Great Siege of 1565.

Toward the west side of the same block is the Church of St. Lawrence, which served as the main church of the order before the Co-Cathedral of St. John in Valletta was completed in 1577. Although its dome was bombed and destroyed in World War II, most of the beautiful pink marble columns survived. Most of the present church dates back to its reconstruction in 1691.

Back in Vittoriosa Square, head for Britannic Street at approximately the northeast corner. Five of the Knights' first auberges (inns divided by langue or language region of origin) were situated here. Today, the first one you see is on your left is the Auberge de Provence et Auvergne, which is now occupied, but marked outside by a plaque. Next door is the Auberge de France, the first auberge in the area. Its layout included an entrance hall and courtyard. Adjacent is the nondescript Auberge d'Aragon. Around the corner on Mistral (or Majjistral) Street, just off the square, is the Auberge d'Angleterre, which was home to the English knights until the Reformation and rise of Protestantism made the existence of Catholic English knights difficult.

At the tip of the Vittoriosa peninsula is Fort St. Angelo, which served as the headquarters of the order during the Great Siege. The fort is believed to have been built over the site of a prehistoric pagan temple. During World War II, the fort was the headquarters of the Royal Navy, which was probably why it was bombed directly by the Axis forces at least 69 times.

Senglea was heavily bombed during World War II; consequently very little of the suburb's original architecture remains. It's worth walking up to the bastions on the tip of the peninsula. Known as Isola Point, it's marked by a garden and a six-windowed lookout that's decorated with stone carvings of large eyes and ears.

Cospicua was also heavily bombed and destroyed in World War II, but its impressive walls—the Cotonera Lines—survived. Commissioned and financed by Grand Master Nicholas Cotoner in 1670, the walls and accompanying bastions were still unfinished by the time of his death in 1680.

There are frequent buses to the Three Cities from the City Gate in Valletta.

Ancient Tombs and Temples Near Valletta

South of Valletta and the 'Three Cities" in the suburb of Paola are two of Malta's most important archeological sites: the Hal Saflieni Hypogeum and the Tarxien Temple ruins.

The Hypogeum is a vast underground labyrinth of chambers, pits, and cubicles cut into the limestone at three levels. This dank, dark complex covers a total area of 8,600 square feet and dates back, at least on the first level, to about 3,000 B.C. The other levels have been dated to about the time of the Tarxien Temples (2500 to 1800 B.C.). A "Sleeping Lady" statuette discovered in the main chamber of the middle level suggests that a fertility cult once existed here. Other parts, such as pits at the bottom level, contained as many as 6,000 bodies of men, women, and children. The walls of a few rooms have spiral and hexagonal designs in red and black. Try the echo chamber, which seems to be effective only with male voices.

This complex descends to a depth of about 40 feet and was accidentally uncovered in 1902 by workers digging the foundations for houses in the neighborhood. Malta's foremost archeologist, Sir Themistocles Zammit, conducted the first excavation work and studies of the site; the mysteries of this complex have yet to be fully understood.

Zammit also worked on the excavations at the Tarxien Temples, which are in a walled garden area just down the street from the Hypogeum. There are three temples, each erected at different times with the oldest dating to about 2500 B.C. Just past the small museum on the temple grounds is the first temple and its bas-relief replicas of farm animals and a fat woman. Spiral carvings grace what are believed to be altars for animal sacrifices.

The second temple is divided into a main hall with three bays or chambers on each side. In the center of the hall is a round orange-yellow hearth where ancient fires seem to have burned, perhaps for cremations. To the right of this hearth is a small room that contains a wall with carved pictures depicting a sow suckling her litter, and bulls.

The third and oldest temple is attached to the second by what used to be a corridor. Because there is a hole in the wall of a small room in this temple, an oracle room was believed to have once existed here. More excavation work needs to be done here.

Both sites are open October 1 to June 15 Monday to Saturday from 8.15 A.M. to 5 P.M. and 8.15 A.M. to 4 P.M. on Sundays; June 16 to September 30 Monday to Saturday 7.45 to 1.30 P.M. Bus 5 comes here from the City Gate in Valletta.

INTO THE COUNTRYSIDE

Marsaxlokk

Southeast of Paola and Valletta, Marsaxlokk (pronounced Mar-sa-schlock) is a small, picturesque fishing village at the northeastern corner of Marsaxlokk bay. It was here that Dragut, an infamous Mediterranean pirate, landed his fleet to assist the Turks in their 1565 siege of Malta. No fortifications were built until the following century, so Dragut and the Turks were practically unopposed in landing here. Fort Delimara was eventually built near Delimara Point south of the village.

A good day hike is possible along the Delimara peninsula with stops at the Punic and Roman Temple of Astarte (the Phoenician goddess of fertility and sexual love) and Hera (the sister and consort of Zeus); Peter's Pool, which is renowned for deep-water rock swimming; and Delimara Point.

Back in Marsaxlokk, with the colorful fishing boats bobbing in the bay and women on the quay selling bright, multi-colored woven net bags and delicate tablecloths, photo opportunities are abundant, so bring your camera.

Marsaxlokk also has a few good fish restaurants across from the quay.

There are frequent buses from the City Gate in Valletta to Marsaxlokk (No. 27, via Zejtun). Bus 26 goes only as far as Zejtun, but you can easily change to a bus for Marsaxlokk.

The Blue Grotto and Ghar Lapsi

Along the southern coast of Malta are the beautiful coastal sites of the Blue Grotto and Ghar Lapsi. The Blue Grotto is at the end of the road from the village of Zurrieq (noted for the festa of St. Catherine at the end of June). It is exactly as its name suggest—a grotto of dark blue water that changes shades with the position of the sun. Fishermen line their boats up in the grotto to take you for about a half-hour excursion through caves near the grotto. The sun's rays seem to brighten up the caves best before 11 A.M., which is good for photographers keen on capturing on film the colorful limestone and coral walls of the caves.

Ghar Lapsi is a tiny fishing village and beach approximately west of the Blue Grotto. The pools surrounded by rocks make wonderful, and occasionally popular, swimming holes.

Buses from Valletta (Nos. 32, 33, and 34) to the Blue Grotto go only as far as Zurrieq. For the remaining 1 1/4 miles to the grotto, you have to walk or take a taxi. For Ghar Lapsi, take a bus from Valletta to Siggiewi (No. 89) and then No. 94 (summer only) to Ghar Lapsi; the rest of the year, you'll have to walk.

Rabat and Mdina

Rabat and Mdina are old charming towns connected to each other by the Howard Gardens about 11 km (7 miles) from Valletta. Mdina is a tiny walled citadel of small palaces, bastions, and a partial moat that is home to about 400 inhabitants. Some of the current residents include several of Malta's old aristocratic families.

This was Malta's first capital and bishopric. St. Publius, Malta's first bishop, was a Roman governor here before being converted to Christianity by St. Paul; the latter stayed in Malta for three months following his shipwreck and is credited with bringing Christianity to Malta.

There are two main entrance gates to Mdina: near the southwest corner is the Greek's Gate and toward the southeast corner is Mdina Gate, the main entrance. Crossing the moat bridge and entering through the Mdina Gate, on your left is the sixteenth-century Torre delle Standardo (Tower of the Standard). It was originally the gatehouse, but today it is the local police station. Directly across from the Torre is the Vilhena Palace and Natural History Museum. Commissioned by eighteenth-century Grand Master Vilhena and built by Giovanni Barbara, it was designed in typical French architectural style, with several courtyards. Today it houses the Natural History Museum with exhibits on Malta's geology, birds, and insects. Facing the palace are the Nunnery and Chapel of St. Benedict.

The palace and museum are open October 1 to June 15 Monday to Saturday from 8.15 A.M. to 5 P.M. and 8.15 A.M. to 4 P.M. on Sundays; June 16 to September 30 Monday to Saturday 7.45 A.M. to 1.30 P.M.

Returning to the police station (Torre delle Standardo), follow Villegaignon Street, the main thoroughfare in Mdina, north through the heart of town. On the left is Casa Inguanez, home of Malta's oldest aristocratic family. The main entrance door on Mesquita Street, the next one up on your left, is a favorite tour stop because of its impressive brass Neptune door knockers.

Continuing along Villegaignon Street past Mesquita Street, on the right is the Testaferrata Palace, which supposedly has a fine art collection, but it's closed to the public.

St. Paul's Square is just past the Palace and dominated on the east side by St. Paul's Cathedral (Co-Cathedral with St. John's of Valletta). The first church on this spot was built in the thirteenth century, but most of the present cathedral was built by Lorenzo Gafà between 1697 and 1702. The façade is a typical baroque balance of vertical and horizontal lines and designs and is topped by an impressive octagonal dome.

Interior details are equally impressive—carefully designed marble slabs cover floor tombs of Malta's bishops and monsignors, a fresco depicting "The shipwreck of St. Paul" in the apse, and a fine silver cross to the left of the apse that was brought by the knights from Rhodes.

Adjacent to the cathedral is the Cathedral Museum with a variety of articles on display that had been saved from the church's treasury, including an extensive coin collection from Carthage almost to the present, the bishop's carriage, vestments, a collection of illuminated choir books dating from the eleventh century, painting from various sixteenth- to eighteenth-century European schools, and engravings from Rembrandt, Van Dyck, Goya, and other artists.

Hours for the museum are October to May, Monday to Saturday from 9 A.M. to 1 P.M. and 1.30 to 4.30 P.M. and the same days the rest of the year but open from 9 A.M. to 1 P.M. and 1.30 to 5 P.M.; always closed on Sundays.

Back on Villegaignon Street, the house at the corner of Holy Cross Street is the Palazzo Santa Sophia, which is supposedly the oldest house in Mdina. On the next block past St. Sophia and St. Roque streets are the Church of the Annunciation (on the left) and the Church of St. Roque. The former's bells attained notoriety in 1798 when they were rung to summon people from the countryside into town to protest French plans to confiscate and sell the church's tapestries.

Toward the end of Villegaignon Street on the right is the Palazzo Fallon, also known as the Norman House. The lower floor was built in the fourteenth and fifteenth centuries and still retains a sense of medieval Malta.

At the end of Villegaignon Street is a bastion esplanade that offers a panoramic view of the surrounding countryside. Valletta is visible in the distance and the great dome of the church of Mosta sits a few miles away.

Rabat is the adjacent, semimodern village "suburb" of Mdina. Just outside Mdina Gate are the main bus terminus and Howard Gardens. At the western edge of the gardens is a museum and restored Roman villa where Roman, Greek, and Carthaginian tomb artifacts and a few interesting mosaic panels are displayed.

In front of the museum and leading to the right is St. Paul Street. Follow this to St. Paul's Church and Grotto; this sixteenth-century edifice is a noteworthy predecessor to St. John's in Valletta. St. Paul supposedly resided in a grotto just outside the church; Grand Master di Pino placed a statue of St. Paul in the grotto.

Catacombs (St. Paul and St. Agatha) down the street from the church and grotto are worth a quick visit; follow the signs. A Christian community is believed to have resided in the area in the fourth and fifth centuries and held various feasts and celebrations in the catacombs. The St. Paul's catacombs form a multilevel labyrinth of chambers, crypts, and graves connected by narrow passageways and staircases cut into the rock. The custom of catacomb burials is believed to have been adopted from Jews from Palestine who settled in Rome. The Jews objected to the Roman practice of cremation.

Bus 80 departs Valletta for Rabat and Mdina every 10 minutes.

Near Rabat

South of Rabat are the Verdala Palace, Buskett Gardens, the village of Dingli, and the imposing Dingli cliffs. To the northeast and visible from Mdina is the small town of Mosta and its famous parish church.

Verdala Palace is a square castle surrounded by a moat and pine forest just east of the road between Buskett Gardens and Rabat. Built in 1586 as a summer residence for the Grand Master and Cardinal de Verdalle, it is now used as an official guesthouse. It isn't open to the public, but permission to enter may sometimes be obtained from the Ministry of Works in Valletta.

Nestled in a small valley, Buskett Gardens is Malta's largest green area, thus a popular area for picnics. On June 28 and 29 , the Gardens are abuzz with the festivities of the Imnarja (or Mnarja), also called the Feast of St. Peter and St. Paul. This is one of the biggest festivals of the year in Malta. Traditionally, it is a harvest festival celebrated with folk music competitions and a fried-rabbit picnic. Horse and donkey races are also held.

Dingli is a small village near Buskett Gardens and the highest point in the islands—a hill 253 m (829 ft) above sea level. From here, there are some decent walks along the Dingli cliffs and northwestward on the trails and secondary roads of a hilly, unpopulated area.

Bus 81 departs Valletta hourly for Dingli, and from there you can walk to Buskett Gardens and the Dingli cliffs.

Mosta is a small town northeast of Rabat and Mdina that is best known for its immense nineteenth-century parish church—the Church of St. Mary. Built with contributions from Mosta's inhabitants between 1833 and 1860, it boasts the fourth largest church dome (a diameter of almost 37 1/2 m, or 123 ft) in Europe and possibly in the world; the third largest is in Xewkija on Gozo. In the sacristy, you'll notice something that appears in no other church in the world—a World War II bomb that is big enough to fit snugly into a bathtub. On April 9, 1942, it fell through part of the dome during church services and didn't explode. It has been defused.

THE ISLAND OF GOZO

Separated from Malta by the North and South Comino channels, the island of Gozo is smaller in area and population, but greener than and just as interesting to visit as Malta.

Only 14 km (9 miles) by 7 km (4 1/2 miles), there are approximately 25,000 Gozitans, as the inhabitants of Gozo call themselves, on the island. Gozitans are predominantly farmers and fishers and considered quite religious. Tomatoes, potatoes, figs, oranges, and melons are the principal crops. Prayer seems to be a principal and favorite activity; there are at least twenty-nine parish churches and probably as many little chapels scattered around the island. For the women, weaving, knitting, and lacemaking also seem to be favorite pastimes and, increasingly, sources of incomes; hand-made Gozitan products have become popular with tourists.

Gozo is only accessible by ferry or private boat from Malta and Comino. All boats land at Mgarr Harbor on the southeast coast of the island. Although it is apt to change with the seasons and fluctuating numbers of tourists, the following is the ferry schedule:

From Mgarr	From Cirkewwa
November to March	
6 A.M.	7 A.M.
7.30 A.M.	8.15 A.M.
9 A.M.	10 A.M.
11 A.M.	12 noon
1 P.M.	2 P.M.
3 P.M.	4 P.M.
5 P.M.	6 P.M.
7 P.M.	8 P.M.
9 P.M.	10 P.M.
April to October	
6 A.M.	7 A.M.
6.45 A.M.	7.30 A.M.
7.30 A.M.	8.15 A.M.
9 A.M.	10 A.M.
11 A.M.	12 noon
1 P.M.	2 P.M.
3 P.M.	4 P.M.
5 P.M.	6 P.M.
7 P.M.	8 P.M.
8 P.M.	9 P.M.
10 P.M.	10.30 P.M.
12 midnight	12.30 A.M.
2 A.M.	2.30 A.M.
4 A.M.	4.30 A.M.

August
Departures every hour between 9 A.M. and 9 P.M. from both points.

From Sa Maison near Valletta, there's a boat daily Monday through Friday departing at 9.30 A.M. (November to June); on Monday, Tuesday, Wednesday, Friday, and Sunday at 9.30 A.M. and 5 P.M. (July to October).

From Mgarr, 5.30 P.M. the same days and months, and 11.45 A.M. and 5.30 P.M. the same days and months.

Bus 45 leaves Valletta daily to connect with the Cirkewwa ferry to Gozo, but see above for the ferry from Sa Maison once or twice daily to Mgarr. At Mgarr, buses meet the ferry and shuttle people to Victoria, Gozo's capital and principal city. There are also many taxis at the ferry landing, so transport shouldn't be a problem.

As capital city, Victoria is the focal point of the island. The British named it Victoria during Queen Victoria's 1897 jubilee, but Gozitans still refer to the city as Rabat, which is what the Arabs named it many centuries ago.

It-Tokk, the tree-shaded central square, is the heart of Victoria with its daily (except Sunday) open-air market, small shops and bars, and war monument. The eighteenth-century St. James Church fills one side of the square and a building of the same century that now houses the tourist office is adjacent.

Set back behind the square are the narrow alleyways, market streets, and classic balconied houses of the "old town." There's also St. George's Square and St. George's Church; the latter is a twentieth-century baroque restoration of the original church, which was built in 1673.

Republic Street, the main street, heads downhill past Main Gate Street—where the bus terminus is located—and Rundle Gardens. The gardens are named after Sir Leslie Rundle, governor of Malta from 1909 to 1915. One of Gozo's biggest events—the August fifteenth Feast of the Assumption—is held in the Gardens.

One of the most significant sights on the island is also its most visible—the citadel. From atop a hill overlooking the town, the ramparts of the citadel offer a commanding view of most of Gozo. The citadel was fortified after Dragut, an infamous Mediterranean pirate, attacked Gozo and kidnapped approximately 6,000 to 7,000 Gozitans for slavery. It proved insufficient, however, against future attacks. The citadel's cathedral now comprises most of the complex. From the outside, it looks almost stark, but inside the marble mosaic slabs covering the tombs on the floor are colorful compensation. It was built between 1697 and 1711 by architect Lorenzo Gafà.

Next to the cathedral is Bondi Palace, which is now the Gozo Museum. The museum's exhibits emphasize the history of Gozo, particularly its prehistoric periods. If you plan to visit the Ggantija Temples near Xaghra, it's a good idea to first come here for an introduction.

Xewkija

Xewkija (pronounced *Shaw-kee-yah*)—Gozo's third largest village—is between Victoria and the Mgarr ferry landing. Its most notable feature is a massive church, started in 1952 and recently completed. Its dome is possibly the third largest church dome in Europe and the rest of the world.

Xaghra

Xaghra (pronounced *Shah-rah*) is about 2 1/4 miles northwest of Victoria. It's known for the nearby prehistoric Ggantija Temples and grottoes of stalagmites and stalactites beneath a few of the houses in town.

The Ggantija Temples are one of the Maltese islands' most impressive prehistoric sites. The larger and older of two temples identified here dates back to 2800 B.C. Several parts of the temple comprise 20-ft-high limestone slabs, which divide the temple grounds into five apses. Swirls have been carved into some of the slabs along with various types of holes. A fireplace hole was believed to have been used for an "eternal" flame, while an oracle hole may have been used for ritual communication with the gods. Toward the rear are apses that may have been accessible only to priests. The smaller temple has similar details but is much less impressive.

The grottoes are an interesting geological phenomenon—colorful underground stalagmites and stalactites. One is called Ninu's Cave and the other Xerri's Cave. Ninu's Cave is located beneath Juliana Attard's house in Xaghra (follow the signs) and accessible via a stairway next to her kitchen. You have to walk through her house to get to the stairway, but Attard seems used to having visitors. After you visit the cave, she sits you down in her kitchen, turns on a tape recounting the story of the cave, and serves coffee and homemade cookies.

Calypso's Cave

On the northeast coast overlooking picturesque Ramla bay is Calypso's Cave, which is literally a hole in the cliff. The cave's legend is more interesting than the cave. Ulysses (Odysseus) supposedly did a bit of cavorting here with the siren of Greek mythology—an insidiously seductive woman who lured ancient mariners in from the sea with her singing. Actually, the cave seems to fit the description of the Ogygia in Homer's *Odyssey*, although most of the surrounding vegetation has long since vanished.

A few other sights worth visiting on Gozo include the inland bay or "sea" of Qawra, which leads to the sea through a natural archway in Dwejra point; Xlendi, a popular village and bay for swimming and walks; and Marsalforn for snorkeling and diving.

INDEX

(A) = Algeria, (M) = Morocco, (MI) = Maltese Islands, (MK) = Marrakesh, and (T) = Tunisia